SEVENTH EDITION

STRATEGIC MANAGEMENT

J. David Hunger

Iowa State University

Thomas L. Wheelen

University of South Florida and
Visiting Professor, Trinity College,
Dublin, Ireland

Prentice Hall
Upper Saddle River, New Jersey 07458

Senior Acquisitions Editor: David A. Shafer
Editor in Chief: Natalie E. Anderson
Executive Marketing Manager: Michael D. Campbell
Managing Editor (Editorial): Jennifer Glennon
Assistant Editor: Michele Foresta
Editorial Assistant: Kim Marsden
Production Supervisor: Nancy Fenton
Managing Editor: James Rigney
Manufacturing Supervisor: Tim McDonald
Text Design: Carol Rose
Production Services: Books By Design, Inc.
Cover Design: Regina Hagen
Illustrator (Interior): Network Graphics; Books By Design, Inc.
Cover Art: © John Still/Photonica
Composition: G & S Typesetters, Inc.

Library of Congress Cataloging-in-Publication Data

Hunger, J. David
    Strategic management / J. David Hunger, Thomas L. Wheelen. — 7th ed.
        p.   cm.
    Includes index.
    ISBN 0-13-087296-2 (pbk.)
    1. Strategic planning.   I. Title.   II. Wheelen, Thomas L.
HD30.28.W429   1999
658.4'012 21—dc21   99-042089
                                                                        CIP

Prentice-Hall International (UK) Limited, London
Prentice-Hall of Australia Pty. Limited, Sydney
Prentice-Hall Canada, Inc., Toronto
Prentice-Hall Hispanoamericana, S.A., Mexico
Prentice-Hall of India Private Limited, New Delhi
Prentice-Hall of Japan, Inc., Tokyo
Pearson Education Asia Pte. Ltd., Singapore
Editora Prentice-Hall do Brasil, Ltda., Rio de Janeiro

Printed in the United States of America

10 9 8 7 6 5 4 3

Dedicated to

Kathy, Tom, and Richard

Betty, Kari and Jeff, Suzi, Lori, Merry, and Smokey: Those for whom this book was written; and to Elizabeth Carey and Jackson S. Hunger: without whom there would be no book; and to Jane Hunger Randal and Jim Hunger: two siblings who actually read this book!!

Special Dedication by Tom Wheelen

In the year 2000, to my family in America, who trace their roots and heritage from Ireland:

- Great Grandparents
    1. David Whelan (1806–1858) and Mary Killan (1822–18xx) of Cork, Ireland
    2. William Layhon and Margaret Shae of Ireland

- Grandparents
    1. Thomas Wheelen (1849–1911) of Cork, Ireland, and Hannah I. Laylon (1863–1934) of Burke, New York
    2. William E. McGrath (1865–1939) of Tipperary, Ireland, and Catherine McCarthy (1867–1932) of Clare, Ireland

- Parents
    Thomas L. Wheelen (1892–1938) of Gardner, Massachusetts, and Kathryn E. McGrath (1895–1972) of Fitchburg, Massachusetts

- Me
    Thomas L. Wheelen (1935–) of Gardner, Massachusetts

- Children
    Kathryn E. Wheelen (1967–) of Fairfax, Virginia
    Thomas L. Wheelen II (1968–) of Fairfax, Virginia
    Richard D. Wheelen (1970–) of Charlottesville, Virginia

Preface

We've written *Strategic Management* to introduce you to a field of inquiry that focuses on the corporation as a whole and its interactions with its environment. The corporate world is in the process of global transformation. Every day brings word of new mergers, acquisitions, outsourcing, downsizing, and strategic alliances. Strategic management takes a panoramic view of this changing corporate terrain and attempts to show how large and small firms can be more effective and efficient not only in today's world, but in tomorrow's as well.

This book has been class-tested in strategy classes and revised based upon feedback from students, reviewers, and instructors. In response to comments, we have emphasized primarily those concepts and techniques that have proven to be most useful in understanding strategic decision-making and in conducting case analysis. Our goal was to make the text as comprehensive as possible without getting bogged down in any one area. Endnote references are provided for those who wish to learn more about any particular topic. This book is organized around a strategic management model that prefaces each key chapter. The model provides a structure for content and for complex case analyses by students.

This text was originally part of a hardcover book titled *Strategic Management and Business Policy, 6th edition*—a 1999 winner of the prestigious McGuffey Award for Excellence and Longevity, given by the Text and Academic Authors Association. Given the strong demand for this hardcover book, we decided to publish the 14 chapters of text (without cases) in this softcover version. The only difference between this edition and the 6th edition of *Strategic Management* are various corrections throughout and some updating of Chapter 14.

Objectives

This book focuses on the following objectives, typically found in most strategic management and business policy courses:

- To develop an understanding of strategic management concepts, research, and theories.

- To develop a framework of analysis to enable a student to identify central issues and problems in complex, comprehensive cases; to suggest alternative courses of action; and to present well-supported recommendations for future action.

- To develop conceptual skills so that a student is able to integrate previously learned aspects of corporations.

- To develop an understanding of the emerging global economy and its potential impact on business activities in any location.

- To develop an understanding of the role of corporate governance in strategic management.

- To develop the ability to analyze and evaluate, both quantitatively and qualitatively, the performance of the people responsible for strategic decisions.

- To bridge the gap between theory and practice by developing an understanding of when and how to apply concepts and techniques learned in earlier courses on marketing, accounting, finance, management, production, and information systems.

- To improve research capabilities necessary to gather and interpret key environmental data.

- To develop a better understanding of the present and future environments in which corporations must function.

- To develop analytical and decision-making skills for dealing with complex conceptual problems in an ethical manner.

This book achieves these objectives by presenting and explaining concepts and theories useful in understanding the strategic management process. It critically analyzes studies in the field of strategy to acquaint the student with the literature of this area and to help develop the student's research capabilities. It also suggests a model of strategic management. It recommends the strategic audit as one approach to the systematic analysis of complex organization-wide issues. The book focuses on the business corporation because of its crucial position in the economic system of the world and in the material development of any society.

How This Book Is Different from Other Strategy Books
In Terms of Concepts

- The firm is conceptualized as a **learning organization** that can learn from its own experience (Chapter 1).

- The typical top-down **orientation** toward strategic management is softened by showing how people at all organizational levels are becoming increasingly involved in strategic management as members of a learning organization (Chapter 1).

- **Corporate governance** is examined in terms of the roles, responsibilities, and interactions of top management and the board of directors and is coupled with **social responsibility and ethics** (Chapter 2).

- **Social responsibility and managerial ethics** are examined in detail in terms of how they affect strategic decision-making (Chapter 2).

- Equal emphasis is placed on **environmental scanning** of the societal environment as well as on the task environment. Topics include forecasting and Miles and Snow's typology in addition to Porter's industry analysis (Chapter 3).

- **Hypercompetition** is discussed in terms of its impact on industry analysis and competitive strategy (Chapters 3 and 5).

- The **resource-based view of the firm** has been expanded to include an examination of core and distinctive competencies (Chapters 4 and 7).

- **Activity-based costing and value-chain analysis** (both industry and firm value chains) are used to identify those activities and functions that can be outsourced or developed to gain competitive advantage (Chapters 3 and 10).

- **Cooperative strategy** (strategic alliances, joint ventures, etc.) is added to competitive strategy and tactics in a separate business strategy chapter (Chapter 5).

- **Corporate strategy** is reconceptualized and presented not only in the traditional sense as portfolio analysis and as directional strategy for the firm as a whole, but also as "parenting" of business units to transfer core competencies (Chapter 6).

- Two chapters deal with issues in **strategy implementation,** such as organizational and job design plus strategy-manager fit, action planning, and corporate culture (Chapters 8 and 9).

- A separate chapter on **evaluation and control** explains the importance of measurement and incentives to organizational performance (Chapter 10).

- Special chapters deal with strategic issues in **managing technology and innovation, entrepreneurial ventures and small businesses,** and **not-for-profit organizations** (Chapters 11, 12, and 13, respectively).

In Terms of Features

- A **strategic management model** runs throughout the first ten chapters as a unifying concept.

- **Key Theory capsules** explain key theories underlying strategic management. This feature adds emphasis to the theories, but does not interrupt the flow of the text material.

- **International issues are integrated throughout** the text chapters where appropriate.

- Two specially boxed features—**21st Century Global Society** and **Strategy in a Changing World**—illustrate not only how the global environment is affecting strategic decisions, but also how strategic concepts are being applied in actual organizations.

- A section on **Global Issues for the 21st Century** highlights how international issues will be affecting strategic management in the future.

- **Projections for the 21st Century** end each chapter by forecasting what the world will be like in 2010.

- A **short case or experiential exercise** focusing on the material covered in each chapter helps the reader to apply strategic concepts to an actual situation.

- A list of **key terms** and the pages in which they are discussed enable the reader to keep track of important concepts as they are introduced in each chapter.

- **Company Spotlight on Maytag Corporation** illustrates the issues in each chapter and serves to integrate the material (Chapters 1–13).

- An **industry matrix** adds to industry analysis by providing a means to summarize strategic factors facing a particular industry (Chapter 3).

- Internal and external strategic factors are emphasized through the use of specially designed **EFAS, IFAS,** and **SFAS tables** (Chapters 3, 4, and 5).

- The **strategic audit,** a way to operationalize the strategic decision-making process, serves as a checklist in case analysis (Chapter 10).

- **Suggestions for in-depth case analysis** provide a complete listing of financial ratios, recommendations for oral and written analysis, and ideas for further research (Chapter 14).

- The **Strategic Audit Worksheet** is based on the time-tested strategic audit and is designed to help students organize and structure daily case preparation in a brief period of time. The worksheet works exceedingly well for checking the level of daily student case preparation—especially for open class discussions of cases (Chapter 14).

Supplements

Supplemental materials are available to the instructor from the publisher. These include an Instructor's Manual, Win/PH Test Manager, video clips, a Web site, and overhead transparencies.

Instructor's Manual

A comprehensive Instructor's Manual has been carefully constructed to accompany this book. To aid in discussing the 14 chapters dealing with strategic management concepts, the TEXT Instructor's Manual includes:

1. *Suggestions for Teaching Strategic Management:* Discusses various teaching methods and includes suggested course syllabi.

2. *Chapter Notes:* Includes summaries of each chapter, suggested answers to discussion questions, suggestions for using end of chapter cases/exercises, plus additional discussion questions (with answers) and lecture modules.

3. *Multiple-Choice Test Questions:* Contains approximately 50 questions for each of the 14 chapters summing to over 700 questions from which to choose.

4. *Transparency Masters:* Includes over 170 transparency masters of figures and tables in the text plus other exhibits.

Instructor's Resource CD-ROM

The Instructor's Resource CD-ROM contains tools to facilitate instructors' lectures and examinations. These include PowerPoint™ Electronic Transparency Masters, a collection of over 170 figures and tables from the text. The instructor may customize these presentations and can present individual slides for student handouts. The Instructor's Manuals have also been added to the Instructor's Resource CD-ROM.

Win/PH Test Manager

Containing all of the questions in the printed Test Item File, Test Manager is a comprehensive suite of tools for testing and assessment. Test Manager allows educators to easily create and distribute tests for their courses, either by printing and distributing through traditional methods, or by on-line delivery via a Local Area Network (LAN) server.

Videos

Video clips featuring cases in this book plus company and industry vignettes for use with various chapters are available free to adopters of this textbook. These video clips can be used to accompany various chapters in the text to provide examples of strategic management issues and concepts. A Video Guide accompanying the video clips includes video summaries and suggestions for classroom use.

PHLIP/CW

Strategic Management, 7/e, is supported by PHLIP (Prentice Hall Learning on the Internet Partnership), the book's companion Web site. An invaluable resource for both instructors and students, PHLIP features a wealth of up-to-date, on-line resources at the touch of a button! A research center, current event articles, interactive study guide, exercises, and additional resources are combined to offer the most advanced text-specific Web site available.

Visit **www.prenhall.com/wheelen**

An alternate Web site you can access is:

http://www.bus.iastate.edu/jdhunger/strategy

Transparencies

NEW! One hundred and thirty professionally prepared overhead transparencies are now available for instructors' use.

Acknowledgments

We are grateful to the people who reviewed this edition for their constructive comments and suggestions. Their thought and effort has resulted in a book far superior to our original manuscript. This was one of the best set of reviewers ever to work on this book.

Kimberly Boal, Texas Tech University
Robert DeFillippi, Suffolk University
Helen Deresky, SUNY at Plattsburgh
Patricia Feltes, Southwest Missouri State University
Calvin Fields, Western Illinois University
Steven Floyd, University of Connecticut
Charles R. Gowen, III, Northern Illinois University
Marilyn Helms, University of Tennessee at Chattanooga
Alan Hoffman, Bentley College
Douglas Micklich, Illinois State University
Ann Morinoni, Lake Superior State University
Rebecca Morris, University of Nebraska at Omaha
George Puia, Indiana State University
Mike Raphael, Central Connecticut State University
Barbara Ribbens, St. Cloud State University
Margaret White, Oklahoma State University

Our thanks go to Patricia Mahtani, Project Manager at Addison Wesley Longman, for her coordination of the work going into this 7th edition. We also thank the many other people at Addison Wesley and Prentice Hall who worked to supervise and market this book. Some of these people are Joyce Cosentino, Marketing Coordinator, and David A. Shafer, Senior Editor. We are especially grateful to Nancy Benjamin of Books By Design, Inc., for her patience, expertise, and even disposition during the copyediting and production process.

We thank Betty Hunger for her preparation of the subject and name indexes. We are also very grateful to Kathy Wheelen for her first-rate administrative support. In addition, we express our appreciation to Dr. Ben Allen, Dean, and Dr. Brad Shrader, Management Department Chair, of Iowa State University's College of Business, for their support and provision of the resources so necessary to produce a textbook. Both of us acknowledge our debt to Dr. William Shenkir and Dr. Frank S. Kaulback, former Deans of the McIntire School of Commerce of the University of Virginia for the provision of a work climate most supportive to the original development of this book.

Lastly, to the many strategy/policy instructors and students who have moaned to us about their problems with the strategy/policy course: we have tried to respond to your problems and concerns as best we could by providing a comprehensive yet usable text. To you, the people who work hard in the strategy/policy trenches, we acknowledge our debt. This book is yours.

Ames, Iowa   J. D. H.
Tampa, Florida   T. L. W.

About the Authors

J. David Hunger, Ph.D. (Ohio State University) is Professor of Strategic Management at Iowa State University. He previously taught at George Mason University, the University of Virginia, and Baldwin-Wallace College. His research interests lie in strategic management, corporate governance, leadership, conflict management, and entrepreneurship. He is currently serving as Academic Director of the Pappajohn Center for Entrepreneurship at Iowa State University. He has worked in management positions for Procter & Gamble, Lazarus Department Store, and the U.S. Army. He has been active as consultant and trainer to business corporations, as well as to state and federal government agencies. He has written numerous articles and cases that have appeared in the *Academy of Management Journal, International Journal of Management, Human Resource Management, Journal of Business Strategies, Case Research Journal, Business Case Journal, Handbook of Business Strategy, Journal of Management Case Studies, Annual Advances in Business Cases, Journal of Retail Banking, SAM Advanced Management Journal,* and *Journal of Management,* among others. Dr. Hunger is a member of the Academy of Management, North American Case Research Association (NACRA), Society for Case Research (SCR), North American Management Society, World Association for Case Method Research and Application (WACRA), and the Strategic Management Society. He is past-President of the Society for Case Research and the Iowa State University Press Board of Directors. He is currently serving as NACRA's Web Master (nacra.net). He is currently serving on the editorial review boards of *SAM Advanced Management Journal, Journal of Business Strategies,* and *Journal of Business Research.* He is also a member of the board of directors of the North American Case Research Association, and the North American Management Society. He is co-author with Thomas L. Wheelen of *Strategic Management and Business Policy, Essentials of Strategic Management, Cases in Strategic Management,* as well as *Strategic Management Cases (PIC: Preferred Individualized Cases)* and a monograph assessing undergraduate business education in the United States. His textbook *Strategic Management and Business Policy* received the McGuffey Award for Excellence and Longevity in 1999 from the Text and Academic Authors Association. Dr. Hunger received the *Best Case Award* given by the McGraw Hill Publishing Company and the Society for Case Research in 1991 for outstanding case development. He is listed in various versions of Who's Who, including *Who's Who in the World.* He was also recognized in 1999 by the Iowa State University College of Business with its Innovation in Teaching Award.

Thomas L. Wheelen, D.B.A., MBA., BS. Cum Laude (George Washington University, Babson College, and Boston College, respectively), is Professor of Strategic Management, University of South Florida, and was formerly the Ralph A. Beeton Professor of Free Enterprise at the McIntire School of Commerce, University of Virginia. He was awarded Fullbright Scholar. He was Visiting Professor at both the University of Arizona and Northeastern University. In 1999, the International Board of Directors of the Society for Advancement of Management (SAM) awarded Dr. Wheelen the Phil Carroll Advancement of Management Award in Strategic Management. He is a graduate of Gardner High School (MA) and Sacred Heart School in 1953 and 1949, respectively. He has worked in management positions for General Electric and the U.S. Navy and has been active as a consultant and trainer to business corporations, as well as to federal and state government agencies. He currently serves on the Board of Directors of Adhice Fund and The Society for Advancement of Management and on the Editorial Board of *SAM Advanced Management Journal.* He is the Associate Editor of *SAM Advanced Management*

Journal. He served on the Board of Directors of Lazer Surgical Software, Inc., and on the *Journal of Management* and *Journal of Management Case Studies.* He is co-author of *Strategic Management and Business Policy, Essentials of Strategic Management, Cases in Strategic Management, Strategic Management and Business Policy—World Version,* and *Strategic Management Cases (PIC: Preferred Individualized Cases)* as well as the *Public Sector* and co-developer of *Financial Analyzer (FAN)* and *Strategic Financial Analyzer* (St. FAN) software. His textbook *Strategic Management and Business Policy* received the McGuffey Award for Excellence and Longevity in 1999 from the Text and Academic Authors Association. He has authored over 40 articles that have appeared in such journals as the *Journal of Management, Business Quarterly, Personnel Journal, SAM Advanced Management Journal, Journal of Retailing, International Journal of Management,* and the *Handbook of Business Strategy.* He has over 130 cases appearing in over 55 text and case books, as well as the *Journal of Management Case Research.* He has served on the board of directors of the Southern Management Association and the Society for the Advancement of Management, as Vice-President-at-large and Vice President of Strategic Management for the Society for the Advancement of Management, and as President of the North American Case Research Association. He is a member of the Academy of Management, Beta Gamma Sigma, Southern Management Association, North American Case Research Association, Society for Advancement of Management, Society for Case Research, Strategic Management Association, and World Association for Case Method Research and Application. He is listed in *Who's Who in Finance and Industry, Who's Who in the South and Southwest,* and *Who's Who in American Education.*

Contents

Part One

INTRODUCTION TO STRATEGIC MANAGEMENT AND BUSINESS POLICY

Chapter 1
Basic Concepts of Strategic Management 1

1.1 The Study of Strategic Management 3
Phases of Strategic Management 3
Benefits of Strategic Management 4
Company Spotlight on Maytag Corporation:
Initiation of Strategic Management at Maytag 5

1.2 Globalization: A Challenge to Strategic Management 6
21st Century Global Society: Regional Trade Associations Replace
National Trade Barriers 7

1.3 Creating a Learning Organization 7

1.4 Basic Model of Strategic Management 8
Environmental Scanning 9
Strategy Formulation 10
Strategy Implementation 14
Evaluation and Control 15
Strategy in a Changing World: Strategic Management at Delta Airlines 16
Feedback/Learning Process 16

1.5   *Initiation of Strategy: Triggering Events 17*

1.6   *Strategic Decision Making 17*
         Strategy in a Changing World: Triggering Event at Iomega Corporation 18
         What Makes a Decision Strategic 18
         Mintzberg's Modes of Strategic Decision-Making 18
         Strategic Decision-Making Process: Aid to Better Decisions 19

1.7   *Global Issues for the 21st Century 21*
         Projections for the 21st Century 22
         Discussion Questions 22
         Key Terms 22
         Strategic Practice Exercise 23
         Notes 23

Chapter 2
Corporate Governance
and Social Responsibility 25

2.1   *Corporate Governance: Role of the Board of Directors 26*
         Responsibilities of the Board 27
         Members of a Board of Directors 29
         Key Theory: Application of Agency Theory to Corporate Governance 31
         **21st Century Global Society: Hoechst AG Adds International
             Members to Its Board** 32
         Nomination and Election of Board Members 33
         Organization of the Board 33
         Trends in Corporate Governance 34

2.2   *Corporate Governance: The Role of Top Management 35*
         Responsibilities of Top Management 35
         **Strategy in a Changing World: Board Qualifications: Diversity or
             Technical Competence?** 36
         Strategy in a Changing World: Executive Leadership at Eastman Kodak 38

2.3   *Social Responsibilities of Strategic Decision Makers 39*
         Responsibilities of a Business Firm 39
         Corporate Stakeholders 41
         Company Spotlight on Maytag Corporation: Location Decision 42
         Strategy in a Changing World: Kathy Lee Gifford Has Some Bad Days 43

2.4   *Ethical Decision Making 43*

Some Reasons for Unethical Behavior 43

Encouraging Ethical Behavior 45

Strategy in a Changing World: Reebok Demands Human Rights Standards from Its Suppliers 46

2.5   🌐 *Global Issues for the 21st Century 48*

Projections for the 21st Century 48

Discussion Questions 49

Key Terms 49

Strategic Practice Exercise 49

Notes 50

Part Two

SCANNING THE ENVIRONMENT

Chapter 3
*Environmental Scanning
and Industry Analysis 52*

3.1   *Environmental Scanning 53*

Identifying External Environmental Variables 54

Identifying External Strategic Factors 58

Key Theory: Using PPP to Identify Potential Markets in Developing Nations 59

3.2   *Industry Analysis: Analyzing the Task Environment 60*

Porter's Approach to Industry Analysis 60

Industry Evolution 65

Categorizing International Industries 65

Company Spotlight on Maytag Corporation: Evolution of the U.S. Major Home Appliance Industry 66

International Risk Assessment 67

Strategic Groups 67

Strategic Types 68

Hypercompetition 69

Strategy in a Changing World: Microsoft Operates in a Hypercompetitive Industry 70

Creating an Industry Matrix 70

3.3   *Industry/Competitive Intelligence 72*

3.4   *Forecasting 73*

Danger of Assumptions 73

Useful Forecasting Techniques 73

21st Century Global Society: Expert Opinion on the Future of Eastern Europe 74

3.5   *Synthesis of External Factors—EFAS 75*

3.6   *Global Issues for the 21st Century 77*

Projections for the 21st Century 77

Discussion Questions 77

Key Terms 78

Strategic Practice Exercise 78

Notes 79

Chapter 4
Internal Scanning:
Organizational Analysis 81

4.1   *A Resource-Based Approach to Organizational Analysis 82*

Using Resources to Gain Competitive Advantage 82

Determining the Sustainability of an Advantage 83

4.2   *Value-Chain Analysis 84*

Industry Value-Chain Analysis 85

Corporate Value-Chain Analysis 86

4.3   *Scanning Functional Resources 87*

Basic Organizational Structures 87

Corporate Culture: The Company Way 89

Strategic Marketing Issues 90

21st Century Global Society: ABB Uses Corporate Culture as a Competitive Advantage 91

Strategic Financial Issues 91

Company Spotlight on Maytag Corporation: Culture as a Key Strength 92

Strategic Research and Development (R&D) Issues 93

Strategy in a Changing World: A Problem of Technology Transfer at Xerox Corporation 95

Strategic Operations Issues 96

Strategic Human Resource (HRM) Issues 98

Strategic Information Systems Issues 100

4.4   The Strategic Audit: A Checklist for Organizational Analysis 100

4.5   Synthesis of Internal Factors—IFAS 101

4.6   Global Issues for the 21st Century 102

Projections for the 21st Century 103

Discussion Questions 103

Key Terms 103

Strategic Practice Exercise 104

Notes 104

Part Three

STRATEGY FORMULATION

Chapter 5
Strategy Formulation: Situation Analysis and Business Strategy 106

5.1   Situational Analysis: SWOT 107

Generating a Strategic Factors Analysis Summary (SFAS) Matrix 107

Finding a Propitious Niche 110

5.2   Review of Mission and Objectives 111

5.3   *Generating Alternative Strategies Using a TOWS Matrix 111*

5.4   *Business Strategies 113*
Porter's Competitive Strategies 113
Strategy in a Changing World: Differentiation Focus Strategy at Morgan Motor Car Company 117
Cooperative Strategies 124
Company Spotlight on Maytag Corporation: Maytag Forms a Joint Venture in China 126
21st Century Global Society: Dean Foods Finds a Joint Venture Partner in Mexico 128

5.5   *Global Issues for the 21st Century 129*
Projections for the 21st Century 130
Discussion Questions 130
Key Terms 130
Strategic Practice Exercise 130
Notes 131

Chapter 6
Strategy Formulation:
Corporate Strategy 132

6.1   *Corporate Strategy 133*

6.2   *Directional Strategy 133*
Growth Strategies 134
Key Theory: Transaction Cost Economics Analyzes Vertical Growth Strategy 137
Company Spotlight on Maytag Corporation: A Growth Strategy of Horizontal Growth Through Acquisitions 139
International Entry Options 140
21st Century Global Society: Daewoo Expands Its Corporate Growth Strategy Internationally 141
Controversies in Directional Growth Strategies 142
Stability Strategies 143
Retrenchment Strategies 144
Strategy in a Changing World: IBM Follows a Turnaround Strategy 145

6.3   *Portfolio Analysis 147*

    BCG Growth-Share Matrix 147

    GE Business Screen 149

    International Portfolio Analysis 150

    Advantages and Limitations of Portfolio Analysis 151

6.4   *Corporate Parenting 152*

    Developing a Corporate Parenting Strategy 153

    Parenting-Fit Matrix 153

    Horizontal Strategy: Corporate Competitive Strategy 155

6.5   *Global Issues for the 21st Century 156*

    Projections for the 21st Century 156

    Discussion Questions 156

    Key Terms 157

    Strategic Practice Exercise 157

    Notes 158

Chapter 7
Strategy Formulation:
Functional Strategy
and Strategic Choice 159

7.1   *Functional Strategy 160*

    Core Competencies 160

    The Sourcing Decision: Where Should Functions Be Housed? 161

    Marketing Strategy 162

    Financial Strategy 164

    **Company Spotlight on Maytag Corporation: Maytag Supports
    Dealers as Part of Its Marketing Strategy** 165

    Research and Development (R&D) Strategy 165

    Operations Strategy 166

    **21st Century Global Society: Whirlpool Adjusts Its Manufacturing
    Strategy to Local Conditions** 168

    Purchasing Strategy 168

    Logistics Strategy 169

    Human Resource Management (HRM) Strategy 170

    Information Systems Strategy 170

7.2   Strategies to Avoid 171

7.3   Strategic Choice: Selection of the Best Strategy 171
　　　Constructing Corporate Scenarios 172
　　　Process of Strategic Choice 176
　　　**Strategy in a Changing World: Intel Makes a Strategic
　　　　Decision** 177

7.4   Development of Policies 177

7.5   Global Issues for the 21st Century 178
　　　Projections for the 21st Century 178
　　　Discussion Questions 179
　　　Key Terms 179
　　　Strategic Practice Exercise 179
　　　Notes 180

Part Four

STRATEGY IMPLEMENTATION AND CONTROL

Chapter 8
*Strategy Implementation:
Organizing for Action 182*

8.1   Strategy Implementation 183

8.2   Who Implements Strategy? 185

8.3   What Must Be Done? 185
　　　Developing Programs, Budgets, and Procedures 185
　　　Achieving Synergy 186

8.4   How Is Strategy to Be Implemented? Organizing for Action 186
　　　Structure Follows Strategy 187

Stages of Corporate Development 188

Strategy in a Changing World: The Founder of the Modem Blocks the Transition to Stage II 191

Organizational Life Cycle 192

Advanced Types of Organizational Structures 192

Company Spotlight on Maytag Corporation: Initiating a Revival Phase 194

Reengineering and Strategy Implementation 197

Designing Jobs to Implement Strategy 198

Key Theory: Designing Jobs with the Job Characteristics Model 199

8.5 *International Issues in Strategy Implementation 199*

21st Century Global Society: The Internet: Instant Entry into the International Marketplace 201

8.6 *Global Issues for the 21st Century 203*

Projections for the 21st Century 203

Discussion Questions 203

Key Terms 204

Strategic Practice Exercise 204

Notes 204

Chapter 9
Strategy Implementation:
Staffing and Directing 206

9.1 *Staffing 207*

Staffing Follows Strategy 208

Selection and Management Development 209

Strategy in a Changing World: Ann Iverson Implements a Turnaround Strategy at Laura Ashley 210

Problems in Retrenchment 211

International Issues in Staffing 212

21st Century Global Society: General Motors Uses Chinese-Americans in Chinese Joint Venture 214

9.2 *Leading 214*

Managing Corporate Culture 214

Company Spotlight on Maytag Corporation: Assimilating Admiral's Culture 218

Action Planning 218
Management By Objectives 220
Total Quality Management 221
International Considerations in Leading 222

9.3   *Global Issues for the 21st Century 223*
21st Century Global Society: Cultural Differences Create
    Implementation Problems in Merger 224
Projections for the 21st Century 225
Discussion Questions 225
Key Terms 225
Strategic Practice Exercise 225
Notes 227

Chapter 10
Evaluation and Control 229

10.1   *Evaluation and Control in Strategic Management 230*

10.2   *Measuring Performance 231*
Appropriate Measures 231
Behavior and Output Controls 231
Activity-Based Costing 233
Primary Measures of Corporate Performance 234
Evaluating Top Management 238
Primary Measures of Divisional and Functional Performance 239
International Measurement Issues 241
Strategy in a Changing World: Seitz Corporation Uses Benchmarking
    in Strategy Implementation 242
21st Century Global Society: European Union's Problems with
    Forming a Single Currency 243

10.3   *Strategic Information Systems 244*

10.4   *Problems in Measuring Performance 245*
Short-Term Orientation 245
Goal Displacement 246
Company Spotlight on Maytag Corporation: The Impact of Hoover
    on Maytag's Financial Performance 247

10.5   *Guidelines for Proper Control 248*

10.6   *Strategic Incentive Management 248*
        Strategy in a Changing World: Southwest Airlines' Corporate
            Culture Makes Control Easier 249

10.7   *Using the Strategic Audit to Evaluate Corporate Performance 251*

10.8   *Global Issues for the 21st Century 259*
        Projections for the 21st Century 260
        Discussion Questions 260
        Key Terms 260
        Strategic Practice Exercise 260
        Notes 261

Part Five

OTHER STRATEGIC ISSUES

Chapter 11
*Strategic Issues in Managing
Technology and Innovation 263*

11.1   *Role of Management 264*
        Strategy in a Changing World: Examples of Innovation Emphasis
            in Mission Statements 265

11.2   *Environmental Scanning 265*
        External Scanning 265
        Internal Scanning 267

11.3   *Strategy Formulation 269*
        Product versus Process R&D 269
        Technology Sourcing 269

21st Century Global Society: The Impact of R&D on Competitive
Advantage in China 270

**Company Spotlight on Maytag Corporation: Importance of Product
and Process R&D in the Major Home Appliance Industry** 272

Importance of Technological Competence 272

Product Portfolio 273

11.4   Strategy Implementation 273

Developing an Innovative Entrepreneurial Culture 273

Organizing for Innovation: Corporate Entrepreneurship 275

**Strategy in a Changing World: DuPont Uses Cross-Functional Teams
to Improve Innovation** 276

11.5   Evaluation and Control 278

11.6   Global Issues for the 21st Century 278

Projections for the 21st Century 279

Discussion Questions 280

Key Terms 280

Strategic Practice Exercise 280

Notes 281

Chapter 12

*Strategic Issues in Entrepreneurial
Ventures and Small Businesses 283*

12.1   Importance of Small Business and Entrepreneurial Ventures 284

Definition of Small-Business Firms and Entrepreneurial
Ventures 284

The Entrepreneur as Strategic Manager 284

12.2   Use of Strategic Planning and Strategic Management 285

Degree of Formality 286

Usefulness of Strategic Management Model 286

Usefulness of Strategic Decision-Making Process 286

12.3   Issues in Environmental Scanning and Strategy Formulation 288

Sources of Innovation 290

21st Century Global Society: Mission and Policies of The Body Shop Reflect Entrepreneur's Personal Values and Experiences 291

Factors Affecting a New Venture's Success 293

Strategy in a Changing World: Cherrill Farnsworth's Entrepreneurial Personality 294

12.4   *Issues in Strategy Implementation 294*

Stages of Small Business Development 295

Company Spotlight on Maytag Corporation: Impact of F. L. Maytag on Maytag Corporation 297

Transfer of Power and Wealth in Family Businesses 298

12.5   *Issues in Evaluation and Control 298*

12.6   *Global Issues for the 21st Century 300*

Projections for the 21st Century 301

Discussion Questions 301

Key Terms 301

Strategic Practice Exercise 302

Notes 303

Chapter 13
Strategic Issues in Not-for-Profit Organizations 305

13.1   *Why Not-for-Profit? 306*

21st Century Global Society: Aspects of Life Most Suited for Not-for-Profits 307

13.2   *Importance of Revenue Source 307*

Sources of Not-for-Profit Revenue 308

Patterns of Influence on Strategic Decision Making 308

Usefulness of Strategic Management Concepts and Techniques 310

13.3   *Impact of Constraints on Strategic Management 310*

Impact on Strategy Formulation 311

Impact on Strategy Implementation 312

Impact on Evaluation and Control 313

13.4   *Popular Not-for-Profit Strategies 313*
Strategic Piggybacking 313
Mergers 314
Strategic Alliances 314

13.5   *Global Issues for the 21st Century 314*
**Strategy in a Changing World: Resources Needed for Successful
Strategic Piggybacking** 315
Projections for the 21st Century 316
Discussion Questions 316
Key Terms 316
Strategic Practice Exercises 316
Notes 317

Part Six

INTRODUCTION TO CASE ANALYSIS

Chapter 14
Suggestions for Case Analysis 319

14.1   *The Case Method 320*

14.2   *Researching the Case Situation 320*

14.3   *Financial Analysis: A Place to Begin 320*
**Strategy in a Changing World: Using the World Wide Web to Obtain
Information** 321
Analyzing Financial Statements 322
Common-Size Statements 324
Z-Value, Index of Sustainable Growth, and Free Cash Flow 326
Strategy in a Changing World: Is Inflation Dead or Just Sleeping? 327
Useful Economic Measures 327

14.4   *Format for Case Analysis: The Strategic Audit 328*
   21st Century Global Society: The Fastest Growing Economies in the
     World 329

14.5   *Global Issues for the 21st Century 331*
   Projections for the 21st Century 332
   Discussion Questions 332
   Key Terms 332
   Strategic Practice Exercise 333

Appendix 14.A   *Resources for Case Library Research 334*

Appendix 14.B   *Suggested Case Analysis Methodology Using the Strategic Audit 336*
   • *Strategic Audit appears on pages 251–258.*

Appendix 14.C   *Example of Student-Written Strategic Audit 340*
   Notes 344

Name Index I-1
Subject Index I-10

STRATEGIC
MANAGEMENT

Chapter 1

Basic Concepts of Strategic Management

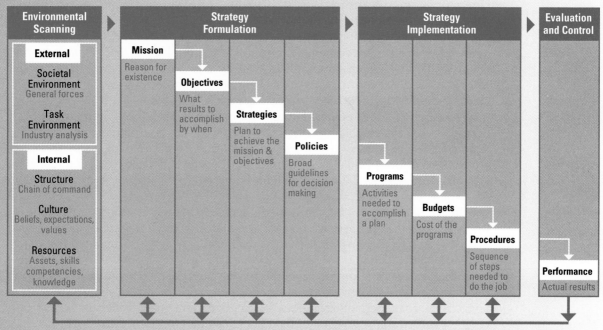

Steven Borsse was fed up. Borsse, who owned his own underwater search business in Sebastian, Florida, had paid $358 in November 1996 for a two-year, prepaid membership with America Online, Inc. (AOL). This package had offered Borsse a real savings compared to the usual monthly cost of $9.95 for the first five hours of use plus $2.95 for each hour thereafter. Unfortunately, in December 1996, AOL began offering a new plan charging $19.95 a month for *unlimited* online time. The attractiveness of the new flat rate plan was such that subscribers flooded AOL's circuits, preventing Borsse and thousands of other AOL customers from getting online. After unsuccessfully trying 20 times in one night to get through to AOL's jammed customer service center, Borsse complained. "It's literally impossible to get on AOL at night. I do business on the Internet, and this has really hurt me."

Founded in 1985 by Steve Case, America Online bragged in its 1996 annual report that it was "the world's first billion-dollar new media company." (See *aol.com* on the World Wide Web.) From its inception, the Dulles, Virginia, company had worked to dominate the developing Internet provider industry through an extremely aggressive growth strategy. Management emphasized saturation marketing by distributing free computer diskettes to almost every person in North America—some people actually received as many as 20 AOL disks in one year! These disks offered a month's free America Online service. Distribution was so intense and so thorough that it became an object of jokes. One cartoon showed an archeologist unearthing an Egyptian mummy only to find an America Online disk inside the coffin!

America Online's fast growth strategy was very successful. AOL's total revenues jumped from a little over $38 million from 182,000 subscribers in 1992 to more than $1 billion with over 6 million subscribers in 1996. By 1996, AOL had become the dominant Internet provider in North America, leaving behind its slower growing competitors, CompuServe, Prodigy, and the Microsoft Network, among others.

AOL introduced its unlimited usage plan on December 1, 1996. Admitting publicly that it would have trouble meeting the added demand, management was eager for market share and decided to go ahead—regardless. Four days later, the system was already overwhelmed. About 75% of the subscribers had changed to the flat rate plan. Customer usage soared from 1.6 million hours online in October to over 4 million hours in January.

Steven Borsse was not alone in being unable to access his AOL Internet connection. AOL became the busy signal heard around the world. Those subscribers lucky to get through stayed online for hours to avoid having to redial. Frustrated customers filed class action law suits for breach of contract against AOL in California and New York. To placate state attorneys general from 36 states, AOL offered to give subscribers refunds and free usage. Unfortunately customers still couldn't get access to AOL to take advantage of these offers. Because subscribers were unable to access AOL to cancel their subscriptions, they continued being charged for the service, or, rather, lack thereof.

AOL founder and Chairman, Steve Case, finally admitted that management had made a big mistake. "I would acknowledge it is a failure. We thought we had a pretty good grasp when we were making projections, but we were wrong." Realizing that the company had to do something to keep from losing its customers to the competition, Case went on to say, "We have made a commitment to our customers. . . . We'll deliver on this commitment, but it will take time." The company was in the process of spending $250 million to expand capacity by June 1997. Until capacity was expanded, management actually resorted to asking subscribers *not* to use the service! Meanwhile, the Microsoft Network, which had begun offering a flat rate in November 1996, was already expanding capacity by 25% to avoid the same problem.[1]

What went wrong? How could such a promising company as America Online make such a critical error? One reason was a lack of strategic management. Decisions were made piecemeal to the disadvantage of the company as a whole. To achieve fast growth, marketing was emphasized over all other business functions. Excellent advertising and promotional programs were implemented without considering how they would affect day-to-day operations. Hungry for market share, management pushed sales far beyond the ability of the company to support both current and new customers. The company had a good strategy for growth, but it failed to properly manage that strategy.

1.1 The Study of Strategic Management

Strategic management is that set of managerial decisions and actions that determines the long-run performance of a corporation. It includes *environmental scanning* (both external and internal), *strategy formulation* (strategic or long-range planning), *strategy implementation*, and *evaluation and control*. The study of strategic management, therefore, emphasizes the monitoring and evaluating of external opportunities and threats in light of a corporation's strengths and weaknesses. Originally called business policy, strategic management incorporates such topics as long-range planning and strategy. **Business policy,** in contrast, has a general management orientation and tends primarily to look inward with its concern for properly integrating the corporation's many functional activities. *Strategic management, as a field of study, incorporates the integrative concerns of business policy with a heavier environmental and strategic emphasis.* Therefore, *strategic management* has tended to replace *business policy* as the preferred name of the field.

Phases of Strategic Management

Many of the concepts and techniques dealing with strategic management have been developed and used successfully by business corporations such as General Electric and the Boston Consulting Group. Over time, business practitioners and academic researchers have expanded and refined these concepts. Initially strategic management was of most use to large corporations operating in multiple industries. Increasing risks of error, costly mistakes, and even economic ruin are causing today's professional managers in all organizations to take strategic management seriously in order to keep their company competitive in an increasingly volatile environment.

As managers attempt to better deal with their changing world, a firm generally evolves through the following four **phases of strategic management**:[2]

Phase 1. *Basic financial planning:* Managers initiate serious planning when they are requested to propose next year's budget. Projects are proposed on the basis of very little analysis, with most information coming from within the firm. The sales force usually provides the small amount of environmental information. Such simplistic operational planning only pretends to be strategic management, yet it is quite time consuming. Normal company activities are often suspended for weeks while managers try to cram ideas into the proposed budget. The time horizon is usually one year.

Phase 2. *Forecast-based planning:* As annual budgets become less useful at stimulating long-term planning, managers attempt to propose five-year plans. They now consider projects that may take more than one year. In addition to internal information, managers gather any available environmental data—usually on an ad hoc basis—and extrapolate current trends five years into the future. This phase is also time consuming, often involving a full month of managerial activity to make sure all the proposed budgets fit together. The process gets very political as managers compete for larger shares of funds. Endless meetings take place to evaluate proposals and justify assumptions. The time horizon is usually three to five years.

Phase 3. *Externally oriented planning (strategic planning):* Frustrated with highly political, yet ineffectual five-year plans, top management takes control of the planning process by initiating strategic planning. The company seeks to increase its responsiveness to changing markets and competition by thinking strategically. Planning is taken out of the hands of lower level managers and concentrated in a planning staff whose task is to develop strategic plans for the corporation. Consultants often provide the sophisticated and innovative techniques that the planning staff uses to gather information and forecast future trends. Ex-military experts develop competitive intelligence units. Upper level managers meet once a year at a resort "retreat" led by key members of the planning staff to evaluate and update the current strategic plan. Such top-down planning emphasizes formal strategy formulation and leaves the implementation issues to lower management levels. Top management typically develops five-year plans with help from consultants but minimal input from lower levels.

Phase 4. *Strategic management:* Realizing that even the best strategic plans are worthless without the input and commitment of lower level managers, top management forms planning groups of managers and key employees at many levels from various departments and workgroups. They develop and integrate a series of strategic plans aimed at achieving the company's primary objectives. Strategic plans now detail the implementation, evaluation, and control issues. Rather than attempting to perfectly forecast the future, the plans emphasize probable scenarios and contingency strategies. The sophisticated annual five-year strategic plan is replaced with strategic thinking at all levels of the organization throughout the year. Strategic information, previously available only centrally to top management, is available via local area networks to people throughout the organization. Instead of a large centralized planning staff, internal and external planning consultants are available to help guide group strategy discussions. Although top management may still initiate the strategic planning process, the resulting strategies may come from anywhere in the organization. Planning is typically interactive across levels and is no longer top down. People at all levels are now involved.

General Electric, one of the pioneers of strategic planning, led the transition from strategic planning to strategic management during the 1980s. By the 1990s, most corporations around the world had also begun the conversion to strategic management.

Until 1978, Maytag Company, the major home appliance manufacturer, could be characterized as being in Phase 1 of strategic management. See the **Company Spotlight on Maytag Corporation** feature to see how this company began making the transition from its budget-oriented planning approach to strategic management. We will follow Maytag throughout much of this text to illustrate concepts and techniques from each chapter.

Benefits of Strategic Management

Research has revealed that organizations that engage in strategic management generally outperform those that do not.[3] The attainment of an appropriate match or "fit" between an organization's environment and its strategy, structure, and processes has positive effects on the organization's performance. For example, a study of the impact of deregulation on U.S. railroads found that those railroads that changed their strategy as their environment changed outperformed those railroads that did not change their strategies.[4]

A survey of nearly 50 corporations in a variety of countries and industries found the three most highly rated benefits of strategic management to be:

- Clearer sense of strategic vision for the firm.

- Sharper focus on what is strategically important.

- Improved understanding of a rapidly changing environment.[5]

COMPANY SPOTLIGHT

Initiation of Strategic Management at Maytag

Maytag Corporation is a successful full-line manufacturer of major home appliances. Beginning with its very successful high-quality washers and dryers, it branched out through acquisitions into cooking appliances (Magic Chef, Hardwick, and Jenn-Air), refrigerators (Admiral), and vacuum cleaners (Hoover). Until 1978, however, the corporation (then known simply as Maytag Company) was strictly a laundry appliances manufacturer. Its only experience with any sort of strategic planning was in preparing the next year's budget!

In 1978, Daniel Krumm, Maytag's CEO, asked Leonard Hadley (at that time the company's Assistant Controller in charge of preparing the annual budget) and two others from manufacturing and marketing to serve as a strategic planning task force. Krumm posed to these three people the question: *"If we keep doing what we're now doing, what will the Maytag Company look like in five years?"* The question was a challenge to answer, especially considering that the company had never done financial modeling and none of the three knew much about strategic planning. Hadley, trained in accounting, worked with a programmer in his MIS section to develop "what if" scenarios. The task force presented its conclusion to the board of directors: A large part of Maytag's profits (the company at that time had the best profit margin in the industry) was coming from products and services with no future. These were repair parts, portable washers and dryers, and wringer washing machines.

This report triggered Maytag's interest in strategic change. After engaging in a series of acquisitions, including Magic Chef, to broaden its product line within the United States and Canada, management became interested in becoming a player in the European major home appliance industry. The trend toward the unification of Europe plus the rapid economic development of the Far East suggested to management that Maytag could no longer survive simply as a specialty appliance manufacturer serving only North America. It subsequently purchased Hoover in 1988 to not only acquire its worldwide strength in floor-care appliances, but also Hoover's strong laundry, cooking, and refrigeration appliance business in the United Kingdom and Australia. Although the strategy appeared to be sound at the time, the corporation later found that it had paid far too much for Hoover's European operations—its plants were outdated and inefficient.

MAYTAG CORPORATION

To be effective, however, strategic management need not always be a formal process. As occurred at Maytag, it can begin with a few simple questions:

1. **Where is the organization now? (Not where do we hope it is!)**

2. **If no changes are made, where will the organization be in one year? two years? five years? ten years? Are the answers acceptable?**

3. **If the answers are not acceptable, what specific actions should management undertake? What are the risks and payoffs involved?**

Studies of the planning practices of actual organizations suggest that the real value of strategic planning may be more in the future orientation of the planning process itself than in any written strategic plan. Small companies, in particular, may plan informally and irregularly. Nevertheless, a recent study of small businesses revealed that even though the degree of formality in strategic planning had no significant impact on a firm's profitability, formal planners had twice the growth rate in sales.[6]

Planning the strategy of large, multidivisional corporations can become complex and time consuming. It often takes slightly more than a year for a large company to move from situation assessment to a final decision agreement. Because of the relatively large number of people affected by a strategic decision in such a firm, a formalized, more sophisticated system is needed to ensure that strategic planning leads to successful performance. Otherwise, top management becomes isolated from developments in the business units, and lower level managers lose sight of the corporate mission and objectives.

1.2 Globalization: A Challenge to Strategic Management

Not too long ago, a business corporation could be successful by focusing only on making and selling goods and services within its national boundaries. International considerations were minimal. Profits earned from exporting products to foreign lands were considered frosting on the cake, but not really essential to corporate success. During the 1960s, for example, most U.S. companies organized themselves around a number of product divisions that made and sold goods *only* in the United States. All manufacturing and sales outside the United States were typically managed through one international division. An international assignment was usually considered a message that the person was no longer promotable and should be looking for another job.

Today, everything has changed. **Globalization,** the internationalization of markets and corporations, has changed the way modern corporations do business. To reach the economies of scale necessary to achieve the low costs, and thus the low prices, needed to be competitive, companies are now thinking of a global (worldwide) market instead of a national market. Nike and Reebok, for example, manufacture their athletic shoes in various countries throughout Asia for sale in every continent. Instead of using one international division to manage everything outside the home country, large corporations are now using matrix structures in which product units are interwoven with country or regional units. International assignments are now considered key for anyone interested in reaching top management. To emphasize the importance of globalization to strategic management, we end each chapter with a special section, *Global Issues for the 21st Century*.

As more industries become global, strategic management is becoming an increasingly important way to keep track of international developments and position the company for long-term competitive advantage. For example, Maytag Corporation purchased Hoover not so much for its vacuum cleaner business, but for its European laundry, cooking, and refrigeration business. Maytag's management realized that a company without a manufacturing presence in the European Union (EU) would be at a competitive disadvantage in the changing major home appliance industry. See the **21st Century Global Society** feature to see how regional trade associations are changing world trade.

Globalization presents a real challenge to the strategic management of business corporations. How can any one group of people in any one company keep track of all the changing technological, economic, political-legal, and sociocultural trends around the world? This is clearly impossible. More and more companies are realizing that they must shift from a vertically organized, top-down type of organization to a more horizontally managed, interactive organization. They are attempting to adapt more quickly to changing conditions by becoming learning organizations.

REGIONAL TRADE ASSOCIATIONS REPLACE NATIONAL TRADE BARRIERS

Previously known as the Common Market and the European Community, the **European Union (EU)** is the most significant trade association in the world. The goal of the EU is the complete economic integration of its 15 member countries— *Austria, Belgium, Denmark, Finland, France, Germany, Greece, Ireland, Italy, Luxembourg, The Netherlands, Portugal, Spain, Sweden,* and the *United Kingdom*—so that goods made in one part of Western Europe can move freely without ever stopping for a customs inspection. One currency, the euro, is eventually to be used throughout the region as members integrate their monetary systems. The steady elimination of barriers to free trade is providing the impetus for a series of mergers, acquisitions, and joint ventures among business corporations. The requirement of at least 60% local content to avoid tariffs is forcing many American and Asian companies to abandon exporting in favor of a strong local presence in Europe. The EU is committed to open membership negotiations with Eastern European countries before the end of the century.

Canada, the *United States,* and *Mexico* are affiliated economically under the **North American Free Trade Agreement (NAFTA)**. The goal of NAFTA is improved trade among the three member countries rather than complete economic integration. Launched in 1994, the agreement requires all three members to remove all tariffs among themselves over 15 years, but they are allowed to have their own tariff arrangements with nonmember countries. Cars and trucks must have 62.5% North American content to qualify for duty-free status. Transportation restrictions and other regulations are being significantly reduced. Some Asian and European corporations are locating operations in one of the countries to obtain access to the entire North American region. Discussions are underway to extend NAFTA farther south to include Chile.

South American countries are also working to harmonize their trading relationships with each other and to form trade associations. The establishment of the **Mercosur** (Mercosul in Portuguese) free-trade area among *Argentina, Brazil, Uruguay,* and *Paraguay* means that a manufacturing presence within these countries is becoming essential to avoid tariffs for nonmember countries. Claiming to be NAFTA's southern counterpart, Mercosur is extending free-trade agreements to Bolivia and Venezuela.

Asia has no comparable regional trade association to match the potential economic power of either NAFTA or the EU. Japan, South Korea, China, and India generally operate as independent economic powers. Nevertheless, the **Association of South East Asian Nations (ASEAN)**—composed of *Brunei, Indonesia, Malaysia, the Philippines, Singapore, Thailand,* and *Vietnam*—is attempting to link its members into a borderless economic zone. With the EU extending eastward and NAFTA extending southward to connect with Mercosur, pressure will build on the independent Asian nations to soon form an expanded version of ASEAN.

Source: D. Fishburn, ed., *The World in 1997* (London: The Economist Group, 1996).

1.3 Creating a Learning Organization

Strategic management has now evolved to the point that its primary value is in helping the organization operate successfully in a dynamic, complex environment. Inland Steel Company, for example, uses strategic planning as a tool to drive organizational change. Managers at all levels are expected to continually analyze the changing steel industry in order to create or modify strategic plans throughout the year.[7] To be competitive in dynamic environments, corporations are having to become less bureaucratic and more flexible. In stable environments such as have existed in years past, a competitive strategy simply involved defining a competitive position and then defending it. As it takes less and less time for one product or technology to replace another, companies are finding that there is no such thing as a permanent competitive advantage. Many agree with Richard D'Aveni (in his book *HyperCompetition*) that any sustainable competitive advantage lies not in doggedly following a centrally managed five-year plan, but in stringing together a series of strategic short-term thrusts (as Intel does by cutting into the sales of its own offerings with periodic introductions of new products).[8] This means that corporations must develop *strategic flexibility*—the ability to shift from one dominant strategy to another.[9]

Strategic flexibility demands a long-term commitment to the development and nurturing of critical resources. It also demands that the company become a **learning organization**—an organization skilled at creating, acquiring, and transferring knowledge, and at modifying its behavior to reflect new knowledge and insights. Learning organizations are skilled at four main activities:

- Solving problems systematically

- Experimenting with new approaches

- Learning from their own experiences and past history as well as from the experiences of others

- Transferring knowledge quickly and efficiently throughout the organization.[10]

Learning organizations avoid stability through continuous self-examination and experimentation. People at all levels, not just top management, need to be involved in strategic management—helping to scan the environment for critical information, suggesting changes to strategies and programs to take advantage of environmental shifts, and working with others to continuously improve work methods, procedures, and evaluation techniques. At Xerox, for example, all employees have been trained in small-group activities and problem-solving techniques. They are expected to use the techniques at all meetings and at all levels, with no topic being off-limits. Research indicates that organizations that are willing to experiment and able to learn from their experiences are more successful than those that do not. For example, in a study of U.S. manufacturers of diagnostic imaging equipment, the most successful firms were those that improved products sold in the United States by incorporating some of what they had learned from their manufacturing and sales experiences in other nations. The less successful firms used the foreign operations primarily as sales outlets, not as important sources of technical knowledge.[11]

1.4   *Basic Model of Strategic Management*

Strategic management consists of four basic elements:

- **environmental scanning**
- **strategy formulation**
- **strategy implementation**
- **evaluation and control**

Figure 1.1 shows simply how these elements interact; Figure 1.2 expands each of these elements and serves as the model for this book. The terms used in Figure 1.2 are explained in the following pages.

Figure 1.1
Basic Elements of the Strategic Management Process

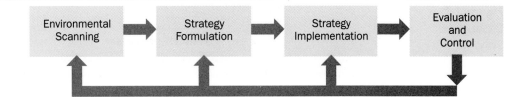

Environmental Scanning

Environmental scanning is the monitoring, evaluating, and disseminating of information from the external and internal environments to key people within the corporation. Its purpose is to identify **strategic factors**—those external and internal elements that will determine the future of the corporation. The simplest way to conduct environmental scanning is through **SWOT Analysis**. SWOT is an acronym used to describe those particular **S**trengths, **W**eaknesses, **O**pportunities, and **T**hreats that are strategic factors for a specific company. The **external environment** consists of variables (**O**pportunities and **T**hreats) that are outside the organization and not typically within the short-run control of top management. These variables form the context within which the corporation exists. Figure 1.3 depicts key environmental variables. They may be general forces and trends within the overall *societal* environment or specific factors that operate within an organization's specific *task* environment—often called its industry. ***(These external variables are defined and discussed in more detail in Chapter 3.)***

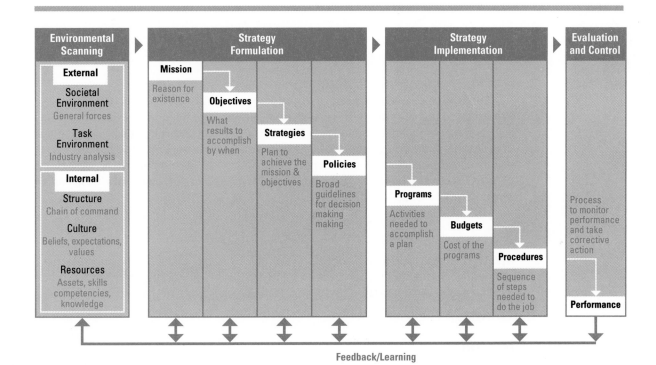

Figure 1.2
Strategic Management Model

Figure 1.3
**Environmental
Variables**

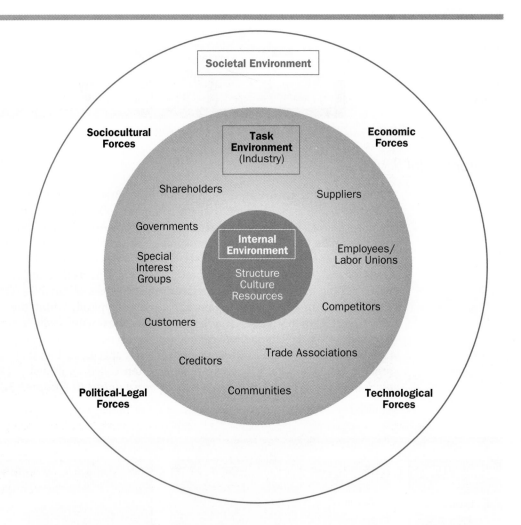

The **internal environment** of a corporation consists of variables (**S**trengths and **W**eaknesses) that are within the organization itself and are not usually within the short-run control of top management. These variables form the context in which work is done. They include the corporation's *structure, culture,* and *resources.* Key strengths form a set of *core competencies* which the corporation can use to gain competitive advantage. ***(These internal variables and core competencies are defined and discussed in more detail in Chapter 4.)***

Strategy Formulation

Strategy formulation is the development of long-range plans for the effective management of environmental opportunities and threats, in light of corporate strengths and weaknesses. It includes defining the corporate *mission,* specifying achievable *objectives,* developing *strategies,* and setting *policy* guidelines.

Mission

An organization's **mission** is the purpose or reason for the organization's existence. It tells what the company is providing to society—either a service like housecleaning or a product like automobiles. A well-conceived mission statement defines the fundamental, unique purpose that sets a company apart from other firms of its type and identifies the scope of the company's operations in terms of products (including services) offered and markets served. It may also include the firm's philosophy about how it does business and treats its employees. It puts into words not only what the company is now, but what it wants to become—management's strategic vision of the firm's future. (Some people like to consider *vision* and *mission* as two different concepts: a mission statement describes what the organization is now; a vision statement describes what the organization would like to become. We prefer to combine these ideas into a single mission statement.)[12] The mission statement promotes a sense of shared expectations in employees and communicates a public image to important stakeholder groups in the company's task environment. *It tells who we are and what we do as well as what we'd like to become.*

One example of a mission statement is that of Maytag Corporation:

> To improve the quality of home life by designing, building, marketing, and servicing the best appliances in the world.

Another classic example is that etched in bronze at Newport News Shipbuilding, unchanged since its founding in 1886:

> We shall build good ships here—at a profit if we can—at a loss if we must—but always good ships.[13]

A mission may be defined narrowly or broadly in scope. An example of a *broad* mission statement is that used by many corporations: *Serve the best interests of shareowners, customers, and employees.* A broadly defined mission statement such as this keeps the company from restricting itself to one field or product line, but it fails to clearly identify either what it makes or which product/markets it plans to emphasize. Because this broad statement is so general, a *narrow* mission statement, such as the preceding one by Maytag emphasizing appliances, is more useful. A narrow mission very clearly states the organization's primary business, but it may limit the scope of the firm's activities in terms of product or service offered, the technology used, and the market served.

Objectives

Objectives are the end results of planned activity. They state *what* is to be accomplished by *when* and should be *quantified* if possible. The achievement of corporate objectives should result in the fulfillment of a corporation's mission. Minnesota Mining & Manufacturing (3M), for example, has set very specific financial objectives for itself:

1. To achieve 10% annual growth in earnings per share.

2. To achieve 20%–25% return on equity.

3. To achieve 27% return on capital employed.

The term "goal" is often used interchangeably with the term "objective." In this book, we prefer to differentiate the two terms. In contrast to an objective, we consider a **goal** as an open-ended statement of what one wants to accomplish with no quantification of what is to be achieved and no time criteria for completion. For example, a simple statement of "increased profitability" is thus a goal, not an objective, because it does not state how much profit the firm wants to make the next year.

Some of the areas in which a corporation might establish its goals and objectives are:

- Profitability (net profits)
- Efficiency (low costs, etc.)
- Growth (increase in total assets, sales, etc.)
- Shareholder wealth (dividends plus stock price appreciation)
- Utilization of resources (ROE or ROI)
- Reputation (being considered a "top" firm)
- Contributions to employees (employment security, wages, diversity)
- Contributions to society (taxes paid, participation in charities, providing a needed product or service)
- Market leadership (market share)
- Technological leadership (innovations, creativity)
- Survival (avoiding bankruptcy)
- Personal needs of top management (using the firm for personal purposes, such as providing jobs for relatives)

Strategies

A **strategy** of a corporation forms a comprehensive master plan stating how the corporation will achieve its mission and objectives. It maximizes competitive advantage and minimizes competitive disadvantage. For example, after Rockwell International Corporation realized that it could no longer achieve its objectives by continuing with its strategy of diversification into multiple lines of businesses, it sold its aerospace and defense units to Boeing. Rockwell instead chose to concentrate on commercial electronics, an area that management felt had greater opportunities for growth.

The typical business firm usually considers three types of strategy: corporate, business, and functional.

1. **Corporate strategy** describes a company's overall direction in terms of its general attitude toward growth and the management of its various businesses and product lines. Corporate strategies typically fit within the three main categories of *stability*, *growth*, and *retrenchment*. For example, Maytag Corporation followed a corporate growth strategy by acquiring other appliance companies in order to have a full line of major home appliances.

2. **Business strategy** usually occurs at the business unit or product level, and it emphasizes improvement of the competitive position of a corporation's products or services in the specific industry or market segment served by that business unit. Business strategies may fit within the two overall categories of *competitive* or *cooperative* strategies. For example, Maytag Corporation uses a differentiation competitive strategy that emphasizes quality for its Maytag brand appliances, but it uses a low-cost competitive strategy for its Magic Chef brand appliances so that it can sell these appliances to cost-conscious home builders.

3. **Functional strategy** is the approach taken by a functional area to achieve corporate and business unit objectives and strategies by maximizing resource productivity. It is concerned with developing and nurturing a *distinctive competence* to provide a company or business unit with a competitive advantage. Examples of functional

Figure 1.4
Hierarchy of Strategy

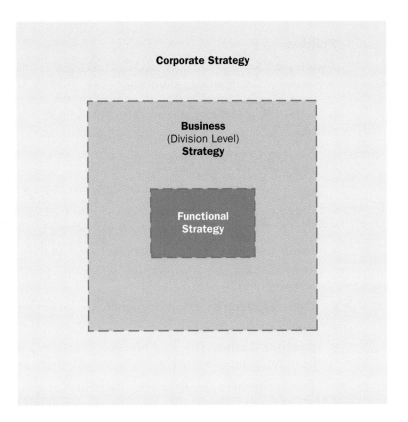

strategies within an R&D department are *technological followership* (imitate the products of other companies) and *technological leadership* (pioneer an innovation). To become more efficient throughout the corporation, Maytag Corporation is converting from a manufacturing strategy of making different types of home appliances under the same brand name in one plant to a more cost-effective strategy of making only one type of appliance (for example, dishwashers) for many brands in a very large plant. Another example of a functional strategy is America Online's marketing strategy of saturating the entire market with a low-priced product (as contrasted with selling a higher priced product to a particular market segment).

Business firms use all three types of strategy simultaneously. A **hierarchy of strategy** is the grouping of strategy types by level in the organization. This hierarchy of strategy is a nesting of one strategy within another so that they complement and support one another. (See Figure 1.4.) Functional strategies support business strategies, which, in turn, support the corporate strategy(ies).

Just as many firms often have no formally stated objectives, many firms have unstated, incremental, or intuitive strategies that have never been articulated or analyzed. Often the only way to spot a corporation's implicit strategies is to look not at what management says, but at what it does. Implicit strategies can be derived from corporate policies, programs approved (and disapproved), and authorized budgets. Programs and divisions favored by budget increases and staffed by managers who are considered to be on the fast promotion track reveal where the corporation is putting its money and its energy.

Policies

A **policy** is a *broad guideline* for decision making that links the formulation of strategy with its implementation. Companies use policies to make sure that employees throughout the firm make decisions and take actions that support the corporation's mission, objectives, and strategies. For example, consider the following company policies:

- **Maytag Company:** Maytag will not approve any cost reduction proposal if it reduces product quality in any way. (This policy supports Maytag's strategy for Maytag brands to compete on quality rather than on price.)

- **3M:** Researchers should spend 15% of their time working on something other than their primary project. (This supports 3M's strong product development strategy.)

- **Intel:** Cannibalize your product line (undercut the sales of your current products) with better products before a competitor does it to you. (This supports Intel's objective of market leadership.)

- **General Electric:** GE must be number one or two wherever it competes. (This supports GE's objective to be number one in market capitalization.)

- **America Online:** The company could have used a policy stating that a new marketing program would not be implemented until proper support was in place.

Policies like these provide clear guidance to managers throughout the organization. **(Strategy formulation is discussed in greater detail in Chapters 5, 6, and 7.)**

Strategy Implementation

Strategy implementation is the process by which strategies and policies are put into action through the development of *programs*, *budgets*, and *procedures*. This process might involve changes within the overall culture, structure, and/or management system of the entire organization. Except when such drastic corporatewide changes are needed, however, the implementation of strategy is typically conducted by middle and lower level managers with review by top management. Sometimes referred to as operational planning, strategy implementation often involves day-to-day decisions in resource allocation.

Programs

A **program** is a statement of the activities or steps needed to accomplish a single-use plan. It makes the strategy action-oriented. It may involve restructuring the corporation, changing the company's internal culture, or beginning a new research effort. For example, consider Intel Corporation, the microprocessor manufacturer. Realizing that Intel would not be able to continue its corporate growth strategy without the continuous development of new generations of microprocessors, management decided to implement a series of programs:

- They formed an alliance with Hewlett-Packard to develop the successor to the Pentium Pro chip.

- They assembled an elite team of engineers and scientists to do long-term, original research into computer chip design.

Another example is AMR's SABRE Group (the computer reservations unit developed by American Airlines), which forged alliances with Microsoft and Time Warner to start selling airline tickets directly to customers on the Internet.

Keep in mind, however, America Online's experience. Be careful of introducing a new program without ensuring its fit with the organization's overall strategies and objectives as well as its impact on the rest of the firm.

Budgets

A **budget** is a statement of a corporation's programs in terms of dollars. Used in planning and control, a budget lists the detailed cost of each program. Many corporations demand a certain percentage return on investment, often called a "hurdle rate," before management will approve a new program. This ensures that the new program will significantly add to the corporation's profit performance and thus build shareholder value. The budget thus not only serves as a detailed plan of the new strategy in action, it also specifies through pro forma financial statements the expected impact on the firm's financial future.

For example, to become a significant global competitor in cars and trucks, the Daewoo Group of Korea budgeted $11 billion over the four-year period from 1996 to 2000 to quadruple its annual production of automobiles to two million vehicles (more than Chrysler Corporation produced). In addition to spending on its new plants in the Czech Republic and Romania, Daewoo budgeted $300 million and $650 million, respectively, to build new plants in Poland and Uzbekistan as part of its European expansion program.[14]

Procedures

Procedures, sometimes termed Standard Operating Procedures (SOP), are a system of sequential steps or techniques that describe in detail how a particular task or job is to be done. They typically detail the various activities that must be carried out in order to complete the corporation's program. For example, Delta Airlines used various procedures to cut costs. To reduce the number of employees, Delta asked technical experts in hydraulics, metal working, avionics, and other trades to design cross-functional work teams. To cut marketing expenses, Delta instituted a cap on travel agent commissions and emphasized sales to bigger accounts. Delta also changed its purchasing and food service procedures. See the **Strategy in a Changing World** feature to see how these procedures supported Delta's objectives and strategy. *(Strategy implementation is discussed in more detail in Chapters 8 and 9.)*

Evaluation and Control

Evaluation and control is the process in which corporate activities and performance results are monitored so that actual performance can be compared with desired performance. Managers at all levels use the resulting information to take corrective action and resolve problems. Although evaluation and control is the final major element of strategic management, it also can pinpoint weaknesses in previously implemented strategic plans and thus stimulate the entire process to begin again.

For evaluation and control to be effective, managers must obtain clear, prompt, and unbiased information from the people below them in the corporation's hierarchy. Using this information, managers compare what is actually happening with what was

STRATEGIC MANAGEMENT AT DELTA AIRLINES

Delta Airlines initiated an aggressive cost-cutting program in April 1994 called "Leadership 7.5" in order to become profitable in a highly competitive industry. Because of deregulation, new competitors, like Southwest Airlines, were able to introduce low-cost strategies to offer extremely cheap fares (and minimal service) to gain market share—resulting in half-filled flights for full-service companies like Delta Airlines. Delta had not turned a profit since 1990 and chose to institute a turnaround strategy (a type of retrenchment corporate strategy) to achieve an objective of reducing annual expenses by $2.1 billion by June 1997 (and make a profit). To fulfill this strategy, management had to change many of the policies for which the company had long prided itself: lifetime employment, high pay, lush in-flight services, and routes to every destination. The "Leadership 7.5" program attempted to reduce the amount of money it spent on each airplane seat from 9.76¢ in 1994 to 7.5¢ in 1997 per flight mile.

The company budgeted $400 million in savings from marketing, $300 million from layoffs,

and $310 million from onboard services. To reduce the number of employees, technical experts in hydraulics, metal-working, avionics, and other trades were asked to design cross-functional work teams. Marketing expenses were cut by instituting a cap on travel agent commissions and emphasizing sales to bigger accounts. In addition to layoffs, purchasing and food service procedures were changed.

The success of Delta Airlines's turnaround strategy can be evaluated by measuring the amount the firm was spending on each airplane seat per flight mile. Before the "Leadership 7.5" program was instituted in April 1994, the cost per seat was 9.76¢. By the end of 1995, it was down to 8.4¢. The program seemed to be working, but Delta needed to reach 7.5¢ by June 1997 to achieve the corporate objectives of reducing annual expenses by $2.1 billion and make a profit.

Source: D. Greising, "It Hurts So Good at Delta," *Business Week* (December 11, 1995), pp. 106–107.

originally planned in the formulation stage. For example, the success of Delta Airlines's turnaround strategy was evaluated in terms of the amount spent on each airplane seat per mile of flight. Before the "Leadership 7.5" program was instituted in April 1994, the cost per seat was 9.76¢. By the end of 1995, it was down to 8.4¢. The program seemed to be working, but it needed to reach 7.5¢ by June 1997 to achieve the company's objective of reducing annual expenses by $2.1 billion.

The evaluation and control of performance completes the strategic management model. Based on performance results, management may need to make adjustments in its strategy formulation, in implementation, or in both. **(*Evaluation and control is discussed in more detail in Chapter 10.*)**

Feedback/Learning Process

Note that the strategic management model depicted in Figure 1.2 includes a feedback/learning process. Arrows are drawn coming out of each part of the model and taking information to each of the previous parts of the model. As a firm or business unit develops strategies, programs, and the like, it often must go back to revise or correct decisions made earlier in the model. For example, poor performance (as measured in evaluation and control) usually indicates that something has gone wrong with either strategy formulation or implementation. It could also mean that a key variable, such as a new competitor, was ignored during environmental scanning and assessment.

1.5 Initiation of Strategy: Triggering Events

After much research, Henry Mintzberg discovered that strategy formulation is typically not a regular, continuous process: "It is most often an irregular, discontinuous process, proceeding in fits and starts. There are periods of stability in strategy development, but also there are periods of flux, of groping, of piecemeal change, and of global change."[15] This view of strategy formulation as an irregular process can be explained by the very human tendency to continue on a particular course of action until something goes wrong or a person is forced to question his or her actions. This period of "strategic drift" may simply result from inertia on the part of the organization or may simply reflect management's belief that the current strategy is still appropriate and needs only some "fine-tuning."

Most large organizations tend to follow a particular strategic orientation for about 15 to 20 years before making a significant change in direction.[16] After this rather long period of fine-tuning an existing strategy, some sort of shock to the system is needed to motivate management to seriously reassess the corporation's situation.

A **triggering event** is something that acts as a stimulus for a change in strategy. Some possible triggering events are:

- **New CEO.** By asking a series of embarrassing questions, the new CEO cuts through the veil of complacency and forces people to question the very reason for the corporation's existence.

- **External intervention.** The firm's bank suddenly refuses to approve a new loan or suddenly demands payment in full on an old one.

- **Threat of a change in ownership.** Another firm may initiate a takeover by buying the company's common stock.

- **Performance gap.** A performance gap exists when performance does not meet expectations. Sales and profits either are no longer increasing or may even be falling.

Iomega Corporation is an example of one company in which a triggering event forced its management to radically rethink what it was doing. See the **Strategy in a Changing World** feature to show how one simple question from the new CEO stimulated a change in strategy at Iomega.

1.6 Strategic Decision Making

The distinguishing characteristic of strategic management is its emphasis on strategic decision making. As organizations grow larger and more complex with more uncertain environments, decisions become increasingly complicated and difficult to make. This book proposes a strategic decision-making framework that can help people make these decisions regardless of their level and function in the corporation.

STRATEGY IN A CHANGING WORLD

TRIGGERING EVENT AT IOMEGA CORPORATION

Iomega Corporation is a successful manufacturer of computer storage devices. Its most popular line of products is the Zip drive, a book-sized, portable storage device that uses a new kind of floppy disk with a capacity of 100 megabytes—equal to about 70 standard floppy disks. Earning $8.5 million on $326.2 million of sales in 1995, the company's stock price escalated from $5 per share in 1995 to $112 (after adjustment for a stock split) in April 1996.

Until Kim Edwards took over as Iomega's CEO in 1993, the company had been an unglamorous provider of niche computer storage products. Soon after he joined the company, Edwards asked his team to name some potential new markets for the company's products. After a long pause, one person said, "The Air Force really likes our Bernoulli Box." Thought Edwards, "Geez, this isn't good." The Bernoulli Box was a powerful storage device, but it was so expensive and specialized that only a few buyers, such as the military, had any use for it. "I realized the company had no clue that there was a mass market out there, waiting for a fun product," commented Edwards. Soon Iomega's engineers developed a series of products to appeal to this mass market: the Zip drive, the Ditto tape backup system, and the Jaz removable hard drive, which holds one gigabyte of data—ten times as much as the Zip.

Source: L. Gomes, "Iomega Adds Zip to Ho-Hum Business of Floppy Disks," *Wall Street Journal* (June 17, 1996), p. B6.

What Makes a Decision Strategic

Unlike many other decisions, **strategic decisions** deal with the long-run future of the entire organization and have three characteristics:

1. **Rare:** Strategic decisions are unusual and typically have no precedent to follow.

2. **Consequential:** Strategic decisions commit substantial resources and demand a great deal of commitment from people at all levels.

3. **Directive:** Strategic decisions set precedents for lesser decisions and future actions throughout the organization.[17]

Mintzberg's Modes of Strategic Decision Making

Some strategic decisions are made in a flash by one person (often an entrepreneur or a powerful chief executive officer) who has a brilliant insight and is quickly able to convince others to adopt his or her idea. Other strategic decisions seem to develop out of a series of small incremental choices that over time push the organization more in one direction than another. According to Henry Mintzberg, the most typical approaches, or modes, of strategic decision making are:[18]

- **Entrepreneurial mode.** Strategy is made by one powerful individual. The focus is on opportunities; problems are secondary. Strategy is guided by the founder's own vision of direction and is exemplified by large, bold decisions. The dominant goal is growth of the corporation. America Online, founded by Steve Case, is an example of this mode of strategic decision making. The company reflects his vision of the Internet provider industry. Although AOL's clear growth strategy is certainly an advantage of the entrepreneurial mode, its tendency to market its products before the company is able to support them is a significant disadvantage.

- **Adaptive mode.** Sometimes referred to as "muddling through," this decision-making mode is characterized by reactive solutions to existing problems, rather than a proactive search for new opportunities. Much bargaining goes on concerning priorities of objectives. Strategy is fragmented and is developed to move the corporation forward incrementally. This mode is typical of most universities, many large hospitals, a large number of governmental agencies, and a surprising number of large corporations. Encyclopaedia Britannica, Inc., operated successfully for many years in this mode, but continued to rely on the door-to-door selling of its prestigious books long after dual career couples made this marketing approach obsolete. Only after it was acquired in 1996 did the company change its marketing strategy to television advertising and Internet marketing. *(See http:// www.eb.com.)* It now offers CD-ROMs in addition to the printed volumes.

- **Planning mode.** This decision-making mode involves the systematic gathering of appropriate information for situation analysis, the generation of feasible alternative strategies, and the rational selection of the most appropriate strategy. It includes both the proactive search for new opportunities and the reactive solution of existing problems. The J. C. Penney Company is an example of the planning mode. After a careful study of shopping trends in the 1980s, the retailing company discontinued its sales of paint, hardware, major appliances, automotive items, and electronics to concentrate on apparel and home furnishings. Declining personal incomes and greater uncertainty in the 1990s led Penney's to emphasize private brands. This new merchandising strategy allowed the company to offer the high quality of goods often found in better department stores at a competitively lower price.[19]

In some instances, a corporation might follow a fourth approach called **logical incrementalism,** which is a synthesis of the planning, adaptive, and, to a lesser extent, the entrepreneurial modes of strategic decision making. As described by Quinn, top management might have a reasonably clear idea of the corporation's mission and objectives, but, in its development of strategies, it chooses to use "an interactive process in which the organization probes the future, experiments and learns from a series of partial (incremental) commitments rather than through global formulations of total strategies."[20] This approach appears to be useful when the environment is changing rapidly and when it is important to build consensus and develop needed resources before committing the entire corporation to a specific strategy.

Strategic Decision-Making Process: Aid to Better Decisions

Good arguments can be made for using either the entrepreneurial or adaptive modes (or logical incrementalism) in certain situations. This book proposes, however, that in most situations the planning mode, which includes the basic elements of the strategic management process, is a more rational and thus better way of making strategic decisions. The planning mode is not only more analytical and less political than are the other modes, but it is also more appropriate for dealing with complex, changing environments.[21] We therefore propose the following eight-step **strategic decision-making process** to improve the making of strategic decisions (see Figure 1.5):

Figure 1.5
Strategic Decision-Making Process

Source: T. L. Wheelen and J. D. Hunger, "Strategic Decision-Making Process," Copyright © 1994 and 1997 by Wheelen and Hunger Associates. Reprinted by permission.

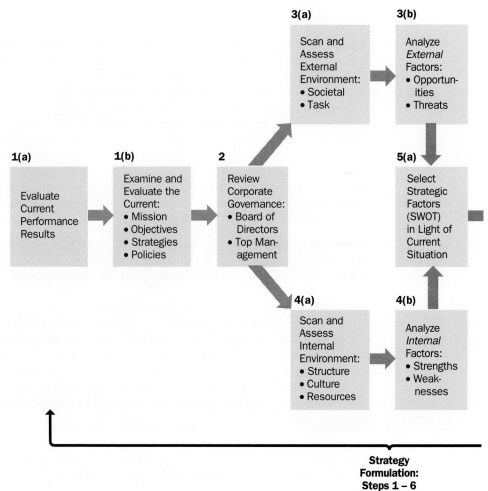

1. **Evaluate current performance results** in terms of (a) return on investment, profitability, and so forth, and (b) the current mission, objectives, strategies, and policies.

2. **Review corporate governance,** that is, the performance of the firm's board of directors and top management.

3. **Scan and assess the external environment** to determine the strategic factors that pose **O**pportunities and **T**hreats.

4. **Scan and assess the internal corporate environment** to determine the strategic factors that are **S**trengths (especially core competencies) and **W**eaknesses.

5. **Analyze strategic (SWOT) factors** to (a) pinpoint problem areas, and (b) review and revise the corporate mission and objectives as necessary.

6. **Generate, evaluate, and select the best alternative strategy** in light of the analysis conducted in *Step 5*.

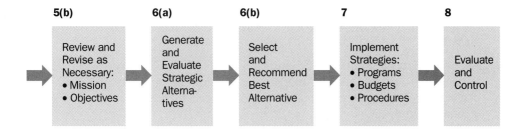

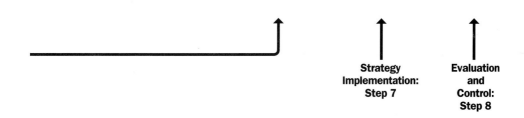

7. Implement selected strategies via programs, budgets, and procedures.

8. Evaluate implemented strategies via feedback systems, and the control of activities to ensure their minimum deviation from plans.

This rational approach to strategic decision making has been used successfully by corporations like Warner-Lambert; Dayton Hudson; Avon Products; Bechtel Group, Inc.; and Taisei Corporation.

● **1.7** *Global Issues for the 21st Century*

- The **21st Century Global Society** feature in this chapter described how nations are forming regional trading associations. These associations act to increase trade among member nations, but make it increasingly difficult to trade between regional blocs. This has significant implications for corporations operating within these regions. Firms need to decide if they will do better as a regional or as a global competitor.

- It is likely that the world will eventually be composed of three dominant trading blocs: one each in Europe, Asia, and the Americas. Because of local content regulations, multinational corporations will need to have meaningful manufacturing and marketing activities in every trading bloc, or else be relegated to just one part of the world.

- Globalization creates opportunities, but it also poses threats to companies that are not able to adapt quickly enough to a more complex and changing environment. As a result, firms are attempting to adopt the characteristics of a learning organization. Thus employees at all levels of the organization will need to have greater access to the information necessary to evaluate company performance and to suggest strategic changes.

- As more people at all levels and units are involved in strategic decision making, there will be a greater need for more access to information, but greater difficulty in dealing with it. Too much information could cause chaos. Coordination may become increasingly difficult.

- Increasing pressure on organizations for a quick response to changing conditions may make it difficult for corporations to engage in the planning mode of strategic management. Even with its faults, the entrepreneurial mode is exceptionally agile.

Projections for the 21st Century

- From 1994 to 2010, the world economy will grow from $26 trillion to $48 trillion.

- From 1994 to 2010, world trade will increase from $4 trillion to $16.6 trillion.[22]

Discussion Questions

1. Why has strategic management become so important to today's corporations?

2. How does strategic management typically evolve in a corporation?

3. What is a learning organization? Is this approach to strategic management better than the more traditional top-down approach?

4. Why are strategic decisions different from other kinds of decisions?

5. When is the planning mode of strategic decision making superior to the entrepreneurial and adaptive modes?

Key Terms

adaptive mode (p. 19)
budget (p. 15)
business policy (p. 3)

business strategy (p. 12)
corporate strategy (p. 12)
entrepreneurial mode (p. 18)

environmental scanning (p. 9)
evaluation and control (p. 15)
external environment (p. 9)

functional strategy (p. 12)
globalization (p. 6)
goals (p. 11)
hierarchy of strategy (p. 13)
internal environment (p. 10)
learning organization (p. 8)
logical incrementalism (p. 19)
mission (p. 10)
objectives (p. 11)

performance gap (p. 17)
phases of strategic management (p. 3)
planning mode (p. 19)
policy (p. 14)
procedures (p. 15)
program (p. 14)
strategic decision-making process (p. 19)

strategic decisions (p. 18)
strategic factors (p. 9)
strategic management (p. 3)
strategy (p. 12)
strategy formulation (p. 10)
strategy implementation (p. 8)
SWOT Analysis (p. 9)
triggering event (p. 17)

Strategic Practice Exercise

Mission statements vary widely from one company to another. Why is one mission statement better than another? Develop some criteria for evaluating a mission statement. Then, do one or both of the following exercises:

1. Evaluate the mission statement of Celestial Seasonings:

   Our mission is to grow and dominate the U.S. specialty tea market by exceeding consumer expectations with the best tasting, 100% natural hot and iced teas, packaged with Celestial art and philosophy, creating the most valued tea experience. Through leadership, innovation, focus, and teamwork, we are dedicated to continuously improving value to our consumers, customers, employees, and stakeholders with a quality-first organization.[23]

2. Find the mission statements of three different organizations, which can be business or not-for-profit. (*Hint:* Check annual reports. They may be in the library or on a company's web page.) Which mission statement is best? Why?

Notes

1. A. Barrett, P. Eng, and K. Rebello, "For $19.95 a Month, Unlimited Headaches for AOL," *Business Week* (January 27, 1997), p. 35; T. Petzinger, Jr., "'Gunning for Growth,' AOL's Steve Case Shot Himself in the Foot," *Wall Street Journal* (January 24, 1997), p. B1; L. Zuckerman, "America Online Moves to Placate Angry Users," (Ames, Iowa) *Daily Tribune* (January 18, 1997), p. B4.

2. F. W. Gluck, S. P. Kaufman, and A. S. Walleck, "The Four Phases of Strategic Management," *Journal of Business Strategy* (Winter 1982), pp. 9–21.

3. C. C. Miller, and L. B. Cardinal, "Strategic Planning and Firm Performance: A Synthesis of More Than Two Decades of Research," *Academy of Management Journal* (December 1994), pp. 1649–1665; P. Pekar, Jr., and S. Abraham, "Is Strategic Management Living Up To Its Promise?" *Long Range Planning* (October 1995), pp. 32–44.

4. K. G. Smith, and C. M. Grimm, "Environmental Variation, Strategic Change and Firm Performance: A Study of Railroad Deregulation," *Strategic Management Journal* (July-August 1987), pp. 363–376.

5. I. Wilson, "Strategic Planning Isn't Dead—It Changed," *Long Range Planning* (August 1994), p. 20.

6. M. A. Lyles, I. S. Baird, J. B. Orris, and D. F. Kuratko, "Formalized Planning in Small Business: Increasing Strategic Choices," *Journal of Small Business Management* (April 1993), pp. 38–50.

7. C. Gebelein, "Strategic Planning: the Engine of Change," *Planning Review* (September/October 1993), pp. 17–19.

8. R. A. D'Aveni, *HyperCompetition* (New York: Free Press, 1994). HyperCompetition is discussed in more detail in Chapter 3.

9. R. S. M. Lau, "Strategic Flexibility: A New Reality for World-Class Manufacturing," *SAM Advanced Management Journal* (Spring 1996), pp. 11–15.

10. D. A. Garvin, "Building a Learning Organization," *Harvard Business Review* (July/August 1993), p. 80. See also P. M. Senge, *The Fifth Discipline: The Art and Practice of the Learning Organization* (New York: Doubleday, 1990).

11. W. Mitchell, J. M. Shaver, and B. Yeung, "Getting There in a Global Industry: Impacts on Performance of Changing International Presence," *Strategic Management Journal* (September 1992), pp. 419–432.

12. See A. Campbell, and S. Yeung, "Brief Case: Mission, Vision, and Strategic Intent," *Long Range Planning* (August

1991), pp. 145-147; S. Cummings and J. Davies, "Mission, Vision, Fusion," *Long Range Planning* (December 1994), pp. 147–150.

13. J. Cosco, "Down To the Sea in Ships," *Journal of Business Strategy* (November/December 1995), p. 48.

14. L. Kraar, "Daewoo's Daring Drive Into Europe," *Fortune* (May 13, 1996), pp. 145–152.

15. H. Mintzberg, "Planning on the Left Side and Managing on the Right," *Harvard Business Review* (July-August 1976), p. 56.

16. This phenomenon of "punctuated equilibrium" describes corporations as evolving through relatively long periods of stability (equilibrium periods) punctuated by relatively short bursts of fundamental change (revolutionary periods). See E. Romanelli and M. L. Tushman, "Organizational Transformation as Punctuated Equilibrium: An Empirical Test," (October 1994), pp. 1141–1166.

17. D. J. Hickson, R. J. Butler, D. Cray, G. R. Mallory, and D. C. Wilson, *Top Decisions: Strategic Decision-Making in Organizations* (San Francisco: Jossey-Bass, 1986), pp. 26–42.

18. H. Mintzberg, "Strategy-Making in Three Modes," *California Management Review* (Winter 1973), pp. 44–53.

19. W. H. Howell, "Leading Strategic Change: Something Old, Something New." *Planning Review* (September/October 1995), pp. 10–12.

20. J. B. Quinn, *Strategies for Change: Logical Incrementalism* (Homewood, Ill.: Irwin, 1980), p. 58.

21. R. L. Priem, A. M. A. Rasheed, and A. G. Kotulic, "Rationality in Strategic Decision Processes, Environmental Dynamism and Firm Performance," *Journal of Management*, Vol. 21, No. 5 (1995), pp. 913–929; J. W. Dean, Jr. and M. P. Sharfman, "Does Decision Process Matter? A Study of Strategic Decision-Making Effectiveness," *Academy of Management Journal* (April 1996), pp. 368–396.

22. J. Warner, "21st Century Capitalism: Snapshot of the Next Century," *Business Week* (November 18, 1994), p. 194.

23. P. Jones and L. Kahaner, *Say It & Live It: 50 Corporate Mission Statements That Hit the Mark* (New York: Currency Doubleday, 1995), p. 53.

Chapter 2

Corporate Governance and Social Responsibility

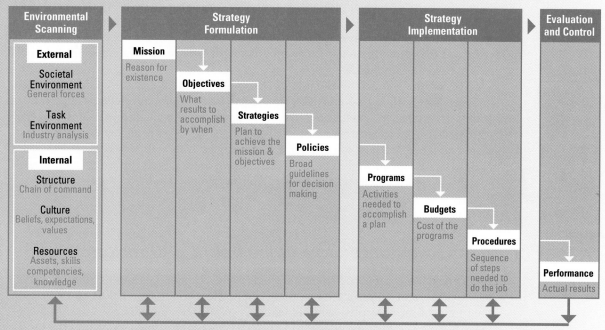

At one time, the Eastman Kodak Company had been one of the most respected companies in the United States and perhaps the world. It was known for its excellent product quality and reliability. From 1983 to 1993, the company fell, however, from the top 10% to the bottom 18% of admired companies. Industry analysts portrayed the firm as bloated, slow-moving, myopic, and incapable of dealing effectively with its falling share of the photographic film market. Top management made strategic decisions based on protecting current products instead of developing future ones. For example, even though Kodak had been one of the first companies to develop a camcorder, management decided not to introduce it because it was costly and might detract from the current sales of its amateur film products. Profits were consistently below expectations. The company incurred billions of dollars in repeated one-time charges as it undertook incremental efforts to streamline and improve its performance.

Kodak's board of directors was extremely concerned with the inability of Chief Executive Officer Kay Whitmore to turn the company around. Whitmore had joined Kodak in 1957 as an engineer and epitomized the company's cautious home-grown management. On August 6, 1993, Kodak's board of directors, led by a group of outside directors, fired Whitmore. Instead of looking internally for a replacement, the board offered the CEO position to George Fisher, then Chairman and CEO of Motorola, Inc. Motorola had long been regarded a well-managed company, known for its dedication to hard work and quality. The board expected Fisher to deliver fast and deep cost cuts. Just four months later, however, Fisher stated that cost cutting alone would not be the answer. He proposed to commit the entire company to growth opportunities in imaging and to divest non-core businesses.[1]

This example illustrates the impact of top management and the board of directors on a firm's performance. Kodak's top managers had traditionally been promoted from within. They became so dedicated to the company's past in chemical imaging that they were unable to perceive a future in electronic imaging. As strategic managers, management had failed to adjust to a changing environment. Although slow to react, the board of directors finally moved to bring in some new blood. Would this be enough to save Kodak and return it to its past position of industry dominance?

2.1 Corporate Governance: Role of the Board of Directors

A **corporation** is a mechanism established to allow different parties to contribute capital, expertise, and labor, for their mutual benefit. The investor/shareholder participates in the profits of the enterprise without taking responsibility for the operations. Management runs the company without being responsible for personally providing the funds. To make this possible, laws have been passed so that shareholders have limited liability and, correspondingly, limited involvement in a corporation's activities. That involvement does include, however, the right to elect directors who have a legal duty to represent the shareholders and protect their interests. As representatives of the shareholders, directors have both the authority and the responsibility to establish basic corporate policies and to ensure that they are followed.[2]

The board of directors has, therefore, an obligation to approve all decisions that might affect the long-run performance of the corporation. This means that the corporation is fundamentally governed by the *board of directors* overseeing *top management*, with the concurrence of the *shareholder*. The term **corporate governance** refers to the relationship among these three groups in determining the direction and performance of the corporation.[3]

Over the past decade, shareholders and various interest groups have seriously questioned the role of the board of directors in corporations. They are concerned that outside board members often lack sufficient knowledge, involvement, and enthusiasm to do an adequate job of providing guidance to top management. For example, when officials of the California Public Employees' Retirement System—a key shareholder group—criticized IBM's board of directors in the early 1990s for not doing more to prevent the company's nosedive in earnings, the four outside members of the board's executive committee admitted that they did not know enough about the company's business to properly evaluate management. Like IBM's top management, they had missed the trend away from mainframe computers to personal computers. Board members actually admitted in the meeting that none of them felt comfortable using a personal computer. According to one director, "Not one of us has a PC in our home or office."[4]

The general public has not only become more aware and more critical of many boards' apparent lack of responsibility for corporate activities, it has begun to push government to demand accountability. As a result, the board as a rubber stamp of the CEO or as a bastion of the "old-boy" selection system is being replaced by more active, more professional boards.

Responsibilities of the Board

Laws and standards defining the responsibilities of boards of directors vary from country to country. For example, board members in Ontario, Canada, face more than 100 provincial and federal laws governing director liability. The United States, however, has no clear national standards or federal laws. Specific requirements of directors vary, depending on the state in which the corporate charter is issued. There is, nevertheless, a developing worldwide consensus concerning the major responsibilities of a board. Interviews with 200 directors from eight countries (Canada, France, Germany, Finland, Switzerland, the Netherlands, United Kingdom, and Venezuela) revealed strong agreement on the following five **board of director responsibilities,** listed in order of importance:

1. Setting corporate strategy, overall direction, mission or vision

2. Hiring and firing the CEO and top management

3. Controlling, monitoring, or supervising top management

4. Reviewing and approving the use of resources

5. Caring for shareholder interests[5]

Directors in the United States must make certain, in addition to the duties just listed, that the corporation is managed in accordance with the laws of the state in which it is incorporated. They must also ensure management's adherence to laws and regulations, such as those dealing with the issuance of securities, insider trading, and other conflict-of-interest situations. They must also be aware of the needs and demands of constituent groups so that they can achieve a judicious balance among the interests of these diverse groups while ensuring the continued functioning of the corporation.

In a legal sense, the board is required to direct the affairs of the corporation but not to manage them. It is charged by law to act with **due care,** or *due diligence*. If a director or the board as a whole fails to act with due care and, as a result, the corporation is in some way harmed, the careless director or directors can be held personally liable for the harm done. This is no small concern given that a recent survey of outside directors revealed that more than 40% have been named as part of a lawsuit against the corporation.[6]

Role of the Board in Strategic Management

How does a board of directors fulfill these many responsibilities? The **role of the board of directors in strategic management** is to carry out three basic tasks:

- **Monitor.** By acting through its committees, a board can keep abreast of developments inside and outside the corporation, bringing to management's attention developments it might have overlooked. A board should at least carry out this task.

- **Evaluate and influence.** A board can examine management's proposals, decisions, and actions; agree or disagree with them; give advice and offer suggestions; outline alternatives. More active boards perform this task in addition to the monitoring one.

- **Initiate and determine.** A board can delineate a corporation's mission and specify strategic options to its management. Only the most active boards take on this task in addition to the two previous ones.

Board of Directors Continuum

A board of directors is involved in strategic management to the extent that it carries out the three tasks of monitoring, evaluating and influencing, and initiating and determining. The **board of directors continuum** shown in Figure 2.1 shows the possible degree of involvement (from low to high) in the strategic management process. As types, boards can range from *phantom boards* with no real involvement to *catalyst boards* with a very high degree of involvement. Research does suggest that active board involvement in strategic management is positively related to corporate financial performance.[7]

Highly involved boards tend to be very active. They take their tasks of monitoring, evaluating, and influencing, plus initiating and determining very seriously; they provide advice when necessary and keep management alert. As depicted in Figure 2.1, their heavy involvement in the strategic management process places them in the active participation or even catalyst positions. At Zenith Electronics Corporation, for example, the board's executive committee of three outsiders meets monthly with Chief Executive Jerry Pearlman to discuss business issues. The board created an oversight system to track 20 performance measures. The CEO must explain to the board any deviation from the corporate plan in any of the variables. The board also linked all top management bonuses exclusively to Zenith's financial performance.[8] Other corporations with actively participating boards are Mead Corporation, Rolm and Haas, Whirlpool, Westinghouse, the Mallinckrodt Group, Dayton-Hudson, and General Motors.

As a board becomes less involved in the affairs of the corporation, it moves farther to the left on the continuum (see Figure 2.1). On the far left are passive phantom or rubber stamp boards that typically never initiate or determine strategy unless a crisis occurs. In these situations, the CEO also serves as Chairman of the Board, personally nominates all directors, and works to keep board members under his or her control by giving them the "mushroom treatment"—*throw manure on them and keep them in the dark!*

Generally, the smaller the corporation, the less active is its board of directors. In an entrepreneurial venture, for example, the privately-held corporation may be 100% owned by the founders—who also manage the company. In this case, there is no need for an active board to protect the interests of the owner-manager shareholders—the interests of the owners and the managers are identical. In this instance, a board is really unnecessary and only meets to satisfy legal requirements. If stock is sold to outsiders to finance growth, however, the board becomes more active. Key investors want seats on the board so they can oversee their investment. To the extent that they still control most of the stock, however, the founders dominate the board. Friends, family members, and key shareholders usually become members, but the board acts primarily as a rubber stamp for any proposals put forward by the owner-managers. This cozy relationship between the board and management should change, however, when the corporation goes public and stock is more widely dispersed. The founders, who are still acting as management, may sometimes make decisions that conflict with the needs of the other share-

Figure 2.1
Board of Directors Continuum

Source: T. L. Wheelen and J. D. Hunger, "Board of Directors Continuum." Copyright © 1994 by Wheelen and Hunger Associates. Reprinted by permission.

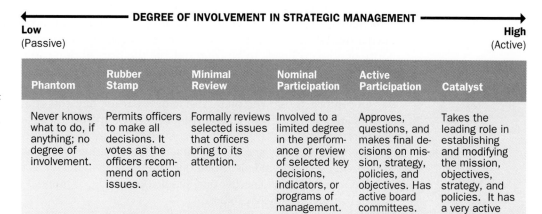

←		DEGREE OF INVOLVEMENT IN STRATEGIC MANAGEMENT			→
Low (Passive)					**High** (Active)
Phantom	**Rubber Stamp**	**Minimal Review**	**Nominal Participation**	**Active Participation**	**Catalyst**
Never knows what to do, if anything; no degree of involvement.	Permits officers to make all decisions. It votes as the officers recommend on action issues.	Formally reviews selected issues that officers bring to its attention.	Involved to a limited degree in the performance or review of selected key decisions, indicators, or programs of management.	Approves, questions, and makes final decisions on mission, strategy, policies, and objectives. Has active board committees. Performs fiscal and management audits.	Takes the leading role in establishing and modifying the mission, objectives, strategy, and policies. It has a very active strategy committee.

holders (especially if the founders own less than 50% of the common stock). In this instance, problems could occur if the board fails to become more active in terms of its roles and responsibilities.

Most large, publicly-owned corporations probably have boards that operate at some point between nominal and active participation. One study of boards ranging from hospitals to Fortune 500 firms found that:

* 30% of the boards actively worked with management to develop strategic direction (**active/catalyst**)

* 30% worked to revise as well as ratify management's proposals (**minimal/ nominal participation**)

* 40% merely ratified management's strategic proposals (**phantom/rubber stamp**).[9]

Members of a Board of Directors

The boards of most publicly owned corporations are composed of both inside and outside directors. **Inside directors** (sometimes called management directors) are typically officers or executives employed by the corporation. **Outside directors** may be executives of other firms but are not employees of the board's corporation. Although there is no clear evidence indicating that a high proportion of outsiders on a board results in improved corporate performance, there is a trend in the United States to increase the number of outsiders on boards. The typical large U.S. corporation has an average of eleven directors, of whom two are insiders.[10] Even though outsiders account for around 80% of the board members in these large U.S. corporations (approximately the same as in Canada), they only account for about 40% of board membership in small U.S. companies. People who favor a high proportion of outsiders state that outside directors are less biased and more likely to evaluate management's performance objectively than are inside directors. This is the main reason why the New York Stock Exchange requires that all companies listed on the exchange have an audit committee composed entirely of independent, outside members. This view is in agreement with **agency theory,** which states that problems arise in corporations because the agents (top management) are not willing to bear responsibility for their decisions unless they own a substantial amount of stock in the corporation. The theory suggests that a majority of a board needs to be from outside the firm so that top management is prevented from acting selfishly to the detriment of the shareholders. See the **Key Theory** feature for fuller discussion of Agency Theory.

In contrast, those who prefer inside over outside directors contend that outside directors are less effective than are insiders because the outsiders are less likely to have the necessary interest, availability, or competency. Directors may sometimes serve on so many boards that they spread their time and interest too thin to actively fulfill their responsibilities. They could also point out that the term "outsider" is too simplistic—some outsiders are not truly objective and should be considered more as insiders than as outsiders. For example, there can be:

1. *Affiliated* directors who, though not really employed by the corporation, handle the legal or insurance work for the company (thus dependent on the current management for a key part of their business).

2. *Retired* directors who used to work for the company, such as the past CEO (partly responsible for much of the corporation's current strategy and probably groomed the current CEO as his or her replacement).

3. *Family* directors who are descendants of the founder and own significant blocks of stock (with personal agendas based on a family relationship with the current CEO).[11]

The majority of outside directors are active or retired CEOs and COOs of other corporations. Others are academicians, attorneys, consultants, former government officials, major shareholders, and bankers. In Germany, bankers are represented on almost every board—primarily because they own large blocks of stock in German corporations. In Denmark, Sweden, Belgium, and Italy, however, investment companies assume this role. For example, the investment company Investor AB casts 42.5% of the Electrolux AB shareholder votes—thus guaranteeing itself positions on the Electrolux board. Nineteen ninety-five surveys of large U.S. corporations found that 69% of the boards had at least one woman director—up from 60% in 1992 and only 11% in 1972 with one-third now having two female directors.[12] Boards having at least one minority member increased from 9% in 1973 to 47% in 1995 (African-American: 34%; Latino: 9%; Asian: 4%).

The globalization of business has not yet had much impact on board membership. One study of U.S. boards found 37 international (non-U.S.) directors on only 30 out of 100 boards surveyed. Of these, five were insiders and 32 were outsiders.[13] The scarcity of international directors may be changing as more corporations increase their operations around the world. See the ●**21st Century Global Society** feature for recent board changes at Hoechst AG.

Outside directors serving on the boards of large U.S. corporations annually earned on average $33,000. Most companies also provided some form of payment through stock options.[14] Directors serving on the boards of small companies usually received much less (around $10,000).

The vast majority of inside directors includes the chief executive officer, chief operating officer, and presidents or vice-presidents of key operating divisions or functional units. Few, if any, inside directors receive any extra compensation for assuming this extra duty. Very rarely does a U.S. board include any lower level operating employees.

KEY THEORY

APPLICATION OF AGENCY THEORY TO CORPORATE GOVERNANCE

Managers of large, modern publicly-held corporations are typically not the owners. In fact, most of today's top managers own only nominal amounts of stock in the corporation they manage. The real owners (shareholders) elect boards of directors who hire managers as their agents to run the firm's day-to-day activities. As suggested in the classic study by Berle and Means, top managers are, in effect, "hired hands" who may very likely be more interested in their personal welfare than that of the shareholders. For example, management might emphasize strategies, such as acquisitions, that increase the size of the firm (to become more powerful and to demand increased pay and benefits) or that diversify the firm into unrelated businesses (to reduce short-term risk and to allow them to put less effort into a core product line that may be facing difficulty), but that result in a reduction in dividends and/or stock price.

Agency theory is concerned with analyzing and resolving two problems that occur in relationships between principals (owners/shareholders) and their agents (top management):

1. *The agency problem* that arises when (a) the desires or objectives of the owners and the agents conflict or (b) it is difficult or expensive for the owners to verify what the agent is actually doing.

2. *The risk sharing problem* that arises when the owners and agents have different attitudes toward risk.

The likelihood that these problems will occur increases when stock is widely held (no one shareholder owns more than a small percentage of the total common stock), when the board of directors is composed of people who know little of the company or who are personal friends of top management, and when a high percentage of board members are inside (management) directors.

To better align the interests of the agents with those of the owners and to increase the corporation's overall performance, agency theory suggests that top management have a significant degree of ownership in the firm and/or have a strong financial stake in its long-term performance. In support of this argument, research does indicate a positive relationship between corporate performance and the amount of stock owned by directors.[15]

Source: For a good summary of agency theory as applied to corporate governance, see J. P. Walsh and J. K. Seward, "On the Efficiency of Internal and External Corporate Control Mechanisms," *Academy of Management Review* (July 1990), pp. 421–458; K. M. Eisenhardt, "Agency Theory: An Assessment and Review," *Academy of Management Review* (January 1989), pp. 57–74; S. L. Oswald and J. S. Jahera, Jr., "The Influence of Ownership on Performance: An Empirical Study," *Strategic Management Journal* (May 1991), pp. 321–326. For background, see also A. A. Berle, Jr. and G. C. Means, *The Modern Corporation and Private Property* (New York: Macmillan, 1932).

Codetermination: Should Employees Serve on Boards?

Codetermination, the inclusion of a corporation's workers on its board, began only recently in the United States. Corporations such as Chrysler, Northwest Airlines, United Airlines (UAL), and Wheeling-Pittsburgh Steel have added representatives from employee associations to their boards as part of union agreements or Employee Stock Ownership Plans (ESOPs). For example, United Airline workers traded 15% in pay cuts for 55% of the company (through an ESOP) and three of the firm's twelve board seats. In this instance, workers represent themselves on the board not so much as employees, but primarily as owners. At Chrysler, however, the United Auto Workers obtained a seat on the board as part of a union contract agreement in exchange for changes in work

21ST CENTURY GLOBAL SOCIETY

HOECHST AG ADDS INTERNATIONAL MEMBERS TO ITS BOARD

The world's biggest chemical firm is based in Germany, but it is increasingly becoming a globally oriented company. For example, two of its six major businesses are located in the United States. Hoechst (pronounced Herkst) now employs more people in the Americas than it does in its home country. According to Chairman Juergen Dormann, "We are not merely a German company with foreign interests. One could almost say we are a nonnational company."

Hoechst expects its sales in the Americas to rise to 40% of the company's total sales by 2000 compared to less than 6% in 1987. To provide an international orientation, Hoechst has added an American and a Brazilian to its nine-member management board. One of their contributions has been to recommend performance-based pay for managers—common in the United States, but very unusual in German corporations.

Source: G. Steinmetz and M. Marshall, "How a Chemical Giant Goes About Becoming a Lot Less German," *Wall Street Journal* (February 18, 1997), pp A1, A14.

rules and reductions in benefits. In situations like this when a director represents an internal stakeholder, critics raise the issue of conflict of interest. Can a member of the board, who is privy to confidential managerial information, function, for example, as a union leader whose primary duty is to fight for the best benefits for his or her members?

Although the movement to place employees on the boards of directors of U.S. companies shows little likelihood of increasing (except through employee stock ownership), the European experience reveals an increasing acceptance of worker participation (without ownership) on corporate boards. Germany pioneered codetermination during the 1950s with a two-tiered system: a *supervisory board* elected by shareholders and employees to approve or decide corporate strategy and policy and a *management board* (composed primarily of top management) appointed by the supervisory board to manage the company's activities. Worker representatives in specific industries such as coal, iron, and steel were given equal status with management on policy-making supervisory boards. In other industries, however, workers only elect one-third of supervisory board membership. At Siemens AG, for example, shareholders only elect ten people to the supervisory board. Employees of Siemens and "dependent" firms elect seven members with employee labor unions electing three more members for a total of ten. This 20-member supervisory board elects a 17-member management board to actually run the company.[16]

Most other western European countries have either passed similar codetermination legislation (as in Sweden, Denmark, Norway, and Austria) or use worker councils to work closely with management (as in Belgium, Luxembourg, France, Italy, Ireland, and the Netherlands). Nevertheless research on German codetermination found that legislation requiring firms to put employee representatives on their boards lowered dividend payments, led to a more conservative investment policy, and reduced firm values.[17]

Interlocking Directorates

CEOs often nominate chief executives (as well as board members) from other firms to membership on their own boards in order to create an interlocking directorate. A *direct*

interlocking directorate occurs when two firms share a director or when an executive of one firm sits on the board of a second firm. An *indirect* interlock occurs when two corporations have directors who also serve on the board of a third firm, such as a bank.

Although the Clayton Act and the Banking Act of 1933 prohibit interlocking directorates by U.S. companies competing in the same industry, interlocking continues to occur in almost all corporations, especially large ones. Interlocking occurs because large firms have a large impact on other corporations; and these other corporations, in turn, have some control over the firm's inputs and marketplace. For example, most large corporations in the United States, Japan, and Germany are interlocked either directly or indirectly with financial institutions.[18] Interlocking directorates are also a useful method for gaining both inside information about an uncertain environment and objective expertise about potential strategies and tactics. Family-owned corporations, however, are less likely to have interlocking directorates than are corporations with highly dispersed stock ownership, probably because family-owned corporations do not like to dilute their corporate control by adding outsiders to boardroom discussions. Nevertheless some evidence indicates that well-interlocked corporations are better able to survive in a highly competitive environment.[19]

Nomination and Election of Board Members

Traditionally the CEO of the corporation decided whom to invite to board membership and merely asked the shareholders for approval in the annual proxy statement. All nominees were usually elected. There are some dangers, however, in allowing the CEO free rein in nominating directors. The CEO might select only board members who, in the CEO's opinion, will not disturb the company's policies and functioning. Given that the average length of service of a U.S. board member is 8.4 years, CEO-friendly, passive boards are likely to result.[20] Directors selected by the CEO often feel that they should go along with any proposal the CEO makes. Thus board members find themselves accountable to the very management they are charged to oversee. Because this is likely to happen, more boards are using a nominating committee to nominate new outside board members for the shareholders to elect. Approximately 73% of Fortune 500 U.S. corporations now use nominating committees to identify potential directors.

Virtually every corporation whose directors serve terms of more than one year divides the board into classes and staggers elections so that only a portion of the board stands for election each year. Arguments in favor of this practice are that it provides continuity by reducing the chance of an abrupt turnover in its membership and that it reduces the likelihood of electing people unfriendly to management (who might be interested in a hostile takeover) through cumulative voting. An argument against staggered boards is that they make it more difficult for concerned shareholders to curb a CEO's power—especially when that CEO is also Chairman of the Board. For example, out of dissatisfaction with the company's recent poor performance and their perception that the board was inactive, two unions supported a shareholder proposal in 1996 to cancel Kmart's staggered board so that the entire board would be elected annually.

Organization of the Board

The size of the board is determined by the corporation's charter and its bylaws in compliance with state laws. Although some states require a minimum number of board members, most corporations have quite a bit of discretion in determining board size. The average large, publicly-held firm has around 11 directors. The average small/medium size privately-held company has approximately seven to eight members.

In 1995, 68% of the top executives of large, U.S. publicly-held corporations held the dual designation of chairman and CEO, a drop from 72% just one year earlier. (The percentage of firms having the Chair/CEO position combined in Canada and the United Kingdom is 43% and 20%, respectively.)[21] The combined Chair/CEO position is being increasingly criticized because of the potential for conflict of interest. The CEO is supposed to concentrate on strategy, planning, external relations, and responsibility to the board. The chairman's responsibility is to ensure that the board and its committees perform their functions as stated in the board's charter. Further, the chairman schedules board meetings and presides over the annual shareholders' meeting. Critics of combining the two offices in one person ask how the board can properly oversee top management if the chairman is also top management. For this reason, the chairman and CEO roles are separated by law in Germany, the Netherlands, and Finland. A similar law is being considered in Britain and Australia. Although the majority of research does suggest that firms that separate the two positions outperform financially those firms that combine the offices, some studies have found no significant difference in operating performance.[22]

Many of those who prefer that the chairman and CEO positions be combined do agree that the outside directors should elect a **lead director.** This person would be consulted by the Chair/CEO regarding board affairs and would coordinate the annual evaluation of the CEO.[23] The lead director position is very popular in the United Kingdom where it originated. Of those U.S. companies combining the chair and CEO positions, 27% currently have a lead director. This is one way to give the board more power without undermining the power of the Chair/CEO.

The most effective boards accomplish much of their work through committees. Although they do not usually have legal duties, most committees are granted full power to act with the authority of the board between board meetings. Typical standing committees are the executive, audit, compensation, finance, and nominating committees. The executive committee is formed from local directors who can meet between board meetings to attend to matters that must be settled quickly. This committee acts as an extension of the board and, consequently, may have almost unrestricted authority in certain areas.

Trends in Corporate Governance

The role of the board of directors in the strategic management of the corporation is likely to be more active in the future. The change will probably be more evolutionary, however, rather than radical or revolutionary. Different boards are at different levels of maturity and will not be changing in the same direction or at the same speed.

Some of today's **trends in governance** that are likely to continue include:

- Institutional investors, such as pension funds, mutual funds, and insurance companies, are becoming active on boards and are putting increasing pressure on top management to improve corporate performance. For example, the California Public Employees' Retirement System (CalPERS), the largest pension system in the United States, annually publishes a list of poorly performing companies, hoping to embarrass management into remedial action.

- As corporations become more global, they will increasingly add international directors to their boards.

- Shareholders are demanding that directors and top managers own more than token amounts of stock in the corporation. Stock is increasingly being used as part of a director's compensation.

- Outside or nonmanagement directors are increasing their numbers and power in publicly-held corporations as CEOs loosen their grip on boards. Outsiders are now taking charge of annual CEO evaluations.

- Boards will continue to take more control of board functions by either splitting the combined Chair/CEO into two separate positions or establishing a lead outside director position.

- Society, in the form of special interest groups, increasingly expects boards of directors to balance the economic goal of profitability with the social needs of society. Issues dealing with workforce diversity and the environment are now reaching the board level. For example, the board of Chase Manhattan Corporation recently questioned top management about its efforts to improve the sparse number of women and minorities in senior management.[24] Although many CEOs are resisting such issues, the battle is only just beginning. See the **Strategy in a Changing World** feature for one CEO's heated argument with a nun regarding her suggestion to add women to his company's board of directors.

2.2   *Corporate Governance: The Role of Top Management*

The top management function is usually conducted by the CEO of the corporation in coordination with the COO (Chief Operating Officer) or president, executive vice-president, and vice-presidents of divisions and functional areas. Even though strategic management involves everyone in the organization, the board of directors holds top management primarily responsible for the strategic management of the firm.[25]

Responsibilities of Top Management

Top management responsibilities, especially those of the CEO, involve getting things accomplished through and with others in order to meet the corporate objectives. Top management's job is thus multidimensional and is oriented toward the welfare of the total organization. Specific top management tasks vary from firm to firm and are developed from an analysis of the mission, objectives, strategies, and key activities of the corporation. The chief executive officer, in particular, must successfully handle two responsibilities crucial to the effective strategic management of the corporation: (1) *provide executive leadership and a strategic vision*, and (2) *manage the strategic planning process*.

Executive Leadership and Strategic Vision

Executive leadership is the directing of activities toward the accomplishment of corporate objectives. Executive leadership is important because it sets the tone for the entire corporation. A **strategic vision** is a description of what the company is capable of becoming. It is often communicated in the mission statement. People in an organization want to have a sense of mission, but only top management is in the position to specify and communicate this strategic vision to the general workforce. Top management's enthusiasm (or lack of it) about the corporation tends to be contagious. The importance of executive leadership is illustrated by John Welch, Jr., the successful Chairman and CEO of General Electric Company (GE). According to Welch: "Good business leaders create a vision, articulate the vision, passionately own the vision, and relentlessly drive it to completion."[26]

STRATEGY IN A CHANGING WORLD

BOARD QUALIFICATIONS: DIVERSITY OR TECHNICAL COMPETENCE?

In her position as Director of Corporate Social Responsibility, Sister Doris Gormley of the Sisters of St. Francis of Philadelphia is responsible for ensuring that investments by her order of nuns—investments selected by professional financial advisers—don't violate the order's principles of social responsibility. The order, composed of 1,000 nuns, has a portfolio that is primarily used to support aging and retired nuns. Among other things, she examines proxy statements (asking shareholders to vote on nominees to the board and other proposals) to ascertain if a corporation's board of directors includes women and minorities. If a corporation does not, she sends it a form letter explaining the order's policy to withhold voting on any nominees or proposals by boards that don't contain qualified women and minorities. The letter, routinely sent each year to about 200 of the corporations in which the order owns stock, says in part:

> We believe that a company is best represented by a Board of qualified Directors reflecting the equality of the sexes, races, and ethnic groups. As women and minorities continue to move into upper level management positions of economic, educational, and cultural institutions, the number of qualified Board candidates also increases.

In the twelve years that Sister Doris has been sending this letter, most companies have responded politely, either explaining why they weren't pursuing board diversity or that they would keep her thoughts in mind when board vacancies occurred.

T. J. Rodgers, CEO of Cypress Semiconductor Corporation, however, took exception to the April 1996 letter. He was so incensed by her suggestion, he wrote her a six-page letter, which he distributed to Cypress shareholders. According to Rodgers, "a 'woman's view' on how to run our semiconductor company does not help us, unless that woman has an advanced technical degree and experience as a CEO." He goes on to say that few women or minorities fit that description. A search for a director "usually yields a male who is 50-plus years old." Rodgers continues by saying:

> You ought to get down from your moral high horse. Your views seem more accurately described as 'politically correct' than 'Christian.' Choosing a Board of Directors based on race and gender is a lousy way to run a company. Cypress will never do it. . . . Bowing to special interest groups is an immoral way to run a company.

In little over a month after writing his response to Sister Doris, Rodgers received over 200 letters—only 15 of which were critical. The chairmen of Hewlett-Packard and Advanced Micro Devices as well as other corporate executives wrote to congratulate him. "Splendid letter," responded economist Milton Friedman.

For her part, Sister Doris was surprised by all the furor. She indicated that her form letter had nothing to do with "political correctness," but simply reflected "concern for the social integrity of business." Because her order owned 7,000 shares of Cypress stock at the time, Sister Doris felt that Rodgers' letter had failed to respect her shareholder rights. Stating that Rodgers' perspective on desired qualifications for a board position were extremely narrow, Sister Doris contended that the company might benefit from the views of other kinds of competent business people. "I would think that in 1996, even in the semiconductor industry, there are beginning to be qualified women and people of color."

Source: E. J. Pollock, "CEO Takes On a Nun in a Crusade Against 'Political Correctness,'" *Wall Street Journal* (July 15, 1996), pp. A1 and A7.

Chief executive officers with a clear strategic vision are often perceived as dynamic and charismatic leaders. For instance, the positive attitude characterizing many well-known industrial leaders—such as Bill Gates at Microsoft, Anita Roddick at The Body Shop, Ted Turner at CNN, Herb Kelleher at Southwest Airlines, and Andy Grove at Intel—has energized their respective corporations. They are able to command respect and to influence strategy formulation and implementation because they tend to have three key characteristics:

1. **The CEO articulates a strategic vision** for the corporation. The CEO envisions the company not as it currently is, but as it can become. The new perspective that the CEO's vision brings to activities and conflicts gives renewed meaning to everyone's work and enables employees to see beyond the details of their own jobs to the functioning of the total corporation.

2. **The CEO presents a role** for others to identify with and to follow. The leader sets an example in terms of behavior and dress. The CEO's attitudes and values concerning the corporation's purpose and activities are clear-cut and constantly communicated in words and deeds.

3. **The CEO communicates high performance standards but also shows confidence in the followers' abilities** to meet these standards. No leader ever improved performance by setting easily attainable goals that provided no challenge. The CEO must be willing to follow through by coaching people.

See the **Strategy in a Changing World** feature to learn how George Fisher provided executive leadership to Kodak.

Manage the Strategic Planning Process

As business corporations adopt more of the characteristics of the learning organization, strategic planning initiatives can now come from any part of an organization. However, unless top management encourages and supports the planning process, strategic management is not likely to result. In most corporations, top management must initiate and manage the strategic planning process. It may do so by first asking business units and functional areas to propose strategic plans for themselves, or it may begin by drafting an overall corporate plan within which the units can then build their own plans. Other organizations engage in concurrent strategic planning in which all the organization's units draft plans for themselves after they have been provided with the organization's overall mission and objectives.

Regardless of the approach taken, the typical board of directors expects top management to manage the overall strategic planning process so that the plans of all the units and functional areas fit together into an overall corporate plan. Top management's job therefore includes the tasks of evaluating unit plans and providing feedback. To do this, it may require each unit to justify its proposed objectives, strategies, and programs in terms of how well they satisfy the organization's overall objectives in light of available resources.[27]

Many large organizations have a **strategic planning staff** charged with supporting both top management and the business units in the strategic planning process. This planning staff typically consists of just under ten people, headed by a senior vice-president or director of corporate planning. The staff's major responsibilities are to:

1. Identify and analyze companywide strategic issues, and suggest corporate strategic alternatives to top management.

STRATEGY IN A CHANGING WORLD

EXECUTIVE LEADERSHIP AT EASTMAN KODAK

When George Fisher replaced Kay Whitmore as CEO of Eastman Kodak in 1993, the outlook for the company was dismal. The workforce had been dispirited by the loss of 40,000 jobs in five downsizings. Despite $10 billion in investments over the past decade, Kodak's nearly 100% U.S. market share in film had fallen to 70%, earnings per share had only grown 12¢, and long-term debt had risen to 66% of capital. Rather than simply cut costs quickly, as expected by the board of directors, Fisher committed the company to new imaging opportunities and the divestment of non-core businesses. He had a new vision for Kodak's future, one in which the company gave up its dedication to chemical-based film technology in favor of new electronic photography. The Wall Street community, however, was not only unimpressed, it questioned Kodak's very ability to undertake meaningful strategic change.

During the next three years, Fisher worked hard to turn Kodak around. He sold unrelated businesses that had been acquired during an earlier diversification and poured money into new product development. He successfully pushed for improvements in quality and efficiency.

Fisher is aware that in addition to obtaining profitable growth from today's chemistry-based photo products, he must ensure that the company is researching, developing, and marketing digital-electronic systems for the future. As a result, he is attempting to boost motivation for growing current products by encouraging the company's employees to innovate, differentiate products from competitors', and be more aggressive internationally. He also supports and encourages new developments in digital imaging that won't even begin to be profitable until 1997.

Nevertheless, during the 1995 fiscal year, Kodak earned a respectable $1.3 billion on sales of $15 billion and debt fell to only 11.5% of capital. In 1996, analyst Alex Henderson even advised clients to buy Eastman Kodak's stock. In 1997, after another year of improved corporate performance, the board increased Fisher's compensation package and extended his contract (which was to have expired in 1998) until 2000. Wall Street is no longer betting against George Fisher!

Source: L. Grant, "The Bears Back Off Kodak," *Fortune* (June 24, 1996), pp. 24–25; E. Nelson, "Eastman Kodak CEO Fisher Extends Employment Contract Through 2000," *Wall Street Journal* (February 27, 1997), p. B9.

2. Work as facilitators with business units to guide them through the strategic planning process.

To fulfill these responsibilities, the planning staff must have an in-depth knowledge of the principal techniques used in the strategic planning process. One recent survey of nearly 50 corporations from a variety of countries and industries listed the most popular strategic planning techniques in order of general usage:

- Core competencies analysis—72%
- Scenario planning—69%
- Benchmarking—56%
- Total Quality Management—44%
- Shareholder value analysis—44%

- Value chain analysis—44%

- Business process redesign (re-engineering)—33%

- Time-based competition—25%[28]

2.3 *Social Responsibilities of Strategic Decision Makers*

Should strategic decision makers be responsible only to shareholders or do they have broader responsibilities? The concept of **social responsibility** proposes that a private corporation has responsibilities to society that extend beyond making a profit. Strategic decisions often affect more than just the corporation. A decision to retrench by closing some plants and discontinuing product lines, for example, affects not only the firm's workforce, but also the communities where the plants are located and the customers with no other source of the discontinued product. Such situations raise questions of the appropriateness of certain missions, objectives, and strategies of business corporations. Managers must be able to deal with these conflicting interests in an ethical manner to formulate a viable strategic plan.

Responsibilities of a Business Firm

What are the responsibilities of a business firm and how much of them must be fulfilled? Milton Friedman and Archie Carroll offer two contrasting views of the responsibilities of business firms to society.

Friedman's Traditional View of Business Responsibility

Urging a return to a laissez-faire worldwide economy with a minimum of government regulation, Milton Friedman argues against the concept of social responsibility. A business person who acts "responsibly" by cutting the price of the firm's product to prevent inflation, or by making expenditures to reduce pollution, or by hiring the hard-core unemployed, according to Friedman, is spending the shareholder's money for a general social interest. Even if the business person has shareholder permission or encouragement to do so, he or she is still acting from motives other than economic and may, in the long run, harm the very society the firm is trying to help. By taking on the burden of these social costs, the business becomes less efficient—either prices go up to pay for the increased costs or investment in new activities and research is postponed. These results negatively affect—perhaps fatally—the long-term efficiency of a business. Friedman thus referred to the social responsibility of business as a "fundamentally subversive doctrine" and stated that:

> There is one and only one social responsibility of business—to use its resources and engage in activities designed to increase its profits so long as it stays within the rules of the game, which is to say, engages in open and free competition without deception or fraud.[29]

Carroll's Four Responsibilities of Business

As shown in Figure 2.2, Archie Carroll proposes that the managers of business organizations have **four responsibilities**: economic, legal, ethical, and discretionary.[30]

Figure 2.2
**Responsibilities
of Business**

Source: Adapted from
A. B. Carroll, "A Three
Dimensional Concep-
tual Model of Corporate
Performance," *Academy
of Management Review*
(October 1979),
p. 499. Reprinted with
permission.

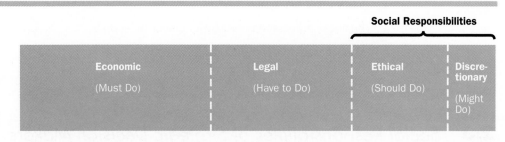

1. **Economic** responsibilities of a business organization's management are to produce goods and services of value to society so that the firm may repay its creditors and shareholders.

2. **Legal** responsibilities are defined by governments in laws that management is expected to obey. For example, U.S. business firms are required to hire and promote people based on their credentials rather than to discriminate on non–job-related characteristics such as race, gender, or religion.

3. **Ethical** responsibilities of an organization's management are to follow the generally held beliefs about behavior in a society. For example, society generally expects firms to work with the employees and the community in planning for layoffs, even though no law may require this. The affected people can get very upset if an organization's management fails to act according to generally prevailing ethical values.

4. **Discretionary** responsibilities are the purely voluntary obligations a corporation assumes. Examples are philanthropic contributions, training the hard-core unemployed, and providing day-care centers. The difference between ethical and discretionary responsibilities is that few people expect an organization to fulfill discretionary responsibilities, whereas many expect an organization to fulfill ethical ones.[31]

Carroll lists these four responsibilities *in order of priority.* A business firm must first make a profit to satisfy its economic responsibilities. To continue in existence, the firm must follow the laws—thus fulfilling its legal responsibilities. To this point Carroll and Friedman are in agreement. Carroll, however, goes further by arguing that business managers have responsibilities beyond the economic and legal ones.

Having satisfied the two basic responsibilities, according to Carroll, the firm should look to fulfilling its social responsibilities. **Social responsibility,** *therefore, includes both ethical and discretionary, but not economic and legal responsibilities.* A firm can fulfill its ethical responsibilities by taking actions that society tends to value but has not yet put into law. When ethical responsibilities are satisfied, a firm can focus on discretionary responsibilities—purely voluntary actions that society has not yet decided are important.

The discretionary responsibilities of today may become the ethical responsibilities of tomorrow. The provision of day-care facilities is, for example, moving rapidly from a discretionary to an ethical responsibility. Carroll suggests that to the extent that business corporations fail to acknowledge discretionary or ethical responsibilities, society, through government, will act, making them legal responsibilities. Government may do this, moreover, without regard to an organization's economic responsibilities. As a result, the organization may have greater difficulty in earning a profit than it would have had if it had voluntarily assumed some ethical and discretionary responsibilities.

Both Friedman and Carroll argue their positions based on the impact of socially responsible actions on a firm's profits. Friedman says that socially responsible actions hurt a firm's efficiency. Carroll proposes that a lack of social responsibility results in increased government regulations, which reduce a firm's efficiency. Research has failed, unfortunately, to consistently support either position. There is no clear relationship between social responsibility and financial performance.[32]

As a matter of fact, refusing to live up to the expectations of society can sometimes pay off. For example, three firms that remained in segregated South Africa during the economic sanctions of the 1980s—Colgate-Palmolive, Johnson & Johnson, and 3M— were damned in shareholder resolutions, college demonstrations, and informal boycotts of their products. They were, however, able to expand their base quickly once apartheid ended and now dominate their South African markets. Firms that lived up to society's expectations by leaving are finding it very difficult to return to South Africa because they are now at a competitive disadvantage. McDonald's, which pulled its operations out of South Africa during apartheid, lost its right to its trademark during the firm's absence.

In contrast, firms that are known to be ethical and socially responsible often enjoy some benefits that may even provide them a competitive advantage. Some examples of these benefits are:

- Their environmental concerns may enable them to charge premium prices and gain brand loyalty (Ben & Jerry's Ice Cream).

- Their trustworthiness may help them generate enduring relationships with suppliers and distributors without needing to spend a lot of time and money policing contracts (Maytag).

- They can attract outstanding employees at less than the market rate (Procter & Gamble).

- They are more likely to be welcomed into a foreign country (Levi Strauss).

- They can utilize the goodwill of public officials for support in difficult times (Minnesota supported Dayton-Hudson's fight to avoid being acquired by Dart Industries of Maryland).

- They are more likely to attract capital infusions from investors who view reputable companies as desirable long-term investments (Rubbermaid).[33]

Corporate Stakeholders

The concept that business must be socially responsible sounds appealing until we ask, "Responsible to whom?" A corporation's task environment includes a large number of groups with interest in a business organization's activities. These groups are referred to as **corporate stakeholders** because they affect or are affected by the achievement of the firm's objectives.[34] Should a corporation be responsible only to some of these groups, or does business have an equal responsibility to all of them?

In any one strategic decision, the interests of one stakeholder group can conflict with another. For example, a business firm's decision to use only recycled materials in its manufacturing process may have a positive effect on environmental groups but a

COMPANY SPOTLIGHT

Location Decision

Throughout its history, Maytag Corporation has tried to act responsibly in light of the various concerns of its many stakeholder groups. Even though the corporation has kept its headquarters in Newton, Iowa, the acquisitions of Magic Chef and Hoover had meant that Maytag Corporation had to view things differently from Maytag Company. The company previously made only Maytag-brand major appliances in Newton, Iowa. The corporation now makes Maytag, Admiral, Magic Chef, Jenn-Air, Hardwick, Norge, and Hoover brand appliances, as well as Dixie-Narco vending machines, throughout North America and the world. Maytag Corporation's top management (many of whom came from Maytag Company) has to consider not only their responsibilities to the stakeholders of Maytag Company, but also their responsibilities to the various stakeholders of Magic Chef, Jenn-Air, Hoover, Admiral, and Dixie-Narco, as well as those stakeholders of the corporation as a whole. This has not been easy.

Maytag's reputation as a good corporate citizen was tarnished in 1990 by its decision to move dishwasher manufacturing from Newton to Jackson, Tennessee. Chairman and CEO Daniel Krumm announced that Maytag would consolidate the manufacturing of all the brands marketed by the corporation into one large, highly efficient plant.

Lonnie White, President of United Auto Workers Local 997 (the bargaining unit representing Maytag Company unionized employees in Newton, Iowa), responded with dismay to top management's decision. "Where is their commitment to the community and the state of Iowa?" asked White. "They can add a facility here in Newton to do the same thing that they're doing in Jackson, Tennessee." Pointing out that Maytag owned plenty of unused land in Newton, White contended that there could be only three reasons management would move dishwasher production to Tennessee: (1) to escape union shop, (2) to reduce wage costs, and (3) to cut benefits. "The Newton dishwasher line is only running one shift. Other lines run two shifts," said White in response to the statement that the line was near capacity. He indicated that the union was not so much concerned with itself as it was with the impact on local communities and the need to avoid "community cannibalism."

MAYTAG CORPORATION

negative effect on shareholder dividends. See the **Company Spotlight on Maytag Corporation** feature for a description of the firm's decision to move dishwasher production from Iowa to a lower wage location. On the one hand, shareholders were generally pleased with the decision because it would lower costs. On the other hand, Iowa officials and local union people were very unhappy at what they called "community cannibalism." Which group's interests should have priority?

Given the wide range of interests and concerns present in any organization's task environment, one or more groups, at any one time, probably will be dissatisfied with an organization's activities—even if management is trying to be socially responsible. As shown in the **Strategy in a Changing World** feature on Kathy Lee Gifford, a company may have some stakeholders of which it is only marginally aware. Therefore, before making a strategic decision, strategic managers should consider how each alternative will affect various stakeholder groups. What seems at first to be the best decision because it appears to be the most profitable may actually result in the worst set of consequences to the corporation.

KATHY LEE GIFFORD HAS SOME BAD DAYS

Should a company be concerned if some of its suppliers in developing countries are abusing their workers, employing child labor, and paying near starvation wages? Many companies would probably say that although such practices are regrettable, the internal practices of other companies (especially in other countries) is not their concern. In 1996, however, a human rights advocacy group accused U.S. clothing manufacturers and retailers Eddie Bauer, J. Crew, Kmart, and Wal-Mart of selling products made by underage Honduran workers under sweatshop conditions. Charles Kernaghan, executive director of the National Labor Committee Education Fund in Support of Worker and Human Rights in Central America, charged television personality Kathy Lee Gifford with supporting Wal-Mart's use of sweatshop suppliers by advertising the clothing.

Upon learning of these practices in the national media, Ms. Gifford and Wal-Mart severed ties with the Honduran plant employing children and with a New York sweatshop producing goods in Gifford's name. Following the uproar, President Clinton announced a labeling agreement with ten manufacturers stating that they would ensure that their products are manufactured under decent conditions and that they will identify clothes not made under these exploitative conditions.

Very little attention was paid by the media to an argument raised by Lucy Martinez-Mont, a professor of economics in Guatemala:

> The likely impact of Ms. Gifford's crusade on Central America frightens me. If it drives businesses to leave the region altogether, it will kill jobs and worsen living conditions for the poor. . . . People choose to work in the maquila shops of their own free will, because these are the best jobs available to them. Given that unemployment compensation is unheard of in Central America, a lousy job is always better than no job at all.[35]

Following the resolution of the sweatshop incidents, Gifford received a letter from a marine ministry association urging her to disassociate herself from the cruise industry (Gifford appears in ads for Carnival Cruise Lines) because of its exploitation of foreign crew members.

2.4   Ethical Decision Making

Some people joke that there is no such thing as "business ethics." They call it an oxymoron—a concept that combines opposite or contradictory ideas. Unfortunately there is some truth to this sarcastic comment. For example, a 1996 survey by the Ethics Resource Center of 1,324 employees of 747 American companies found that 48% of employees surveyed said that they had engaged in one or more unethical and/or illegal actions during the past year. The most common questionable behavior involved cutting corners on quality (16%), covering up incidents (14%), abusing or lying about sick days (11%), and lying to or deceiving customers (9%). Some 56% of workers reported pressure to act unethically or illegally on the job.[36]

Some Reasons for Unethical Behavior

Why are many business people perceived to be acting unethically? It may be that the involved people are not even aware that they are doing something questionable. There is no worldwide standard of conduct for business people. Cultural norms and values vary between countries and even between different geographic regions and ethnic groups within a country. For example, what is considered in one country to be a bribe to expedite service is sometimes considered in another country to be normal business practice.

Another possible reason for what is often perceived to be unethical behavior lies in differences in values between business people and key stakeholders. Some business people may believe profit maximization is the key goal of their firm, whereas concerned interest groups may have other priorities, such as the hiring of minorities and women or the safety of their neighborhoods. Of the six values measured by the Allport-Vernon-Lindzey Study of Values test (*aesthetic, economic, political, religious, social,* and *theoretical*), both U.S. and British executives consistently score highest on economic and political values and lowest on social and religious ones. This is similar to the value profile of managers from Japan, Korea, India, and Australia, as well as those of American business school students. U.S. Protestant ministers, in contrast, score highest on religious and social values and very low on economic values.[37]

This difference in values can make it difficult for one group of people to understand another's actions. For example, even though some people feel that the advertising of cigarettes (especially to youth) is unethical, the people managing these companies respond that they are simply offering a product—"*Let the buyer beware*" is a traditional saying in free market capitalism. They argue that customers in a free market democracy have the right to choose how they spend their money and live their lives. Social progressives may contend that business people working in tobacco, alcoholic beverages, and gambling industries are acting unethically by making and advertising products with potentially dangerous and expensive side effects, such as cancer, alcoholism, and addiction. People working in these industries could respond by asking if it is ethical for people who don't smoke, drink, or gamble to reject another person's right to do so.

Moral Relativism

Some people justify their seeming unethical positions by arguing that there is no one absolute code of ethics and that morality is relative. Simply put, **moral relativism** claims that morality is relative to some personal, social, or cultural standard and that there is no method for deciding whether one decision is better than another.

Adherents of moral relativism may believe that all moral decisions are deeply personal and that individuals have the right to run their own lives; each person should be allowed to interpret situations and act on his or her own moral values. They may also argue that social roles carry with them certain obligations to those roles only. A manager in charge of a department, for example, must put aside his or her personal beliefs and do instead what the role requires, that is, act in the best interests of the department. They could also argue that a decision is legitimate if it is common practice regardless of other considerations ("Everyone's doing it"). Some propose that morality itself is relative to a particular culture, society, or community. People should therefore "understand" the practices of other countries, but not judge them. If the citizens of another country share certain norms and customs, what right does an outsider have to criticize them?

Although these arguments make some sense, moral relativism could enable a person to justify almost any sort of decision or action, so long as it is not declared illegal.

Kohlberg's Levels of Moral Development

Another reason why some business people might be seen as unethical is that they may have no well-developed personal sense of ethics. A person's ethical behavior will be affected by his or her level of moral development, certain personality variables, and such situational factors as the job itself, the supervisor, and the organizational culture.[38] Kohlberg proposes that a person progresses through three levels of moral development.[39] Similar in some ways to Maslow's hierarchy of needs, the individual moves from total self-centeredness to a concern for universal values. Kohlberg's three levels are as follows:

1. **The preconventional level** is characterized by a concern for *self*. Small children and others who have not progressed beyond this stage evaluate behaviors on the basis of personal interest—avoiding punishment or quid pro quo.

2. **The conventional level** is characterized by considerations of society's *laws* and *norms*. Actions are justified by an external code of conduct.

3. **The principled level** is characterized by a person's adherence to an *internal moral code*. The individual at this level looks beyond norms or laws to find universal values or principles.

Kohlberg places most people in the conventional level, with less than 20% of U.S. adults in the principled level of development.[40]

Encouraging Ethical Behavior

Following Carroll's work, if business people do not act ethically, government will be forced to pass laws regulating their actions—and usually increasing their costs. For self interest, if for no other reason, managers should be more ethical in their decision making. One way to do that is by encouraging codes of ethics. Another is by providing guidelines for ethical behavior.

Codes of Ethics

Codes of ethics specify how an organization expects its employees to behave while on the job. Developing codes of ethics can be a useful way to promote ethical behavior, especially for people who are operating at Kohlberg's conventional level of moral development. Such codes are currently being used by about half of American business corporations. According to a report by the Business Roundtable, an association of CEOs from 200 major U.S. corporations, the importance of a code is that it (1) clarifies company expectations of employee conduct in various situations and (2) makes clear that the company expects its people to recognize the ethical dimensions in decisions and actions.[41]

Various studies do indicate that an increasing number of companies are developing codes of ethics and implementing ethics training workshops and seminars. However, research also indicates that when faced with a question of ethics, managers tend to ignore codes of ethics and try to solve their dilemma on their own.[42] To combat this tendency, the management of a company that wants to improve its employees' ethical behavior should not only develop a comprehensive code of ethics, but also communicate the code in its training programs, performance appraisal system, in policies and procedures, and through its own actions. It may also want to do the same for those companies with which it does business. For example, Reebok International has developed a set of production standards for the manufacturers that supply the company with its athletic shoes on a contract basis. See the **Strategy in a Changing World** feature for Reebok's human rights standards.

STRATEGY IN A CHANGING WORLD

REEBOK DEMANDS HUMAN RIGHTS STANDARDS FROM ITS SUPPLIERS

Reebok International, the well-known athletic shoe company, contracts with independent companies in Asia to manufacture all of its footwear products. Although low cost and high-quality production are important to Reebok, the company is also concerned with the human rights record of its suppliers. Consequently it requires its suppliers to follow the following Human Rights Production Standards:

- **Non-Discrimination.** Reebok will seek business partners that do not discriminate in hiring and employment practices on grounds of race, color, national origin, gender, religion, or political or other opinion.

- **Working Hours/Overtime.** Reebok will seek business partners who do not require more than 60-hour work weeks on a regularly scheduled basis, except for appropriately compensated overtime in compliance with local laws, and will favor business partners who use 48-hour work weeks as their maximum normal requirement.

- **Forced or Compulsory Labor.** Reebok will not work with business partners that use forced or other compulsory labor, including labor that was required as a means of political coercion or as punishment for peacefully expressing political views, in the manufacture of its products. Reebok will not purchase materials that were produced by forced prison or other compulsory labor and will terminate business relationships with any sources found to utilize such labor.

- **Fair Wages.** Reebok will seek business partners who share a commitment to the better-ment of wage and benefit levels that address the basic needs of workers and their families so far as is possible and appropriate in light of national practices and conditions. Reebok will not select business partners that pay less than the minimum wage required by local law or that pay less than prevailing local industry practices (whichever was higher).

- **Child Labor.** Reebok will not work with business partners that use child labor. The term "child" generally refers to a person who was less than 14 years of age, or younger than the age for completing compulsory education if that age was higher than 14. In countries where the law defines "child" to include individuals who were older than 14, Reebok will apply that definition.

- **Freedom of Association.** Reebok will seek business partners that share its commitment to the right of employees to establish and join organizations of their own choosing. Reebok will seek to assure that no employee was penalized because of his or her nonviolent exercise of this right. Reebok recognizes and respects the right of all employees to organize and bargain collectively.

- **Safe and Healthy Work Environment.** Reebok will seek business partners that strive to assure employees a safe and healthy workplace and that do not expose workers to hazardous conditions.

Source: Reebok International, Ltd., "Reebok Human Rights Production Standards," company document.

Guidelines for Ethical Behavior

According to Von der Embse and Wagley, **ethics** is defined as the consensually accepted standards of behavior for an occupation, trade, or profession. **Morality,** in contrast, is the precepts of personal behavior based on religious or philosophical grounds. **Law** refers to formal codes that permit or forbid certain behaviors and may or may not en-force ethics or morality.[43] Given these definitions, how do we arrive at a comprehensive statement of ethics to use in making decisions in a specific occupation, trade, or profession? A starting point for such a code of ethics is to consider the *three basic approaches to ethical behavior:*[44]

1. **Utilitarian approach:** This approach proposes that actions and plans should be judged by their consequences. People should therefore behave in such a way that will produce the greatest benefit to society and produce the least harm or the lowest cost. A problem with this approach is the difficulty in recognizing all the benefits and the costs of any particular decision. It is likely that only the most obvious stake-holders may be considered, and others may be "conveniently" forgotten.

2. **Individual rights approach:** This approach proposes that human beings have certain fundamental rights that should be respected in all decisions. A particular de-cision or behavior should be avoided if it interferes with the rights of others. A prob-lem with this approach is in defining "fundamental rights." The U.S. Constitution includes a Bill of Rights that may or may not be accepted throughout the world. The approach can also encourage selfish behavior when a person defines a personal need or want as a "right."

3. **Justice approach:** This approach proposes that decision makers be equitable, fair, and impartial in the distribution of costs and benefits to individuals and groups. It follows the principles of *distributive justice* (people who are similar on relevant di-mensions such as job seniority should be treated in the same way) and *fairness* (lib-erty should be equal for all persons). The justice approach can also include the concepts of *retributive justice* (punishment should be proportional to the "crime") and *compensatory justice* (wrongs should be compensated in proportion to the of-fense). Affirmative action issues such as reverse discrimination are examples of con-flicts between distributive and compensatory justice.

Cavanagh proposes that we solve ethical problems by asking the following three questions regarding an act or decision:

1. **Utility:** Does it optimize the satisfactions of all stakeholders?

2. **Rights:** Does it respect the rights of the individuals involved?

3. **Justice:** Is it consistent with the canons of justice?

For example, is padding an expense account ethical or not? Using the utility crite-rion, this action increases the company's costs and thus does not optimize benefits for shareholders or customers. Using the rights approach, a person has no right to the money (otherwise we wouldn't call it "padding"). Using the justice criterion, salary and commissions constitute ordinary compensation, but expense accounts only compensate a person for expenses incurred in doing his or her job—expenses that the person would not normally incur except in doing this job.[45]

Another approach to resolving ethical dilemmas is by applying the logic of the philosopher Immanual Kant. Kant presents two principles (called categorical impera-tives) to guide our actions:

1. *A person's action is ethical only if that person is willing for that same action to be taken by everyone who is in a similar situation.* This is same as the *Golden Rule:* Treat others as you would like them to treat you. For example, padding an expense account would be considered ethical if the person were also willing for everyone to do the same if

he or she were the boss. Because it is very doubtful that any manager would be pleased with expense account padding, the action must be considered unethical.

2. *A person should never treat another human being simply as a means, but always as an end.* This means that an action is morally wrong for a person if that person uses others merely as means for advancing his or her own interests. To be moral, the act should not restrict another people's actions so that they are left disadvantaged in some way.[46]

2.5 *Global Issues for the 21st Century*

- The **21st Century Global Society** feature in this chapter described a German-based corporation adding non-Germans to its board of directors. As business firms become increasingly global, their boards of directors may need to become more international in terms of their composition and orientation.

- Although codetermination seems to be primarily a European experience, it is likely that employees at all levels will continue to become more involved in strategic management.

- When making and approving strategic decisions, boards of directors will find that they must consider the interests of *all* key stakeholders and not just those of the people who own stock in the corporation. To avoid unwanted government interference, boards must ensure that management's actions do not antagonize any important stakeholders.

- Questions of diversity in the workplace and the human rights of employees are beginning to impact strategic decision making. Companies such as Reebok and Nike have been criticized for paying low wages to female workers in emerging economies.

- The ability to articulate a strategic vision and motivate people to achieve it may soon be the most important characteristic required of a chief executive officer.

- As business firms become increasingly multinational in scope, they will need to justify their strategic and operational decisions on a basis other than self-interest through moral relativism.

Projections for the 21st Century

- From 1994 to 2010, the world population will grow from 5.607 billion to 7.32 billion.

- From 1994 to 2010, the number of nations will increase from 192 to 202.[47]

Discussion Questions

1. Does a corporation really need a board of directors?

2. What recommendations would you make to improve the effectiveness of today's boards of directors?

3. What is the relationship between corporate governance and social responsibility?

4. What is your opinion of Reebok's production standards of human rights for its suppliers? What would Milton Friedman say? Contrast his view with Archie Carroll's view.

5. Does a company have to act selflessly to be considered socially responsible? For example, when building a new plant, a corporation voluntarily invested in additional equipment enabling it to reduce its pollution emissions beyond any current laws. Knowing that it would be very expensive for its competitors to do the same, the firm lobbied the government to make pollution regulations more restrictive on the entire industry. Is this company socially responsible? Were its managers acting ethically?

Key Terms

active board (p. 29)
agency theory (p. 30)
board of directors continuum (p. 28)
board of director responsibilities (p. 27)
board role in strategic management (p. 27)
Carroll's four responsibilities (p. 39)
catalyst board (p. 29)
codes of ethics (p. 45)
codetermination (p. 31)
corporate governance (p. 26)
corporate stakeholders (p. 41)

corporation (p. 26)
due care (p. 27)
ethics (p. 46)
executive leadership (p. 35)
individual rights approach (p. 47)
inside directors (p. 29)
interlocking directorate (p. 33)
justice approach (p. 47)
law (p. 46)
lead director (p. 34)
levels of moral development (p. 44)
minimal participation board (p. 29)
moral relativism (p. 44)

morality (p. 46)
nominal participation board (p. 29)
outside directors (p. 29)
phantom board (p. 29)
rubber stamp board (p. 29)
social responsibility (p. 40)
strategic planning staff (p. 37)
strategic vision (p. 35)
top management responsibilities (p. 35)
trends in governance (p. 34)
utilitarian approach (p. 47)

Strategic Practice Exercise

How far should people in a business firm go in gathering competitive intelligence? Where do *you* draw the line?

Evaluate each of the following approaches that a business firm could use to gather information about competition. For each approach, mark your feeling about its appropriateness: **1** *(definitely not appropriate)*, **2** *(probably not appropriate)*, **3** *(undecided)*, **4** *(probably appropriate)*, or **5** *(definitely appropriate)*.

The business firm should try to get useful information about competitors by:

_____ Careful study of trade journals.

_____ Wiretapping the telephones of competitors.

_____ Posing as a potential customer to competitors.

_____ Getting loyal customers to put out a phoney "request for proposal" soliciting competitors' bids.

_____ Buying competitors' products and taking them apart.

_____ Hiring management consultants who have worked for competitors.

_____ Rewarding competitors' employees for useful "tips."

_____ Questioning competitors' customers and/or suppliers.

_____ Buying and analyzing competitors' garbage.

_____ Advertising and interviewing for nonexistent jobs.

_____ Taking public tours of competitors' facilities.

_____ Releasing false information about the company in order to confuse competitors.

_____ Questioning competitors' technical people at trade shows and conferences.

_____ Hiring key people away from competitors.

_____ Analyzing competitors' labor union contracts.

_____ Having employees date persons who work for competitors.

_____ Studying aerial photographs of competitors' facilities.

After marking each of the preceding approaches, compare your responses to those of other people in your class. For each approach, the *people marking 4 or 5 should say why they thought this particular act would be appropriate. Those who marked 1 or 2 should then state why they thought this act would be inappropriate.*

What does this tell us about ethics and socially responsible behavior?

_____

Source: Developed from W. A. Jones, Jr. and N. B. Bryan, Jr., "Business Ethics and Business Intelligence: An Empirical Study of Information-Gathering Alternatives," *International Journal of Management* (June 1995), pp. 204–208.

Notes

1. J. A. Kidney, *Eastman Kodak Company* (December 5, 1995).
2. A. G. Monks, and N. Minow, *Corporate Governance* (Cambridge, Mass.: Blackwell Business, 1995), pp. 8–32.
3. *Ibid.*, p. 1.
4. J. H. Dobrzynski, "These Board Members Aren't IBM-Compatible," *Business Week* (August 2, 1992), p. 23.
5. A. Demb, and F. F. Neubauer, "The Corporate Board: Confronting the Paradoxes," *Long Range Planning* (June 1992), p. 13. These results are supported by a 1995 Korn/Ferry International survey in which chairmen and directors agreed that strategy and management succession, in that order, are the most important issues the board expects to face.
6. L. Light, "Why Outside Directors Have Nightmares," *Business Week* (October 23, 1996), p. 6.
7. W. Q. Judge, Jr., and C. P. Zeithaml, "Institutional and Strategic Choice Perspectives on Board Involvement in the Strategic Choice Process," *Academy of Management Journal* (October 1992), 766–794; J. A. Pearce II, and S. A. Zahra, "Effective Power-Sharing Between the Board of Directors and the CEO," *Handbook of Business Strategy, 1992/93 Yearbook* (Boston: Warren, Gorham, and Lamont, 1992), pp. 1.1–1.16.
8. J. H. Dobrzynski, "How to Handle a CEO," *Business Week* (February 21, 1994), pp. 64–65.
9. Judge and Zeithaml.
10. Statistics on boards of directors are taken from *23rd Annual Board of Directors Study* (New York: Korn/Ferry International, 1996); *Corporate Directors' Compensation, 1996 Edition* (New York: Conference Board, 1995); *Corporate Boards: CEO Selection, Evaluation and Succession* (New York: Conference Board, 1995) and were gathered during 1995.
11. See S. Finkelstein, and D. C. Hambrick, *Strategic Leadership: Top Executives and Their Impact on Organizations* (St. Paul: West, 1996), p. 213.
12. Reported by Korn/Ferry International and J. S. Lublin, "Survey Finds More Fortune 500 Firms Have At Least Two Female Directors," *Wall Street Journal* (September 25, 1995), p. A5.
13. T. J. Neff, "Boards Make Steady Progress in Key Areas," *Directors & Boards* (Summer 1994), p. 54.
14. According to 1995 proxy information gathered by Korn/Ferry International and surveys by The Conference Board.
15. D. J. McLaughlin, "The Director's Stake in the Enterprise," *Directors & Boards* (Winter 1994), pp. 53–59; R. Stobaugh, "The Positive Effects of Stock Ownership," *Directors & Boards* (Spring 1996), pp. 33–34.
16. R. E. Berenbeim, *Corporate Boards: CEO Selection, Evaluation and Succession: A Research Report* (New York: The Conference Board, 1995), p. 15.
17. L. H. Clark, Jr., "What Economists Say About Business—and Baboons," *Wall Street Journal* (June 7, 1983), p. 33. Article summarizes a research paper presented to the Interlaken Seminar on Analysis and Ideology, Interlaken, Switzerland, 1983.
18. M. L. Gerlach, "The Japanese Corporate Network: A Blockmodel Analysis," *Administrative Science Quarterly* (March 1992), pp. 105–139.
19. J. A. C. Baum, and C. Oliver, "Institutional Linkages and Organizational Mortality," *Administrative Science Quarterly* (June 1991) pp. 187–218; J. P. Sheppard, "Strategy and Bankruptcy: An Exploration into Organizational Death," *Journal of Management* (Winter 1994), pp. 795–833.
20. D. O'Neal, and H. Thomas, "Developing the Strategic Board," *Long Range Planning* (June 1996), p. 317.
21. The Conference Board reported that although 18% had an outsider as chair, 9% had another employee as chair.
22. See P. L. Rechner, and D. R. Dalton, "CEO Duality and Organizational Performance: A Longitudinal Analysis," *Strategic Management Journal* (February 1991), pp. 155–160 and C. M. Daily and D. R. Dalton, "Corporate Governance and the Bankrupt Firm: An Empirical Assessment," *Strategic Management Journal* (October 1994), pp. 643–654 for evidence favoring separation of Chair and CEO positions.

See also B. R. Baliga, R. C. Moyer, and R. S. Rao, "CEO Duality and Firm Performance: What's the Fuss?" *Strategic Management Journal* (January 1996), pp. 41–53 and A. Campbell, "The Cost of Independent Chairmen," *Long Range Planning* (December 1995), pp. 107–108 for evidence against separating the combined Chair/CEO position.

23. M. Lipton, and J. W. Lorsch, "The Lead Director," *Directors & Boards* (Spring 1993), pp. 28–31.

24. J. S. Lublin, "Texaco Case Causes a Stir in Boardrooms," *Wall Street Journal* (November 22, 1996), p. B1.

25. For an in-depth analysis of top management, see Finkelstein and Hambrick.

26. N. Tichy, and R. Charan, "Speed, Simplicity, Self-Confidence: An Interview with Jack Welch," *Harvard Business Review* (September-October 1989), p. 113.

27. For an in-depth guide to conducting the strategic planning process, see C. D. Fogg, *Team-Based Strategic Planning* (New York: AMACOM, 1994).

28. I. Wilson, "Strategic Planning Isn't Dead—It Changed," *Long Range Planning* (August 1994), pp. 12–24.

29. M. Friedman, "The Social Responsibility of Business Is to Increase Its Profits," *New York Times Magazine* (September 13, 1970), pp. 30, 126–127; and *Capitalism and Freedom* (Chicago: University of Chicago Press, 1963), p. 133.

30. A. B. Carroll, "A Three-Dimensional Conceptual Model of Corporate Performance," *Academy of Management Review* (October 1979), pp. 497–505.

31. Carroll refers to discretionary responsibilities as philanthropic responsibilities in A. B. Carroll, "The Pyramid of Corporate Social Responsibility: Toward the Moral Management of Organizational Stakeholders," *Business Horizons* (July-August 1991), pp. 39–48.

32. P. Rechner, and K. Roth, "Social Responsibility and Financial Performance: A Structural Equation Methodology," *International Journal of Management* (December 1990), pp. 382–391; K. E. Aupperle, A. B. Carroll, and J. D. Hatfield, "An Empirical Examination of the Relationship Between Corporate Social Responsibility and Profitability," *Academy of Management Journal* (June 1985), p. 459.

33. S. Preece, C. Fleisher, and J. Toccacelli, "Building a Reputation Along the Value Chain at Levi Strauss," *Long Range Planning* (December 1995), pp. 88–98; J. B. Barney and M. H. Hansen, "Trustworthiness as a Source of Competitive Advantage," *Strategic Management Journal* (Special Winter Issue, 1994), pp. 175–190.

34. R. E. Freeman, and D. R. Gilbert, *Corporate Strategy and the Search for Ethics* (Englewood Cliffs, N.J.: Prentice-Hall, 1988), p. 6.

35. L. Martinez-Mont, "Sweatshops Are Better Than No Shops," *Wall Street Journal* (June 25, 1996), p. A14.

36. "Nearly Half of Workers Take Unethical Actions—Survey," *Des Moines Register* (April 7, 1997), p. 18B.

37. K. Kumar, "Ethical Orientation of Future American Executives: What the Value Profiles of Business School Students Portend," *SAM Advanced Management Journal* (Autumn 1995), pp. 32–36, 47; M. Gable, and P. Arlow, "A Comparative Examination of the Value Orientations of British and American Executives," *International Journal of Management* (September 1986), pp. 97–106; W. D. Guth, and R. Tagiuri, "Personal Values and Corporate Strategy," *Harvard Business Review* (September-October 1965), pp. 126–127; G. W. England, "Managers and Their Value Systems: A Five Country Comparative Study," *Columbia Journal of World Business* (Summer 1978), p. 35.

38. L. K. Trevino, "Ethical Decision Making in Organizations: A Person-Situation Interactionist Model," *Academy of Management Review* (July 1986), pp. 601–617.

39. L. Kohlberg, "Moral Stage and Moralization: The Cognitive-Development Approach," in *Moral Development and Behavior,* edited by T. Lickona (New York: Holt, Rinehart & Winston, 1976).

40. Trevino, p. 606.

41. J. Keogh, ed., *Corporate Ethics: A Prime Business Asset* (New York: The Business Roundtable, 1988), p. 5.

42. G. F. Kohut, and S. E. Corriher, "The Relationship of Age, Gender, Experience and Awareness of Written Ethics Policies to Business Decision Making," *SAM Advanced Management Journal* (Winter 1994), pp. 32–39.

43. T. J. Von der Embse, and R. A. Wagley, "Managerial Ethics: Hard Decisions on Soft Criteria," *SAM Advanced Management Journal* (Winter 1988), p. 6.

44. G. F. Cavanagh, *American Business Values,* 3rd ed. (Englewood Cliffs, N.J.: Prentice Hall, 1990), pp. 186–199.

45. *Ibid.,* pp. 195–196.

46. I. Kant, "The Foundations of the Metaphysic of Morals," in *Ethical Theory: Classical and Contemporary Readings,* 2d ed., by L. P. Pojman (Belmont, Calif.: Wadsworth Publishing, 1995), pp. 255–279.

47. J. Warner, "21st Century Capitalism: Snapshot of the Next Century," *Business Week* (November 18, 1994), p. 194.

Chapter 3

Environmental Scanning and Industry Analysis

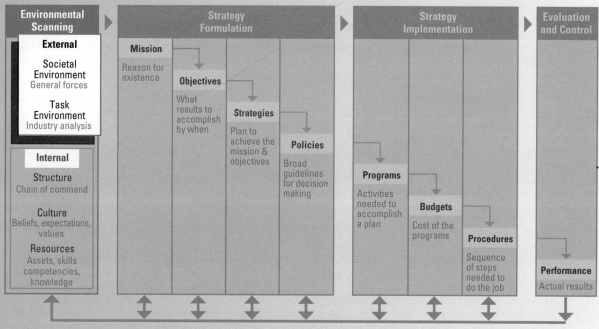

The decades of the 1960s and 1970s were exciting days for Tupperware, the company that originated airtight, easy-to-use plastic food-storage containers. Housewives gathered ten at a time in each others' homes to socialize and play games at Tupperware parties. The local Tupperware lady demonstrated and sold new products at these parties. The party concept as a marketing and distribution device was a huge success—company sales nearly doubled every five years.

During this same time period, however, the company's environment changed—with serious implications for Tupperware. By 1980, divorce was more common and more women had full-time jobs. More customers were single, childless, and working outside the home. As a result, Tupperware parties began to lose their popularity. Tupperware's North American sales slipped from 60% to 40% of the market, in contrast to Rubbermaid's increase from 5% to 40% of units sold during this same time period. The number of Tupperware dealers dropped from 32,000 to 24,000. By the early 1990s, most American women had either no idea how to find Tupperware or no desire to go to a Tupperware party. About 40% of the company's sales were from people who skipped the parties but sent orders along with friends who attended. Still hoping that these environmental changes were only temporary, management refused to change its marketing system. Tupperware's president actually predicted that before the end of the 1990s, the party concept would return to popularity because women and families will be spending more time at home—a forecast that by 1996 showed no indication of occurring. In contrast, Rubbermaid and other competitors, who had switched to marketing their containers in grocery and discount stores, continued to grow at the expense of Tupperware.[1]

Contrast Tupperware's experience with that of Chefs Unlimited, a company founded in 1992 by Dodd and Michelle Aldred of Raleigh, North Carolina. As husband and wife veterans of the restaurant industry, they knew how difficult it was to work long hours and still allow time to prepare home-cooked meals. That was one reason why people were spending more at restaurants during the 1990s. (The percentage of food dollars spent away from home increased from 36% in 1980 to 44% in 1995.) The Aldreds felt that many people were beginning to tire with eating out and would be willing to pay for a quality meal eaten in their own home. They offered people the opportunity to order entrees for either a one- or two-week period. Doing their own cooking in a 3,000 square foot commercial kitchen, the Aldreds delivered meals to customers for subsequent reheating. Although more expensive, these meals were of higher quality than the typical frozen dinner. By 1996, Chefs Unlimited was so successful catering to modern families that the Aldreds were planning to air express their meals to a nationwide audience the next year. Meanwhile, the U.S. Personal Chef Association was predicting the number of personal chef entrepreneurs in the United States and Canada to increase from 1,000 in 1996 to 5,000 in 2001.[2]

The Tupperware example shows how quickly a pioneering company can become an also-ran by failing to adapt to environmental change or, even worse, by failing to create change. The Chefs Unlimited example shows how a changing environment can create new opportunities at the same time it destroys old ones. The lesson is simple. To be successful over time, an organization needs to be in tune with its external environment. There must be a *strategic fit* between what the environment wants and what the corporation has to offer, as well as between what the corporation needs and what the environment can provide.

Current predictions are that the environment for all organizations will become even more uncertain as the world enters the twenty-first century.[3] **Environmental uncertainty** is the degree of *complexity* plus the degree of *change* existing in an organization's external environment. Environmental uncertainty is a threat to strategic managers because it hampers their ability to develop long-range plans and to make strategic decisions to keep the corporation in equilibrium with its external environment.

3.1 Environmental Scanning

Before an organization can begin strategy formulation, it must scan the external environment to identify possible opportunities and threats and its internal environment for strengths and weaknesses. **Environmental scanning** is the monitoring, evaluating, and disseminating of information from the external and internal environments to key people within the corporation. A corporation uses this tool to avoid strategic surprise and to ensure its long-term health. Research has found a positive relationship between environmental scanning and profits.[4]

Identifying External Environmental Variables

In undertaking environmental scanning, strategic managers must first be aware of the many variables within a corporation's societal and task environments. The **societal environment** includes general forces that do not directly touch on the short-run activities of the organization but that can, and often do, influence its long-run decisions. These, shown in Figure 1.3 on page 10, are as follows:

- **Economic** forces that regulate the exchange of materials, money, energy, and information.

- **Technological** forces that generate problem-solving inventions.

- **Political-legal** forces that allocate power and provide constraining and protecting laws and regulations.

- **Sociocultural** forces that regulate the values, mores, and customs of society.

The **task environment** includes those elements or groups that directly affect the corporation and, in turn, are affected by it. These are governments, local communities, suppliers, competitors, customers, creditors, employees/labor unions, special-interest groups, and trade associations. A corporation's task environment is typically the industry within which that firm operates. **Industry analysis** refers to an in-depth examination of key factors within a corporation's task environment. Both the societal and task environments must be monitored to detect the strategic factors that are likely to have a strong impact on corporate success or failure.

Scanning the Societal Environment

The number of possible strategic factors in the societal environment is very high. The number becomes enormous when we realize that, generally speaking, each country in the world can be represented by its own unique set of societal forces—some of which are very similar to neighboring countries and some of which are very different.

For example, even though Korea and China share Asia's Pacific Rim area with Thailand, Taiwan, and Hong Kong (sharing many similar cultural values), they have very different views about the role of business in society. It is generally believed in Korea and China (and to a lesser extent in Japan) that the role of business is primarily to contribute to national development; whereas in Hong Kong, Taiwan, and Thailand (and to a lesser extent in the Philippines, Indonesia, Singapore, and Malaysia), the role of business is primarily to make profits for the shareholders.[5] Such differences may translate into different trade regulations and varying difficulty in the **repatriation of profits** (transferring profits from a foreign subsidiary to a corporation's headquarters) from one group of Pacific Rim countries to another.

Monitoring Societal Trends As noted in Table 3.1, large corporations categorize the societal environment in any one geographic region into four areas and focus their scanning in each area on trends with corporatewide relevance. Obviously trends in any one area may be very important to the firms in one industry but of lesser importance to firms in other industries.

Table 3.1 **Some Important Variables in the Societal Environment**

Economic	Technological	Political-Legal	Sociocultural
GDP trends	Total government spending for R&D	Antitrust regulations	Lifestyle changes
Interest rates	Total industry spending for R&D	Environmental protection laws	Career expectations
Money supply	Focus of technological efforts	Tax laws	Consumer activism
Inflation rates	Patent protection	Special incentives	Rate of family formation
Unemployment levels	New products	Foreign trade regulations	Growth rate of population
Wage/price controls	New developments in technology transfer from lab to marketplace	Attitudes toward foreign companies	Age distribution of population
Devaluation/revaluation		Laws on hiring and promotion	Regional shifts in population
Energy availability and cost	Productivity improvements through automation	Stability of government	Life expectancies
Disposable and discretionary income			Birth rates

Trends in the *economic* part of the societal environment can have an obvious impact on business activity. For example, an increase in interest rates means fewer sales of major home appliances. *Why?* Because a rising interest rate tends to be reflected in higher mortgage rates. Because higher mortgage rates increase the cost of buying a house, the demand for new and used houses tends to fall. Because most major home appliances are sold when people change houses, a reduction in house sales soon translates into a decline in sales of refrigerators, stoves, and dishwashers and reduced profits for everyone in that industry.

Changes in the *technological* part of the societal environment can also have a great impact on multiple industries. For example, improvements in computer microprocessors have not only led to the widespread use of home computers, but also to better automobile engine performance in terms of power and fuel economy through the use of microprocessors to monitor fuel injection.

Trends in the *political-legal* part of the societal environment have a significant impact on business firms. For example, periods of strict enforcement of U.S. antitrust laws directly affect corporate growth strategy. As large companies find it more difficult to acquire another firm in the same or in a related industry, they are typically driven to diversify into unrelated industries.[6] In Europe, the formation of the European Union has led to an increase in merger activity across national boundaries.

Demographic trends are part of the *sociocultural* aspect of the societal environment. The demographic bulge in the U.S. population caused by the "baby boom" in the 1950s strongly affects market demand in many industries. For example, between 1995 and 2005, an average of 4,400 Americans will turn 50 every day. This over-50 age group has become the fastest growing age group in all developed countries. Companies with an eye on the future can find many opportunities offering products and services to the growing number of "woofies" (well-off old folks)—defined as people over 50 with money to spend. These people are very likely to purchase recreational vehicles, take ocean cruises, and enjoy leisure sports such as boating, fishing, and bowling, in addition to needing financial services and health care.

This trend can mean increasing sales for firms like Winnebago (RVs), Carnival Cruise Lines, and Brunswick (sports equipment), among others.[7] To attract older customers, retailers will need to place seats in their larger stores so aging shoppers can rest. Washrooms need to be more accessible. Signs need to be larger. Restaurants need to raise the level of lighting so people can read their menus. Home appliances need simpler and larger controls. Already, the market for road bikes is declining as sales for tread mills and massagers for aching muscles increase.

Seven sociocultural trends in the United States that are helping to define what North America and the world will look like at the beginning of the next century are:

1. **Increasing environmental awareness.** Recycling and conservation are becoming more than slogans. Busch Gardens, for example, eliminated the use of disposable styrofoam trays in favor of washing and reusing plastic trays.

2. **Growth of the seniors market.** As their numbers increase, people over age 55 will become an even more important market. Already some companies are segmenting the senior population into Young Matures, Older Matures, and the Elderly—each having a different set of attitudes and interests.

3. **Generation Y boomlet.** Born after 1980 to the boomer and X generations, this cohort may end up being as large as the boomer generation. In 1957, the peak year of the postwar boom, 4.3 million babies were born. In 1990, there were 4.2 million births. By the mid 1990s, elementary schools were becoming overcrowded.[8] The U.S. census bureau projects generation Y to crest at 30.8 million births by 2005.

4. **Decline of the mass market.** Niche markets are beginning to define the marketers' environment. People want products and services that are adapted more to their personal needs. For example, Estee Lauder's "All Skin" and Maybelline's "Shades of You" line of cosmetic products are specifically made for African-American women. "Mass customization"—the making and marketing of products tailored to a person's requirements (Dell Computers)—is replacing the mass production and marketing of the same product in some markets.

5. **Pace and location of life.** Instant communication via facsimile machines, car telephones, and overnight mail enhances efficiency, but it also puts more pressure on people. Merging the personal computer with the communication and entertainment industry through telephone lines, satellite dishes, and cable television increases consumers' choices and allows workers to leave overcrowded urban areas for small towns and "telecommute" via personal computers and modems.

6. **Changing household.** Single-person households could become the most common household type in the United States after the year 2005. By 2005, only households composed of married couples with no children will be larger.[9] Although the Y generation baby boomlet may alter this estimate, a household clearly will no longer be the same as it was once portrayed in "The Brady Bunch" in the 1970s or even "The Cosby Show" in the 1980s.

7. **Diversity of workforce and markets.** Minority groups are increasing as a percentage of the total U.S. population. From 1996 to 2050, group percentages are expected by the U.S. Census Bureau to change as follows: *Whites*—from 83% to 75%; *Blacks*—from 13% to 15%; *Asian*—from 4% to 9%; *American Indian*—slight increase. *Hispanics*, which can be of any race, are projected to grow from 10% to 25% during this time period.[10] Traditional minority groups are increasing their numbers in the workforce and are being identified as desirable target markets. For example, the South Dekalb Mall in Atlanta, Georgia, recently restyled itself as an "Afrocentric retail center" in response to the rapid growth of the African-American 18-to-34 age group.[11]

Table 3.2 **Some Important Variables in International Societal Environments**

Economic	Technological	Political-Legal	Sociocultural
Economic development	Regulations on technology transfer	Form of government	Customs, norms, values
Per capita income	Energy availability/cost	Political ideology	Language
Climate	Natural resource availability	Tax laws	Demographics
GDP trends	Transportation network	Stability of government	Life expectancies
Monetary and fiscal policies	Skill level of work force	Government attitude toward foreign companies	Social institutions
Unemployment level	Patent-trademark protection	Regulations on foreign ownership of assets	Status symbols
Currency convertibility	Information-flow infrastructure	Strength of opposition groups	Life-style
Wage levels		Trade regulations	Religious beliefs
Nature of competition		Protectionist sentiment	Attitudes toward foreigners
Membership in regional economic associations		Foreign policies	Literacy level
		Terrorist activity	Human rights
		Legal system	Environmentalism

International Societal Considerations Each country or group of countries in which a company operates presents a whole new societal environment with a different set of economic, technological, political-legal, and sociocultural variables for the company to face. International societal environments vary so widely that a corporation's internal environment and strategic management process must be very flexible. Cultural trends in Germany, for example, have resulted in the inclusion of worker representatives in corporate strategic planning. Differences in societal environments strongly affect the ways in which a **multinational corporation (MNC),** a company operating in multiple countries, conducts its marketing, financial, manufacturing, and other functional activities. For example, the existence of regional associations like the European Union, the North American Free Trade Zone, and Mercosur in South America has a significant impact on the competitive "rules of the game" both for those MNCs operating within and for those MNCs wanting to enter these areas.

To account for the many differences among societal environments from one country to another, consider Table 3.2. It includes a list of economic, technological, political-legal, and sociocultural variables for any particular country or region. For example, an important economic variable for any firm investing in a foreign country is currency convertibility. Without convertibility, a company operating in Russia cannot convert its profits from rubles to dollars. In terms of sociocultural variables, many Asian cultures (especially China) are less concerned with the values of human rights than are European and North American cultures. Some Asians actually contend that American companies are trying to impose Western human rights requirements on them in an attempt to make Asian products less competitive by raising their costs.[12]

Before planning its strategy for a particular international location, a company must scan the particular country environment(s) in question for opportunities and threats, and compare these with its own organizational strengths and weaknesses. For example, to operate successfully in a global industry such as automobiles, tires, electronics, or watches, a company must be prepared to establish a significant presence in the three developed areas of the world known collectively as the **Triad**. This term was coined by the Japanese management expert, Kenichi Ohmae, and it refers to the three developed markets of Japan, North America, and Western Europe, which now form a single market with common needs.[13] Focusing on the Triad is essential for an MNC pursuing success in a global industry, according to Ohmae, because close to 90% of all high–value-added, high-technology manufactured goods are produced and consumed in North America, Western Europe, and Japan. Ideally a company should have a significant presence in each of these regions so that it can produce and market its products simultaneously in all three areas. Otherwise, it will lose competitive advantage to Triad-oriented MNCs. No longer can an MNC develop and market a new product in one part of the world before it exports it to other developed countries.

Focusing only on the developed nations, however, causes a corporation to miss important market opportunities in the developing nations of the world. Although these nations may not have developed to the point that they have significant demand for a broad spectrum of products, they may very likely be on the threshold of rapid growth in the demand for specific products. This would be the ideal time for a company to enter this market—before competition is established. The key is to be able to identify the "trigger point" when demand for a particular product or service is ready to boom. See the **Key Theory** feature for an in-depth explanation of a technique to identify the optimum time to enter a particular market in a developing nation.

Scanning the Task Environment

As shown in Figure 3.1, a corporation's scanning of the environment will include analyses of all the relevant elements in the task environment. These analyses take the form of individual reports written by various people in different parts of the firm. At Procter & Gamble (P&G), for example, people from each of the brand management teams work with key people from the sales and market research departments to research and write a "competitive activity report" each quarter on each of the product categories in which P&G competes. People in purchasing also write similar reports concerning new developments in the industries that supply P&G. These and other reports are then summarized and transmitted up the corporate hierarchy for top management to use in strategic decision making. If a new development is reported regarding a particular product category, top management may then send memos asking people throughout the organization to watch for and report on developments in related product areas. The many reports resulting from these scanning efforts, when boiled down to their essentials, act as a detailed list of external strategic factors.

Identifying External Strategic Factors

Why do companies often respond differently to the same environmental changes? One reason is because of differences in the ability of managers to recognize and understand external strategic issues and factors. Few firms can successfully monitor all important external factors. Even though managers agree that strategic importance determines what variables are consistently tracked, they sometimes miss or choose to ignore crucial new developments.[14] Personal values of a corporation's managers as well as the success of current strategies are likely to bias both their perception of what is important to monitor in the external environment and their interpretations of what they perceive.[15]

In Tupperware's case, even though a number of top managers were generally aware that women were leaving the house in favor of careers, they chose to discount its importance in the marketing of the company's products. This willingness to reject unfamiliar

KEY THEORY

USING PPP TO IDENTIFY POTENTIAL MARKETS IN DEVELOPING NATIONS

Research by the Deloitte & Touche Consulting Group reveals that the demand for a specific product increases exponentially at certain points in a country's development. Identifying this trigger point of demand is thus critical to entering emerging markets at the best time—the time when enough people have enough money to buy what a company has to sell, but before competition is established. This can be done by using the concept of **purchasing power parity (PPP),** which measures the cost in dollars of the U.S.–produced equivalent volume of goods that an economy produces.

PPP offers an estimate of the material wealth a nation can purchase, rather than the financial wealth it creates as typically measured by Gross Domestic Product (GDP). As a result, restating a nation's GDP in PPP terms reveals much greater spending power than market exchange rates would suggest. For example, a shoe shine costing $5 to $10 in New York City can be purchased for 50¢ in Mexico City. Consequently the people of Mexico City can enjoy the same standard of living (with respect to shoe shines) as people in New York City with only 5% to 10% of the money. Correcting for PPP restates all Mexican shoe shines at their U.S. purchase value of $5. If one million shoe shines were purchased in Mexico last year, using the PPP model would effectively increase Mexican GDP by $5 million–$10 million. Using PPP, China becomes the world's second largest economy after the United States, with Brazil, Mexico, and India moving ahead of Canada into the top ten world markets.

Trigger points identify when demand for a particular product is about to rapidly increase in a country. This can be a very useful technique to identify when to enter a new market in a developing nation. Trigger points vary for different products. For example, an apparent trigger point for long-distance telephone services is at $7,500 in GDP per capita—a point when demand for telecommunications services increases rapidly. Once national wealth surpasses $15,000 per capita, demand increases at a much slower rate with further increases in wealth. The trigger point for life insurance is around $8,000 in GDP per capita. At this point, the demand for life insurance increases between 200% and 300% above those countries with GDP per capita below the trigger point.

Source: Summarized from D. Fraser and M. Raynor, "The Power of Parity," *Forecast* (May/June, 1996), pp. 8–12.

as well as negative information is called **strategic myopia.**[16] If a firm needs to change its strategy, it might not be gathering the appropriate external information to change strategies successfully.

One way to identify and analyze developments in the external environment is to use the **issues priority matrix** (Figure 3.2) in this way:

1. Identify a number of likely trends emerging in the societal and task environments. These are strategic environmental issues—those important trends that, if they occur, determine what the industry or the world will look like.

2. Assess the probability of these trends actually occurring from low to high.

3. Attempt to ascertain the likely impact (from low to high) of each of these trends on the corporation being examined.

A corporation's **external strategic factors** are those key environmental trends that are judged to have both a *medium to high probability of occurrence* and a *medium to*

Figure 3.1
Scanning the External Environment

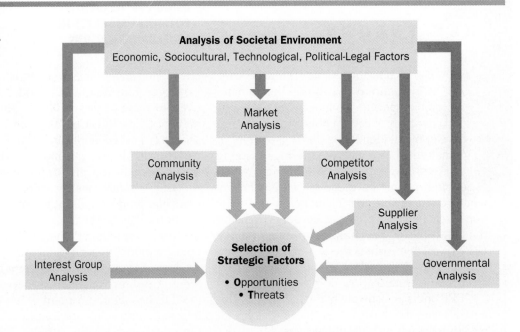

high probability of impact on the corporation. The issues priority matrix can then be used to help managers decide which environmental trends should be merely scanned (low priority) and which should be monitored as strategic factors (high priority). Those environmental trends judged to be a corporation's strategic factors are then categorized as *opportunities* and *threats* and are included in strategy formulation.

3.2 Industry Analysis: Analyzing the Task Environment

An **industry** is a group of firms producing a similar product or service, such as soft drinks or financial services. An examination of the important stakeholder groups, such as suppliers and customers, in a particular corporation's task environment is a part of industry analysis.

Porter's Approach to Industry Analysis

Michael Porter, an authority on competitive strategy, contends that a corporation is most concerned with the intensity of competition within its industry. The level of this intensity is determined by basic competitive forces, which are depicted in Figure 3.3. "The collective strength of these forces," he contends, "determines the ultimate profit potential in the industry, where profit potential is measured in terms of long-run return on invested capital."[17] In carefully scanning its industry, the corporation must assess the importance to its success of each of the six forces: *threat of new entrants, rivalry among existing firms, threat of substitute products or services, bargaining power of buyers, bargaining power of suppliers, and relative power of other stakeholders.*[18] The stronger each of these forces, the more limited companies are in their ability to raise prices and earn greater profits. Although Porter mentions only five forces, a sixth—other stakeholders—is added here to reflect

Figure 3.2
Issues Priority
Matrix

Source: Adapted from L. L. Lederman, "Foresight Activities in the U.S.A.: Time for a Reassessment?" *Long-Range Planning* (June 1984), p. 46. Copyright © 1984 by Pergamon Press, Ltd. Reprinted by permission.

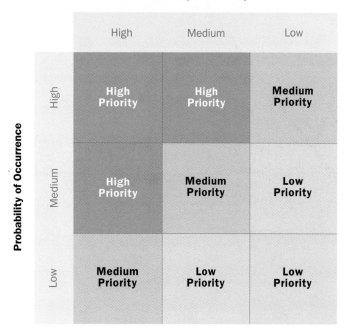

the power that governments, local communities, and other groups from the task environment wield over industry activities.

Using the model in Figure 3.3, a high force can be regarded as a threat because it is likely to reduce profits. A low force, in contrast, can be viewed as an opportunity because it may allow the company to earn greater profits. In the short run, these forces act as constraints on a company's activities. In the long run, however, it may be possible for a company, through its choice of strategy, to change the strength of one or more of the forces to the company's advantage.

A strategist can analyze any industry by rating each competitive force as *high, medium,* or *low* in strength. For example, the athletic shoe industry could be currently rated as follows: rivalry is high (Nike, Reebok, Adidas, and Converse are strong competitors), threat of potential entrants is low (industry is reaching maturity), threat of substitutes is low (other shoes don't provide support for sports activities), bargaining power of suppliers is medium but rising (suppliers in Asian countries are increasing in size and ability), bargaining power of buyers is medium to low (advertising is more important than distribution channels), threat of other stakeholders is medium to high (government regulations and human rights concerns are growing). Based on current trends in each of these competitive forces, the industry appears to be increasing in its level of competitive intensity—meaning profit margins will likely fall for the industry as a whole.

Threat of New Entrants

New entrants to an industry typically bring to it new capacity, a desire to gain market share, and substantial resources. They are, therefore, threats to an established corporation. The threat of entry depends on the presence of entry barriers and the reaction that can be expected from existing competitors. An **entry barrier** is an obstruction that

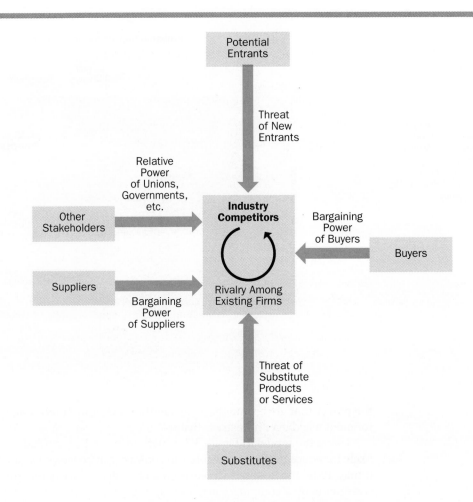

Figure 3.3
Forces Driving
Industry Competition

Source: Adapted/
reprinted with permission of The Free Press,
an imprint of Simon &
Schuster, from *Competitive Strategy: Techniques
for Analyzing Industries
and Competitors* by
Michael E. Porter.
Copyright © 1980 by
The Free Press.

makes it difficult for a company to enter an industry. For example, no new domestic automobile companies have been successfully established in the United States since the 1930s because of the high capital requirements to build production facilities and to develop a dealer distribution network. Some of the possible barriers to entry are:

- **Economies of Scale.** Scale economies in the production and sale of mainframe computers, for example, gave IBM a significant cost advantage over any new rival.

- **Product Differentiation.** Corporations like Procter & Gamble and General Mills, which manufacture products like Tide and Cheerios, create high entry barriers through their high levels of advertising and promotion.

- **Capital Requirements.** The need to invest huge financial resources in manufacturing facilities in order to produce computer microprocessors creates a significant barrier to entry to any competitor for Intel.

- **Switching Costs.** Once a software program like Excel or Word becomes established in an office, office managers are very reluctant to switch to a new program because of the high training costs.

- **Access to Distribution Channels.** Small entrepreneurs often have difficulty obtaining supermarket shelf space for their goods because large retailers charge for space on their shelves and give priority to the established firms who can pay for the advertising needed to generate high customer demand.

- **Cost Disadvantages Independent of Size.** Microsoft's development of the first widely adopted operating system (MS-DOS) for the IBM-type personal computer gave it a significant advantage over potential competitors. Its introduction of Windows helped to cement that advantage.

- **Government Policy.** Governments can limit entry into an industry through licensing requirements by restricting access to raw materials, such as off-shore oil drilling sites.

Rivalry Among Existing Firms

In most industries, corporations are mutually dependent. A competitive move by one firm can be expected to have a noticeable effect on its competitors and thus may cause retaliation or counterefforts. For example, the entry by mail order companies such as Dell and Gateway into a PC industry previously dominated by IBM, Apple, and Compaq increased the level of competitive activity to such an extent that any price reduction or new product introduction is now quickly followed by similar moves from other PC makers. According to Porter, intense rivalry is related to the presence of several factors, including:

- **Number of Competitors.** When competitors are few and roughly equal in size, such as in the U.S. auto and major home appliance industries, they watch each other carefully to make sure that any move by another firm is matched by an equal countermove.

- **Rate of Industry Growth.** Any slowing in passenger traffic tends to set off price wars in the airline industry because the only path to growth is to take sales away from a competitor.

- **Product or Service Characteristics.** Many people choose a videotape rental store based on location, variety of selection, and pricing because they view videotapes as a *commodity*—a product whose characteristics are the same regardless of who sells it.

- **Amount of Fixed Costs.** Because airlines must fly their planes on a schedule regardless of the number of paying passengers for any one flight, they offer cheap standby fares whenever a plane has empty seats.

- **Capacity.** If the only way a manufacturer can increase capacity is in a large increment by building a new plant (as in the paper industry), it will run that new plant at full capacity to keep its unit costs as low as possible—thus producing so much that the selling price falls throughout the industry.

- **Height of Exit Barriers.** Exit barriers keep a company from leaving an industry. The brewing industry, for example, has a low percentage of companies that leave the industry because breweries are specialized assets with few uses except for making beer.

- **Diversity of Rivals.** Rivals that have very different ideas of how to compete are likely to cross paths often and unknowingly challenge each other's position.

Threat of Substitute Products or Services

Substitute products are those products that appear to be different but can satisfy the same need as another product. For example, the fax is a substitute for Fed Ex,

Nutrasweet is a substitute for sugar, and bottled water is a substitute for a cola. According to Porter, "Substitutes limit the potential returns of an industry by placing a ceiling on the prices firms in the industry can profitably charge."[19] To the extent that switching costs are low, substitutes may have a strong effect on an industry. Tea can be considered a substitute for coffee. If the price of coffee goes up high enough, coffee drinkers will slowly begin switching to tea. The price of tea thus puts a price ceiling on the price of coffee. Sometimes a difficult task, the identification of possible substitute products or services means searching for products or services that can perform the same function, even though they may not appear to be easily substitutable.

Bargaining Power of Buyers

Buyers affect an industry through their ability to force down prices, bargain for higher quality or more services, and play competitors against each other. A buyer or a group of buyers is powerful if some of the following factors hold true:

- A buyer purchases a large proportion of the seller's product or service (for example, oil filters purchased by a major automaker).

- A buyer has the potential to integrate backward by producing the product itself (for example, a newspaper chain could make its own paper).

- Alternative suppliers are plentiful because the product is standard or undifferentiated (for example, motorists can choose among many gas stations).

- Changing suppliers costs very little (for example, office supplies are easy to find).

- The purchased product represents a high percentage of a buyer's costs, thus providing an incentive to shop around for a lower price (for example, gasoline purchased for resale by convenience stores makes up half their costs).

- A buyer earns low profits and is thus very sensitive to costs and service differences (for example, grocery stores have very small margins).

- The purchased product is unimportant to the final quality or price of a buyer's products or services and thus can be easily substituted without affecting the final product adversely (for example, electric wire bought for use in lamps).

Bargaining Power of Suppliers

Suppliers can affect an industry through their ability to raise prices or reduce the quality of purchased goods and services. A supplier or supplier group is powerful if some of the following factors apply:

- The supplier industry is dominated by a few companies, but it sells to many (for example, the petroleum industry).

- Its product or service is unique and/or it has built up switching costs (for example, word processing software).

- Substitutes are not readily available (for example, electricity).

- Suppliers are able to integrate forward and compete directly with their present customers (for example, a microprocessor producer like Intel can make PCs).

- A purchasing industry buys only a small portion of the supplier group's goods and services and is thus unimportant to the supplier (for example, sales of lawn mower tires are less important to the tire industry than are sales of auto tires).

Relative Power of Other Stakeholders

A sixth force should be added to Porter's list to include a variety of stakeholder groups from the task environment. Some of these groups are governments (if not explicitly included elsewhere), local communities, creditors (if not included with suppliers), trade associations, special-interest groups, and shareholders. The importance of these stakeholders varies by industry. For example, environmental groups in Maine, Michigan, Oregon, and Iowa successfully fought to pass bills outlawing disposable bottles and cans, and thus deposits for most drink containers are now required. This effectively raised costs across the board, with the most impact on the marginal producers who could not internally absorb all of these costs.

Industry Evolution

Over time most industries evolve through a series of stages from growth through maturity to eventual decline. The strength of each of the six forces mentioned earlier varies according to the stage of industry evolution. The industry life cycle is useful for explaining and predicting trends among the six forces driving industry competition. For example, when an industry is new, people often buy the product regardless of price because it fulfills a unique need. This is probably a **fragmented industry**—no firm has large market share and each firm serves only a small piece of the total market in competition with others (for example, Chinese restaurants). As new competitors enter the industry, prices drop as a result of competition. Companies use the experience curve (to be discussed in Chapter 4) and economies of scale to reduce costs faster than the competition. Companies integrate to reduce costs even further by acquiring their suppliers and distributors. Competitors try to differentiate their products from one another's in order to avoid the fierce price competition common to a maturing industry.

By the time an industry enters maturity, products tend to become more like commodities. This is now a **consolidated industry**—dominated by a few large firms, each of which struggles to differentiate its products from the competition. As buyers become more sophisticated over time, purchasing decisions are based on better information. Price becomes a dominant concern, given a minimum level of quality and features. One example of this trend is the videocassette recorder industry. By the 1990s, VCRs had reached the point where there were few major differences among them. Consumers realized that because slight improvements cost significantly more money, it made little sense to pay more than the minimum for a VCR. The same is true of gasoline.

As an industry moves through maturity toward possible decline, its products' growth rate of sales slows and may even begin to decrease. To the extent that exit barriers are low, firms will begin converting their facilities to alternate uses or will sell them to another firm. The industry tends to consolidate around fewer but larger competitors. As in the case of the U.S. major home appliance industry described in the **Company Spotlight on Maytag Corporation** feature, the industry changed from being a fragmented industry (pure competition) composed of hundreds of appliance manufacturers in the industry's early years to a consolidated industry (mature oligopoly) composed of five companies (including Maytag) controlling over 98% of U.S. appliance sales. A similar consolidation was occurring in European major home appliances during the 1990s.

Categorizing International Industries

World industries vary on a continuum from multidomestic to global (see Figure 3.4).[20] **Multidomestic industries** are specific to each country or group of countries. This type of international industry is a collection of essentially domestic industries, like retailing

In 1945, there were approximately 300 major home appliance manufacturers in the United States. By 1996, however, the "big five"—Whirlpool, General Electric, A.B. Electrolux (*no* relation to Electrolux Corporation, a U.S. company selling Electrolux brand vacuum cleaners), Maytag, and Raytheon—controlled over 98% of the U.S. market. The consolidation of the industry over the period was a result of fierce domestic competition. Emphasis on quality and durability coupled with strong price competition drove the surviving firms to increased efficiencies and a strong concern for customer satisfaction.

Prior to World War II, most appliance manufacturers produced a limited line of appliances deriving from one successful product. General Electric made refrigerators. Maytag focused on washing machines. Hotpoint produced electric ranges. Each offered variations of its basic product, but not until 1945 did firms begin to offer full lines of various appliances. By 1955, the major appliance industry began experiencing overcapacity, leading to mergers and acquisitions and a proliferation of national and private brands. Product reliability improved even though real prices (adjusted for inflation) declined about 10%.

Acknowledging that the U.S. major home appliance industry had reached maturity—future U.S. unit sales were expected to grow only 1%–2% annually on average for the foreseeable future—U.S. appliance makers decided to expand into Europe (where unit sales were expected to grow 5% annually). With Whirlpool's acquisition of the appliance business of Philips (The Netherlands), GE's joint venture with GEC (United Kingdom), AB Electrolux's (Sweden) purchase of White in the United States, and Maytag's acquisition of Hoover (vacuum cleaners worldwide plus major home appliances in the UK), the level of competition increased dramatically in both Europe and North America during the 1990s. In addition, rapid economic growth in Asia as well as in Mexico and South America had tremendous implications for the emerging global appliance industry. Environmental scanning and industry analysis had to be international in scope if a firm was to succeed in the 21st century.

and insurance. The activities in a subsidiary of a multinational corporation (MNC) in this type of industry are essentially independent of the activities of the MNC's subsidiaries in other countries. In each country, the MNC tailors its products or services to the very specific needs of consumers in that particular country.

Global industries, in contrast, operate worldwide, with MNCs making only small adjustments for country-specific circumstances. A global industry is one in which an MNC's activities in one country are significantly affected by its activities in other countries. MNCs produce products or services in various locations throughout the world and sell them, making only minor adjustments for specific country requirements. Examples of global industries are commercial aircraft, television sets, semiconductors, copiers, automobiles, watches, and tires. The largest industrial corporations in the world in terms of dollar sales are, for the most part, multinational corporations operating in global industries.

The factors that tend to determine whether an industry will be primarily multidomestic or primarily global are:

1. *Pressure for coordination* within the multinational corporations operating in that industry.

2. *Pressure for local responsiveness* on the part of individual country markets.

Figure 3.4
Continuum of
International
Industries

Multidomestic ◄───► Global

Industry in which companies tailor their products to
the specific needs of consumers in a particular country.
• Retailing
• Insurance
• Banking

Industry in which companies manufacture and sell the same
products, with only minor adjustments made for individual
countries around the world.
• Automobiles
• Tires
• Television sets

To the extent that the pressure for coordination is strong and the pressure for local responsiveness is weak for multinational corporations within a particular industry, that industry will tend to become global. In contrast, when the pressure for local responsiveness is strong and the pressure for coordination is weak for multinational corporations in an industry, that industry will tend to be multidomestic. Between these two extremes lie a number of industries with varying characteristics of both multidomestic and global industries. The dynamic tension between these two factors is contained in the phrase: *Think globally, but act locally*.

International Risk Assessment

Some firms, such as American Can Company and Mitsubishi Trading Company, develop elaborate information networks and computerized systems to evaluate and rank investment risks. Small companies can hire outside consultants such as Chicago's Associated Consultants International or Boston's Arthur D. Little, Inc., to provide political-risk assessments. Among the many systems that exist to assess political and economic risks are the Political System Stability Index, the Business Environment Risk Index, Business International's Country Assessment Service, and Frost and Sullivan's World Political Risk Forecasts.[21] Business International provides subscribers with continuously updated information on conditions in 63 countries. A Boston company called International Strategies offers an Export Hotline (800 USA-XPORT) that faxes information to callers for only the cost of the call.[22] Regardless of the source of data, a firm must develop its own method of assessing risk. It must decide on its most important risk factors and then assign weights to each.

Strategic Groups

A **strategic group** is a set of business units or firms that "pursue similar strategies with similar resources."[23] Categorizing firms in any one industry into a set of strategic groups is very useful as a way of better understanding the competitive environment.[24] Because a corporation's structure and culture tend to reflect the kinds of strategies it follows, companies or business units belonging to a particular strategic group within the same industry tend to be strong rivals and tend to be more similar to each other than to competitors in other strategic groups within the same industry.

For example, although McDonald's and Olive Garden are a part of the same restaurant industry, they have different missions, objectives, and strategies, and thus belong to different strategic groups. They generally have very little in common and pay little attention to each other when planning competitive actions. Burger King and Hardee's, however, have a great deal in common with McDonald's in terms of their similar strategy of producing a high volume of low-priced meals targeted for sale to the average family. Consequently they are strong rivals and are organized to operate similarly.

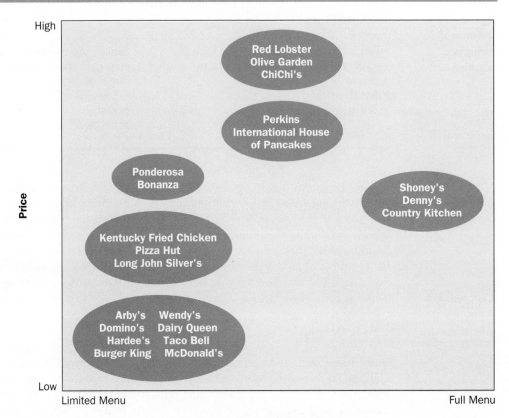

Figure 3.5
Mapping Strategic Groups in the U.S. Restaurant Chain Industry

Strategic groups in a particular industry can be *mapped* by plotting the market positions of industry competitors on a two-dimensional graph using two strategic variables as the vertical and horizontal axes. (See Figure 3.5.)

1. Select two broad characteristics, such as price and menu, that differentiate the companies in an industry from one another.

2. Plot the firms using these two characteristics as the dimensions.

3. Draw a circle around those companies that are closest to one another as one strategic group, varying the size of the circle in proportion to the group's share of total industry sales. (You could also name each strategic group in the restaurant industry with an identifying title, such as quick fast food or buffet style service.)

Other dimensions, such as quality and degree of vertical integration, can also be used in additional graphs of the restaurant industry to gain a better understanding of how the various firms in the industry compete. Keep in mind, however, that when choosing the two dimensions, they should not be highly correlated; otherwise, the circles on the map will simply lie along the diagonal, providing very little new information other than the obvious.

Strategic Types

In analyzing the level of competitive intensity within a particular industry or strategic group, it is useful to characterize the various competitors for predictive purposes. A **strategic type** is a category of firms based on a common strategic orientation and a combination of structure, culture, and processes consistent with that strategy. According to Miles and Snow, competing firms within a single industry can be categorized on the basis of their general strategic orientation into one of four basic types.[25] This distinction helps explain why companies facing similar situations behave differently and why they continue to do so over a long period of time. These general types have the following characteristics:

- **Defenders** are companies with a limited product line that *focus on improving the efficiency of their existing operations*. This cost orientation makes them unlikely to innovate in new areas. An example is the Adolph Coors Company, which for many years emphasized production efficiency in its one Colorado brewery and virtually ignored marketing.

- **Prospectors** are companies with fairly broad product lines that *focus on product innovation and market opportunities*. This sales orientation makes them somewhat inefficient. They tend to emphasize creativity over efficiency. An example is the Miller Brewing Company, which successfully promoted "light" beer and generated aggressive, innovative advertising campaigns, but had to close a brand-new brewery when management overestimated market demand.

- **Analyzers** are corporations that *operate in at least two different product-market areas*, one stable and one variable. In the stable areas, efficiency is emphasized. In the variable areas, innovation is emphasized. An example is Anheuser-Busch, which can take a defender orientation to protect its massive market share in U.S. beer and a prospector orientation to generate sales in its amusement parks.

- **Reactors** are corporations that *lack a consistent strategy-structure-culture relationship*. Their (often ineffective) responses to environmental pressures tend to be piecemeal strategic changes. An example is the Pabst Brewing Company, which, because of numerous takeover attempts, has been unable to generate a consistent strategy to keep its sales from dropping.

Dividing the competition into these four categories enables the strategic manager not only to monitor the effectiveness of certain strategic orientations, but also to develop scenarios of future industry developments (discussed later in this chapter).

Hypercompetition

Most industries today are facing an ever-increasing level of environmental uncertainty. They are becoming more complex and more dynamic. Industries that used to be multidomestic are becoming global. New flexible, aggressive, innovative competitors are moving into established markets to rapidly erode the advantages of large previously dominant firms. Distribution channels vary from country to country and are being altered daily through the use of sophisticated information systems. Closer relationships with suppliers are being forged to reduce costs, increase quality, and gain access to new technology. Companies learn to quickly imitate the successful strategies of market leaders, and it becomes harder to sustain any competitive advantage for very long. Consequently, the level of competitive intensity is increasing in most industries.

Richard D'Aveni contends that as this type of environmental turbulence reaches more industries, competition becomes **hypercompetition**. According to D'Aveni:

> In hypercompetition the frequency, boldness, and aggressiveness of dynamic movement by the players accelerates to create a condition of constant disequilibrium and change. Market stability is threatened by short product life cycles, short product design cycles, new

MICROSOFT OPERATES IN A HYPERCOMPETITIVE INDUSTRY

Microsoft is a hypercompetitive firm operating in a hypercompetitive industry. It has used its dominance in operating systems (DOS and Windows) to move into a very strong position in application programs like word processing and spreadsheets (Word and Excel). Even though Microsoft held 90% of the market for personal computer operating systems in 1992, it still invested millions in developing the next generation—Windows 95 and Windows NT. Instead of trying to protect its advantage in the profitable DOS operating system, Microsoft actively sought to replace DOS with various versions of Windows. Before hypercompetition, most experts argued against cannibalization of a company's own product line because it destroys a very profitable product instead of harvesting it like a "cash cow." According to this line of thought, a company would be better off defending its older products. New products would only be introduced if it could be proven that they would not take sales away from current products. Microsoft was one of the first companies to disprove this argument against cannibalization.

Bill Gates, Microsoft's co-founder, Chairman, and CEO, realized that if his company didn't replace its own DOS product line with a better product, someone else would (such as IBM with OS/2 Warp). He knew that success in the software industry depends not so much on company size but on moving aggressively to the next competitive advantage before a competitor does. "This is a hypercompetitive market," explained Gates. "Scale is not all positive in this business. Cleverness is the position in this business." By 1997, Microsoft still controlled over 90% of operating systems software and had achieved a dominant position in applications software as well.

Source: R. A. D'Aveni, *HyperCompetition* (New York: Free Press, 1994), p. 2.

technologies, frequent entry by unexpected outsiders, repositioning by incumbents, and tactical redefinitions of market boundaries as diverse industries merge. In other words, environments escalate toward higher and higher levels of uncertainty, dynamism, heterogeneity of the players and hostility.[26]

In hypercompetitive industries such as computers, competitive advantage comes from an up-to-date knowledge of environmental trends and competitive activity coupled with a willingness to risk a current advantage for a possible new advantage. Companies must be willing to *cannibalize* their own products (replacing popular products before competitors do so) in order to sustain their competitive advantage. As a result, industry or competitive intelligence has never been more important. See the **Strategy in a Changing World** feature to see how Microsoft is operating in the hypercompetitive industry of computer software. (Hypercompetition is discussed in more detail in Chapter 5.)

Creating an Industry Matrix

An **industry matrix** summarizes the external strategic factors (opportunities and threats) facing a particular industry. As shown in Table 3.3, the matrix gives a weight for each factor based on how important that factor is to the future of the industry. The matrix also specifies how well various competitors in the industry are responding to each factor. To generate an industry matrix using two industry competitors (called A and B), complete the following steps for the industry being analyzed:

Table 3.3 **Industry Matrix**

Strategic Factors	Weight	Company A Rating	Company A Weighted Score	Company B Rating	Company B Weighted Score
1	2	3	4	5	6
Total	1.00				

Source: T. L. Wheelen and J. D. Hunger, "Industry Matrix." Copyright © 1997 by Wheelen and Hunger Associates. Reprinted by permission.

- In **Column 1** (*Strategic Factors*) list the eight to ten most important opportunities and threats facing the industry as a whole.

- In **Column 2** (*Weight*) assign a weight to each factor from **1.0** (*Most Important*) to **0.0** (*Not Important*) based on that factor's probable impact on the overall industry's future success. **(All weights must sum to 1.0 regardless of the number of strategic factors.)**

- In **Column 3** (*Company A Rating*) examine a particular company within the industry—for example, Company A. Assign a rating to each factor from **5** (*Outstanding*) to **1** (*Poor*) based on Company A's current response to that particular factor. Each rating is a judgment regarding how well that company is currently dealing with each strategic factor.

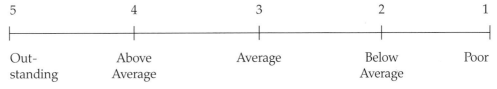

- In **Column 4** (*Company A Weighted Score*) multiply the *weight* in **Column 2** for each factor times its rating in **Column 3** to obtain that factor's *weighted score* for Company A. This results in a weighted score for each factor ranging from **5.0** (*Outstanding*) to **1.0** (*Poor*) with 3.0 as the *average.*

- In **Column 5** (*Company B Rating*) examine a second company within the industry—in this case, Company B. Assign a rating to each factor from **5** (*Outstanding*) to **1** (*Poor*) based on Company B's current response to each particular factor.

- In **Column 6** (*Company B Weighted Score*) multiply the *weight* in **Column 2** for each factor times its rating in **Column 5** to obtain that factor's *weighted score* for Company B.

Finally, add the weighted scores for all the factors in **Columns 4** and **6** to determine the total weighted scores for companies A and B. The *total weighted score* indicates how well each company is responding to current and expected factors in the industry's environment. The industry matrix can be expanded to include all the major competitors within an industry simply by adding two additional columns for each additional competitor.

3.3 Industry/Competitive Intelligence

Much external environmental scanning is done on an informal and individual basis. Information is obtained from a variety of sources—customers, suppliers, bankers, consultants, publications, personal observations, subordinates, superiors, and peers. For example, scientists and engineers working in a firm's R&D lab can learn about new products and competitors' ideas at professional meetings; someone from the purchasing department, speaking with supplier-representatives' personnel, may also uncover valuable bits of information about a competitor. A study of product innovation in the scientific instrument and machine tool industries found that 80% of all product innovations were initiated by the customer in the form of inquiries and complaints.[27] In these industries, the sales force and service departments must be especially vigilant.

Industry (or **competitive**) **intelligence** is a formal program of gathering information on a company's competitors. Only 7% of large U.S. corporations have fully developed intelligence programs. In contrast, all Japanese corporations involved in international business and most large European companies have active intelligence programs.[28] This situation is changing, however. At General Mills, for example, all employees have been trained to recognize and tap sources of competitive information. Janitors no longer simply place orders with suppliers of cleaning materials, they also ask about relevant practices at competing firms!

Most corporations rely on outside organizations to provide them with environmental data. Firms such as A. C. Nielsen Co. provide subscribers with bimonthly data on brand share, retail prices, percentages of stores stocking an item, and percentages of stock-out stores. Strategists can use this data to spot regional and national trends as well as to assess market share. Information on market conditions, government regulations, competitors, and new products can be bought from "information brokers" such as FIND/SVP and Finsbury Data Services. Company and industry profiles are generally available from the Reference Press at Hoover's On Line site on the World Wide Web (*http://www.hoovers.com*). Many business corporations have established their own in-house libraries and computerized information systems to deal with the growing mass of available information.

Some companies, however, choose to use industrial espionage or other intelligence-gathering techniques to get their information straight from their competitors. Theft of proprietary R&D has risen 260% from 1985 to 1995. Using current or former competitors' employees and by using private contractors, some firms attempt to steal trade secrets, technology, business plans, and pricing strategies.[29] For example, Avon Products hired private investigators to retrieve from a public dumpster documents (some of them shredded) that Mary Kay Corporation had thrown away. Even Procter & Gamble, which defends itself like a fortress from information leaks, is vulnerable. A competitor was able to learn the precise launch date of a concentrated laundry detergent in Europe when one of its people visited the factory where machinery was being made. Simply asking a few questions about what a certain machine did, whom it was for, and when it would be delivered was all that was necessary.

3.4 Forecasting

Environmental scanning provides reasonably hard data on the present situation and current trends, but intuition and luck are needed to accurately predict if these trends will continue. The resulting forecasts are, however, usually based on a set of assumptions that may or may not be valid.

Danger of Assumptions

Faulty underlying assumptions are the most frequent cause of forecasting errors. Nevertheless many managers who formulate and implement strategic plans rarely consider that their success is based on a series of assumptions. Many long-range plans are simply based on projections of the current situation. One example of what can happen when a corporate strategy rests on the very questionable assumption that the future will simply be an extension of the present is that of Tupperware. Management not only assumed in the 1960s and 1970s that Tupperware parties would continue being an excellent distribution channel, its faith in this assumption also blinded it to information about America's changing lifestyles and their likely impact on sales. Even in the 1990s, when Tupperware executives realized that their extrapolated sales forecasts were no longer justified, they were unable to improve their forecasting techniques until they changed their assumptions.

Useful Forecasting Techniques

Various techniques are used to forecast future situations. Each has its proponents and critics. A study of nearly 500 of the world's largest corporations revealed trend extrapolation to be the most widely practiced form of forecasting—over 70% use this technique either occasionally or frequently.[30] Simply stated, **extrapolation** is the extension of present trends into the future. It rests on the assumption that the world is reasonably consistent and changes slowly in the short run. Time-series methods are approaches of this type; they attempt to carry a series of historical events forward into the future. The basic problem with extrapolation is that a historical trend is based on a series of patterns or relationships among so many different variables that a change in any one can drastically alter the future direction of the trend. As a rule of thumb, the further back into the past you can find relevant data supporting the trend, the more confidence you can have in the prediction.

Brainstorming, expert opinion, and statistical modeling are also very popular forecasting techniques. **Brainstorming** is a nonquantitative approach requiring simply the presence of people with some knowledge of the situation to be predicted. The basic ground rule is to propose ideas without first mentally screening them. No criticism is allowed. Ideas tend to build on previous ideas until a consensus is reached. This is a good technique to use with operating managers who have more faith in "gut feel" than in more quantitative "number-crunching" techniques. **Expert opinion** is a nonquantitative technique in which experts in a particular area attempt to forecast likely developments. This type of forecast is based on the ability of a knowledgeable person(s) to construct probable future developments based on the interaction of key variables. See the ⬤**21st Century Global Society** feature for a prediction of the immediate future of Eastern Europe based on expert opinion. **Statistical modeling** is a quantitative technique that attempts to discover causal or at least explanatory factors that link two or more time series together. Examples of statistical modeling are regression analysis and other econometric methods. Although very useful in the grasping of historic trends, statistical modeling, like trend extrapolation, is based on historical data. As the patterns of

21ST CENTURY GLOBAL SOCIETY

EXPERT OPINION ON THE FUTURE OF EASTERN EUROPE

Based on his many years in the region, Edward Lucas, Eastern European correspondent for *The Economist*, predicted the likely future of a number of Eastern European nations. According to Lucas, it will soon become clear that the entrenched political and economic system in these countries would be a form of "crony capitalism," in which the communist elites have made a quiet shift from power to wealth. Although they will overtly support capitalism, political connections will be crucial for anyone wanting to do serious business. Output will rise, but according to Lucas, the amount will be based on some key factors: a nation's competitive advantage and its political and financial institutions. The region's current competitive advantage lay in cheap labor and high skills, but these are already being eroded.

A crucial distinction will thus emerge between those nations that keep their education system intact (as in Estonia, Czech Republic, and Slovenia) and where they are practically collapsing (as in Kazakhstan and Georgia). In addition, the likelihood of high taxes, capricious customs rules, and irresponsible politicians reinforced by public apathy in some countries will lead to a bad investment climate. Lucas made country-by-country predictions based on his score of some key factors ranging from 5=Outstanding to 1=Deplorable with a mid-point of 3=Tolerable.

	Democracy	Economic Performance	Internal Stability	Relations with Neighbors	Human Rights	Overall Outlook
Albania	2	3	3	3	2	Good
Azerbaijan	2	3	2	2	2	Good
Belarus	1	1	2	3	1	Poor
Bosnia-Herzegovina	2	1	1	1	2	Poor
Czech Republic	4	4	5	4	4	Good
Estonia	4	5	3	2	3	Good
Georgia	2	2	2	2	2	Good
Hungary	4	4	4	5	4	Good
Poland	4	5	4	5	4	Good
Serbia-Montenegro	1	1	2	1	1	Poor
Slovenia	4	4	5	4	4	Good
Tajikistan	1	1	1	2	1	Poor

Source: E. Lucas, "The Good Life After Communism," *The World in 1997* (London: The Economist Group, 1996), p. 42.

relationships change, the accuracy of the forecast deteriorates. Other forecasting techniques, such as *cross-impact analysis (CIA)* and *trend-impact analysis (TIA)*, have not established themselves successfully as regularly employed tools.

Scenario writing appears to be the most widely used forecasting technique after trend extrapolation. Originated by Royal Dutch Shell, scenarios are focused descriptions of different likely futures presented in a narrative fashion. The scenario thus may be merely a written description of some future state, in terms of key variables and issues, or it may be generated in combination with other forecasting techniques.

An **industry scenario** is a forecasted description of a particular industry's likely future. Such a scenario is developed by analyzing the probable impact of future societal forces on key groups in a particular industry. The process may operate as follows:[31]

1. Examine possible shifts in the societal variables globally.

2. Identify uncertainties in each of the six forces of the task environment (for example, potential entrants, competitors, likely substitutes, buyers, suppliers, and other key stakeholders).

3. Make a range of plausible assumptions about future trends.

4. Combine assumptions about individual trends into internally consistent scenarios.

5. Analyze the industry situation that would prevail under each scenario.

6. Determine the sources of competitive advantage under each scenario.

7. Predict competitors' behavior under each scenario.

8. Select the scenarios that are either most likely to occur or most likely to have a strong impact on the future of the company. Use these scenarios in strategy formulation.

3.5 Synthesis of External Factors—EFAS

After strategic managers have scanned the societal and task environments and identified a number of likely external factors for their particular corporation, they may want to refine their analysis of these factors using a form such as that given in Table 3.4. The **EFAS Table** (*External Factors Analysis Summary*) is one way to organize the external factors into the generally accepted categories of opportunities and threats as well as to analyze how well a particular company's management (rating) is responding to these specific factors in light of the perceived importance (weight) of these factors to the company. To generate an EFAS Table for the company being analyzed, complete the following steps:

- In **Column 1** (*External Factors*), list the eight to ten most important opportunities and threats facing the company.

- In **Column 2** (*Weight*), assign a weight to each factor from **1.0** (*Most Important*) to **0.0** (*Not Important*) based on that factor's probable impact on a particular company's current strategic position. The higher the weight, the more important is this factor to the current and future success of the company. **(All weights must sum to 1.0 regardless of the number of strategic factors.)**

- In **Column 3** (*Rating*), assign a rating to each factor from **5** (*Outstanding*) to **1** (*Poor*) based on that particular company's current response to that particular factor. Each rating is a judgment regarding how well the company is currently dealing with each external factor.

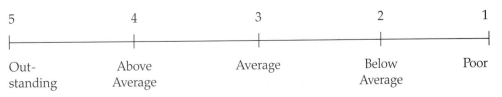

Table 3.4   External Factor Analysis Summary (EFAS): Maytag as Example

External Factors	Weight	Rating	Weighted Score	Comments
	1	2	3	4	5
Opportunities				
• Economic integration of European Community	.20	4	.80	Acquisition of Hoover
• Demographics favor quality appliances	.10	5	.50	Maytag quality
• Economic development of Asia	.05	1	.05	Low Maytag presence
• Opening of Eastern Europe	.05	2	.10	Will take time
• Trend to "Super Stores"	.10	2	.20	Maytag weak in this channel
Threats				
• Increasing government regulations	.10	4	.40	Well positioned
• Strong U.S. competition	.10	4	.40	Well positioned
• Whirlpool and Electrolux strong globally	.15	3	.45	Hoover weak globally
• New product advances	.05	1	.05	Questionable
• Japanese appliance companies	.10	2	.20	Only Asian presence is Australia
Total Scores	1.00		3.15	

Notes:

1. List opportunities and threats (5–10 each) in column 1.
2. Weight each factor from 1.0 (Most Important) to 0.0 (Not Important) in Column 2 based on that factor's probable impact on the company's strategic position. **The total weights must sum to 1.00.**
3. Rate each factor from 5 (Outstanding) to 1 (Poor) in Column 3 based on the company's response to that factor.
4. Multiply each factor's weight times its rating to obtain each factor's weighted score in Column 4.
5. Use Column 5 (comments) for rationale used for each factor.
6. Add the weighted scores to obtain the total weighted score for the company in Column 4. This tells how well the company is responding to the strategic factors in its external environment.

Source: T. L. Wheelen and J. D. Hunger, "External Strategic Factors Analysis Summary (EFAS)." Copyright © 1991 by Wheelen and Hunger Associates. Reprinted by permission.

- In **Column 4** (*Weighted Score*), multiply the *weight* in **Column 2** for each factor times its *rating* in **Column 3** to obtain that factor's *weighted score*. This results in a weighted score for each factor ranging from **5.0** (*Outstanding*) to **1.0** (*Poor*) with **3.0** as *average*.

- In **Column 5** (*Comments*), note why a particular factor was selected and how its weight and rating were estimated.

Finally, add the weighted scores for all the external factors in **Column 4** to determine the total weighted score for that particular company. The **total weighted score** indicates how well a particular company is responding to current and expected factors in its external environment. The score can be used to compare that firm to other firms in its industry. *The total weighted score for an average firm in an industry is always 3.0.*

As an example of this procedure, Table 3.4 includes a number of external factors for Maytag Corporation with corresponding weights, ratings, and weighted scores provided. This table is appropriate for 1995 *before* Maytag sold its European and Australian operations. Note that Maytag's total weight is 3.15, meaning that the corporation is slightly above average in the major home appliance industry.

● **3.6** *Global Issues for the 21st Century*

- The **21st Century Global Society** feature in this chapter explained how the economic outlook for some countries in Eastern Europe is poor, even though the region, as a whole, has great promise. Those countries that are able to build on their quality educational system and relatively low wages with solid political and financial institutions should be able to attract foreign investment and joint ventures.

- Increasing environmental uncertainty means that environmental scanning will become an important part of everyone's job. For companies to remain competitive, they will need to develop better methods of gathering, evaluating, and disseminating intelligence to those who need it.

- To manage strategically, organizations will have to become more attuned to the concerns of the many stakeholder groups who are affected by the company's actions. Shareholders will be only one part of the equation.

- The distinction made between the *developed* and *developing* nations will slowly begin to fade as the developing nations take on a greater proportion of world trade. The economic growth of the next century will be in Asia and Latin America, not in Western Europe or northern North America.

- As more industries become hypercompetitive, strategy will become increasingly short term in orientation—thus creating a paradox: Can strategic management exist with only a short-term time horizon?

Projections for the 21st Century

- From 1994 to 2010, the number of people living in poverty will increase from 3.7 billion to 3.9 billion.

- From 1994 to 2010, the average number of children per woman will decrease from 3.2 to 2.7.[32]

Discussion Questions

1. Discuss how a development in a corporation's societal environment can affect the corporation through its task environment.

2. According to Porter, what determines the level of competitive intensity in an industry?

3. According to Porter's discussion of industry analysis, is Pepsi Cola a substitute for Coca-Cola?

4. How can a decision maker identify strategic factors in the corporation's external international environment?

5. Compare and contrast trend extrapolation with the writing of scenarios as forecasting techniques.

Key Terms

brainstorming (p. 73)
consolidated industry (p. 65)
EFAS Table (p. 75)
entry barriers (p. 61)
environmental scanning (p. 53)
environmental uncertainty (p. 53)
expert opinion (p. 73)
external strategic factors (p. 59)
extrapolation (p. 73)
fragmented industry (p. 65)
global industry (p. 66)

hypercompetition (p. 69)
industry (p. 60)
industry analysis (p. 54)
industry intelligence (p. 72)
industry matrix (p. 70)
industry scenario (p. 75)
issues priority matrix (p. 59)
multidomestic industry (p. 65)
multinational corporation (MNC)
 (p. 57)
new entrants (p. 61)

purchasing power parity (p. 59)
repatriation of profits (p. 54)
scenario writing (p. 74)
societal environment (p. 54)
statistical modeling (p. 73)
strategic group (p. 67)
strategic myopia (p. 59)
strategic type (p. 68)
substitute products (p. 63)
task environment (p. 54)
the Triad (p. 58)

Strategic Practice Exercise

What are the forces driving industry competition in the airline industry? Read the following paragraphs. Using Porter's approach to industry analysis, evaluate each of the six forces to ascertain what drives the level of competitive intensity in this industry.

In recent years, the airline industry has become increasingly competitive. Since being deregulated during the 1970s in the United States, long established airlines such as Pan American and Eastern have gone out of business as new upstarts like US West and Southwest have successfully entered the market. It appeared that almost anyone could buy a few used planes to serve the smaller cities that the larger airlines no longer wanted to serve. These low-cost, small-capacity commuter planes were able to make healthy profits in these markets where it was too expensive to land large jets. Rail and bus transportation either did not exist or was undesirable in many locations. Eventually the low-cost local commuter airlines expanded service to major cities and grabbed market share from the majors by offering cheaper fares with no-frills service. In order to be competitive with these lower cost upstarts, United Airlines and Northwest Airlines offered stock in the company and seats on the board of directors to their unionized employees in exchange for wage and benefit reductions. Delta and American Airlines, among other major carriers, reduced their costs by instituting a cap on travel agent commissions. Travel agencies were livid at this cut in their livelihood, but they needed the airlines' business in order to offer customers a total travel package.

Globally it seemed as though every nation had to have its own airline for national prestige. These state-owned airlines were expensive, but the governments subsidized them with money and supporting regulations. For example, a foreign airline was normally only allowed to fly into one of a country's airports—forcing travelers to switch to the national airline to go to other cities. During the 1970s and 1980s, however, many countries began privatizing their airlines as governments tried to improve their budgets. To be viable in an increasingly global industry, national or regional airlines were forced to form alliances and even purchase an airline in another country or region. For example, the Dutch KLM Airline acquired half interest in the U.S Northwest Airlines in order to obtain not only U.S. destinations, but also Northwest's Asian travel routes, thus making it one of the few global airlines.

Costs were still relatively high for all of the world's major airlines because of the high cost of new airplanes. Just one new jet plane cost anywhere from $25 million to $100 million. By the 1990s, only three airframe manufacturers provided almost all of the commercial airliners: Boeing, Airbus, and McDonnell Douglas. Major airlines were forced to purchase new planes because they were more fuel efficient, safer, and easier to maintain. Airlines that chose to stay with an older fleet of planes had to deal with higher fuel and maintenance costs—factors that often made it cheaper to buy new planes.

1. Evaluate each of the forces driving competition in the airline industry:

Threat of New Entrants	High, Medium, or Low? _____
Rivalry Among Existing Firms	High, Medium, or Low? _____
Threat of Substitutes	High, Medium, or Low? _____
Bargaining Power of Buyers/Distributors	High, Medium, or Low? _____
Bargaining Power of Suppliers	High, Medium, or Low? _____
Relative Power of Other Stakeholders	High, Medium, or Low? _____

2. *Which of these forces is changing?* What will this mean to the overall level of competitive intensity in the airline industry in the future? Would you invest or look for a job in this industry?

Notes

1. L. M. Grossman, "Families Have Changed But Tupperware Keeps Holding Its Parties," *Wall Street Journal* (July 21, 1992), pp. A1, A13.

2. D. Phillips, "Special Delivery," *Entrepreneur* (September 1996), pp. 98–100; B. Saporito, "What's For Dinner?" *Fortune* (May 15, 1995), pp. 50–64.

3. S. H. Haeckel, "Adaptive Enterprise Design: The Sense-and-Respond Model," *Planning Review* (May/June 1995), pp. 6–13, 42.

4. J. B. Thomas, S. M. Clark, and D. A. Gioia, "Strategic Sensemaking and Organizational Performance: Linkages Among Scanning, Interpretation, Action, Outcomes," *Academy of Management Journal* (April 1993), pp. 239–270; M. A. Reynolds, G. Lindstrom, and C. Despres, "Strategy, Performance and the Use of Environmental Information: Evidence from a Computer Simulation," *American Business Review* (January 1994), pp. 45–52.

5. P. Lasserre, and J. Probert, "Competing on the Pacific Rim: High Risks and High Returns," *Long Range Planning* (April 1994), pp. 12–35.

6. A. Shleifer, and R. W. Viskny, "Takeovers in the 1960s and the 1980s: Evidence and Implications," in *Fundamental Issues in Strategy: A Research Agenda*, edited by R. P. Rumelt, D. E. Schendel, and D. J. Teece (Boston: Harvard Business School Press, 1994), pp. 403–418.

7. J. Wyatt, "Playing the Woofie Card," *Fortune* (February 6, 1995), pp. 130–132.

8. J. Greco, "Meet Generation Y," *Forecast* (May/June, 1996), pp. 48–54; J. Fletcher, "A Generation Asks: 'Can the Boom Last?'" *Wall Street Journal* (June 14, 1996), p. B10.

9. "Alone in America," *The Futurist* (September-October 1995), pp. 56–57.

10. "Population Growth Slowing as Nation Ages," *The (Ames, IA) Daily Tribune* (March 14, 1996), p. A7.

11. L. M. Grossman, "After Demographic Shift, Atlanta Mall Restyles Itself as Black Shopping Center," *Wall Street Journal* (February 26, 1992), p. B1.

12. J. Naisbitt, *Megatrends Asia* (New York: Simon & Schuster, 1996), p. 79.

13. K. Ohmae, "The Triad World View," *Journal of Business Strategy* (Spring 1987), pp. 8–19.

14. B. K. Boyd, and J. Fulk, "Executive Scanning and Perceived Uncertainty: A Multidimensional Model," *Journal of Management*, Vol. 22, No. 1 (1996), pp. 1–21.

15. R. A. Bettis and C. K. Prahalad, "The Dominant Logic: Retrospective and Extension," *Strategic Management Journal* (January 1995), pp. 5–14; J. M. Stofford and C. W. F. Baden-Fuller, "Creating Corporate Entrepreneurship," *Strategic Management Journal* (September 1994), pp. 521–536.

16. H. I. Ansoff, "Strategic Management in a Historical Perspective," in *International Review of Strategic Management*, Vol. 2, No. 1 (1991), edited by D. E. Hussey (Chichester, England: Wiley, 1991), p. 61.

17. M. E. Porter, *Competitive Strategy* (New York: Free Press, 1980), p. 3.

18. This summary of the forces driving competitive strategy is taken from Porter, *Competitive Strategy*, pp. 7–29.

19. *Ibid.*, p. 23.

20. M. E. Porter, "Changing Patterns of International Competition," *California Management Review* (Winter 1986), pp. 9–40.

21. T. N. Gladwin, "Assessing the Multinational Environment for Corporate Opportunity," in *Handbook of Business Strategy*, edited by W. D. Guth (Boston: Warren, Gorham and Lamont, 1985), pp. 7.28–7.41.

22. B. Holstein, "An Export Service of Great Import," *Business Week* (September 28, 1992), p. 138.

23. K. J. Hatten, and M. L. Hatten, "Strategic Groups, Asymmetrical Mobility Barriers, and Contestability," *Strategic Management Journal* (July-August 1987), p. 329.

24. A. Fiegenbaum, and H. Thomas, "Strategic Groups as Reference Groups: Theory, Modeling and Empirical Examination of Industry and Competitive Strategy," *Strategic Management Journal* (September 1995), pp. 461–476.

25. R. E. Miles, and C. C. Snow, *Organizational Strategy, Structure, and Process* (New York: McGraw-Hill, 1978).

26. R. A. D'Aveni, *HyperCompetition* (New York: The Free Press, 1994), pp. xiii–xiv.

27. R. T. Pascale, "Perspective on Strategy: The Real Story Behind Honda's Success," *California Management Review* (Spring 1981), p. 70.

28. L. Kahaner, *Competitive Intelligence* (New York: Simon & Schuster, 1996).

29. "Spooks Should Scare Corporate America," *Journal of Business Strategy* (July/August 1995), pp. 14–15; "Tips from Top Spies," *Journal of Business Strategy* (September/October 1996), p. 6.

30. H. E. Klein, and R. E. Linneman, "Environmental Assessment: An International Study of Corporate Practices," *Journal of Business Strategy* (Summer 1984), p. 72.

31. This process of scenario development is adapted from M. E. Porter, *Competitive Advantage* (New York: Free Press, 1985), pp. 448–470.

32. J. Warner, "21st Century Capitalism: Snapshot of the Next Century," *Business Week* (November 18, 1994), p. 194.

Chapter 4

Internal Scanning:
Organizational Analysis

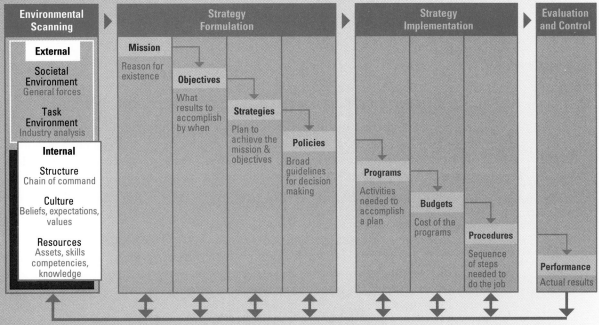

Environmental Scanning	Strategy Formulation	Strategy Implementation	Evaluation and Control

Environmental Scanning

External

Societal Environment
General forces

Task Environment
Industry analysis

Internal

Structure
Chain of command

Culture
Beliefs, expectations, values

Resources
Assets, skills competencies, knowledge

Strategy Formulation

Mission

Reason for existence

Objectives

What results to accomplish by when

Strategies

Plan to achieve the mission & objectives

Policies

Broad guidelines for decision making

Strategy Implementation

Programs

Activities needed to accomplish a plan

Budgets

Cost of the programs

Procedures

Sequence of steps needed to do the job

Evaluation and Control

Performance

Actual results

Feedback/Learning

United Airlines is a very successful, full-service international airline. It was not happy, however, about losing its traditional market share dominance in California to upstart Southwest Airlines. To regain this lucrative market, it took direct aim at Southwest in 1994 by launching on the West Coast its own low-cost carrier, Shuttle by United. It tried to imitate what it thought were Southwest's advantages. It used a fleet of Boeing 737s, the same plane Southwest used. It was able to obtain looser union work rules and a lower wage scale from those at its United Airlines' parent. To compete effectively, the Shuttle aimed to reduce United's cost of flying from the main airline's 10.5¢ to 7.4¢ per passenger mile. It planned to fly planes longer, speed up passenger boarding and takeoffs, and reduce idle time on the ground. By February 1996, however, Shuttle by United had only been able to reduce its costs to 8¢ per passenger mile contrasted with

Southwest's 7.1¢. To keep from losing money, the Shuttle was forced to raise fares and to pull out of all routes that did not connect with the carrier's hubs in San Francisco and Los Angeles. Its rate from San Francisco to Southern California was often $30 more than was Southwest's rate of $69. After 16 months of competition, Southwest had not only regained traffic it had lost initially to the Shuttle, but had actually increased its share of the California market! In addition to Southwest's low costs, it had a well-earned reputation for flying passengers safely to their destination on time. Even United's most loyal customers were taking Southwest for short flights. According to David Kliman, Director of Travel Management for Fireman's Fund Insurance of San Francisco, "We have a real bias to United all things being equal. But when fares are different, we book Southwest because it's cheaper."[1]

What gave Southwest Airlines this kind of advantage in a very competitive industry? So far no U.S. airline seems able to copy the secret of its success.

4.1 A Resource-Based Approach to Organizational Analysis

Scanning and analyzing the external environment for opportunities and threats is not enough to provide an organization a competitive advantage. Analysts must also look within the corporation itself to identify **internal strategic factors**—those critical *strengths* and *weaknesses* that are likely to determine if the firm will be able to take advantage of opportunities while avoiding threats. This internal scanning is often referred to as **organizational analysis** and is concerned with identifying and developing an organization's resources.

A **resource** is an asset, competency, process, skill, or knowledge controlled by the corporation. A resource is a strength if it provides a company with a competitive advantage. It is something the firm does or has the potential to do particularly well relative to the abilities of existing or potential competitors. A resource is a weakness if it is something the corporation does poorly or doesn't have the capacity to do although its competitors have that capacity. Barney, in his **VRIO framework** of analysis, proposes four questions to evaluate each of a firm's key resources:

1. **Value:** Does it provide competitive advantage?

2. **Rareness:** Do other competitors possess it?

3. **Imitability:** Is it costly for others to imitate?

4. **Organization:** Is the firm organized to exploit the resource?

If the answer to these questions is "yes" for a particular resource, that resource is considered a strength and a distinctive competence.[2]

Evaluate the importance of these resources to ascertain if they are internal strategic factors—those particular strengths and weaknesses that will help determine the future of the company. This can be done by comparing measures of these resources with measures of (1) *the company's past performance,* (2) *the company's key competitors,* and (3) *the industry as a whole.* To the extent that a resource (such as a firm's financial situation) is significantly different from the firm's own past, its key competitors, or the industry average, the resource is likely to be a strategic factor and should be considered in strategic decisions.

Using Resources to Gain Competitive Advantage

Proposing that a company's sustained competitive advantage is primarily determined by its resource endowments, Grant proposes a five-step, resource-based approach to strategy analysis.

1. Identify and classify the firm's resources in terms of strengths and weaknesses.

2. Combine the firm's strengths into specific capabilities. **Corporate capabilities** (often called **core competencies**) are the things that a corporation can do exceedingly well. When these capabilities/competencies are superior to those of competitors, they are often called **distinctive competencies.**

3. Appraise the profit potential of these resources and capabilities in terms of their potential for sustainable competitive advantage and the ability to harvest the profits resulting from the use of these resources and capabilities.

4. Select the strategy that best exploits the firm's resources and capabilities relative to external opportunities.

5. Identify resource gaps and invest in upgrading weaknesses.[3]

As indicated in Step 2, when an organization's resources are combined, they form a number of capabilities. In the earlier example, Southwest Airlines has two identifiable capabilities: low costs per passenger mile, and the capability for energizing its people to provide safe, on-time flight service.

Determining the Sustainability of an Advantage

Just because a firm is able to use its resources and capabilities to develop a competitive advantage does not mean it will be able to sustain it. Two characteristics determine the sustainability of a firm's distinctive competency(ies): durability and imitability.

Durability is the rate at which a firm's underlying resources and capabilities (core competencies) depreciate or become obsolete. New technology can make a company's core competency obsolete or irrelevant. For example, Intel's skills in using basic technology developed by others to manufacture and market quality microprocessors was a crucial capability until management realized that the firm had taken current technology as far as possible with the Pentium chip. Without basic R&D of its own, it would slowly lose its competitive advantage to others.

Imitability is the rate at which a firm's underlying resources and capabilities (core competencies) can be duplicated by others. To the extent that a firm's distinctive competency gives it competitive advantage in the marketplace, competitors will do what they can to imitate that set of skills and capabilities. Competitors' efforts may range from reverse engineering to hiring employees from the competitor to outright patent infringement. A core competency can be easily imitated to the extent that it is transparent, transferable, and replicable.

- **Transparency**—the speed with which other firms can understand the relationship of resources and capabilities supporting a successful firm's strategy. For example, Gillette has always supported its dominance in the marketing of razors with excellent R&D. A competitor could never understand how the Sensor razor was produced simply by taking one apart. Gillette's Sensor razor design was very difficult to copy, partially because the manufacturing equipment needed to produce it was so expensive and complicated.

- **Transferability**—the ability of competitors to gather the resources and capabilities necessary to support a competitive challenge. For example, it may be very difficult for a wine maker to duplicate a French winery's key resources of land and climate, especially if the imitator is located in Iowa.

- **Replicability**—the ability of competitors to use duplicated resources and capabilities to imitate the other firm's success. For example, even though many companies

Figure 4.1
Continuum of Resource Sustainability

Source: Suggested by J. R. Wiliams, "How Sustainable Is Your Competitive Advantage?" *California Management Review* (Spring 1992), p. 33.

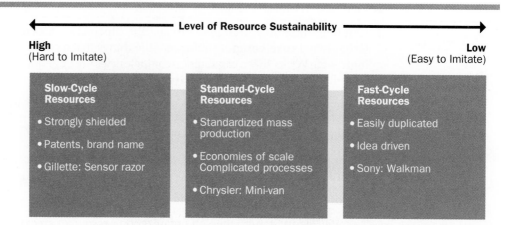

have tried to imitate Procter & Gamble's success with brand management by hiring brand managers away from P&G, they have often failed to duplicate P&G's success. The competitors failed to identify less visible P&G coordination mechanisms or to realize that P&G's brand management style conflicted with the competitor's own corporate culture.[4]

An organization's resources and capabilities can be placed on a continuum to the extent they are durable and can't be imitated (that is, aren't transparent, transferable, or replicable) by another firm. This **continuum of sustainability** is depicted in Figure 4.1. At one extreme are *slow-cycle resources,* which are sustainable because they are shielded by patents, geography, strong brand names, and the like. These resources and capabilities are distinctive competencies because they provide a sustainable competitive advantage. Gillette's Sensor razor is a good example of a product built around slow-cycle resources. The other extreme includes *fast-cycle resources,* which face the highest imitation pressures because they are based on a concept or technology that can be easily duplicated, such as Sony's Walkman. To the extent that a company has fast-cycle resources, the primary way it can compete successfully is through increased speed from lab to marketplace. Otherwise, it has no real sustainable competitive advantage.

With its low-cost position, reputation for safe, on-time flights, and its dedicated workforce, Southwest Airlines has successfully built a sustainable competitive advantage based on relatively slow-cycle resources—resources that are durable and can't be easily imitated because they lack transparency, transferability, and replicability.

4.2 Value-Chain Analysis

A good way to begin an organizational analysis is to ascertain where a firm's products are located in the overall value chain. A **value chain** is a linked set of value-creating activities beginning with basic raw materials coming from suppliers, moving on to a series of value-added activities involved in producing and marketing a product or service, and ending with distributors getting the final goods into the hands of the ultimate consumer. See Figure 4.2 for an example of a typical value chain for a manufactured product. The focus of value-chain analysis is to examine the corporation in the context of the overall chain of value-creating activities, of which the firm may only be a small part.

Figure 4.2
Typical Value Chain for a Manufactured Product

Source: Suggested by J. R. Galbraith, "Strategy and Organization Planning," in *The Strategy Process: Concepts, Contexts, Cases,* 2nd ed., edited by H. Mintzberg and J. B. Quinn (Englewood Cliffs, N.J.: Prentice Hall, 1991), p. 316.

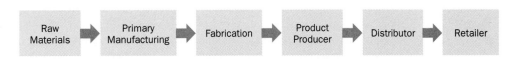

Very few corporations include a product's entire value chain, although Ford Motor Company did when it was run by its founder, Henry Ford I. During the 1920s and 1930s, the company owned its own iron mines, ore-carrying ships, and a small rail line to bring ore to its mile-long River Rouge plant in Detroit. Visitors to the plant would walk along an elevated walkway where they could watch iron ore being dumped from the rail cars into huge furnaces. The resulting steel was poured and rolled out onto a moving belt to be fabricated into auto frames and parts while the visitors watched in awe. As a group of visitors walked along the walkway, they observed an automobile being built piece by piece. Reaching the end of the moving line, the finished automobile was driven out of the plant into a vast adjoining parking lot. Ford trucks would then load the cars for delivery to dealers. Although the Ford dealers were not employees of the company, they had almost no power in the arrangement. Dealerships were awarded by the company and taken away if a dealer was at all disloyal. Ford Motor Company at that time was completely vertically integrated, that is, it controlled (usually by ownership) every stage of the value chain from the iron mines to the retailers.

Industry Value-Chain Analysis

The value chains of most industries can be split into two segments, *upstream* and *downstream* halves. In the petroleum industry, for example, upstream refers to oil exploration, drilling, and moving the crude oil to the refinery, and downstream refers to refining the oil plus the transporting and marketing of gasoline and refined oil to distributors and gas station retailers. Even though most large oil companies are completely integrated, they often vary in the amount of expertise they have at each part of the value chain. Texaco, for example, has its greatest expertise downstream in marketing and retailing. Others, such as British Petroleum, are more dominant in upstream activities like exploration.

In analyzing the complete value chain of a product, note that even if a firm operates up and down the entire industry chain, it usually has an area of primary expertise where its primary activities lie. A company's **center of gravity** is the part of the chain that is most important to the company and the point where its greatest expertise and capabilities lie—its core competencies. According to Galbraith, a company's center of gravity is usually the point at which the company started. After a firm successfully establishes itself at this point by obtaining a competitive advantage, one of its first strategic moves is to move forward or backward along the value chain in order to reduce costs, guarantee access to key raw materials, or to guarantee distribution.[5] This process is called *vertical integration.*

In the paper industry, for example, Weyerhauser's center of gravity is in the raw materials and primary manufacturing parts of the value chain in Figure 4.2. Weyerhauser's expertise is in lumbering and pulp mills, which is where the company started. It integrated forward by using its wood pulp to make paper and boxes, but its greatest capability still lay in getting the greatest return from its lumbering activities. In contrast, Procter & Gamble is primarily a consumer products company that also owned timberland and operated pulp mills. Its expertise is in the product producer and marketer distributor parts of the Figure 4.2 value chain. P & G purchased these assets to guarantee access to the large quantities of wood pulp it needed to expand its disposable diaper, toilet tissue, and napkin products. P & G's strongest capabilities have always been in the downstream activities of product development, marketing, and brand management. It has never been as efficient in upstream paper activities as Weyerhauser. It had no real distinctive competence on that part of the value chain. When paper supplies became more plentiful (and competition got rougher), P & G gladly sold its land and mills to focus more on that part of the value chain where it could provide the greatest value at the lowest cost—creating and marketing innovative consumer products.

Corporate Value-Chain Analysis

Each corporation has its own internal value chain of activities. See Figure 4.3 for an example of a corporate value chain. Porter proposes that a manufacturing firm's **primary activities** usually begin with *inbound logistics* (raw materials handling and warehousing), go through an *operations process* in which a product is manufactured, and continue on to *outbound logistics* (warehousing and distribution), *marketing and sales*, and finally to *service* (installation, repair, and sale of parts). Several **support activities,** such as *procurement* (purchasing), *technology development* (R&D), *human resource management*, and *firm infrastructure* (accounting, finance, strategic planning), ensure that the primary value-chain activities operate effectively and efficiently. Each of a company's product lines has its own distinctive value chain. Because most corporations make several different products or services, an internal analysis of the firm involves analyzing a series of different value chains.

The systematic examination of individual value activities can lead to a better understanding of a corporation's strengths and weaknesses. According to Porter, "Differences among competitor value chains are a key source of competitive advantage."[6] Corporate value chain analysis involves the following steps:

1. Examine each product line's value chain in terms of the various activities involved in producing that product or service. Which activities can be considered strengths or weaknesses?

2. Examine the "linkages" within each product line's value chain. **Linkages** are the connections between the way one value activity (for example, marketing) is performed and the cost of performance of another activity (for example, quality control). In seeking ways for a corporation to gain competitive advantage in the marketplace, the same function can be performed in different ways with different results. For example, quality inspection of 100% of output by the workers themselves instead of the usual 10% by quality control inspectors might increase production costs, but that increase could be more than offset by the savings obtained from reducing the number of repair people needed to fix defective products and increasing the amount of salespeople's time devoted to selling instead of exchanging already-sold, but defective, products.

3. Examine the potential synergies among the value chains of different product lines or business units. Each value element, such as advertising or manufacturing, has an inherent economy of scale in which activities are conducted at their lowest possible cost per unit of output. If a particular product is not being produced at a high enough level to reach economies of scale in distribution, another product could be used to share the same distribution channel. This is an example of **economies of**

**Figure 4.3
A Corporation's
Value Chain**

Source: Adapted/
reprinted with the per-
mission of the The Free
Press, an imprint of Si-
mon & Schuster, from
*Competitive Advantage:
Creating and Sustaining
Superior Performance* by
Michael E. Porter, p. 37.
Copyright © 1985 by
Michael E. Porter.

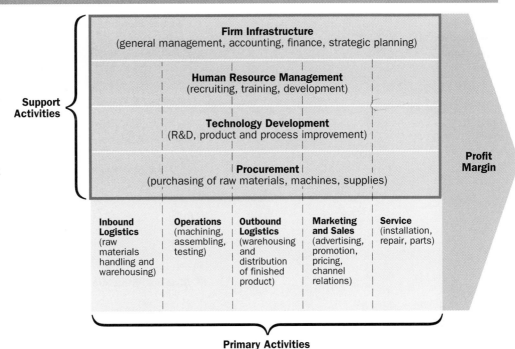

scope, which result when the value chains of two separate products or services share activities, such as the same marketing channels or manufacturing facilities. For example, the cost of joint production of multiple products can be less than the cost of separate production.

4.3   Scanning Functional Resources

The simplest way to begin an analysis of a corporation's value chain is by carefully examining its traditional functional areas for strengths and weaknesses. Functional resources include not only the financial, physical, and human assets in each area, but also the ability of the people in each area to formulate and implement the necessary functional objectives, strategies, and policies. The resources include the knowledge of analytical concepts and procedural techniques common to each area as well as the ability of the people in each area to use them effectively. If used properly, these resources serve as strengths to carry out value-added activities and support strategic decisions. In addition to the usual business functions of marketing, finance, R&D, operations, human resources, and information systems, we also discuss structure and culture as key parts of a business corporation's value chain.

Basic Organizational Structures

Although there is an almost infinite variety of structural forms, certain basic types predominate in modern complex organizations. Figure 4.4 illustrates three basic **organizational structures.** The conglomerate structure is a variant of divisional structure and is

Figure 4.4
Basic Structures of Corporations

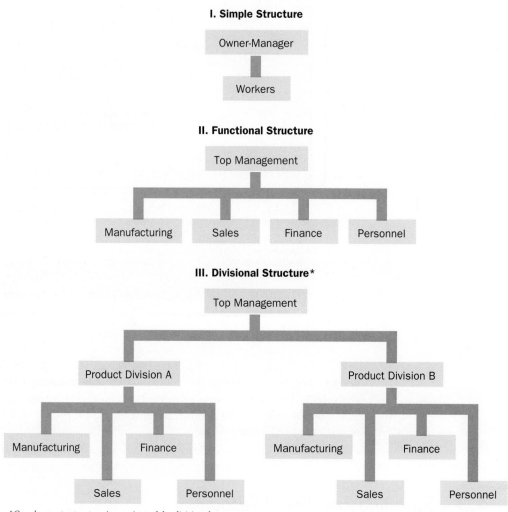

I. Simple Structure

Owner-Manager

Workers

II. Functional Structure

Top Management

Manufacturing   Sales   Finance   Personnel

III. Divisional Structure*

Top Management

Product Division A   Product Division B

Manufacturing   Finance   Manufacturing   Finance

Sales   Personnel   Sales   Personnel

*Conglomerate structure is a variant of the divisional structure.

thus not depicted as a fourth structure. Generally speaking, each structure tends to support some corporate strategies over others.

- **Simple structure** has no functional or product categories and is appropriate for a small, entrepreneur-dominated company with one or two product lines that operates in a reasonably small, easily identifiable market niche. Employees tend to be generalists and jacks-of-all-trades.

- **Functional structure** is appropriate for a medium-sized firm with several product lines in one industry. Employees tend to be specialists in the business functions important to that industry, such as manufacturing, marketing, finance, and human resources.

- **Divisional structure** is appropriate for a large corporation with many product lines in several related industries. Employees tend to be functional specialists organized according to product/market distinctions. General Motors, for example, groups its various auto lines into the separate divisions of Chevrolet, Pontiac,

Oldsmobile, Buick, and Cadillac. Management attempts to find some synergy among divisional activities through the use of committees and horizontal linkages.

- **Strategic business units (SBUs)** are a recent modification to the divisional structure. Strategic business units are divisions or groups of divisions composed of independent product-market segments that are given primary responsibility and authority for the management of their own functional areas. An SBU may be of any size or level, but it must have (1) *a unique mission*, (2) *identifiable competitors*, (3) *an external market focus*, and (4) *control of its business functions*.[7] The idea is to decentralize on the basis of strategic elements rather than on the basis of size, product characteristics, or span of control and to create horizontal linkages among units previously kept separate. For example, rather than organize products on the basis of packaging technology like frozen foods, canned foods, and bagged foods, General Foods organized its products into SBUs on the basis of consumer-oriented menu segments: breakfast food, beverage, main meal, dessert, and pet foods.

- **Conglomerate structure** is appropriate for a large corporation with many product lines in several unrelated industries. A variant of the divisional structure, the conglomerate structure (sometimes called a *holding company*) is typically an assemblage of legally independent firms (subsidiaries) operating under one corporate umbrella but controlled through the subsidiaries' boards of directors. The unrelated nature of the subsidiaries prevents any attempt at gaining synergy among them.

If the current basic structure of a corporation does not easily support a strategy under consideration, top management must decide if the proposed strategy is feasible or if the structure should be changed to a more advanced structure such as the matrix or network. (Advanced structural designs are discussed in Chapter 7.)

Corporate Culture: The Company Way

There is an oft-told story of a person new to a company asking an experienced co-worker what an employee should do when a customer calls. The old-timer responded: "There are three ways to do any job—the right way, the wrong way, and the company way. Around here, we always do things the company way." In most organizations, the "company way" is derived from the corporation's culture. **Corporate culture** is the collection of *beliefs, expectations,* and *values* learned and shared by a corporation's members and transmitted from one generation of employees to another. The corporate culture generally reflects the values of the founder(s) and the mission of the firm. It gives a company a sense of identity: "This is who we are. This is what we do. This is what we stand for." The culture includes the dominant orientation of the company, such as research and development at Hewlett-Packard, customer service at Nordstrom's, or product quality at Maytag. It often includes a number of informal work rules (forming the "company way") that employees follow without question. These work practices over time become part of a company's unquestioned tradition.

Corporate culture has two distinct attributes, intensity and integration.[8] **Cultural intensity** is the degree to which members of a unit accept the norms, values, or other culture content associated with the unit. This shows the culture's depth. Organizations with strong norms promoting a particular value, such as quality at Maytag, have intensive cultures, whereas new firms (or those in transition) have weaker, less intensive cultures. Employees in an intensive culture tend to exhibit consistent behavior, that is, they tend to act similarly over time. **Cultural integration** is the extent to which units throughout an organization share a common culture. This is the culture's breadth.

Organizations with a pervasive dominant culture may be hierarchically controlled and power oriented, such as a military unit, and have highly integrated cultures. All employees tend to hold the same cultural values and norms. In contrast, a company that is structured into diverse units by functions or divisions usually exhibits some strong subcultures (for example, R&D versus manufacturing) and a less integrated corporate culture.

Corporate culture fulfills several important functions in an organization:

1. Conveys a sense of identity for employees.

2. Helps generate employee commitment to something greater than themselves.

3. Adds to the stability of the organization as a social system.

4. Serves as a frame of reference for employees to use to make sense out of organizational activities and to use as a guide for appropriate behavior.[9]

Corporate culture shapes the behavior of people in the corporation. Because these cultures have a powerful influence on the behavior of people at all levels, they can strongly affect a corporation's ability to shift its strategic direction. A strong culture should not only promote survival, but it should also create the basis for a superior competitive position. See the **21st Century Global Society** feature to see how the Swiss company ABB Asea Brown Boveri AG uses its corporate culture to obtain competitive advantage. To the extent that a corporation's distinctive competence is embedded in an organization's culture, it will be very hard for a competitor to imitate it.[10]

A change in mission, objectives, strategies, or policies is not likely to be successful if it is in opposition to the accepted culture of the firm. Foot-dragging and even sabotage may result, as employees fight to resist a radical change in corporate philosophy. Like structure, if an organization's culture is compatible with a new strategy, it is an internal strength. But if the corporate culture is not compatible with the proposed strategy, it is a serious weakness. See the **Company Spotlight on Maytag Corporation** feature for how its corporate culture affects the company's orientation and activities.

Strategic Marketing Issues

The marketing manager is the company's primary link to the customer and the competition. The manager, therefore, must be especially concerned with the market position and marketing mix of the firm.

Market Position and Segmentation

Market position deals with the question, "Who are our customers?" It refers to the selection of specific areas for marketing concentration and can be expressed in terms of market, product, and geographical locations. Through market research, corporations are able to practice **market segmentation** with various products or services so that managers can discover what niches to seek, which new types of products to develop, and how to ensure that a company's many products do not directly compete with one another.

Marketing Mix

The **marketing mix** refers to the particular combination of key variables under the corporation's control that can be used to affect demand and to gain competitive advantage. These variables are *product*, *place*, *promotion*, and *price*. Within each of these four variables

21ST CENTURY GLOBAL SOCIETY

ABB USES CORPORATE CULTURE AS A COMPETITIVE ADVANTAGE

Zurich-based ABB Asea Brown Boveri AG is a worldwide builder of power plants, electrical equipment, and industrial factories in 140 countries. By establishing one set of values throughout its global operations, ABB's management believes that the company will gain an advantage over its rivals Siemens AG of Germany, France's Alcatel-Alsthom NV, and the U.S.'s General Electric Company.

Percy Barnevik, Swedish Chairman of ABB, managed the 1988 merger that created ABB from Sweden's Asea AB and Switzerland's BBC Brown Boveri Ltd. At that time both companies were far behind the world leaders in electrical equipment and engineering. Barnevik introduced his concept of a company with no geographic base—one that had many "home" markets that could draw on expertise from around the globe. To do this, he created a set of 500 global managers who could adapt to local cultures while executing ABB's global strategies. These people are multilingual and move around each of ABB's 5,000 profit cen-

ters in 140 countries. Their assignment is to cut costs, improve efficiency, and integrate local businesses with the ABB world view.

ABB requires local business units, such as Mexico's motor factory, to report both to one of ABB's traveling global managers and to a business area manager who sets global motor strategy for ABB. When the goals of the local factory conflict with worldwide priorities, it is up to the global manager to resolve it.

Few multinational corporations are as successful as ABB in getting global strategies to work with local operations. In agreement with the resource-based view of the firm, Barnevik states, "Our strength comes from pulling together. . . . If you can make this work real well, then you get a competitive edge out of the organization which is very, very difficult to copy."

Source: J. Guyon, "ABB Fuses Units With One Set of Values," *Wall Street Journal* (October 2, 1996), p. A15.

are several subvariables, listed in Table 4.1, that should be analyzed in terms of their effects on divisional and corporate performance.

Product Life Cycle

One of the most useful concepts in marketing, insofar as strategic management is concerned, is that of the product life cycle. As depicted in Figure 4.5, the **product life cycle** is a graph showing time plotted against the dollar sales of a product as it moves from introduction through growth and maturity to decline. This concept enables a marketing manager to examine the marketing mix of a particular product or group of products in terms of its position in its life cycle.

Strategic Financial Issues

The financial manager must ascertain the best sources of funds, uses of funds, and control of funds. Cash must be raised from internal or external (local and global) sources and allocated for different uses. The flow of funds in the operations of the organization must be monitored. To the extent that a corporation is involved in international activities, currency fluctuations must be dealt with to ensure that profits aren't wiped out by the rise or fall of the dollar versus the yen, deutsche mark, and other currencies. Bene-

COMPANY SPOTLIGHT

Culture as a Key Strength

F. L. Maytag, founder of the company, made a direct impact on Maytag Corporation's philosophy of management. He strongly valued (among other things) a commitment to quality, promotion from within, dedication to hard work, and an emphasis on performance. For example, in the company's first year of operation, almost half the products sold were defective in some way. In F. L. Maytag's words: "It was then that we learned that *nothing was actually 'sold' until it was in the hands of a satisfied user,* no matter if it had been paid for." His insistence on fixing or purchasing back the faulty products resulted in losses for the new company. The resulting commitment to quality became a key aspect of the corporate culture and a strength of the organization.

In the 1990s, Maytag Corporation still reflected F. L. Maytag's beliefs that hard work and performance are more important than management perquisites. For example, the corporate headquarters is housed on the second floor of a relatively small and modest building. Built in 1961, the Newton, Iowa, building also housed Maytag Company administrative offices on the first floor. Responding to a comment from outside observers that the corporation had spartan offices, Leonard Hadley, then–Chief Operating Officer, looked around at his rather small, windowless office and said, "See for yourself. We want to keep corporate staff to a minimum." Hadley felt that the headquarters' location, coupled with the fact that most of the corporate officers had originally been with the Maytag Company, resulted in an overall top management concern for product quality and financial conservatism.

Maytag purchased Magic Chef partially to obtain access to Admiral's refrigeration operations. Maytag needed Admiral to help it build a high-quality Maytag brand refrigerator. Unfortunately there were some doubts about Admiral's ability to produce quality products. Prior to its acquisition, Admiral had been owned by three different corporations. These previous owners had invested very little into the operation, and production quality had dropped significantly. Employee morale was low. When Leonard Hadley first visited Admiral's facilities in Galesburg, Illinois, to discuss the design of a Maytag line of refrigerators, employees wondered how Admiral was going to be integrated in the new Maytag Corporation. When Admiral personnel asked Hadley when the name on the plant water tower would be changed from Admiral to Maytag, Hadley responded: *"When you earn it!"* This story is widely told throughout Maytag Corporation not only to show Maytag's commitment to quality, but also to show how acquired companies were expected to also adopt this value.

MAYTAG CORPORATION

fits in the form of returns, repayments, or products and services must be given to the sources of outside financing. All these tasks must be handled in a way that complements and supports overall corporate strategy.

Financial Leverage

The mix of externally generated short-term and long-term funds in relation to the amount and timing of internally generated funds should be appropriate to the corporate objectives, strategies, and policies. The concept of **financial leverage** (the ratio of total debt to total assets) is helpful in describing how debt is used to increase the earnings available to common shareholders. When the company finances its activities by sales of bonds or notes instead of through stock, the earnings per share are boosted: the interest

Table 4.1   **Marketing Mix Variables**

Product	Place	Promotion	Price
Quality	Channels	Advertising	List price
Features	Coverage	Personal selling	Discounts
Options	Locations	Sales promotion	Allowances
Style	Inventory	Publicity	Payment periods
Brand name	Transport		Credit terms
Packaging			
Sizes			
Services			
Warranties			
Returns			

Source: Philip Kotler, *Marketing Management: Analysis, Planning, and Control,* 4th ed. (Englewood Cliffs, N.J.: Prentice-Hall, 1980), p. 89. Copyright © 1980. Reprinted by permission of Prentice-Hall, Inc.

paid on the debt reduces taxable income, but fewer shareholders share the profits than if the company had sold more stock to finance its activities. The debt, however, does raise the firm's break-even point above what it would have been if the firm had financed from internally generated funds only. High leverage may therefore be perceived as a corporate strength in times of prosperity and ever-increasing sales, or as a weakness in times of a recession and falling sales. This is because leverage acts to magnify the effect on earnings per share of an increase or decrease in dollar sales.

Capital Budgeting

Capital budgeting is the analyzing and ranking of possible investments in fixed assets such as land, buildings, and equipment in terms of the additional outlays and additional receipts that will result from each investment. A good finance department will be able to prepare such capital budgets and to rank them on the basis of some accepted criteria or *hurdle rate* (for example, years to pay back investment, rate of return, or time to break-even point) for the purpose of strategic decision making.

Strategic Research and Development (R&D) Issues

The R&D manager is responsible for suggesting and implementing a company's technological strategy in light of its corporate objectives and policies. The manager's job, therefore, involves (1) choosing among alternative new technologies to use within the corporation, (2) developing methods of embodying the new technology in new products and processes, and (3) deploying resources so that the new technology can be successfully implemented.

R&D Intensity, Technological Competence, and Technology Transfer

The company must make available the resources necessary for effective research and development. A company's **R&D intensity** (its spending on R&D as a percentage of sales revenue) is a principal means of gaining market share in global competition. The amount spent on R&D often varies by industry. For example, the U.S. computer software indus-

Figure 4.5
Product Life Cycle

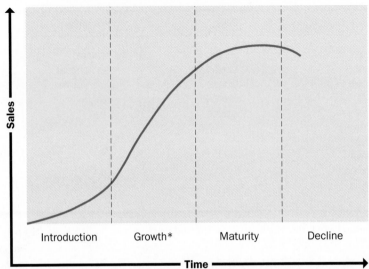

* The right end of the Growth stage is often called Competitive Turbulence because of price and distribution competition that shakes out the weaker competitors. For further information, see C. R. Wasson, *Dynamic Competitive Strategy and Product Life Cycles,* 3rd ed. (Austin, Tex.: Austin Press, 1978).

try spends an average of 13.5% of its sales dollar for R&D, whereas the paper and forest products industry spends only 1.0%.[11] A good rule of thumb for R&D spending is that a corporation should spend at a "normal" rate for that particular industry unless its strategic plan calls for unusual expenditures.

Simply spending money on R&D or new projects does not mean, however, that the money will produce useful results. For example, Pharmacia Upjohn spent more of its revenues on research than any other company in any industry (18%), but it was ranked low in innovation.[12] A company's R&D unit should be evaluated for **technological competence** in both the development and the use of innovative technology. Not only should the corporation make a consistent research effort (as measured by reasonably constant corporate expenditures that result in usable innovations), it should also be proficient in managing research personnel and integrating their innovations into its day-to-day operations. If a company is not proficient in **technology transfer**, the process of taking a new technology from the laboratory to the marketplace, it will not gain much advantage from new technological advances. For example, Xerox Corporation has been criticized for failing to take advantage of various innovations (such as the mouse and the graphical user interface for personal computers) developed originally in its sophisticated Palo Alto Research Center. See the **Strategy in a Changing World** feature for a classic example of how Apple Computer's ability to imitate a core competency of Xerox gave it a competitive advantage (sustainable until Microsoft launched Windows 3.0).

R&D Mix

Basic R&D is conducted by scientists in well-equipped laboratories where the focus is on theoretical problem areas. The best indicators of a company's capability in this area are its patents and research publications. **Product R&D** concentrates on marketing and is concerned with product or product-packaging improvements. The best measurements of ability in this area are the number of successful new products introduced and the per-

A PROBLEM OF TECHNOLOGY TRANSFER AT XEROX CORPORATION

In the mid 1970s, Xerox Corporation's Palo Alto Research Center (PARC) had developed Alto, a new type of computer with some innovative features. Although Alto was supposed to serve as a research prototype, it became so popular among PARC personnel that some researchers began to develop Alto as a commercial product. Unfortunately this put PARC into direct conflict with Xerox's product development group, which was at the same time developing a rival machine called the Star. Because the Star was in line with the company's expressed product development strategy, top management, who placed all its emphasis on the Star, ignored Alto.

In 1979, Steve Jobs, co-founder of Apple Computer, Inc., made a now-legendary tour of the normally very secretive PARC. Researchers gave Jobs a demonstration of the Alto. Unlike the computers that Apple was then building, Alto had the power of a minicomputer. Its user-friendly software generated crisp text and bright graphics. Jobs fell in love with the machine. He promptly asked Apple's engineers to duplicate the look and feel of Alto. The result was the Macintosh—a personal computer that soon revolutionized the industry.

centage of total sales and profits coming from products introduced within the past five years. **Engineering** (or **process**) **R&D** is concerned with engineering, concentrating on quality control, and the development of design specifications and improved production equipment. A company's capability in this area can be measured by consistent reductions in unit manufacturing costs and by the number of product defects.

Most corporations will have a mix of basic, product, and process R&D, which varies by industry, company, and product line. The balance of these types of research is known as the **R&D mix** and should be appropriate to the strategy being considered and to each product's life cycle. For example, it is generally accepted that product R&D normally dominates the early stages of a product's life cycle (when the product's optimal form and features are still being debated), whereas process R&D becomes especially important in the later stages (when the product's design is solidified and the emphasis is on reducing costs and improving quality).

Impact of Technological Discontinuity on Strategy

The R&D manager must determine when to abandon present technology and when to develop or adopt new technology. Richard Foster of McKinsey and Company states that the displacement of one technology by another (**technological discontinuity**) is a frequent and strategically important phenomenon. Such a discontinuity occurs when a new technology cannot simply be used to enhance the current technology, but actually substitutes for that technology to yield better performance. For each technology within a given field or industry, according to Foster, the plotting of product performance against research effort/expenditures on a graph results in an S-shaped curve. He describes the process depicted in Figure 4.6:

> Early in the development of the technology a knowledge base is being built and progress requires a relatively large amount of effort. Later, progress comes more easily. And then, as the

Figure 4.6
Technological Discontinuity

Source: P. Pascarella, "Are You Investing in the Wrong Technology?" *Industry Week* (July 25, 1983), p. 38. Copyright © 1983 Penton/IPC. All rights reserved. Reprinted by permission.

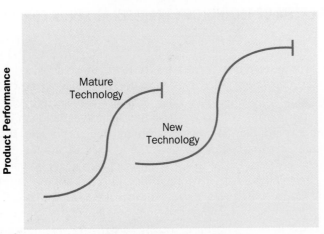

What the S-Curves Reveal

In the corporate planning process, it is generally assumed that incremental progress in technology will occur. But past developments in a given technology cannot be extrapolated into the future, because every technology has its limits. The key to competitiveness is to determine when to shift resources to a technology with more potential.

limits of that technology are approached, progress becomes slow and expensive. That is when R&D dollars should be allocated to technology with more potential. That is also—not so incidentally—when a competitor who has bet on a new technology can sweep away your business or topple an entire industry.[13]

The presence of a technological discontinuity in the world's steel industry during the 1960s explains why the large capital expenditures by U.S. steel companies failed to keep them competitive with the Japanese firms that adopted the new technologies. As Foster points out, "History has shown that as one technology nears the end of its S-curve, competitive leadership in a market generally changes hands."[14]

Strategic Operations Issues

The primary task of the operations (manufacturing or service) manager is to develop and operate a system that will produce the required number of products or services, with a certain quality, at a given cost, within an allotted time. Many of the key concepts and techniques popularly used in manufacturing can be applied to service businesses.

In very general terms, manufacturing can be intermittent or continuous. In **intermittent systems** (job shops), the item is normally processed sequentially, but the work and sequence of the process vary. An example is an auto body repair shop. At each location, the tasks determine the details of processing and the time required for them. These job shops can be very labor intensive. For example, a job shop usually has little automated machinery and thus a small amount of fixed costs. It has a fairly low break-even point, but its variable cost line (composed of wages and costs of special parts) has a relatively steep slope. Because most of the costs associated with the product are variable (many employees earn piece-rate wages), a job shop's variable costs are higher than those of automated firms. Its advantage over other firms is that it can operate at low levels and still be profitable. After a job shop's sales reach break-even, however, the huge variable costs as a percentage of total costs keep the profit per unit at a relatively low level. In terms of strategy, this firm should look for a niche in the marketplace for which it can produce and sell a reasonably small quantity of goods.

In contrast, **continuous systems** are those laid out as lines on which products can be continuously assembled or processed. An example is an automobile assembly line. A firm using continuous systems invests heavily in fixed investments such as automated processes and highly sophisticated machinery. Its labor force, relatively small but highly skilled, earns salaries rather than piece-rate wages. Consequently this firm has a high amount of fixed costs. It also has a relatively high break-even point, but its variable cost line rises slowly. Its advantage is that once it reaches break-even, its profits rise faster than do those of less automated firms. It reaps benefits from economies of scale. In terms of strategy, this firm needs to find a high-demand niche in the marketplace for which it can produce and sell a large quantity of goods. However, this type of firm is likely to suffer huge losses during a recession. During an economic downturn, the firm with less automation and thus less leverage is more likely to survive comfortably because a drop in sales primarily affects variable costs. It is often easier to lay off labor than to sell off specialized plants and machines.

Experience Curve

A conceptual framework that many large corporations have used successfully is the experience curve (originally called the learning curve). The **experience curve** suggests that unit production costs decline by some fixed percentage (commonly 20%–30%) each time the total accumulated volume of production in units doubles. The actual percentage varies by industry and is based on many variables: the amount of time it takes a person to learn a new task, scale economies, product and process improvements, and lower raw materials costs, among others. For example, in an industry with an 85% experience curve, a corporation might expect a 15% reduction in unit costs for every doubling of volume. The total costs per unit can be expected to drop from $100 when the total production is 10 units, to $85 ($100 × 85%) when production increases to 20 units, and to $72.25 ($85 × 85%) when it reaches 40 units. Achieving these results often means investing in R&D and fixed assets; higher fixed costs and less flexibility thus result. Nevertheless the manufacturing strategy is one of building capacity ahead of demand in order to achieve the lower unit costs that develop from the experience curve. On the basis of some future point on the experience curve, the corporation should price the product or service very low to preempt competition and increase market demand. The resulting high number of units sold and high market share should result in high profits, based on the low unit costs.

Management commonly uses the experience curve in estimating the production costs of (1) a product never before made with the present techniques and processes or (2) current products produced by newly introduced techniques or processes. The concept was first applied in the airframe industry and can be applied in the service industry as well. For example, a cleaning company can reduce its costs per employee by having its workers use the same equipment and techniques to clean many adjacent offices in one office building rather than just cleaning a few offices in multiple buildings. Although many firms have used experience curves extensively, an unquestioning acceptance of the industry norm (such as 80% for the airframe industry or 70% for integrated circuits) is very risky. The experience curve of the industry as a whole might not hold true for a particular company for a variety of reasons.

Flexible Manufacturing for Mass Customization

Recently the use of large, continuous, mass-production facilities to take advantage of experience-curve economies has been criticized. The use of Computer-Assisted Design and Computer-Assisted Manufacturing (CAD/CAM) and robot technology means that learning times are shorter and products can be economically manufactured in small, customized batches in a process called **mass customization**—the low-cost production of individually customized goods and services.[15] **Economies of scope** (in which common parts of the manufacturing activities of various products are combined to gain economies even though small numbers of each product are made) replace **economies of scale** (in which unit costs are reduced by making large numbers of the same product) in flexible manufacturing. **Flexible manufacturing** permits the low-volume output of custom-tailored products at relatively low unit costs through economies of scope. It is thus possible to have the cost advantages of continuous systems with the customer-oriented advantages of intermittent systems.

Strategic Human Resource (HRM) Issues

The primary task of the manager of human resources is to improve the match between individuals and jobs. A good HRM department should know how to use attitude surveys and other feedback devices to assess employees' satisfaction with their jobs and with the corporation as a whole. HRM managers should also use job analysis to obtain job description information about what each job needs to accomplish in terms of quality and quantity. Up-to-date job descriptions are essential not only for proper employee selection, appraisal, training, and development for wage and salary administration, and for labor negotiations, but also for summarizing the corporatewide human resources in terms of employee-skill categories. Just as a company must know the number, type, and quality of its manufacturing facilities, it must also know the kinds of people it employs and the skills they possess. The best strategies are meaningless if employees do not have the skills to carry them out or if jobs cannot be designed to accommodate the available workers. Hewlett-Packard, for example, uses employee profiles to ensure that it has the right mix of talents to implement its planned strategies.

Use of Teams

Management is beginning to realize that it must be more flexible in its utilization of employees in order for human resources to be a strength. Human resource managers, therefore, need to be knowledgeable about work options such as part-time work, job sharing, flex-time, extended leaves, and contract work, and especially about the proper use of teams. Over two-thirds of large U.S. companies are successfully using **autonomous work teams** in which a group of people work together without a supervisor to plan, coordinate, and evaluate their own work. Nevertheless only 10% of workers are currently in these teams.[16] Northern Telecom found productivity and quality to increase with work teams to such an extent that it was able to reduce the number of quality inspectors by 40%.[17]

As a way to move a product more quickly through its development stage, companies like Motorola, Chrysler, NCR, Boeing, and General Electric have begun using *cross-functional* work teams. Instead of developing products in a series of steps—beginning with a request from sales, which leads to design, then to engineering and on to purchasing, and finally to manufacturing (and often resulting in a costly product rejected by the customer)—companies are tearing down the traditional walls separating the departments so that people from each discipline can get involved in projects early on. In a process called **concurrent engineering,** the once-isolated specialists now work side by side and compare notes constantly in an effort to design cost-effective products with features customers want. Taking this approach enabled Chrysler Corporation to reduce its product development cycle from 60 to 36 months.[18]

Union Relations and Temporary Workers

If the corporation is unionized, a good human resource manager should be able to work closely with the union. Although union membership in the United States has dropped to less than 10% of private sector workers in the mid 1990s from over 23% in the 1970s, unions still represent around 20% of workers in manufacturing in the United States.[19] To save jobs, U.S. unions are increasingly willing to support employee involvement programs designed to increase worker participation in decision making.

Outside the United States, the average proportion of unionized workers among major industrialized nations is around 50%. European unions tend to be militant, politically oriented, and much less interested in working with management to increase efficiency. Nationwide strikes can occur quickly. Japanese unions are typically tied to individual companies and are usually supportive of management. These differences among countries have significant implications for the management of multinational corporations.

To increase flexibility, avoid layoffs, and reduce labor costs, corporations are using more temporary workers. According to a survey of 93 major multinational corporations (MNCs), 35% of the MNCs expect "contingent" workers to account for at least 10% of their workforce by the year 2000. For example, one out of five French workers were on a temporary or part-time contract in 1996.[20] Labor unions are concerned that companies are using temps to avoid hiring unionized workers. According to John Kinloch, vice-president of Communications Workers of America local 1058, "Corporations are trying to create a disposable workforce with low wages and no benefits."[21]

Quality of Work Life and Human Diversity

Human resource departments have found that to reduce employee dissatisfaction and unionization efforts (or, conversely, to improve employee satisfaction and existing union relations), they must consider the quality of work life in the design of jobs. Partially a reaction to the traditionally heavy emphasis on technical and economic factors in job design, **quality of work life** emphasizes improving the human dimension of work. The knowledgeable human resource manager, therefore, should be able to improve the corporation's quality of work life by (1) introducing participative problem solving, (2) restructuring work, (3) introducing innovative reward systems, and (4) improving the work environment. It is hoped that these improvements will lead to a more participative corporate culture and thus higher productivity and quality products.

Human diversity refers to the mix in the workplace of people from different races, cultures, and backgrounds. This is a hot issue in HRM. Realizing that the demographics are changing toward an increasing percentage of minorities and women in the U.S. workforce, companies are now concerned with hiring and promoting people without regard to ethnic background. Good human resource managers should be working to ensure that people are treated fairly on the job and not harassed by prejudiced co-workers or managers. According to one survey of 645 companies, 74% are concerned with issues in diversity and one-third believe that diversity will affect their corporate strategies.[22]

An organization's human resources are especially important in today's world of global communication and transportation systems. Advances in technology are copied almost immediately by competitors around the world. People are not as willing to move to other companies in other countries. This means that the only long-term resource advantage remaining to corporations operating in the industrialized nations may lie in the area of skilled human resources.

Strategic Information Systems Issues

The primary task of the manager of information systems (IS) is to design and manage the flow of information in an organization in ways that improve productivity and decision making. Information must be collected, stored, and synthesized in such a manner that it will answer important operating and strategic questions. This function is growing in importance.

A corporation's information system can be a strength or a weakness in all three elements of strategic management. It can not only aid in environmental scanning and in controlling a company's many activities, it can also be used as a strategic weapon in gaining competitive advantage. For example, American Hospital Supply (AHS), a leading manufacturer and distributor of a broad line of products for doctors, laboratories, and hospitals, developed an order entry distribution system that directly linked the majority of its customers to AHS computers. The system was successful because it simplified ordering processes for customers, reduced costs for both AHS and the customer, and allowed AHS to provide pricing incentives to the customer. As a result, customer loyalty was high and AHS's share of the market became large.

A trend in corporate information systems is the increasing use of the Internet for marketing and intranets for internal communication. For example, Federal Express found that by allowing customers to directly access its package-tracking database via the Fed Ex Web site instead of their having to ask a human operator, the company saved up to $2 million annually.[23] An **intranet** is an information network within an organization that also has access to the external worldwide Internet. The percentage of large and midsize firms using an intranet soared to 55% in 1996 from just 11% the previous year. Intranets typically begin as ways to provide employees with company information such as lists of product prices, fringe benefits, and company policies. The networks are then gradually extended to major suppliers and customers. Few companies have taken the next step—to allow employees, customers, and suppliers to conduct business on the Internet in a completely automated manner.[24] By connecting these groups, companies hope to obtain a competitive advantage by reducing the time needed to design and bring new products to market, slashing inventories, customizing manufacturing, and entering new markets.[25]

4.4 The Strategic Audit: A Checklist for Organizational Analysis

One way of conducting an organizational analysis to ascertain a company's strengths and weakness is by using the **Strategic Audit found in Table 10.5 in Chapter 10.** The audit provides a checklist of questions by area of concern. For example, Part IV of the audit examines corporate structure, culture, and resources. It looks at resources in terms of the functional areas of marketing, finance, R&D, operations, human resources, and information systems, among others.

4.5 Synthesis of Internal Factors—IFAS

After strategists have scanned the internal organizational environment and identified factors for their particular corporation, they may want to summarize their analysis of these factors using a form such as that given in Table 4.2. This **IFAS Table** (*Internal Factor Analysis Summary*) is one way to organize the internal factors into the generally accepted categories of strengths and weaknesses as well as to analyze how well a particular company's management is responding to these specific factors in light of the perceived importance of these factors to the company. Except for its internal orientation, this IFAS Table is built the same way as the EFAS Table described in Chapter 3 (in Table 3.4). To use the IFAS Table, complete the following steps:

- In **Column 1** (*Internal Strategic Factors*), list the eight to ten most important strengths and weaknesses facing the company.

- In **Column 2** (*Weight*), assign a weight to each factor from **1.0** (*Most Important*) to **0.0** (*Not Important*) based on that factor's probable impact on a particular company's current strategic position. The higher the weight, the more important is this factor to the current and future success of the company. *All weights must sum to 1.0 regardless of the number of factors.*

- In **Column 3** (*Rating*), assign a rating to each factor from **5** (*Outstanding*) to **1** (*Poor*) based on management's current response to that particular factor. Each rating is a judgment regarding how well the company's management is currently dealing with each internal factor.

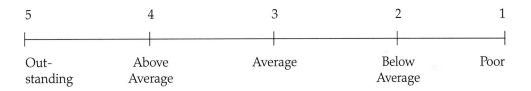

- In **Column 4** (*Weighted Score*), multiply the *weight* in **Column 2** for each factor times its *rating* in Column 3 to obtain that factor's *weighted score*. This results in a weighted score for each factor ranging from **5.0** (*Outstanding*) to **1.0** (*Poor*) with 3.0 as *Average*.

- In **Column 5** (*Comments*), note why a particular factor was selected and how its weight and rating were estimated.

Finally, add the weighted scores for all the internal factors in Column 4 to determine the total weighted score for that particular company. The *total weighted score* indicates how well a particular company is responding to current and expected factors in its internal environment. The score can be used to compare that firm to other firms in its industry. *The total weighted score for an average firm in an industry is always 3.0.*

As an example of this procedure, Table 4.2 includes a number of internal factors for Maytag Corporation with corresponding weights, ratings, and weighted scores provided. This table is appropriate for 1995 *before* Maytag sold its European and Australian operations. Note that Maytag's total weighted score is 3.05, meaning that the corporation is about average compared to the strengths and weaknesses of others in the major home appliance industry.

Table 4.2 Internal Factor Analysis Summary (IFAS): Maytag as Example

Internal Factors	Weight	Rating	Weighted Score	Comments
	1	2	3	4	5
Strengths				
• Quality Maytag culture	.15	5	.75	Quality key to success
• Experienced top management	.05	4	.20	Know appliances
• Vertical integration	.10	4	.40	Dedicated factories
• Employee relations	.05	3	.15	Good, but deteriorating
• Hoover's international orientation	.15	3	.45	Hoover name in cleaners
Weaknesses				
• Process-oriented R&D	.05	2	.10	Slow on new products
• Distribution channels	.05	2	.10	Superstores replacing small dealers
• Financial position	.15	2	.30	High debt load
• Global positioning	.20	2	.40	Hoover weak outside the United Kingdom and Australia
• Manufacturing facilities	.05	4	.20	Investing now
Total Scores	1.00		3.05	

Notes:
1. List strengths and weaknesses (5–10 each) in Column 1.
2. Weight each factor from 1.0 (Most Important) to 0.0 (Not Important) in Column 2 based on that factor's probable impact on the company's strategic position. **The total weights must sum to 1.00.**
3. Rate each factor from 5 (Outstanding) to 1 (Poor) in Column 3 based on the company's response to that factor.
4. Multiply each factor's weight times its rating to obtain each factor's weighted score in Column 4.
5. Use Column 5 (comments) for rationale used for each factor.
6. Add the weighted scores to obtain the total weighted score for the company in Column 4. This tells how well the company is responding to the strategic factors in its internal environment.

Source: T. L. Wheelen and J. D. Hunger, "Internal Strategic Factor Analysis Summary (IFAS)." Copyright © 1991 by Wheelen and Hunger Associates. Reprinted by permission.

🌐 4.6 Global Issues for the 21st Century

- The **21st Century Global Society** feature in this chapter illustrated how business corporations are hiring a more diverse workforce with multilingual abilities in order to gain competitive advantage in a global environment. A number of firms, from American Express to Delta Airlines, have established international service centers in Utah, for example, because of the high level of multilingual talent within the state. Primarily because Mormons have sent their young people on missions around the world, the people of Utah can collectively speak 90% of the world's written languages. According to Fred Ball, head of a local Chamber of Commerce, "I can make one phone call and get a foreign language speaker in 30 minutes."[26]

- As more and more industries become hypercompetitive, it will become harder to sustain a competitive advantage unless a company has a distinctive competency that is not only durable but also hard to imitate. Durability has little value, however, in a global industry during a time of technological discontinuity.

- Expect an increasing number of corporations to contract various functions to suppliers or distributors in an effort to reduce costs and be globally competitive. For example, the manufacturing of athletic shoes is now exclusively done by Asian contractors for Nike, Reebok, and other global competitors. Corporations are downsizing in an attempt to focus on those parts of the industry value chain where they have distinctive competencies.

- Although the SBU structure has become widespread in most large corporations around the world, such a decentralized structure makes it difficult to take advantage of a corporation's core competencies. This problem will increase as more industries become global with longer communication and logistical networks.

- Expect corporate culture and human resources to increase in importance in hypercompetitive global industries. New products and new technologies are easier to duplicate than are the *intangible* aspects of corporate culture and human resources.

- Autonomous work teams should lead not only to greater efficiency through a reduction of supervisors, but also to greater effectiveness as work teams act to integrate functional specialties at the task level rather than at managerial levels. With supervisors no longer available to deal with disagreements, work teams will need increased training in conflict management.

Projections for the 21st Century

- From 1994 to 2010, the average income per capita in the *developed* nations will rise from $16,610 to $22,802.

- From 1994 to 2010, the average income per capita in the *developing* nations will increase from $950 to $2,563.[27]

Discussion Questions

1. What is the relevance of the resource-based view of the firm to strategic management in a global environment?

2. How can value-chain analysis help identify a company's strengths and weaknesses?

3. In what ways can a corporation's structure and culture be internal strengths or weaknesses?

4. What are the pros and cons of management's using the experience curve to determine strategy?

5. How might a firm's management decide whether it should continue to invest in current known technology or in new, but untested technology? What factors might encourage or discourage such a shift?

Key Terms

autonomous work teams (p. 98)
basic R&D (p. 94)
capital budgeting (p. 93)
center of gravity (p. 85)
concurrent engineering (p. 99)
continuous systems (p. 97)
continuum of sustainability (p. 84)

core competencies (p. 83)
corporate capabilities (p. 83)
corporate culture (p. 89)
cultural integration (p. 89)
cultural intensity (p. 89)
distinctive competencies (p. 83)
durability (p. 83)

economies of scale (p. 98)
economies of scope (p. 86)
engineering (or process) R&D (p. 95)
experience curve (p. 97)
financial leverage (p. 92)
flexible manufacturing (p. 98)

human diversity (p. 99)
IFAS Table (p. 101)
imitability (p. 83)
intermittent systems (p. 96)
internal strategic factors (p. 82)
intranet (p. 100)
linkages (p. 86)
market position (p. 90)
market segmentation (p. 90)
marketing mix (p. 90)

mass customization (p. 98)
organizational analysis (p. 82)
organizational structures (p. 87)
primary activities (p. 86)
product life cycle (p. 91)
product R&D (p. 94)
quality of work life (p. 99)
R&D intensity (p. 93)
R&D mix (p. 95)
resource (p. 82)

strategic business units (SBUs) (p. 89)
support activities (p. 86)
technological competence (p. 94)
technological discontinuity (p. 95)
technology transfer (p. 94)
value chain (p. 84)
VRIO framework (p. 82)
value-chain linkages (p. 86)

Strategic Practice Exercise

Does your college or university have a corporate culture? If it has survived for more than a decade, it probably has one. What are its characteristics? How intense is it? How well integrated?

Before the next class, interview a long-time employee and find some tangible items (like a mission statement, printed philosophy, or honor system policies) that illustrate the culture of your school. What aspect of the culture does your item illustrate? Try to answer the following questions:

____ 1. What are some key beliefs or values that faculty, staff (including administrators), and students share?

____ 2. Is there a story that people tell one another to illustrate a key value of the school? How long ago did this event occur?

____ 3. Does the school have a dominant orientation regarding teaching, research, and service? What does it communicate to its key stakeholders? Is it truthful or just advertising what it thinks stakeholders want from it?

____ 4. Are there any work practices that have become part of the school's unquestioned tradition, but no one seems to know why things are done that way?

Discuss in class what you have discovered. Do your fellow students agree with you? Is there anything about your school's culture you would like to see changed? Why?

Notes

1. S. McCartney, and M. J. McCarthy, "Southwest Flies Circles Around United's Shuttle," *Wall Street Journal* (February 20, 1996), pp. B1 and B8.
2. J. B. Barney, *Gaining and Sustaining Competitive Advantage* (Reading, Mass.: Addison-Wesley, 1997), pp. 145–164.
3. R. M. Grant, "The Resource-Based Theory of Competitive Advantage: Implications for Strategy Formulation," *California Management Review* (Spring 1991), pp. 114–135.
4. *Ibid*, pp. 123–128.
5. J. R. Galbraith, "Strategy and Organization Planning," in *The Strategy Process: Concepts, Contexts, and Cases*, 2nd ed., edited by H. Mintzberg and J. B. Quinn (Englewood Cliffs, N.J.: Prentice Hall, 1991), pp. 315–324.
6. M. Porter, *Competitive Advantage: Creating and Sustaining Superior Performance* (New York: The Free Press, 1985), p. 36.
7. M. Leontiades, "A Diagnostic Framework for Planning," *Strategic Management Journal* (January-March 1983), p. 14.
8. D. M. Rousseau, "Assessing Organizational Culture: The Case for Multiple Methods," in *Organizational Climate and Culture*, edited by B. Schneider (San Francisco: Jossey-Bass, 1990), pp. 153–192.
9. L. Smircich, "Concepts of Culture and Organizational Analysis," *Administrative Science Quarterly* (September 1983), pp. 345–346.
10. Barney, p. 155.
11. "R&D Scoreboard," *Business Week* (June 27, 1994), pp. 81–103.
12. B. O'Reilly, "The Secrets of America's Most Admired Corporations: New Ideas and New Products," *Fortune* (March 3, 1997), p. 62.
13. P. Pascarella, "Are You Investing in the Wrong Technology?" *Industry Week* (July 25, 1983), p. 37.
14. *Ibid.*, p. 38.
15. B. J. Pine, *Mass Customization: The New Frontier in Business Competition* (Boston: Harvard Business School Press, 1993).
16. B. Dumaine, "The Trouble with Teams," *Fortune* (September 5, 1994), p. 86.

17. A. Versteeg, "Self-Directed Work Teams Yield Long-Term Benefits," *Journal of Business Strategy* (November/December 1990), pp. 9–12.

18. R. Sanchez, "Strategic Flexibility in Product Competition," *Strategic Management Journal* (Summer 1995), p. 147.

19. The percentage of unionized government employees is 38.7%. See "Uncle Sam Gompers," *Wall Street Journal* (October 25, 1994), p. A20.

20. G. Koretz, "U.S. Labor Gets Flexible," *Business Week* (January 15, 1996), p. 22; J. Templeman, M. Trinephi, and S. Toy, "A Continent Swarming with Temps," *Business Week* (April 8, 1996), p. 54.

21. D. L. Boroughs, "The New Migrant Workers," *U.S. News & World Report* (July 4, 1994), p. 53.

22. D. S. Hames, "Training in the Land of Doone: An Exercise in Understanding Cultural Differences," *Journal of Management Education* (May 1996), p. 258.

23. A. Cortese, "Here Comes the Intranet," *Business Week* (February 26, 1996), p. 76.

24. B. Richards, "Inside Story," *Wall Street Journal* (June 17, 1996), p. R23.

25. D. Bartholomew, "Blue-Collar Computing," *InformationWeek* (June 19, 1995), pp. 34–43.

26. S. B. Donnelly, "The State of Many Tongues," *Time* (April 13, 1992), p. 51.

27. J. Warner, "21st Century Capitalism: Snapshot of the Next Century," *Business Week* (November 18, 1994), p 194.

Chapter 5

Strategy Formulation: Situation Analysis and Business Strategy

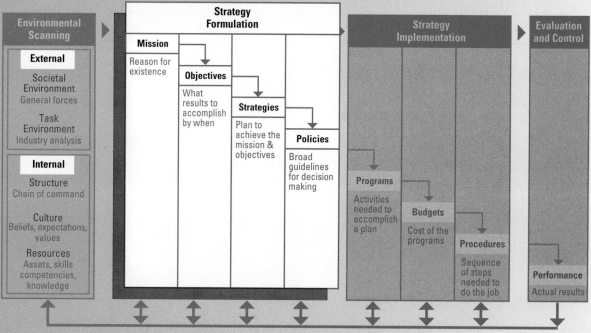

When Donald Lamberti incorporated Casey's General Stores in 1967 in Des Moines, Iowa, he formulated a strategy unknown at that time in the convenience store industry. Instead of targeting the large, growing metropolitan areas of the eastern, western, and southern United States where potential sales were high, he chose to focus on the small towns in the agricultural heartland of the Midwest. Contrary to all the conventional wisdom arguing against beginning a business in a declining market, Lamberti avoided direct competition with Seven-Eleven and moved into these increasingly ignored small markets. The company expanded its offerings from just gasoline and basic groceries to include fast food and bakeries. In many small midwestern towns, Casey's was now the only retail business left. These were towns too small for even Wal-Mart to covet. Like any convenience store, prices were somewhat higher than in larger, more specialized stores in the cities. But small-town people did not want to have to drive 10 to 20 miles for a loaf of bread or a pizza.

By autumn 1996, Casey's was opening an average of six new convenience stores a month for a total of just over 1,000 stores in the upper midwestern United States. At a time when other convenience stores were struggling to show a profit and avoid bankruptcy, Casey's recorded continuing growth and profitability. (*For further information, see Caseys.com on the World Wide Web.*)

Casey's General Stores is successful because its strategic managers formulated a new strategy designed to give it an advantage in a very competitive industry. Casey's is an example of a differentiation focus competitive strategy in which a company focuses on a particular market area to provide a differentiated product or service. This strategy is one of the business competitive strategies discussed in this chapter.

5.1   *Situational Analysis: SWOT*

Strategy formulation is often referred to as strategic planning or long-range planning and is concerned with developing a corporation's mission, objectives, strategies, and policies. It begins with situation analysis: the process of finding a strategic fit between external opportunities and internal strengths while working around external threats and internal weaknesses. As shown in the Strategic Decision-Making Process in Figure 1.5, this is step 5(a): analyzing strategic factors in light of the current situation using SWOT analysis. **SWOT** is an acronym used to describe the particular **S**trengths, **W**eaknesses, **O**pportunities, and **T**hreats that are strategic factors for a specific company. SWOT analysis should not only result in the identification of a corporation's **distinctive competencies**—the particular capabilities and resources that a firm possesses and the superior way in which they are used—but also in the identification of opportunities that the firm is not currently able to take advantage of due to a lack of appropriate resources.

Generating a Strategic Factors Analysis Summary (SFAS) Matrix

The **SFAS (Strategic Factors Analysis Summary) Matrix** summarizes an organization's strategic factors by combining the *external* factors from the EFAS Table with the *internal* factors from the IFAS Table. The EFAS and IFAS examples given of Maytag Corporation (as it was in 1995) in Tables 3.4 and 4.2 list a total of 20 internal and external factors. These are too many factors for most people to use in strategy formulation. The SFAS Matrix requires the strategic decision maker to condense these strengths, weaknesses, opportunities, and threats into fewer than ten strategic factors. This is done by reviewing and revising the weight given each factor. The revised weights reflect the priority of each factor as a determinant of the company's future success. The highest weighted EFAS and IFAS factors should appear in the SFAS Matrix.

As shown in Figure 5.1, you can create an SFAS Matrix by following these steps:

- In the **Key Strategic Factors** column (column 1), list the most important EFAS and IFAS items. After each factor, indicate whether it is a strength (S), weakness (W), opportunity (O), or threat (T).

- In the **Weight** column (column 2), enter the weights for all of the internal and external strategic factors. As with the EFAS and IFAS Tables presented earlier, the **weight column must still total 1.00**. *This means that the weights calculated earlier for EFAS and IFAS will probably have to be adjusted.*

Table 4.2   Internal Factor Analysis Summary (IFAS): Maytag as Example (Selection of Strategic Factors)*

Internal Strategic Factors	Weight	Rating	Weighted Score	Comments
	1	2	3	4	5
Strengths				
S1 Quality Maytag culture	.15	5	.75	Quality key to success
S2 Experienced top management	.05	4	.20	Know appliances
S3 Vertical integration	.10	4	.40	Dedicated factories
S4 Employee relations	.05	3	.15	Good, but deteriorating
S5 Hoover's international orientation	.15	3	.45	Hoover name in cleaners
Weaknesses				
W1 Process-oriented R&D	.05	2	.10	Slow on new products
W2 Distribution channels	.05	2	.10	Superstores replacing small dealers
W3 Financial position	.15	2	.30	High debt load
W4 Global positioning	.20	2	.40	Hoover weak outside the United Kingdom and Australia
W5 Manufacturing facilities	.05	4	.20	Investing now
Total	1.00		3.05	

Table 3.4   External Factor Analysis Summary (EFAS): Maytag as Example (Selection of Strategic Factors)*

External Strategic Factors	Weight	Rating	Weighted Score	Comments
	1	2	3	4	5
Opportunities				
O1 Economic integration of European Community	.20	4	.80	Acquisition of Hoover
O2 Demographics favor quality appliances	.10	5	.50	Maytag quality
O3 Economic development of Asia	.05	1	.05	Low Maytag presence
O4 Opening of Eastern Europe	.05	2	.10	Will take time
O5 Trend to "Super Stores"	.10	2	.20	Maytag weak in this channel
Threats				
T1 Increasing government regulations	.10	4	.40	Well positioned
T2 Strong U.S. competition	.10	4	.40	Well positioned
T3 Whirlpool and Electrolux strong globally	.15	3	.45	Hoover weak globally
T4 New product advances	.05	1	.05	Questionable
T5 Japanese appliance companies	.10	2	.20	Only Asian presence is Australia
Total	1.00		3.15	

*The most important external and internal factors are identified in the EFAS and IFAS tables as shown here by shading these factors.

Figure 5.1 **Strategic Factor Analysis Summary (SFAS) Matrix**

Key Strategic Factors (Select the most important opportunities/threats from EFAS, Table 3.4 and the most important strengths and weaknesses from IFAS, Table 4.2)	1 Weight	3 Rating	4 Weighted Score	Duration 5 SHORT	INTERMEDIATE	LONG	6 Comments
S1 Quality Maytag culture (S)	.10	5	.50			X	Quality key to success
S3 Hoover's international orientation (S)	.10	3	.30		X		Name recognition
W3 Financial position (W)	.10	2	.20		X		High debt
W4 Global positioning (W)	.15	2	.30			X	Only in N.A., U.K., and Australia
O1 Economic integration of European Community (O)	.10	4	.40			X	Acquisition of Hoover
O2 Demographics favor quality (O)	.10	5	.50		X		Maytag quality
O5 Trend to super stores (O + T)	.10	2	.20	X			Weak in this channel
T3 Whirlpool and Electrolux (T)	.15	3	.45	X			Dominate industry
T5 Japanese appliance companies (T)	.10	2	.20			X	Asian presence
Total Score	**1.00**		**3.05**				

Notes:
1. List each of your key strategic features developed in your IFAS and EFAS tables in Column 1.
2. Weight each factor from 1.0 (Most Important) to 0.0 (Not Important) in Column 2 based on that factor's probable impact on the company's strategic position. **The total weights must sum to 1.00.**
3. Rate each factor from 5 (Outstanding) to 1 (Poor) in Column 3 based on the company's response to that factor.
4. Multiply each factor's weight times its rating to obtain each factor's weighted score in Column 4.
5. For duration in Column 5, check appropriate column (short term—less than 1 year; intermediate—1 to 3 years; long term—over 3 years.)
6. Use Column 6 (comments) for rationale used for each factor.

Source: T. L. Wheelen and J. D. Hunger, "Strategic Factors Analysis Summary (SFAS)." Copyright © 1997 by Wheelen and Hunger Associates. Reprinted by permission.

- In the **Rating** column (column 3), enter the ratings of how the company's management is responding to each of the strategic factors. These ratings will probably (but not always) be the same as those listed in the EFAS and IFAS Tables.

- In the **Weighted Score** column (column 4), calculate the weighted scores as done earlier for EFAS and IFAS.

- In the new **Duration** column (column 5), depicted in Figure 5.1, indicate short-term (less than one year), intermediate-term (one to three years), or long-term (three years and beyond).

- In the **Comments** column (column 6), repeat or revise your comments for each strategic factor from the previous EFAS and IFAS Tables.

The resulting SFAS Matrix is a listing of the firm's external and internal strategic factors in one table. The example given is that of Maytag Corporation in 1995 *before the firm sold its European and Australian operations.* The SFAS Matrix includes only the most important factors gathered from environmental scanning and thus provides the information essential for strategy formulation.

Finding a Propitious Niche

One desired outcome of analyzing strategic factors is identifying a niche where an organization can use its core competencies to take advantage of a particular market opportunity. A niche is a need in the marketplace that is currently unsatisfied. The goal is to find a **propitious niche**—an extremely favorable niche—that is so well suited to the firm's internal and external environment that other corporations are not likely to challenge or dislodge it.[1] A niche is propitious to the extent that it currently is just large enough for one firm to satisfy its demand. After a firm has found and filled that niche, it is not worth a potential competitor's time or money to also go after the same niche.

Finding such a niche is not always easy. A firm's management must be always looking for a **strategic window**, that is, a unique market opportunity that is available only for a particular time. The first firm through a strategic window can occupy a propitious niche and discourage competition (if the firm has the required internal strengths). One company that has successfully found a propitious niche is Frank J. Zamboni & Company, the manufacturer of the machines that smooth the ice at ice skating rinks. Frank Zamboni invented the unique tractor-like machine in 1949 and no one has found a substitute for what it does. Before the machine was invented, people had to clean and scrape the ice by hand to prepare the surface for skating. Now hockey fans look forward to intermissions just to watch "the Zamboni" slowly drive up and down the ice rink turning rough, scraped ice into a smooth mirror surface—almost like magic. So long as Zamboni's company is able to produce the machines in the quantity and quality desired at a reasonable price, it's not worth another company's while to go after Frank Zamboni & Company's propitious niche.

As the niche grows, so can the company within that niche—by increasing its operations' capacity or through alliances with larger firms. The key is to identify a market opportunity in which the first firm to reach that market segment can obtain and keep dominant market share. For example, Church & Dwight was the first company in the United States to successfully market sodium bicarbonate for use in cooking. Its Arm & Hammer brand baking soda is still found in 95% of all U.S. households. The propitious niche concept is crucial to the software industry. Small initial demand in emerging markets allows new entrepreneurial ventures to go after niches too small to be noticed by established companies. When Microsoft developed its first disk operating system (DOS) in 1980 for IBM's personal computers, for example, the demand for such open systems software was very small—a small niche for a then very small Microsoft. The company was able to fill that niche and to successfully grow with it.

Niches can also change—sometimes faster than a firm can adapt to that change. A company may discover in its situation analysis that it needs to invest heavily in its capabilities to keep them competitively strong in a changing niche. Cummins Engine took this approach when it realized that it did not have what was needed to take advantage of a developing opportunity in the diesel engine market. It invested $1 billion—more than three times the market value of its stock—in two new lines of engines in the early 1980s. Ten years later, eager customers such as Ford and Chrysler were purchasing so many of the fuel-efficient motors for their trucks that Cummins had to build a second plant to meet demand. "Competence has given us an economic opportunity," explained CEO Henry Schacht. In retrospect, the CEO pointed out that if in 1981 the company had not chosen to invest heavily, "we would be in decline if not out of business."[2]

5.2   *Review of Mission and Objectives*

A reexamination of an organization's current mission and objectives must be made before alternative strategies can be generated and evaluated. Even when formulating strategy, decision makers tend to concentrate on the alternatives—the action possibilities—rather than on a mission to be fulfilled and objectives to be achieved. This tendency is so attractive because it is much easier to deal with alternative courses of action that exist right here and now than to really think about what you want to accomplish in the future. The end result is that we often choose strategies that set our objectives for us, rather than having our choices incorporate clear objectives and a mission statement.

Problems in performance can derive from an inappropriate statement of mission, which may be too narrow or too broad. If the mission does not provide a common thread (a unifying theme) for a corporation's businesses, managers may be unclear about where the company is heading. Objectives and strategies might be in conflict with each other. Divisions might be competing against one another, rather than against outside competition—to the detriment of the corporation as a whole.

A company's objectives can also be inappropriately stated. They can either focus too much on short-term operational goals or be so general that they provide little real guidance. There may be a gap between planned and achieved objectives. When such a gap occurs, either the strategies have to be changed to improve performance or the objectives need to be adjusted downward to be more realistic. Consequently objectives should be constantly reviewed to ensure their usefulness. This is what happened at Toyota Motor Corporation when top management realized that its "Global 10" objective of aiming for 10% of the global vehicle market by the end of the century was no longer feasible. Emphasis was then shifted from market share to profits. Interestingly, at the same time that both Toyota and General Motors were deemphasizing market share as a key corporate objective, Ford Motor Company was stating that it wanted to be Number One in sales worldwide. No longer content with being in second place, Alexander Trotman, Ford's Chairman of the Board, contends: "Have you ever seen a team run out on the field and say, 'We're going to be No. 2'"?[3]

5.3   *Generating Alternative Strategies Using a TOWS Matrix*

Thus far we have discussed how a firm uses SWOT analysis to assess its situation. *SWOT can also be used to generate a number of possible alternative strategies.* The **TOWS Matrix** (TOWS is just another way of saying SWOT) illustrates how the external opportunities and threats facing a particular corporation can be matched with that company's internal strengths and weaknesses to result in four sets of possible strategic alternatives. (See Figure 5.2.) This is a good way to use brainstorming to create alternative strategies that might not otherwise be considered. It forces strategic managers to create various kinds of growth as well as retrenchment strategies. It can be used to generate corporate as well as business strategies.

To generate a TOWS Matrix for Maytag Corporation in 1995, for example, use the *External Factor Analysis Summary* (EFAS) listed in Table 3.4 from Chapter 3 and the *Internal Factor Analysis Summary* (IFAS) listed in Table 4.2 from Chapter 4. To build Figure 5.3, take the following steps:

Figure 5.2
TOWS Matrix

Source: Adapted from *Long-Range Planning*, April 1982, H. Weihrich, "The TOWS Matrix—A Tool for Situational Analysis" p. 60. Copyright 1982, with kind permission from H. Weihrich and Elsevier Science Ltd. The Boulevard, Langford Lane, Kidlington OX5 1GB, UK.

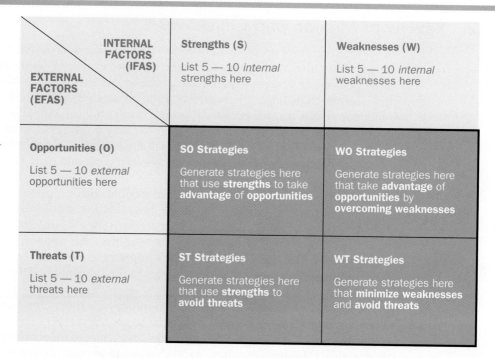

1. In the **Opportunities** (**O**) block, list the external opportunities available in the company's or business unit's current and future environment from the *EFAS Table* (Table 3.4).

2. In the **Threats** (**T**) block, list the external threats facing the company or unit now and in the future from the *EFAS Table* (Table 3.2).

3. In the **Strengths** (**S**) block, list the specific areas of current and future strength for the company or unit from the *IFAS Table* (Table 4.2).

4. In the **Weaknesses** (**W**) block, list the specific areas of current and future weakness for the company or unit from the *IFAS Table* (Table 4.2).

5. Generate a series of possible strategies for the company or business unit under consideration based on particular combinations of the four sets of strategic factors:

   • **SO Strategies** are generated by thinking of ways in which a company or business unit could use its strengths to take advantage of opportunities.

   • **ST Strategies** consider a company's or unit's strengths as a way to avoid threats.

   • **WO Strategies** attempt to take advantage of opportunities by overcoming weaknesses.

   • **WT Strategies** are basically defensive and primarily act to minimize weaknesses and avoid threats.

The TOWS Matrix is very useful for generating a series of alternatives that the decision makers of a company or business unit might not otherwise have considered. It can be used for the corporation as a whole (as was done in Figure 5.3 with Maytag Corporation before it sold Hoover Europe), or it can be used for a specific business unit within a corporation (like Hoover's floor care products). Nevertheless the TOWS Matrix is only one of many ways to generate alternative strategies. Another approach is to evaluate each business unit within a corporation in terms of possible competitive and cooperative strategies.

5.4 Business Strategies

Business strategy focuses on improving the competitive position of a company's or business unit's products or services within the specific industry or market segment that the company or business unit serves. Business strategy can be competitive (battling against all competitors for advantage) and/or cooperative (working with one or more competitors to gain advantage against other competitors). Just as corporate strategy asks *what* industry(ies) the company should be in, business strategy asks *how* the company or its units should compete or cooperate in each industry.

Porter's Competitive Strategies

Competitive strategy raises the following questions:

- Should we compete on the basis of low cost (and thus price), or should we differentiate our products or services on some basis other than cost, such as quality or service?

- Should we compete head to head with our major competitors for the biggest but most sought-after share of the market, or should we focus on a niche in which we can satisfy a less sought-after but also profitable segment of the market?

Michael Porter proposes two "generic" competitive strategies for outperforming other corporations in a particular industry: lower cost and differentiation.[4] These strategies are called generic because they can be pursued by any type or size of business firm, even by not-for-profit organizations.

- **Lower cost strategy** is the ability of a company or a business unit to design, produce, and market a comparable product more efficiently than its competitors.

- **Differentiation strategy** is the ability to provide unique and superior value to the buyer in terms of product quality, special features, or after-sale service.

Porter further proposes that a firm's competitive advantage in an industry is determined by its **competitive scope**, that is, the breadth of the company's or business unit's target market. Before using one of the two generic competitive strategies (lower cost or differentiation), the firm or unit must choose the range of product varieties it will produce, the distribution channels it will employ, the types of buyers it will serve, the geographic areas in which it will sell, and the array of related industries in which it will also compete. This should reflect an understanding of the firm's unique resources. Simply put, a company or business unit can choose a *broad target* (that is, aim at the middle of the mass market) or a *narrow target* (that is, aim at a market niche). Combining these two types of target markets with the two competitive strategies results in the four variations of generic strategies depicted in Figure 5.4. When the lower cost and differentiation strategies have a broad mass-market target, they are simply called *cost leadership* and *differentiation*. When they are focused on a market niche (narrow target), however, they are called *cost focus* and *differentiation focus*.

Table 4.2 Internal Factor Analysis Summary (IFAS): Maytag as Example

Internal Strategic Factors	Weight	Rating	Weighted Score	Comments
	1	2	3	4	5
Strengths				
S1 Quality Maytag culture	.15	5	.75	Quality key to success
S2 Experienced top management	.05	4	.20	Know appliances
S3 Vertical integration	.10	4	.40	Dedicated factories
S4 Employee relations	.05	3	.15	Good, but deteriorating
S5 Hoover's international orientation	.15	3	.45	Hoover name in cleaners
Weaknesses				
W1 Process-oriented R&D	.05	2	.10	Slow on new products
W2 Distribution channels	.05	2	.10	Superstores replacing small dealers
W3 Financial position	.15	2	.30	High debt load
W4 Global positioning	.20	2	.40	Hoover weak outside the United Kingdom and Australia
W5 Manufacturing facilities	.05	4	.20	Investing now
Total	1.00		3.05	

Table 3.4 External Factor Analysis Summary (EFAS): Maytag as Example

External Strategic Factors	Weight	Rating	Weighted Score	Comments
	1	2	3	4	5
Opportunities				
O1 Economic integration of European Community	.20	4	.80	Acquisition of Hoover
O2 Demographics favor quality appliances	.10	5	.50	Maytag quality
O3 Economic development of Asia	.05	1	.05	Low Maytag presence
O4 Opening of Eastern Europe	.05	2	.10	Will take time
O5 Trend to "Super Stores"	.10	2	.20	Maytag weak in this channel
Threats				
T1 Increasing government regulations	.10	4	.40	Well positioned
T2 Strong U.S. competition	.10	4	.40	Well positioned
T3 Whirlpool and Electrolux strong globally	.15	3	.45	Hoover weak globally
T4 New product advances	.05	1	.05	Questionable
T5 Japanese appliance companies	.10	2	.20	Only Asian presence is Australia
Total	1.00		3.15	

Figure 5.3   **Generating a TOWS Matrix for Maytag Corporation**

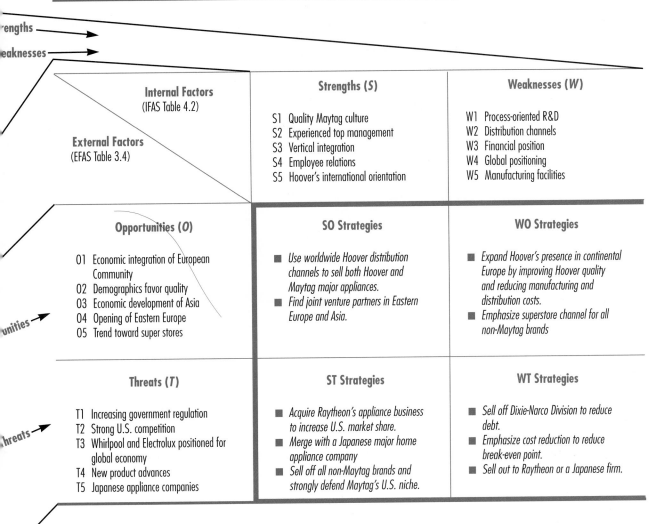

Internal Factors (IFAS Table 4.2) External Factors (EFAS Table 3.4)	**Strengths (S)** S1 Quality Maytag culture S2 Experienced top management S3 Vertical integration S4 Employee relations S5 Hoover's international orientation	**Weaknesses (W)** W1 Process-oriented R&D W2 Distribution channels W3 Financial position W4 Global positioning W5 Manufacturing facilities
Opportunities (O) O1 Economic integration of European Community O2 Demographics favor quality O3 Economic development of Asia O4 Opening of Eastern Europe O5 Trend toward super stores	**SO Strategies** ■ *Use worldwide Hoover distribution channels to sell both Hoover and Maytag major appliances.* ■ *Find joint venture partners in Eastern Europe and Asia.*	**WO Strategies** ■ *Expand Hoover's presence in continental Europe by improving Hoover quality and reducing manufacturing and distribution costs.* ■ *Emphasize superstore channel for all non-Maytag brands*
Threats (T) T1 Increasing government regulation T2 Strong U.S. competition T3 Whirlpool and Electrolux positioned for global economy T4 New product advances T5 Japanese appliance companies	**ST Strategies** ■ *Acquire Raytheon's appliance business to increase U.S. market share.* ■ *Merge with a Japanese major home appliance company* ■ *Sell off all non-Maytag brands and strongly defend Maytag's U.S. niche.*	**WT Strategies** ■ *Sell off Dixie-Narco Division to reduce debt.* ■ *Emphasize cost reduction to reduce break-even point.* ■ *Sell out to Raytheon or a Japanese firm.*

Cost leadership is a low-cost competitive strategy that aims at the broad mass market and requires "aggressive construction of efficient-scale facilities, vigorous pursuit of cost reductions from experience, tight cost and overhead control, avoidance of marginal customer accounts, and cost minimization in areas like R&D, service, sales force, advertising, and so on."[5] Because of its lower costs, the cost leader is able to charge a lower price for its products than its competitors and still make a satisfactory profit. Some companies successfully following this strategy are Wal-Mart, Alamo Rent-A-Car, Southwest Airlines, Timex, and Gateway 2000. Having a low-cost position also gives a company or business unit a defense against rivals. Its lower costs allow it to continue to earn profits during times of heavy competition. Its high market share means that it will have high bargaining power relative to its suppliers (because it buys in large quantities). Its low price will also serve as a barrier to entry because few new entrants will be able to match the leader's cost advantage. As a result, cost leaders are likely to earn above-average returns on investment.

Differentiation is aimed at the broad mass market and involves the creation of a product or service that is perceived throughout its industry as unique. The company or

Figure 5.4
Porter's Generic Competitive Strategies

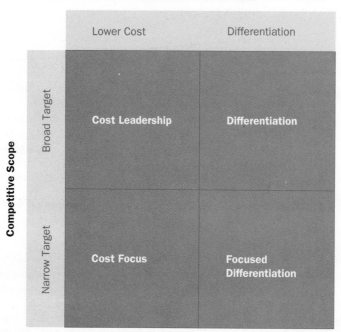

business unit may then charge a premium for its product. This specialty can be associated with design or brand image, technology, features, dealer network, or customer service. Differentiation is a viable strategy for earning above-average returns in a specific business because the resulting brand loyalty lowers customers' sensitivity to price. Increased costs can usually be passed on to the buyers. Buyer loyalty also serves as an entry barrier—new firms must develop their own distinctive competence to differentiate their products in some way in order to compete successfully. Examples of the successful use of a differentiation strategy are Walt Disney Productions, Maytag appliances, Nike athletic shoes, and Mercedes-Benz automobiles. Research does suggest that a differentiation strategy is more likely to generate higher profits than is a low-cost strategy because differentiation creates a better entry barrier. A low-cost strategy is more likely, however, to generate increases in market share.[6]

Cost focus is a low-cost competitive strategy that focuses on a particular buyer group or geographic market and attempts to serve only this niche, to the exclusion of others. In using cost focus, the company or business unit seeks a cost advantage in its target segment. A good example of this strategy is Fadal Engineering. Fadal focuses its efforts on building and selling no-frills machine tools to small manufacturers. Fadal achieved cost focus by keeping overhead and R&D to a minimum and by focusing its marketing efforts strictly on its market niche. The cost focus strategy is valued by those who believe that a company or business unit that focuses its efforts is better able to serve its narrow strategic target more efficiently than can its competition. It does, however, require a tradeoff between profitability and overall market share.

Differentiation focus, like cost focus, concentrates on a particular buyer group, product line segment, or geographic market. This is the strategy successfully followed by Casey's General Stores, Morgan Motor Car Company (manufacturer of classic British sports cars), and local health food stores. In using differentiation focus, the company or business unit seeks differentiation in a targeted market segment. This strategy is valued

◀ *STRATEGY IN A CHANGING WORLD*

DIFFERENTIATION FOCUS STRATEGY AT MORGAN MOTOR CAR COMPANY

By focusing on the values of traditional British, top-down, sports car motoring, the Morgan Motor Car Company has successfully found a way to differentiate itself from all competitors. Once competing with the respected British marques of MG, Triumph, Austin-Healey, Jaguar, and Aston Martin, the Morgan is now the sole occupant of a small, but durable propitious niche. Founded in 1919 by Henry F. S. Morgan, the company continues to use the same factory in England's West Midlands to produce automobiles seemingly unchanged from those produced before World War II. Although Morgans (known as "mogs" by admirers) have state-of-the-art engines with fuel injection, electronic ignition, and pollution control devices, the basic front-end suspension design has remained relatively unchanged since the company's founder built the first Morgan by hand in 1908. Although the chassis is based on a simple steel frame, the body is still constructed on a hand-built wooden frame of specially aged ash. The Morgan's hand-cut body panel must be fitted by hand onto the car.

The company makes three models, ranging in price from $35,000 to $50,000. The company has no long-term debt and enjoys steady growth in sales and profits. Sports cars with reputations comparable to that of the Morgan sell for $150,000 and up. For the person wanting a personalized car, the Morgan is available in 35,000 hand-painted colors. The company employs just enough skilled workers to build ten cars a week for an annual capacity of fewer than 500 cars. Because the company receives about 600 to 800 new orders each year, the current waiting list for a new Morgan is about 2,500 to 5,000 cars—about 10 years' production! The firm's response to a rapidly changing automobile industry seems perfectly tuned to staying in its propitious niche. According to Charles Morgan, grandson of the founder, "We . . . believe the Morgan policy of gradual and carefully considered change will enable us to maintain the car's qualities and unique appeal, and thereby ensure its survival for the foreseeable future."

Source: P. G. Goulet and A. Rappaport, "The Morgan Motor Car Company: The Last of the Great Independents," in Wheelen and Hunger, *Strategic Management and Business Policy*, 5th ed. (Reading, Mass.: Addison-Wesley, 1995), pp. 1126–1138.

by those who believe that a company or a unit that focuses its efforts is better able to serve the special needs of a narrow strategic target more effectively than can its competition. See the **Strategy in a Changing World** feature for Morgan Motors' ability to prosper in a changing global industry by sticking to British tradition.

Risks in Competitive Strategies

No one competitive strategy is guaranteed to achieve success, and some companies that have successfully implemented one of Porter's competitive strategies have found that they could not sustain the strategy. As shown in Table 5.1, each of the generic strategies has its risks. For example, a company following a differentiation strategy must ensure that the higher price it charges for its higher quality is not priced too far above the competition, otherwise customers will not see the extra quality as worth the extra cost. This is what is meant in Table 5.1 by the term **cost proximity.** Procter & Gamble's use of R&D and advertising to differentiate its products had been very successful for many years until customers in the value-conscious 1990s turned to cheaper private brands. As a result, P & G was forced to reduce costs until it could get prices back in line with customer expectations.

Table 5.1   **Risks of Generic Competitive Strategies**

Risks of Cost Leadership	Risks of Differentiation	Risks of Focus
Cost leadership is not sustained: • Competitors imitate. • Technology changes. • Other bases for cost leadership erode. Proximity in differentiation is lost.	Differentiation is not sustained: • Competitors imitate. • Bases for differentiation become less important to buyers. Cost proximity is lost.	The focus strategy is imitated: The target segment becomes structurally unattractive: • Structure erodes. • Demand disappears. Broadly targeted competitors overwhelm the segment: • The segment's differences from other segments narrow. • The advantages of a broad line increase. New focusers subsegment the industry.
Cost focusers achieve even lower cost in segments.	Differentiation focusers achieve even greater differentiation in segments.	

Source: Adapted/reprinted with permission of The Free Press, an imprint of Simon & Schuster, from *Competitive Advantage: Creating and Sustaining Superior Performance* by Michael E. Porter, p. 21. Copyright © 1985 by Michael E. Porter.

Issues in Competitive Strategies

Porter argues that to be successful, a company or business unit must achieve one of the preceding generic competitive strategies. Otherwise, the company or business unit is **stuck in the middle** of the competitive marketplace with no competitive advantage and is doomed to below-average performance. An example of a company stuck in the middle was Tandy Corporation. Tandy's strategy of selling personal computers to the average person had failed to generate the large amount of sales and profits top management had desired. Its computers had neither the exciting new features found on Compaq's products nor the low price of the PC clones like those sold through the mail by Dell or Gateway. Sales were stagnating. Attempting to increase its sales to business through its GRID Systems subsidiary while keeping up its Radio Shack sales, Tandy was confronted with the dilemma of trying to be all things to all people—and failing. Deciding at last that computers were distracting it from its primary business of consumer electronics retailing, management sold the company's computer operations to AST Research.

Research generally supports Porter's contention that a firm that fails to achieve a generic strategy is going to be stuck in the middle with no competitive advantage. But what about companies that attempt to achieve both a low-cost *and* a high differentiation position? The Japanese auto companies of Toyota, Nissan, and Honda are often presented as examples of successful firms able to achieve both of these generic strategies. Although Porter agrees that it is possible for a company or a business unit to achieve low cost and differentiation simultaneously, he argues that this state is often temporary. Porter does admit, however, that many different kinds of potentially profitable competitive strategies exist. Although there is generally room for only one company to successfully pursue the mass market cost leadership strategy (because it is so dependent on achieving dominant market share), there is room for an almost unlimited number of differentiation and focus strategies (depending on the range of possible desirable features and the number of identifiable market niches). Quality, alone, has eight different dimensions—each with the potential of providing a product with a competitive advantage (see Table 5.2).

Table 5.2 **The Eight Dimensions of Quality**

1. Performance.	Primary operating characteristics, such as a washing machine's cleaning ability.
2. Features.	"Bells and whistles," like cruise control in a car, that supplement the basic functions.
3. Reliability.	Probability that the product will continue functioning without any significant maintenance.
4. Conformance.	Degree to which a product meets standards. When a customer buys a product out of the warehouse, it will perform identically to that viewed on the showroom floor.
5. Durability.	Number of years of service a consumer can expect from a product before it significantly deteriorates. Differs from reliability in that a product can be durable, but still need a lot of maintenance.
6. Serviceability.	Product's ease of repair.
7. Aesthetics.	How a product looks, feels, sounds, tastes, or smells.
8. Perceived Quality.	Product's overall reputation. Especially important if there are no objective, easily used measures of quality.

Source: Adapted from D. A. Garvin, *Managing Quality: The Strategic and Competitive Edge* (New York: Free Press, 1988).

Most entrepreneurial ventures follow focus strategies. The successful ones differentiate their product from those of other competitors in the areas of quality and service, and they focus the product on customer needs in a segment of the market, thereby achieving a dominant share of that part of the market. Adopting guerrilla warfare tactics, these companies go after opportunities in market niches too small to justify retaliation from the market leaders.

Industry Structure and Competitive Strategy

Although each of Porter's generic competitive strategies may be used in any industry, certain strategies are more likely to succeed than others in some instances. In a **fragmented industry**, for example, where many small- and medium-sized local companies compete for relatively small shares of the total market, focus strategies will likely predominate. Fragmented industries are typical for products in the early stages of their life cycle. If few economies are to be gained through size, no large firms will emerge and entry barriers will be low—allowing a stream of new entrants into the industry. Chinese restaurants and funeral homes are examples. Over 85% of funeral homes in the United States are independently owned.[7]

If a company is able to overcome the limitations of a fragmented market, however, it can reap the benefits of a broadly targeted cost leadership or differentiation strategy. Until Pizza Hut was able to use advertising to differentiate itself from local competitors, the pizza fast-food business was a fragmented industry composed primarily of locally owned pizza parlors, each with its own distinctive product and service offering. Subsequently Domino's used the cost leader strategy to achieve U.S. national market share. Currently Sears is attempting to dominate the traditionally fragmented household repair and home improvement industry. Operating on the assumption that people have less time to fix things around the house, Sears is spending $30 million to emphasize "the service side of Sears" tied to "one phone call to Sears Home Central (800) 4-Repair."[8]

As an industry matures, fragmentation is overcome and the industry tends to become a **consolidated industry** dominated by a few large companies. Although many industries begin fragmented, battles for market share and creative attempts to overcome local or niche market boundaries often increase the market share of a few companies. After product standards become established for minimum quality and features, competition shifts to a greater emphasis on cost and service. Slower growth, overcapacity, and knowledgeable buyers combine to put a premium on a firm's ability to achieve cost leadership or differentiation along the dimensions most desired by the market. Research and development shifts from product to process improvements. Overall product quality improves, and costs are reduced significantly.

The industry has now become one in which cost leadership and differentiation tend to be combined to various degrees. A firm can no longer gain high market share simply through low price. The buyers are more sophisticated and demand a certain minimum level of quality for price paid. The same is true for firms emphasizing high quality. Either the quality must be high enough and valued by the customer enough to justify the higher price or the price must be dropped (through lowering costs) to compete effectively with the lower priced products. This consolidation is taking place worldwide in the automobile, airline, and home appliance industries.

Hypercompetition and Competitive Strategy

In his book *HyperCompetition*, D'Aveni proposes that it is becoming increasingly difficult to sustain a competitive advantage for very long. "Market stability is threatened by short product life cycles, short product design cycles, new technologies, frequent entry by unexpected outsiders, repositioning by incumbents, and tactical redefinitions of market boundaries as diverse industries merge."[9] Consequently a company or business unit must constantly work to improve its competitive advantage. It is not enough to be just the lowest cost competitor. Through continuous improvement programs, competitors are usually working to lower their costs as well. Firms must find new ways not only to reduce costs further, but also to add value to the product or service being provided.

The same is true of a firm or unit that is following a differentiation strategy. Maytag Company (a unit of Maytag Corporation), for example, was successful for many years by offering the most durable brand in major home appliances. It was able to charge the highest prices for Maytag brand washing machines. When other competitors improved the quality of their products, however, it became increasingly harder for customers to justify Maytag's significantly higher price. Consequently Maytag Company was forced not only to add new features to its products, but also to reduce costs through improved manufacturing processes so that its prices were no longer out of line with those of the competition.

D'Aveni contends that when industries become **hypercompetitive,** they tend to go through escalating stages of competition. Firms initially compete on cost and quality until an abundance of high-quality, low-priced goods result. This occurred in the U.S. major home appliance industry by 1980. In a second stage of competition, the competitors move into untapped markets. Others usually imitate these moves until the moves become too risky or expensive. This epitomized the major home appliance industry during the 1980s and 1990s as firms moved first to Europe and then into Asia and South America.

According to D'Aveni, firms then raise entry barriers to limit competitors. Economies of scale, distribution agreements, and strategic alliances make it all but impossible for a new firm to enter the major home appliance industry by the turn of the century. After the established players have entered and consolidated all new markets, the next stage is for the remaining firms to attack and destroy the strongholds of other firms. Maytag's 1995 decision to divest its European division and concentrate on improving its position in North America could be a prelude to building a North American stronghold while Whirlpool, GE, and Electrolux are distracted by European and worldwide investments. Eventually, according to D'Aveni, the remaining large global competitors work their way to a situation of perfect competition in which no one has any advantage and profits are minimal.

Before hypercompetition, strategic initiatives provided competitive advantage for many years, perhaps for decades. This is no longer the case. According to D'Aveni, as industries become hypercompetitive, there is no such thing as a sustainable competitive advantage. Successful strategic initiatives in this type of industry typically last only months to a few years. According to D'Aveni, the only way a firm in this kind of dynamic industry can sustain any competitive advantage is through a continuous series of multiple short-term initiatives aimed at replacing a firm's current successful products with the next generation of products before the competitors can do so. Intel and Microsoft are taking this approach in the hypercompetitive computer industry.

Hypercompetition views competition, in effect, as a distinct series of ocean waves on what used to be a fairly calm stretch of water. As industry competition becomes more intense, the waves grow higher and require more dexterity to handle. Although a strategy is still needed to sail from point A to point B, more turbulent water means that a craft must continually adjust course to suit each new large wave. One danger of D'Aveni's concept of hypercompetition, however, is that it may lead to an overemphasis on short-term tactics (to be discussed in the next section) over long-term strategy. Too much of an orientation on the individual waves of hypercompetition could cause a company to focus too much on short-term temporary advantage and not enough on achieving its long-term objectives through building sustainable competitive advantage.

Which Competitive Strategy Is Best?

Before selecting one of Porter's generic competitive strategies for a company or business unit, management should assess its feasibility in terms of company or business unit resources and capabilities. Porter lists some of the commonly required skills and resources, as well as organizational requirements, in Table 5.3.

Competitive Tactics

A **tactic** is a specific operating plan detailing how a strategy is to be implemented in terms of *when* and *where* it is to be put into action. By their nature, tactics are narrower in their scope and shorter in their time horizon than are strategies. Tactics, therefore, may be viewed (like policies) as a link between the formulation and implementation of strategy. Some of the tactics available to implement competitive strategies are **timing tactics** (when) and **market location tactics** (where).

Timing Tactics: When to Compete

The first company to manufacture and sell a new product or service is called the **first mover** (or pioneer). Some of the advantages of being a first mover are that the company is able to establish a reputation as an industry leader, move down the learning curve to assume the cost leader position, and earn temporarily high profits from buyers who value the product or service very highly. A successful first mover can also set the standard for all subsequent products in the industry. A company that sets the standard "locks in" customers and is then able to offer further products based on that standard.[10] Microsoft was able to do this in software with its Windows operating system, and Netscape garnered over 80% share of the Internet browser market by being first to commercialize the product successfully.

Being a first mover does, however, have its disadvantages. These disadvantages can be, conversely, advantages enjoyed by late mover firms. **Late movers** may be able to imitate the technological advances of others (and thus keep R&D costs low), keep risks

Table 5.3 **Requirements for Generic Competitive Strategies**

Generic Strategy	Commonly Required Skills and Resources	Common Organizational Requirements
Overall Cost Leadership	• Sustained capital investment and access to capital • Process engineering skills • Intense supervision of labor • Products designed for ease of manufacture • Low-cost distribution system	• Tight cost control • Frequent, detailed control reports • Structured organization and responsibilities • Incentives based on meeting strict quantitative targets.
Differentiation	• Strong marketing abilities • Product engineering • Creative flair • Strong capability in basic research • Corporate reputation for quality or technological leadership • Long tradition in the industry or unique combination of skills drawn from other businesses • Strong cooperation from channels	• Strong coordination among functions in R&D, product development, and marketing • Subjective measurement and incentives instead of quantitative measures • Amenities to attract highly skilled labor, scientists, or creative people
Focus	• Combination of the above policies directed at the particular strategic target	• Combination of the above policies directed at the particular strategic target

Source: Adapted/reprinted with permission of The Free Press, an imprint of Simon & Schuster, from *Competitive Strategy: Techniques for Analyzing Industries and Competitors* by Michael E. Porter, pp. 40–41. Copyright © 1980 by The Free Press.

down by waiting until a new market is established, and take advantage of the first mover's natural inclination to ignore market segments. Once Netscape had established itself as the standard for Internet browsers, Microsoft used its huge resources to directly attack Netscape's position. It did not want Netscape to also set the standard in the developing and highly lucrative intranet market inside corporations.

Market Location Tactics: Where to Compete

A company or business unit can implement a competitive strategy either offensively or defensively. An **offensive tactic** usually takes place in an established competitor's market location. A defensive tactic usually takes place in the firm's own current market position as a defense against possible attack by a rival.[11]

Offensive Tactics Some of the methods used to attack a competitor's position are:

- **Frontal Assault.** The attacking firm goes head to head with its competitor. It matches the competitor in every category from price to promotion to distribution channel. To be successful, the attacker must not only have superior resources, but also the willingness to persevere. This is generally a very expensive tactic and may serve to awaken a sleeping giant (as MCI and Sprint did to AT&T in long distance telephone service), depressing profits for the whole industry.

- **Flanking Maneuver.** Rather than going straight for a competitor's position of strength with a frontal assault, a firm may attack a part of the market where the competitor is weak. Cyrix Corporation followed this tactic with its entry into the microprocessor market—a market then almost totally dominated by Intel. Rather than going directly after Intel's microprocessor business, Cyrix developed a math coprocessor for Intel's 386 chip that would run 20 times faster than Intel's micro-processor. To be successful, the flanker must be patient and willing to carefully expand out of the relatively undefended market niche or else face retaliation by an established competitor.

- **Bypass Attack.** Rather than directly attacking the established competitor frontally or on its flanks, a company or business unit may choose to change the rules of the game. This tactic attempts to cut the market out from under the established defender by offering a new type of product that makes the competitor's product unnecessary. For example, instead of competing directly against Microsoft's Windows 95 operating system, Netscape chose to use Java "applets" in its Internet browser so that an operating system and specialized programs were no longer necessary to run applications on a personal computer.

- **Encirclement.** Usually evolving out of a frontal assault or flanking maneuver, encirclement occurs as an attacking company or unit encircles the competitor's position in terms of products or markets or both. The encircler has greater product variety (a complete product line ranging from low to high price) and/or serves more markets (it dominates every secondary market). Microsoft is following this tactic as it attacks Netscape's Internet browser business with its "embrace and extend" strategy. By embracing Netscape's use of cross-platform Internet applets and quickly extending it into multiple applications, Microsoft attempted to dominate the browser market.

- **Guerrilla Warfare.** Instead of a continual and extensive resource-expensive attack on a competitor, a firm or business unit may choose to "hit and run." Guerrilla warfare is characterized by the use of small, intermittent assaults on different market segments held by the competitor. In this way, a new entrant or small firm can make some gains without seriously threatening a large, established competitor and evoking some form of retaliation. To be successful, the firm or unit conducting guerrilla warfare must be patient enough to accept small gains and to avoid pushing the established competitor to the point that it must respond or else lose face. Microbreweries, which make beer for sale to local customers, use this tactic against national brewers like Anheuser-Busch.

Defensive Tactics According to Porter, **defensive tactics** aim to lower the probability of attack, divert attacks to less threatening avenues, or lessen the intensity of an attack. Instead of increasing competitive advantage per se, they make a company's or business unit's competitive advantage more sustainable by causing a challenger to conclude that an attack is unattractive. These tactics deliberately reduce short-term profitability to ensure long-term profitability.[12]

- **Raise Structural Barriers.** Entry barriers act to block a challenger's logical avenues of attack. Some of the most important according to Porter are to:

    (1) offer a full line of products in every profitable market segment to close off any entry points;

    (2) block channel access by signing exclusive agreements with distributors;

    (3) raise buyer switching costs by offering low-cost training to users;

    (4) raise the cost of gaining trial users by keeping prices low on items new users are most likely to purchase;

    (5) increase scale economies to reduce unit costs;

(6) foreclose alternative technologies through patenting or licensing;

(7) limit outside access to facilities and personnel;

(8) tie up suppliers by obtaining exclusive contracts or purchasing key locations;

(9) avoid suppliers that also serve competitors; and

(10) encourage the government to raise barriers such as safety and pollution standards or favorable trade policies.

- **Increase Expected Retaliation.** This tactic is any action that increases the perceived threat of retaliation for an attack. For example, management may strongly defend any erosion of market share by drastically cutting prices or matching a challenger's promotion through a policy of accepting any price-reduction coupons for a competitor's product. This counterattack is especially important in markets that are very important to the defending company or business unit. For example, when Clorox Company challenged Procter & Gamble Company in the detergent market with Clorox Super Detergent, P&G retaliated by test marketing its liquid bleach, Lemon Fresh Comet, in an attempt to scare Clorox into retreating from the detergent market.

- **Lower the Inducement for Attack.** A third type of defensive tactic is to reduce a challenger's expectations of future profits in the industry. Like Southwest Airlines, a company can deliberately keep prices low and constantly invest in cost-reducing measures. With prices kept very low, there is little profit incentive for a new entrant.

Cooperative Strategies

Competitive strategies and tactics are used to gain competitive advantage within an industry by *battling against* other firms. These are not, however, the only business strategy options available to a company or business unit for competing successfully within an industry. **Cooperative strategies** can also be used to gain competitive advantage within an industry by *working with* other firms.

Collusion

The two general types of cooperative strategies are collusion and strategic alliances. **Collusion** is the active cooperation of firms within an industry to reduce output and raise prices in order to get around the normal economic law of supply and demand. Collusion may be *explicit*, in which firms cooperate through direct communication and negotiation, or *tacit*, in which firms cooperate indirectly through an informal system of signals. Explicit collusion is illegal in most countries. For example, Archer Daniels Midland (ADM), the large U.S. agricultural products firm, has been accused of conspiring with its competitors to limit the sales volume and raise the price of the food additive lysine. Executives from three Japanese and South Korean lysine manufacturers admitted meeting in hotels in major cities throughout the world to form a "lysine trade association." By the end of 1996, the three companies had been fined more than $20 million by the U.S. federal government. Although ADM had earlier agreed to pay $25 million to settle a lawsuit on behalf of 600 lysine customers, U.S. federal prosecutors sought a grand jury indictment of the company and two of its senior executives.[13]

Collusion can also be tacit, in which there is no direct communication among competing firms. According to Barney, tacit collusion in an industry is most likely to be successful if (1) there are a small number of identifiable competitors, (2) costs are similar among firms, (3) one firm tends to act as the "price leader," (4) there is a common industry culture that accepts cooperation, (5) sales are characterized by a high frequency of small orders, (6) large inventories and order backlogs are normal ways of dealing with fluctuations in demand, and (7) there are high entry barriers to keep out new competitors.[14]

Even tacit collusion can, however, be illegal. For example, when General Electric wanted to ease price competition in the steam turbine industry, it widely advertised its prices and publicly committed not to sell below these prices. Customers were even told that if GE reduced turbine prices in the future, it would give customers a refund equal to the price reduction. GE's message was not lost on Westinghouse, the major competitor in steam turbines. Both prices and profit margins remained stable for the next ten years in this industry. The U.S. Department of Justice then sued both firms for engaging in "conscious parallelism" (following each other's lead to reduce the level of competition) in order to reduce competition.

Strategic Alliances

A **strategic alliance** is a partnership of two or more corporations or business units to achieve strategically significant objectives that are mutually beneficial.[15] Alliances between companies or business units have become a fact of life in modern business. Some alliances are very short term, only lasting long enough for one partner to establish a beachhead in a new market. Others are more long lasting and may even be the prelude to a full merger between two companies.

Companies or business units may form a strategic alliance for a number of reasons, including:

1. **To obtain technology and/or manufacturing capabilities.** For example, Intel formed a partnership with Hewlett-Packard to use HP's capabilities in RISC technology in order to develop the successor to Intel's Pentium microprocessor.

2. **To obtain access to specific markets.** Rather than buy a foreign company or build breweries of its own in other countries, Anheuser-Busch chose to license the right to brew and market Budweiser to other brewers, such as Labatt in Canada, Modelo in Mexico, and Kirin in Japan.

3. **To reduce financial risk.** For example, because the costs of developing a new large jet airplane were becoming too high for any one manufacturer, Boeing, Aerospatiale of France, British Aerospace, Construcciones Aeronáuticas of Spain, and Deutsche Aerospace of Germany planned a joint venture to design such a plane.

4. **To reduce political risk.** To gain access to China while ensuring a positive relationship with the often restrictive Chinese government, Maytag Corporation formed a joint venture with the Chinese appliance maker, RSD. See the **Company Spotlight on Maytag Corporation** feature to learn what both companies hoped to obtain from this strategic alliance.

5. **To achieve or ensure competitive advantage.** General Motors and Toyota formed Nummi Corporation as a joint venture to provide Toyota a manufacturing facility in the United States and GM access to Toyota's low-cost, high-quality manufacturing expertise.[16]

Cooperative arrangements between companies and business units fall along a continuum from weak and distant to strong and close. (See Figure 5.5.) The types of alliances range from mutual service consortia to joint ventures and licensing arrangements to value-chain partnerships.[17]

COMPANY SPOTLIGHT

Maytag Forms a Joint Venture in China

Asia had become the world's second largest home appliance market (after Europe) by the mid 1990s and opportunities were still emerging. China and India, in particular, offered phenomenal growth opportunities. For example, the saturation level of washing machines (percentage of homes having a washer) in China was only 10% compared to 54% in Mexico and 75% in the United States. Although Japanese and Korean appliance manufacturers dominated the Asian market overall, the industry was still fragmented with no single dominant company in terms of market share. Matsushita was the overall market leader in Asia, but it had a market share of less than 10% outside Japan. U.S. and European appliance manufacturers were using acquisitions and joint ventures to establish a presence in this part of the world. AB Electrolux was establishing a full line of appliance facilities in China and India, among other Asian locations. In addition to its distributors in Australia, Malaysia, Japan, Singapore, Thailand, and Taiwan, Whirlpool established joint ventures in China and India. General Electric had part ownership of Philcor in the Philippines and a joint venture with Godrej & Boyce, India's largest appliance maker.

Realizing the vast potential of the Chinese market, Maytag Corporation formed two joint ventures in 1996 with Hefei Rongshida Group Corporation, known as RSD, to manufacturer and market washing machines and refrigerators. RSD was among the market leaders in China in laundry products and was a widely recognized brand throughout the country. It produced about 1.1 million washers in 1995 out of a total of 9.5 million sold in China. Maytag invested $35 million in a joint laundry products facility to sell washers and dryers throughout the country and some Pacific Rim areas. To help RSD enter the refrigerator business, Maytag invested another $35 million in the construction of a jointly-owned refrigeration products facility in the city of Hefei. Maytag owned 50.5% of both joint ventures through two wholly-owned subsidiaries. According to Leonard Hadley, Maytag Corporation's Chairman and CEO: "This is a focused investment for Maytag aimed at profitable growth in a market that is growing at double-digit rates."

MAYTAG CORPORATION

Mutual Service Consortia   A **mutual service consortium** is a partnership of similar companies in similar industries who pool their resources to gain a benefit that is too expensive to develop alone, such as access to advanced technology. For example, IBM of the United States, Toshiba of Japan, and Siemens of Germany formed a consortium to develop new generations of computer chips. As part of this alliance, IBM offered Toshiba its expertise in chemical mechanical polishing to help develop a new manufacturing process using ultraviolet lithography to etch tiny circuits in silicon chips. IBM then transferred the new technology to a facility in the United States.[18]

In another example, General Motors, Procter & Gamble, and six other companies purchased $20 million of equity in a small artificial intelligence company called Teknowledge. GM hoped that Teknowledge's expert systems software would help it to design cars and to prepare factory schedules. The other members of the consortium had similar hopes. The mutual service consortia is a fairly weak and distant alliance. There is very little interaction or communication among the partners.

Joint Venture   A **joint venture** is a "cooperative business activity, formed by two or more separate organizations for strategic purposes, that creates an independent busi-

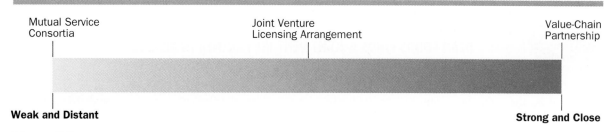

Mutual Service
Consortia

Joint Venture
Licensing Arrangement

Value-Chain
Partnership

Weak and Distant

Strong and Close

Figure 5.5
Continuum of
Strategic Alliances

Source: Suggested by
R. M. Kanter, "Collaborative Advantage: The
Art of Alliances," *Harvard Business Review*
(July-August 1994), pp.
96–108.

ness entity and allocates ownership, operational responsibilities, and financial risks and rewards to each member, while preserving their separate identity/autonomy."[19] Along with licensing arrangements, joint ventures lay at the mid-point of the continuum and are formed to pursue an opportunity that needs a capability from two companies or business units, such as the technology of one and the distribution channels of another.

Joint ventures are the most popular form of strategic alliance. They often occur because the companies involved do not want to or cannot legally merge permanently. Joint ventures provide a way to temporarily combine the different strengths of partners to achieve an outcome of value to both. For example, the pharmaceutical firm Merck & Company agreed with the chemical giant DuPont Company to form, under joint ownership, a new company called DuPont Merck Pharmaceutical Company. Merck provided the new company with its foreign marketing rights to some prescription medicines plus some cash. In return, Merck got access to all of DuPont's experimental drugs and its small but productive research operation.

Extremely popular in international undertakings because of financial and political-legal constraints, joint ventures are a convenient way for corporations to work together without losing their independence. See the 🌐 **21st Century Global Society** feature for an example of such a joint venture between a U.S. and a Mexican company.

Disadvantages of joint ventures include loss of control, lower profits, probability of conflicts with partners, and the likely transfer of technological advantage to the partner. Joint ventures are often meant to be temporary, especially by some companies who may view them as a way to rectify a competitive weakness until they can achieve long-term dominance in the partnership. Partially for this reason, joint ventures have a high failure rate.[20] Research does indicate, however, that joint ventures tend to be more successful when both partners have equal ownership in the venture and are mutually dependent on each other for results.[21]

Licensing Arrangement A **licensing arrangement** is an agreement in which the licensing firm grants rights to another firm in another country or market to produce and/or sell a product. The licensee pays compensation to the licensing firm in return for technical expertise. Licensing is an especially useful strategy if the trademark or brand name is well known, but the MNC does not have sufficient funds to finance its entering the country directly. Anheuser-Busch is using this strategy to produce and market Budweiser beer in the United Kingdom, Japan, Israel, Australia, Korea, and the Philippines. This strategy also becomes important if the country makes entry via investment either difficult or impossible. The danger always exists, however, that the licensee might develop its competence to the point that it becomes a competitor to the licensing firm. Therefore, a company should never license its distinctive competence, even for some short-run advantage.

21st Century Global Society

DEAN FOODS FINDS A JOINT VENTURE PARTNER IN MEXICO

Half of all the citizens of Mexico are under the age of 18. To the management of the Chicago-based Dean Foods Company, this meant that Mexico was a potential market for milk and milk products. The country had withstood a chronic shortage of fresh milk due to government-set price ceilings, which reduced the incentive for local producers to provide the product. When trade barriers began dropping in 1991, Dean's El Paso dairy teamed with a Mexican distributor to truck milk and ice cream to border towns. By 1992, Mexico consumed one-third of that dairy's output. Dean also began purchasing broccoli and cauliflower from Mexico for its processing plants in Texas and New Mexico. The company assigned two of its corporate staff people to research the Mexican market. Based on their findings, Dean Foods planned to first emphasize dairy products and then vegetables. The company would eventually like to sell products that aren't native to Mexico, such as canned sweet corn, peas, and green beans.

Although Dean Foods could buy an existing Mexican dairy or simply export products from the United States, the company decided to ask its current dairy products distributor if it would be interested in a joint venture. Dean's managers toured the distributor's facilities; the distributor's managers toured one of Dean Foods' plants in Rockford, Illinois. Even with a joint venture, huge problems still existed. For example, only about half of all households in Mexico had refrigerators. Instead of selling milk in gallon jugs, Dean Foods would need to use small cartons. Some supermarkets turned off their electricity overnight. Dean Foods would have to set up refrigerated cases in supermarkets and pay the stores to maintain the electricity 24 hours a day. Because dairy farms were scarce in Mexico, Dean Foods would probably have to encourage the development of new ones. The company would probably also have to establish special quality control standards because 40% of all milk sold in the country was unpasteurized.

For Howard Dean, CEO of the company, the allure of Mexico was not in shifting plants to cut labor costs, but in the market potential for his products. "We've got to move quickly. The opportunity is now," concluded the grandson of the company's founder.

Source: L. Therrein and S. Baker, "Market Share Con Leche?" *Business Week* (Reinventing America, 1992 edition), p. 122.

Value-Chain Partnership The **value-chain partnership** is a strong and close alliance in which one company or unit forms a long-term arrangement with a key supplier or distributor for mutual advantage. Value-chain partnerships are becoming extremely popular as more companies and business units outsource activities that were previously done within the company or business unit. For example, DuPont contracts out project engineering and design to Morrison Knudsen; AT&T, its credit card processing to Total System Services; Northern Telecom, its electronic component manufacturing to Comptronix; and Eastman Kodak, its computer support services to Businessland.

Another example of a value-chain partnership is the long-term relationship between a company or business unit with a supplier or distributor. To improve the quality of parts it purchases, companies in the U.S. auto industry, for example, have decided to work more closely with fewer suppliers and to involve them more in product design decisions. Such partnerships are also a way for a firm to acquire new technology to use in its own products. For example, Maytag Company was approached by one of its suppliers, Honeywell's Microswitch Division, which offered its expertise in fuzzy logic technology—a technology Maytag did not have at that time. The resulting partnership in product development resulted in Maytag's new IntelliSense™ dishwasher. Unlike previous dishwashers that the operator had to set, Maytag's fuzzy logic dishwasher automatically selected the proper cleaning cycle based on a series of factors such as the amount of dirt and presence of detergent.

According to Paul Ludwig, business development manager for Honeywell's Microswitch division, "Had Maytag not included us on the design team, we don't believe the two companies would have achieved the same innovative solution, nor would we have completed the project in such a short amount of time."[22] The benefits of such relationships do not just accrue to the purchasing firm. Research suggests that suppliers who engage in long-term relationships are more profitable than suppliers with multiple short-term contracts.[23]

5.5   *Global Issues for the 21st Century*

- The **21st Century Global Society** feature in this chapter illustrated how Dean Foods formed a joint venture with its Mexican distributor in order to expand its business in Mexico. Even though individual joint ventures are often short-lived, this type of strategic alliance is an extremely popular way of expanding globally. As countries become less fearful of foreign-based multinational corporations, they may begin to allow more cross-border mergers and acquisitions in addition to strategic alliances.

- As a corporation becomes more involved internationally, it will need to constantly review the appropriateness of its current mission and objectives. The huge investment required to become a global competitor means that return on investment objectives will need to be reduced while other objectives are expanded.

- One set of business strategies may not be sufficient for success in a global industry. A company may need to tailor its business strategies to each nation in which it operates.

- To be competitive in a global industry, companies are discovering that they must raise the quality of their products and reduce the prices. Although this does not mean that a company must follow both a differentiation and a low-cost strategy simultaneously, it does mean that international competition usually requires a higher level of performance in terms of cost and quality than does domestic competition.

- As more industries become increasingly global and hypercompetitive, fewer companies will survive unless they are able to adapt to changing conditions. For example, European companies in 1997 were falling behind many U.S. and some Asian companies in the use of networked personal computers. According to Intel CEO Andy Grove, European companies "operate like old-line U.S. companies did ten years ago." He warned of a "growing technology deficit."[24]

Projections for the 21st Century

- From 1994 to 2010, the average life expectancy for women will rise from 67 to 71 and for men will increase from 63 to 67.

- From 1994 to 2010, the number of AIDS cases worldwide will increase from 20 million to 38 million.[25]

Discussion Questions

1. What industry forces might cause a propitious niche to disappear?

2. Is it possible for a company or business unit to follow a cost leadership strategy and a differentiation strategy simultaneously? Why or why not?

3. Is it possible for a company to have a sustainable competitive advantage when its industry becomes hypercompetitive?

4. What are the advantages and disadvantages of being a first mover in an industry? Give some examples of first mover and late mover firms. Were they successful?

5. Why are most strategic alliances temporary?

Key Terms

business strategy (p. 113)
collusion (p. 124)
competitive scope (p. 113)
competitive strategy (p. 113)
consolidated industry (p. 119)
cooperative strategies (p. 124)
cost focus (p. 116)
cost leadership (p. 115)
cost proximity (p. 117)
defensive tactics (p. 123)
differentiation (p. 115)
differentiation focus (p. 116)

differentiation strategy (p. 113)
distinctive competencies (p. 107)
first mover (p. 121)
fragmented industry (p. 119)
hypercompetitive (p. 120)
joint venture (p. 126)
late mover (p. 121)
licensing arrangement (p. 127)
lower cost strategy (p. 113)
market location tactics (p. 121)
mutual service consortium (p. 126)
offensive tactics (p. 122)

propitious niche (p. 110)
SFAS Matrix (p. 107)
SO, ST, WO, WT Strategies (p. 112)
strategic alliances (p. 125)
strategic window (p. 110)
stuck in the middle (p. 118)
SWOT (p. 107)
tactics (p. 121)
timing tactics (p. 121)
TOWS Matrix (p. 111)
value-chain partnership (p. 128)

Strategic Practice Exercise

Read the following paragraph about a successful company in a newly emerging business. What should this company do if it wants to continue competing successfully in the future? Form a group with 3–4 other people in your class. Consider the questions posed at the end of the paragraph. Compare your group's recommendations with those of other groups.

E*Trade Group, Inc., was a pioneer in the on-line trading of securities. Led by CEO Christos Cotsakos, the discount brokerage firm had the largest volume of Internet trades—2,500 daily during 1996. Seventy-five percent of its business was conducted online. Even though only 80,000 investors traded online in 1996, that number was expected to grow to 1.3 million in just two years. E*Trade has been successful not only by being the first on the Internet, but also by charging only $12 per trade. Revenue, totaling $23.3 million in 1995, has grown an average of 125% annually since 1991. While E*Trade was preparing to go public, it was dealing with several problems. A computer hardware failure in May 1996 left many customers unable to access their accounts for 2½ hours. That led to a $1.7 million payment to clients who lost money in the market. An increase in accounts from 38,000 to 65,000, with trading volume tripling from 50 million to 170 million shares during the first five months of 1996, left the company struggling to keep up. Established brokerage firms, such as Charles Schwab and Fidelity Investments, were reducing their commissions and gearing up to compete for a share of this emerging Internet market.[26]

1. What competitive strategy is E*Trade following?

2. Does E*Trade have a sustainable competitive advantage?

3. Given the increasing level of competition in this industry, what do you think E*Trade should do to continue competing successfully?

Notes

1. W. H. Newman, "Shaping the Master Strategy of Your Firm," *California Management Review,* Vol. 9, No. 3 (1967), pp. 77–88.
2. K. Kelly, "Henry Schacht," *The 1993 Business Week 1000* (1993), p. 80.
3. R. L. Simpson, and O. Suris, "Alex Trotman's Goal: To Make Ford No. 1 in World Auto Sales," *Wall Street Journal* (July 18, 1995), p. A5.
4. M. E. Porter, *Competitive Strategy* (New York: The Free Press, 1980), pp. 34–41 as revised in M. E. Porter, *The Competitive Advantage of Nations* (New York: The Free Press, 1990), pp. 37–40.
5. Porter, *Competitive Strategy,* p. 35.
6. R. E. Caves, and P. Ghemawat, "Identifying Mobility Barriers," *Strategic Management Journal* (January 1992), pp. 1–12.
7. R. Tomsho, "Funeral Parlors Become Big Business," *Wall Street Journal* (September 18, 1996), pp. B1 & B4.
8. G. Buck, "If It Ain't Broke, Don't Fix It! It Is? Call Sears," *Des Moines Register* (March 2, 1997), p. G3.
9. R. A. D'Aveni, *HyperCompetition* (New York: The Free Press, 1994), pp. xiii–xiv.
10. Some refer to this as the economic concept of "increasing returns." Instead of reaching a point of diminishing returns when a product saturates a market and the curve levels off, the curve continues to go up as the company takes advantage of setting the standard to spin off new products that use the new standard to achieve higher performance than competitors. See J. Alley, "The Theory That Made Microsoft," *Fortune* (April 29, 1996), pp. 65–66.
11. Summarized from various articles by L. Fahey in *The Strategic Management Reader,* edited by L. Fahey (Englewood Cliffs, N.J.: Prentice-Hall, 1989), pp. 178–205.
12. This information on defensive tactics is summarized from M. E. Porter, *Competitive Advantage* (New York: Free Press, 1985), pp. 482–512.
13. T. M. Burton, "Archer-Daniels Faces a Potential Blow As Three Firms Admit Price-Fixing Plot," *Wall Street Journal* (August 28, 1996), pp. A3 & A6; R. Henkoff, "The ADM Tale Gets Even Stranger," *Fortune* (May 13, 1996), pp. 113–120.
14. Much of the content on cooperative strategies was summarized from J. B. Barney, *Gaining and Sustaining Competitive Advantage* (Reading, Mass.: Addison-Wesley, 1997), pp. 255–278.
15. E. A. Murray, Jr., and J. F. Mahon, "Strategic Alliances: Gateway to the New Europe?" *Long Range Planning* (August 1993), p. 103.
16. *Ibid,* pp. 105–106.
17. R. M. Kanter, "Collaborative Advantage: The Art of Alliances," *Harvard Business Review* (July-August 1994), pp. 96–108.
18. B. Bremner, Z. Schiller, T. Smart, and W. J. Holstein, "Keiretsu Connections," *Business Week* (July 22, 1996), pp. 52–54.
19. R. P. Lynch, *The Practical Guide to Joint Ventures and Corporate Alliances* (New York: John Wiley and Sons, 1989), p. 7.
20. One study of 880 alliances revealed only 45% were felt to be successful by both parties and 40% of the cases failed to last four years. See B. J. James, "Strategic Alliances," in *International Review of Strategic Management,* Vol. 2, No. 2, edited by D. E. Hussey (New York: John Wiley & Sons, 1992), pp. 63–72.
21. L. L. Blodgett, "Factors in the Instability of International Joint Ventures: An Event History Analysis," *Strategic Management Journal* (September 1992), pp. 475–481; J. Bleeke and D. Ernst, "The Way to Win in Cross-Border Alliances," *Harvard Business Review* (November-December 1991), pp. 127–135; J. M. Geringer, "Partner Selection Criteria for Developed Country Joint Ventures," in *International Management Behavior,* 2nd ed., edited by H. W. Lane and J. J. DiStephano (Boston: PWS-Kent, 1992), pp. 206–216.
22. S. Stevens, "Speeding the Signals of Change," *Appliance* (February 1995), p. 7.
23. K. Z. Andrews, "Manufacturer/Supplier Relationships: The Supplier Payoff," *Harvard Business Review* (September-October 1995), pp. 14–15.
24. D. Kirkpatrick, "Europe's Technology Gap Is Getting Scary," *Fortune* (March 17, 1997), pp. 26–27.
25. J. Warner, "21st Century Capitalism: Snapshot of the Next Century," *Business Week* (November 18, 1994), p. 194.
26. L. Himelstein, "This Virtual Broker Has Real Competition," *Business Week* (July 22, 1996), pp. 91–92.

Chapter 6

Strategy Formulation:
Corporate Strategy

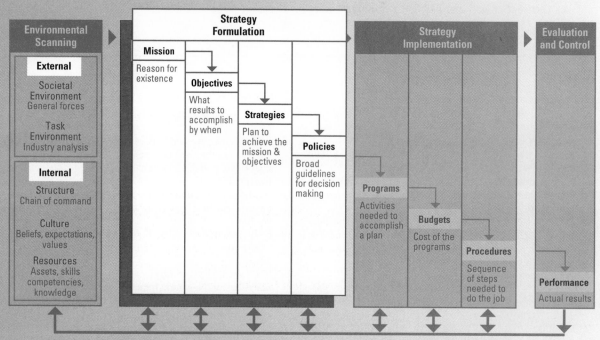

| Environmental Scanning | Strategy Formulation | | | | Strategy Implementation | | | Evaluation and Control |

Environmental Scanning

External

Societal Environment
General forces

Task Environment
Industry analysis

Internal

Structure
Chain of command

Culture
Beliefs, expectations, values

Resources
Assets, skills competencies, knowledge

Strategy Formulation

Mission
Reason for existence

Objectives
What results to accomplish by when

Strategies
Plan to achieve the mission & objectives

Policies
Broad guidelines for decision making

Strategy Implementation

Programs
Activities needed to accomplish a plan

Budgets
Cost of the programs

Procedures
Sequence of steps needed to do the job

Evaluation and Control

Performance
Actual results

Feedback/Learning

When Lewis Platt became CEO of Hewlett-Packard Company in the early 1990s, he soon realized that the company was in danger of missing critical opportunities. Computers, communications, and consumer electronics were rapidly converging into one interrelated industry. Unfortunately Hewlett-Packard was not involved in the strategic alliances and acquisitions that other companies were using to take advantage of this development. A close look internally at Hewlett-Packard's strengths revealed a unique mix of core technologies that no single competitor could match. HP offered a broad and well-regarded family of computers; it was a leader in test and measurement instruments; and it was strong in computer networking. Management proposed that the company blend these three technologies to create new product categories.

Following this idea, Hewlett-Packard developed a diagnostic system for Ford Motor Company's dealers that combined instruments that monitor a car's internal operations with an HP computer. HP also began developing other products that could take advantage of its core competencies—video servers, interactive TV devices, digital cable TV decoders, video printers, interactive notepads, health monitors, and a physician's workstation, among others. It also formed a partnership with Intel Corporation to develop next-generation processors using HP's RISC expertise. According to Platt, the Intel relationship is "the key, the heart" of HP's hardware future. This strategy is already paying off for the company in terms of increased sales and profits.[1]

6.1   Corporate Strategy

Corporate strategy deals with three key issues facing the corporation as a whole:

1. The firm's overall orientation toward growth, stability, or retrenchment (*directional strategy*)

2. The industries or markets in which the firm competes through its products and business units (*portfolio strategy*)

3. The manner in which management coordinates activities and transfers resources and cultivates capabilities among product lines and business units (*parenting strategy*)

Corporate strategy is primarily about the choice of direction for the firm as a whole.[2] This is true whether the firm is a small, one-product company or a large multinational corporation. In a large multibusiness company, however, corporate strategy is also about managing various product lines and business units for maximum value. In this instance, corporate headquarters must play the role of the organizational "parent," in that it must deal with various product and business unit "children." Even though each product line or business unit has its own competitive or cooperative strategy that it uses to obtain it own competitive advantage in the marketplace, the corporation must coordinate these different business strategies so that the corporation as a whole succeeds as a "family."[3]

Corporate strategy, therefore, includes decisions regarding the flow of financial and other resources to and from a company's product lines and business units. Through a series of coordinating devices, a company transfers skills and capabilities developed in one unit to other units that need such resources. In this way, it attempts to obtain synergies among numerous product lines and business units so that the corporate whole is greater than the sum of its individual business unit parts.[4] All corporations, from the smallest company offering one product in only one industry to the largest conglomerate operating in many industries with many products must, at one time or another, consider one or more of these issues.

To deal with each of the key issues, this chapter is organized into **three parts** that examine corporate strategy in terms of *directional strategy* (orientation toward growth), *portfolio analysis* (coordination of cash flow among units), and *corporate parenting* (building corporate synergies through resource sharing and development).

6.2   Directional Strategy

Just as every product or business unit must follow a business strategy to improve its competitive position, every corporation must decide its orientation toward growth by asking the following three questions:

- Should we expand, cut back, or continue our operations unchanged?

- Should we concentrate our activities within our current industry or should we diversify into other industries?

- If we want to grow and expand nationally and/or globally, should we do so through *internal* development or through *external* acquisitions, mergers, or strategic alliances?

A corporation's **directional strategy** is composed of three general orientations (sometimes called grand strategies):

- **Growth strategies** expand the company's activities.

- **Stability strategies** make no change to the company's current activities.

- **Retrenchment strategies** reduce the company's level of activities.

Having chosen the general orientation (such as growth), a company's managers can select from several more specific corporate strategies such as concentration within one product line/industry or diversification into other products/industries. (See Figure 6.1.) These strategies are useful both to corporations operating in only one industry with one product line and to those operating in many industries with many product lines.

Growth Strategies

By far the most widely pursued corporate directional strategies are those designed to achieve growth in sales, assets, profits, or some combination. Companies that do business in expanding industries must grow to survive. Continuing growth means increasing sales and a chance to take advantage of the experience curve to reduce the per-unit cost of products sold, thereby increasing profits. This cost reduction becomes extremely important if a corporation's industry is growing quickly and competitors are engaging in price wars in attempts to increase their shares of the market. Firms that have not reached "critical mass" (that is, gained the necessary economy of large-scale production) will face large losses unless they can find and fill a small, but profitable, niche where higher prices can be offset by special product or service features. That is why Motorola, Inc., continued to spend large sums on the product development of cellular phones, pagers, and two-way radios, despite a serious drop in profits. According to Motorola's Chairman George Fisher, "What's at stake here is leadership." Even though the industry was changing quickly, the company was working to avoid the erosion of its market share by jumping into new wireless markets as quickly as possible. Continuing as the market leader in this industry would almost guarantee Motorola enormous future returns.

A corporation can grow internally by expanding its operations both globally and domestically, or it can grow externally through mergers, acquisitions, and strategic alliances. A **merger** is a transaction involving two or more corporations in which stock is exchanged, but from which only one corporation survives. Mergers usually occur between firms of somewhat similar size and are usually "friendly." The resulting firm is likely to have a name derived from its composite firms. One example is the merging of Allied Corporation and Signal Companies to form Allied Signal. An **acquisition** is the purchase of a company that is completely absorbed as an operating subsidiary or division of the acquiring corporation. Examples are Procter & Gamble's acquisition of Richardson-Vicks, known for its Oil of Olay and Vidal Sassoon brands, and Noxell Cor-

Section 6.2 Directional Strategy

Figure 6.1
Corporate Direc-tional Strategies

- **GROWTH**
  Concentration
    Vertical Growth
    Horizontal Growth
  Diversification
    Concentric
    Conglomerate

- **STABILITY**
    Pause/Proceed with Caution
    No Change
    Profit

- **RETRENCHMENT**
    Turnaround
    Captive Company
    Sell-Out/Divestment
    Bankruptcy/Liquidation

poration, known for Noxema and Cover Girl. Acquisitions usually occur between firms of different sizes and can be either friendly or hostile. Hostile acquisitions are often called takeovers. A **strategic alliance** is a partnership of two or more corporations or business units to achieve strategically significant objectives that are mutually beneficial. See Chapter 5 for a detailed discussion of strategic alliances.

Growth is a very attractive strategy for two key reasons:

- Growth based on increasing market demand may mask flaws in a company—flaws that would be immediately evident in a stable or declining market. A growing flow of revenue into a highly leveraged corporation can create a large amount of **organization slack** (unused resources) that can be used to quickly resolve problems and conflicts between departments and divisions. Growth also provides a big cushion for a turnaround in case a strategic error is made. Larger firms also have more bargaining power than do small firms and are more likely to obtain support from key stakeholders in case of difficulty.

- A growing firm offers more opportunities for advancement, promotion, and interesting jobs. Growth itself is exciting and ego-enhancing for CEOs. The marketplace and potential investors tend to view a growing corporation as a "winner" or "on the move." Executive compensation tends to get bigger as an organization increases in size. Large firms are also more difficult to acquire than are smaller ones; thus an executive's job is more secure.

The two basic growth strategies are **concentration** on the current product line(s) in one industry and **diversification** into other product lines in other industries.

Concentration

If a company's current product lines have real growth potential, concentration of resources on those product lines makes sense as a strategy for growth. The two basic concentration strategies are vertical growth and horizontal growth. Growing firms in a growing industry tend to choose these strategies before they try diversification.

Vertical Growth Vertical growth can be achieved by taking over a function previously provided by a supplier or by a distributor. The company, in effect, grows by making its own supplies and/or by distributing its own products. This growth can be achieved either *internally* by expanding current operations or *externally* through acquisitions. Henry Ford, for example, used internal company resources to build his River Rouge Plant outside Detroit. The manufacturing process was integrated to the point that iron ore entered one end of the long plant and finished automobiles rolled out the other end into a huge parking lot. In contrast, DuPont, the huge chemical company, chose the external route to vertical growth by acquiring Conoco for the oil DuPont needed to produce synthetic fabrics.

Vertical growth results in **vertical integration**—the degree to which a firm operates vertically in multiple locations on an industry's value chain from extracting raw materials to manufacturing to retailing. More specifically, assuming a function previously provided by a *supplier* is called **backward integration** (going backward on an industry's value chain), whereas assuming a function previously provided by a *distributor* is labeled **forward integration** (going forward on an industry's value chain). Micron, for example, used forward integration when it expanded out of its successful memory manufacturing business to make and market its own personal computers.

Vertical growth is a logical strategy for a corporation or business unit with a strong competitive position in a highly attractive industry—especially when technology is predictable and markets are growing.[5] To keep and even improve its competitive position, the company may use backward integration to minimize resource acquisition costs and inefficient operations as well as forward integration to gain more control over product distribution. The firm, in effect, builds on its distinctive competence by expanding along the industry's value chain to gain greater competitive advantage.

Although backward integration is usually more profitable than forward integration, it can reduce a corporation's strategic flexibility. The resulting encumbrance of expensive assets that might be hard to sell could create an *exit barrier,* preventing the corporation from leaving that particular industry. When sales of its autos were declining, General Motors, for example, resorted to offering outside parts suppliers the use of its idle factories and workers.

Transaction cost economics proposes that vertical integration is more efficient than contracting for goods and services in the marketplace when the transaction costs of buying goods on the open market become too great. When highly vertically integrated firms become excessively large and bureaucratic, however, the costs of managing the internal transactions may become greater than simply purchasing the needed goods externally—thus justifying outsourcing over vertical integration. See the **Key Theory** feature for more information on transaction cost economics.

Harrigan proposes that a company's degree of vertical integration can range from total ownership of the value chain needed to make and sell a product to no ownership at all.[6] Under **full integration**, a firm internally makes 100% of its key supplies and completely controls its distributors. Large oil companies such as British Petroleum, Royal Dutch Shell, and Texaco are fully integrated. If a corporation does not want the disadvantages of full vertical integration, it may choose either taper or quasi-integration strategies. With **taper integration**, a firm internally produces less than half of its own requirements and buys the rest from outside suppliers. In terms of distributors, it sells part of its goods through company-owned stores and the rest through general wholesalers. With **quasi-integration**, a company does not make any of its key supplies, but purchases most of its requirements from outside suppliers that are under its partial control. For example, by purchasing 20% of the common stock of In Focus Systems, Motorola guaranteed its access to In Focus' revolutionary technology and enabled Motorola to establish a joint venture with In Focus to manufacture flat-panel video displays.[7] An example of forward quasi-integration would be a large pharmaceutical firm that acquires part interest in a

KEY THEORY

Why do corporations use vertical growth to permanently own suppliers or distributors when they could simply purchase individual items when needed on the open market? Transaction cost economics is a branch of institutional economics that attempts to answer this question. Beginning with work by Coase and extended by Williamson, transaction cost economics proposes that ownership of resources through vertical growth is more efficient than contracting for goods and services in the marketplace when the transaction costs of buying goods on the open market become too great. Transaction costs include the basic costs of drafting, negotiating, and safeguarding a market agreement (a contract) as well as the later managerial costs when the agreement is creating problems (goods aren't being delivered on time or quality is lower than needed), renegotiation costs (costs of meetings and phone calls), and the costs of settling disputes (lawyers' fees and court costs).

According to Williamson, three conditions must be met before a corporation will prefer internalizing a vertical transaction through ownership over contracting for the transaction in the marketplace: (1) a high level of uncertainty must surround the transaction; (2) assets involved in the transaction must be highly specialized to the transaction; and (3) the transaction must occur frequently. If there is a high level of uncertainty, it will be impossible to write a contract covering all contingencies and it is likely that the contractor will act opportunistically to exploit any gaps in the written agreement—thus creating problems and increasing costs. If the assets being

contracted for are highly specialized (goods or services with few alternate uses), there are likely to be few alternative suppliers—thus allowing the contractor to take advantage of the situation and increase costs. The more frequent the transactions, the more opportunity for the contractor to demand special treatment and thus increase costs further.

Vertical integration is not always more efficient than the marketplace, however. When highly vertically integrated firms become excessively large and bureaucratic, the costs of managing the internal transactions may become greater than simply purchasing the needed goods externally—thus justifying outsourcing over ownership. The usually hidden management costs (excessive layers of management, endless committee meetings needed for interdepartmental coordination, and delayed decision making due to excessively detailed rules and policies) add to the internal transaction costs—thus reducing the effectiveness and efficiency of vertical integration. The decision to own or to contract is, therefore, based on the particular situation surrounding the transaction and the ability of the corporation to manage the transaction internally both effectively and efficiently.

Sources: O. E. Williamson and S. G. Winter, eds., *The Nature of the Firm: Origins, Evolution, and Development* (New York: Oxford University Press, 1991); E. Mosakowski, "Organizational Boundaries and Economic Performance: An Empirical Study of Entrepreneurial Computer Firms," *Strategic Management Journal* (February 1991), pp. 115–133; P. S. Ring and A. H. Van De Ven, "Structuring Cooperative Relationships Between Organizations," *Strategic Management Journal* (October 1992), pp. 483–498.

drugstore chain in order to guarantee that its drugs have access to the distribution channel. Purchasing part interest in a key supplier or distributor usually provides a company with a seat on the other firm's board of directors, thus guaranteeing the acquiring firm both information and control. A company may not want to invest in suppliers or distributors, but it still wants to guarantee access to needed supplies or distribution channels. In this case, it may use contractual agreements. **Long-term contracts** are agreements between two separate firms to provide agreed-upon goods and services to each other for a specified period of time. This cannot really be considered to be vertical integration unless the contract specifies that the supplier or distributor cannot have a similar relationship with a competitive firm. In this case, the supplier or distributor is really a "captive company" that, although officially independent, does most of its business with the contracted firm and is formally tied to the other company through a long-term contract.

During the 1990s, there has been a movement away from vertical growth strategies (and thus vertical integration) toward cooperative contractual relationships with suppliers and even with competitors. These relationships range from **outsourcing**, in which resources are purchased from outsiders through long-term contracts instead of being made in-house (for example, Hewlett-Packard buys all its laser engines from Canon for HP's laser jet printers), to strategic alliances, in which partnerships, technology licensing agreements, and joint ventures supplement a firm's capabilities (for example, Toshiba has used strategic alliances with GE, Siemens, Motorola, and Ericsson to become one of the world's leading electronic companies).[8]

Horizontal Growth   Horizontal growth can be achieved by expanding the firm's products into other geographic locations and/or by increasing the range of products and services offered to current markets. In this case, the company expands sideways at the same location on the industry's value chain. For example, Dell Computers followed a horizontal growth strategy when it extended its mail order business to the European continent. A company can grow horizontally through internal development or externally through acquisitions or strategic alliances with another firm in the same industry.

Horizontal growth results in **horizontal integration**—the degree to which a firm operates in multiple geographic locations at the same point in an industry's value chain. Horizontal integration for a firm may range from full to partial ownership to long-term contracts. For example, KLM, the Dutch airline, purchased a controlling stake (partial ownership) in Northwest Airlines to obtain access to American and Asian markets. KLM was unable to acquire all of Northwest's stock because of U.S. government regulations forbidding foreign ownership of a domestic airline (for defense reasons). Many small commuter airlines engage in long-term contracts with major airlines in order to offer a complete arrangement for travelers. For example, Mesa Airlines arranged a five-year agreement with United Airlines to be listed on United's computer reservations as United Express through the Denver airport. See also the **Company Spotlight on Maytag Corporation** feature for a discussion of Maytag's use of horizontal growth through acquisitions.

Diversification Strategies

When an industry consolidates and becomes mature, most of the surviving firms have reached the limits of growth using vertical and horizontal growth strategies. Unless the competitors are able to expand internationally into less mature markets (as was the case in the major home appliance industry), they may have no choice but to diversify into different industries if they want to continue growing. The two basic diversification strategies are concentric and conglomerate.

Concentric (Related) Diversification   Growth through **concentric diversification** into a related industry may be a very appropriate corporate strategy when a firm has a strong competitive position but industry attractiveness is low. By focusing on the characteristics that have given the company its distinctive competence, the company uses those very strengths as its means of diversification. The firm attempts to secure strategic fit in a new industry where the firm's product knowledge, its manufacturing capabilities, and the

COMPANY SPOTLIGHT

A Growth Strategy Of Horizontal Growth Through Acquisitions

Maytag management realized in 1978 that the company would be unable to continue competing effectively in the U.S. major home appliance industry if it remained only a high-quality niche manufacturer of automatic washers and dryers. The industry was rapidly consolidating around those appliance companies with a complete line of products at all price and quality levels in all three key lines of "white goods": laundry (washers and dryers), cooking (stoves and ovens), and cooling (refrigerators and freezers) appliances. Previously most companies made appliances deriving from one or two successful products: General Electric made refrigerators; Maytag focused on washing machines; and Hotpoint produced electric ranges. A company would fill the gaps in its line by putting its own brand name on products it purchased from other manufacturers. This was done because stoves could not be made in a plant making refrigerators and vice versa. Purchasing from others was cheaper than building a new plant. To keep unit costs low, companies had to build larger plants than its own sales justified (to obtain economies of scale). To keep the plants running at close to 100% capacity (thus keeping unit costs as low as possible), a firm would produce other brands' products through contracts until its own brand's sales caught up with plant capacity. Nevertheless it was significantly cheaper to be vertically integrated than to buy appliances from another appliance company, especially a competitor. The need to own plants in all three lines of white goods led to a series of acquisitions and mergers within the industry—growth through horizontal integration throughout the United States and Canada.

Maytag's top management concluded that it would soon have to acquire other companies or risk being bought out itself. Given the long time-frame needed to acquire the technology as well as the manufacturing and marketing expertise necessary to produce and sell these other lines of appliances, Maytag chose to grow externally by acquiring Jenn-Air and Magic Chef in the mid 1980s. It was thus able to obtain Jenn-Air's popular down-draft ranges and Magic Chef's gas stoves and other appliances plus Admiral's refrigeration facilities—products Maytag needed to be a full-line home appliance manufacturer. Similarly Maytag's management concluded that the best way to ensure a global presence in major home appliances was to purchase Hoover, the well-known vacuum cleaner company with a solid position in white goods in Europe and Australia. Competitors like GE, Whirlpool, and AB Electrolux were growing through horizontal integration across the globe. Maytag felt that it needed to be part of this growth.

MAYTAG CORPORATION

marketing skills it used so effectively in the original industry can be put to good use.[9] The corporation's products or processes are related in some way: they possess some common thread. The search is for **synergy**, the concept that two businesses will generate more profits together than they could separately. The point of commonality may be similar technology, customer usage, distribution, managerial skills, or product similarity.

The firm may choose to diversify concentrically through either internal or external means. American Airlines, for example, has diversified both internally and externally out of the increasingly unprofitable airline business into a series of related businesses run by the parent company AMR Corporation. Building on the expertise of its SABRE Travel Information Network, it built a computer reservations system for the French high-speed rail network and for the tunnel under the English Channel.

Conglomerate (Unrelated) Diversification When management realizes that the current industry is unattractive and that the firm lacks outstanding abilities or skills that it could easily transfer to related products or services in other industries, the most likely strategy is **conglomerate diversification**—diversifying into an industry unrelated to its current one. Rather than maintaining a common thread throughout their organization, strategic managers who adopt this strategy are primarily concerned with financial considerations of cash flow or risk reduction.

The emphasis in conglomerate diversification is on financial considerations rather than on the product-market synergy common to concentric diversification. A cash-rich company with few opportunities for growth in its industry might, for example, move into another industry where opportunities are great, but cash is hard to find. Another instance of conglomerate diversification might be when a company with a seasonal and, therefore, uneven cash flow purchases a firm in an unrelated industry with complementing seasonal sales that will level out the cash flow. CSX management considered the purchase of a natural gas transmission business (Texas Gas Resources) by CSX Corporation (a railroad-dominated transportation company) to be a good fit because most of the gas transmission revenue was realized in the winter months—the railroads' lean period.

International Entry Options

In today's world, growth usually has international implications. A corporation can select from several strategic options the most appropriate method for it to use in entering a foreign market or establishing manufacturing facilities in another country. The options vary from simple exporting to acquisitions to management contracts. As in the case of KLM's purchase of stock in Northwest Airlines, this can be a part of the corporate strategies previously discussed. See the 🌐 **21st Century Global Society** feature to see how the South Korean firm Daewoo is using multiple international entry options in a horizontal growth strategy. Some of the more popular options for international entry are as follows:

- **Exporting. Exporting,** shipping goods produced in the company's home country to other countries for marketing, is a good way to minimize risk and experiment with a specific product. The company could choose to handle all critical functions itself, or it could contract these functions to an export management company. Exporting is becoming increasingly popular for small businesses because of fax machines, 800 numbers, and overnight air express services, which reduce the once formidable costs of going international.

- **Licensing.** Under a **licensing** agreement, the licensing firm grants rights to another firm in the host country to produce and/or sell a product. The licensee pays compensation to the licensing firm in return for technical expertise. This is an especially useful strategy if the trademark or brand name is well known, but the company does not have sufficient funds to finance its entering the country directly. Anheuser-Busch is using this strategy to produce and market Budweiser beer in the United Kingdom, Japan, Israel, Australia, Korea, and the Philippines. This strategy also becomes important if the country makes entry via investment either difficult or impossible. The danger always exists, however, that the licensee might develop its competence to the point that it becomes a competitor to the licensing firm. Therefore, a company should never license its distinctive competence, even for some short-run advantage.

- **Joint Ventures.** The rate of **joint venture** formation between U.S. companies and international partners has been growing 27% annually since 1985.[10] Companies often form joint ventures to combine the resources and expertise needed to develop

21ST CENTURY GLOBAL SOCIETY

DAEWOO EXPANDS ITS CORPORATE GROWTH STRATEGY INTERNATIONALLY

Daewoo, the South Korean conglomerate, is spending $18 billion to become the world's largest consumer electronics company and one of the top ten automakers by 2002. It has formed joint ventures with companies in the emerging markets of Vietnam, Poland, and Uzbekistan. In 1997, it introduced new car models in Europe and entered the U.S. auto market for the first time. Daewoo also hopes to acquire France's Thomson Multimedia and become the biggest seller of television sets in the United States.

Daewoo's low-price products using fairly simple technology have sold well in emerging nations. Management is concerned, however, that the company does not yet have the technology to compete with established U.S. and Japanese competitors. As a result, it has tripled its auto engineering staff at its Worthing Technical Center (purchased in 1992) in the United Kingdom. It

is also working to improve the quality of its electronics at its color television plant in Kumi, South Korea.

Chairman Kim Woo Choong believes Daewoo can make the money-losing French television maker Thomson Multimedia profitable in two years. "We will have full economies of scale, so we can invest more in research and development," states Mr. Kim. Skeptics doubt if Daewoo has both the money and the capabilities needed to make meaningful inroads into markets in the developed nations. Kim responded that it is a goal worth attaining. "No one believed that we could make so much progress. Now, nobody's laughing."

Source: M. Schuman, "Daewoo Lifts Its Sights to U.S. and Europe," *Wall Street Journal* (March 3, 1997), p. A15.

new products or technologies. It also enables a firm to enter a country that restricts foreign ownership. The corporation can enter another country with fewer assets at stake and thus lower risk. For example, because the costs of developing a new large jet were becoming too high for any one manufacturer, Boeing, Aerospatiale of France, British Aerospace, Construcciones Aeronáuticas of Spain, and Deutsche Aerospace of Germany planned a joint venture to design such a plane. A joint venture may be an association between a company and a firm in the host country or a government agency in that country. A quick method of obtaining local management, it also reduces the risks of expropriation and harassment by host country officials.

- **Acquisitions.** A relatively quick way to move into an international area is through **acquisitions**—purchasing another company already operating in that area. Synergistic benefits can result if the company acquires a firm with strong complementary product lines and a good distribution network. Maytag Corporation's acquisition of Hoover gave it entry into Europe through Hoover's strength in home appliances in the United Kingdom and in its vacuum cleaner distribution centers on the European continent. To expand into North America, the Swedish appliance maker, A.B. Electrolux, purchased the major home appliance operations of White Consolidated Industries and renamed them Frigidaire. Research does suggest that wholly-owned subsidiaries are more successful in international undertakings than are strategic alliances, such as joint ventures.[11] In some countries, however, acquisitions can be difficult to arrange because of a lack of available information about potential candidates. Government restrictions on ownership, such as the U.S. requirement that limits foreign ownership of U.S. airlines to 49% of nonvoting and 25% of voting stock, can also discourage acquisitions.

- **Green-Field Development.** If a company doesn't want to purchase another company's problems along with its assets (as Japan's Bridgestone did when it acquired Firestone in the United States) it may choose **green-field development**—building its own manufacturing plant and distribution system. This is usually a far more complicated and expensive operation than acquisition, but it allows a company more freedom in designing the plant, choosing suppliers, and hiring a workforce. For example, Nissan, Honda, and Toyota built auto factories in rural areas of Great Britain and then hired a young workforce with no experience in the industry.

- **Production Sharing.** Coined by Peter Drucker, the term **production sharing** means the process of combining the higher labor skills and technology available in the developed countries with the lower-cost labor available in developing countries. The current trend is to move data processing and programming activities "offshore" to places such as Ireland, India, Barbados, Jamaica, the Philippines, and Singapore where wages are lower, English is spoken, and telecommunications are in place.

- **Turnkey Operations. Turnkey operations** are typically contracts for the construction of operating facilities in exchange for a fee. The facilities are transferred to the host country or firm when they are complete. The customer is usually a government agency of, for example, a Middle Eastern country that has decreed that a particular product must be produced locally and under its control. For example, Fiat built an auto plant in Russia to produce an older model of Fiat under a Russian brand name. MNCs that perform turnkey operations are frequently industrial equipment manufacturers that supply some of their own equipment for the project and that commonly sell replacement parts and maintenance services to the host country. They thereby create customers as well as future competitors.

- **BOT Concept.** The **BOT** (build, operate, transfer) concept is a variation of the turnkey operation. Instead of turning the facility (usually a power plant or toll road) over to the host country when completed, the company operates the facility for a fixed period of time during which it earns back its investment, plus a profit. It then turns the facility over to the government at little or no cost to the host country.[12]

- **Management Contracts.** A large corporation operating throughout the world is likely to have a large amount of management talent at its disposal. **Management contracts** offer a means through which a corporation may use some of its personnel to assist a firm in a host country for a specified fee and period of time. Management contracts are common when a host government expropriates part or all of a foreign-owned company's holdings in its country. The contracts allow the firm to continue to earn some income from its investment and keep the operations going until local management is trained.

Controversies in Directional Growth Strategies

Is vertical growth better than horizontal growth? Is concentric diversification better than conglomerate diversification? Although the research is not in complete agreement, growth into areas related to a company's current product lines is generally more successful than is growth into completely unrelated areas. For example, one study of various growth projects examined how many were considered successful, that is, still in existence after 22 years. The results were: vertical growth, 80%; horizontal growth, 50%; concentric diversification, 35%; and conglomerate diversification, 28%.[13]

In terms of diversification strategies, research suggests that the relationship between relatedness and performance is curvilinear. If a new business is very similar to that of the acquiring firm, it adds little new to the corporation and only marginally improves performance. If the new business is completely different from the acquiring company's businesses, there may be very little potential for any synergy. If, however, the new business provides new resources and capabilities in a different, but similar, business, the likelihood of a significant performance improvement is high.[14]

Is internal growth better than external growth? Corporations can follow the growth strategies of either concentration or diversification through the internal development of new products and services, or through external acquisitions, mergers, and strategic alliances. Although not yet conclusive, the research indicates that firms that grow through acquisitions do not perform financially as well as firms that grow through internal means.[15] Other research indicates, however, that acquisitions have a higher survival rate than do new internally generated business ventures.[16]

Stability Strategies

A corporation may choose stability over growth by continuing its current activities without any significant change in direction. Although sometimes viewed as a lack of strategy, the stability family of corporate strategies can be appropriate for a successful corporation operating in a reasonably predictable environment.[17] They are very popular with small business owners who have found a niche and are happy with their success and the manageable size of their firms. Stability strategies can be very useful in the short run, but they can be dangerous if followed for too long (as many small-town businesses discovered when Wal-Mart came to town). Some of the more popular of these strategies are the pause/proceed with caution, no change, and profit strategies.

Pause/Proceed with Caution Strategy

A **pause/proceed with caution strategy** is, in effect, a timeout—an opportunity to rest before continuing a growth or retrenchment strategy. It is a very deliberate attempt to make only incremental improvements until a particular environmental situation changes. It is typically conceived as a *temporary strategy* to be used until the environment becomes more hospitable or to enable a company to consolidate its resources after prolonged rapid growth. This was the strategy Dell Computer Corporation followed in 1993 after its growth strategy had resulted in more growth than it could handle. Explained CEO Michael Dell, "We grew 285% in two years, and we're having some growing pains." Selling personal computers by mail enabled it to underprice Compaq Computer and IBM, but it could not keep up with the needs of the $2 billion, 5,600-employee company selling PCs in 95 countries. Dell was not giving up on its growth strategy; it was merely putting it temporarily in limbo until the company could hire new managers, improve the structure, and build new facilities.

No Change Strategy

A **no change strategy** is a decision to do nothing new—a choice to continue current operations and policies for the foreseeable future. Rarely articulated as a definite strategy, a no change strategy's success depends on a lack of significant change in a corporation's situation. The relative stability created by the firm's modest competitive position in an industry facing little or no growth encourages the company to continue on its current course, making only small adjustments for inflation in its sales and profit objectives. There are no obvious opportunities or threats nor much in the way of significant strengths or weaknesses. Few aggressive new competitors are likely to enter such an industry. The corporation has probably found a reasonably profitable and stable niche for its products. Unless the industry is undergoing consolidation, the relative comfort a company in this situation experiences is likely to encourage the company to follow a no change strategy in which the future is expected to continue as an extension of the present. Most small-town businesses probably follow this strategy before Wal-Mart moves into their areas.

Profit Strategy

A **profit strategy** is a decision to do nothing new in a worsening situation, but instead to act as though the company's problems are only temporary. The profit strategy is an attempt to artificially support profits when a company's sales are declining by reducing investment and short-term discretionary expenditures. Rather than announcing the company's poor position to shareholders and the investment community at large, top management may be tempted to follow this very seductive strategy. Blaming the company's problems on a hostile environment (such as anti-business government policies, unethical competitors, finicky customers, and/or greedy lenders), management defers investments and/or cuts expenses (such as R&D, maintenance, and advertising) to stabilize profits during this period. It may even sell one of its product lines for the cash flow benefits. Obviously the profit strategy is useful only to help a company get through a temporary difficulty. Unfortunately the strategy is seductive and if continued long enough will lead to a serious deterioration in a corporation's competitive position. The profit strategy is thus usually top management's passive, short-term, and often self-serving response to the situation.

Retrenchment Strategies

A company may pursue retrenchment strategies when it has a weak competitive position in some or all of its product lines resulting in poor performance—sales are down and profits are becoming losses. These strategies impose a great deal of pressure to improve performance. In an attempt to eliminate the weaknesses that are dragging the company down, management may follow one of several retrenchment strategies ranging from turnaround or becoming a captive company to selling out, bankruptcy, or liquidation.

Turnaround Strategy

The **turnaround strategy** emphasizes the improvement of operational efficiency and is probably most appropriate when a corporation's problems are pervasive, but not yet critical. Analogous to a weight reduction diet, the two basic phases of a turnaround strategy are contraction and consolidation.[18]

Contraction is the initial effort to quickly "stop the bleeding" with a general across-the-board cutback in size and costs. The second phase, *consolidation*, implements a program to stabilize the now-leaner corporation. To streamline the company, plans are developed to reduce unnecessary overhead and to make functional activities cost-justified. This is a crucial time for the organization. If the consolidation phase is not conducted in a positive manner, many of the best people leave the organization. If, however, all employees are encouraged to get involved in productivity improvements, the firm is likely to emerge from this retrenchment period a much stronger and better organized company. It has improved its competitive position and is able once again to expand the business. See the **Strategy in a Changing World** feature for a description of IBM's effective use of the turnaround strategy.

STRATEGY IN A CHANGING WORLD

IBM FOLLOWS A TURNAROUND STRATEGY

During the 1970s and 1980s, IBM dominated the computer industry worldwide. It was the market leader in both large mainframe and small personal computers. Along with Apple Computer, IBM set the standard for all personal computers. Even now—when IBM no longer dominates the field—personal computers are still identified as being either Apple or IBM-style PCs.

IBM's problems came to a head in the early 1990s. The company's computer sales were falling. More companies were choosing to replace their large, expensive mainframe computers with personal computers, but they weren't buying the PCs from IBM. An increasing number of firms like Hewlett-Packard, Dell, Gateway, and Compaq had entered the industry. They offered IBM-style PC "clones" that were considerably cheaper and often more advanced than IBM's PCs. IBM's falling revenues meant corporate losses in 1992 and 1993. Industry experts perceived the company as a bureaucratic dinosaur that could no longer adapt to changing conditions. Its stock price fell to $40 with no end in sight.

IBM's board of directors hired a new CEO, Louis Gerstner, to lead a corporate turnaround strategy at "Big Blue" (the nickname IBM earned from its rigid dress code policies). To stop the flow of red ink, the company violated its long-held "no layoffs" policy by reducing its workforce 40%. Under Gerstner, IBM reorganized its sales force around specific industries such as retailing and banking. Decision making was made easier. Previously, according to Joseph Formichelli, a top executive with the PC division, he "had to go through seven layers to get things done." Firing incompetent employees could take a year, "so

you pawned them off on another group." Strategy presentations were hashed over so many times "they got watered down to nothing." Under Gerstner, however, formal presentations were no longer desired. The emphasis switched to quicker decision making and a stronger customer orientation.

In 1987, customers had been forced to wait five to seven years for a new mainframe series. Now IBM produces a new line almost every year. Gerstner personally talks with at least one customer every day. The company's PC business, which had lost market share and generated huge losses in the early 1990s, has become profitable. Its market share rose almost one point to 8.9% in 1996—second place in global market share. Its stock price topped $140 by the end of 1996. Customers have been pleased with the company's improved products and better customer service. "Over the last couple of years they have been going out of their way to have a contact person you could call with any issue," reported Linda Wiersema, Chief Information Officer at LTV Corporation's LTV Steel unit.

The corporation still has a long way to go to complete its turnaround. Even though revenue increased 40% over the past decade, profits increased only 3.2%. In 1996, IBM's revenue increased just 5.6% compared to 19% at Hewlett-Packard and 29% at Intel. According to Chief Financial Officer Richard Thoman, "We've done a lot, but we still have a lot to do."

Source: B. Ziegler, "Gerstner's IBM Revival: Impressive, Incomplete," *Wall Street Journal* (March 25, 1997), pp. B1, B4.

Captive Company Strategy

A **captive company strategy** is the giving up of independence in exchange for security. A company with a weak competitive position may not be able to engage in a full-blown turnaround strategy. The industry may not be sufficiently attractive to justify such an effort from either the current management or from investors. Nevertheless a company in this situation faces poor sales and increasing losses unless it takes some action.

Management desperately searches for an "angel" by offering to be a captive company to one of its larger customers in order to guarantee the company's continued existence with a long-term contract. In this way, the corporation may be able to reduce the scope of some of its functional activities, such as marketing, thus reducing costs significantly. The weaker company gains certainty of sales and production in return for becoming heavily dependent on one firm for at least 75% of its sales. For example, to become the sole supplier of an auto part to General Motors, Simpson Industries of Birmingham, Michigan, agreed to let a special team from GM inspect its engine parts facilities and books and interview its employees. In return, nearly 80% of the company's production was sold to GM through long-term contracts.[19]

Sell-Out/Divestment Strategy

If a corporation with a weak competitive position in this industry is unable either to pull itself up by its bootstraps or to find a customer to which it can become a captive company, it may have no choice but to **sell out** and leave the industry completely. The sell-out strategy makes sense if management can still obtain a good price for its shareholders by selling the entire company to another firm. For example, Johnson Products, a pioneer in hair care products for African-American and other ethnic markets, found that over time it had lost its competitive position to larger cosmetics companies who had entered Johnson Products' niche. After numerous attempts to turn the company around, the Johnson family finally decided to sell out to Ivax Corporation while they could still get a decent price for the firm.

If the corporation has multiple business lines and it chooses to sell off a division with low growth potential, this is called **divestment**. Monsanto is one example of a company using this strategy. Founded in 1901, Monsanto recently realized that the very chemical business for which it had been known was hurting its growth as a corporation. The chemical division's performance had been overshadowed in the past ten years by advances in biotechnology and agricultural products such as Roundup. Divestment seemed a viable decision in 1997.

Bankruptcy/Liquidation Strategy

When a company finds itself in the worst possible situation with a poor competitive position in an industry with few prospects, management has only a few alternatives—all of them distasteful. Because no one is interested in buying a weak company in an unattractive industry, the firm must pursue a bankruptcy or liquidation strategy. **Bankruptcy** involves giving up management of the firm to the courts in return for some settlement of the corporation's obligations. Top management hopes that once the court decides the claims on the company, the company will be stronger and better able to compete in a more attractive industry. Wang Laboratories, Inc., took this approach in 1992. Founded by An Wang, the company had been unable to make the transition from word processors to personal computers and finally collapsed after the death of its founder. The company emerged from bankruptcy in 1993 under a court-supervised reorganization plan requiring that the company focus on office software.

In contrast to bankruptcy, which seeks to perpetuate the corporation, **liquidation** is the termination of the firm. Because the industry is unattractive and the company too weak to be sold as a going concern, management may choose to convert as many saleable assets as possible to cash, which is then distributed to the shareholders after all obligations are paid. The benefit of liquidation over bankruptcy is that the board of directors, as representatives of the shareholders, together with top management make the decisions instead of turning them over to the court, which may choose to ignore share-holders completely.

At times, top management must be willing to select one of these less desirable re-trenchment strategies. Unfortunately, many top managers are unwilling to admit that their company has serious weaknesses for fear that they may be personally blamed. Even worse, top management may not even perceive that crises are developing. When these top managers do eventually notice trouble, they are prone to attribute the problems to temporary environmental disturbances and tend to follow profit strategies. Even when things are going terribly wrong, top management is greatly tempted to avoid liquidation in the hope of a miracle. Thus, a corporation needs a strong board of directors who, to safeguard shareholders' interests, can tell top management when to quit.

6.3 Portfolio Analysis

Chapter 5 dealt with how individual product lines and business units can gain competitive advantage in the marketplace by using competitive and cooperative strategies. Companies with multiple product lines or business units must also ask themselves how these various products and business units should be managed to boost overall corporate performance.

- How much of our time and money should we spend on our best products and business units to ensure that they continue to be successful?

- How much of our time and money should we spend developing new costly products, most of which will never be successful?

One of the most popular aids to developing corporate strategy in a multibusiness corporation is portfolio analysis. Although its popularity has dropped since the 1970s and 1980s when over half of the largest business corporations used portfolio analysis, it is still used by 27% of Fortune 500 firms in corporate strategy formulation.[20] Portfolio analysis puts corporate headquarters into the role of an internal banker. In **portfolio analysis**, top management views its product lines and business units as a series of investments from which it expects a profitable return. The product lines/business units form a portfolio of investments that top management must constantly juggle to ensure the best return on the corporation's invested money. Two of the most popular approaches are the BCG Growth-Share Matrix and GE Business Screen. This concept can also be used to develop strategies for international markets.

BCG Growth-Share Matrix

The **BCG (Boston Consulting Group) Growth-Share Matrix** depicted in Figure 6.2 is the simplest way to portray a corporation's portfolio of investments. Each of the corporation's product lines or business units is plotted on the matrix according to both the growth rate of the industry in which it competes and its relative market share. A unit's relative competitive position is defined as its market share in the industry divided by that of the largest other competitor. By this calculation, a relative market share above 1.0 belongs to the market leader. The business growth rate is the percentage of market growth, that is, the percentage by which sales of a particular business unit classification of products have increased. The matrix assumes that, other things being equal, a growing market is attractive.

Figure 6.2
BCG Growth-
Share Matrix

Source: B. Hedley,
"Strategy and the
Business Portfolio,"
Long Range Planning
(February 1997), p. 12.
Reprinted with
permission.

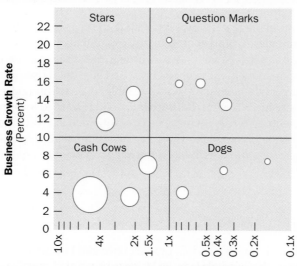

The line separating areas of high and low relative competitive position is set at 1.5 times. A product line or business unit must have relative strengths of this magnitude to ensure that it will have the dominant position needed to be a "star" or "cash cow." On the other hand, a product line or unit having a relative competitive position less than 1.0 has "dog" status.[21] Each product or unit is represented in Figure 6.2 by a circle. The area of the circle represents the relative significance of each business unit or product line to the corporation in terms of assets used or sales generated.

The BCG Growth-Share Matrix has a lot in common with the product life cycle. As a product moves through its life cycle, it is categorized into one of four types for the purpose of funding decisions:

- **Question marks** (sometimes called "problem children" or "wildcats") are new products with the potential for success, but they need a lot of cash for development. If such a product is to gain enough market share to become a market leader and thus a star, money must be taken from more mature products and spent on a question mark.

- **Stars** are market leaders typically at the peak of their product life cycle and are usually able to generate enough cash to maintain their high share of the market. When their market growth rate slows, stars become cash cows.

- **Cash cows** typically bring in far more money than is needed to maintain their market share. In this declining stage of their life cycle, these products are "milked" for cash that will be invested in new question marks. Question marks unable to obtain a dominant market share (and thus become stars) by the time the industry growth rate inevitably slows become dogs.

- **Dogs** have low market share and do not have the potential (because they are in an unattractive industry) to bring in much cash. According to the BCG Growth-Share Matrix, dogs should be either sold off or managed carefully for the small amount of cash they can generate.

Underlying the BCG Growth-Share Matrix is the concept of the experience curve (discussed in Chapter 4). The key to success is assumed to be market share. Firms with the highest market share tend to have a cost leadership position based on economies of scale, among other things. If a company is able to use the experience curve to its advantage, it should be able to manufacture and sell new products at a price low enough to garner early market share leadership (assuming no successful imitation by competitors). Once the product becomes a star, it is destined to be very profitable, considering its inevitable future as a cash cow.

Having plotted the current positions of its product lines or business units on a matrix, a company can project their future positions, assuming no change in strategy. Present and projected matrixes can thus be used to help identify major strategic issues facing the organization. The goal of any company is to maintain a balanced portfolio so it can be self-sufficient in cash and always working to harvest mature products in declining industries to support new ones in growing industries.

The BCG Growth-Share Matrix is a very well-known portfolio concept with some clear advantages. It is quantifiable and easy to use. Cash cows, dogs, and stars are an easy to remember way to refer to a corporation's business units or products. Unfortunately the BCG Growth-Share Matrix also has some serious limitations:

- The use of highs and lows to form four categories is too simplistic.

- The link between market share and profitability is not necessarily strong. Low-share businesses can also be profitable.

- Growth rate is only one aspect of industry attractiveness.

- Product lines or business units are considered only in relation to one competitor: the market leader. Small competitors with fast-growing market shares are ignored.

- Market share is only one aspect of overall competitive position.

GE Business Screen

General Electric, with the assistance of the McKinsey and Company consulting firm, developed a more complicated matrix. As depicted in Figure 6.3, the **GE Business Screen** includes nine cells based on long-term industry attractiveness and business strength/competitive position. The GE Business Screen, in contrast to the BCG Growth-Share Matrix, includes much more data in its two key factors than just business growth rate and comparable market share. For example, at GE, industry attractiveness includes market growth rate, industry profitability, size, and pricing practices, among other possible opportunities and threats. Business strength or competitive position includes market share as well as technological position, profitability, and size, among other possible strengths and weaknesses.[22]

The individual product lines or business units are identified by a letter and plotted as circles on the GE Business Screen. The area of each circle is in proportion to the size of the industry in terms of sales. The pie slices within the circles depict the market share of each product line or business unit.

To plot product lines or business units on the GE Business Screen, follow these four steps:

Step 1. Select criteria to rate the industry for each product line or business unit. Assess overall industry attractiveness for each product line or business unit on a scale from 1 (very unattractive) to 5 (very attractive).

Step 2. Select the key factors needed for success in each product line or business unit. Assess business strength/competitive position for each product line or business unit on a scale of 1 (very weak) to 5 (very strong).

Figure 6.3
General Electric's Business Screen

Source: Adapted from *Strategic Management in GE*, Corporate Planning and Development, General Electric Corporation. Used by permission of General Electric Company.

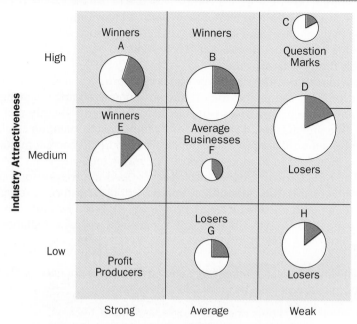

Step 3. Plot each product line's or business unit's current position on a matrix like that depicted in Figure 6.3.

Step 4. Plot the firm's future portfolio assuming that present corporate and business strategies remain unchanged. Is there a performance gap between projected and desired portfolios? If so, this gap should serve as a stimulus to seriously review the corporation's current mission, objectives, strategies, and policies.

Overall the nine-cell GE Business Screen is an improvement over the BCG Growth-Share Matrix. The GE Business Screen considers many more variables and does not lead to such simplistic conclusions. It recognizes, for example, that the attractiveness of an industry can be assessed in many different ways (other than simply using growth rate), and it thus allows users to select whatever criteria they feel are most appropriate to their situation. This portfolio matrix, however, does have some shortcomings:

- It can get quite complicated and cumbersome.

- The numerical estimates of industry attractiveness and business strength/competitive position give the appearance of objectivity, but they are in reality subjective judgments that may vary from one person to another.

- It cannot effectively depict the positions of new products or business units in developing industries.

International Portfolio Analysis

To aid international strategic planning, portfolio analysis can be applied to international markets.[23] Two factors form the axes of the matrix in Figure 6.4. A **country's attractiveness** is composed of its market size, the market rate of growth, the extent and type of government regulation, and economic and political factors. A **product's competitive**

Figure 6.4
Portfolio Matrix for Plotting Products by Country

Source: G. D. Harrell and R. O. Kiefer, "Multinational Strategic Market Portfolios," *MSU Business Topics* (Winter 1981), p. 7. Reprinted by permission.

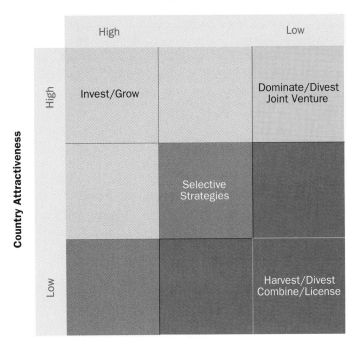

strength is composed of its market share, product fit, contribution margin, and market support. Depending on where a product fits on the matrix, it should either receive more funding or be harvested for cash.

Portfolio analysis might not be useful, however, to corporations operating in a global industry rather than a multidomestic one. In discussing the importance of global industries, Porter argues against the use of portfolio analysis on a country-by-country basis:

> In a global industry, however, managing international activities like a portfolio will undermine the possibility of achieving competitive advantage. In a global industry, a firm must in some way integrate its activities on a worldwide basis to capture the linkage among countries.[24]

Advantages and Limitations of Portfolio Analysis

Portfolio analysis is commonly used in strategy formulation because it offers certain *advantages*:

- It encourages top management to evaluate each of the corporation's businesses individually and to set objectives and allocate resources for each.

- It stimulates the use of externally oriented data to supplement management's judgment.

- It raises the issue of cash flow availability for use in expansion and growth.

- Its graphic depiction facilitates communication.

Portfolio analysis does, however, have some very real *limitations* that have caused some companies to reduce their use of this approach:

- It is not easy to define product/market segments.

- It suggests the use of standard strategies that can miss opportunities or be impractical.

- It provides an illusion of scientific rigor when in reality positions are based on subjective judgments.

- Its value-laden terms like cash cow and dog can lead to self-fulfilling prophecies.

- It is not always clear what makes an industry attractive or where a product is in its life cycle.

- Naively following the prescriptions of a portfolio model may actually reduce corporate profits if they are used inappropriately. For example, General Mills' Chief Executive H. Brewster Atwater cites his company's Bisquick brand of flour as a product that would have been written off years ago based on portfolio analysis. "This product is 57 years old. By all rights it should have been overtaken by newer products. But with the proper research to improve the product and promotion to keep customers excited, it's doing very well."[25]

6.4 *Corporate Parenting*

Campbell, Goold, and Alexander, authors of *Corporate-Level Strategy: Creating Value in the Multibusiness Company*, contend that corporate strategists must address two crucial questions:

- What businesses should this company own and why?

- What organizational structure, management processes, and philosophy will foster superior performance from the company's business units?[26]

Portfolio analysis attempts to answer these questions by examining the attractiveness of various industries and by managing business units for cash flow, that is, by using cash generated from mature units to build new product lines. Unfortunately portfolio analysis fails to deal with the question of what industries a corporation should enter or with how a corporation can attain synergy among its product lines and business units. As suggested by its name, portfolio analysis tends to primarily view matters financially, regarding business units and product lines as separate and independent investments.

Corporate parenting, in contrast, views the corporation in terms of resources and capabilities that can be used to build business unit value as well as generate synergies across business units. According to Campbell, Goold, and Alexander:

> Multibusiness companies create value by influencing—or parenting—the businesses they own. The best parent companies create more value than any of their rivals would if they owned the same businesses. Those companies have what we call *parenting advantage.*[27]

Corporate parenting generates corporate strategy by focusing on the core competencies of the parent corporation and on the value created from the relationship between the parent and its businesses. In the form of corporate headquarters, the parent has a great deal of power in this relationship. If there is a good fit between the parent's skills and resources and the needs and opportunities of the business units, the corporation is likely to create value. If, however, there is not a good fit, the corporation is likely to destroy value.[28] This approach to corporate strategy is useful not only in deciding what new businesses to acquire, but also in choosing how each existing business unit should be best managed. The primary job of corporate headquarters is, therefore, to obtain synergy among the business units by providing needed resources to units, transferring skills and capabilities among the units, and by coordinating the activities of shared unit functions to attain economies of scope (as in centralized purchasing).[29]

Developing a Corporate Parenting Strategy

Campbell, Goold, and Alexander recommend that the search for appropriate corporate strategy involves three analytical steps.

First, examine each business unit (or target firm in the case of acquisition) in terms of its critical success factors. **Critical success factors** are those elements of a company that determine its strategic success or failure. They emphasize its distinctive competence to ensure competitive advantage. Critical success factors will likely vary from company to company and from one business unit to another. People in the business units probably identified the critical success factors when they were generating business strategies for their units.

Second, examine each business unit (or target firm) in terms of areas in which performance can be improved. These are considered to be parenting opportunities. For example, two business units might be able to gain economies of scope by combining their sales forces. In another instance, a unit may have good, but not great, manufacturing and logistics skills. A parent company having world-class expertise in these areas can improve that unit's performance. The corporate parent could also transfer some people from one business unit having the desired skills to another unit in need of those skills. People at corporate headquarters may, because of their experience in many industries, spot areas where improvements are possible that even people in the business unit may not have noticed. Unless specific areas are significantly weaker than the competition, people in the business units may not even be aware that these areas could be improved, especially if each business unit only monitors its own particular industry.

Third, analyze how well the parent corporation fits with the business unit (or target firm). Corporate headquarters must be aware of its own strengths and weaknesses in terms of resources, skills, and capabilities. To do this, the corporate parent must ask if it has the characteristics that fit the parenting opportunities in each business unit. It must also ask if there is a misfit between the parent's characteristics and the critical success factors of each business unit.

Parenting-Fit Matrix

Campbell, Goold, and Alexander further recommend the use of a **parenting-fit matrix** which summarizes the various judgments regarding corporate/business unit fit for the corporation as a whole. Instead of describing business units in terms of their growth potential, competitive position, or industry structure, such a matrix emphasizes their fit with the corporate parent. As shown in Figure 6.5, the parenting-fit matrix is composed of two dimensions: the *positive contributions* that the parent can make and the *negative effects* the parent can make. The combination of these two dimensions creates five different positions—each with its own implications for corporate strategy.

Heartland Businesses

According to Campbell, Goold, and Alexander, business units that lie in the top right corner of the matrix should be at the heart of the corporation's future. These **heartland businesses** have opportunities for improvement by the parent, and the parent understands their critical success factors well. These businesses should have priority for all corporate activities.

Figure 6.5
Parenting-Fit Matrix

Source: Adapted from M. Alexander, A. Campbell, and M. Goold, "A New Model for Reforming the Planning Review Process," *Planning Review* (January/February 1995), p. 17. Reprinted with permission from Planning Reveiw, © 1995 The Planning Forum..

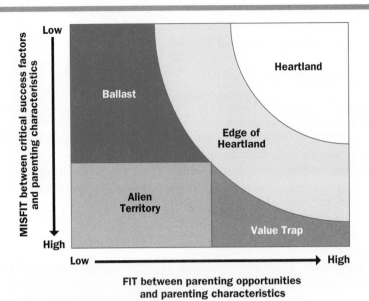

FIT between parenting opportunities
and parenting characteristics

Edge-of-Heartland Businesses

For **edge-of-heartland businesses**, some parenting characteristics fit the business, but others do not. The parent may not have all the characteristics needed by a unit, or the parent may not really understand all of the unit's critical success factors. For example, a unit in this area may be very strong in creating its own image through advertising—a critical success factor in its industry (such as in perfumes). The corporate parent may, however, not have this strength and tends to leave this to its advertising agency. If the parent forced the unit to abandon its own creative efforts in favor of using the corporation's favorite ad agency, the unit may flounder. Such business units are likely to consume much of the parent's attention, as the parent tries to understand them better and transform them into heartland businesses. In this instance, the parent needs to know when to interfere in business unit activities and strategies and when to keep at arm's length.

Ballast Businesses

Ballast businesses fit very comfortably with the parent corporation but contain very few opportunities to be improved by the parent. This is likely to be the case in units that have been with the corporation for many years and have been very successful. The parent may have added value in the past, but it can no longer find further parenting opportunities. Like cash cows, ballast businesses may be important sources of stability and earnings. They can, however, also be a drag on the corporation as a whole by slowing growth and distracting the parent from more productive activities. Some analysts might put IBM's mainframe business units in this category. Because there is always a danger that environmental changes could move a ballast business unit into alien territory, corporate decision makers should consider divesting this unit as soon as they can get a price that exceeds the expected value of future cash flows.

Alien Territory Businesses

Alien territory businesses have little opportunity to be improved by the corporate parent, and a misfit exists between the parenting characteristics and the units' critical success factors. There is little potential for value creation, but high potential for value destruction on the part of the parent. These units are usually small and are often remnants of past experiments with diversification, businesses acquired as part of a larger purchase, or pet projects of senior managers. Even though corporate headquarters may admit that there is little fit, there may be reasons for keeping a unit: it is currently profitable, there are few buyers, the parent has made commitments to the unit's managers, or it is a favorite of the chairman. Because the corporate parent is probably destroying value in its attempts to improve fit, Campbell, Goold, and Alexander recommend that the corporation divest this unit while it still has value.

Value Trap Businesses

Value trap businesses fit well with parenting opportunities, but they are a misfit with the parent's understanding of the units' critical success factors. This is where corporate headquarters can make its biggest error. It mistakes what it sees as opportunities for ways to improve the business unit's profitability or competitive position. For example, in its zeal to make the unit a world-class manufacturer (because the parent has world-class manufacturing skills), it may not notice that the unit is primarily successful because of its unique product development and niche marketing expertise. The potential for possible gain blinds the parent to the downside risks of doing the wrong thing and destroying the unit's core competencies.

Horizontal Strategy: Corporate Competitive Strategy

A **horizontal strategy** is a corporate strategy that cuts across business unit boundaries to build synergy across business units and to improve the competitive position of one or more business units. When used to build synergy, it acts like a parenting strategy. When used to improve the competitive position of one or more business units, it can be thought of as a corporate competitive strategy. Large multibusiness corporations often compete against other large multibusiness firms in a number of markets. These **multipoint competitors** are firms that compete with each other not only in one business unit, but also in a number of business units. At one time or another, a cash-rich competitor may choose to build its own market share in a particular market to the disadvantage of another corporation's business unit. Although each business unit has primary responsibility for its own business strategy, it may sometimes need some help from its corporate parent, especially if the competitor business unit is getting heavy financial support from its corporate parent. In this instance, corporate headquarters develops a horizontal strategy to coordinate the various goals and strategies of related business units.[30]

For example, Procter & Gamble, Kimberly-Clark, Scott Paper, and Johnson and Johnson compete with one another in varying combinations of consumer paper products, from disposable diapers to facial tissue. If (purely hypothetically) Johnson and Johnson had just developed a toilet tissue with which it chose to challenge Procter & Gamble's high-share Charmin brand in a particular district, it might charge a low price for its new brand to build sales quickly. Procter & Gamble might not choose to respond to this attack on its share by cutting prices on Charmin. Because of Charmin's high market share, Procter & Gamble would lose significantly more sales dollars in a price war than Johnson and Johnson would with its initially low-share brand. To retaliate, Procter & Gamble might thus challenge Johnson and Johnson's high-share baby shampoo with Procter & Gamble's own low-share brand of baby shampoo in a different district. Once Johnson and Johnson had perceived Procter & Gamble's response, it might choose to stop challenging Charmin so that Procter & Gamble would stop challenging Johnson and Johnson's baby shampoo.

⚫ **6.5** *Global Issues for the 21st Century*

- The **21st Century Global Society** feature in this chapter illustrates how the South Korean firm Daewoo is using a combination of international entry options to become a global player in both the automobile and consumer electronics industries. Expect more Asian corporations to become major world players in the coming decades.

- The international implications of corporate growth strategies are increasing. Even if a firm is not planning to enter an international market, many of its suppliers and some of its manufacturing will probably be located in other nations.

- A disadvantage of a vertical growth strategy for a corporation operating in a global industry is that its functional value chain will be spread over the world, making logistics and communication especially important. A natural disaster or national revolution in any part of the world could temporarily halt the production of a company's products worldwide.

- Conglomerate diversification has been criticized as providing less value than has concentric diversification, primarily because it is more difficult to keep track of unrelated business units than related ones. Partially because of this, many companies are currently divesting units unrelated to their primary business. As more corporations become involved in international operations through acquisitions, strategic alliances, and other options (thus complicating management further), expect conglomerate diversification to become even less popular.

- Expect corporate parenting to become the dominant model in corporate strategy for evaluating business units and working to achieve synergies across unit boundaries. The parenting concept is based on the idea of the corporation as a learning organization that can transfer knowledge, skills, resources, and capabilities from a high-performing to an under-performing unit.

Projections for the 21st Century

- From 1994 to 2010, the number of wired telephone lines in the world will increase from 607 million to 1.4 billion.

- From 1994 to 2010, the number of wireless telephone lines in the world will increase from 34 million to 1.3 billion.[31]

Discussion Questions

1. How does horizontal growth differ from vertical growth as a corporate strategy? From concentric diversification?

2. What are the tradeoffs between an internal and an external growth strategy? Which approach is best as an international entry strategy?

3. Is stability really a strategy or just a term for no strategy?

4. Compare and contrast SWOT analysis with portfolio analysis.

5. How is corporate parenting different from portfolio analysis? How is it alike? Is it a useful concept in a global industry?

Key Terms

acquisition (p. 134, 141)
alien territory businesses (p. 154)
backward integration (p. 136)
ballast businesses (p. 154)
bankruptcy (p. 146)
BCG Growth-Share Matrix (p. 147)
BOT (p. 142)
captive company strategy (p. 145)
cash cows (p. 148)
concentration (p. 135)
concentric diversification (p. 138)
conglomerate diversification (p. 140)
corporate parenting (p. 152)
corporate strategy (p. 133)
country's attractiveness (p. 150)
critical success factors (p. 153)
directional strategy (p. 134)
diversification (p. 135)
divestment (p. 146)
dogs (p. 148)
edge-of-heartland businesses
    (p. 154)
exporting (p. 140)

forward integration (p. 136)
full integration (p. 136)
GE Business Screen (p. 149)
green-field development
    (p. 142)
growth strategies (p. 134)
heartland businesses (p. 153)
horizontal growth (p. 138)
horizontal integration (p. 138)
horizontal strategy (p. 155)
joint ventures (p. 140)
licensing (p. 140)
liquidation (p. 146)
long-term contracts (p. 137)
management contracts (p. 142)
merger (p. 134)
multipoint competitors (p. 155)
no change strategy (p. 143)
organization slack (p. 135)
outsourcing (p. 138)
parenting-fit matrix (p. 153)
pause/proceed with caution
    strategy (p. 143)

portfolio analysis (p. 147)
production sharing (p. 142)
product's competitive strength
    (p. 150-151)
profit strategy (p. 144)
quasi-integration (p. 136)
question marks (p. 148)
retrenchment strategies (p. 134)
sell out (p. 146)
stability strategies (p. 134)
stars (p. 148)
strategic alliance (p. 135)
synergy (p. 139)
taper integration (p. 136)
transaction cost economics
    (p. 136)
turnaround strategy (p. 144)
turnkey operations (p. 142)
value trap businesses (p. 155)
vertical growth (p. 135)
vertical integration (p. 136)

Strategic Practice Exercise

Read the following example of a company that has had its share of successes and failures in a very unique industry. Consider the questions at the end of the paragraph and discuss them with others.

> KinderCare Learning Centers had been founded to take advantage of the increasing numbers of dual-career couples who were turning to day-care centers to watch their children while they were at work. In comparison to some centers that were nothing more than babysitting services providing only minimal attention to the needs of the children, Kinder-Care offered pleasant surroundings staffed by well-trained personnel. Soon KinderCare had over 1,000 centers in almost 40 states in the United States. Not satisfied with its success, however, KinderCare's top management decided to take advantage of its relationship with working parents to diversify into the somewhat related businesses of banking, insurance, and retailing. Financed through junk bonds, the strategy failed to bring in enough cash to pay for its implementation. After years of losses, the company was driven to bankruptcy in the

late 1980s. It emerged from bankruptcy in 1993, divested itself of its acquisitions and pledged to stay away from diversification. The new CEO initiated a concentration strategy with an emphasis on horizontal growth. KinderCare opened its first center catering expressly to commuters in a renovated supermarket near the Metro line to Chicago. It also offered to build child-care centers for big employers or to run existing facilities for a fee. It opened its first overseas center in Britain. By 1996, the company was earning $21.7 million on revenues of $506.5 million with centers in 38 states and the United Kingdom.[32]

___ What did this company do right?

___ What mistakes did it make?

___ Do you think it made the right decision to grow internationally?

___ Should it expand further? If so, what corporate strategy should it use?

Notes

1. R. D. Hof, "Hewlett-Packard Digs Deep for a Digital Future," *Business Week* (October 18, 1993), pp. 72–75; B. Gillooly, "HP's New Course," *InformationWeek* (March 20, 1996), pp. 45–56.

2. R. P. Rumelt, D. E. Schendel, and D. J. Teece, "Fundamental Issues in Strategy," in *Fundamental Issues in Strategy: A Research Agenda,* edited by R. P. Rumelt, D. E. Schendel, and D. J. Teece (Boston: HBS Press, 1994), p. 42.

3. This analogy of corporate parent and business unit children was initially proposed by A. Campbell, M. Goold, and M. Alexander. See "Corporate Strategy: The Quest for Parenting Advantage," *Harvard Business Review* (March-April, 1995), pp. 120–132.

4. M. E. Porter, "From Competitive Strategy to Corporate Strategy," in *International Review of Strategic Management*, Vol. 1, edited by D. E. Husey (Chicester, England: John Wiley & Sons, 1990), p. 29.

5. J. W. Slocum, Jr., M. McGill, and D. T. Lei, "The New Learning Strategy: Anytime, Anything, Anywhere," *Organizational Dynamics* (Autumn 1994), p. 36.

6. K. R. Harrigan, *Strategies for Vertical Integration* (Lexington, Mass.: Lexington Books, D. C. Heath, 1983), pp. 16–21.

7. L. Grant, "Partners in Profit," *U. S. News and World Report* (September 20, 1993), pp. 65–66.

8. For a discussion of the pros and cons of contracting versus vertical integration, see J. T. Mahoney, "The Choice of Organizational Form: Vertical Financial Ownership Versus Other Methods of Vertical Integration," *Strategic Management Journal* (November 1992), pp. 559–584.

9. A. Y. Ilinich, and C. P. Zeithaml, "Operationalizing and Testing Galbraith's Center of Gravity Theory," *Strategic Management Journal* (June 1995), pp. 401–410.

10. S. Sherman, "Are Strategic Alliances Working?" *Fortune* (September 21, 1992), p. 77.

11. B. Voss, "Strategic Federations Frequently Falter in Far East," *Journal of Business Strategy* (July/August 1993), p. 6; S. Douma, "Success and Failure in New Ventures," *Long Range Planning* (April 1991), pp. 54–60.

12. J. Naisbitt, *Megatrends Asia* (New York: Simon & Schuster, 1996), p. 143.

13. J. M. Pennings, H. Barkema, and S. Douma, "Organizational Learning and Diversification," *Academy of Management Journal* (June 1994), pp. 608–640.

14. C. C. Markides, "Consequences of Corporate Refocusing: Ex Ante Evidence," *Academy of Management Journal* (June 1992), pp. 398–412; M. Lubatkin, and S. Chatterjee, "Extending Modern Portfolio Theory into the Domain of Corporate Diversification: Does It Apply?" *Academy of Management Journal* (February 1994), pp. 109–136; J. S. Harrison, M. A. Hitt, R. E. Hoskisson, and R. D. Ireland, "Synergies and Post-Acquisition Performance: Differences Versus Similarities in Resource Allocations," *Journal of Management* (March 1991), pp. 173–190; J. Robins, and M. F. Wiersema, "A Resource-Based Approach to the Multibusiness Firm: Empirical Analysis of Portfolio Interrelationships and Corporate Financial Performance," *Strategic Management Journal* (May 1995), pp. 277–299.

15. W. B. Carper, "Corporate Acquisitions and Shareholder Wealth: A Review and Exploratory Analysis," *Journal of Management* (December 1990), pp. 807–823; P. G. Simmonds, "Using Diversification as a Tool for Effective Performance," *Handbook of Business Strategy, 1992/93 Yearbook,* edited by H. E. Glass and M. A. Hovde (Boston: Warren, Gorham & Lamont, 1992), pp. 3.1–3.7; B. T. Lamont and C. A. Anderson, "Mode of Corporate Diversification and Economic Performance," *Academy of Management Journal* (December 1985), pp. 926–936.

16. J. M. Pennings, H. Barkema, and S. Douma, "Organizational Learning and Diversification," *Academy of Management Journal* (June 1994), pp. 608–640.

17. A. Inkpen, and N. Choudhury, "The Seeking of Strategy Where It Is Not: Towards a Theory of Strategy Absence," *Strategic Management Journal* (May 1995), pp. 313–323.

18. J. A. Pearce II and D. K. Robbins, "Retrenchment Remains the Foundation of Business Turnaround," *Strategic Management Journal* (June 1994), pp. 407–417.

19. J. B. Treece, "U.S. Parts Makers Just Won't Say 'Uncle,'" *Business Week* (August 10, 1987), pp. 76–77.

20. B. C. Reimann, and A. Reichert, "Portfolio Planning Methods for Strategic Capital Allocation: A Survey of Fortune 500 Firms," *International Journal of Management* (March 1996), pp. 84–93; D. K. Sinha, "Strategic Planning in the Fortune 500," *Handbook of Business Strategy, 1991/92 Yearbook,* edited by H. E. Glass and M. A. Hovde (Boston: Warren Gorham & Lamont, 1991), p. 9.6.

21. B. Hedley, "Strategy and the Business Portfolio," *Long Range Planning* (February 1977), p. 9.

22. R. G. Hamermesh, *Making Strategy Work* (New York: John Wiley and Sons, 1986), p. 14.

23. G. D. Harrell, and R. O. Kiefer, "Multinational Strategic Market Portfolios," *MSU Business Topics* (Winter 1981), p. 5.

24. M. E. Porter, "Changing Patterns of International Competition," *California Management Review* (Winter 1986), p. 12.

25. J. J. Curran, "Companies That Rob the Future," *Fortune* (July 4, 1988), p. 84.

26. A. Campbell, M. Goold, and M. Alexander, *Corporate-Level Strategy: Creating Value in the Multibusiness Company* (New York: John Wiley & Sons, 1994).

27. A. Campbell, M. Goold, and M. Alexander, "Corporate Strategy: The Quest for Parenting Advantage," *Harvard Business Review* (March-April 1995), p. 121.

28. *Ibid.*, p. 122.

29. D. J. Collis, "Corporate Strategy in Multibusiness Firms," *Long Range Planning* (June 1996), pp. 416–418; D. Lei, M. A. Hitt, and R. Bettis, "Dynamic Core Competencies Through Meta-Learning and Strategic Context," *Journal of Management,* Vol. 22, No. 4 (1996), pp. 549–569.

30. M. E. Porter, *Competitive Advantage* (New York: Free Press, 1985), pp. 317–382.

31. J. Warner, "21st Century Capitalism: Snapshot of the Next Century," *Business Week* (November 18, 1994), p. 194.

32. S. Lipin, "KKR, On Buying Spree, to Acquire KinderCare," *Wall Street Journal* (October 4, 1996), p. A3.

Chapter 7

Strategy Formulation: Functional Strategy and Strategic Choice

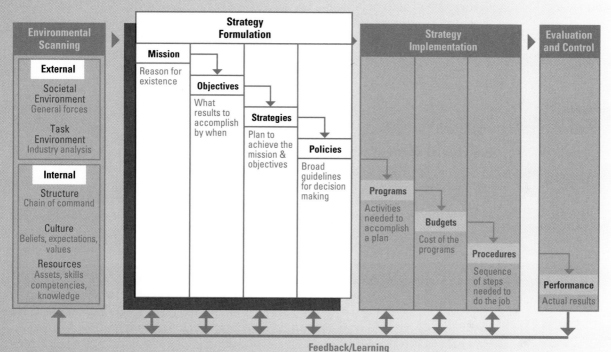

For almost 150 years, the Church & Dwight Company has been building market share on a brand name whose products are in 95% of all U.S. households. Yet if you asked the average person what products this company made, few would know. Although Church & Dwight may not be a household name, the company's ubiquitous orange box of Arm & Hammer[1] brand baking soda is cherished throughout North America. Church & Dwight is a classic example of a marketing functional strategy called product development. Shortly after its introduction in 1878, Arm & Hammer Baking Soda became a fundamental item on the pantry shelf as people found many uses for sodium bicarbonate other than baking, such as cleaning, deodorizing, and tooth brushing. Hearing of the many uses people were finding for its product, the company advertised that its baking soda was good not only for baking, but also for deodorizing refrigerators—simply by leaving an open box in the refrigerator. In a brilliant marketing move, the firm then suggested that consumers buy the product and throw it away—deodorize a kitchen sink by dumping Arm & Hammer baking soda down the drain! The company did not stop here. It looked for other uses of its sodium bicarbonate in new products. Church & Dwight has achieved consistent growth in sales and earnings through the use of "line extensions"—putting the Arm & Hammer brand first on baking soda, then on laundry detergents, toothpaste, and deodorants. By the mid 1990s, Church & Dwight had become a significant competitor in markets previously dominated only by giants like Procter & Gamble, Lever Brothers, and Colgate—using only one brand name. Was there a limit to this growth? Was there a point at which these continuous line extensions would begin to eat away at the integrity of the Arm & Hammer name?

7.1 Functional Strategy

Functional strategy is the approach a functional area takes to achieve corporate and business unit objectives and strategies by maximizing resource productivity. It is concerned with developing and nurturing a distinctive competence to provide a company or business unit with a competitive advantage. For example, just as a multidivisional corporation has several business units, each with its own business strategy, each business unit has its own set of departments, each with its own functional strategy.

The orientation of the functional strategy is dictated by its parent business unit's strategy. For example, a business unit following a competitive strategy of differentiation through high quality needs a manufacturing functional strategy that emphasizes expensive, quality assurance processes over cheaper, high-volume production; a human resource functional strategy that emphasizes the hiring and training of a highly skilled, but costly, workforce; and a marketing functional strategy that emphasizes distribution channel "pull" using advertising to increase consumer demand over "push" using promotional allowances to retailers. If a business unit were to follow a low-cost competitive strategy, however, a different set of functional strategies would be needed to support the business strategy.

Core Competencies

As defined earlier in Chapter 4, a **core competency** is something that a corporation can do exceedingly well. It is a key strength. It may also be called a **core capability** because it includes a number of constituent skills. When these competencies or capabilities are superior to those of the competition, they are called **distinctive competencies**. Although it is typically not an asset in the accounting sense, it is a very valuable capability—it does not "wear out." In general, the more core competencies are used, the more refined they get and the more valuable they become. To be considered a *distinctive* competency, the competency must meet three tests:

1. **Customer Value:** It must make a disproportionate contribution to customer-perceived value.

2. **Competitor Unique:** It must be unique and superior to competitor capabilities.

3. **Extendibility:** It must be something that can be used to develop new products/services or enter new markets.[2]

Even though a distinctive competency is certainly considered a corporation's key strength, a key strength is not always considered to be a distinctive competency. As competitors attempt to imitate another company's competence in a particular functional area, what was once a distinctive competency becomes a minimum requirement to compete in the industry.[3] Even though the competency may still be a core competency and thus a strength, it is no longer unique. For example, when Maytag Company alone had high-quality products, Maytag's ability to make exceedingly reliable and durable washing machines was a distinctive competency. As other appliance makers imitated its quality control and design processes, this continued to be a key strength (that is, a core competency and a strategic factor) of Maytag, but it was less and less a distinctive competency.

Where do these competencies come from? A corporation can gain access to a distinctive competency in four ways:

- It may be an asset endowment, such as a key patent, coming from the founding of the company—Xerox grew on the basis of its original copying patent.

- It may be acquired from someone else—Whirlpool bought a worldwide distribution system when it purchased Philips's appliance division.

- It may be shared with another business unit or alliance partner—Apple Computer worked with a design firm to create the special appeal of its Apple II and Mac computers.

- It may be carefully built and accumulated over time within the company—Honda carefully extended its expertise in small motor manufacturing from motorcycles to autos and lawnmowers.[4]

For a functional strategy to have the best chance of success, it should be built on a distinctive competency residing within that functional area. If a corporation does not have a distinctive competency in a particular functional area, that functional area could be a candidate for outsourcing.

The Sourcing Decision: Where Should Functions Be Housed?

Where should a function be housed? Should it be integrated within the organization or purchased from an outside contractor? **Outsourcing** is purchasing from someone else a product or service that had been previously provided internally. For example, DuPont contracts out project engineering and design to Morrison Knudsen; AT&T contracts its credit card processing to Total System Services; Northern Telecom, its electronic component manufacturing to Comptronix; and Eastman Kodak, its computer support services to Businessland. Outsourcing is becoming an increasingly important part of strategic decision making and an important way to increase efficiency and often quality. Firms competing in global industries must in particular search worldwide for the most appropriate suppliers. In a study of 30 firms, outsourcing resulted on average in a 9% reduction in costs and a 15% increase in capacity and quality.[5]

Management services and information systems were the first functional areas to be heavily outsourced. In a 1995 survey of 314 large U.S. firms, 26% outsourced benefits administration, 87% outsourced recordkeeping, and 59% outsourced administration and service.[6] Approximately 20% of U.S. companies now use some form of information technology outsourcing.[7] Sales, marketing, and customer service are now becoming likely candidates for outsourcing.[8] For example, United Parcel Service has turned to outside sources to run 65 customer service "call centers" employing 5,000 people.[9]

Sophisticated strategists, according to Quinn, are no longer thinking just of market share or vertical integration as the keys to strategic planning:

> Instead they concentrate on identifying those few core service activities where the company has or can develop: (1) a continuing strategic edge and (2) long-term streams of new products to satisfy future customer demands. They develop these competencies in greater depth than anyone else in the world. Then they seek to eliminate, minimize, or outsource activities where the company cannot be preeminent, unless those activities are essential to support or protect the chosen areas of strategic focus.[10]

The key to outsourcing is to purchase from outside only those activities that are not key to the company's distinctive competencies. Otherwise, the company may give up the very capabilities that made it successful in the first place—thus putting itself on the road to eventual decline. Therefore, in determining functional strategy, the strategist must:

- Identify the company's or business unit's core competencies.

- Ensure that the competencies are continually being strengthened.

- Manage the competencies in such a way that best preserves the competitive advantage they create.

An outsourcing decision depends on the fraction of total value added that the activity under consideration represents and by the amount of potential competitive advantage in that activity for the company or business unit. See a proposed outsourcing matrix in Figure 7.1. A firm should consider outsourcing any activity or function that has low potential for competitive advantage. If that activity constitutes only a small part of the total value of the firm's products or services, it should be purchased on the open market (assuming that quality providers of the activity are plentiful). If, however, the activity contributes highly to the company's products or services, the firm should purchase it through long-term contracts with trusted suppliers or distributors. A firm should always produce at least some of the activity or function (taper vertical integration) if that activity has the potential for providing the company some competitive advantage. Full vertical integration should only be considered, however, when that activity or function adds significant value to the company's products or services in addition to providing competitive advantage.

Outsourcing does, however, have some disadvantages. For example, GE's introduction of a new washing machine was delayed three weeks by production problems at a supplier's company to whom it had contracted out key work. Some companies have found themselves locked into long-term contracts with outside suppliers that are no longer competitive.[11] Some authorities propose that the cumulative effects of continued outsourcing steadily reduces a firm's ability to learn new skills and to develop new core competencies.[12] A study of 30 firms with outsourcing experience revealed that unsuccessful outsourcing efforts had three common characteristics:

- The firms' finance and legal departments and their vendors dominated the decision process.

- Vendors were not prequalified based on total capabilities.

- Short-term benefits dominated decision making.[13]

Marketing Strategy

Marketing strategy deals with pricing, selling, and distributing a product. Using a **market development** strategy, a company or business unit can (1) capture a larger share of an existing market for current products through market saturation and market penetra-

**Figure 7.1
Proposed
Outsourcing
Matrix**

Source: J. D. Hunger
and T. L. Wheelen,
"Proposed Outsourcing
Matrix." Copyright ©
1996 by Wheelen and
Hunger Associates.
Reprinted by
permission.

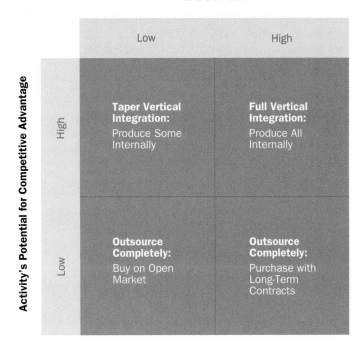

tion or (2) develop new markets for current products. Consumer product giants such as Procter & Gamble, Colgate-Palmolive, and Unilever are experts at using advertising and promotion to implement a market saturation/penetration strategy to gain the dominant market share in a product category. As seeming masters of the product life cycle, these companies are able to extend product life almost indefinitely through "new and improved" variations of product and packaging that appeal to most market niches. These companies also follow the second market development strategy by taking a successful product they market in one part of the world and marketing it elsewhere. Noting the success of their presoak detergents in Europe, for example, both P&G and Colgate successfully introduced this type of laundry product to North America under the trade names of Biz and Axion.

Using the **product development** strategy, a company or unit can (1) develop new products for *existing markets* or (2) develop new products for *new markets*. Church & Dwight has had great success following the first product development strategy by developing new products to sell to its current customers. Acknowledging the widespread appeal of its Arm & Hammer brand baking soda, the company generated new uses for its sodium bicarbonate by reformulating it as toothpaste, deodorant, and detergent. The company has also successfully followed the second product development strategy by developing pollution reduction products (using sodium bicarbonate compounds) for sale to coal-fired electric utility plants.

There are numerous other marketing strategies. For advertising and promotion, for example, a company or business unit can choose between a "push" or a "pull" marketing strategy. Many large food and consumer products companies in the United States and Canada have followed a **push strategy** by spending a large amount of money on trade promotion in order to gain or hold shelf space in retail outlets. Trade promotion includes discounts, in-store special offers, and advertising allowances designed to "push" products through the distribution system. The Kellogg Company recently decided to change its emphasis from a push to a **pull strategy**, in which advertising "pulls" the products through the distribution channels. The company now spends more money on consumer advertising designed to build brand awareness so that shoppers will ask for the products. Research has indicated that a high level of advertising (a key part of a pull strategy) is most beneficial to leading brands in a market.[14]

Other marketing strategies deal with distribution and pricing. Should a company use distributors and dealers to sell its products or should it sell directly to retailers? Gateway 2000, noted for only selling computers directly to the customer via telephone, decided in 1996 to sell "Destination," its combination computer television set, through CompUSA and Nobody Beats the Wiz chains of retail stores. The product was so novel that people were unwilling to buy the product unless they could personally view it in action. Another example was Sears Roebuck's decision to market brands of major home appliances other than its own Kenmore brand. Most appliance makers were very happy to sell their products through Sears' "Brand Central." After all, Sears sold one out of every four major home appliances sold in the United States. Maytag Corporation, however, had its reservations about changing its traditional distribution channels. As shown in the **Company Spotlight on Maytag Corporation** feature, the corporation chose not to sell its Maytag brand home appliances through Sears because management did not want to alienate existing Maytag dealers.

When pricing a new product, a company or business unit can follow one of two strategies. For new-product pioneers, **skim pricing** offers the opportunity to "skim the cream" from the top of the demand curve with a high price while the product is novel and competitors are few. **Penetration pricing**, in contrast, attempts to hasten market development and offers the pioneer the opportunity to use the experience curve to gain market share with a low price and dominate the industry. Depending on corporate and business unit objectives and strategies, either of these choices may be desirable to a particular company or unit. Penetration pricing is, however, more likely than skim pricing to raise a unit's operating profit in the long term.[15]

Financial Strategy

Financial strategy examines the financial implications of corporate and business-level strategic options and identifies the best financial course of action. It can also provide competitive advantage through a lower cost of funds and a flexible ability to raise capital to support a business strategy. Financial strategy usually attempts to maximize the financial value of the firm.

The tradeoff between achieving the desired debt-to-equity ratio and relying on internal long-term financing via cash flow is a key issue in financial strategy. Many small- and medium-sized companies such as Urschel Laboratories try to avoid all external sources of funds in order to avoid outside entanglements and to keep control of the company within the family. Many financial analysts believe, however, that only by financing through long-term debt can a corporation use financial leverage to boost earnings per share—thus raising stock price and the overall value of the company.

The desired level of current versus long-term investments has become a strategic issue. Although most companies usually choose to invest cash instead of hoarding it (to obtain a better return on investment), there are some exceptions. During the mid 1990s, U.S. auto companies together held more than $30 million in cash in short-term U.S. Treasury and corporate instruments. In past years, the auto firms had used cash earned during prosperous times to diversify into financial services, car rental, and aerospace companies. When the inevitable downturn occurred, the auto firms had been forced to divest their acquisitions and cut product development programs. This time, managers in

COMPANY SPOTLIGHT

Maytag Supports Dealers as Part of Its Marketing Strategy

In the late 1980s, Sears instituted its new "Brand Central" format to sell white goods. In addition to offering its own private brands, the retail giant planned to offer nationally known brands such as General Electric, Whirlpool, Amana, Jenn-Air, and Speedqueen. Except for its Jenn-Air products, Maytag Corporation chose not to join Sears' Brand Central concept. Some industry experts thought this to be a strange decision given that Sears alone sold one out of every four U.S. major home appliances. Why would Maytag ignore this key sales outlet?

Leonard Hadley, Chief Operating Officer of Maytag Corporation at the time, explained that the company did not want to antagonize its carefully nurtured appliance dealers who had always considered Sears their major retail competition. Maytag Company's emphasis on quality and higher price rather than market share as its business competitive strategy made the Maytag brand more dependent on appliance dealers than either General Electric or Whirlpool were. In addition, some Maytag people feared that Sears might use the Maytag brand's image to attract customers into the stores, but then persuade them to buy a less-expensive Sears brand carrying a higher markup.

MAYTAG CORPORATION

all three U.S. auto companies decided to save their money to get through the next recession. In response to arguments from financial analysts and shareholders that cash was not a very productive asset, Ford's Treasurer, Malcolm MacDonald, responded that the corporation wanted immediate access to cash for strategic reasons.[16]

A very popular financial strategy is the leveraged buy out (LBO). In a **leveraged buy out**, a company is acquired in a transaction financed largely by debt—usually obtained from a third party, such as an insurance company. Ultimately the debt is paid with money generated from the acquired company's operations or by sales of its assets. The acquired company, in effect, pays for its own acquisition! Management of the LBO is then under tremendous pressure to keep the highly leveraged company profitable. Unfortunately the huge amount of debt on the acquired company's books may actually cause its eventual decline unless it goes public once again.

The management of dividends to shareholders is an important part of a corporation's financial strategy. Corporations in fast-growing industries such as computers and computer software often do not declare dividends. They use the money they might have spent on dividends to finance rapid growth. If the company is successful, its growth in sales and profits is reflected in a higher stock price—eventually resulting in a hefty capital gain when shareholders sell their common stock. Other corporations such as electric utilities that do not face rapid growth must support the value of their stock by offering generous and consistent dividends.

Research and Development (R&D) Strategy

R&D strategy deals with product and process innovation and improvement. It also deals with the appropriate mix of different types of R&D (basic, product, or process) and with the question of how new technology should be accessed—internal development, external acquisition, or through strategic alliances.

Table 7.1 Research and Development Strategy and Competitive Advantage

	Technological Leadership	Technological Followership
Cost Advantage	Pioneer the lowest cost product design. Be the first firm down the learning curve. Create low-cost ways of performing value activities.	Lower the cost of the product or value activities by learning from the leader's experience. Avoid R&D costs through imitation.
Differentiation	Pioneer a unique product that increases buyer value. Innovate in other activities to increase buyer value.	Adapt the product or delivery system more closely to buyer needs by learning from the leader's experience.

Source: Adapted/reprinted with the permission of The Free Press, an imprint of Simon & Schuster, from *Competitive Advantage: Creating and Sustaining Superior Performance* by Michael E. Porter, p. 181. Copyright © 1985 by Michael E. Porter.

One of the R&D choices is to be either a **technological leader** in which one pioneers an innovation or a **technological follower** in which one imitates the products of competitors. Porter suggests that deciding to become a technological leader or follower can be a way of achieving either overall low cost or differentiation. (See Table 7.1.)

One example of an effective use of the *leader* R&D functional strategy to achieve a differentiation competitive advantage is Nike, Inc. Nike spends more than most in the industry on R&D to differentiate the performance of its athletic shoes from that of its competitors. As a result, its products have become the favorite of the serious athlete. An example of the use of the *follower* R&D functional strategy to achieve a low-cost competitive advantage is Dean Foods Company. "We're able to have the customer come to us and say, 'If you can produce X, Y, and Z product for the same quality and service, but at a lower price and without that expensive label on it, you can have the business,'" says Howard Dean, president of the company.[17]

An increasing number of companies are working with their suppliers to help them keep up with changing technology. They are beginning to realize that a firm cannot be competitive technologically only through internal development. For example, Chrysler Corporation's skillful use of parts suppliers to design everything from car seats to drive shafts has enabled it to spend consistently less money than its competitors to develop new car models. Strategic technology alliances are one way to combine the R&D capabilities of two companies. As mentioned earlier in Chapter 5, Maytag Company worked with one of its suppliers to apply fuzzy logic technology to its new IntelliSense™ dishwasher. The partnership enabled Maytag to complete the project in a shorter amount of time than if it had tried to do it alone.[18]

Operations Strategy

Operations strategy determines how and where a product or service is to be manufactured, the level of vertical integration in the production process, the deployment of physical resources, and relationships with suppliers. It should also deal with the optimum level of technology the firm should use in its operations processes. See the 🌐 **21st Century Global Society** feature to see how differences in national conditions can lead to differences in product design and manufacturing facilities from one country to another.

Advanced Manufacturing Technology (AMT) is revolutionizing operations world-wide and should continue to have a major impact as corporations strive to integrate diverse business activities using computer integrated design and manufacturing (CAD/CAM) principles. The use of CAD/CAM, flexible manufacturing systems, computer numerically controlled systems, automatically guided vehicles, robotics, manufacturing resource planning (MRP II), optimized production technology, and just-in-time contribute to increased flexibility, quick response time, and higher productivity. Such investments also act to increase the company's fixed costs and could cause significant problems if the company is unable to achieve economies of scale or scope.

A firm's manufacturing strategy is often affected by a product's life cycle. As the sales of a product increase, there will be an increase in production volume ranging from lot sizes as low as one in a **job shop** (one-of-a-kind production using skilled labor) through **connected line batch flow** (components are standardized; each machine functions like a job shop but is positioned in the same order as the parts are processed) to lot sizes as high as 100,000 or more per year for **flexible manufacturing systems** (parts are grouped into manufacturing families to produce a wide variety of mass-produced items) and **dedicated transfer lines** (highly automated assembly lines making one mass-produced product using little human labor). According to this concept, the product becomes standardized into a commodity over time in conjunction with increasing demand. Flexibility thus gives way to efficiency.[19] This concept of eventual reduced flexibility is, however, being increasingly challenged by the new concept of mass customization.

Increasing competitive intensity in many industries has forced companies to switch from traditional mass production using dedicated transfer lines to a continuous improvement production strategy. A **mass production** system was an excellent method to produce a large amount of low-cost, standard goods and services. Employees worked on narrowly defined, repetitious tasks under close supervision in a bureaucratic and hierarchical structure. Quality, however, often tended to be fairly low. Learning how to do something better was the prerogative of management; workers were expected only to learn what was assigned to them. This system tended to dominate manufacturing until the 1970s. Under the **continuous improvement** system developed by Japanese firms, empowered cross-functional teams strive constantly to improve production processes. Managers become more like coaches. The result is a large quantity of low-cost, standard goods and services, but with high quality. The key to continuous improvement is the acknowledgment that workers' experience and knowledge can help managers solve production problems and contribute toward tightening variances and reducing errors. Because continuous improvement enables firms to use the same low-cost competitive strategy as do mass production firms but at a significantly higher level of quality, it is rapidly replacing mass production as an operations strategy.

According to B. Joseph Pine in his book *Mass Customization: The New Frontier in Business Competition*, a number of companies are now experimenting with **mass customization** as an operations strategy.[20] In contrast to continuous improvement, mass customization requires flexibility and quick responsiveness. Appropriate for an ever-changing environment, mass customization requires that people, processes, units, and technology reconfigure themselves to give customers exactly what they want, when they want it. Managers coordinate independent, capable individuals. An efficient linkage system is crucial. The result is low-cost, high-quality, customized goods and services. Mass customization is having a significant impact on product development. Under a true mass customization system, no one knows exactly what the next customer will want. Therefore, no one can know exactly what product the company will be creating/producing next. Because it is becoming increasingly difficult to predict what product-market opportunity will

WHIRLPOOL ADJUSTS ITS MANUFACTURING STRATEGY TO LOCAL CONDITIONS

To better penetrate the growing markets in developing nations, Whirlpool decided to build a "world washer." This new type of washing machine was to be produced in Brazil, Mexico, and India. Lightweight, with substantially fewer parts than its U.S. counterpart, its performance was to be equal to or better than anything on the world market while being competitive in price with the most popular models in these markets. The goal was to develop a complete product, process, and facility design package that could be used in different countries with low initial investment. Originally the plan had been to make the same low-cost washer in identical plants in each of the three countries.

Significant differences in each of the three countries forced Whirlpool to change its product design to suit each nation's situation. According to Lawrence Kremer, Senior Vice-President of Global Technology and Operations, "Our Mexican affiliate, Vitromatic, has porcelain and glassmaking capabilities. Porcelain baskets made sense for them. Stainless steel became the preferred material for the others." Costs also affected decisions. "In India, for example, material costs may run as much as 200% to 800% higher than elsewhere, while labor and overhead costs are comparatively minimal," added Kremer. Another consideration were the garments to be washed in each country. For example, saris—the 18-foot lengths of cotton or silk with which Indian women drape themselves—needed special treatment in an Indian washing machine, forcing additional modifications.

Manufacturing facilities also varied from country to country. Brastemp, Whirlpool's Brazilian partner, built its plant of precast concrete to address the problems of high humidity. In India, however, the construction crew cast the concrete, allowed it to cure, and then using chain, block, and tackle, five or six men raised each three-ton slab into place. Instead of using one building, Mexican operations used two, one housing the flexible assembly lines and stamping operations, and an adjacent facility housing the injection molding and extrusion processes.

Source: A. A. Ullmann, "Whirlpool Corporation, 1993: A Metamorphosis," in Wheelen and Hunger, *Strategic Management and Business Policy,* 5th ed. (Reading, Mass.: Addison-Wesley, 1995), pp. 713–715.

open up next, it is harder to create a long-term vision of the company's products. Companies using mass customization often say "anything," "anywhere," and "any time." Peter Kann, CEO of Dow Jones, describes his company as providing "business and financial news and information however, wherever, and whenever customers want to receive it."[21] Another example of mass customization is the new "Personal Pair" system Levi Strauss introduced to combat the growing competition from private label jeans. The customer is measured at one of the company's Personal Pair outlets, the measurements are sent to Levi's by computer, and the made-to-order jeans arrive a few days later. The jeans cost about $10 more than an off-the-shelf pair.[22]

Purchasing Strategy

Purchasing strategy deals with obtaining the raw materials, parts, and supplies needed to perform the operations function. Some purchasing choices are multiple, sole, and parallel sourcing. Under **multiple sourcing**, the purchasing company orders a particular part from several vendors. Multiple sourcing has traditionally been considered superior to other purchasing approaches because (1) it forces suppliers to compete for the business of an important buyer, thus reducing purchasing costs; and (2) if one supplier could not deliver, another usually could, thus guaranteeing that parts and supplies would always be on hand when needed. Multiple sourcing was one way a purchasing firm could control the relationship with its suppliers. So long as suppliers could provide evidence that they could meet the product specifications, they were kept on the purchaser's list of acceptable vendors for specific parts and supplies. Unfortunately the common practice of accepting the lowest bid often compromised quality.

W. Edward Deming, a well-known management consultant, strongly recommended sole sourcing as the only manageable way to obtain high supplier quality. **Sole sourcing** relies on only one supplier for a particular part. Given his concern with designing quality into a product in its early stages of development, Deming argued that the buyer should work closely with the supplier at all stages. This reduces both cost and time spent on product design as well as improving quality. It can also simplify the purchasing company's production process by using the *just-in-time (JIT)* concept of the purchased parts arriving at the plant just when they are needed rather than keeping inventories. The concept of sole sourcing is being taken one step further in *JIT II*, in which vendor sales representatives actually have desks next to the purchasing company's factory floor, attend production status meetings, visit the R&D lab, and analyze the purchasing company's sales forecasts. These in-house suppliers then write sales orders for which the purchasing company is billed. Developed by Lance Dixon at Bose Corporation, JIT II is also being used at IBM, Honeywell, and Ingersoll-Rand. Karen Dale, purchasing manager for Honeywell's office supplies, said she was very concerned about confidentiality when JIT II was first suggested to her. Now she has five suppliers working with her 20 buyers and reports few problems.[23]

Sole sourcing reduces transactions costs and builds quality by having purchaser and supplier work together as partners rather than as adversaries. Sole sourcing means that more companies are going to have longer relationships with fewer suppliers. For example, the average computer company obtained 80% of its material from 22 suppliers in 1995 compared to 31 suppliers in 1992.[24] Sole sourcing does, however, have its limitations. If a supplier is unable to deliver a part, the purchaser has no alternative but to delay production. Multiple suppliers can provide the purchaser with better information about new technology and performance capabilities. The limitations of sole sourcing have led to the development of parallel sourcing. In **parallel sourcing,** two suppliers are the sole suppliers of two different parts, but they are also backup suppliers for each other's parts. In case one vendor cannot supply all of its parts on time, the other vendor would be asked to make up the difference.[25]

Logistics Strategy

Logistics strategy deals with the flow of products into and out of the manufacturing process. During the 1990s, two trends were evident: centralization and outsourcing. To gain logistical synergies across business units, corporations began centralizing logistics in the headquarters group. This centralized logistics group usually contains specialists with expertise in different transportation modes such as rail or trucking. They work to aggregate shipping volumes across the entire corporation to gain better contracts with shippers. Companies like Amoco Chemical, Georgia-Pacific, Marriott, and Union Carbide view the logistics function as an important way to differentiate themselves from the competition, to add value, and to reduce costs. As in purchasing, long-term relationships between carriers and shippers coupled with sophisticated information systems are part of this logistics strategy.[26]

Many companies have found that outsourcing of logistics reduces costs and improves delivery time. For example, Hewlett-Packard contracted with Roadway Logistics to manage its in-bound raw materials warehousing in Vancouver, Canada. Nearly 140 Roadway employees replaced 250 HP workers, who were transferred to other HP activities. According to George Gecowets, Executive Director of the Council of Logistics Management, increasing global competition should motivate U.S. companies to increase their outsourcing of the logistics function from 12% in 1995 to as much as 30% in a few years.[27]

Human Resource Management (HRM) Strategy

HRM strategy, among other things, addresses the issue of whether a company or business unit should hire a large number of low-skilled employees who receive low pay, perform repetitive jobs, and most likely quit after a short time (the McDonald's restaurant strategy) or hire skilled employees who receive relatively high pay and are cross-trained to participate in *self-managed work teams*. As work increases in complexity, the more suited it is for teams, especially in the case of innovative product development efforts. A recent survey of 476 Fortune 1000 U.S. companies revealed that although only 7% of their workforce was organized into self-managed teams, half the companies reported that they would be relying significantly more on them in the years ahead.[28] Research indicates that the use of work teams leads to increased quality and productivity.[29]

Many North American and European companies are not only using an increasing amount of part-time and *temporary employees*, they are also experimenting with leasing temporary employees from employee leasing companies. To reduce costs and obtain increased flexibility, companies in the United States hired around two million temporary workers in 1994 (up from 600 thousand in 1984).[30] This number is expected to double by the end of the century.

Companies are finding that having a *diverse workforce* can be a competitive advantage. DuPont, for example, found that a group of African-American employees were able to create promising new markets for its agricultural products by focusing on black farmers. DuPont's use of multinational teams has helped the company develop and market products internationally. McDonald's has discovered that older workers perform as well, if not better, than younger employees. According to Edward Rensi, CEO of McDonald's USA: "We find these people to be particularly well motivated, with a sort of discipline and work habits hard to find in younger employees."[31]

Information Systems Strategy

Corporations are increasingly adopting **information systems strategies** in that they are turning to information systems technology to provide business units with competitive advantage. When Federal Express first provided its customers with *PowerShip* computer software to store addresses, print shipping labels, and track package location, its sales jumped significantly. UPS soon followed with its own *MaxiShips* software. Viewing its information system as a distinctive competency, Federal Express continued to push for further advantage against UPS by using its web site to enable customers to track their packages.

Many companies are also attempting to use information systems to form closer relationships with both their customers and suppliers through sophisticated intranets. For example, General Electric's Trading Process Network allows suppliers to electronically download GE's requests for proposals, view diagrams of parts specifications, and communicate with GE purchasing managers. According to Robert Livingston, GE's head of worldwide sourcing for the Lighting Division, going on the web reduces processing time by one-third.[32]

7.2   Strategies to Avoid

Several strategies, which could be considered corporate, business, or functional, are very dangerous. Managers who have made a poor analysis or lack creativity may be trapped into considering some of the following **strategies to avoid:**

- **Follow the Leader.** Imitating a leading competitor's strategy might seem to be a good idea, but it ignores a firm's particular strengths and weaknesses and the possibility that the leader may be wrong. Fujitsu Ltd., the world's second-largest computer maker, was driven since the 1960s by the sole ambition of catching up to IBM. Like IBM, Fujitsu competed primarily as a mainframe computer maker. So devoted was it to catching IBM, however, that it failed to notice that the mainframe business was reaching maturity and by the 1990s was no longer growing.

- **Hit Another Home Run.** If a company is successful because it pioneered an extremely successful product, it tends to search for another superproduct that will ensure growth and prosperity. Like betting on long shots at the horse races, the probability of finding a second winner is slight. Polaroid spent a lot of money developing an "instant" movie camera, but the public ignored it.

- **Arms Race.** Entering into a spirited battle with another firm for increased market share might increase sales revenue, but that increase will probably be more than offset by increases in advertising, promotion, R&D, and manufacturing costs. Since the deregulation of airlines, price wars and rate "specials" have contributed to the low profit margins or bankruptcy of many major airlines such as Eastern and Continental.

- **Do Everything.** When faced with several interesting opportunities, management might tend to leap at all of them. At first, a corporation might have enough resources to develop each idea into a project, but money, time, and energy are soon exhausted as the many projects demand large infusions of resources.

- **Losing Hand.** A corporation might have invested so much in a particular strategy that top management is unwilling to accept its failure. Believing that it has too much invested to quit, the corporation continues to throw "good money after bad." Pan American Airlines, for example, chose to sell its Pan Am Building and Intercontinental Hotels, the most profitable parts of the corporation, to keep its money-losing airline flying. Continuing to suffer losses, the company followed this strategy of shedding assets for cash, until it had sold off everything and went bankrupt.

7.3   Strategic Choice: Selection of the Best Strategy

After the *pros* and *cons* of the potential strategic alternatives have been identified and evaluated, one must be selected for implementation. By now, it is likely that many feasible alternatives will have emerged. How is the best strategy determined?

Perhaps the most important criterion is the ability of the proposed strategy to deal with the specific strategic factors developed earlier in the SWOT analysis. If the alternative doesn't take advantage of environmental opportunities and corporate strengths, and lead away from environmental threats and corporate weaknesses, it will probably fail.

Another important consideration in the selection of a strategy is the ability of each alternative to satisfy agreed-on objectives with the least resources and the fewest negative side effects. It is, therefore, important to develop a tentative implementation plan so that the difficulties that management is likely to face are addressed. This should be done in light of societal trends, the industry, and the company's situation based on the construction of scenarios.

Constructing Corporate Scenarios

Corporate scenarios are *pro forma* balance sheets and income statements that forecast the effect each alternative strategy and its various programs will likely have on division and corporate return on investment. In a survey of Fortune 500 firms, 84% reported using computer simulation models in strategic planning. Most of these were simply spreadsheet-based simulation models dealing with "what if" questions.[33]

The recommended scenarios are simply extensions of the industry scenarios discussed in Chapter 3. If, for example, industry scenarios suggest the probable emergence of a strong market demand in a specific country for certain products, a series of alternative strategy scenarios can be developed. The alternative of acquiring another firm having these products in that country can be compared with the alternative of a green-field development (building new operations in that country). Using three sets of estimated sales figures (optimistic, pessimistic, and most likely) for the new products over the next five years, the two alternatives can be evaluated in terms of their effect on future company performance as reflected in its probable future financial statements. *Pro forma* (estimated future) balance sheets and income statements can be generated with spreadsheet software, such as Lotus 1-2-3 or Excel, on a personal computer.

To construct a scenario, follow these steps:

- **First**, use *industry scenarios* (discussed earlier in Chapter 3) to develop a set of assumptions about the task environment (in the specific country under consideration). For example, 3M requires the general manager of each business unit to describe annually what his or her industry will look like in 15 years. List *optimistic, pessimistic,* and *most likely* assumptions for key economic factors such as the GDP (Gross Domestic Product), CPI (Consumer Price Index), and prime interest rate, and for other key external strategic factors such as governmental regulation and industry trends. *This needs to be done for every country/region in which the corporation has significant operations that will be affected by each strategic alternative.* These same underlying assumptions should be listed for each of the alternative scenarios to be developed.

- **Second**, develop *common-size financial statements* (discussed in Chapter 10) for the company's or business unit's previous years, to serve as the basis for the trend analysis projections of pro forma financial statements. Use the *Scenario Box* form in Table 7.2.
  - (a) Use the historical common-size percentages to estimate the level of revenues, expenses, and other categories in estimated pro forma statements for future years.
  - (b) Develop for each strategic alternative a set of *optimistic, pessimistic,* and *most likely* assumptions about the impact of key variables on the company's future financial statements.
  - (c) Forecast three sets of sales and cost of goods sold figures for at least five years into the future.
  - (d) Analyze historical data and make adjustments based on the environmental assumptions listed earlier. Do the same for other figures that can vary significantly.
  - (e) Assume for other figures that they will continue in their historical relationship to sales or some other key determining factor. Plug in expected inventory levels, accounts receivable, accounts payable, R&D expenses, advertising and promotion expenses, capital expenditures, and debt payments (assuming that debt is used to finance the strategy), among others.

Table 7.2 **Scenario Box for Use in Generating Financial Pro Forma Statements**

Factor	Last Year	Historical Average	Trend Analysis	Projections[1] 19—			19—			19—			Comments
				O	P	ML	O	P	ML	O	P	ML	
GDP													
CPI													
Other													
Sales units													
Dollars													
COGS													
Advertising and marketing													
Interest expense													
Plant expansion													
Dividends													
Net profits													
EPS													
ROI													
ROE													
Other													

Note:
1. **O** = Optimistic; **P** = Pessimistic; **ML** = Most Likely.

Source: T. L. Wheelen and J. D. Hunger. Copyright © 1993 by Wheelen and Hunger Associates. Reprinted by permission.

(f) Consider not only historical trends, but also programs that might be needed to implement each alternative strategy (such as building a new manufacturing facility or expanding the sales force).

- **Third**, construct detailed **pro forma financial statements** for each strategic alternative.
    (a) List the actual figures from this year's financial statements in the left column of the spreadsheet.
    (b) List to the right of this column the optimistic figures for years one through five.
    (c) Go through this same process with the same strategic alternative, but now list the pessimistic figures for the next five years.
    (d) Do the same with the most likely figures.
    (e) Develop a similar set of *optimistic* (O), *pessimistic* (P), and *most likely* (ML) pro forma statements for the second strategic alternative. This process generates six different pro forma scenarios reflecting three different situations (O, P, and ML) for two strategic alternatives.
    (f) Calculate financial ratios and common-size income statements, and balance sheets to accompany the pro formas.
    (g) Compare the assumptions underlying the scenarios with these financial statements and ratios to determine the feasibility of the scenarios. For example, if cost of goods sold drops from 70% to 50% of total sales revenue in the pro forma income statements, this drop should result from a change in the production process or a shift to cheaper raw materials or labor costs, rather than from a failure to keep the cost of goods sold in its usual

percentage relationship to sales revenue when the predicted statement was developed.

The result of this detailed scenario construction should be anticipated net profits, cash flow, and net working capital for each of three versions of the two alternatives for five years into the future. A strategist might want to go further into the future if the strategy is expected to have a major impact on the company's financial statements beyond five years. The result of this work should provide sufficient information on which forecasts of the likely feasibility and probable profitability of each of the strategic alternatives could be based.

Obviously these scenarios can quickly become very complicated, especially if three sets of acquisition prices and development costs are calculated. Nevertheless this sort of detailed "what if" analysis is needed to realistically compare the projected outcome of each reasonable alternative strategy and its attendant programs, budgets, and procedures. Regardless of the quantifiable pros and cons of each alternative, the actual decision will probably be influenced by several subjective factors like those described in the following sections.

Management's Attitude Toward Risk

The attractiveness of a particular strategic alternative is partially a function of the amount of risk it entails. **Risk** is composed not only of the *probability* that the strategy will be effective, but also of the *amount of assets* the corporation must allocate to that strategy and the *length of time* the assets will be unavailable for other uses. Because of variation among countries in terms of customs, regulations, and resources, companies operating in global industries must deal with a greater amount of risk than firms operating only in one country. The greater the assets involved and the longer they are committed, the more likely top management is to demand a high probability of success.

This might be one reason that innovations seem to occur more often in small firms than in large, established corporations. The small firm managed by an entrepreneur is willing to accept greater risk than would a large firm of diversified ownership run by professional managers. It is one thing to take a chance if you are the primary shareholder and are not concerned with periodic changes in the value of the company's common stock. It is something else if the corporation's stock is widely held and acquisition-hungry competitors or takeover artists surround the company like sharks every time the company's stock price falls below some external assessment of the firm's value!

Pressures from the External Environment

The attractiveness of a strategic alternative is affected by its perceived compatibility with the key stakeholders in a corporation's task environment. Creditors want to be paid on time. Unions exert pressure for comparable wage and employment security. Governments and interest groups demand social responsibility. Shareholders want dividends. All of these pressures must be considered in the selection of the best alternative.

Strategic managers should ask four questions to assess the importance of stakeholder concerns in a particular decision:

1. What stakeholders are most crucial for corporate success?

2. How much of what they want are they likely to get under this alternative?

3. What are they likely to do if they don't get what they want?

4. What is the probability that they will do it?

Strategy makers should be better able to choose strategic alternatives that minimize external pressures and maximize the probability of gaining stakeholder support. In addition, top management can propose a **political strategy** to influence its key stakeholders. Some of the most commonly used political strategies are constituency building, political action committee contributions, advocacy advertising, lobbying, and coalition building.

Pressures from the Corporate Culture

If a strategy is incompatible with the corporate culture, the likelihood of its success is very low. Foot-dragging and even sabotage will result as employees fight to resist a radical change in corporate philosophy. Precedents from the past tend to restrict the kinds of objectives and strategies that can be seriously considered. The "aura" of the founders of a corporation can linger long past their lifetimes because their values have been imprinted on a corporation's members.

In evaluating a strategic alternative, the strategy makers must consider **corporate culture pressures** and assess the strategy's compatibility with the corporate culture. If there is little fit, management must decide if it should:

*   Take a chance on ignoring the culture.

*   Manage around the culture and change the implementation plan.

*   Try to change the culture to fit the strategy.

*   Change the strategy to fit the culture.

Further, a decision to proceed with a particular strategy without a commitment to change the culture or manage around the culture (both very tricky and time consuming) is dangerous. Nevertheless restricting a corporation to only those strategies that are completely compatible with its culture might eliminate from consideration the most profitable alternatives. (See Chapter 9 for more information on managing corporate culture.)

Needs and Desires of Key Managers

Even the most attractive alternative might not be selected if it is contrary to the needs and desires of important top managers. Personal characteristics and experience do affect a person's assessment of an alternative's attractiveness.[34] A person's ego may be tied to a particular proposal to the extent that all other alternatives are strongly lobbied against. As a result, he or she may have unfavorable forecasts altered so that they are more in agreement with the desired alternative.[35] A key executive might influence other people in top management to favor a particular alternative so that objections to it are ignored. For example, Nextel's CEO, Daniel Akerson, decided that the best place to locate the corporation's 500-person national headquarters would be the Washington, D.C., area, close to his own home.[36]

There is a tendency to maintain the status quo, which means that decision makers continue with existing goals and plans beyond the point when an objective observer would recommend a change in course. Some executives show a self-serving tendency to attribute the firm's problems not to their own poor decisions, but to environmental events out of their control such as government policies or a poor economic climate.[37] Negative information about a particular course of action to which a person is committed may be ignored because of a desire to appear competent or because of strongly held values regarding consistency. It may take a crisis or an unlikely event to cause strategic decision makers to seriously consider an alternative they had previously ignored or discounted.[38] For example, it wasn't until the CEO of ConAgra, a multinational food products company, had a heart attack that ConAgra started producing the Healthy Choice line of low-fat, low-cholesterol, low-sodium frozen-food entrees.

Process of Strategic Choice

There is an old story at General Motors:

> At a meeting with his key executives, CEO Alfred Sloan proposed a controversial strategic decision. When asked for comments, each executive responded with supportive comments and praise. After announcing that they were all in apparent agreement, Sloan stated that they were not going to proceed with the decision. Either his executives didn't know enough to point out potential downsides of the decision, or they were agreeing to avoid upsetting the boss and disrupting the cohesion of the group. The decision was delayed until a debate could occur over the pros and cons.[39]

Strategic choice is the evaluation of alternative strategies and selection of the best alternative. There is mounting evidence that when an organization is facing a dynamic environment, the best strategic decisions are not arrived at through **consensus** when everyone agrees on one alternative. They actually involve a certain amount of heated disagreement, and even conflict. This is certainly the case for firms operating in a global industry. See the **Strategy in a Changing World** feature for how Intel made a decision of critical significance to its future. Because unmanaged conflict often carries a high emotional cost, authorities in decision making propose that strategic managers use "programmed conflict" to raise different opinions, regardless of the personal feelings of the people involved.[40] Two techniques help strategic managers avoid the consensus trap that Alfred Sloan found:

1. **Devil's Advocate.** The devil's advocate originated in the medieval Roman Catholic Church as a way of ensuring that impostors were not canonized as saints. One trusted person was selected to find and present all reasons why the person should *not* be canonized. When applied to strategic decision making, the **devil's advocate** (who may be an individual or a group) is assigned to identify potential pitfalls and problems with a proposed alternative strategy in a formal presentation.

2. **Dialectical Inquiry.** The dialectic philosophy, which can be traced back to Plato and Aristotle and more recently to Hegel, involves combining two conflicting views—the *thesis* and the *antithesis*—into a *synthesis*. When applied to strategic decision making, **dialectical inquiry** requires that two proposals using different assumptions be generated for each alternative strategy under consideration. After advocates of each position present and debate the merits of their arguments before key decision makers, either one of the alternatives or a new compromise alternative is selected as the strategy to be implemented.

Research generally supports the conclusion that both the devil's advocate and dialectical inquiry are equally superior to consensus in decision making, especially when the firm's environment is dynamic. The debate itself, rather than its particular format, appears to improve the quality of decisions by formalizing and legitimizing constructive conflict and by encouraging critical evaluation. Both lead to better assumptions and recommendations and to a higher level of critical thinking among the people involved.[41]

STRATEGY IN A CHANGING WORLD

INTEL MAKES A STRATEGIC DECISION

The board of directors of Intel Corporation met in 1991 to decide the future of the company. They were being asked to vote on a proposal to commit $5 billion to making the next generation of microprocessor chip—five times the amount previously needed for the 486 chip and 50 times that for the earlier 386 chip. By 1991, Intel was already the world's largest manufacturer of microprocessors, the brains of personal computers. Its latest chip, the 486, was just beginning to take off. Its successor, the Pentium, was still in design. Intel's CEO, Andy Grove, received the startling estimate of the capital spending needed to make the Pentium just before the start of the board meeting. Grove hastily drew the spending curve on graph paper as the directors looked on.

In looking back on that board meeting, Grove remarked, "I remember people's eyes looking at that chart and getting big. I wasn't even sure I believed those numbers at the time." The proposal committed the company to building new factories—something Intel had been slow to do during the 1980s. According to Intel director Arthur Rock, a wrong decision would mean that the company would end up with a killing amount of overcapacity. "You had to have faith," said Rock. Based on Grove's presentation, the board decided to take the gamble. As a result, Intel's manufacturing expansion consumed $10 billion from 1991 through 1995. It was, however, timed perfectly for the boom in personal computer sales. Although rivals Motorola and IBM also began to add manufacturing capacity, none has been able to yet match the cash generated by Intel's 75% share of the microprocessor business. In this one crucial decision, Intel was able to turn the spiraling cost of competition into a competitive weapon.

Source: D. Clark, "All the Chips: A Big Bet Made Intel What It Is Today; Now It Wagers Again," *Wall Street Journal* (June 6, 1995), pp. A1, A5.

7.4 Development of Policies

The selection of the best strategic alternative is not the end of strategy formulation. The organization must now engage in **developing policies**. Policies define the broad guidelines for implementation. Flowing from the selected strategy, policies provide guidance for decision making and actions throughout the organization. At General Electric, for example, Chairman Welch insists that GE be Number One or Number Two wherever it competes. This policy gives clear guidance to managers throughout the organization. Another example of such a policy is Casey's General Stores' policy that a new service or product line may be added to its stores only when the product or service can be justified in terms of increasing store traffic.

Policies tend to be rather long lived and can even outlast the particular strategy that created them. Interestingly these general policies—such as "The customer is always right" or "Research and development should get first priority on all budget requests"—can become, in time, part of a corporation's culture. Such policies can make the implementation of specific strategies easier. They can also restrict top management's strategic options in the future. Thus a change in strategy should be followed quickly by a change in policies. Managing policy is one way to manage the corporate culture.

● *7.5* *Global Issues for the 21st Century*

- The **21st Century Global Society** feature in this chapter illustrates how Whirlpool adjusted its manufacturing strategy to suit local conditions in different parts of the world. Corporations operating internationally will constantly need to deal with the tradeoffs involved in producing one uniform, low-cost product for sale in all countries or producing a series of higher cost products modified to individual country tastes.

- For core competencies to be distinctive competencies, they must be superior to those of the competition. As more industries become hypercompetitive (discussed in Chapter 3), it will be increasingly difficult to keep a core competence distinctive. These resources are likely either to be imitated or made obsolete by new technologies.

- Outsourcing has become an important issue in all industries, especially in global industries such as automobiles where cost competition is fierce. General Motors, for example, was faced with a strike by its Canadian unions during 1996 when it wanted to outsource some operations. The Canadian unions were very concerned that such outsourcing would reduce union employment and increase the number of low-paying jobs. Expect this issue to continue in importance throughout the world as more industries become global.

- Just as a competitive strategy may need to vary from one region of the world to another, functional strategies may need to vary from region to region. When Mr. Donut expanded into Japan, for example, it had to market donuts not as breakfast, but as snack food. Because the Japanese had no breakfast coffee and donut custom, they preferred to eat the donuts in the afternoon or evening. Mr. Donut restaurants were thus located near railroad stations and supermarkets. All signs were in English to appeal to the Western interests of the Japanese.

- Even though shifting costly functions to the developing countries (either through outsourcing or transferring operations) has become an accepted way to reduce human resource costs, such a functional strategy is creating some problems. The United Nations enacted a convention in 1973 that called on nations to set 15 as the basic minimum work age, with 13 being the minimum for light work and 18 the minimum for hazardous work. Although many countries have ratified some parts of the agreement, some developing nations are ignoring it. Citing that as many as 250 million children between the ages of 5 and 14 work in low-paying jobs, the International Labor Organization is working to outlaw the practice beginning in 2000.[42]

Projections for the 21st Century

- From 1994 to 2010, the number of desktop PCs worldwide will double from 132 million to 278 million.

- From 1994 to 2010, the number of mobile PCs worldwide will more than triple from 18 million to 47 million.[43]

Discussion Questions

1. How can a corporation identify its core competencies? Its distinctive competencies?

2. When should a corporation or business unit outsource a function or activity?

3. Why is penetration pricing more likely than skim pricing to raise a company's or a business unit's operating profit in the long run?

4. How does mass customization support a business unit's competitive strategy?

5. What is the relationship of policies to strategies?

Key Terms

connected line batch flow (p. 167)
consensus (p. 176)
continuous improvement (p. 167)
core capability (p. 160)
core competency (p. 160)
corporate culture pressures (p. 175)
corporate scenarios (p. 172)
dedicated transfer lines (p. 167)
developing policies (p. 177)
devil's advocate (p. 176)
dialectical inquiry (p. 176)
distinctive competency (p. 160)
financial strategy (p. 164)
flexible manufacturing
    systems (p. 167)

functional strategy (p. 160)
HRM strategy (p. 170)
information systems strategy (p. 170)
job shop (p. 167)
leveraged buy out (p. 165)
logistics strategy (p. 169)
market development (p. 162)
marketing strategy (p. 162)
mass customization (p. 167)
mass production (p. 167)
multiple sourcing (p. 168)
operations strategy (p. 166)
outsourcing (p. 161)
parallel sourcing (p. 169)
penetration pricing (p. 164)

political strategy (p. 175)
pro forma financial statements (p. 173)
product development (p. 163)
pull strategy (p. 164)
purchasing strategy (p. 168)
push strategy (p. 163)
R&D strategy (p. 165)
risk (p. 173)
skim pricing (p. 164)
sole sourcing (p. 169)
strategic choice (p. 176)
strategies to avoid (p. 171)
technological follower (p. 166)
technological leader (p. 166)

Strategic Practice Exercise

Read the following example of a company that is attempting to use its functional expertise in information system technology to obtain a competitive advantage in its industry. Do you think it will succeed?

In October 1996 Federal Express (FedEx) announced plans to give away its "BusinessLink" software early in 1997 to enable thousands of companies to buy and sell goods on the Internet. The system was to allow businesses to tap into FedEx's central computer to build web sites promoting their goods on the World Wide Web. Customers would be able to view the catalogue on-line and order goods, pay for them, and arrange delivery—through FedEx, of course! FedEx had a highly regarded web site for

tracking its own delivery system, but this was its first venture into offering companies a way of doing business electronically.

FedEx planned to charge customers a transaction fee each time Federal Express processed an order made through the system. This fee was to average less than the average of a "few dollars" made to telephone order centers. There might also be a small setup fee when each customer went on-line. The company declined to specify how many customers it expected to sign up, except to say that it hoped to see thousands of software packages in use during 1997. The prime candidates were perceived to be rapidly growing businesses that already supplied a substantial volume of products to other businesses and whose products had a short shelf life. In 1996, approximately 425,000 customers shipped via FedEx using its Internet web site or other software.

At the time, analysts viewed FedEx's move as an unorthodox attempt to stake out a position on the crowded frontier of Internet commerce—an area predicted to grow from $40 million in 1995 to perhaps hundreds of billions of dollars in a decade. By offering free software and an easy route to Internet business, FedEx apparently hoped to lock up customers by using the software to capture shipping business. Critics thought the strategy to be far afield for a business based on moving parcels via airplanes and trucks. They remembered when FedEx introduced Zap Mail, a way to transmit document facsimiles, in the 1980s. The introduction of inexpensive fax machines forced FedEx to abandon Zap Mail, at a cost of $190 million.

Nevertheless FedEx executives were committed to doing something radical. The company had not been having the same rate of growth recently enjoyed by UPS, its major rival. Although not abandoning its primary logistics business, executives contended that the future of the company was in BusinessLink. According to Laurie Tucker, Senior Vice-President of Logistics and Electronic Commerce: "You're not going to see us going out buying up property and building million-square-foot warehouses. Been there. Done that."

Interestingly both AT&T and Microsoft also thought Internet commerce to be a good opportunity. Within the same month that FedEx announced its plan, AT&T and Microsoft announced their intentions to develop and provide software allowing Internet transactions.[44]

____ Does Federal Express need to have a core competency in information systems technology to achieve its strategy?

____ What are the pros and cons of FedEx's BusinessLink software strategy?

____ Will BusinessLink have any impact on FedEx's primary logistics business of moving packages?

____ What are the odds that FedEx will succeed with BusinessLink?

Notes

1. Arm & Hammer is a registered trademark of Church & Dwight Company, Inc.
2. G. Hamel, and S. K. Prahalad, *Competing for the Future* (Boston: Harvard Business School Press, 1994), pp. 202–207.
3. *Ibid*, p. 211.
4. P. J. Verdin, and P. J. Williamson, "Core Competencies, Competitive Advantage and Market Analysis: Forging the Links," in *Competence-Based Competition*, edited by G. Hamel and A. Heene (New York: John Wiley and Sons, 1994), pp. 83–84.
5. B. Kelley, "Outsourcing Marches On," *Journal of Business Strategy* (July/August 1995), p. 40.
6. T. A. Stewart, "Taking On the Last Bureaucracy," *Fortune* (January 15, 1996), pp. 105–106.
7. J. W. Verity, "Let's Order Out for Technology," *Business Week* (May 13, 1996), p. 47.
8. "Taking Outsourcing to Higher Strategic Levels," *1996 Strategic Outsourcing Conference* (The Conference Board: New York City, June 13, 1996).
9. R. Frank, "Efficient UPS Tries to Increase Efficiency," *Wall Street Journal* (May 24, 1995), pp. B1, B4.
10. J. B. Quinn, "The Intelligent Enterprise: A New Paradigm," *Academy of Management Executive* (November 1992), pp. 48–63.
11. J. A. Byrne, "Has Outsourcing Gone Too Far?" *Business Week* (April 1, 1996), pp. 26–28.
12. D. Lei, and M. A. Hitt, "Strategic Restructuring and Outsourcing: The Effect of Mergers and Acquisitions and LBOs on Building Firm Skills and Capabilities," *Journal of Management*, Vol. 21, No. 5 (1995), pp. 835–859.
13. Kelley, "Outsourcing Marches On," p. 40.
14. S. M. Oster, *Modern Competitive Analysis,* 2d ed. (New York: Oxford University Press, 1994), p. 93.
15. W. Redmond, "The Strategic Pricing of Innovative Products," *Handbook of Business Strategy, 1992/1993 Yearbook,* edited by H. E. Glass and M. A. Hovde (Boston: Warren, Gorham and Lamont, 1992), pp. 16.1–16.13.
16. G. Stern, and R. L. Simison, "Big Three Auto Companies Are Parked on a Cash Cache Exceeding $30 Billion," *Wall Street Journal* (February 7, 1996), p. A2.
17. T. Due, "Dean Foods Thrives on Regional Off-Brand Products," *Wall Street Journal* (September 17, 1987), p. A6.
18. S. Stevens, "Speeding the Signals of Change," *Appliance* (February 1995), p. 7.
19. J. R. Williams, and R. S. Novak, "Aligning CIM Strategies to Different Markets," *Long Range Planning* (February 1990), pp. 126–135.
20. B. J. Pine, *Mass Customization: The New Frontier in Business Competition* (Boston: Harvard Business School Press, 1993).
21. B. J. Pine II, B. Victor, and A. C. Boynton, "Making Mass Customization Work," *Harvard Business Review* (September-October 1993), p. 119.
22. G. Hamel, "Strategy as Revolution," *Harvard Business Review* (July-August, 1996), p. 73.
23. F. R. Bleakley, "Some Companies Let Supplies Work on Site and Even Place Orders," *Wall Street Journal* (January 13, 1995), pp. A1, A6.

24. "Quality News," *The Quality Observer* (March 1996), p. 24.

25. J. Richardson, "Parallel Sourcing and Supplier Performance in the Japanese Automobile Industry," *Strategic Management Journal* (July 1993), pp. 339–350.

26. T. Richman, "Logistics Management: How 20 Best-Practice Companies Do It," *Harvard Business Review* (September-October 1995), pp. 11–12.

27. J. Bigness, "In Today's Economy, There Is Big Money To Be Made in Logistics," *Wall Street Journal* (September 6, 1995), pp. A1, A9.

28. B Dumaine, "Who Needs a Boss?" *Fortune* (May 7, 1990), pp. 52–60.

29. R. D. Banker, J. M. Field, R. G. Schroeder, and K. K. Sinha, "Impact of Work Teams on Manufacturing Performance: A Longitudinal Field Study," *Academy of Management Journal* (August 1996), pp. 867–890.

30. M. Cadden, and B. Laird, "Rising Market for Temps," *USA Today* (May 8, 1995), p. B1; J. Fierman, "The Contingency Work Force," *Fortune* (January 24, 1994), pp. 30–36.

31. K. Labich, "Making Diversity Pay," *Fortune* (September 9, 1996), pp. 177–180.

32. T. Smart, "Jack Welch's Cyber-Czar," *Business Week* (August 5, 1996), p. 83.

33. D. K. Sinha, "Strategic Planning in the Fortune 500," *Handbook of Business Strategy, 1991/1992 Yearbook,* edited by H. E. Glass and M. A. Hovde (Boston: Warren, Gorham and Lamont, 1991), pp. 9.6–9.8.

34. B. B. Tyler, and H. K. Steensma. "Evaluating Technological Collaborative Opportunities: A Cognitive Modeling Perspective," *Strategic Management Journal* (Summer 1995), pp. 43–70.

35. C. S. Galbraith, and G. B. Merrill, "The Politics of Forecasting: Managing the Truth," *California Management Review* (Winter 1996), pp. 29–43.

36. M. Leuchter, "The Rules of the Game," *Forecast* (May/June 1996), pp. 16–23.

37. V. L. Barker III, and P. S. Barr, "Why Is Performance Declining and What Road Leads to Recovery? An Empirical Examination of the Link Between Top Management Causal Attributions and Strategic Change During Turnaround Attempts," paper presented to *Academy of Management,* Dallas, Texas (August 1994).

38. J. Ross, and B. M. Staw, "Organizational Escalation and Exit: Lessons from the Shoreham Nuclear Power Plant," *Academy of Management Journal* (August 1993), pp. 701–732; P. W. Mulvey, J. F. Veiga, and P. M. Elsass, "When Teammates Raise a White Flag," *Academy of Management Executive* (February 1996), pp. 40–49.

39. R. A. Cosier, and C. R. Schwenk, "Agreement and Thinking Alike: Ingredients for Poor Decisions," *Academy of Management Executive* (February 1990), p. 69.

40. A. C. Amason, "Distinguishing the Effects of Functional and Dysfunctional Conflict On Strategic Decision Making: Resolving a Paradox for Top Management Teams," *Academy of Management Journal* (February 1996), pp. 123–148.

41. D. M. Schweiger, W. R. Sandberg, and P. L. Rechner, "Experiential Effects of Dialectical Inquiry, Devil's Advocacy, and Consensus Approaches to Strategic Decision Making," *Academy of Management Journal* (December 1989), pp. 745–772; G. Whyte, "Decision Failures: Why They Occur and How to Prevent Them," *Academy of Management Executive* (August 1991), pp. 23–31; R. L. Priem, D. A. Harrison, and N. K. Muir, "Structured Conflict and Consensus Outcomes in Group Decision Making," *Journal of Management,* Vol. 21, No. 4 (1995), pp. 691–710.

42. "30 Nations Want Rules to Restrict Child Labor," *St. Petersburg Times* (February 27, 1997), p. 6E.

43. J. Warner, "21st Century Capitalism: Snapshot of the Next Century," *Business Week* (November 18, 1994), p. 194.

44. Based on information in D. A. Blackmon, "FedEx Plans to Establish a Marketplace in Cyberspace," *Wall Street Journal* (October 9, 1996), p. B4.

Chapter 8

Strategy Implementation:
Organizing for Action

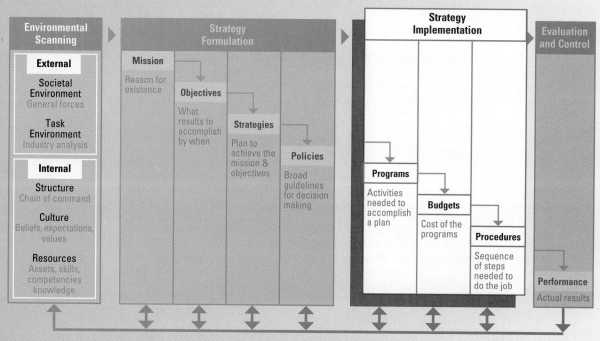

Feedback/Learning

Pepsico, Inc., the maker of Pepsi Cola, was not pleased with only having 10% of the soft drink market in Brazil—the third largest soft-drink market in the world after the United States and Mexico. Coca-Cola, in contrast, controlled more than 50% of the market. Coke had successfully consolidated its many independent local bottlers into a set of regional bottlers that worked well together. The new regional Coke bottlers had close local connections, large capital budgets, and a solid distribution system. To combat Coke's entrenched position, Pepsico formulated an ambitious growth strategy in 1994. It wanted to achieve at least 20% share of Brazil's main urban markets by selling more than 250 million cases annually. To manage this growth strategy, Pepsico selected Charles Beach as its partner. After successfully building Pepsico's market shares in both Puerto Rico and Argentina, Beach was offered the Brazilian franchise as well. Beach used his bottling company, Buenos Aires Embotelladora SA (known simply as Baesa) to expand soft drink production and market share. With Pepsico's encouragement, Baesa built four Brazilian plants with a total capacity of 250 million cases of soft drinks—more than twice Pepsico's highest amount of sales in Brazil. Rather than distributing its products via beer trucks (as did most of the soft-drink companies in Brazil), Baesa built its own distribution fleet by purchasing 700 new trucks. The company introduced four new flavors of its Kas line of juice-based sodas that Pepsico had formulated especially for Brazil—offering them not just in the usual returnable bottles, but also in cans and plastic containers. To the amazement of analysts, Baesa and Pepsico pledged to have the Brazilian operations running within a year.

Operating problems plagued the company from the start. The new bottling plants were often forced to close down lines because of rushed installation and insufficient employee training. Baesa found itself discarding ten times as many bent or punctured cans as did its competitors. Management turnover was a serious problem. Many managers were unable to keep up with Baesa's fast pace and Beach's conflicting signals. At one point, Beach fired more than 20 executives who had been hired from other multinationals after they had been on the job only three months! Even though Baesa's debt had increased from $15.4 million in 1993 (before the Brazilian expansion) to $374 million in 1995, it planned to purchase two additional Brazilian bottling plants. By 1996, Baesa's debt reached $745 million.

In May 1996, Pepsico announced that Beach had been relieved of operational responsibility and that it would assume control of Baesa's operations. In August, Baesa announced a quarterly loss of $250 million. The bottler defaulted on $34 million in debt payments. Sales had not met expectations. In addition to selling some of its franchises, Baesa closed one of its new plants and laid off more than 1,500 workers. Pepsico's aggressive Brazilian growth strategy had failed. According to Craig Weatherup, Pepsico's new head of global beverages, "I guess we got a little ahead of our headlights. We may have gone too fast."[1]

8.1   Strategy Implementation

Strategy implementation is the sum total of the activities and choices required for the execution of a strategic plan. It is *the process by which strategies and policies are put into action through the development of programs, budgets, and procedures.* Although implementation is usually considered after strategy has been formulated, implementation is a key part of strategic management. Strategy formulation and strategy implementation should thus be considered as two sides of the same coin. Poor implementation has been blamed for a number of strategic failures. For example, half of all acquisitions fail to achieve what was expected of them, and one out of four international ventures do not succeed.[2] Pepsico's failed expansion in Brazil is one example of how a good strategy can result in a disaster through poor strategy implementation.

To begin the implementation process, strategy makers must consider these questions:

- *Who* are the people who will carry out the strategic plan?

- *What* must be done to align the company's operations in the new intended direction?

- *How* is everyone going to do what is needed?

These questions and similar ones should have been addressed initially when the pros and cons of strategic alternatives were analyzed. They must also be addressed again before appropriate implementation plans can be made. Unless top management can answer these basic questions satisfactorily, even the best planned strategy is unlikely to provide the desired outcome.

A survey of 93 Fortune 500 firms revealed that over half of the corporations experienced the following ten problems when they attempted to implement a strategic change. These problems are listed in order of frequency.

1. Implementation took more time than originally planned.

2. Unanticipated major problems arose.

3. Activities were ineffectively coordinated.

4. Competing activities and crises took attention away from implementation.

5. The involved employees had insufficient capabilities to perform their jobs.

6. Lower-level employees were inadequately trained.

7. Uncontrollable external environmental factors created problems.

8. Departmental managers provided inadequate leadership and direction.

9. Key implementation tasks and activities were poorly defined.

10. The information system inadequately monitored activities.[3]

Pepsico experienced almost all of these problems in its Brazilian expansion—all except the first one. Pepsico's "ready, fire, aim" corporate culture would not tolerate a slow deliberate implementation process. Most of its Brazilian problems resulted from the corporation's unwillingness to implement its strategy at anything but breakneck speed.

- Pepsico selected a relatively inexperienced manager to implement its expansion strategy. In a hurry to begin implementation, it failed to question Charles Beach's past. As a manager at a North Carolina Coca-Cola bottler, Beach had pleaded no contest in 1987 to a price-fixing charge. Beach's optimistic aggressiveness fit well with Pepsico's high-pressured, fast-moving corporate culture.

- Pepsico pushed Beach too fast. After building the Puerto Rican franchise, Beach was awarded the Argentina franchise in 1989. By 1994, Beach had been awarded the entire Southern Cone of South America—ten times the size of the market he had managed the year before. In contrast, Coca-Cola seasons even its largest bottlers over several years, letting them add to their territory slowly. According to one Salomon Brothers analyst, "Beach was a good operator, but he didn't have the management experience to take on the whole Southern Cone in one year."

- Both Pepsico and Beach's Baesa company assumed that a hard-hitting, fast-moving expansion strategy would make up for any slippage in implementation details. Over one year's time, Baesa built four new state-of-the-art bottling plants and a completely new distribution system to sell untested soft-drink products. People were hired quickly and put into key positions with insufficient training. No time was allowed to develop and coordinate implementation procedures. Even the infusion of money and talent from Pepsico was unable to keep the Brazilian operations from deteriorating into chaos.[4]

8.2   Who Implements Strategy?

Depending on how the corporation is organized, those who implement strategy will probably be a much more diverse set of people than those who formulate it. In most large, multi-industry corporations, the implementers are everyone in the organization. Vice-presidents of functional areas and directors of divisions or SBUs work with their subordinates to put together large-scale implementation plans. Plant managers, project managers, and unit heads put together plans for their specific plants, departments, and units. Therefore, every operational manager down to the first-line supervisor and every employee is involved in some way in the implementing of corporate, business, and functional strategies.

Many of the people in the organization who are crucial to successful strategy implementation probably have little to do with the development of the corporate and even business strategy. Therefore, they might be entirely ignorant of the vast amount of data and work that went into the formulation process. Unless changes in mission, objectives, strategies, and policies and their importance to the company are communicated clearly to all operational managers, there can be a lot of resistance and foot-dragging. Managers might hope to influence top management into abandoning its new plans and returning to its old ways. This is one reason why involving people from all organizational levels in the formulation and in the implementation of strategy tends to result in better organizational performance.

8.3   What Must Be Done?

The managers of divisions and functional areas work with their fellow managers to develop programs, budgets, and procedures for the implementation of strategy. They also work to achieve synergy among the divisions and functional areas in order to establish and maintain a company's distinctive competence.

Developing Programs, Budgets, and Procedures

Programs

The purpose of a **program** is to make the strategy action-oriented. For example, assume Ajax Continental chose forward vertical integration as its best strategy for growth. It purchased existing retail outlets from another firm (Jones Surplus) instead of building its own. To integrate the new stores into the company, various programs would now have to be developed:

1. A restructuring program to move the Jones Surplus stores into Ajax Continental's marketing chain of command so that store managers report to regional managers, who report to the merchandising manager, who reports to the vice-president in charge of marketing.

2. An advertising program. ("Jones Surplus is now a part of Ajax Continental. Prices are lower. Selection is better.")

3. A training program for newly hired store managers and for those Jones Surplus managers the corporation has chosen to keep.

4. A program to develop reporting procedures that will integrate the Jones Surplus stores into Ajax Continental's accounting system.

5. A program to modernize the Jones Surplus stores and to prepare them for a "grand opening."

Budgets

After programs have been developed, the **budget** process begins. Planning a budget is the last real check a corporation has on the feasibility of its selected strategy. An ideal strategy might be found to be completely impractical only after specific implementation programs are costed in detail.

Procedures

After the program, divisional, and corporate budgets are approved, standard operating **procedures (SOPs)** must be developed. They typically detail the various activities that must be carried out to complete a corporation's programs. Once in place, they must be updated to reflect any changes in technology as well as in strategy. In the case of Ajax Corporation's acquisition of Jones Surplus' retail outlets, new operating procedures must be established for, among others, in-store promotions, inventory ordering, stock selection, customer relations, credits and collections, warehouse distribution, pricing, paycheck timing, grievance handling, and raises and promotions. These procedures ensure that the day-to-day store operations will be consistent over time (that is, next week's work activities will be the same as this week's) and consistent among stores (that is, each store will operate in the same manner as the others). For example, to ensure that its policies are carried out to the letter in every one of its fast-food retail outlets, McDonald's has done an excellent job of developing very detailed procedures (and policing them!).

Achieving Synergy

One of the goals to be achieved in strategy implementation is synergy between and among functions and business units. This is the reason why corporations commonly reorganize after an acquisition. **Synergy** is said to exist for a divisional corporation if the return on investment (ROI) of each division is greater than what the return would be if each division were an independent business. The acquisition or development of additional product lines is often justified on the basis of achieving some advantages of scale in one or more of a company's functional areas. For example, when Ralston Purina acquired Union Carbide's Eveready and Energizer lines of batteries, Ralston's CEO argued that his company would earn better profit margins on batteries than Union Carbide because of Ralston's expertise in developing and marketing branded consumer products. Ralston Purina felt it could lower the costs of the batteries by taking advantage of synergies in advertising, promotion, and distribution.

8.4   How Is Strategy to Be Implemented? Organizing for Action

Before plans can lead to actual performance, a corporation should be appropriately organized, programs should be adequately staffed, and activities should be directed toward achieving desired objectives. (*Organizing activities are reviewed briefly in this chapter; staffing, directing, and control activities are discussed in Chapters 9 and 10.*)

Any change in corporate strategy is very likely to require some sort of change in the way an organization is structured and in the kind of skills needed in particular positions. Managers must, therefore, closely examine the way their company is structured in order to decide what, if any, changes should be made in the way work is accomplished. Should activities be grouped differently? Should the authority to make key decisions be centralized at headquarters or decentralized to managers in distant locations? Should the company be managed like a "tight ship" with many rules and controls, or "loosely" with few rules and controls? Should the corporation be organized into a "tall" structure with many layers of managers, each having a narrow span of control (that is, few employees per supervisor) to better control his or her subordinates; or should it be organized into a "flat" structure with fewer layers of managers, each having a wide span of control (that is, more employees per supervisor) to give more freedom to his or her subordinates? For example, Ford had a fairly tall structure with 15 layers of managers, whereas Toyota had a relatively flat structure (for an automaker) composed of seven layers. Was Toyota's or Ford's structure "better"?

Structure Follows Strategy

In a classic study of large U.S. corporations such as DuPont, General Motors, Sears, and Standard Oil, Alfred Chandler concluded that **structure follows strategy**—that is, changes in corporate strategy lead to changes in organizational structure.[5] He also concluded that organizations follow a pattern of development from one kind of structural arrangement to another as they expand. According to Chandler, these structural changes occur because the old structure, having been pushed too far, has caused inefficiencies that have become too obviously detrimental to bear. Chandler, therefore, proposed the following as the sequence of what occurs:

1. New strategy is created.

2. New administrative problems emerge.

3. Economic performance declines.

4. New appropriate structure is invented.

5. Profit returns to its previous level.

Chandler found that in their early years, corporations such as DuPont tend to have a centralized functional organizational structure that is well suited to producing and selling a limited range of products. As they add new product lines, purchase their own sources of supply, and create their own distribution networks, they become too complex for highly centralized structures. To remain successful, this type of organization needs to shift to a decentralized structure with several semiautonomous divisions (referred to in Chapter 4 as divisional structure).

Alfred P. Sloan, past CEO of General Motors, detailed how GM conducted such structural changes in the 1920s.[6] He saw decentralization of structure as "centralized policy determination coupled with decentralized operating management." After top management had developed a strategy for the total corporation, the individual divisions (Chevrolet, Buick, and so on) were free to choose how to implement that strategy. Patterned after DuPont, GM found the decentralized multidivisional structure to be extremely effective in allowing the maximum amount of freedom for product development. Return on investment was used as a financial control. (*This measure is discussed in more detail in Chapter 10.*)

Research generally supports Chandler's proposition that structure follows strategy (as well as the reverse proposition that structure influences strategy).[7] As mentioned earlier, changes in the environment tend to be reflected in changes in a corporation's strategy, thus leading to changes in a corporation's structure. Strategy, structure, and the environment need to be closely aligned; otherwise, organizational performance will likely suffer.[8] For example, a business unit following a differentiation strategy needs more freedom from headquarters to be successful than does another unit following a low-cost strategy.[9]

Although it is agreed that organizational structure must vary with different environmental conditions, which, in turn, affect an organization's strategy, there is no agreement about an optimal organizational design. What was appropriate for DuPont and General Motors in the 1920s might not be appropriate today. Firms in the same industry do, however, tend to organize themselves similarly. For example, automobile manufacturers tend to emulate General Motors' divisional concept, whereas consumer-goods producers tend to emulate the brand-management concept (a type of matrix structure) pioneered by Procter & Gamble Company. The general conclusion seems to be that firms following similar strategies in similar industries tend to adopt similar structures.

Stages of Corporate Development

Successful corporations tend to follow a pattern of structural development as they grow and expand. Beginning with the simple structure of the entrepreneurial firm (in which everybody does everything), they usually (if they are successful) get larger and organize along functional lines with marketing, production, and finance departments. With continuing success, the company adds new product lines in different industries and organizes itself into interconnected divisions. The differences among these three structural **stages of corporate development** in terms of typical problems, objectives, strategies, reward systems and other characteristics are specified in detail in Table 8.1.

Stage I: Simple Structure

Stage I is typified by the entrepreneur, who founds the company to promote an idea (product or service). The entrepreneur tends to make all the important decisions personally and is involved in every detail and phase of the organization. The Stage I company has little formal structure, which allows the entrepreneur to directly supervise the activities of every employee (see Figure 4.4 for an illustration of the simple, functional, and divisional structures). Planning is usually short range or reactive. The typical managerial functions of planning, organizing, directing, staffing, and controlling are usually performed to a very limited degree, if at all. The greatest strengths of a Stage I corporation are its flexibility and dynamism. The drive of the entrepreneur energizes the organization in its struggle for growth. Its greatest weakness is its extreme reliance on the entrepreneur to decide general strategies as well as detailed procedures. If the entrepreneur falters, the company usually flounders. This is often referred to as a **crisis of leadership**.[10]

Stage I describes Oracle Corporation, the computer software firm, under the management of its co-founder and CEO Lawrence Ellison. The company adopted a pioneering approach to retrieving data called structured query language (SQL). When IBM made SQL its standard, Oracle's success was assured. Unfortunately Ellison's technical wizardry was not sufficient to manage the company. Often working at home, he lost sight of details outside his technical interests. Although the company's sales were rapidly increasing, its financial controls were so weak that management had to restate an entire year's results to rectify irregularities. After the company recorded its first loss, Ellison hired a set of functional managers to run the company while he retreated to focus on new product development.

Table 8.1   **Factors Differentiating Stage I, II, and III Companies**

Function	Stage I	Stage II	Stage III
1. Sizing up: Major problems	Survival and growth dealing with short-term operating problems.	Growth, rationalization, and expansion of resources, providing for adequate attention to product problems.	Trusteeship in management and investment and control of large, increasing, and diversified resources. Also, important to diagnose and take action on problems at division level.
2. Objectives	Personal and subjective.	Profits and meeting functionally oriented budgets and performance targets.	ROI, profits, earnings per share.
3. Strategy	Implicit and personal; exploitation of immediate opportunities seen by owner-manager.	Functionally oriented moves restricted to "one product" scope; exploitation of one basic product or service field.	Growth and product diversification; exploitation of general business opportunities.
4. Organization: Major characteristic of structure	One unit, "one-man show."	One unit, functionally specialized group.	Multiunit general staff office and decentralized operating divisions.
5. (a) Measurement and control	Personal, subjective control based on simple accounting system and daily communication and observation.	Control grows beyond one person; assessment of functional operations necessary; structured control systems evolve.	Complex formal system geared to comparative assessment of performance measures, indicating problems and opportunities and assessing management ability of division managers.
5. (b) Key performance indicators	Personal criteria, relationships with owner, operating efficiency, ability to solve operating problems.	Functional and internal criteria such as sales, performance compared to budget, size of empire, status in group, personal relationships, etc.	More impersonal application of comparisons such as profits, ROI, P/E ratio, sales, market share, productivity, product leadership, personnel development, employee attitudes, public responsibility.
6. Reward-punishment system	Informal, personal, subjective; used to maintain control and divide small pool of resources to provide personal incentives for key performers.	More structured; usually based to a greater extent on agreed policies as opposed to personal opinion and relationships.	Allotment by "due process" of a wide variety of different rewards and punishments on a formal and systematic basis. Companywide policies usually apply to many different classes of managers and workers with few major exceptions for individual cases.

Source: D. H. Thain, "Stages of Corporate Development," *Business Quarterly* (Winter 1969), p. 37. Copyright © 1969 by *Business Quarterly*. Reprinted by permission.

Stage II: Functional Structure

Stage II is the point when the entrepreneur is replaced by a team of managers who have functional specializations. The transition to this stage requires a substantial managerial style change for the chief officer of the company, especially if he or she was the Stage I entrepreneur. He or she must learn to delegate; otherwise, having additional staff members yields no benefits to the organization. The previous example of Lawrence Ellison's retreat from top management at Oracle Corporation to new product development manager is one way that technically brilliant founders are able to get out of the way of the newly empowered functional managers. Once into Stage II, the corporate strategy favors protectionism through dominance of the industry, often through vertical and horizontal growth. The great strength of a Stage II corporation lies in its concentration and specialization in one industry. Its great weakness is that all of its eggs are in one basket.

By concentrating on one industry while that industry remains attractive, a Stage II company, like Oracle Corporation in computer software, can be very successful. Once a functionally structured firm diversifies into other products in different industries, however, the advantages of the functional structure break down. A **crisis of autonomy** can now develop, in which people managing diversified product lines need more decision-making freedom than top management is willing to delegate to them. The company needs to move to a different structure.

Stage III: Divisional Structure

Stage III is typified by the corporation's managing diverse product lines in numerous industries; it decentralizes the decision-making authority. These organizations grow by diversifying their product lines and expanding to cover wider geographical areas. They move to a divisional structure with a central headquarters and decentralized operating divisions—each division or business unit is a functionally organized Stage II company. They may also use a conglomerate structure if top management chooses to keep its collection of Stage II subsidiaries operating autonomously.

Recently divisions have been evolving into strategic business units (SBUs) to better reflect product-market considerations. Headquarters attempts to coordinate the activities of its operating divisions or SBUs through performance- and results-oriented control and reporting systems, and by stressing corporate planning techniques. The units are not tightly controlled but are held responsible for their own performance results. Therefore, to be effective, the company has to have a decentralized decision process. The greatest strength of a Stage III corporation is its almost unlimited resources. Its most significant weakness is that it is usually so large and complex that it tends to become relatively inflexible. General Electric, DuPont, and General Motors are Stage III corporations.

Stage IV: Beyond SBUs

Even with its evolution into strategic business units during the 1970s and 1980s, the divisional form is not the last word in organization structure. Under conditions of (1) increasing environmental uncertainty, (2) greater use of sophisticated technological production methods and information systems, (3) the increasing size and scope of worldwide business corporations, (4) a greater emphasis on multi-industry competitive strategy, and (5) a more educated cadre of managers and employees, new advanced forms of organizational structure have emerged and are continuing to emerge during the latter half of the twentieth century. The *matrix* and the *network* are two possible candidates for a fourth stage in corporate development—a stage that not only emphasizes horizontal over vertical connections between people and groups, but also organizes work around temporary projects in which sophisticated information systems support collaborative activities.

Blocks to Changing Stages

Corporations often find themselves in difficulty because they are blocked from moving into the next logical stage of development. Blocks to development may be internal (such as lack of resources, lack of ability, or a refusal of top management to delegate decision

THE FOUNDER OF THE MODEM BLOCKS THE TRANSITION TO STAGE II

Dennis Hayes is legendary not only for inventing the personal computer modem, but also for driving his company into bankruptcy. Hayes and retired partner Dale Heatherington founded Hayes Microcomputer Products 20 years ago when they invented a device that allowed personal computers to communicate with each other through telephone lines. Business boomed from $4.8 million in sales in 1981 to $150 million in 1985. When competitors developed low-cost modems, Hayes delayed until the early 1990s to respond with its own low-priced version. Sales and profits plummeted. Hayes lost its dominant position to U.S. Robotics. Management problems mounted. Creditors and potential investors looking into the company's books and operations found them a shambles. According to one investment banker, "The factory was in complete disarray." The company reported its first loss in 1994, by which time the company had nearly $70 million in debt. In November 1994, Hayes applied for protection from creditors under Chapter 11 of the U.S. Bankruptcy Code.

Still under the leadership of its founder, the company underwent a turnaround during 1995.

Still in second place with a 9.3% market share of modem sales in North America, Dennis Hayes put his company up for sale. He turned down a bid of $140 million from rival Diamond Multimedia Systems and instead accepted only $30 million for 49% of the company from Asian investors. Although the offer required Mr. Hayes to relinquish the title of chief executive, Hayes would still be a part of the company. He explained his decision as deriving from his unwillingness to completely let go of his baby. "I'll be able to have input, through the board and as chairman, that will best use my abilities. What I was concerned about was that someone would come in and . . . slash a part of the company without understanding how it fit in." Somewhat resigned to a lesser role, yet pleased to still have his name on the company, Dennis Hayes has finally accepted the need to let others help him manage the company. "Now I can hand over those day-to-day operations," smiled Hayes.

Source: D. McDermott, "Asians Rejuvenate Hayes Microcomputer," *Wall Street Journal* (May 6, 1996), p. A10.

making to others) or they may be external (such as economic conditions, labor shortages, and lack of market growth). For example, Chandler noted in his study that the successful founder/CEO in one stage was rarely the person who created the new structure to fit the new strategy, and that, as a result, the transition from one stage to another was often painful. This was true of General Motors Corporation under the management of William Durant, Ford Motor Company under Henry Ford I, Polaroid Corporation under Edwin Land, Apple Computer under Steven Jobs, and Hayes Microcomputer Products under Dennis Hayes. (See the **Strategy in a Changing World** feature for what happened to the inventor of the modem.)

This difficulty in moving to a new stage is compounded by the founder's tendency to maneuver around the need to delegate by carefully hiring, training, and grooming his or her own team of managers. The team tends to maintain the founder's influence throughout the organization long after the founder is gone. This is what happened at Walt Disney Productions when the family continued to emphasize Walt's policies and plans long after he was dead. Although this may often be an organization's strength, it may also be a weakness—to the extent that the culture supports the status quo and blocks needed change.

Organizational Life Cycle

Instead of considering stages of development in terms of structure, the organizational life cycle approach places the primary emphasis on the dominant issue facing the corporation. Organizational structure is only a secondary concern. The **organizational life cycle** describes how organizations grow, develop, and eventually decline. It is the organizational equivalent of the product life cycle in marketing. These stages are *Birth* (Stage I), *Growth* (Stage II), *Maturity* (Stage III), *Decline* (Stage IV), and *Death* (Stage V). The impact of these stages on corporate strategy and structure is summarized in Table 8.2. Note that the first three stages of the organizational life cycle are similar to the three commonly accepted stages of corporate development mentioned previously. The only significant difference is the addition of Decline and Death stages to complete the cycle. Even though a company's strategy may still be sound, its aging structure, culture, and processes may be such that they prevent the strategy from being executed properly—thus the company moves into Decline.

Movement from Growth to Maturity to Decline and finally to Death is not, however, inevitable. A *Revival* phase may occur sometime during the Maturity or Decline stages. The corporation's life cycle can be extended by managerial and product innovations.[11] This often occurs during the implementation of a turnaround strategy. At Maytag Corporation, for example, the Revival phase was initiated in the 1970s under the leadership of Daniel Krumm while Maytag was still in its Maturity stage of development. As pointed out in the **Company Spotlight on Maytag Corporation** feature, the transition from aggressive growth to a rather passive and complacent maturity in the 1950s and 1960s left the company vulnerable to competitive advances and the possibility of being acquired.

Unless a company is able to resolve the critical issues facing it in the Decline stage, it is likely to move into Stage V, corporate death—also known as bankruptcy. This is what happened to Pan American Airlines, Macy's Department Stores, Baldwin-United, Eastern Airlines, Colt's Manufacturing, Orion Pictures, and Wheeling-Pittsburgh Steel, as well as to many other firms. As in the cases of Johns-Manville, International Harvester, and Macy's—all of which went bankrupt—a corporation might nevertheless rise like a phoenix from its own ashes and live again under the same or a different name. The company may be reorganized or liquidated, depending on individual circumstances. Unfortunately less than 20% of firms entering Chapter 11 bankruptcy in the U.S. emerge as going concerns; the rest are forced into liquidation.[12]

Few corporations will move through these five stages in order. Some corporations, for example, might never move past Stage II. Others, like General Motors, might go directly from Stage I to Stage III. A large number of entrepreneurial ventures jump from Stage I or II directly into Stage IV or V. Hayes Microcomputer Products, for example, went from a Growth to a Decline stage under its founder Dennis Hayes. The key is to be able to identify indications that a firm is in the process of changing stages and to make the appropriate strategic and structural adjustments to ensure that corporate performance is maintained or even improved. Only time will tell if Hayes Microcomputer Products' new investors will be able to work with Dennis Hayes to take the company through a Revival phase—and successfully move it back to a growing, professionally managed Stage II firm.

Advanced Types of Organizational Structures

The basic structures (simple, functional, divisional, and conglomerate) were discussed earlier in Chapter 4 and summarized under the first three stages of corporate development. A new strategy may require more flexible characteristics than the traditional functional or divisional structure can offer. Today's business organizations are becoming less

Table 8.2   **Organizational Life Cycle**

	Stage I	Stage II	Stage III[1]	Stage IV	Stage V
Dominant Issue	Birth	Growth	Maturity	Decline	Death
Popular Strategies	Concentration in a niche	Horizontal and vertical growth	Concentric and conglomerate diversification	Profit strategy followed by retrenchment	Liquidation or bankruptcy
Likely Structure	Entrepreneur-dominated	Functional management emphasized	Decentralization into profit or investment centers	Structural surgery	Dismemberment of structure

Note:
1. An organization may enter a *Revival Phase* either during the Maturity or Decline Stages and thus extend the organization's life.

centralized with a greater use of cross-functional work teams. Table 8.3 depicts some of the changing structural characteristics of modern corporations. Although many variations and hybrid structures contain these characteristics, two forms stand out: the *matrix structure* and the *network structure*.

Matrix Structure

Most organizations find that organizing around either functions (in the functional structure) or around products and geography (in the divisional structure) provides an appropriate organizational structure. The matrix structure, in contrast, may be very appropriate when organizations conclude that neither functional nor divisional forms, even when combined with horizontal linking mechanisms like strategic business units, are right for their situations. In **matrix structures**, functional and product forms are combined simultaneously at the same level of the organization. (See Figure 8.1.) Employees have two superiors, a product or project manager and a functional manager. The "home" department—that is, engineering, manufacturing, or sales—is usually functional and is reasonably permanent. People from these functional units are often assigned temporarily to one or more product units or projects. The product units or projects are usually temporary and act like divisions in that they are differentiated on a product-market basis.

Pioneered in the aerospace industry, the matrix structure was developed to combine the stability of the functional structure with the flexibility of the product form. The matrix structure is very useful when the external environment (especially its technological and market aspects) is very complex and changeable. It does, however, produce conflicts revolving around duties, authority, and resource allocation. To the extent that the goals to be achieved are vague and the technology used is poorly understood, a continuous battle for power between product and functional managers is likely. The matrix structure is often found in an organization or within an SBU when the following three conditions exist:

- Ideas need to be cross-fertilized across projects or products.

- Resources are scarce.

- Abilities to process information and to make decisions need to be improved.[13]

Davis and Lawrence, authorities on the matrix form of organization, propose that *three distinct phases* exist in the development of the matrix structure.[14]

COMPANY SPOTLIGHT

Initiating a Revival Phase

Maytag Company expanded during the 1920s into a national company. In terms of the organizational life cycle, this was Maytag Company's *Growth stage*. Throughout the 1920s and 1930s, Maytag Company had an average U.S. market share of over 40% in washing machines. During the Great Depression of the 1930s, Maytag never suffered a loss. By World War II, Maytag had become the most successful washing machine company in the U.S. and had reached its *Maturity stage*. Unfortunately the innovative genius and entrepreneurial drive of the company's early years were no longer present. In the 1950s, Bendix, a newcomer to the industry, introduced an automatic washing machine that used an automatic spin cycle instead of a hand-cranked wringer to squeeze excess rinse water out of clothes. Maytag, however, was reluctant to convert to automatic washers. This reluctance cost the company its leadership of the industry. By 1954, Maytag's share of the U.S. washer market had dropped to only 8%. It continued through the 1960s as a relatively small (compared to its competition), but profitable company.

Taking over as company president in 1972, Daniel Krumm was not satisfied with Maytag's situation. Although the company had added products to its original line of washers, Krumm saw Maytag as merely a successful niche manufacturer in a maturing U.S. market and vulnerable to aggressive actions by larger competitors. Consequently Maytag's management adopted a strategy to become a full-line manufacturer and develop a stronger position in the U.S. appliance industry. The decision was made to grow by acquisition within the appliance industry. The *Revival phase* of Maytag's organizational life had begun.

In 1981, Maytag purchased Hardwick Stove, followed by Jenn-Air a year later, and Magic Chef in 1986. These acquisitions provided Maytag Corporation a full line of home appliances in the key three categories of laundry, cooking, and refrigeration appliances. This revitalized the firm and enabled it to solidify its position as one of the "Big Five" U.S. major home appliance manufacturers. It then began to look for growth opportunities in other parts of the world.

MAYTAG CORPORATION

1. *Temporary cross-functional task forces* are initially used when a new product line is being introduced. A project manager is in charge as the key horizontal link. Chrysler has extensively used this approach in product development.

2. *Product/brand management.* If the cross-functional task forces become more permanent, the project manager becomes a product or brand manager and a second phase begins. In this arrangement, function is still the primary organizational structure, but *product or brand managers act as the integrators of semipermanent products or brands*. Considered by many a key to the success of Procter & Gamble, brand management has been widely imitated by other consumer products firms around the world.

3. *Mature matrix.* The third and final phase of matrix development involves a *true dual-authority structure*. Both the functional and product structures are permanent. All employees are connected to both a vertical functional superior and a horizontal product manager. Functional and product managers have equal authority and must work well together to resolve disagreements over resources and priorities. TRW Systems, the aerospace company, is an example of a company that uses a mature matrix.

Table 8.3   **Changing Structural Characteristics of Modern Corporations**

Old Organizational Design	New Organizational Design
One large corporation	Mini-business units & cooperative relationships
Vertical communication	Horizontal communication
Centralized top-down decision making	Decentralized participative decision making
Vertical integration	Outsourcing & virtual organizations
Work/quality teams	Autonomous work teams
Functional work teams	Cross-functional work teams
Minimal training	Extensive training
Specialized job design focused on individual	Value-chain team-focused job design

Source: Adapted from B. Macy and H. Izumi, "Organizational Change, Design, and Work Innovation: A Meta-Analysis of 131 North American Field Studies—1961–1991," *Research in Organizational Change and Development*, Vol. 7, JAI Press (1993), p. 298. Reprinted with permission of JAI Press, Inc., Greenwich, CT and London, England.

Network Structure

A newer and somewhat more radical organizational design, the **network structure** (see Figure 8.1) is an example of what could be termed a "nonstructure" by its virtual elimination of in-house business functions. Many activities are outsourced. A corporation organized in this manner is often called a *virtual organization* because it is composed of a series of project groups or collaborations linked by constantly changing nonhierarchical, cobweb-like networks.[15] The network structure becomes most useful when the environment of a firm is unstable and is expected to remain so. Under such conditions, there is usually a strong need for innovation and quick response. Instead of having salaried employees, it may contract with people for a specific project or length of time. Long-term contracts with suppliers and distributors replace services that the company could provide for itself through vertical integration. Electronic markets and sophisticated information systems reduce the transaction costs of the marketplace, thus justifying a "buy" over a "make" decision. Rather than being located in a single building or area, an organization's business functions are scattered worldwide. The organization is, in effect, only a shell, with a small headquarters acting as a "broker," electronically connected to some completely owned divisions, partially owned subsidiaries, and other independent companies. In its ultimate form, the network organization is a series of independent firms or business units linked together by computers in an information system that designs, produces, and markets a product or service.[16]

An example of a complete network organization is Just Toys. The New York City company licenses characters like Disney's Little Mermaid, Hanna-Barbera's Flintstones, and Marvel Entertainment's Spiderman to make bendable polyvinyl chloride figures called Bend-Ems. The manufacturing and administrative work for Bend-Ems is contracted out. The company only employs 30 employees. If a toy isn't selling well, production can be reduced and shipments stopped almost immediately. It would take Mattel and Hasbro months to react in a similar situation.

Other companies like Nike, Reebok, and Benetton use the network structure in their operations function by subcontracting manufacturing to other companies in low-cost locations around the world. For control purposes, the Italian-based Benetton maintains what it calls an "umbilical cord" by assuring production planning for all its subcontractors, planning materials requirements for them, and providing them with bills of labor and standard prices and costs, as well as technical assistance to make sure their quality is up to Benetton's standards.

Figure 8.1
Matrix and Network Structures

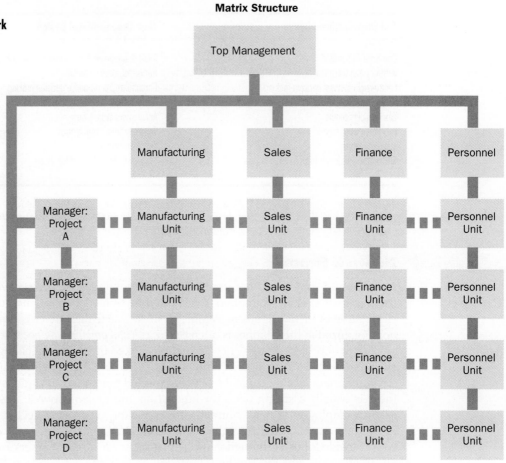

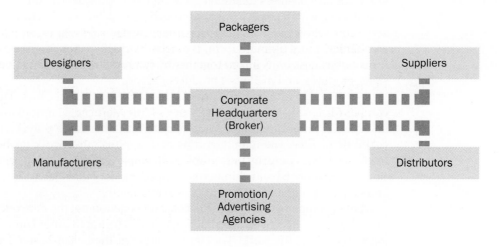

The network organization structure provides an organization with increased flexibility and adaptability to cope with rapid technological change and shifting patterns of international trade and competition. It allows a company to concentrate on its distinctive competencies, while gathering efficiencies from other firms who are concentrating their efforts in their areas of expertise. The network does, however, have disadvantages. The availability of numerous potential partners can be a source of trouble. Contracting out functions to separate suppliers/distributors may keep the firm from discovering any synergies by combining activities. If a particular firm overspecializes on only a few functions, it runs the risk of choosing the wrong functions and thus becoming noncompetitive.

Reengineering and Strategy Implementation

A recent approach to strategy implementation used to improve operations is called reengineering. **Reengineering** is the radical redesign of business processes to achieve major gains in cost, service, or time. It is not in itself a type of structure, but it is an effective way to implement a turnaround strategy.

Reengineering strives to break away from the old rules and procedures that develop and become ingrained in every organization over the years. These may be a combination of policies, rules, and procedures that have never been seriously questioned because they were established years earlier. These may range from "Credit decisions are made by the credit department" to "Local inventory is needed for good customer service." These rules of organization and work design were based on assumptions about technology, people, and organizational goals that may no longer be relevant. Rather than attempting to fix existing problems through minor adjustments and fine-tuning existing processes, the key to reengineering is to ask "If this were a new company, how would we run this place?"

Michael Hammer, who popularized the concept, suggests the following principles for reengineering:

- **Organize around outcomes, not tasks.** Design a person's or a department's job around an objective or outcome instead of a single task or series of tasks.

- **Have those who use the output of the process perform the process.** With computer-based information systems, processes can now be reengineered so that the people who need the result of the process can do it themselves.

- **Subsume information-processing work into the real work that produces the information.** People or departments that produce information can also process it for use instead of just sending raw data to others in the organization to interpret.

- **Treat geographically dispersed resources as though they were centralized.** With modern information systems, companies can provide flexible service locally while keeping the actual resources in a centralized location for coordination purposes.

- **Link parallel activities instead of integrating their results.** Instead of having separate units perform different activities that must eventually come together, have them communicate while they work so that *they* can do the integrating.

- **Put the decision point where the work is performed, and build control into the process.** The people who do the work should make the decisions and be self-controlling.

- **Capture information once and at the source.** Instead of having each unit develop its own database and information processing activities, the information can be put on a network so that all can access it.[17]

Several companies have had success with reengineering. For example, Pratt & Whitney, a jet engine manufacturer, used reengineering to overhaul its inefficient assembly lines. Independent product centers were established to replace old, mile-long "flow lines" to support an efficient work flow. In each center, old clusters of identical machines were regrouped into new clusters of different machines that together could manufacture one engine part in a simple continuous flow. Employees were cross-trained so that every person could operate every machine. This effort saved the company $5 billion and resulted in a 70% faster manufacturing process.[18] Nevertheless, because reengineering is almost always accompanied by a significant amount of pain, it is estimated that between 50% and 70% of reengineering efforts fail to achieve their goals.[19]

Designing Jobs to Implement Strategy

Organizing a company's activities and people to implement strategy involves more than simply redesigning a corporation's overall structure; it also involves redesigning the way jobs are done. With the increasing emphasis on reengineering, many companies are beginning to rethink their work processes with an eye toward phasing unnecessary people and activities out of the process. Process steps that had traditionally been performed sequentially can be improved by performing them concurrently using cross-functional work teams. Harley-Davidson, for example, has managed to reduce total plant employment by 25% while reducing by 50% the time needed to build a motorcycle. Restructuring through fewer people requires broadening the scope of jobs and encouraging teamwork. The design of jobs and subsequent job performance are, therefore, increasingly being considered as sources of competitive advantage.

Job design refers to the study of individual tasks in an attempt to make them more relevant to the company and to the employee(s). To minimize some of the adverse consequences of task specialization, corporations have turned to new job design techniques: **job enlargement** (combining tasks to give a worker more of the same type of duties to perform), **job rotation** (moving workers through several jobs to increase variety), and **job enrichment** (altering the jobs by giving the worker more autonomy and control over activities). The **job characteristics model** is a good example of job enrichment. (See the **Key Theory** feature.) Although each of these methods has its adherents, no one method seems to work in all situations.

A good example of modern job design is the introduction of team-based production by Corning, Inc., the glass manufacturer, in its Blacksburg, Virginia, plant. With union approval, Corning reduced job classifications from 47 to 4 to enable production workers to rotate jobs after learning new skills. The workers were divided into 14-member teams that, in effect, managed themselves. The plant had only two levels of management: Plant Manager Robert Hoover and two line leaders who only advised the teams. Employees worked demanding 12½ hour shifts, alternating three-day and four-day weeks. The teams made managerial decisions, imposed discipline on fellow workers, and were required to learn three "skill modules" within two years or else lose their jobs. As a result of this new job design, a Blacksburg team, made up of workers with interchangeable skills, can retool a line to produce a different type of filter in only ten minutes—six times faster than workers in a traditionally designed filter plant. The Blacksburg plant earned a $2 million profit in its first eight months of production, instead of losing the $2.3 million projected for the start-up period. The plant performed so well that Corning's top management acted to convert the company's 27 other factories to team-based production.[20]

KEY THEORY

DESIGNING JOBS WITH THE JOB CHARACTERISTICS MODEL

The job characteristics model is an advanced approach to job design based on the belief that tasks can be described in terms of certain objective characteristics and that these characteristics affect employee motivation. In order for the job to be motivating, (1) the worker needs to feel a sense of responsibility, feel the task to be meaningful, and receive useful feedback on his or her performance, and (2) the job has to satisfy needs that are important to the worker. The model proposes that managers follow five principles for redesigning work:

1. *Combine tasks* to increase task variety and to enable workers to identify with what they are doing.

2. *Form natural work units* to make a worker more responsible and accountable for the performance of the job.

3. *Establish client relationships* so the worker will know what performance is required and why.

4. *Vertically load the job* by giving workers increased authority and responsibility over their activities.

5. *Open feedback channels* by providing workers with information on how they are performing.

Research supports the job characteristics model as a way to improve job performance through job enrichment. Although there are several other approaches to job design, practicing managers seem increasingly to follow the prescriptions of this model as a way of improving productivity and product quality.

Source: J. R. Hackman and G. R. Oldham, *Work Redesign* (Reading, Mass.: Addison-Wesley, 1980), pp. 135–141; G. Johns, J. L. Xie, and Y. Fang, "Mediating and Moderating Effects in Job Design," *Journal of Management* (December 1992), pp. 657–676; R. W. Griffin, "Effects of Work Redesign on Employee Perceptions, Attitudes, and Behaviors: A Long-Term Investigation," *Academy of Management Journal* (June 1991), pp. 425–435.

8.5 International Issues in Strategy Implementation

An international company is one that engages in any combination of activities, from exporting/importing to full-scale manufacturing, in foreign countries. The **multinational corporation (MNC)**, in contrast, is a highly developed international company with a deep involvement throughout the world, plus a worldwide perspective in its management and decision making. For a multinational corporation to be considered global, it must manage its worldwide operations as if they were totally interconnected. This approach works best when the industry has moved from being multidomestic (each country's industry is essentially separate from the same industry in other countries; an example is retailing) to global (each country is a part of one worldwide industry; an example is consumer electronics).

Strategic alliances, such as joint ventures and licensing agreements, between a multinational company (MNC) and a local partner in a host country are becoming increasingly popular as a means by which a corporation can gain entry into other countries, especially less developed countries. The key to the successful implementation of these strategies is the selection of the local partner. Each party needs to assess not only the strategic fit of each company's project strategy, but also the fit of each company's respective resources. A successful joint venture may require as much as two years of prior contacts between both parties.

The design of an organization's structure is strongly affected by the company's stage of development in international activities and the types of industries in which the company is involved. The issue of centralization versus decentralization becomes especially important for a multinational corporation operating in both multidomestic and global industries.

Stages of International Development

Corporations operating internationally tend to evolve through five common stages, both in their relationships with widely dispersed geographic markets and in the manner in which they structure their operations and programs. These **stages of international development** are:

- **Stage 1 (Domestic Company).** The primarily domestic company exports some of its products through local dealers and distributors in the foreign countries. The impact on the organization's structure is minimal because an export department at corporate headquarters handles everything.

- **Stage 2 (Domestic Company with Export Division).** Success in Stage 1 leads the company to establish its own sales company with offices in other countries to eliminate the middlemen and to better control marketing. Because exports have now become more important, the company establishes an export division to oversee foreign sales offices.

- **Stage 3 (Primarily Domestic Company with International Division).** Success in earlier stages leads the company to establish manufacturing facilities in addition to sales and service offices in key countries. The company now adds an international division with responsibilities for most of the business functions conducted in other countries.

- **Stage 4 (Multinational Corporation with Multidomestic Emphasis).** Now a full-fledged multinational corporation, the company increases its investments in other countries. The company establishes a local operating division or company in the host country, such as Ford of Britain, to better serve the market. The product line is expanded, and local manufacturing capacity is established. Managerial functions (product development, finance, marketing, and so on) are organized locally. Over time, the parent company acquires other related businesses, broadening the base of the local operating division. As the subsidiary in the host country successfully develops a strong regional presence, it achieves greater autonomy and self-sufficiency. The operations in each country are, nevertheless, managed separately as if each is a domestic company.

- **Stage 5 (Multinational Corporation with Global Emphasis).** The most successful multinational corporations move into a fifth stage in which they have worldwide personnel, R&D, and financing strategies. Typically operating in a global industry, the MNC denationalizes its operations and plans product design, manufacturing, and marketing around worldwide considerations. Global considerations now dominate organizational design. The global MNC structures itself in a matrix form around some combination of geographic areas, product lines, and functions. All managers are now responsible for dealing with international as well as domestic issues.

Research provides some support for the stages of international development concept, but it does not necessarily support the preceding sequence of stages. For example,

THE INTERNET: INSTANT ENTRY INTO THE INTERNATIONAL MARKETPLACE

A few years ago, The Doll Collection was a barely profitable neighborhood retail shop in Louisville, Kentucky, with a staff of three people. Looking for an inexpensive way to boost its sales, one of the employees, Jason Walters, suggested putting a web page on the Internet. After spending two weeks learning the Internet computer language, html, Walters designed a simple site showcasing well-known dolls like Barbie and Madam Alexander to attract buyers. Employees of The Doll Collection were amazed by the response—much of which came from outside North America. Sales jumped 375%. By 1997, the shop had become a global retailer, marketing Barbie and Madam Alexander dolls to people in almost every country, including Japan, China, and Australia. (Try The Doll Collection's web site at *http://www.dollpage.com.*)

This story is no isolated example. The transaction value of goods and services purchased using the Internet is predicted to rise from $100 million in 1995 to $186 billion by the turn of the century. Even though 75% of web users live in North America, it is becoming a global phenom-

enon. New translation software is being developed to make the web more accessible to non-English speaking users. The World Trade Organization is working on a free trade framework for telecommunications. The European Union has set a January 1998 deadline for the full opening of its telecom markets in the majority of its member countries. Companies are expected to use the Internet to expand brand identification, access markets worldwide, and communicate effectively with customers. Soon e-mail transmitted over the Internet will rival the telephone and replace the fax machine. Videoconferencing will enable people to hold virtual meetings with people in different parts of the globe. If nothing else, the growth of the Internet is providing impetus for the globalization of 21st-century society.

Source: L. Beresford, "Global Smarts: Toy Story," *Entrepreneur* (February 1997), p. 38; W. Gates, "The Internet Grows Out of Nappies," *The World in 1997* (London: The Economist Group, 1996), p. 103; J. Chalmers, "Telecom Titans," *The World in 1997* (London: The Economist Group, 1996), p. 104–106.

a company may initiate production and sales in multiple countries without having gone through the steps of exporting or having local sales subsidiaries. In addition, any one corporation can be at different stages simultaneously, with different products in different markets at different levels. Firms may also leapfrog across stages to a global emphasis. The widespread growth of the Internet is changing the way business is being done internationally. See the 🌐 **21st Century Global Society** feature for an example of how the Internet is enabling companies of all sizes to access the increasingly global marketplace. Nevertheless the stages concept provides a useful way to illustrate some of the structural changes corporations undergo when they increase their involvement in international activities.

Centralization versus Decentralization

A basic dilemma a multinational corporation faces is how to organize authority centrally so that it operates as a vast interlocking system that achieves synergy, and at the same time decentralize authority so that local managers can make the decisions necessary to meet the demands of the local market or host government. To deal with this problem, MNCs tend to structure themselves either along product groups or geographic areas.

Figure 8.2
Geographic Area Structure for a Multinational Corporation

*Note: Because of space limitations, product groups for only Europe and Asia are shown here.

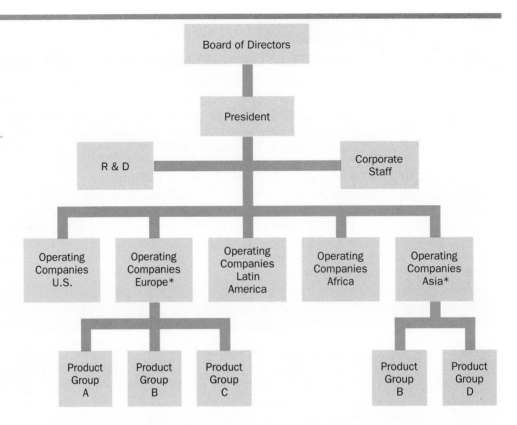

They may even combine both in a matrix structure—the design chosen by 3M Corporation and Asea Brown Boveri (ABB), among others.[21] One side of 3M's matrix represents the company's product divisions; the other side includes the company's international country and regional subsidiaries.

Two examples of the usual international structures are Nestlé and American Cyanamid. Nestlé's structure is one in which significant power and authority have been decentralized to geographic entities. This structure is similar to that depicted in Figure 8.2, in which each geographic set of operating companies has a different group of products. In contrast, American Cyanamid has a series of centralized product groups with worldwide responsibilities. To depict Cyanamid's structure, the geographical entities in Figure 8.2 would have to be replaced by product groups or strategic business units.

The **product-group structure** of American Cyanamid enables the company to introduce and manage a similar line of products around the world. This enables the corporation to *centralize* decision making along product lines and to reduce costs. The **geographic-area structure** of Nestlé, in contrast, allows the company to tailor products to regional differences and to achieve regional coordination. This *decentralizes* decision making to the local subsidiaries. As industries move from being multidomestic to more globally integrated, multinational corporations are increasingly switching from the geographic-area to the product-group structure. Texaco, Inc., for example, changed to a product-group structure in 1996 by consolidating its international, U.S., and new business opportunities under each line of business at its White Plains, New York, headquarters. According to Chairman Peter Bijur, "By placing groups which will perform similar work in the same location, they will be able to share information, ideas, and resources more readily—and move critical information throughout the organization."[22]

Simultaneous pressures for decentralization to be locally responsive and centralization to be maximally efficient are causing interesting structural adjustments in most large corporations. This is what is meant by the phrase "Think globally, act locally." Companies are attempting to decentralize those operations that are culturally oriented and closest to the customers—manufacturing, marketing, and human resources. At the same time, the companies are consolidating less visible internal functions, such as research and development, finance, and information systems, where there can be significant economies of scale.

8.6 Global Issues for the 21st Century

- The **21st Century Global Society** feature in this chapter illustrates how the Internet is changing the way business is being conducted around the world. Small, local businesses can now access the international marketplace in a way undreamed of previously. The growth of the Internet is likely to stimulate the growth of an increasingly global society.

- Strategy implementation is likely to become an even more important issue to corporations engaging in international operations. Pepsico's bad experience in South America is one reason why, compared to the internationally successful Coca Cola, the company is struggling internationally.

- Strategic business units have become the most popular structural design in today's large multidivisional corporations. With more companies becoming multinational, expect them to take on many of the characteristics of the matrix and network organization.

- Many U.S. corporations have gone through the renewal phase of the organizational life cycle during the 1980s and 1990s by converting to more flexible organizational structures with cross-functional activities. This is making them more competitive in global industries. Most European corporations have yet to enter this phase and are beginning to lose their competitive advantages. Expect reengineering, job redesign, and other change techniques to soon become popular in Europe.

- As more industries become global, expect multinational corporations to adopt the matrix organization structure focusing on a centralized product group with various functions being decentralized to various regions for maximum efficiency and effectiveness.

Projections for the 21st Century

- From 1994 to 2010, the number of automobiles produced in the developed countries will increase from 20 million to 30 million vehicles.

- From 1994 to 2010, the number of automobiles produced in the emerging market nations will jump from 8 million to 30 million vehicles.[23]

Discussion Questions

1. How should a corporation attempt to achieve synergy among functions and business units?

2. How should an owner-manager prepare a company for its movement from Stage I to Stage II?

3. How can a corporation keep from sliding into the Decline stage of the organizational life cycle?

4. Is reengineering just another management fad or does it offer something of lasting value?

5. What are the advantages and disadvantages of the network structure?

Key Terms

budget (p. 186)
crisis of autonomy (p. 190)
crisis of leadership (p. 188)
divisional structure (p. 190)
functional structure (p. 189)
geographic-area structure (p. 201)
job characteristics model (p. 198)
job design (p. 198)
job enlargement (p. 198)
job enrichment (p. 198)

job rotation (p. 198)
matrix structure (p. 193)
multinational corporation (MNC) (p. 199)
network structure (p. 195)
organizational life cycle (p. 192)
procedures (p. 186)
product-group structure (p. 202)
program (p. 185)
reengineering (p. 197)

simple structure (p. 186)
SOPs (p. 186)
stages of corporate development (p. 188)
stages of international develop-ment (p. 200)
strategy implementation (p. 183)
structure follows strategy (p. 187)
synergy (p. 186)

Strategic Practice Exercise

One of today's trends is for large corporations to divide themselves into smaller units, eliminate layers of middle managers, and outsource many activities previously done internally—in order to better implement their strategies. One such company is Dana Corporation, a $5 billion auto-parts manufacturer. A big supplier to the large U.S., European, and Japanese automakers, Dana likes to operate as a series of small units. Only a handful of Dana's 120 plants employ more than 200 people. When a division of the company gets too big, it simply splits in half. "Plant managers should know the name and personal circumstances of everyone," insisted Dana Chairman Southwood Morcott.[24]

____ What kind of organizational structure does Dana use?

____ What is Dana Corporation trying to accomplish by breaking itself into a series of small units?

____ By keeping plant size so small, isn't Dana giving up economies of scale and thus potential cost advantages?

____ Would Dana be better off divesting many of its business units and using a network structure to contract for its supplies and raw materials in the marketplace?

Notes

1. R. Frank, and J. Friedland, "How Pepsi's Charge Into Brazil Fell Short of Its Ambitious Goals," *Wall Street Journal* (August 30, 1996), pp. A1, A6.

2. J. W. Gadella, "Avoiding Expensive Mistakes in Capital Investment," *Long Range Planning* (April 1994), pp. 103–110; B. Voss, "World Market Is Not for Everyone," *Journal of Business Strategy* (July/August 1993), p. 4.

3. L. D. Alexander, "Strategy Implementation: Nature of the Problem," *International Review of Strategic Management,*

Vol. 2, No. 1, edited by D. E. Hussey (New York: John Wiley & Sons, 1991), pp. 73–113.

4. Frank and Friedland.

5. A. D. Chandler, *Strategy and Structure* (Cambridge, Mass.: MIT Press, 1962).

6. A. P. Sloan, Jr., *My Years with General Motors* (Garden City, N.Y.: Doubleday, 1964).

7. T. L. Amburgey, and T. Dacin, "As the Left Foot Follows the Right? The Dynamics of Strategic and Structural

Change," *Academy of Management Journal* (December 1994), pp. 1427–1452; M. Ollinger, "The Limits of Growth of the Multidivisional Firm: A Case Study of the U.S. Oil Industry from 1930–90," *Strategic Management Journal* (September 1994), pp. 503–520.

8. D. F. Jennings, and S. L. Seaman, "High and Low Levels of Organizational Adaptation: An Empirical Analysis of Strategy, Structure, and Performance," *Strategic Management Journal* (July 1994), pp. 459–475.

9. A. K. Gupta, "SBU Strategies, Corporate-SBU Relations, and SBU Effectiveness in Strategy Implementation," *Academy of Management Journal* (September 1987), pp. 477–500.

10. L. E. Greiner, "Evolution and Revolution as Organizations Grow," *Harvard Business Review* (July-August 1972), pp. 37–46.

11. D. Miller, and P. H. Friesen, "A Longitudinal Study of the Corporate Life Cycle," *Management Science* (October 1984), pp. 1161–1183.

12. H. Tavakolian, "Bankruptcy: An Emerging Corporate Strategy," *SAM Advanced Management Journal* (Spring 1995), p. 19.

13. L. G. Hrebiniak, and W. F. Joyce, *Implementing Strategy* (New York: Macmillan, 1984), pp. 85–86.

14. S. M. Davis, and P. R. Lawrence, *Matrix* (Reading, Mass.: Addison-Wesley, 1977), pp. 11–24.

15. J. G. March, "The Future Disposable Organizations and the Rigidities of Imagination," *Organization* (August/November 1995), p. 434.

16. For more information on managing a network organization, see G. Lorenzoni and C. Baden-Fuller, "Creating a Strategic Center to Manage a Web of Partners," *California Management Review* (Spring 1995), pp. 146–163.

17. Summarized from M. Hammer, "Reengineering Work: Don't Automate, Obliterate," *Harvard Business Review* (July-August 1990), pp. 104–112.

18. J. Champy, *Managing Successful Reengineering* (Boston: HBS Management Productions, 1995). This is a videotape.

19. T. A. Stewart, "Reengineering: The Hot New Managing Tool," *Fortune* (August 23, 1993), pp. 41–42.

20. J. Hoerr, "Sharpening Minds for a Competitive Edge," *Business Week* (December 17, 1990), pp. 72–78.

21. C. A. Bartlett, and S. Ghoshal, "Beyond the M-Form: Toward a Managerial Theory of the Firm," *Strategic Management Journal* (Winter 1993), pp. 23–46.

22. A. Sullivan, "Texaco Revamps Executive Structure to Focus on Business, Not Geography," *Wall Street Journal* (October 3, 1996), p. B15.

23. J. Warner, "21st Century Capitalism: Snapshot of the Next Century," *Business Week* (November 18, 1994), p. 194.

24. R. A. Melcher, "How Goliaths Can Act Like Davids," *Business Week* (Enterprise 1993), p. 195.

Chapter 9

Strategy Implementation: Staffing and Directing

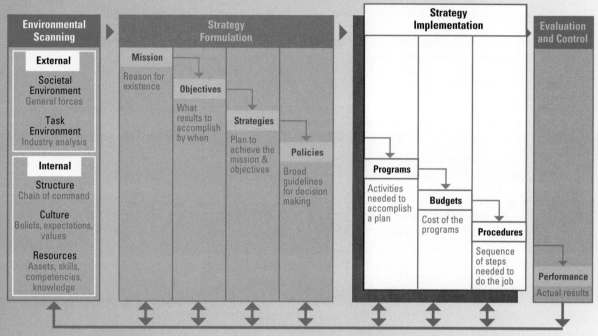

Environmental Scanning

External

Societal Environment
General forces

Task Environment
Industry analysis

Internal

Structure
Chain of command

Culture
Beliefs, expectations, values

Resources
Assets, skills, competencies, knowledge

Strategy Formulation

Mission

Reason for existence

Objectives

What results to accomplish by when

Strategies

Plan to achieve the mission & objectives

Policies

Broad guidelines for decision making

Strategy Implementation

Programs

Activities needed to accomplish a plan

Budgets

Cost of the programs

Procedures

Sequence of steps needed to do the job

Evaluation and Control

Performance

Actual results

Feedback/Learning

Have you heard of Enterprise Rent-A-Car? You won't find it at the airport with Hertz, Avis, or National car rental operations. Yet Enterprise owns more cars and operates in more locations than Hertz. The company accounts for over 20% of the $15 billion per year U.S. car rental market compared to 17% for Hertz and 12% for Avis. In ignoring the highly competitive airport market, Enterprise has chosen a differentiation competitive strategy by marketing to people in need of a spare car. Instead of locating many cars at a few high-priced locations at airports, Enterprise sets up inexpensive offices throughout metropolitan areas. As a result, cars are rented for 30% less than they cost at airports. As soon as one branch office grows to about 150 cars, the company opens another rental office a few miles away. People are increasingly renting from Enterprise even when their current car works fine. According to CEO Andy Taylor, "We call it a 'virtual car.' Small-business people who have to pick up clients call us when they want something better than their own car." Why is Enterprise able to follow this competitive strategy so successfully without attracting Hertz and Avis into its market?

The secret to Enterprise's success is its well-executed strategy implementation. Clearly laid out programs, budgets, and procedures support the company's competitive strategy by making Enterprise stand out in the mind of the consumer. When a new rental office opens, employees spend time developing relationships with the service managers of every auto dealership and body shop in the area. Enterprise employees bring pizza and doughnuts to workers at the auto garages across the country. Enterprise forms agreements with dealers to provide replacements for cars brought in for service. At major accounts, the company actually staffs an office at the dealership and has cars parked outside so customers don't have to go to an Enterprise office to complete paperwork.

One key to implementation at Enterprise is staffing—through hiring and promoting a certain kind of person. Virtually every Enterprise employee is a college graduate, usually from the bottom half of the class. According to COO Donald Ross, "We hire from the half of the college class that makes the upper half possible. We want athletes, fraternity types—especially fraternity presidents and social directors. People people." These new employees begin as management trainees in the $20,000–$25,000 salary range. Instead of regular raises, their pay is tied to branch office profits.

Another key to implementation at Enterprise is leading—through specifying clear performance objectives and promoting a team-oriented corporate culture. The company stresses promotion from within. Every Enterprise employee, including top executives, starts at the bottom. As a result, a bond of shared experience connects all employees and managers. To reinforce a cohesive culture of camaraderie, senior executives routinely do "grunt work" at branch offices. Even Andy Taylor, the CEO, joins the work. "We were visiting an office in Berkeley and it was mobbed, so I started cleaning cars," says Taylor. "As it was happening, I wondered if it was a good use of my time, but the effect on morale was tremendous." Because the financial results of every branch office and every region are available to all, the collegial culture stimulates good-natured competition. "We're this close to beating out Middlesex," grins Woody Erhardt, an area manager in New Jersey. "I want to pound them into the ground. If they lose, they have to throw a party for us, and we get to decide what they wear."[1]

This example from Enterprise Rent-A-Car illustrates how a competitive strategy must be implemented with carefully considered programs in order to succeed. This chapter discusses strategy implementation in terms of staffing and leading. *Staffing* focuses on the selection and use of employees. *Leading* emphasizes the use of programs to better align employee interests and attitudes with a new strategy.

9.1   Staffing

The implementation of new strategies and policies often calls for new human resource management priorities and a different use of personnel. Such **staffing** issues can involve hiring new people with new skills, firing people with inappropriate or substandard skills, and/or training existing employees to learn new skills.

If growth strategies are to be implemented, new people may need to be hired and trained. Experienced people with the necessary skills need to be found for promotion to newly created managerial positions. When a corporation follows a growth through acquisition strategy, it may find that it needs to replace several managers in the acquired company. Research by Walsh of 102 companies following an acquisition revealed that the percentage of the acquired company's top management team that either quit or was asked to leave was 26% after the first year and 61% after five years.[2]

If a corporation adopts a retrenchment strategy, however, a large number of people may need to be laid off or fired; and top management, as well as the divisional managers, needs to specify the criteria to be used in making these personnel decisions. Should employees be fired on the basis of low seniority or on the basis of poor performance? Sometimes corporations find it easier to close an entire division than to choose which individuals to fire.

Staffing Follows Strategy

As in the case of structure, staffing requirements are likely to follow a change in strategy. For example, promotions should be based not only on current job performance, but also on whether a person has the skills and abilities to do what is needed to implement the new strategy.

Hiring and Training Requirements Change

Having formulated a new strategy, a corporation may find that it needs to either hire different people or retrain current employees to implement the new strategy. Consider the introduction of team-based production at Corning's filter plant mentioned earlier in Chapter 8. Employee selection and training were crucial to the success of the new manufacturing strategy. Plant Manager Robert Hoover sorted through 8,000 job applications before hiring 150 people with the best problem-solving ability and a willingness to work in a team setting. Those selected received extensive training in technical and interpersonal skills. During the first year of production, 25% of all hours worked were devoted to training at a cost of $750,000.[3]

One way to implement a company's business strategy, such as overall low cost, is through training and development. One study of 155 manufacturing firms revealed that those with training programs had 19% higher productivity than did those without such a program. Another study found that a doubling of formal training per employee resulted in a 7% reduction in scrap.[4] Training is especially important for a differentiation strategy emphasizing quality or customer service. For example, Motorola, with annual sales of $17 billion, spends 4% of its payroll on training by providing at least 40 hours of training a year to its employees. It hopes to quadruple that within a few years at an annual cost of $600 million. There is a very strong connection between strategy and training at Motorola. For example, after setting a goal to reduce product development cycle time, Motorola created a course to teach its employees how to accomplish that goal. The company is especially concerned with attaining the highest quality possible in all its operations. Realizing that it couldn't hit quality targets with poor parts, Motorola developed a class for its suppliers on statistical process control. The company estimates that every $1 it spends on training delivers $30 in productivity gains within three years.[5]

Training is also important when implementing a retrenchment strategy. As suggested earlier, successful downsizing means that the company has to invest in its remaining employees. General Electric's Aircraft Engine Group used training to maintain its share of the market even though it had cut its workforce from 42,000 to 33,000 between 1991 and 1993.[6]

Matching the Manager to the Strategy

The most appropriate type of general manager needed to effectively implement a new corporate or business strategy depends on the desired strategic direction of that firm or business unit. Executives with a particular mix of skills and experiences may be classified as an **executive type** and paired with a specific corporate strategy. For example, a corporation following a concentration strategy emphasizing vertical or horizontal growth would probably want an aggressive new chief executive with a great deal of experience in that particular industry—a ***dynamic industry expert***. A diversification strategy, in contrast, might call for someone with an analytical mind who is highly knowledgeable in other industries and can manage diverse product lines—an ***analytical portfolio manager***. A corporation choosing to follow a stability strategy would probably want as its CEO a ***cautious profit planner***, a person with a conservative style, a production or engineering background, and experience with controlling budgets, capital expenditures, inventories, and standardization procedures. Weak companies in a relatively attractive industry tend to turn to a type of challenge-oriented executive known as the ***turnaround specialist*** to save the company. See the **Strategy in a Changing World** feature for a description of Ann Iverson, one such turnaround specialist. If a company cannot be saved, a **professional liquidator** might be called on by a bankruptcy court to close the firm and liquidate its assets. Research tends to support the conclusion that as a firm's environment changes, it tends to change the type of top executive to implement a new strategy.[7]

This approach is in agreement with Chandler, who proposed in Chapter 8 that the most appropriate CEO of a company changes as a firm moves from one stage of development to another. Because priorities certainly change over an organization's life, successful corporations need to select managers who have skills and characteristics appropriate to the organization's particular stage of development and position in its life cycle. For example, founders of firms tend to have functional backgrounds in technological specialties; whereas successors tend to have backgrounds in marketing and administration.[8]

Other studies have found a link between the type of CEO and the firm's overall strategic type. For example, successful prospector firms tended to be headed by CEOs from research/engineering and general management backgrounds. High performance defenders tended to have CEOs with accounting/finance, manufacturing/production, and general management experience. Analyzers tended to have CEOs with a marketing/sales background.[9]

A study of 173 firms over a 25-year period revealed that CEOs in these companies tended to have the same functional specialization as the former CEO, especially when the past CEO's strategy continued to be successful. This may be a pattern for successful corporations.[10] In particular, it explains why so many prosperous companies tend to recruit their top executives from one particular area. At Procter & Gamble (a good example of an analyzer firm), for example, the route to the CEO's position has always been through brand management with a strong emphasis on marketing. In other firms, the route may be through manufacturing, marketing, accounting, or finance—depending on what the corporation has always considered its key area (and its overall strategic orientation).

Selection and Management Development

Selection and development are important not only to ensure that people with the right mix of skills and experiences are initially hired, but also to help them grow on the job so that they might be prepared for future promotions.

ANN IVERSON IMPLEMENTS A TURNAROUND STRATEGY AT LAURA ASHLEY

When Sir Bernard Ashley visited a North Carolina shopping mall to see a prototype of an expanded Laura Ashley store, he was amazed and delighted. As the company's largest shareholder and co-founder, Ashley was well aware of how poorly the $512 million apparel and home furnishings company has fared since his wife Laura died in 1985. Unlike other Ashley shops, this one was packed with customers. "I almost cried, it was so marvelous," he exclaimed.

The credit for this change belongs to Ann Iverson. Since becoming CEO in July 1995, she had replaced most of top management, cut the payroll, slashed costs, and proposed an aggressive U.S. expansion plan. "I'm the kind of person who has a steamroller behind her back," explained Iverson. The board of directors of Laura Ashley Holdings PLC selected Iverson because of her ability to implement a turnaround strategy. Earlier Iverson had helped improve the profits of British Home Stores, a division of Storehouse PLC. She then moved to the CEO position of Storehouse's Mothercare Ltd. and introduced attractions such as talking trees and singing clocks to lure children and their mothers back into the stores. When Mothercare became profitable, she joined Melville Corporation in the United States to run its Kay-Bee Toy & Hobby Shops. At the same time, she agreed to serve on the Laura Ashley board of directors. Her in-depth knowledge of retailing soon led the board to pick her to manage the company.

Iverson is a hands-on manager. She answers her own phone and gets into discussions regarding what kind of wood flooring should be used in the stores. To save expenses, she moved headquarters into a converted London bus depot. Acknowledging the dated Victorian look of the company's apparel, Iverson hired a new clothes designer, Basha Cohen, to freshen the line, but keep the flowing, romantic look. She also expanded the size of the stores to 7,200 from 2,500 square feet to expand home furnishings. One of her objectives is to increase revenue from home furnishings to 65% from its current 50% of total sales by the end of the decade. The company's wallpaper, bedspreads, linens, and curtains are less dependent on changing fashions than is its apparel line, with its floral prints and long, girlish dresses. Since Iverson's appointment as CEO, the company's stock has more than doubled to $3.20 per share. If her turnaround strategy succeeds, Iverson could earn $5.2 million over a three-year period.

Source: J. Flynn, and C. Power, "Giving Laura Ashley a Yank," *Business Week* (May 27, 1996), p. 147.

Executive Succession: Insiders versus Outsiders

Executive succession is the process of replacing a key top manager. Given that almost half of all CEOs are replaced within five years, it is important that the firm plan for this eventuality.[11] It is especially important for a company that usually promotes from within to prepare its current managers for promotion. Prosperous firms tend to look outside for CEO candidates only if they have no obvious internal candidates. Firms in trouble, however, tend to choose outsiders to lead them. For example, one study of 22 firms undertaking a turnaround strategy over a 13-year period found that the CEO was replaced in all but two companies. Of 27 changes of CEO (several firms had more than one CEO during this period), only seven were insiders—20 were outsiders.[12] The probability of an outsider being chosen to lead a firm in difficulty increases if there is no internal heir apparent, the last CEO was fired, and if the board of directors is composed of a large percentage of outsiders.[13] Boards realize that the best way to force a change in strategy is to hire a new CEO with no connections to the current strategy.

Identifying Abilities and Potential

A company can identify and prepare its people for important positions in several ways. One approach is to establish a sound **performance appraisal system** to identify good performers with promotion potential. A survey of 34 corporate planners and human resource executives from 24 large U.S. corporations revealed that approximately 80% made some attempt to identify managers' talents and behavioral tendencies so that they could place a manager with a likely fit to a given competitive strategy.[14] A company should examine its human resource system to ensure not only that people are being hired without regard to their racial, ethnic, or religious background, but also that they are being identified for training and promotion in the same manner. Management diversity could be a competitive advantage in a multiethnic world.

Many large organizations are using **assessment centers** to evaluate a person's suitability for an advanced position. Corporations such as AT&T, Standard Oil, IBM, Sears, and GE have successfully used assessment centers. Because each is specifically tailored to its corporation, these assessment centers are unique. They use special interviews, management games, in-basket exercises, leaderless group discussions, case analyses, decision-making exercises, and oral presentations to assess the potential of employees for specific positions. Promotions into these positions are based on performance levels in the assessment center. Many assessment centers have been able to accurately predict subsequent job performance.

Job rotation—moving people from one job to another—is also used in many large corporations to ensure that employees are gaining the appropriate mix of experiences to prepare them for future responsibilities. Rotating people among divisions is one way that the corporation can improve the level of organizational learning. For example, companies that pursue related diversification strategies through internal development make greater use of interdivisional transfers of people than do companies that grow through unrelated acquisitions. Apparently the companies that grow internally attempt to transfer important knowledge and skills throughout the corporation in order to achieve some sort of synergy.[15]

Problems in Retrenchment

Downsizing (sometimes called "rightsizing") refers to the planned elimination of positions or jobs. This program is often used to implement retrenchment strategies. Because the financial community is likely to react favorably to announcements of downsizing from a company in difficulty, such a program may provide some short-term benefits such as raising the company's stock price. If not done properly, however, downsizing may result in less, rather than more, productivity. One study of downsizing revealed that at 20 out of 30 automobile-related U.S. industrial companies, either the wrong jobs were eliminated or blanket offers of early retirement prompted managers, even those considered invaluable, to leave. After the layoffs, the remaining employees had to do not only their, work, but also the work of the people who had gone. Because the survivors often didn't know how to do the departeds' work, morale and productivity plummeted.[16] In addition, cost-conscious executives tend to defer maintenance, skimp on training, delay new product introductions, and avoid risky new businesses—all of which leads to lower sales and eventually to lower profits.

A good retrenchment strategy can thus be implemented well in terms of organizing, but poorly in terms of staffing. A situation can develop in which retrenchment feeds on itself and acts to further weaken instead of strengthening the company. Research indicates that companies undertaking cost-cutting programs are four times more likely than others to cut costs again, typically by reducing staff.[17] In contrast, successful downsizing firms undertake a strategic reorientation, not just a bloodletting of employees. Research shows that when companies use downsizing as part of a larger restructuring program to narrow company focus, they enjoy better performance.[18]

Consider the following guidelines that have been proposed for successful downsizing:

- **Eliminate unnecessary work instead of making across-the-board cuts.** Spend the time to research where money is going and eliminate the task, not the workers, if it doesn't add value to what the firm is producing. Reduce the number of administrative levels rather than the number of individual positions. Look for interdependent relationships before eliminating activities. Identify and protect core competencies.

- **Contract out work that others can do cheaper.** For example, Bankers Trust of New York contracts out its mail room and printing services and some of its payroll and accounts payable activities to a division of Xerox. Outsourcing may be cheaper than vertical integration.

- **Plan for long-run efficiencies.** Don't simply eliminate all postponable expenses, such as maintenance, R&D, and advertising, in the unjustifiable hope that the environment will become more supportive. Continue to hire, grow, and develop—particularly in critical areas.

- **Communicate the reasons for actions.** Tell employees not only why the company is downsizing, but also what the company is trying to achieve. Promote educational programs.

- **Invest in the remaining employees.** Because most "survivors" in a corporate downsizing will probably be doing different tasks from what they were doing before the change, firms need to draft new job specifications, performance standards, appraisal techniques, and compensation packages. Additional training is needed to ensure that everyone has the proper skills to deal with expanded jobs and responsibilities. Empower key individuals/groups and emphasize team building. Identify, protect, and mentor people with leadership talent.

- **Develop value-added jobs to balance out job elimination.** When no other jobs are currently available within the organization to transfer employees to, management must consider other staffing alternatives. Harley-Davidson, for example, worked with the company's unions to find other work for surplus employees by moving work into Harley plants that was previously done by suppliers.[19]

International Issues in Staffing

Because of cultural differences, managerial style and human resource practices must be tailored to fit the particular situations in other countries. Most multinational corporations (MNCs) attempt to fill managerial positions in their subsidiaries with well-qualified citizens of the host countries. Unilever and IBM take this approach to international staffing. This policy serves to placate nationalistic governments and to better attune management practices to the host country's culture. The danger in using primarily foreign nationals to staff managerial positions in subsidiaries is the increased likelihood of suboptimization (the local subsidiary ignores the needs of the larger parent corporation). This makes it difficult for a multinational corporation to meet its long-term, worldwide objectives. To a local national in an MNC subsidiary, the corporation as a whole is an abstraction. Communication and coordination across subsidiaries become more difficult. As it becomes harder to coordinate the activities of several international subsidiaries, an MNC will have serious problems operating in a global industry.

Another approach to staffing the managerial positions of multinational corporations is to use people with an "international" orientation, regardless of their country of origin or host country assignment. This is a widespread practice among European firms. For example, Electrolux, a Swedish firm, had a French director in its Singapore factory. Using third-country "nationals" can allow for more opportunities for promotion than does Unilever's policy of hiring local people, but it can also result in more misunderstandings and conflicts with the local employees and with the host country's government.

To improve organizational learning, many multinational corporations are providing their managers with international assignments lasting as long as five years. Upon their return to headquarters, these expatriates will have an in-depth understanding of the company's operations in another part of the world. This has value to the extent that these employees communicate this understanding to others in decision-making positions. Unfortunately not all corporations appropriately manage international assignments. One mistake is failing to educate the person about the customs in other countries. While out of the country, a person may be overlooked for an important promotion (out of sight, out of mind). Upon his or her return to the home country, co-workers may deprecate the out-of-country experience as a waste of time. To improve their chances of success using expatriates, multinational corporations are now putting more emphasis on intercultural training for those managers being sent on an assignment to a foreign country. This training is one of the commonly cited reasons for the lower expatriate failure rates—6% or less—for European and Japanese MNCs, which have emphasized cross-cultural experiences, compared with a 35% failure rate for U.S.-based MNCs.[20]

Multinational corporations with a high level of international interdependence among activities need to provide their managers with significant international assignments and experiences as part of their training and development. Such assignments provide future corporate leaders with a series of valuable international contacts in additional to a better personal understanding of international issues and global linkages among corporate activities.[21] Daniel Krumm, for example, was Maytag Corporation's CEO when the corporation acquired Hoover to expand its international operations. One of Krumm's earlier assignments had been five years in Belgium and Germany as manager of Maytag's European operations. Executive recruiters report that compared to 1990, a greater percentage of major corporations are now requiring candidates to have international experience.[22]

U.S. corporations are also attempting to take advantage of immigrants and their children to staff key positions when negotiating entry into another country and when selecting an executive to manage the company's new foreign operations. For example, when General Motors wanted to learn more about business opportunities in China, it turned to its Chinese-American employees. See the 🌐 **21st Century Global Society** feature to learn how Shirley Young, a Chinese-American, helped negotiate a joint venture with a Chinese company to manufacture midsize Buicks in Shanghai.

Staffing international positions with immigrants or descendants of immigrants from that country may not necessarily be appropriate. AT&T, for example, has had mixed results with relocating around 50 ethnic employees to their home countries. The person may not understand the country's business practices because they either left long ago or never lived there. Local employees, in turn, often resent the newcomers' "foreign" manners and higher pay.[23]

21ST CENTURY GLOBAL SOCIETY

GENERAL MOTORS USES CHINESE-AMERICANS IN CHINESE JOINT VENTURE

Shirley Young, a Vice-President of Marketing at General Motors, was instrumental in helping GM negotiate a $1 billion joint venture with Shanghai Automotive to build a Buick plant in China. Uniquely qualified for this assignment, Young had been born in Shanghai, had relatives in China, and was fluent in Chinese. Her father, a hero in China, had been that country's Consul General to the Philippines during World War II. When GM wanted to establish links with China in 1992, it asked Young to help its people become acquainted with influential people in China's government and industrial circles. Young and other Chinese-Americans formed a committee to ad-vise GM on relations with China. Although just a part of a larger team of GM employees working on the joint venture, Young coached GM employees on Chinese customs and traditions. Rather than eating together after transacting business, for example, she suggested that GM follow the Chinese practice of dining first. "These are little things that are just differences in the way each one looks at the world," says Ms. Young. "My being Chinese helps in that regard."

Source: G. Stern, "GM Executive's Ties to Native Country Help Auto Maker Clinch Deal in China," *Wall Street Journal* (November 2, 1995), p. B7.

9.2 Leading

Implementation also involves **leading** people to use their abilities and skills most effectively and efficiently to achieve organizational objectives. Without direction, people tend to do their work according to their personal view of what tasks should be done, how, and in what order. They may approach their work as they have in the past or emphasize those tasks that they most enjoy—regardless of the corporation's priorities. This can create real problems, particularly if the company is operating internationally and must adjust to customs and traditions in other countries. This direction may take the form of management leadership, communicated norms of behavior from the corporate culture, or agreements among workers in autonomous work groups. It may also be accomplished more formally through action planning, or through programs such as Management By Objectives and Total Quality Management.

Managing Corporate Culture

Because an organization's culture can exert a powerful influence on the behavior of all employees, it can strongly affect a company's ability to shift its strategic direction. A problem for a strong culture is that a change in mission, objectives, strategies, or policies is not likely to be successful if it is in opposition to the accepted culture of the company. Corporate culture has a strong tendency to resist change because its very reason for existence often rests on preserving stable relationships and patterns of behavior. For example, the male-dominated, Japanese-centered corporate culture of the giant Mitsubishi Corporation has created problems for the company as it tries to implement its growth strategy in North America. The alleged sexual harassment of its female employees by male supervisors resulted in a law suit by the U.S. Equal Employment Opportunity

Commission and a boycott of the company's automobiles by the National Organization for Women in 1996.[24]

There is no one best corporate culture. An optimal culture is one that best supports the mission and strategy of the company of which it is a part. This means that, like structure and staffing, *corporate culture should support the strategy.* Unless strategy is in complete agreement with the culture, any significant change in strategy should be followed by a modification of the organization's culture. Although corporate culture can be changed, it may often take a long time and it requires much effort. A key job of management involves **managing corporate culture.** In doing so, management must evaluate what a particular change in strategy means to the corporate culture, assess if a change in culture is needed, and decide if an attempt to change the culture is worth the likely costs.

Assessing Strategy-Culture Compatibility

When implementing a new strategy, a company should take the time to assess **strategy-culture compatibility.** (See Figure 9.1.) Consider the following questions regarding the corporation's culture:

1. **Is the planned strategy compatible with the company's current culture?** If *yes*, full steam ahead. Tie organizational changes into the company's culture by identifying how the new strategy will achieve the mission better than the current strategy does. *If not . . .*

2. **Can the culture be easily modified to make it more compatible with the new strategy?** If *yes*, move forward carefully by introducing a set of culture-changing activities such as minor structural modifications, training and development activities, and/or hiring new managers who are more compatible with the new strategy. When Procter & Gamble's top management decided to implement a strategy aimed at reducing costs, for example, it made some changes in how things were done, but it did not eliminate its brand-management system. The culture adapted to these modifications over a couple years and productivity increased. *If not . . .*

3. **Is management willing and able to make major organizational changes and accept probable delays and a likely increase in costs?** If *yes*, manage around the culture by establishing a new structural unit to implement the new strategy. At General Motors, for example, top management realized the company had to make some radical changes to be more competitive. Because the current structure, culture, and procedures were very inflexible, management decided to establish a completely new division (GM's first new division since 1918) called Saturn to build its new auto. In cooperation with the United Auto Workers, an entirely new labor agreement was developed, based on decisions reached by consensus. Carefully selected employees received from 100 to 750 hours of training, and a whole new culture was built piece by piece. *If not . . .*

4. **Is management still committed to implementing the strategy?** If *yes*, find a joint-venture partner or contract with another company to carry out the strategy. *If not,* **formulate a different strategy.**

Managing Cultural Change Through Communication

Communication is key to the effective management of change. Rationale for strategic changes should be communicated to workers not only in newsletters and speeches, but

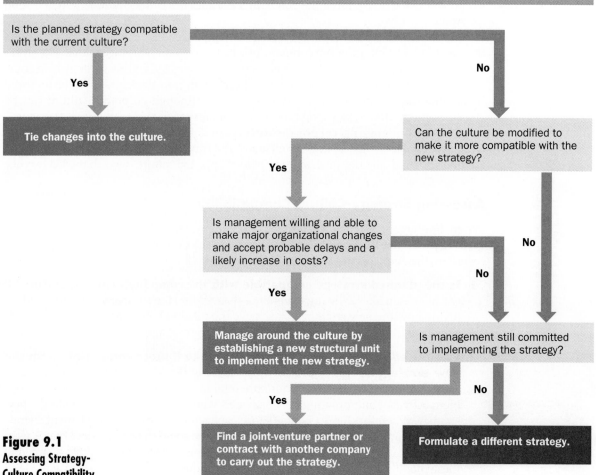

Figure 9.1
Assessing Strategy-Culture Compatibility

also in training and development programs. Companies in which major cultural changes have taken place successfully had the following characteristics in common:

- The CEO and other top managers had a strategic vision of what the company could become and communicated this vision to employees at all levels. The current performance of the company was compared to that of its competition and constantly updated.

- The vision was translated into the key elements necessary to accomplish that vision. For example, if the vision called for the company to become a leader in quality or service, aspects of quality and service were pinpointed for improvement and appropriate measurement systems were developed to monitor them. These measures were communicated widely through contests, formal and informal recognition, and monetary rewards, among other devices.[25]

Managing Diverse Cultures Following an Acquisition

When merging with or acquiring another company, top management must give some consideration to a potential clash of corporate cultures. It's dangerous to assume that the firms can simply be integrated into the same reporting structure. The greater the gap between the cultures of the acquired firm and the acquiring firm, the faster executives in the acquired firm quit their jobs and valuable talent is lost.

Figure 9.2
Methods of Managing the Culture of an Acquired Firm

Source: A. Nahavardi and A. R. Malekzadeh, "Accultutation in Mergers and Acquisitions," *Academy of Management Review* (January 1988), p. 83. Copyright © 1988 by the Academy of Management. Reprinted by permission.

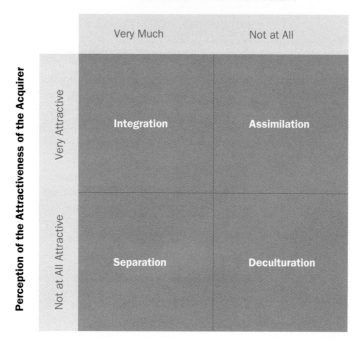

How Much Members of the Acquired Firm Value Preservation of Their Own Culture

	Very Much	Not at All
Very Attractive	Integration	Assimilation
Not at All Attractive	Separation	Deculturation

Perception of the Attractiveness of the Acquirer

There are four general methods of managing two different cultures. (See Figure 9.2.) The choice of which method to use should be based on (1) *how much members of the acquired firm value preserving their own culture* and (2) *how attractive they perceive the culture of the acquirer to be.*[26]

1. **Integration** involves a relatively balanced give-and-take of cultural and managerial practices between the merger partners, and no strong imposition of cultural change on either company. It merges the two cultures in such a way that the separate cultures of both firms are preserved in the resulting culture. This is what occurred when the Seaboard and Chesapeake & Ohio railroads merged to form CSX Corporation. The top executives were so concerned that both cultures be equally respected that they kept referring to the company as a "partnership of equals."

2. **Assimilation** involves the domination of one organization over the other. The domination is not forced, but it is welcomed by members of the acquired firm, who may feel for many reasons that their culture and managerial practices have not produced success. The acquired firm surrenders its culture and adopts the culture of the acquiring company. The **Company Spotlight on Maytag Corporation** feature describes this method of acculturation when Admiral, a subsidiary of Magic Chef, joined Maytag Corporation.

3. **Separation** is characterized by a separation of the two companies' cultures. They are structurally separated, without cultural exchange. In the Shearson-American Express merger, both parties agreed to keep the fast-paced Shearson completely separate from the planning-oriented American Express. This approach allowed American Express to easily divest Shearson once it discovered that the merger was not working.

Maytag's corporate culture had been dominated almost from the beginning of the company by the concept of quality. Maytag employees took great pride in being known as the "dependability people." Over the years, Maytag Company consistently advertised that their repairmen were "lonely" because Maytag products rarely, if ever, needed repair.

Admiral's history had, however, been quite different. Prior to Maytag's purchase of Magic Chef (and thus Admiral) in 1986, Admiral had been owned by three different corporations. Its manufacturing plant in Galesburg, Illinois, had deteriorated to a dismal level by the time Maytag acquired it. Refrigerators sometimes rolled off the assembly line with screws driven in crooked and temperature balances askew!

Maytag's management had always wanted to have its own Maytag brand refrigerator. That was one reason why it purchased Magic Chef. But it was worried that Admiral might not be able to produce a quality product to Maytag's specifications. To improve Admiral's quality, Maytag's top management decided to integrate Admiral directly into Maytag Company operations. As a result, all Admiral functional departments, except

marketing, reported directly to the Maytag Company president.

Under the direction of Leonard Hadley, while he was serving as Maytag Company President, a project was initiated to design and manufacture a refrigerator for the Maytag brand at the Admiral plant. When Hadley first visited Admiral's facilities to discuss the design of a Maytag line of refrigerators, Admiral personnel asked Hadley when the name on their plant's water tower would be changed from Admiral to Maytag. Hadley (acknowledging Maytag's cultural concerns regarding quality) responded: "When you earn it."

The refrigerator resulting from the Maytag-Admiral collaboration was a huge success. The project crystallized corporate management's philosophy for forging synergies among the Maytag companies, while simultaneously allowing the individual expertise of those units to flourish. Admiral's employees were willing to accept the dominance of Maytag's strong quality-oriented culture because they respected it. In turn, they expected to be treated with some respect for their tradition of skill in refrigeration technology.

MAYTAG CORPORATION

4. **Deculturation** involves the disintegration of one company's culture resulting from unwanted and extreme pressure from the other to impose its culture and practices. This is the most common and most destructive method of dealing with two different cultures. It is often accompanied by much confusion, conflict, resentment, and stress. Such a merger typically results in poor performance by the acquired company and its eventual divestment. This is what happened when AT&T acquired NCR Corporation in 1990 for its computer business. It replaced NCR managers with an AT&T management team, reorganized sales, forced employees to adhere to the AT&T code of values (called the "Common Bond"), and even dropped the proud NCR name (successor to National Cash Register) in favor of a sterile GIS (Global Information Solutions) nonidentity. By 1995, AT&T was forced to take a $1.2 billion loss and lay off 10,000 people.[27] The NCR unit was put up for sale in 1996.

Action Planning

Activities can be directed toward accomplishing strategic goals through action planning. At a minimum, an **action plan** states what actions are going to be taken, by whom,

Table 9.1   **Example of an Action Plan**

Action Plan for Jan Lewis, Advertising Manager, Ajax Continental

---

Program Objective: To Run a New Advertising and Promotion Campaign for the Combined Jones Surplus/Ajax Continental Retail Stores for the Coming Christmas Season Within a Budget of $XX.

Program Activities:
1. Identify Three Best Ad Agencies for New Campaign.
2. Ask Three Ad Agencies to Submit a Proposal for a New Advertising and Promotion Campaign for Combined Stores.
3. Agencies Present Proposals to Marketing Manager.
4. Select Best Proposal and Inform Agencies of Decision.
5. Agency Presents Winning Proposal to Top Management.
6. Ads Air on TV and Promotions Appear in Stores.
7. Measure Results of Campaign in Terms of Viewer Recall and Increase in Store Sales.

Action Steps	Responsibility	Start-End
1. A. Review previous programs	Lewis & Carter	1/1–2/1
B. Discuss with boss	Lewis & Smith	2/1–2/3
C. Decide on 3 agencies	Lewis	2/4
2. A. Write specifications for ad	Lewis	1/15–1/20
B. Assistant writes ad request	Carter	1/20–1/30
C. Contact ad agencies	Lewis	2/5–2/8
D. Send request to 3 agencies	Carter	2/10
E. Meet with agency acct. execs	Lewis & Carter	2/16–2/20
3. A. Agencies work on proposals	Acct. Execs	2/23–5/1
B. Agencies present proposals	Carter	5/1–5/15
4. A. Select best proposal	Lewis	5/15–5/20
B. Meet with winning agency	Lewis	5/22–5/30
C. Inform losers	Carter	6/1
5. A. Fine-tune proposal	Acct. Exec	6/1–7/1
B. Presentation to management	Lewis	7/1–7/3
6. A. Ads air on TV	Lewis	9/1–12/24
B. Floor displays in stores	Carter	8/20–8/30
7. A. Gather recall measures of ads	Carter	9/1–12/24
B. Evaluate sales data	Carter	1/1–1/10
C. Prepare analysis of campaign	Carter	1/10–2/15

---

during what timeframe, and with what expected results. After a program has been selected to implement a particular strategy, an action plan should be developed to put the program in place. See Table 9.1 for an example of an action plan for a new advertising and promotion program.

Take the example of a company choosing forward vertical integration through the acquisition of a retailing chain as its growth strategy. Now that it owns its own retail outlets, it must integrate the stores into the company. One of the many programs it would have to develop is a new advertising program for the stores. The resulting action plan to develop a new advertising program should include much of the following information:

1. Specific actions to be taken to make the program operational. One action might be to contact three reputable advertising agencies and ask them to prepare a proposal for a new radio and newspaper ad campaign based on the theme "Jones Surplus is now a part of Ajax Continental. Prices are lower. Selection is better."

2. **Dates to begin and end each action.** Time would have to be allotted not only to select and contact three agencies, but to allow them sufficient time to prepare a detailed proposal. For example, allow one week to select and contact the agencies plus three months for them to prepare detailed proposals to present to the company's marketing director. Also allow some time to decide which proposal to accept.

3. **Person (identified by name and title) responsible for carrying out each action.** List someone—such as Jan Lewis, advertising manager—who can be put in charge of the program.

4. **Person responsible for monitoring the timeliness and effectiveness of each action.** Indicate that Jan Lewis is responsible for ensuring that the proposals are of good quality and are priced within the planned program budget. She will be the primary company contact for the ad agencies and will report on the progress of the program once a week to the company's marketing director.

5. **Expected financial and physical consequences of each action.** Estimate when a completed ad campaign will be ready to show top management and how long it will take after approval to begin to air the ads. Estimate also the expected increase in store sales over the six-month period after the ads are first aired. Indicate if "recall" measures will be used to help assess the ad campaign's effectiveness plus how, when, and by whom the recall data will be collected and analyzed.

6. **Contingency plans.** Indicate how long it will take to get an acceptable ad campaign to show top management if none of the initial proposals is acceptable.

Action plans are important for several reasons. First, action plans serve as a link between strategy formulation and evaluation and control. Second, the action plan specifies what needs to be done differently from the way operations are currently carried out. Third, during the evaluation and control process that comes later, an action plan helps in both the appraisal of performance and in the identification of any remedial actions, as needed. In addition, the explicit assignment of responsibilities for implementing and monitoring the programs may contribute to better motivation.

Management By Objectives

Management By Objectives (MBO) is an organizationwide approach to help ensure purposeful action toward desired objectives. MBO links organizational objectives and the behavior of individuals. Because it is a system that links plans with performance, it is a powerful implementation technique.

The MBO process involves:

1. Establishing and communicating organizational objectives.

2. Setting individual objectives (through superior-subordinate interaction) that help implement organizational ones.

3. Developing an action plan of activities needed to achieve the objectives.

4. Periodically (at least quarterly) reviewing performance as it relates to the objectives and including the results in the annual performance appraisal.

MBO provides an opportunity for the corporation to connect the objectives of people at each level to those at the next higher level. MBO, therefore, acts to tie together corprate, business, and functional objectives, as well as the strategies developed to achieve them.

One of the real benefits of MBO is that it can reduce the amount of internal politics operating within a large corporation. Political actions within a firm can cause conflict and create divisions between the very people and groups who should be working together to implement strategy. People are less likely to jockey for position if the company's mission and objectives are clear and they know that the reward system is based not on game playing, but on achieving clearly communicated, measurable objectives.

Total Quality Management

Total Quality Management (TQM) is an operational philosophy committed to *customer satisfaction* and *continuous improvement*. TQM is committed to quality/excellence and to being the best in all functions. TQM has four objectives:

1. Better, less variable quality of the product and service.

2. Quicker, less variable response in processes to customer needs.

3. Greater flexibility in adjusting to customers' shifting requirements.

4. Lower cost through quality improvement and elimination of non–value adding work.[28]

Because TQM aims to reduce costs and improve quality, it can be used as a program to implement both an overall low-cost or a differentiation business strategy. About 92% of manufacturing companies and 69% of service firms have implemented some form of quality management practices.[29]

According to TQM, faulty processes, not poorly motivated employees, are the cause of defects in quality. The program involves a significant change in corporate culture, requiring strong leadership from top management, employee training, empowerment of lower level employees (giving people more control over their work), and teamwork for it to succeed in a company. TQM emphasizes prevention, not correction. Inspection for quality still takes place, but the emphasis is on improving the process to prevent errors and deficiencies. Thus quality circles or quality improvement teams are formed to identify problems and to suggest how to improve the processes that may be causing the problems.

TQM's essential *ingredients* are:

- **An intense focus on customer satisfaction.** Everyone (not just people in the sales and marketing departments) understands that their jobs exist only because of customer needs. Thus all jobs must be approached in terms of how it will affect customer satisfaction.

- **Internal as well as external customers.** An employee in the shipping department may be the internal customer of another employee who completes the assembly of a product, just as a person who buys the product is a customer of the entire company. An employee must be just as concerned with pleasing the internal customer as in satisfying the external customer.

- **Accurate measurement of every critical variable in a company's operations.** This means that employees have to be trained in what to measure, how to measure, and how to interpret the data. A rule of TQM is "you only improve what you measure."

- **Continuous improvement of products and services.** Everyone realizes that operations need to be continuously monitored to find ways to improve products and services.

- **New work relationships based on trust and teamwork.** Important is the idea of *empowerment*—giving employees wide latitude in how they go about in achieving the company's goals. Research indicates that the key to TQM success lies in executive commitment, an open organizational culture, and employee empowerment.[30]

International Considerations in Leading

In a study of 53 different national cultures, Hofstede found that each nation's unique culture could be identified using five dimensions. He found that national culture is so influential that it tends to overwhelm even a strong corporate culture. In measuring the differences among these **dimensions of national culture** from country to country, he was able to explain why a certain management practice might be successful in one nation, but fail in another.[31]

1. **Power distance (PD)** is the *extent to which a society accepts an unequal distribution of power in organizations.* Malaysia and Mexico scored highest, whereas Germany and Austria scored lowest. People in those countries scoring high on this dimension tend to prefer autocratic to more participative managers.

2. **Uncertainty avoidance (UA)** is the *extent to which a society feels threatened by uncertain and ambiguous situations.* Greece and Japan scored highest on disliking ambiguity, whereas the United States and Singapore scored lowest. People in those nations scoring high on this dimension tend to want career stability, formal rules, and clear-cut measures of performance.

3. **Individualism-collectivism (I-C)** is the *extent to which a society values individual freedom and independence of action compared with a tight social framework and loyalty to the group.* The United States and Canada scored highest on individualism, whereas Mexico and Guatemala scored lowest. People in those nations scoring high on individualism tend to value individual success through competition, whereas people scoring low on individualism (thus high on collectivism) tend to value group success through collective cooperation.

4. **Masculinity-femininity (M-F)** is the *extent to which society is oriented toward money and things* (which Hofstede labels masculine) *or toward people* (which Hofstede labels feminine). Japan and Mexico scored highest on masculinity, whereas France and Sweden scored lowest (thus highest on femininity). People in those nations scoring high on masculinity tend to value clearly defined sex roles where men dominate and to emphasize performance and independence, whereas people scoring low on masculinity (and thus high on femininity) tend to value equality of the sexes where power is shared and to emphasize the quality of life and interdependence.

5. **Long-term orientation (LT)** is the *extent to which society is oriented toward the long versus the short term.* Hong Kong and Japan scored highest on long-term orientation, whereas Pakistan scored the lowest. A long-term time orientation emphasizes the importance of hard work, education, and persistence as well as the importance of thrift. Nations with a long-term time orientation should value strategic planning and other management techniques with a long-term payback.

These dimensions of national culture may help to explain why some management practices work well in some countries, but not in others. For example, Management By Objectives (MBO), which originated in the United States, has succeeded in Germany, according to Hofstede, because the idea of replacing the arbitrary authority of the boss with the impersonal authority of mutually agreed-upon objectives fits the low power distance that is a dimension of the German culture. It has failed in France, however, because the French are used to high power distances—to accepting orders from a highly personalized authority. In addition, some of the difficulties experienced by U.S. companies in using Japanese-style quality circles in Total Quality Management may stem from the extremely high value U.S. culture places on individualism. The differences between the U.S and Mexico on power distance (Mexico 104 vs. U.S. 46) and individualism-collectivism (U.S. 91 vs. Mexico 30) dimensions may help explain why some companies operating in both countries have difficulty adapting to the differences in customs.[32]

When one successful company in one country merges with another successful company in another country, the clash of corporate cultures is compounded by the clash of national cultures. In Maytag's case, the acquisition of Hoover's North American vacuum cleaner business created few problems because the quality-oriented corporate cultures were so similar. Problems arose when Maytag executives began interacting with their Hoover Europe colleagues in the United Kingdom. Maytag people were viewed by the British as demanding and "rigid," whereas the Hoover-Europe people were viewed as more laid back and "collegial." With cross-border mergers and acquisitions increasing to 6,377 by 1996, the management of cultures is becoming a key issue in strategy implementation.[33] See the ● **21st Century Global Society** feature to learn how differences in national and corporate cultures created conflict when Upjohn Company of the U.S. and Pharmacia AB of Sweden merged.

Multinational corporations must pay attention to the many differences in cultural dimensions around the world and adjust their management practices accordingly. Cultural differences can easily go unrecognized by a headquarters staff that may interpret these differences as personality defects, whether the people in the subsidiaries are locals or expatriates. Hofstede and Bond conclude: "Whether they like it or not, the headquarters of multinationals are in the business of multicultural management."[34]

●**9.3** *Global Issues for the 21st Century*

- The first **21st Century Global Society** feature in this chapter illustrates how General Motors is using the diversity of its workforce to help it obtain entry into China. This is one reason why those companies hiring people of all races, religions, and national backgrounds will have an advantage in the world of the future.

- The second **21st Century Global Society** feature illustrates the difficulty of merging two companies—not only because of differences in corporate, but also in national culture. With the number of cross-border mergers and acquisitions increasing, expect companies to value international work experience more highly.

- Given the importance of technology in global business, companies will need to spend more time and money hiring skilled labor and training these employees to deal with emerging technologies.

- Differences in corporate and national cultures may explain why many companies prefer to work with a local partner in a strategic alliance rather than simply

21ST CENTURY GLOBAL SOCIETY

CULTURAL DIFFERENCES CREATE IMPLEMENTATION PROBLEMS IN MERGER

When Upjohn Pharmaceuticals of Kalamazoo, Michigan, and Pharmacia AB of Stockholm, Sweden, merged in 1995, employees of both sides were optimistic for the newly formed Pharmacia & Upjohn, Inc. Both companies were second-tier competitors fighting for survival in a global industry. Together, the firms would create a global company that could compete scientifically with its bigger rivals.

Because Pharmacia had acquired an Italian firm in 1993, it also had a large operation in Milan. American executives scheduled meetings throughout the summer of 1996—only to cancel them when their European counterparts could not attend. Although it was common knowledge in Europe that most Swedes take the entire month of July for vacation and that Italians take off all of August, this was not common knowledge in Michigan. Differences in management styles became a special irritant. Swedes were used to an open system with autonomous work teams. Executives sought the whole group's approval before making an important decision. Upjohn executives followed the more traditional American top-down approach. Upon taking command of the newly merged firm, Dr. Zabriskie (who had been Upjohn's CEO), divided the company into departments reporting to the new London headquarters. He required frequent reports, budgets, and staffing updates. The Swedes reacted negatively to this top-down management hierarchical style. "It was degrading," said Stener Kvinnsland, head of Pharmacia's cancer research in Italy before he quit the new company.

The Italian operations baffled the Americans, even though the Italians felt comfortable with a hierarchical management style. Italy's laws and unions made layoffs difficult. Italian data and accounting were often inaccurate. Because the Americans didn't trust the data, they were constantly asking for verification. In turn, the Italians were concerned that the Americans were trying to take over Italian operations. At Upjohn, all workers were subject to testing for drug and alcohol abuse. Upjohn also banned smoking. At Pharmacia's Italian business center, however, waiters poured wine freely every afternoon in the company dining room. Pharmacia's boardrooms were stocked with humidors for executives who smoked cigars during long meetings. After a brief attempt to enforce Upjohn's policies, the company dropped both of the no-drinking and no-smoking policies for European workers.

Although the combined company had cut annual costs by $200 million, overall costs of the merger reached $800 million, some $200 million more than projected. Nevertheless, Jan Eckberg, CEO of Pharmacia before the merger, remained confident of the new company's ability to succeed. He admitted, however, that "we have to make some smaller changes to release the full power of the two companies."

Source: R. Frank and T. M. Burton, "Cross-Border Merger Results in Headaches for a Drug Company," *Wall Street Journal* (February 4, 1997), pp. A1, A12.

acquiring a company in another country. Alliances may be similar to a courtship period between two large companies and, if successful, may lead to an eventual merger.

- Improvements in communications (satellites, cell phones, Internet) and logistics are making it easier to interact with people of other nations. As more industries become global, it is possible that differences in national culture may become less important.

Nations do, however, want to keep some of their differences, yet be part of the world community. The British want to remain British. The same is true of the Chinese, the Italians, and the Canadians. Multinational corporations will be forced to deal with this paradox so long as different peoples want to be a part of a larger community, yet have their differences respected.

Projections for the 21st Century

- From 1994 to 2010, movie screens will increase in the United States from 25,105 to 74,114.

- From 1994 to 2010, movie screens will grow worldwide from 86,902 to 162,766.[35]

Discussion Questions

1. What skills should a person have for managing a business unit following a differentiation strategy? Why? What should a company do if no one is available internally and the company has a policy of promotion from within?

2. When should someone from outside the company be hired to manage the company or one of its business units?

3. What are some ways to implement a retrenchment strategy without creating a lot of resentment and conflict with labor unions?

4. How can corporate culture be changed?

5. Why is an understanding of national cultures important in strategic management?

Key Terms

action plan (p. 218)
assessment centers (p. 211)
assimilation (p. 217)
deculturation (p. 218)
dimensions of national culture (p. 222)
downsizing (p. 211)
executive succession (p. 210)
executive type (p. 209)
individualism-collectivism (I-C) (p. 222)

integration (p. 217)
international staffing (p. 212)
job rotation (p. 211)
leading (p. 214)
long-term orientation (LT) (p. 222)
Management By Objectives (MBO) (p. 220)
managing corporate culture (p. 215)
masculinity-femininity (M-F) (p. 222)

performance appraisal system (p. 211)
power distance (PD) (p. 222)
professional liquidator (p. 209)
separation (p. 217)
staffing (p. 207)
staffing follows strategy (p. 208)
strategy-culture compatibility (p. 215)
Total Quality Management (TQM) (p. 221)
turnaround specialist (p. 209)
uncertainty avoidance (UA) (p. 222)

Strategic Practice Exercise

Staffing involves finding the person with the right blend of characteristics, such as personality, training, and experience, to implement a particular strategy. Based on psychologist Carl Jung's work, Isabel Myers and Katheryn Briggs developed a way to measure two key dimensions of an individual's personality: (1) sensing and intuition and (2) thinking and feeling. Data about the world are obtained along a continuum with sensing at one end and intuition at the other. A **sensing person** *strives for logic and order.* An **intuitive in-**

dividual *works according to inspiration, flashes of insight, and hunches.* Judgments about the world are applied along a continuum with thinking at one end and feeling at the other. The **thinking person** *makes assessments in a logical and analytical manner.* A **feeling person** *makes assessments based on values and subjective emotions.* Engage in the following exercise to assess these characteristics of your personality and their impact on your decision making.

1. Fill out the form. Respond to the following 20 items in terms of your personal concerns and behavior. For each item, indicate which of the two alternative statements (*A or B*) is most characteristic of you. **Distribute 5 points between each set of two statements.** You may put all 5 points on A and none on B, or you may put some points on A and the rest on B. *The amount of points for each item (A and B) should sum to 5.*

		A B
1. Are you more	(a) pragmatic (b) idealistic	A B
2. Are you more impressed by	(a) standards (b) sentiments	A B
3. Are you more interested in that which	(a) convinces you by facts (b) emotionally moves you	A B
4. It is worse to be	(a) impractical (b) having a boring routine	A B
5. Are you more attracted to	(a) a person with good common sense (b) a creative person	A B
6. In judging others, are you more swayed by	(a) the rules (b) the situation	A B
7. Are you more interested in	(a) what has happened (b) what can happen	A B
8. Do you more often have	(a) presence of mind (b) warm emotions	A B
9. Are you more frequently	(a) a realistic sort of person (b) an imaginative sort of person	A B
10. Are you more	(a) faithful (b) logical	A B
11. Are you more	(a) action-oriented (b) creation-oriented	A B
12. Which guides you more	(a) your brain (b) your heart	A B
13. Do you take pride in your	(a) realistic outlook (b) imaginative ability	A B
14. Which is more of a personal compliment	(a) you are consistent in your reasoning (b) you are considerate of others	A B
15. Are you more drawn to	(a) basics (b) implications	A B
16. Is it better to be	(a) fair (b) sentimental	A B
17. Would you rather spend time with	(a) realistic people (b) imaginative people	A B
18. Would you describe yourself as	(a) hard (b) soft	A B
19. Would your friends say that you are	(a) someone who is filled with new ideas (b) someone who is a realist	A B
20. It is better to be called a person who shows	(a) feelings (b) reasonable consistency	A B

2. Score the form. Enter the numbers for your response to each item in the appropriate column of the following chart. Then add each of the four columns to obtain a total for each. **Circle** the *highest* of the **S** or **N** column totals. Then **circle** the *highest* of the **T** or **F** column totals. S = sensation. N = intuitive. T = thinking. F = feeling. This will tell you which of the *four decision-making styles you tend to favor:* **Sensation-Thinking (ST), Sensation-Feeling (SF), Intuitive-Thinking (NT),** or **Intuitive-Feeling (IF).**

Item #	A	B	Item #	A	B
1			2		
3			4		
5			6		
7			8		
9			10		
11			12		
13			14		
15			16		
17			18		
19			20		
Totals					
	S = Sensation	N = Intuitive		T = Thinking	F = Feeling

3. Form groups to do the exercise. Form into groups of about 4–6 people based on your decision-making style. Each group should be composed of people with the same decision-making style (**ST**, **SF**, **NT**, or **NF**). Your assignment is to form a new business venture. You have 30 minutes to discuss this in your group. When 30 minutes is over, a spokesperson from each group should present each group's ideas.

4. Analyze the group differences. How did the groups differ in terms of their ideas for a new venture? How did each group handle the assignment? What does this tell you about how staffing should follow strategy?

———————————

Source: Questionnaire taken from D. Hellriegel, J. W. Slocum, and R. W. Woodman, *Organizational Behavior*, 7th ed. (Cincinatti: South-Western, 1995), pp. 108–134. Reprinted by permission. Exercise suggested by F. Ramsoomair, "Relating Theoretical Concepts to Life in the Classroom: Applying the Myers-Briggs Type Indicator," *Journal of Management Education* (February 1994), pp. 111–116.

Notes

1. B. O'Reilly, "The Rent-A-Car Jocks Who Made Enterprise #1," *Fortune* (October 28, 1996), pp. 125–128.
2. J. P. Walsh, "Doing a Deal: Merger and Acquisition Negotiations and Their Impact Upon Target Company Top Management Turnover," *Strategic Management Journal* (July-August 1989), pp. 307–322.
3. J. Hoerr, "Sharpening Minds for a Competitive Edge," *Business Week* (December 17, 1990), pp. 72–78.
4. *High Performance Work Practices and Firm Performance* (Washington, D.C.: U.S. Department of Labor, Office of the American Workplace, 1993), pp. i, 4.
5. K. Kelly, "Motorola: Training for the Millennium," *Business Week* (March 28, 1996), pp. 158–161.
6. R. Henkoff, "Companies That Train Best," *Fortune* (March 22, 1993), pp. 62–75.
7. A. S. Thomas, and K. Ramaswamy, "Environmental Change and Management Staffing: A Comment," *Journal of Management* (Winter 1993), pp. 877–887; J. P. Guthrie, C. M. Grimm, and K. G. Smith, "Environmental Change and Management Staffing: An Empirical Study," *Journal of Management* (December 1991), pp. 735–748.
8. R. Drazin, and R. K. Kazanjian, "Applying the Del Technique to the Analysis of Cross-Classification Data: A Test of CEO Succession and Top Management Team Development," *Academy of Management Journal* (December 1993), pp. 1374–1399; W. E. Rothschild, "A Portfolio of Strategic

Leaders," *Planning Review* (January/February 1996), pp. 16–19.

9. J. A. Parnell, "Functional Background and Business Strategy: The Impact of Executive-Strategy Fit on Performance," *Journal of Business Strategies* (Spring 1994), pp. 49–62.

10. M. Smith and M. C. White, "Strategy, CEO Specialization, and Succession," *Administrative Science Quarterly* (June 1987), pp. 263–280.

11. C. M. Farkas, and S. Wetlaufer, "The Ways Chief Executive Officers Lead," *Harvard Business Review* (May/June, 1996), p. 110.

12. C. Gopinath, "Turnaround: Recognizing Decline and Initiating Intervention," *Long Range Planning* (December 1991), pp. 96–101.

13. K. B. Schwartz, and K. Menon, "Executive Succession in Failing Firms," *Academy of Management Journal* (September 1985), pp. 680–686; A. A. Cannella, Jr., and M. Lubatkin, "Succession as a Sociopolitical Process: Internal Impediments to Outsider Selection," *Academy of Management Journal* (August 1993), pp. 763–793; W. Boeker and J. Goodstein, "Performance and Succession Choice: The Moderating Effects of Governance and Ownership," *Academy of Management Journal* (February 1993), pp. 172–186.

14. P. Lorange, and D. Murphy, "Bringing Human Resources Into Strategic Planning: System Design Characteristics," in *Strategic Human Resource Management,* edited by C. J. Fombrun, N. M. Tichy, and M. A. Devanna (New York: John Wiley and Sons, 1984), pp. 281–283.

15. R. A. Pitts, "Strategies and Structures for Diversification," *Academy of Management Journal* (June 1997), pp. 197–208.

16. B. O'Reilly, "Is Your Company Asking Too Much?" *Fortune* (March 12, 1990), p. 41.

17. *Wall Street Journal* (December 22, 1992), p. B1.

18. G. D. Bruton, J. K. Keels, and C. L. Shook, "Downsizing the Firm: Answering the Strategic Questions," *Academy of Management Executive* (May 1996), pp. 38–45.

19. M. A. Hitt, B. W. Keats, H. F. Harback, and R. D. Nixon, "Rightsizing: Building and Maintaining Strategic Leadership and Long-Term Competitiveness," *Organizational Dynamics* (Autumn 1994), pp. 18–32.

20. R. L. Tung, *The New Expatriates* (Cambridge, Mass.: Ballinger, 1988); J. S. Black, M. Mendenhall, and G. Oddou, "Toward a Comprehensive Model of International Adjustment: An Integration of Multiple Theoretical Perspectives," *Academy of Management Review* (April 1991), pp. 291–317.

21. K. Roth, "Managing International Interdependence: CEO Characteristics in a Resource-Based Framework," *Academy of Management Journal* (February 1995), pp. 200–231.

22. J. S. Lublin, "An Overseas Stint Can Be a Ticket to the Top," *Wall Street Journal* (January 29, 1996), pp. B1, B2.

23. J. S. Lublin, "Is Transfer to Native Land a Passport to Trouble?" *Wall Street Journal* (June 3, 1996), pp. B1, B5.

24. P. Elstrom, and S. V. Brull, "Mitsubishi's Morass," *Business Week* (June 3, 1996), p. 35.

25. G. G. Gordon, "The Relationship of Corporate Culture to Industry Sector and Corporate Performance," in *Gaining Control of the Corporate Culture,* edited by R. H. Kilmann, M. J. Saxton, R. Serpa, and Associates (San Francisco: Jossey-Bass, 1985), p. 123; T. Kono, "Corporate Culture and Long-Range Planning," *Long Range Planning* (August 1990), pp. 9–19.

26. A. R. Malekzadeh, and A. Nahavandi, "Making Mergers Work by Managing Cultures," *Journal of Business Strategy* (May/June 1990), pp. 53–57; A. Nahavandi, and A. R. Malekzadeh, "Acculturation in Mergers and Acquisitions," *Academy of Management Review* (January 1988), pp. 79–90.

27. J. J. Keller, "Why AT&T Takeover of NCR Hasn't Been a Real Bell Ringer," *Wall Street Journal* (September 19, 1995), pp. A1, A5.

28. R. J. Schonberger, "Total Quality Management Cuts a Broad Swath—Through Manufacturing and Beyond," *Organizational Dynamics* (Spring 1992), pp. 16–28.

29. S. S. Masterson, and M. S. Taylor, "Total Quality Management and Performance Appraisal: An Integrative Perspective," *Journal of Quality Management,* Vol. 1, No. 1 (1996), pp. 67–89.

30. T. C. Powell, "Total Quality Management as Competitive Advantage: A Review and Empirical Study," *Strategic Management Journal* (January 1995), pp. 15–37.

31. G. Hofstede, *Cultures and Organizations: Software of the Mind* (London: McGraw-Hill, 1991); G. Hofstede and M. H. Bond, "The Confucius Connection: From Cultural Roots to Economic Growth," *Organizational Dynamics* (Spring 1988), pp. 5–21; R. Hodgetts, "A Conversation with Geert Hofstede," *Organizational Dynamics* (Spring 1993), pp. 53–61.

32. See Hofstede and Bond, "The Confucius Connection," pp. 12–13.

33. R. Frank, and T. M. Burton, "Cross-Border Merger Results in Headaches for a Drug Company," *Wall Street Journal* (February 4, 1997), p. A1.

34. Hofstede and Bond, "The Confucius Connection," p. 20.

35. J. Warner, "21st Century Capitalism: Snapshot of the Next Century," *Business Week* (November 18, 1994), p. 194.

Chapter 10

Evaluation and Control

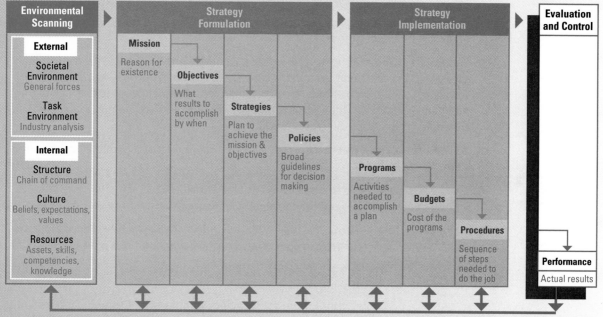

During the spring of 1992, Jim Cannavino, the manager in charge of IBM's personal computer business, insisted that his was the most profitable PC business in the world. Unfortunately his comment was based on the very strange way IBM allocated its costs to products. For example, IBM's system of accounting allocated all of a particular technology's R&D spending to the first group that used the technology; other IBM units then were able to use that technology free. As IBM found itself facing declining profits, it changed its cost allocation system to one that was more realistic. By the fall of 1992, IBM disclosed that its PC business was actually unprofitable. IBM's competitors commented that the business had probably been losing money on and off for years—IBM just didn't know it![1]

The **evaluation and control process** ensures that the company is achieving what it set out to accomplish. It compares performance with desired results and provides the feedback necessary for management to evaluate results and take corrective action, as needed. This process can be viewed as a five-step feedback model, as depicted in Figure 10.1.

1. **Determine what to measure.** Top managers and operational managers need to specify what implementation processes and results will be monitored and evaluated. The processes and results must be capable of being measured in a reasonably objective and consistent manner. The focus should be on the most significant elements in a process—the ones that account for the highest proportion of expense or the greatest number of problems. Measurements must be found for all important areas, regardless of difficulty.

2. **Establish standards of performance.** Standards used to measure performance are detailed expressions of strategic objectives. They are *measures* of acceptable performance results. Each standard usually includes a **tolerance range**, which defines acceptable deviations. Standards can be set not only for final output, but also for intermediate stages of production output.

3. **Measure actual performance.** Measurements must be made at predetermined times.

4. **Compare actual performance with the standard.** If actual performance results are within the desired tolerance range, the measurement process stops here.

5. **Take corrective action.** If actual results fall outside the desired tolerance range, action must be taken to correct the deviation. The following questions must be answered:

   a. Is the deviation only a chance fluctuation?

   b. Are the processes being carried out incorrectly?

   c. Are the processes appropriate to the achievement of the desired standard? Action must be taken that will not only correct the deviation, but will also prevent its happening again.

Top management is often better at the first two steps of the control model than it is in the last three follow-through steps. It tends to establish a control system and then delegate the implementation to others. This can have unfortunate results.

10.1 *Evaluation and Control in Strategic Management*

Evaluation and control information consists of performance data and activity reports (gathered in Step 3 of Figure 10.1). If undesired performance results because the strategic management processes were inappropriately used, operational managers must know about it so that they can correct the employee activity. Top management need not be involved. If, however, undesired performance results from the processes themselves, top managers, as well as operational managers, must know about it so that they can develop new implementation programs or procedures.

Evaluation and control information must be relevant to what is being monitored. The IBM example demonstrates how inappropriate data clouded the perceptions of the PC unit's manager and may have led to poor strategic decision making. Evaluation and control is not an easy process. One of the obstacles to effective control is the difficulty in developing appropriate measures of important activities and outputs.

Figure 10.1
Evaluation and
Control Process

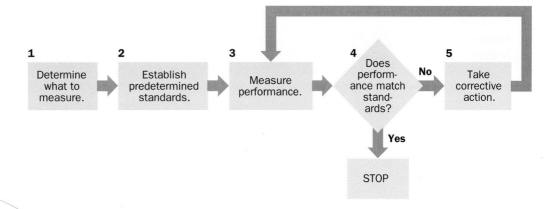

An application of the control process to strategic management is depicted in Figure 10.2. It provides strategic managers with a series of questions to use in evaluating an implemented strategy. Such a strategy review is usually initiated when a gap appears between a company's financial objectives and the expected results of current activities. After answering the proposed set of questions, a manager should have a good idea of where the problem originated and what must be done to correct the situation.

10.2 Measuring Performance

Performance is the end result of activity. Which measures to select to assess performance depends on the organizational unit to be appraised and the objectives to be achieved. The objectives that were established earlier in the strategy formulation part of the strategic management process (dealing with profitability, market share, and cost reduction, among others) should certainly be used to measure corporate performance once the strategies have been implemented.

Appropriate Measures

Some measures, such as return on investment (ROI), are appropriate for evaluating the corporation's or division's ability to achieve a profitability objective. This type of measure, however, is inadequate for evaluating additional corporate objectives such as social responsibility or employee development. Even though profitability is a corporation's major objective, ROI can be computed only *after* profits are totaled for a period. It tells what happened after the fact—not what *is* happening or what *will* happen. A firm, therefore, needs to develop measures that predict *likely* profitability. These are referred to as **steering controls** because they measure variables that influence future profitability. One example of this type of control is the use of control charts in Statistical Process Control (SPC). In SPC, workers and managers maintain charts and graphs detailing quality and productivity on a daily basis. They are thus able to make adjustments to the system before it gets out of control.[2]

Behavior and Output Controls

Controls can be established to focus either on actual performance results (output) or on the activities that generate the performance (behavior). **Behavior controls** specify *how*

Figure 10.2
Evaluating an
Implemented
Strategy

Source: Jeffery A. Schmidt, "The Strategic Review," *Planning Review* (July/August 1988), p. 15. Copyright © 1988 by The Planning Forum, Oxford, Ohio.

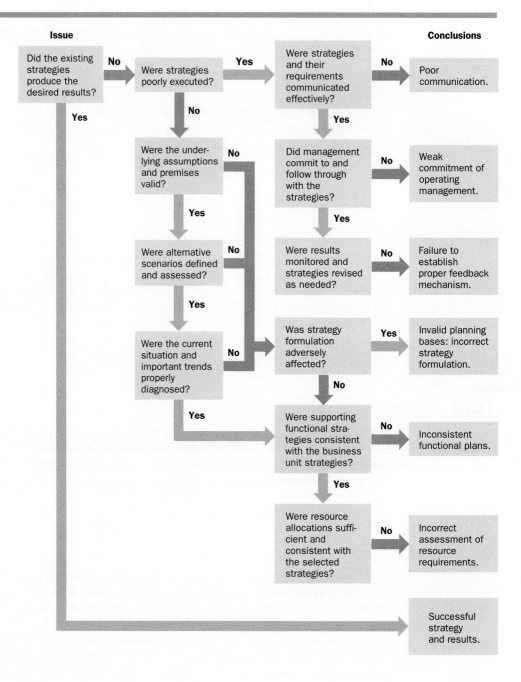

something is to be done through policies, rules, standard operating procedures, and or-ders from a superior. **Output controls** specify *what* is to be accomplished by focusing on the end result of the behaviors through the use of objectives and performance targets or milestones.

Behavior and output controls are not interchangeable. Behavior controls (such as following company procedures, making sales calls to potential customers, and getting to work on time) are most appropriate when performance results are hard to measure but the cause-effect connection between activities and results is clear. Output controls (such as sales quotas, specific cost reduction or profit objectives, and surveys of customer satisfaction) are most appropriate when specific output measures have been agreed on but the cause-effect connection between activities and results is not clear.

One example of an increasingly popular behavior control is the **ISO 9000 Standards Series** on quality management and assurance developed by the International Standards Association of Geneva, Switzerland. The ISO 9000 series (composed of five sections from 9000 to 9004) is a way of objectively documenting a company's high level of quality operations. ISO 9000 and 9004 contain guidelines for use with the other sections; 9001 is the most comprehensive standard; 9002 is less stringent; 9003 is only used for inspecting and testing procedures. A company wanting certification would probably document its process for product introductions, among other things. ISO 9001 would require this firm to separately document design input, design process, design output, and design verification—a large amount of work.

Many corporations view ISO 9000 certification as assurance that a supplier sells quality products. Firms such as DuPont, Hewlett-Packard, and 3M have facilities registered to ISO standards. Companies in over 60 countries, including Canada, Mexico, Japan, the United States (including the entire U.S. auto industry), and the European Union, are requiring ISO 9000 certification of their suppliers. In one survey of manufacturing executives, 51% of the executives found that certification increased their international competitiveness. Other executives noted that it signaled their commitment to quality and gave them a strategic advantage over noncertified competitors.[3]

Activity-Based Costing

Activity-based costing (ABC) is a new accounting method for allocating indirect and fixed costs to individual products or product lines based on the value-added activities going into that product.[4] This accounting method is thus very useful in doing a *value-chain analysis* of a firm's activities for making outsourcing decisions. Traditional cost accounting, in contrast, focuses on valuing a company's inventory for financial reporting purposes. To obtain a unit's cost, cost accountants typically add direct labor to the cost of materials. Then they compute overhead from rent to R&D expenses, based on the number of direct labor hours it takes to make a product. To obtain unit cost, they divide the total by the number of items made during the period under consideration.

Traditional cost accounting is useful when direct labor accounts for most of total costs and a company produces just a few products requiring the same processes. This may have been true of companies during the early part of the twentieth century, but it is no longer relevant today when overhead may account for as much as 70% of manufacturing costs. The appropriate allocation of indirect costs and overhead has thus become crucial for decision making. As mentioned at the beginning of this chapter, the use of traditional cost accounting at IBM blinded management to the true costs of its PC business. As PCs became a larger part of IBM's sales during the 1980s, corporate profits actually declined!

ABC accounting allows accountants to charge costs more accurately than the traditional method because it allocates overhead far more precisely. For example, imagine a production line in a pen factory where black pens are made in high volume and blue pens in low volume. Assume it takes eight hours to retool (reprogram the machinery) to shift production from one kind of pen to the other. The total costs include supplies (the same for both pens), the direct labor of the line workers, and factory overhead. In this instance, a very significant part of the overhead cost is the cost of reprogramming the machinery to switch from one pen to another. If the company produces ten times as many black pens as blue pens, ten times the cost of the reprogramming expenses will be allocated to the black pens as to the blue pens under traditional cost accounting methods. This approach underestimates, however, the true cost of making the blue pens (like IBM's personal computers).

ABC accounting, in contrast, first breaks down pen manufacturing into its activities. It is then very easy to see that it is the activity of changing pens that triggers the cost of retooling. The ABC accountant calculates an average cost of setting up the machinery and charges it against each batch of pens that requires retooling regardless of the size of the run. Thus a product carries only those costs for the overhead it actually consumes. Management is now able to discover that its blue pens cost almost twice as much as do the black pens. Unless the company is able to charge a higher price for its blue pens, it cannot make a profit on these pens. Unless there is a strategic reason why it must offer blue pens (such as a key customer who must have a small number of blue pens with every large order of black pens or a marketing trend away from black to blue pens), the company will earn significantly greater profits if it completely stops making blue pens.[5]

Activity-based costing can be used in many types of industries. For example, a bakery may use standard costs to allocate costs to products and to price customers' orders. Under the traditional standard cost system, overhead costs such as selling, advertising, warehousing, shipping, and administration are allocated to products and spread over the entire customer base. Under a traditional standard cost system, a bakery would allocate order handling charges on a percentage of sales basis. When this is done, profitable accounts tend to subsidize unprofitable ones—without anyone's knowledge. What is ignored is that the amount of time and expense spent processing an order is usually the same, regardless of whether the order is for 200 or 2000 donuts. The cost driver is not the number of cases ordered but the number of separate sales orders that must be processed. By assigning costs based on the number of orders that have to be processed, instead of by the dollar value of the order, the bakery can calculate a much more accurate cost for processing each customer's order. This information is crucial if management is to assess the profitability of different customers and to make strategic decisions regarding growth or retrenchment.[6]

Primary Measures of Corporate Performance

The days when simple financial measures such as ROI or EPS were used alone to assess overall corporate performance are coming to an end. Analysts now recommend a broad range of methods to evaluate the success or failure of a strategy. Some of these methods are stakeholder measures, shareholder value, and the balanced scorecard approach. Even though each of these methods has its supporters as well as detractors, the current trend is clearly toward more complicated financial measures and an increasing use of nonfinancial measures of corporate performance.[7] For example, research indicates that companies pursuing strategies founded on innovation and new product development now tend to favor nonfinancial over financial measures.[8]

Traditional Financial Measures

The most commonly used measure of corporate performance (in terms of profits) is **return on investment (ROI)**. It is simply the result of dividing net income before taxes by total assets. Although using ROI has several advantages, it also has several distinct limitations. (See Table 10.1.) Although ROI gives the impression of objectivity and precision, it can be easily manipulated.

Table 10.1   **Advantages and Limitations of Using ROI as a Measure of Corporate Performance**

Advantages

1. ROI is a single comprehensive figure influenced by everything that happens.
2. It measures how well the division manager uses the property of the company to generate profits. It is also a good way to check on the accuracy of capital investment proposals.
3. It is a common denominator that can be compared with many entities.
4. It provides an incentive to use existing assets efficiently.
5. It provides an incentive to acquire new assets only when doing so would increase the return.

Limitations

1. ROI is very sensitive to depreciation policy. Depreciation write-off variances between divisions affect ROI performance. Accelerated depreciation techniques increase ROI, conflicting with capital budgeting discounted cash-flow analysis.
2. ROI is sensitive to book value. Older plants with more depreciated assets have relatively lower investment bases than newer plants (note also the effect of inflation), thus increasing ROI. Note that asset investment may be held down or assets disposed of in order to increase ROI performance.
3. In many firms that use ROI, one division sells to another. As a result, transfer pricing must occur. Expenses incurred affect profit. Since, in theory, the transfer price should be based on the total impact on firm profit, some investment center managers are bound to suffer. Equitable transfer prices are difficult to determine.
4. If one division operates in an industry that has favorable conditions and another division operates in an industry that has unfavorable conditions, the former division will automatically "look" better than the other.
5. The time span of concern here is short range. The performance of division managers should be measured in the long run. This is top management's timespan capacity.
6. The business cycle strongly affects ROI performance, often despite managerial performance.

Source: "Advantages and Limitations of ROI as a Measure of Corporate Performance" from *Organizational Policy and Strategic Management: Text and Cases,* 2nd ed. by James M. Higgins, copyright © 1984 by The Dryden Press. Reproduced by permission of the publisher.

Earnings per share (EPS), dividing net earnings by the amount of common stock, also has several deficiencies as an evaluation of past and future performance. First, because alternative accounting principles are available, EPS can have several different but equally acceptable values, depending on the principle selected for its computation. Second, because EPS is based on accrual income, the conversion of income to cash can be near term or delayed. Therefore, EPS does not consider the time value of money. **Return on equity (ROE),** dividing net income by total equity, also has its share of limitations because it is also derived from accounting-based data. In addition, EPS and ROE are often unrelated to a company's stock price. Because of these and other limitations, EPS and ROE by themselves are not adequate measures of corporate performance.

Stakeholder Measures

Each stakeholder has its own set of criteria to determine how well the corporation is performing. These criteria typically deal with the direct and indirect impact of corporate activities on stakeholder interests. Top management should establish one or more simple **stakeholder measures** for each stakeholder category so that it can keep track of stakeholder concerns. (See Table 10.2.)

Shareholder Value

Because of the belief that accounting-based numbers such as return on investment, return on equity, and earnings per share are not reliable indicators of a corporation's economic value, many corporations are using shareholder value as a better measure of corporate performance and strategic management effectiveness. Real **shareholder value** can be defined as the present value of the anticipated future stream of cash flows from the business plus the value of the company if liquidated. Arguing that the purpose

Table 10.2 **A Sample Scorecard for "Keeping Score" with Stakeholders**

Stakeholder Category	Possible Near-Term Measures	Possible Long-Term Measures
Customers	Sales ($ and volume) New customers Number of new customer needs met ("tries")	Growth in sales Turnover of customer base Ability to control price

Suppliers	Cost of raw material
	Delivery time
	Inventory
	Availability of raw material
		Growth rates of:
		   Raw material costs
		   Delivery time
		   Inventory
		New ideas from suppliers

Financial community	EPS Stock price Number of "buy" lists ROE	Ability to convince Wall Street of strategy Growth in ROE
Employees	Number of suggestions Productivity Number of grievances	Number of internal promotions Turnover
Congress	Number of new pieces of legislation that affect the firm Access to key members and staff	Number of new regulations that affect industry Ratio of "cooperative" vs. "competitive" encounters
Consumer advocate (CA)	Number of meetings Number of "hostile" encounters Number of times coalitions formed Number of legal actions	Number of changes in policy due to C. A. Number of C. A.-initiated "calls for help"
Environmentalists	Number of meetings Number of hostile encounters Number of times coalitions formed Number of EPA complaints Number of legal actions	Number of changes in policy due to environmentalists Number of environmentalist "calls for help"

Source: R. E. Freeman, *Strategic Management: A Stakeholder Approach* (Boston: Ballinger Publishing Company, 1984), p. 179. Copyright © 1984 by R. E. Freeman. Reprinted by permission.

of a company is to increase shareholder wealth, shareholder value analysis concentrates on cash flow as the key measure of performance. The value of a corporation is thus the value of its cash flows discounted back to their present value, using the business's cost of capital as the discount rate. As long as the returns from a business exceed its cost of capital, the business will create value and be worth more than the capital invested in it.

The New York consulting firm Stern Stewart & Company devised and popularized two shareholder value measures: economic value added (EVA) and market value added (MVA). Well-known companies, such as Coca-Cola, General Electric, AT&T, Whirlpool, Quaker Oats, Eli Lily, Georgia-Pacific, Polaroid, Sprint, Teledyne, and Tenneco have adopted MVA and/or EVA as the best yardstick for corporate performance. According to Sprint's CFO, Art Krause, "Unlike EPS, which measures accounting results, MVA gauges true economic performance."[9]

Economic value added (EVA) has become an extremely popular shareholder value method of measuring corporate and divisional performance and may be on its way to replacing ROI as the standard performance measure. EVA measures the difference between the pre-strategy and post-strategy value for the business. Simply put, EVA is after-tax operating profit minus the total annual cost of capital.

- The annual cost of borrowed capital is the interest charged by the firm's banks and bondholders.

- To calculate the cost of equity, assume that shareholders generally earn about 6% more on stocks than on government bonds. If long-term treasury bills are selling at 7.5%, the firm's cost of equity should be 13.5%—more if the firm is in a risky industry. *A corporation's overall cost of capital is the weighted-average cost of the firm's debt and equity capital.*

- Total the amount of capital invested in the business, including buildings, machines, computers, and investments in R&D and training (allocating costs annually over their useful life).

- Multiply the firm's total capital by the weighted-average cost of capital.

- Compare that figure to pretax operating earnings. If the difference is positive, the strategy (and the management employing it) is generating value for the shareholders. If it is negative, the strategy is destroying shareholder value. [10]

Roberto Goizueta, CEO of Coca Cola, explains, "We raise capital to make concentrate, and sell it at an operating profit. Then we pay the cost of that capital. Shareholders pocket the difference."[11] Unlike ROI, ROE, or ROS, one of EVA's most powerful properties is its strong relationship to stock price.[12] Managers can improve their company's or business unit's EVA by: (1) earning more profit without using more capital, (2) using less capital, and (3) investing capital in high-return projects.

Market value added (MVA) measures the stock market's estimate of the net present value of a firm's past and expected capital investment projects. To calculate MVA,

1. First add all the capital that has been put into a company—from shareholders, bondholders, and retained earnings.

2. Reclassify certain accounting expenses, such as R&D, to reflect that they are actually investments in future earnings. This provides the firm's total capital. So far, this is the same approach taken in calculating EVA.

3. Using the current stock price, total the value of all outstanding stock, adding it to the company's debt. This is the company's market value. If the company's market value is greater than all the capital invested in it, the firm has a positive MVA—meaning that management (and the strategy it is following) has created wealth. In some cases, however, the market value of the company is actually less than the capital put into it—shareholder wealth is being destroyed.

Coca-Cola and General Electric tend to have the highest MVAs. In 1993, IBM had the lowest MVA of 200 large U.S. firms—a negative $23.7 billion. In 1995, that honor went to General Motors with a negative MVA of $17,803 billion. Studies have shown that EVA is a predictor of MVA. Consecutive years of positive EVA generally lead to a soaring MVA.[13] Research also reveals that CEO turnover is significantly correlated with MVA and EVA, whereas ROA and ROE are not. This suggests that EVA and MVA are more appropriate measures of the market's evaluation of a firm's strategy and its management than are the traditional measures of corporate performance.[14]

Balanced Scorecard Approach: Using Key Performance Measures

Rather than evaluate a corporation using a few financial measures, Kaplan and Norton argue for a "balanced scorecard," including nonfinancial as well as financial measures.[15]

The **balanced scorecard** combines financial measures that tell the results of actions already taken with operational measures on customer satisfaction, internal processes, and the corporation's innovation and improvement activities—the drivers of future financial performance. Management should develop goals or objectives in each of four areas:

1. **Financial:** How do we appear to shareholders?

2. **Customer:** How do customers view us?

3. **Internal Business Perspective:** What must we excel at?

4. **Innovation and Learning:** Can we continue to improve and create value?

Each goal in each area (for example, avoiding bankruptcy in the financial area) is then assigned one or more measures, as well as a target and an initiative. These measures can be thought of as **key performance measures**—measures that are essential for achieving a desired strategic option.[16] For example, a company could include cash flow, quarterly sales growth, and ROE as measures for success in the financial area. It could include market share (competitive position goal) and percentage of new sales coming from new products (customer acceptance goal) as measures under the customer perspective. It could include cycle time and unit cost (manufacturing excellence goal) as measures under the internal business perspective. It could include time to develop next generation products (technology leadership objective) under the innovation and learning perspective.

Evaluating Top Management

Through its strategy, audit, and compensation committees, a board of directors closely evaluates the job performance of the CEO and the top management team. Of course, it is concerned primarily with overall corporate profitability as measured quantitatively by return on investment, return on equity, earnings per share, and shareholder value. The absence of short-run profitability certainly contributes to the firing of any CEO. The board, however, is also concerned with other factors.

Members of the compensation committees of today's boards of directors generally agree that a CEO's ability to establish strategic direction, build a management team, and provide leadership are more critical in the long run than are a few quantitative measures. The board should evaluate top management not only on the typical output-oriented quantitative measures, but also on behavioral measures–factors relating to its strategic management practices. Unfortunately it is estimated that less than 30% of companies systematically evaluate their CEO's performance.[17]

The specific items that a board uses to evaluate its top management should be derived from the objectives that both the board and top management agreed on earlier. If better relations with the local community and improved safety practices in work areas were selected as objectives for the year (or for five years), these items should be included in the evaluation. In addition, other factors that tend to lead to profitability might be included, such as market share, product quality, or investment intensity.

Management audits are very useful to boards of directors in evaluating management's handling of various corporate activities. Management audits have been developed to evaluate activities such as corporate social responsibility, functional areas such as the marketing department, and divisions such as the international division, as well as to evaluate the corporation itself in a strategic audit. The strategic audit is explained in detail later in this chapter.

Primary Measures of Divisional and Functional Performance

Companies use a variety of techniques to evaluate and control performance in divisions, SBUs, and functional areas. If a corporation is composed of SBUs or divisions, it will use many of the same performance measures (ROI or EVA, for instance) that it uses to assess overall corporate performance. To the extent that it can isolate specific functional units such as R&D, the corporation may develop responsibility centers. It will also use typical functional measures such as market share and sales per employee (marketing), unit costs and percentage of defects (operations), percentage of sales from new products and number of patents (R&D), and turnover and job satisfaction (HRM).

During strategy formulation and implementation, top management approves a series of programs and supporting **operating budgets** from its business units. During evaluation and control, actual expenses are contrasted with planned expenditures and the degree of variance is assessed. This is typically done on a monthly basis. In addition, top management will probably require **periodic statistical reports** summarizing data on such key factors as the number of new customer contracts, volume of received orders, and productivity figures.

Responsibility Centers

Control systems can be established to monitor specific functions, projects, or divisions. Budgets are one type of control system that is typically used to control the financial indicators of performance. **Responsibility centers** are used to isolate a unit so that it can be evaluated separately from the rest of the corporation. Each responsibility center, therefore, has its own budget and is evaluated on its use of budgeted resources. It is headed by the manager responsible for the center's performance. The center uses resources (measured in terms of costs or expenses) to produce a service or a product (measured in terms of volume or revenues). There are five major types of responsibility centers. The type is determined by the way the corporation's control system measures these resources and services or products.

1. **Standard cost centers.** Primarily used in manufacturing facilities, standard (or expected) costs are computed for each operation on the basis of historical data. In evaluating the center's performance, its total standard costs are multiplied by the units produced. The result is the expected cost of production, which is then compared to the actual cost of production.

2. **Revenue centers.** Production, usually in terms of unit or dollar sales, is measured without consideration of resource costs (for example, salaries). The center is thus judged in terms of effectiveness rather than efficiency. The effectiveness of a sales region, for example, is determined by comparing its actual sales to its projected or previous year's sales. Profits are not considered because sales departments have very limited influence over the cost of the products they sell.

3. **Expense centers.** Resources are measured in dollars without consideration for service or product costs. Thus budgets will have been prepared for *engineered* expenses (those costs that can be calculated) and for *discretionary* expenses (those costs that can be only estimated). Typical expense centers are administrative, service, and research departments. They cost an organization money, but they only indirectly contribute to revenues.

4. **Profit centers.** Performance is measured in terms of the difference between revenues (which measure production) and expenditures (which measure resources). A

profit center is typically established whenever an organizational unit has control over both its resources and its products or services. By having such centers, a company can be organized into divisions of separate product lines. The manager of each division is given autonomy to the extent that she or he is able to keep profits at a satisfactory (or better) level.

Some organizational units that are not usually considered potentially autonomous can, for the purpose of profit center evaluations, be made so. A manufacturing department, for example, can be converted from a standard cost center (or expense center) into a profit center: it is allowed to charge a **transfer price** for each product it "sells" to the sales department. The difference between the manufacturing cost per unit and the agreed-upon transfer price is the unit's "profit."

Transfer pricing is commonly used in vertically integrated corporations and can work well when a price can be easily determined for a designated amount of product. Even though most experts agree that market-based transfer prices are the best choice, only 30%–40% of companies use market price to set the transfer price. (Of the rest, 50% use cost; 10%–20% use negotiation.)[18] When a price cannot be set easily, however, the relative bargaining power of the centers, rather than strategic considerations, tends to influence the agreed-upon price. Top management has an obligation to make sure that these political considerations do not overwhelm the strategic ones. Otherwise, profit figures for each center will be biased and provide poor information for strategic decisions at both corporate and divisional levels.

5. **Investment centers.** Because many divisions in large manufacturing corporations use significant assets to make their products, their asset base should be factored into their performance evaluation. Thus it is insufficient to focus only on profits, as in the case of profit centers. An investment center's performance is measured in terms of the difference between its resources and its services or products. For example, two divisions in a corporation made identical profits, but one division owns a $3 million plant, whereas the other owns a $1 million plant. Both make the same profits, but one is obviously more efficient: the smaller plant provides the shareholders with a better return on their investment. The most widely used measure of investment center performance is return on investment (ROI).

Most single-business corporations, such as Apple Computer, tend to use a combination of cost, expense, and revenue centers. In these corporations, most managers are functional specialists and manage against a budget. Total profitability is integrated at the corporate level. Multidivisional corporations with one dominating product line, such as Anheuser-Busch, which have diversified into a few businesses but which still depend on a single product line (such as beer) for most of their revenue and income, generally use a combination of cost, expense, revenue, plus profit centers. Multidivisional corporations, such as General Electric, tend to emphasize investment centers—although in various units throughout the corporation other types of responsibility centers are also used. One problem with using responsibility centers, however, is that the separation needed to measure and evaluate a division's performance can diminish the level of cooperation among divisions that is needed to attain synergy for the corporation as a whole. (This problem is discussed later in this chapter under "Suboptimization.")

Using Benchmarking to Evaluate Performance

According to Xerox Corporation, the company that pioneered this concept in the United States, **benchmarking** is "the continual process of measuring products, services, and practices against the toughest competitors or those companies recognized as industry leaders."[19] Benchmarking, an increasingly popular program, is based on the concept that it makes no sense to reinvent something that someone else is already using. It involves openly learning how others do something better than one's own company so that one not only can imitate, but perhaps even improve on their current techniques. The benchmarking process usually involves the following steps:

- **Identify the area or process to be examined.** It should be an activity that has the potential to determine a business unit's competitive advantage.

- **Find behavioral and output measures of the area or process and obtain measurements.**

- **Select an accessible set of competitors and best-in-class companies against which to benchmark.** These may very often be companies that are in completely different industries, but perform similar activities. For example, when Xerox wanted to improve its order fulfillment, it went to L. L. Bean, the successful mail order firm, to learn how it achieved excellence in this area.

- **Calculate the differences among the company's performance measurements and those of the best-in-class and determine *why* the differences exist.**

- **Develop tactical programs for closing performance gaps**.

- **Implement the programs and then compare the resulting new measurements with those of the best-in-class companies.**

Benchmarking has been found to produce best results in companies that are already well managed. Apparently poorer performing firms tend to be overwhelmed by the discrepancy between their performance and the benchmark—and tend to view the benchmark as too difficult to reach.[20] Nevertheless, a recent survey by Bain & Company of 460 companies of various sizes across all U.S. industries indicated that over 70% were using benchmarking in either a major or limited manner.[21] Manco, Inc., a small Cleveland-area producer of duct tape regularly benchmarks itself against Wal-Mart, Rubbermaid, and Pepsico to enable it to better compete with giant 3M. The American Productivity & Quality Center, a Houston research group, recently established a "best practices database" of 600 leading techniques from 250 companies.[22] See the **Strategy in a Changing World** feature to see how Seitz Corporation used benchmarking to implement its turnaround strategy.

International Measurement Issues

The three most widely used techniques for international performance evaluation are *return on investment, budget analysis,* and *historical comparisons*. In one study, 95% of the corporate officers interviewed stated that they use the same evaluation techniques for foreign and domestic operations. Rate of return was mentioned as the single most important measure. [23] However, ROI can cause problems when it is applied to international operations: Because of foreign currencies, different rates of inflation, different tax laws, and the use of transfer pricing, both the net income figure and the investment base may be seriously distorted.[24]

A study of 79 MNCs revealed that **international transfer pricing** from one country unit to another is primarily used *not* to evaluate performance, but to minimize taxes.[25] For example, the U.S. Internal Revenue Service contends that many Japanese firms doing business in the United States artificially inflate the value of U.S. deliveries in order to

STRATEGY IN A CHANGING WORLD

SEITZ CORPORATION USES BENCHMARKING IN STRATEGY IMPLEMENTATION

Seitz Corporation of Torrington, Connecticut, was a family-owned company that grew from a garage-based tool shop into a major supplier of the gears and bearings that circulate paper in copiers and dot matrix printers. By the mid 1980s, however, laser and ink jet printers were starting to replace dot matrix printers. Seitz was forced to lay off all but 80 employees as sales dropped significantly. Facing greater losses, management embarked on a major overhaul, using benchmarking. After first identifying the firms and the activities for study, they proceeded to adopt several of the practices that were examined. Among the measures incorporated were techniques to re-

duce new-product-to-market cycle time and just-in-time manufacturing. Cycle time was reduced from around nine weeks to three weeks. The use of just-in-time cut inventories—thus increasing floor space by 30%. With these and other improvements, Seitz's annual revenue reached a record $21 million by 1992 and employment climbed back to 190 people. Seitz's management group agreed that benchmarking had been key in implementing its turnaround strategy.

Source: H. Rothman, "You Need Not Be Big to Benchmark," *Nation's Business* (December 1992), p. 64.

reduce the profits and thus the taxes of their American subsidiaries.[26] Parts made in a subsidiary of a Japanese MNC in a low-tax country like Singapore can be shipped to its subsidiary in a high-tax country like the U.S. at such a high price that the U.S. subsidiary reports very little profit (and thus pays few taxes), while the Singapore subsidiary reports a very high profit (but also pays few taxes because of the lower tax rate). A Japanese MNC can, therefore, earn more profit worldwide by reporting less profit in high-tax countries and more profit in low-tax countries. Transfer pricing is an important factor, given that 56% of all trade in the triad and one-third of all international trade is composed of intercompany transactions.[27] Transfer pricing can thus be one way the parent company can reduce taxes and "capture profits" from a subsidiary. Other common ways of transferring profits to the parent company (often referred to as the **repatriation of profits**) are through dividends, royalties, and management fees.[28]

Transfer pricing and the repatriation of profits are complicated by constantly fluctuating currency exchange rates among nations. To make it easier for goods, services, and profits to move easily across the national borders of its member nations, the European Union is attempting to form a new economic and monetary union by 1998. The goal is to have one common currency, the *euro*, managed by a central bank. To be a part of this economic and monetary union, European Union members must meet four convergence criteria:

1. Government debt no larger than 60% of a country's GDP.

2. Government deficit no greater than 3% of GDP.

3. An inflation rate not exceeding 3.1%.

4. Government bonds yielding 8.5%.[29]

See the 🌍 **21st Century Global Society** feature to see how well each country was meeting the criteria in 1997.

Authorities in international business recommend that the control and reward systems used by a global MNC be different from those used by a multidomestic MNC.[30]

21st Century Global Society

EUROPEAN UNION'S PROBLEMS WITH FORMING A SINGLE CURRENCY

In the 1992 Maastricht treaty, the members of the European Union agreed to form an economic and monetary union in which there would be one currency, the euro, managed by a central bank. A single currency would allow goods, services, and profits to move easily across the national borders of the Union's member nations. To be a part of this economic and monetary union, members agreed to meet four criteria by 1998:

1. government debt no larger than 60% of a country's GDP;

2. government deficit no greater than 3% of GDP;

3. an inflation rate not exceeding 3.1%; and

4. government bonds yielding 8.5%. The following table shows how well each member country was meeting these criteria in 1997.

Only one member country (Luxembourg) in 1997 seemed able to meet all of these standards. Even Germany, the traditional economic powerhouse of Europe, was in difficulty. Some of the member countries were considering the exclusion of Italy and other Mediterranean countries until 2001 or 2002 because of their poor recent economic history. Spain, Portugal, and Italy were, however, in no mood to accept such a delay. It seemed likely that the move to a single European currency might be delayed until the end of the century.

Source: Table taken from "A Little EMU Enlightenment," *The Economist* (February 22, 1997), p. 88. Reprinted by permission. Other information from "Sweating for That Euro," *The Economist* (February 15, 1997), pp. 45–46.

Criteria[1]	Govt Debt as % of GDP	Govt Deficit as % of GDP	Inflation Rate %	Govt Bond Yield %
	no greater than 60	*no greater than* 3.0	*no greater than* 3.1	*no greater than* 8.5
Luxembourg	7	1.2	1.9	5.6
Austria	74	3.0	2.2	5.9
Belgium	127	3.0	1.5	6.7
Britain	59	4.0	2.8	8.3
Denmark	70	0.5	2.5	7.8
Finland	62	2.5	1.4	7.0
France	58	3.7	2.0	5.8
Ireland	80	2.8	3.0	7.4
Netherlands	78	2.4	2.3	5.8
Sweden	80	2.8	2.4	8.2
Germany	62	3.4	2.0	5.7
Portugal	72	3.5	2.8	8.0
Spain	70	3.5	3.0	8.0
Italy	125	4.3	3.0	8.8
Greece	108	6.2	7.5	13.0

Note:
1. Shaded areas indicate where criteria are not currently met.

The *multidomestic MNC* should use loose controls on its foreign units. The management of each geographic unit should be given considerable operational latitude, but it should be expected to meet some performance targets. Because profit and ROI measures are often unreliable in international operations, it is recommended that the MNC's top management, in this instance, emphasize budgets and nonfinancial measures of performance such as market share, productivity, public image, employee morale, and relations with the host country government.[31] Multiple measures should be used to differentiate between the worth of the subsidiary and the performance of its management.

The *global MNC*, however, needs tight controls over its many units. To reduce costs and gain competitive advantage, it is trying to spread the manufacturing and marketing operations of a few fairly uniform products around the world. Therefore, its key operational decisions must be centralized. Its environmental scanning must include research not only into each of the national markets in which the MNC competes, but also into the "global arena" of the interaction between markets. Foreign units are thus evaluated more as cost centers, revenue centers, or expense centers than as investment or profit centers because MNCs operating in a global industry do not often make the entire product in the country in which it is sold.

10.3 Strategic Information Systems

Before performance measures can have any impact on strategic management, they must first be communicated to those people responsible for formulating and implementing strategic plans. Strategic information systems can perform this function. They can be computer-based or manual, formal or informal. One of the key reasons given for the bankruptcy of International Harvester was the inability of the corporation's top management to precisely determine its income by major class of similar products. Because of this inability, management kept trying to fix ailing businesses and was unable to respond flexibly to major changes and unexpected events. In contrast, one of the key reasons for the success of Toys "R" Us has been management's use of the company's sophisticated information system to control purchasing decisions. Cash registers in the 300-plus U.S. Toys "R" Us stores transmit information daily to computers at the company's headquarters. Consequently managers know every morning exactly how many of each item have been sold the day before, how many have been sold so far in the year, and how this year's sales compare to last year's. The information system allows all reordering to be done automatically by computers without any managerial input. It also allows the company to experiment with new toys without committing to big orders in advance. In effect, the system allows the customers to decide through their purchases what gets reordered.

Multinational corporations are adopting a complex software system called R/3 from the German company SAP AG. The **R/3 software system** integrates and automates order taking, credit checking, payment verification, and book balancing. Because of R/3's ability to use a common information system throughout a company's many operations around the world, it is becoming the business information systems' global standard. Microsoft, for example, is using R/3 to replace a tangle of 33 financial tracking systems in 26 subsidiaries. Even though it cost the company $25 million and took 10 months to install, R/3 annually saves Microsoft $18 million. Coca Cola uses the R/3 system to enable a manager in Atlanta to use her personal computer to check the latest sales of 20-ounce bottles of Coke Classic in India. Owens-Corning envisions that its R/3 system will allow sales people to learn what is available at any plant or warehouse and to quickly assemble orders for customers.

R/3 is, nevertheless, not for every company. The system is extremely complicated and demands a high level of standardization throughout a corporation. Its demanding nature often forces companies to change the way they do business. Over the two-year period of installing R/3, Owens-Corning had to completely overhaul its operations. Because R/3 was incompatible with Apple Computer's very organic corporate culture, the company was only able to apply it to its order management and financial operations, but not to manufacturing. Dell Computer canceled its R/3 project after the installation budget reached $150 million and the system was still unable to handle Dell's sales volume.[32]

At the divisional or SBU level of a corporation, the information system should be used to support, reinforce, or enlarge its business-level strategy through its decision support system. An SBU pursuing a strategy of *overall cost leadership* could use its information system to reduce costs either by improving labor productivity or improving the use of other resources such as inventory or machinery. Merrill Lynch took this approach when it developed PRISM software to provide its 500 U.S. retail offices with quick access to financial information in order to boost brokers' efficiency. Another SBU, in contrast, might want to pursue a *differentiation* strategy. It could use its information system to add uniqueness to the product or service and contribute to quality, service, or image through the functional areas. Federal Express wanted to use superior service to gain a competitive advantage. It invested significantly in several types of information systems to measure and track the performance of its delivery service. Together, these information systems gave Federal Express the fastest error-response time in the overnight delivery business.

Increasingly, corporations are connecting their internal information networks (intranets) to other firms via "extranets" to implement strategic decisions and monitor their results. For example, Chicago-based Navistar no longer maintains a tire-and-rim inventory at its Springfield, Ohio, truck assembly plant. That responsibility is now being handled electronically by Goodyear Tire & Rubber, one of Navistar's suppliers. A Goodyear office in New York receives Navistar's manufacturing schedule and tire-and-rim requirements by electronic data interchange. The information is then sent to a Goodyear plant in Ohio where tires are mounted on rims. The completed assemblies are shipped to Navistar's Springfield plant—arriving just eight hours ahead of when they are needed. [33]

10.4 *Problems in Measuring Performance*

The measurement of performance is a crucial part of evaluation and control. The lack of quantifiable objectives or performance standards and the inability of the information system to provide timely and valid information are two obvious control problems. Without objective and timely measurements, it would be extremely difficult to make operational, let alone strategic, decisions. Nevertheless, the use of timely, quantifiable standards does not guarantee good performance. The very act of monitoring and measuring performance can cause side effects that interfere with overall corporate performance. Among the most frequent negative side effects are a short-term orientation and goal displacement.

Short-Term Orientation

Top executives report that in many situations they analyze *neither* the long-term implications of present operations on the strategy they have adopted *nor* the operational impact of a strategy on the corporate mission. Long-run evaluations are often not conducted because executives (1) don't realize their importance, (2) believe that short-run considerations are more important than long-run considerations, (3) aren't personally evaluated on a long-term basis, or (4) don't have the time to make a long-run analysis. [34] There is no real justification for the first and last "reasons." If executives realize the importance of long-run evaluations, they make the time needed to conduct them. Even though many chief executives point to immediate pressures from the investment community and to short-term incentive and promotion plans to support the second and third reasons, evidence does not always support their claims. [35]

Nevertheless, there are times when the stock market does not value a particular strategic investment. See the **Company Spotlight on Maytag Corporation** feature for the response of the investment community to Maytag's acquisition and subsequent divestiture of Hoover (in terms of Maytag's stock market price).

Many accounting-based measures do, however, encourage a **short-term orientation**. Table 10.1 indicates that one of the limitations of ROI as a performance measure is its short-term nature. In theory, ROI is not limited to the short run, but in practice it is often difficult to use this measure to realize long-term benefits for the company. Because managers can often manipulate both the numerator (earnings) and the denominator (investment), the resulting ROI figure can be meaningless. Advertising, maintenance, and research efforts can be reduced. Mergers can be undertaken that will do more for this year's earnings (and next year's paycheck) than for the division's or corporation's future profits. (Research of 55 firms that engaged in major acquisitions revealed that even though the firms performed poorly after the acquisition, the acquiring firms' top management still received significant increases in compensation!) [36] Expensive retooling and plant modernization can be delayed as long as a manager can manipulate figures on production defects and absenteeism.

Goal Displacement

Monitoring and measuring of performance (if not carefully done) can actually result in a decline in overall corporate performance. **Goal displacement** is the confusion of means with ends and occurs when activities originally intended to help managers attain corporate objectives become ends in themselves—or are adapted to meet ends other than those for which they were intended. Two types of goal displacement are behavior substitution and suboptimization.

Behavior Substitution

Behavior substitution refers to a phenomenon when people substitute activities that do not lead to goal accomplishment for activities that do lead to goal accomplishment because the wrong activities are being rewarded. Managers, like most people, tend to focus more of their attention on those behaviors that are clearly measurable than on those that are not. Employees often receive little to no reward for engaging in hard-to-measure activities such as cooperation and initiative. However, easy-to-measure activities might have little to no relationship to the desired good performance. Rational people, nevertheless, tend to work for the rewards that the system has to offer. Therefore, people tend to substitute behaviors that are recognized and rewarded for those behaviors that are ignored, without regard to their contribution to goal accomplishment. A U.S. Navy quip sums up this situation: "What you inspect (or reward) is what you get." In 1992, Sears, Roebuck & Co. thought that it would improve employee productivity by tying performance to rewards. It, therefore, paid commissions to its auto shop employees as a percentage of each repair bill. Behavior substitution resulted as employees altered their behavior to fit the reward system. The result was overbilled customers, charges for work never done, and a scandal that tarnished Sears' reputation. [37]

The law governing the effect of measurement on behavior seems to be that *quantifiable measures drive out nonquantifiable measures.*

COMPANY SPOTLIGHT

The Impact of Hoover on Maytag's Financial Performance

When Maytag Corporation purchased Hoover for its international appliance business, Maytag's debt soared to $923 million from $134 million just nine months earlier. Maytag's total outstanding shares swelled to 105 million from 75 million during the same time period. Interest payments leaped to $70 million in 1989 from $20 million the year before.

The corporation no longer had the best profit margin in the industry. Return on equity had been over 25% before the Magic Chef merger in 1986, peaked at over 30% in 1988, and was nearly halved to 18.3% in 1989 after the Hoover acquisition. By 1991, Maytag was earning just 8% on equity. In 1992, for the first time since the 1920s, the company showed a net loss. The stock price had dropped from $26.50 per share in 1988 to $13 in 1993. Shareholders were extremely unhappy with the company's performance and stated their feelings in the 1993 annual meeting. One angry stockholder asked CEO Leonard Hadley (who was conducting the meeting): "*How long will it be before earnings get back to the 1988 level of $1.77 per share from continuing operations? And along with that,*" he added, "*why should we have any confidence in your answer, given the performance of the past five years?*"

Even though Maytag showed a profit in 1994, the stock price only rose to around $15 a share— far below the $29 per share that one financial analyst thought it was worth. Some investment analysts thought the corporation might soon be forced to sell Hoover or have no choice but to sell out to a competitor by the end of the decade.

Maytag finally decided to divest its Australian operations in December 1994 and its Hoover Europe operations in May 1995. In retrospect, management was forced to admit that Maytag had paid far too much for a very marginal European business. Neither the Australian nor the European operations had provided any profits until recently—and then only relatively small amounts. Selling off the overseas operations had meant big after-tax book losses and meant that Maytag reported another loss in 1995. The sales had, however, provided the cash for the corporation to reduce its heavy debt load. As a result, Maytag's stock price rose to $19 per share by February 1996. Financial analysts realized that without the various write-offs, the corporation would have shown a healthy profit in 1995. Nevertheless, Maytag's stock price continued to fluctuate around $20 per share throughout 1996—lower than what many analysts thought the corporation might actually be worth.

Suboptimization

Suboptimization refers to the phenomenon when a unit optimizes its goal accomplishment to the detriment of the organization as a whole. The emphasis in large corporations on developing separate responsibility centers can create some problems for the corporation as a whole. To the extent that a division or functional unit views itself as a separate entity, it might refuse to cooperate with other units or divisions in the same corporation if cooperation could in some way negatively affect its performance evaluation. The competition between divisions to achieve a high ROI can result in one division's refusal to share its new technology or work process improvements. One division's attempt to optimize the accomplishment of its goals can cause other divisions to fall behind and thus negatively affect overall corporate performance. One common example of suboptimization occurs when a marketing department approves an early shipment date to a customer as a means of getting an order and forces the manufacturing department into overtime production for this one order. Production costs are raised, which reduces the manufacturing department's overall efficiency. The end result might be that, although marketing achieves its sales goal, the corporation as a whole fails to achieve its expected profitability.

10.5 Guidelines for Proper Control

In designing a control system, top management should remember that *controls should follow strategy*. Unless controls ensure the use of the proper strategy to achieve objectives, there is a strong likelihood that dysfunctional side effects will completely undermine the implementation of the objectives. The following guidelines are recommended:

1. **Control should involve only the minimum amount of information** needed to give a reliable picture of events. Too many controls create confusion. Focus on the **critical success factors**: *those 20% of the factors that determine 80% of the results.*

2. **Controls should monitor only meaningful activities and results**, regardless of measurement difficulty. If cooperation between divisions is important to corporate performance, some form of qualitative or quantitative measure should be established to monitor cooperation.

3. **Controls should be timely** so that corrective action can be taken before it is too late. Steering controls, controls that monitor or measure the factors influencing performance, should be stressed so that advance notice of problems is given.

4. **Long-term and short-term controls should be used.** If only short-term measures are emphasized, a short-term managerial orientation is likely.

5. **Controls should aim at pinpointing exceptions.** Only those activities or results that fall outside a predetermined tolerance range should call for action.

6. **Emphasize the reward of meeting or exceeding standards** rather than punishment for failing to meet standards. Heavy punishment of failure typically results in goal displacement. Managers will "fudge" reports and lobby for lower standards.

To the extent that the culture complements and reinforces the strategic orientation of the firm, there is less need for an extensive formal control system. In their book *In Search of Excellence*, Peters and Waterman state that "the stronger the culture and the more it was directed toward the marketplace, the less need was there for policy manuals, organization charts, or detailed procedures and rules. In these companies, people way down the line know what they are supposed to do in most situations because the handful of guiding values is crystal clear."[38] The **Strategy in a Changing World** feature illustrates how the corporate culture at Southwest Airlines enabled the company to achieve its strategic objectives without a lot of detailed rules, regulations, and costly reporting procedures.

10.6 Strategic Incentive Management

To ensure congruence between the needs of the corporation as a whole and the needs of the employees as individuals, management and the board of directors should develop an incentive program that rewards desired performance. This reduces the likelihood of *agency problems* (when employees act to feather their own nest instead of

SOUTHWEST AIRLINES' CORPORATE CULTURE MAKES CONTROL EASIER

What is the secret behind Southwest Airlines's highly productive workforce that enables the company to achieve its low-cost competitive strategy even when it is expanding across the United States? Instead of using a lot of rules and inspectors, it uses corporate culture to ensure quality low-cost performance.

Colleen Barrett, the No. 2 executive at Southwest Airlines, is the keeper of the corporate culture. Though the airline doubled in size from 1991 to 1995, Barrett has devised ways to preserve Southwest's small company work ethic and its "can-do" spirit. Personifying the "empowerment" concept, Barrett gives employees freedom from centralized policies and constantly reinforces the message that employees should be treated like customers. She celebrates workers who go above and beyond the call of duty.

According to Barrett, job applicants are often misled by Southwest's zany reputation. "People get this image—fun, different, party place, Herb's (Founder and CEO Herb Kellehher) half nuts," she explains. "We have to remind them first and foremost, you have to work." Finding young, industrious workers who fit Southwest's culture is

so difficult that the company interviews 50 applicants for every open position.

Fearing that the company might be losing its small company, underdog spirit, Barrett formed a culture committee. When Southwest was having problems with workers at its Los Angeles International Airport station, the culture committee swung into action. It dispatched employees to fill in for local supervisors so the supervisors could address morale and efficiency problems. That station is now considered one of Southwest's most efficient.

Barrett believes that building loyalty builds better performance. Employees are well paid compared to other airlines. Celebrations, ranging from spontaneous "fun sessions" to Christmas parties, are an important part of work. At the same time, employees are expected to work harder than their counterparts at other airlines. This approach has enabled Southwest to avoid the bureaucracy and mediocrity that develop in companies that have outgrown their entrepreneurial roots.

Source: S. McCartney, "Airline Industry's Top-Ranked Woman Keeps Southwest's Small-Fry Spirit Alive," *Wall Street Journal* (November 30, 1995), pp. B1–B2.

building shareholder value) mentioned earlier in Chapter 2. Incentive plans should be linked in some way to corporate and divisional strategy. For example, a survey of 600 business units indicates that the pay mix associated with a growth strategy emphasizes bonuses and other incentives over salary and benefits, whereas the pay mix associated with a stability strategy has the reverse emphasis.[39] Research does indicate that SBU managers having long-term performance elements in their compensation program favor a long-term perspective and thus greater investments in R&D, capital equipment, and employee training.[40]

The following three approaches are tailored to help match measurements and rewards with explicit strategic objectives and timeframes.[41]

1. **Weighted-factor method.** This method is particularly appropriate for measuring and rewarding the performance of top SBU managers and group level executives when performance factors and their importance vary from one SBU to another. One corporation's measurements might contain the following variations: the performance of high-growth SBUs is measured in terms of market share, sales growth, designated future payoff, and progress on several future-oriented strategic projects; the

Table 10.3 **Weighted-Factor Approach to Strategic Incentive Management**

Strategic Business Unit Category	Factor	Weight
High Growth	Return on assets	10%
	Cash flow	0%
	Strategic-funds programs (developmental expenses)	45%
	Market-share increase	45%
		100%
Medium Growth	Return on assets	25%
	Cash flow	25%
	Strategic-funds programs (developmental expenses)	25%
	Market-share increase	25%
		100%
Low Growth	Return on assets	50%
	Cash flow	50%
	Strategic-funds programs (developmental expenses)	0%
	Market-share increase	0%
		100%

Source: Reprinted by permission of the publisher from "The Performance Measurement and Reward System: Critical to Strategic Management," by Paul J. Stonich, from *Organizational Dynamics* (Winter 1984), p. 51. Copyright © 1984 by American Management Association, New York. All rights reserved.

performance of low-growth SBUs, in contrast, is measured in terms of ROI and cash generation; and the performance of medium-growth SBUs is measured for a combination of these factors. (Refer to Table 10.3.)

2. **Long-term evaluation method.** This method compensates managers for achieving objectives set over a multiyear period. An executive is promised some company stock or "performance units" (convertible into money) in amounts to be based on long-term performance. An executive committee, for example, might set a particular objective in terms of growth in earnings per share during a five-year period. The giving of awards would be contingent on the corporation's meeting that objective within the designated time. Any executive who leaves the corporation before the objective is met receives nothing. The typical emphasis on stock price makes this approach more applicable to top management than to business unit managers.

3. **Strategic-funds method.** This method encourages executives to look at developmental expenses as being different from expenses required for current operations. The accounting statement for a corporate unit enters strategic funds as a separate entry below the current ROI. It is, therefore, possible to distinguish between those expense dollars consumed in the generation of current revenues and those invested in the future of the business. Therefore, the manager can be evaluated on both a short- and a long-term basis and has an incentive to invest strategic funds in the future. (See Table 10.4.)

An effective way to achieve the desired strategic results through a reward system is to combine the three approaches:

1. Segregate strategic funds from short-term funds, as is done in the strategic-funds method.

Table 10.4   Strategic-Funds Approach to an SBU's Profit-and-Loss Statement

Sales	$12,300,000
Cost of sales	−6,900,000
Gross margin	$ 5,400,000
General and administrative expenses	−3,700,000
Operating profit (return on sales)	$ 1,700,000
Strategic funds (development expenses)	−1,000,000
Pretax profit	$ 700,000

Source: Reprinted by permission of the publisher from "The Performance Measurement and Reward System: Critical to Strategic Management," by Paul J. Stonich, from *Organizational Dynamics* (Winter 1984), p. 51. Copyright © 1984 by American Management Association, New York. All rights reserved.

2. Develop a weighted-factor chart for each SBU.

3. Measure performance on three bases: The pretax profit indicted by the strategic-funds approach, the weighted factors, and the long-term evaluation of the SBUs' and the corporation's performance.

General Electric and Westinghouse are two firms using a version of these measures.

10.7   *Using the Strategic Audit to Evaluate Corporate Performance*

The **strategic audit** provides a checklist of questions, by area or issue, that enables a systematic analysis of various corporate functions and activities to be made. (See Table 10.5.) It is a type of management audit and is extremely useful as a diagnostic tool to pinpoint corporatewide problem areas and to highlight organizational strengths and weaknesses.[42] The strategic audit can help determine why a certain area is creating problems for a corporation and help generate solutions to the problem.

The strategic audit is not an all-inclusive list, but it presents many of the critical questions needed for a detailed strategic analysis of any business corporation. Some questions or even some areas might be inappropriate for a particular company; in other cases, the questions may be insufficient for a complete analysis. However, each question in a particular area of the strategic audit can be broken down into an additional series of subquestions. Develop these subquestions when they are needed.

The strategic audit summarizes the key topics in the Strategic Management Model discussed in Chapters 1 through 10. As you look through the major headings of the audit in Table 10.5, note that it identifies by chapter, section, and page numbers where information about each topic can be found.

The strategic audit puts into action the strategic decision-making process illustrated in Figure 1.5 on pages 20-21. The headings in the audit are the same as those shown in Figure 1.5:

1. Evaluate current performance results

2. Review corporate governance

3. Scan and assess the *external* environment

4. Scan and assess the *internal* environment

5. Analyze strategic factors using SWOT

6. Generate and evaluate strategic alternatives

7. Implement strategies

8. Evaluate and control

Table 10.5 Strategic Audit of a Corporation

I. Current Situation

A. Current Performance   See Section 10.2 on pages 234–238.

How did the corporation perform the past year overall in terms of return on investment, market share, and profitability?

B. Strategic Posture   See Section 1.3 on pages 10–14.

What are the corporation's current mission, objectives, strategies, and policies?

1. Are they clearly stated or are they merely implied from performance?

2. **Mission:** What business(es) is the corporation in? Why?

3. **Objectives:** What are the corporate, business, and functional objectives? Are they consistent with each other, with the mission, and with the internal and external environments?

4. **Strategies:** What strategy or mix of strategies is the corporation following? Are they consistent with each other, with the mission and objectives, and with the internal and external environments?

5. **Policies:** What are they? Are they consistent with each other, with the mission, objectives, and strategies, and with the internal and external environments?

6. Do the current mission, objectives, strategies, and policies reflect the corporation's international operations—whether global or multidomestic?

II. Corporate Governance

A. Board of Directors   See Section 2.1 on pages 26–35.

1. Who are they? Are they internal or external?

2. Do they own significant shares of stock?

3. Is the stock privately held or publicly traded? Are there different classes of stock with different voting rights?

4. What do they contribute to the corporation in terms of knowledge, skills, background, and connections? If the corporation has international operations, do board members have international experience?

5. How long have they served on the board?

6. What is their level of involvement in strategic management? Do they merely rubber-stamp top management's proposals or do they actively participate and suggest future directions?

Source: T. L. Wheelen and J. D. Hunger, "Strategic Audit of a Corporation." Copyright © 1982 by Wheelen and Hunger Associates. Reprinted by permission. Revised 1988, 1991, 1994, and 1997.

Table 10.5   **Strategic Audit of a Corporation** *(continued)*

B. Top Management   *See Sections 2.2 to 2.4 on pages 35–48.*

1. What person or group constitutes top management?

2. What are top management's chief characteristics in terms of knowledge, skills, background, and style? If the corporation has international operations, does top management have international experience? Are executives from acquired companies considered part of the top management team?

3. Has top management been responsible for the corporation's performance over the past few years? How many managers have been in their current position for less than 3 years? Were they internal promotions or external hires?

4. Has it established a systematic approach to strategic management?

5. What is its level of involvement in the strategic management process?

6. How well does top management interact with lower level managers and with the board of directors?

7. Are strategic decisions made ethically in a socially responsible manner?

8. Is top management sufficiently skilled to cope with likely future challenges?

III. External Environment: Opportunities and Threats (SW**OT**)

A. Societal Environment   *See Section 3.1 on pages 53–60.*

1. What general environmental forces are currently affecting both the corporation and the industries in which it competes? Which present current or future threats? Opportunities? *See Table 3.1 on page 55.*

   a) Economic
   b) Technological
   c) Political-legal
   d) Sociocultural

2. Are these forces different in other regions of the world?

B. Task Environment   *See Section 3.2 on pages 60–72.*

1. What forces drive industry competition? Are these forces the same globally or do they vary from country to country?

   a) Threat of new entrants
   b) Bargaining power of buyers
   c) Threat of substitute products or services
   d) Bargaining power of suppliers
   e) Rivalry among competing firms
   f) Relative power of unions, governments, special interest groups, etc.

2. What key factors in the immediate environment (that is, customers, competitors, suppliers, creditors, labor unions, governments, trade associations, interest groups, local communities, and shareholders) are currently affecting the corporation? Which are current or future threats? Opportunities?

Table 10.5   Strategic Audit of a Corporation *(continued)*

C. Summary of External Factors   *See EFAS Table on pages 75–76.*

Which of these forces and factors are the most important to the corporation and to the industries in which it competes at the present time? Which will be important in the future?

IV. Internal Environment: Strengths and Weaknesses (**SW**OT)

A. Corporate Structure   *See Sections 4.3 and 8.4 on pages 87–89 and 192–197.*

1. How is the corporation structured at present?

   a) Is the decision-making authority centralized around one group or decentralized to many units?
   b) Is it organized on the basis of functions, projects, geography, or some combination of these?

2. Is the structure clearly understood by everyone in the corporation?

3. Is the present structure consistent with current corporate objectives, strategies, policies, and programs as well as with the firm's international operations?

4. In what ways does this structure compare with those of similar corporations?

B. Corporate Culture   *See Section 4.3 on pages 89–90.*

1. Is there a well-defined or emerging culture composed of shared beliefs, expectations, and values?

2. Is the culture consistent with the current objectives, strategies, policies, and programs?

3. What is the culture's position on important issues facing the corporation (that is, on productivity, quality of performance, adaptability to changing conditions, and internationalization)?

4 Is the culture compatible with the employees' diversity of backgrounds?

5. Does the company take into consideration the values of each nation's culture in which the firm operates?

C. Corporate Resources

1. Marketing   *See Section 4.3 on pages 90–91.*

   a) What are the corporation's current marketing objectives, strategies, policies, and programs?
      i) Are they clearly stated, or merely implied from performance and/or budgets?
      ii) Are they consistent with the corporation's mission, objectives, strategies, policies, and with internal and external environments?
   b) How well is the corporation performing in terms of analysis of market position and marketing mix (that is, product, price, place, and promotion) in both domestic and international markets? What percentage of sales comes from foreign operations?
      i)   What trends emerge from this analysis?
      ii) What impact have these trends had on past performance and how will they probably affect future performance?
      iii) Does this analysis support the corporation's past and pending strategic decisions?
      iv) Does marketing provide the company with a competitive advantage?

Table 10.5   Strategic Audit of a Corporation (continued)

c) How well does this corporation's marketing performance compare with that of similar corporations?
d) Are marketing managers using accepted marketing concepts and techniques to evaluate and improve product performance? (Consider product life cycle, market segmentation, market research, and product portfolios.)
e) Does marketing adjust to the conditions in each country in which it operates?
f) What is the role of the marketing manager in the strategic management process?

2. Finance   *See Sections 4.3 and 14.3 on pages 91–93 and 320–326.*

a) What are the corporation's current financial objectives, strategies, policies, and programs?
  i) Are they clearly stated or merely implied from performance and/or budgets?
  ii) Are they consistent with the corporation's mission, objectives, strategies, policies, and with internal and external environments?

b) How well is the corporation performing in terms of financial analysis? (Consider ratios, common size statements, and capitalization structure.)
  i) What trends emerge from this analysis?
  ii) Are there any significant differences when statements are calculated in constant versus reported dollars?
  iii) What impact have these trends had on past performance and how will they probably affect future performance?
  iv) Does this analysis support the corporation's past and pending strategic decisions?
  v) Does finance provide the company with a competitive advantage?

c) How well does this corporation's financial performance compare with that of similar corporations?
d) Are financial managers using accepted financial concepts and techniques to evaluate and improve current corporate and divisional performance? (Consider financial leverage, capital budgeting, ratio analysis, and managing foreign currencies.)
e) Does finance adjust to the conditions in each country in which the company operates?
f) What is the role of the financial manager in the strategic management process?

3. Research and Development (R&D)   *See Section 4.3 on pages 93–96.*

a) What are the corporation's current R&D objectives, strategies, policies, and programs?
  i) Are they clearly stated, or merely implied from performance and/or budgets?
  ii) Are they consistent with the corporation's mission, objectives, strategies, policies, and with internal and external environments?
  iii) What is the role of technology in corporate performance?
  iv) Is the mix of basic, applied, and engineering research appropriate given the corporate mission and strategies?
  v) Does R&D provide the company with a competitive advantage?

b) What return is the corporation receiving from its investment in R&D?
c) Is the corporation competent in technology transfer? Does it use concurrent engineering and cross-functional work teams in product and process design?
d) What role does technological discontinuity play in the company's products?
e) How well does the corporation's investment in R&D compare with the investments of similar corporations?
f) Does R&D adjust to the conditions in each country in which the company operates?
g) What is the role of the R&D manager in the strategic management process?

Table 10.5   **Strategic Audit of a Corporation** *(continued)*

4. Operations and Logistics   *See Section 4.3 on pages 96–98.*

a) What are the corporation's current manufacturing/service objectives, strategies, policies, and programs?

   i)   Are they clearly stated, or merely implied from performance and/or budgets?

   ii) Are they consistent with the corporation's mission, objectives, strategies, policies, and with internal and external environments?

b) What is the type and extent of operations capabilities of the corporation? How much is done domestically versus internationally? Is the amount of outsourcing appropriate to be competitive? Is purchasing being handled appropriately?

   i)   If product-oriented, consider plant facilities, type of manufacturing system (continuous mass production, intermittent job shop, or flexible manufacturing), age and type of equipment, degree and role of automation and/or robots, plant capacities and utilization, productivity ratings, availability and type of transportation.

   ii) If service-oriented, consider service facilities (hospital, theater, or school buildings), type of operations systems (continuous service over time to same clientele or intermittent service over time to varied clientele), age and type of supporting equipment, degree and role of automation and/or use of mass communication devices (diagnostic machinery, video-tape machines), facility capacities and utilization rates, efficiency ratings of professional/service personnel, availability and type of transportation to bring service staff and clientele together.

c) Are manufacturing or service facilities vulnerable to natural disasters, local or national strikes, reduction or limitation of resources from suppliers, substantial cost increases of materials, or nationalization by governments?

d) Is there an appropriate mix of people and machines, in manufacturing firms, or of support staff to professionals, in service firms?

e) How well does the corporation perform relative to the competition? Is it balancing inventory costs (warehousing) with logistical costs (just-in-time)? Consider costs per unit of labor, material, and overhead; downtime; inventory control management and/or scheduling of service staff; production ratings; facility utilization percentages; and number of clients successfully treated by category (if service firm) or percentage of orders shipped on time (if product firm).

   i)   What trends emerge from this analysis?

   ii) What impact have these trends had on past performance and how will they probably affect future performance?

   iii) Does this analysis support the corporation's past and pending strategic decisions?

   iv) Does operations provide the company with a competitive advantage?

f) Are operations managers using appropriate concepts and techniques to evaluate and improve current performance? Consider cost systems, quality control and reliability systems, inventory control management, personnel scheduling, TQM, learning curves, safety programs, and engineering programs that can improve efficiency of manufacturing or of service.

g) Does operations adjust to the conditions in each country in which it has facilities?

h) What is the role of the operations manager in the strategic management process?

5. Human Resources Management (HRM)   *See Section 4.3 on pages 98–100.*

a) What are the corporation's current HRM objectives, strategies, policies, and programs?

   i)   Are they clearly stated, or merely implied from performance and/or budgets?

Table 10.5 Strategic Audit of a Corporation *(continued)*

ii) Are they consistent with the corporation's mission, objectives, strategies, policies, and with internal and external environments?

b) How well is the corporation's HRM performing in terms of improving the fit between the individual employee and the job? Consider turnover, grievances, strikes, layoffs, employee training, and quality of work life.

i) What trends emerge from this analysis?

ii) What impact have these trends had on past performance and how will they probably affect future performance?

iii) Does this analysis support the corporation's past and pending strategic decisions?

iv) Does HRM provide the company with a competitive advantage?

c) How does this corporation's HRM performance compare with that of similar corporations?

d) Are HRM managers using appropriate concepts and techniques to evaluate and improve corporate performance? Consider the job analysis program, performance appraisal system, up-to-date job descriptions, training and development programs, attitude surveys, job design programs, quality of relationship with unions, and use of autonomous work teams.

e) How well is the company managing the diversity of its workforce?

f) Does HRM adjust to the conditions in each country in which the company operates? Does the company have a code of conduct for HRM in developing nations? Are employees receiving international assignments to prepare them for managerial positions?

g) What is the role of the HRM manager in the strategic management process?

6. Information Systems (IS)   *See Section 4.3 on page 100.*

a) What are the corporation's current IS objectives, strategies, policies, and programs?

i) Are they clearly stated, or merely implied from performance and/or budgets?

ii) Are they consistent with the corporation's mission, objectives, strategies, policies, and with internal and external environments?

b) How well is the corporation's IS performing in terms of providing a useful database, automating routine clerical operations, assisting managers in making routine decisions, and providing information necessary for strategic decisions?

i) What trends emerge from this analysis?

ii) What impact have these trends had on past performance and how will they probably affect future performance?

iii) Does this analysis support the corporation's past and pending strategic decisions?

iv) Does IS provide the company with a competitive advantage?

c) How does this corporation's IS performance and stage of development compare with that of similar corporations?

d) Are IS managers using appropriate concepts and techniques to evaluate and improve corporate performance? Do they know how to build and manage a complex database, conduct system analyses, and implement interactive decision-support systems?

e) Does the company have a global IS? Does it have difficulty with getting data across national boundaries?

f) What is the role of the IS manager in the strategic management process?

D. Summary of Internal Factors   *See IFAS Table on pages 101–102.*

Which of these factors are the most important to the corporation and to the industries in which it competes at the present time? Which will be important in the future?

Table 10.5 **Strategic Audit of a Corporation** (continued)

V. Analysis of Strategic Factors (SWOT) See Sections 5.1 and 5.2 on pages 107–111.

A. Situational Analysis See SFAS Table on pages 108–110.

What are the most important internal and external factors (**Strengths, Weaknesses, Opportunities, Threats**) that strongly affect the corporation's present and future performance? List five to ten *strategic factors.*

B. Review of Mission and Objectives See Section 5.2 on page 111.

1. Are the current mission and objectives appropriate in light of the key strategic factors and problems?

2. Should the mission and objectives be changed? If so, how?

3. If changed, what will the effects on the firm be?

VI. Strategic Alternatives and Recommended Strategy

A. Strategic Alternatives See Sections 5.3, 5.4, 6.2, and 7.1 on pages 111–129, 133–147 and 162–170.

1. Can the current or revised objectives be met by the simple, more careful implementing of those strategies presently in use (for example, fine-tuning the strategies)?

2. What are the major feasible alternative strategies available to this corporation? What are the pros and cons of each? Can corporate scenarios be developed and agreed upon?
   a) Consider *cost leadership* and *differentiation* as business strategies.
   b) Consider *stability, growth,* and *retrenchment* as corporate strategies.
   c) Consider any functional strategic alternatives that might be needed for reinforcement of an important corporate or business strategic alternative.

B. Recommended Strategy See Sections 7.3 and 7.4 on pages 171–177.

1. Specify which of the strategic alternatives you are recommending for the corporate, business, and functional levels of the corporation. Do you recommend different business or functional strategies for different units of the corporation?

2. Justify your recommendation in terms of its ability to resolve both long- and short-term problems and effectively deal with the strategic factors.

3. What **policies** should be developed or revised to guide effective implementation?

VII. Implementation See Chapters 8 and 9.

A. What kinds of **programs** (for example, restructuring the corporation or instituting TQM) should be developed to implement the recommended strategy?

Table 10.5   **Strategic Audit of a Corporation** (continued)

1. Who should develop these programs?

2. Who should be in charge of these programs?

B. Are the programs financially feasible? Can pro forma **budgets** be developed and agreed upon? Are priorities and timetables appropriate to individual programs?

C. Will new standard operating **procedures** need to be developed?

VIII. Evaluation and Control   See Chapter 10.

A. Is the current information system capable of providing sufficient feedback on implementation activities and performance? Can it measure *critical success factors*?

1. Can performance results be pinpointed by area, unit, project, or function?

2. Is the information timely?

B. Are adequate control measures in place to ensure conformance with the recommended strategic plan?

1. Are appropriate standards and measures being used?

2. Are reward systems capable of recognizing and rewarding good performance?

● **10.8** Global Issues for the 21st Century

- The **21st Century Global Society** feature in this chapter illustrates how difficult it is for a regional trading bloc to form a single currency for its member countries. Although the reality of the euro may be delayed until the turn of the century, its inevitable appearance may serve as an impetus to other trading blocs, such as NAFTA, to also move to a single currency among member nations.

- The International Standards Organization is going beyond ISO 9000 to develop ISO 14000, which focuses on environmental standards. Given the high level of environmental concern in the developed nations, this set of standards may eventually rival ISO 9000 in its global impact on business activities.

- The balanced scorecard approach to evaluating performance is increasingly being accepted by corporations. One benefit of this approach is its emphasis on evaluating the ability of the corporation to learn from its experience, especially in international activities. Given that "what you inspect is what you get," the balanced scorecard should help improve the learning capabilities of organizations.

- Activity-based costing (ABC) supports value-chain analysis by identifying the value provided by each step in a firm's value chain of activities. A clear understanding of each activity's or function's value can help in outsourcing decisions. As more industries become global, firms will need ABC to evaluate the efficiency of their operations in different parts of the world.

- The continuing evolution of European, American, and Asian trade blocs means that companies will need to have a presence in each bloc in order to be internationally competitive and to avoid customs duties. Given that at least one-third of all international trade takes place internally among individual units of multinational corporations, transfer pricing will continue to be a contentious issue for most countries and most multinational corporations.

Projections for the 21st Century

- From 1994 to 2010, the number of miles traveled by air will double from 1.5 trillion to 3 trillion.

- From 1994 to 2010, the number of credit card transactions will increase from 1.5 trillion to 2 trillion.[43]

Discussion Questions

1. Is Figure 10.1 a realistic model of the evaluation and control process?

2. What are some examples of behavior controls? Output controls?

3. Is EVA an improvement over ROI, ROE, or EPS?

4. How much faith can a manager place in a transfer price as a substitute for a market price in measuring a profit center's performance?

5. Is the evaluation and control process appropriate for a corporation that emphasizes creativity? Are control and creativity compatible?

Key Terms

activity-based costing (ABC) (p. 233)
balanced scorecard (p. 238)
behavior controls (p. 231)
behavior substitution (p. 246)
benchmarking (p. 240)
critical success factors (p. 248)
earnings per share (EPS) (p. 235)
economic value added (EVA) (p. 236)
evaluation and control information (p. 230)
evaluation and control process (p. 230)

goal displacement (p. 246)
international transfer pricing (p. 241)
ISO 9000 Standards Series (p. 233)
key performance measures (p. 238)
long-term evaluation method (p. 250)
management audits (p. 238)
market value added (MVA) (p. 237)
operating budgets (p. 239)
output controls (p. 232)
performance (p. 231)
periodic statistical reports (p. 239)
R/3 software system (p. 244)

repatriation of profits (p. 242)
responsibility centers (p. 239)
return on equity (ROE) (p. 235)
return on investment (ROI) (p. 234)
shareholder value (p. 235)
short-term orientation (p. 246)
stakeholder measures (p. 235)
steering controls (p. 231)
strategic audit (p. 251)
strategic-funds method (p. 250)
suboptimization (p. 247)
tolerance range (p. 230)
transfer prices (p. 240)
weighted-factor method (p. 249)

Strategic Practice Exercise

Have you ever heard a person say that something "was built like a Mack truck?" The Mack name and bulldog mascot are among the most recognized trademarks in the world. As recently as 1980, Mack held more than 20% of the North American heavy-duty truck market and employed 17,000 people. By the late 1980s, however, its well-known slogan was beginning to ring hollow. Market share dipped to 13% in 1989 and employment fell to 6,500 people. The company lost $185 million in that year—followed by four more years of losses. According to Elios Pascual, Chairman, President, and Chief Executive Officer of Mack Trucks Inc., of Allentown, Pennsylvania, "Our quality was suffering, but we didn't know how badly because we weren't really measuring it. Our pride had deteriorated into an arrogance that blinded us to the severity of the situation." What had happened to such a well-known and previously successful company?

In analyzing the situation, Chairman Pascual felt that the most important reason for this drop was the disappearance of the kind of teamwork that had built the company. "Mack had become tied into a segregated, departmental organization that discouraged people from talking to one another. The disconnection and frustration were apparent everywhere—from suppliers to employees." Coordination processes fell apart. For example, some 1,200 partially assembled trucks at the company's Winnsboro, South Carolina, plant had to be parked in nearby fields while the plant waited for needed parts. Relations with labor (represented by the United Auto Workers union) became so bad that when the new general manager of Mack's Macungie, Pennsylvania, assembly plant visited the operation in 1990, an angry employee threw a bolt at him!

Pascual reported, "By 1991 the company was hovering near bankruptcy and we needed teamwork more than ever. It was at that point that we decided that unless we got everyone involved in the game, it would soon be over."[44]

1. What could have been some of the causes of the problems at Mack Trucks?

2. If you were the CEO of Mack Trucks in 1991, what would you do to improve the situation and stop the string of losses?

Notes

1. P. B. Carroll, "The Failures of Central Planning—at IBM," *Wall Street Journal* (January 28, 1993), p. A14.
2. D. Pickton, M. Starkey, and M. Bradford, "Understand Business Variation for Improved Business Performance," *Long Range Planning* (June 1996), pp. 412–415.
3. A. M. Hormozi, "Understanding and Implementing ISO 9000: A Manager's Guide," *SAM Advanced Management Journal* (Autumn 1995), pp. 4–11.
4. J. K. Shank, and V. Govindarajan, *Strategic Cost Management* (New York: The Free Press, 1993).
5. T. P. Pare, "A New Tool For Managing Costs," *Fortune* (June 14, 1993), pp. 124–129.
6. T. R. V. Davis, and B. L. Darling, "ABC in a Virtual Corporation," *Management Accounting* (October 1996), pp. 18–26.
7. C. K. Brancato, *New Corporate Performance Measures* (New York: The Conference Board, 1995).
8. C. D. Ittner, D. F. Larcker, and M. V. Rajan, "The Choice of Performance Measures in Annual Bonus Contracts," Working paper reported by K. Z. Andrews in "Executive Bonuses," *Harvard Business Review* (January-February 1996), pp. 8–9.
9. S. Tully, "America's Best Wealth Creators," *Fortune* (November 28, 1994), p. 143.
10. G. B. Stewart III, "EVA Works—But Not If You Make These Common Mistakes," *Fortune* (May 1, 1995), pp. 117–118.
11. S. Tully, "The Real Key to Creating Wealth," *Fortune* (September 20, 1993), p. 38.
12. K. Lehn, and A. K. Makhija, "EVA & MVA As Performance Measures and Signals for Strategic Change," *Strategy & Leadership* (May/June 1996), pp. 34–38.
13. A. B. Fisher, "Creating Stockholder Wealth: Market Value Added," *Fortune* (December 11, 1995), pp. 105–116.
14. Lehn and Makhija, p. 37.
15. R. S. Kaplan, and D. P. Norton, "Using the Balanced Scorecard as a Strategic Management System," *Harvard Business Review* (January-February 1996), pp. 75–85; R. S. Kaplan, and D. P. Norton, "The Balanced Scorecard—Measures That Drive Performance," *Harvard Business Review* (January-February, 1992), pp. 71–79.
16. C. K. Brancato, *New Performance Measures* (New York: The Conference Board, 1995).
17. J. S. Lublin, "Corporate Chiefs Polish Their Relations with Directors," *Wall Street Journal* (October 15, 1993), p. B1.
18. Z. U. Khan, S. K. Chawla, M. F. Smith, and M. F. Sharif, "Transfer Pricing Policy Issues in Europe 1992," *International Journal of Management* (September 1992), pp. 230–241.
19. H. Rothman, "You Need Not Be Big to Benchmark," *Nation's Business* (December 1992), p. 64.
20. C. W. Von Bergen, and B. Soper, "A Problem With Benchmarking: Using Shaping as a Solution," *SAM Advanced Management Journal* (Autumn 1995), pp. 16–19.
21. "Tool Usage Rates," *Journal of Business Strategy* (March/April 1995), p. 12.
22. G. Fuchsberg, "Here's Help in Finding Corporate Role Models," *Wall Street Journal* (June 1, 1993), p. B1.
23. S. M. Robbins, and R. B. Stobaugh, "The Bent Measuring Stick for Foreign Subsidiaries," *Harvard Business Review* (September-October 1973), p. 82.
24. J. D. Daniels, and L. H. Radebaugh, *International Business*, 5th ed. (Reading, Mass.: Addison-Wesley, 1989), pp. 673–674.

25. W. A. Johnson, and R. J. Kirsch, "International Transfer Pricing and Decision Making in United States Multinationals," *International Journal of Management* (June 1991), pp. 554–561.

26. "Fixing the Bottom Line," *Time* (November 23, 1992), p. 20.

27. T. A. Stewart, "The New Face of American Power," *Fortune* (July 26, 1993), p. 72; G. P. Zachary, "Behind Stocks' Surge Is an Economy in Which Big U.S. Firms Thrive," *Wall Street Journal* (November 22, 1995), pp. A1, A5.

28. J. M. L. Poon, R. Ainuddin, and H. Affrim, "Management Policies and Practices of American, British, European, and Japanese Subsidiaries in Malaysia: A Comparative Study," *International Journal of Management* (December 1990), pp. 467–474.

29. "A Little EMU Enlightenment," *The Economist* (February 22, 1997), p. 88.

30. C. W. L. Hill, P. Hwang, and W. C. Kim, "An Eclectic Theory of the Choice of International Entry Mode," *Strategic Management Journal* (February 1990), pp. 117–128; D. Lei, J. W. Slocum, Jr., and R. W. Slater, "Global Strategy and Reward Systems: The Key Roles of Management Development and Corporate Culture," *Organizational Dynamics* (Autumn 1990), pp. 27–41; W. R. Fannin, and A. F. Rodriques, "National or Global?—Control vs. Flexibility," *Long Range Planning* (October 1986), pp. 84–188.

31. A. V. Phatak, *International Dimensions of Management,* 2nd ed. (Boston: Kent, 1989), pp. 155–157.

32. J. B. White, D. Clark, and S. Ascarelli, "This German Software Is Complex, Expensive—and Wildly Popular," *Wall Street Journal* (March 14, 1997), pp. A1, A8.

33. B. Richards, "The Business Plan," *Wall Street Journal* (November 11, 1996), p. R10.

34. R. M. Hodgetts, and M. S. Wortman, *Administrative Policy,* 2nd ed. (New York: John Wiley and Sons, 1980), p. 128.

35. J. R. Wooldridge, and C. C. Snow, "Stock Market Reaction to Strategic Investment Decisions," *Strategic Management Journal* (September 1990), pp. 353–363.

36. D. R. Schmidt, and K. L. Fowler, "Post-Acquisition Financial Performance and Executive Compensation," *Strategic Management Journal* (November-December 1990), pp. 559–569.

37. W. Zellner, E. Schine, and G. Smith, "Trickle-Down Is Trickling Down at Work," *Business Week* (March 18, 1996), p. 34.

38. T. J. Peters, and R. H. Waterman, *In Search of Excellence* (New York: HarperCollins, 1982), pp. 75–76.

39. D. B. Balkin, and L. R. Gomez-Mejia, "Matching Compensation and Organizational Strategies," *Strategic Management Journal* (February 1990), pp. 153–169.

40. C. S. Galbraith, "The Effect of Compensation Programs and Structure on SBU Competitive Strategy: A Study of Technology-Intensive Firms," *Strategic Management Journal* (July 1991), pp. 353–370.

41. P. J. Stonich, "The Performance Measurement and Reward System: Critical to Strategic Management," *Organizational Dynamics* (Winter 1984), pp. 45–57.

42. G. Donaldson, "A New Tool for Boards: The Strategic Audit," *Harvard Business Review* (July-August 1995), pp. 99–107.

43. J. Warner, "21st Century Capitalism: Snapshot of the Next Century," *Business Week* (November 18, 1994), p. 194.

44. E. Pascual, "Mack Learns the Error of False Pride," *Wall Street Journal* (July 11, 1994), p. A10.

Chapter 11

Strategic Issues in Managing Technology and Innovation

The DuPont Company has long been known for its excellence in basic corporate research. In the early 1990s, for example, it led the nation's chemical companies in patents applied for and granted. The company spent more than $13 billion on chemical and related research during the 1980s, but management admitted that the company failed to develop much in the way of major innovations. "They've been like the space program: the technology is great, but where's the payoff?" commented industry analyst John Garcia. CEO Edgar Woolard admitted that the company took too long to "convert research into products that can benefit our customers." In major established products, the company lost ground to competitors that spent more on improving manufacturing. Customers who wanted changes in Zytel nylon-resin products often had to wait six months for an answer. DuPont had become a secure place to work, said Woolard, but "we have too much bureaucracy running these businesses."

According to Joseph Miller, director of DuPont's polymers research, the emphasis in R&D was to find another "big bang" like its invention of nylon. As a result, the company introduced a series of new products—excellently designed, but rejected by the marketplace. Among them were Kevlar, stronger than steel, but too expensive for widespread usage; Corfam, a synthetic leather that didn't "breathe" and thus made shoes uncomfortable (costing DuPont $250 million); Qiana, a synthetic silk that was ignored because of increasing interest in natural fibers; plus many millions spent unsuccessfully on electronic imaging and pharmaceuticals. To focus "more intensity on customer needs," CEO Woolard announced that the company was shifting about 30% of its research budget (approximately $400 million annually) toward speeding new products to customers.[1]

This example from DuPont illustrates how a successful, established company can have difficulty in developing and marketing new products when it fails to make technology a part of its strategic management process. Companies that aren't knowledgeable about strategically managing technology and innovation have the potential to destroy the very capabilities that originally provided them with distinctive competence. In this chapter, we examine strategic issues in technology and innovation as they impact environmental scanning, strategy formulation, strategy implementation, and evaluation and control.

11.1   Role of Management

Due to increased competition and accelerated product development cycles, innovation and the management of technology is becoming crucial to corporate success. Approximately half the profits of all U.S. companies come from products launched in the previous 10 years.[2] What is less obvious is how a company can generate a significant return from investment in R&D as well as an overall sense of enthusiasm for innovative behavior and risk taking. One way is to include innovation in the corporation's mission statement. See the **Strategy in a Changing World** feature for some examples from well-known companies. Another way is by establishing policies that support the innovative process. For example, 3M has set a policy of generating at least 25% of its revenue from products introduced in the preceding three years. To support this policy, this $13 billion corporation annually spends nearly $1 billion.[3]

The importance of technology and innovation must be emphasized by people at the very top and reinforced by people throughout the corporation. If top management and the board are not interested in these topics, managers below them tend to echo their lack of interest. When Akio Morita, Chairman of Sony Corporation, visited the United Kingdom, he expressed disbelief at the number of accountants leading that country's companies. Uncomfortable because they lacked familiarity with science or technology, these top managers too often limited their role to approving next year's budget. Constrained by what the company could afford and guided by how much the competition was spending, they perceived R&D as a line expense item instead of as an investment in the future.[4]

Management has an obligation to not only encourage new product development, but also to develop a system to ensure that technology is being used most effectively with the consumer in mind. A study by Chicago consultants Kuczmarski & Associates of 11,000 new products marketed by 77 manufacturing, service, and consumer-product firms revealed that only 56% of all newly introduced products were still being sold five years later. Only one in 13 new product ideas ever made it into test markets. Although some authorities argue that this percentage of successful new products needs to be improved, others contend that too high a percentage means that a company isn't taking the risks necessary to develop a really new product.[5]

The importance of top management's providing appropriate direction is exemplified by Chairman Morita's statement of his philosophy for Sony Corporation:

> The key to success for Sony, and to everything in business, science, and technology for that matter, is never to follow the others. . . . Our basic concept has always been this—to give new convenience, or new methods, or new benefits, to the general public with our technology.

▶ ▶ ▶ ▶ ▶ *STRATEGY IN A CHANGING WORLD*

EXAMPLES OF INNOVATION EMPHASIS IN MISSION STATEMENTS

To emphasize the importance of technology, creativity, and innovation to overall future corporate success, some well-known firms have added sections to this effect in their published mission statements. Some of these are listed here.

AT&T: "We believe innovation is the engine that will keep us vital and growing. Our culture embraces creativity, seeks different perspectives and risks pursuing new opportunities. We create and rapidly convert technology into products and services, constantly searching for new ways to make technology more useful to customers."

General Mills: "Innovation is the principal driver of growth. . . . To be first among our competitors, we must constantly challenge the status quo and be willing to experiment. . . . Our motivation system will strongly reward successful risk-taking, while not penalizing an innovative idea that did not work."

Gerber: "[The mission will be achieved by] investing in continued product and body-of-

knowledge, innovation, and research in the areas of infant nutrition, care, and development."

Gillette: "We will invest in and master the key technologies vital to category success."

Hallmark: "[We believe] that creativity and quality—in our concept, products and services—are essential to our success."

Intel: "To succeed we must maintain our innovative environment. We strive to: embrace change, challenge the status quo, listen to all ideas and viewpoints, encourage and reward informed risk taking, and learn from our successes and mistakes."

Merck & Co.: "We are dedicated to achieving the highest level of scientific excellence and commit our research to maintaining human health and improving the quality of life."

Source: P. Jones and L. Kahaner, *Say It and Live It: The 50 Corporate Mission Statements That Hit the Mark* (New York: Currency Doubleday, 1995).

Morita and his co-founder, Masuru Ibuka, always looked for ways to turn ideas into clear targets. Says Morita, "When Ibuka was first describing his idea for the Betamax videocassette, he gave the engineers a paperback book and said, 'Make it this size.' Those were his only instructions."[6]

11.2 Environmental Scanning

External Scanning

Corporations need to continually scan their external societal and task environments for new developments in technology that may have some application to their current or potential products.

Technology Research

Motorola, a company well known for its ability to invest in profitable new technologies and manufacturing improvements, has a sophisticated scanning system. Its intelligence department monitors the latest technology developments introduced at scientific conferences, in journals, and in trade gossip. This information helps it build "technology roadmaps" that assess where breakthroughs are likely to occur, when they can be incorporated into new products, how much money their development will cost, and which of the developments is being worked on by the competition.[7]

Focusing one's scanning efforts too closely on one's own industry is dangerous. Most new developments that threaten existing business practices and technologies do not come from existing competitors or even from within traditional industries.[8] A new technology that can substitute for an existing technology at a lower cost and provide higher quality can change the very basis for competition in an industry. Consider, for example, the impact of Internet technology on the personal computer software industry. Microsoft Corporation had ignored the developing Internet technology while the company battled successfully with IBM, Lotus, and WordPerfect to dominate operating system software via Windows 95 as well as word processing and spreadsheet programs via Microsoft Office. Ironically, just as Microsoft introduced its new Windows 95 operating system, newcomer Netscape used Java applets in its user-friendly, graphically oriented browser program with the potential to make operating systems unnecessary. By the time Microsoft realized this threat to its business, Netscape had already established itself as the industry standard for browsers. Microsoft was forced to spend huge amounts of time and resources trying to catch up to Netscape's dominant market share with its own Internet Explorer browser.

Disadvantages of Market Research

Contrasted with **technology research** engaged in by Motorola and other companies, traditional **market research** may not always provide useful information on new product directions. According to Sony executive Kozo Ohsone, "When you introduce products that have never been invented before, what good is market research?" For example, Hal Sperlich took the concept of the minivan from Ford to Chrysler when Ford refused to develop the concept. According to Sperlich,

> [Ford] lacked confidence that a market existed because the product didn't exist. The auto industry places great value on historical studies of market segments. Well, we couldn't prove there was a market for the minivan because there was no historical segment to cite. In Detroit most product-development dollars are spent on modest improvements to existing products, and most market research money is spent on studying what customers like among available products. In ten years of developing the minivan we never once got a letter from a housewife asking us to invent one. To the skeptics, that proved there wasn't a market out there.[9]

A heavy emphasis on being customer-driven could actually prevent companies from developing innovative new products. A study of the impact of **technological discontinuity** (explained earlier in Chapter 4) in various industries revealed that the leading firms failed to switch to the new technology *not* because management was ignorant of the new development, but rather because they listened too closely to their current customers. In all of these firms, a key task of management was to decide which of the many product and development programs continually being proposed to them should receive financial resources. The criterion used for the decision was the total return perceived in each project, adjusted by the perceived riskiness of the project. Projects targeted at the known needs of key customers in established markets consistently won the most resources. Sophisticated systems for planning and compensation favored this type of project every time. As a result, the leading companies continued to use the established technology to make the products its current customers demanded, allowing smaller entrepreneurial competitors to develop the new, more risky technology.[10]

Because the market for the innovative products based on the new technology was fairly small at first, new ventures had time to fine-tune product design, build sufficient manufacturing capacity, and establish the product as the industry standard (as Netscape did with its Internet browser). As the marketplace began to embrace the new standard, the customers of the leading companies began to ask for products based on the new technology. Although some established manufacturers were able to defend their market share positions through aggressive product development and marketing activity (as Microsoft did against Netscape), many firms, finding that the new entrants had developed insurmountable advantages in manufacturing cost and design experience, were forced out of the market. Even the established manufacturers that converted to the new technology were unable to win a significant share of the new market.[11]

Instead of standard market research to test the potential of innovative products, some successful companies are using speed and flexibility to gain market information. These companies developed their products by "probing" potential markets with early versions of the products, learning from the probes, and probing again.[12] For example, Seiko's only market research is surprisingly simple. The company introduces hundreds of new models of watches into the marketplace. It makes more of the models that sell; it drops those that don't.

The consulting firm Arthur D. Little found that the use of standard market research techniques has only resulted in a success rate of 8% for new cereals—92% of all new cereals fail. As a result, innovative firms, such as Keebler and the leading cereal makers, are reducing their expenditures for market research and working to reduce the cost of launching new products by making their manufacturing processes more flexible.[13]

Internal Scanning

In addition to scanning the external environment, strategists should also assess their company's ability to innovate effectively by asking the following questions:

1. Has the company developed the resources needed to try new ideas?

2. Do the managers allow experimentation with new products or services?

3. Does the corporation encourage risk taking and tolerate mistakes?

4. Are people more concerned with new ideas or with defending their turf?

5. Is it easy to form autonomous project teams?[14]

In addition to answering these questions, strategists should assess how well company resources are internally allocated and evaluate the organization's ability to develop and transfer new technology in a timely manner into the generation of innovative products and services.

Resource Allocation Issues

The company must make available the resources necessary for effective research and development. Research indicates that a company's **R&D intensity** (its spending on R&D as a percentage of sales revenue) is a principal means of gaining market share in global competition.[15] The amount of money spent on R&D often varies by industry. For example, the computer software and drug industries spend an average of 11% to 13% of their sales dollar for R&D. Others, such as the food and the containers and packaging industries, spend less than 1%. A good rule of thumb for R&D spending is that a corporation should spend at a "normal" rate for that particular industry, unless its competitive strategy dictates otherwise.[16] Research indicates that consistency in R&D strategy and resource allocation across lines of business improves corporate performance by enabling the firm to better develop synergies among product lines and business units.[17]

Simply spending money on R&D or new projects does not, however, guarantee useful results. One study found that although large firms spent almost twice as much per R&D patent than did smaller firms, the smaller firms used more of their patents. The innovation rate of small businesses was 322 innovations per million employees versus 225 per million for large companies.[18] One explanation for this phenomenon is that large firms tend to spend development money to increase the efficiency of existing performance with a primary goal of reducing costs and downsizing. In contrast, small firms tend to apply technology to improving effectiveness with a goal of improving quality and customer satisfaction.[19] Other studies reveal that the maximum innovator in various industries often was the middle-sized firm. These firms were generally more effective and efficient in technology transfer. Very small firms often do not have sufficient resources to exploit new concepts, whereas the bureaucracy present in large firms rewards consistency over creativity.[20] From these studies, Hitt, Hoskisson, and Harrison propose the existence of an inverted U-shaped relationship between size and innovation. According to Hitt et al., "This suggests that organizations are flexible and responsive up to some threshold size but encounter inertia after that point."[21]

Sometimes most of the firms in an industry can waste their R&D spending. For example, between 1950 and 1979, the U.S. steel industry spent 20% more on plant maintenance and upgrading for each ton of production capacity added or replaced than did the Japanese steel industry. Nevertheless the top managements of U.S. steel firms failed to recognize and adopt two breakthroughs in steelmaking—the basic oxygen furnace and continuous casting. Their hesitancy to adopt new technology caused them to lose the world steel market.[22]

Time to Market Issues

In addition to money, another important consideration in the effective management of research and development is **time to market**. A decade ago, the time from inception to profitability of a specific R&D program was generally accepted to be 7 to 11 years. According to Karlheinz Kaske, CEO of Siemens AG, however, the time available to complete the cycle is getting shorter. Companies no longer can assume that competitors will allow them the number of years needed to recoup their investment. In the past, Kaske says, "ten to fifteen years went by before old products were replaced by new ones . . . now, it takes only four or five years."[23] Time to market is an important issue because *60% of patented innovations are generally imitated within four years at 65% of the cost of innovation.*[24] In the 1980s, Japanese auto manufacturers gained incredible competitive advantage over U.S. manufacturers by reducing new products' time to market to only three years. (U.S. auto companies needed five years.)[25]

Andy Grove, CEO of Intel, agrees with the increasing importance of time to market as a competitive weapon by stating, "Ultimately 'speed' is the only weapon we have." With $5 billion in annual sales, the company spends $1.2 billion a year on plant and equipment and $800 million on R&D. Intel is no longer content to introduce one or two new-generation microprocessors annually and a completely new family of computer microchips every four years. Previously Intel would introduce a new family of chips (such as the 386) only when the current market was sufficiently saturated with one family of chips (such as the 286). The advent of lower cost microprocessor clone manufacturers, such as Cyrix and AMD, meant that Intel had to give up the 386 market prematurely to focus on the emerging 486 market in 1992. The introduction of the Pentium (586 chip) microprocessor followed quickly in 1993, the Pentium Pro in 1995, and the Pentium II in

1997. Intel plans to continue developing new chip families every two years. Grove believes that this fast pace of development will keep chip cloners from ever catching up with Intel.[26]

11.3   Strategy Formulation

Research and development strategy deals not only with the decision to be a leader or a follower in terms of technology and market entry (discussed earlier in Chapter 7 under R&D strategy), but also with the source of the technology. Should a company develop its own technology or purchase it from others? The strategy also takes into account a company's particular mix of basic versus applied and product versus process R&D (discussed earlier in Chapter 4). The particular mix should suit the level of industry development and the firm's particular corporate and business strategies. The 🌐 **21st Century Global Society** feature illustrates how a company's competence in different aspects of R&D can affect its competitive strategy and its ability to successfully enter new markets. R&D strategy in a large corporation also deals with the proper balance of its product portfolio based on the life cycle of the products.

Product versus Process R&D

As illustrated in Figure 11.1, the proportion of product and process R&D tends to vary as a product moves along its life cycle. In the early stages, **product innovations** are most important because the product's physical attributes and capabilities most affect financial performance. Later, **process innovations** such as improved manufacturing facilities, increasing product quality, and faster distribution become important to maintaining the product's economic returns. Generally product R&D has been key to achieving differentiation strategies, whereas process R&D has been at the core of successful cost leadership strategies.

Historically, U.S. corporations have not been as skillful at process innovations as have German and Japanese companies. The primary reason has been a function of the amount of money invested in each form of R&D. U.S. firms spend, on the average, 70% of their R&D budgets on product R&D and only 30% on process R&D; German firms, 50% on each form; and Japanese firms, 30% on product and 70% on process R&D.[27] The emphasis by U.S. major home appliance manufacturers on process over product R&D may be one reason why they have such a strong position in the industry worldwide. (See the **Company Spotlight on Maytag Corporation** feature.)

Technology Sourcing

Technology sourcing, typically a make-or-buy decision, can be important in a firm's R&D strategy. Although in-house R&D has traditionally been an important source of technical knowledge for companies, firms can also tap the R&D capabilities of competitors, suppliers, and other organizations through contractual agreements (such as licensing, R&D agreements, and joint ventures). One example is Matsushita's licensing of Iomega's zip drive technology in 1996 so that Matshusita could also manufacture and sell removable cartridges for personal computers. When technological cycles were longer, a company was more likely to choose an independent R&D strategy not only because it gave the firm a longer lead time before competitors copied it, but also because it was more profitable in the long run. In today's world of shorter innovation life cycles and global competition, a company may no longer have the luxury of waiting to reap a long-term profit.

21ST CENTURY GLOBAL SOCIETY

THE IMPACT OF R&D ON COMPETITIVE ADVANTAGE IN CHINA

China is one of the ten largest economies in the world. Average income has tripled since 1978 for most rural people. Urban incomes have risen even faster, as the country's economy has grown at an annual rate of 9% in real terms for the past 15 years. As income increases, people are using it to improve their standard of living.

China is the world's fastest growing and potentially most profitable market for bathroom fixture manufacturers. Western-style toilets, which are easier to keep clean and use less water than the traditional Chinese fixtures, have become the standard in thousands of new apartment and office buildings. Two globally oriented companies attempting to dominate this lucrative market are American Standard of the United States and Toto Ltd. of Japan. Both design their products in their home country, manufacture them in Thailand using low-cost labor, and then ship the products to China for sale.

Product design has a significant impact on each company's competitive strategy in China. Toto has an advantage in one part of the design process because its designers in Japan use computers to generate models from blocks of foam. Engineering design is its distinctive competency. Blueprints can be in the hands of factory engineers in four weeks. In contrast, American Standard's process takes two months, on average. Models are crafted by hand by Jack Kaiser, an acknowledged design expert, and six associates. The personal touch is part of Standard's distinctive competency. Although the designers domi-

nate the process, they work closely with marketing and production to develop a product to suit consumers' needs. In contrast, Toto's engineers dominate the process—building for production, but limiting creativity and neglecting markets in other countries. This limits Toto's ability to successfully enter a new market with unusual needs.

Toto dominates the luxury bathroom market in China, but it has been slow to adapt to the fast-growing low end of the market. "To ask a Japanese engineer to make something cheaper is harder than to ask him to make something better," explained Thibault Danjou, a Toto marketing manager. American Standard has another advantage in its flexible manufacturing facility in Thailand. It only stocks 14 days' worth of inventory. Its production process is flexible enough to produce to order. Toto, in contrast, has a much more rigid production process and must keep two months' inventory on hand. American Standard can also fill odd size orders that Toto finds too difficult to fill. In selling new-style toilets to China, manufacturers must customize toilets to line up with existing sewage pipes. Selling close to half of the bathroom fixtures imported into China, American Standard is certainly cleaning up!

Source: S. Glain, "Top Toilet Makers from U.S. and Japan Vie for Chinese Market," *Wall Street Journal* (December 19, 1996), pp. A1, A11; "Deng's China: The Last Emperor," *The Economist* (February 22, 1997), pp. 21–25.

During a time of technological discontinuity in an industry, a company may have no choice but to purchase the new technology from others if it wants to remain competitive. For example, Ford Motor Company paid $100 million for 10.8% of the common stock of Cummins Engine Co., an expert in diesel engine technology. In return for its money, Ford got exclusive access to Cummins's truck engine technology. This allowed Ford to forgo the $300 million expense of designing a new engine on its own to meet U.S. emission standards.[28]

Firms that are unable to finance alone the huge costs of developing a new technology may coordinate their R&D with other firms through a **strategic alliance**. By the

Figure 11.1
Product and Process R&D in the Innovation Life Cycle

Source: Adapted from M. L. Patterson, "Lessons from the Assembly Line," *Journal of Business Strategy* (May/June 1993), p. 43. Permission granted by Faulkner & Gray, Eleven Penn Plaza, NY, NY 10001.

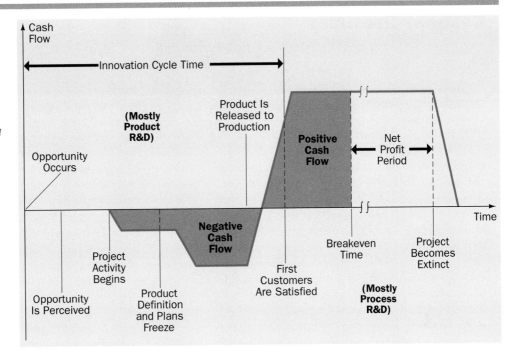

1990s, more than 150 cooperative alliances involving 1,000 companies were operating in the United States and many more were operating throughout Europe and Asia.[29] These alliances can be (a) *joint programs or contracts* to develop a new technology, (b) *joint ventures* establishing a separate company to take a new product to market, or (c) *minority investments* in innovative firms wherein the innovator obtains needed capital and the investor obtains access to valuable research. For example, Hewlett-Packard Company formed an alliance in 1996 with Microsoft, Oracle, and Netscape Communications to create an "electronic business framework" to bring together several Internet-related technologies. Some of their goals are to develop the remote installation and upgrading of software by network administrators, systems for secure electronic payments over the Internet, and integrate the Internet with telephone-based services such as telemarketing and customer service.

When should a company buy or license technology from others instead of developing it internally? Following the resource-based view of the firm discussed previously in Chapter 4, a company should *buy* technologies that are commonly available, but *make* (and protect) those that are rare, valuable, hard to imitate, and having no close substitutes. In addition, *outsourcing technology may be appropriate when:*

- The technology is of low significance to competitive advantage.
- The supplier has proprietary technology.
- The supplier's technology is better and/or cheaper and reasonably easy to integrate into the current system.
- The company's strategy is based on system design, marketing, distribution, and service—not on development and manufacturing.
- The technology development process requires special expertise.
- The technology development process requires new people and new resources.[30]

COMPANY SPOTLIGHT

Importance of Product and Process R&D in the Major Home Appliance Industry

Product innovation is being used in the major home appliance industry to provide consumers with new products as well as to add newer functions and features to existing products. The microwave oven was the last completely new product in this industry. Fuzzy logic technology is now being used to provide more effective, consumer-friendly appliances. Japanese appliance makers were the first to use this new technology to replace the many selector switches on an appliance with one start button. With fuzzy logic, a sophisticated set of electronic sensors and self-diagnostic software could measure the amount of detergent placed in a washing machine, check water temperature, gauge the amount of dirt on clothes, and decide not only how long the wash and rinse cycles should run, but also how vigorous the agitator should swish the water to get the clothes clean. By 1996, most major home appliance manufacturers had added fuzzy logic technology to top-end appliances in at least one of their product categories. Whirlpool added fuzzy logic to its VIP series of microwave ovens. Maytag did the same to its Intellisense™ line of dishwashers.

Process innovation for more efficient manufacturing of current products (as compared to new product development) has dominated research and development efforts in the U.S. major home appliance industry since the 1950s. Even though a refrigerator or a washing machine still looks and acts very much the same today as it did in the 1950s, it is built in a far different and more efficient manner. The components inside the appliances are being produced in highly automated plants using computer integrated manufacturing processes. An example of this emphasis on product simplification was Maytag's "Dependable Drive" washer transmission, which was designed to have 40.6% fewer parts than the transmission it replaced. Fewer parts meant simplified manufacturing and less chance of a breakdown. The result was lower manufacturing costs and higher product quality.

Most industry analysts agreed that continual process improvements have kept U.S. major home appliance manufacturers dominant in their industry. The emphasis on quality and durability, coupled with a reluctance to make major design changes simply for the sake of change, resulted in products with an average life expectancy of 20 years for refrigerators and 15 years for washers and dryers. Even though quality has improved significantly over the past 20 years, the average washer, dryer, and refrigerator cost no more than they did 20 years ago and yet last almost twice as long. If only the same could be said of the automobile industry!

MAYTAG CORPORATION

Importance of Technological Competence

Firms that emphasize growth through acquisitions over internal development tend to be less innovative in the long run.[31] Research suggests that companies must have at least a minimal R&D capability if they are to correctly assess the value of technology developed by others. R&D creates a capacity in a firm to assimilate and exploit new knowledge. This is called a company's **absorptive capacity** and is a valuable by-product of routine in-house R&D activity.[32] Further, without this capacity, firms could become locked out in their ability to assimilate the technology at a later time.

Those corporations that do purchase an innovative technology must have the **technological competence** to make good use of it. Some companies that introduce the latest technology into their processes do not adequately assess the competence of their people to handle it. For example, a survey conducted in the United Kingdom found that 44% of all companies that started to use robots met with initial failure, and that 22% of these firms abandoned the use of robots altogether, mainly because of inadequate technological knowledge and skills.[33] One U.S. company built a new plant equipped with computer-integrated manufacturing and statistical process controls, but the employees could not operate the equipment because 25% of them were illiterate.[34]

Product Portfolio

Developed by Hofer and based on the product life cycle, the 15-cell **product/market evolution matrix** (shown in Figure 11.2) depicts the types of developing products that cannot be easily shown on other portfolio matrixes. Products are plotted in terms of their competitive positions and their stages of product/market evolution. As on the GE Business Screen, the circles represent the sizes of the industries involved, and the pie wedges represent the market shares of the firm's business product lines. Present and future matrixes can be developed to identify strategic issues. In response to Figure 11.2, for example, we could ask why product B does not have a greater share of the market, given its strong competitive position. We could also ask why the company only has one product in the developmental stage. A limitation of this matrix is that the product life cycle does not always hold for every product. Many products, for example, do not inevitably fall into decline but (like Tide detergent and Colgate toothpaste) are revitalized and put back on a growth track.

11.4   Strategy Implementation

If a corporation decides to develop innovations internally, it must make sure that its corporate system and culture are suitable for such a strategy. It must make sufficient resources available for new products, provide collaborative structures and processes, and incorporate innovation into its overall corporate strategy.[35] It must ensure that its R&D operations are managed appropriately. It must establish procedures to support all five **stages of new product development**. (See Table 11.1.) If, like most large corporations, the culture is too bureaucratic and rigid to support entrepreneurial projects, top management must reorganize so that innovative projects can be free to develop.

Developing an Innovative Entrepreneurial Culture

To create a more innovative corporation, top management must develop an entrepreneurial culture—one that is open to the transfer of new technology into company activities and products and services. The company must be flexible and accepting of change. It should include a willingness to withstand a certain percentage of product failures on the way to success. Such a culture has been noted in 3M Corporation and Texas Instruments, among others. Research and development in these companies is managed quite differently from traditional methods. First, employees are dedicated to a particular project outcome rather than to innovation in general. Second, employees are often responsible for all functional activities and for all phases of the innovation process. Time is allowed to be sacrificed from regular duties to spend on innovative ideas. If the ideas are feasible, employees are temporarily reassigned to help develop them. They may become project champions who fight for resources to make the project a success. Third, these internal ventures are often separated from the rest of the company to provide them with greater independence, freedom for short-term pressures, different rewards, improved visibility, and access to key decision makers.[36]

Figure 11.2
Product/Market Evolution Portfolio Matrix

Source: C. W. Hofer and D. Schendel, *Strategy Formulation: Analytical Concepts* (St. Paul, Minn,: West Publishing Co., 1978), p. 34. From C. W. Hofer, "Conceptual Constructs for Formulating Corporate and Business Strategies" (Dover, Mass.: Case Publishing), no. BP-0041, p. 3. Copyright © 1977 by Charles W. Hofer. Reprinted by permission.

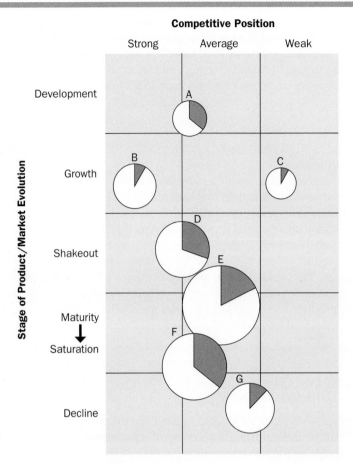

The innovative process often involves individuals at different organizational levels who fulfill three different types of entrepreneurial roles: product champion, sponsor, and orchestrator. A **product champion** is a person who generates a new idea and supports it through many organizational obstacles. A **sponsor** is usually a department manager who recognizes the value of the idea, helps obtain funding to develop the innovation, and facilitates its implementation. An **orchestrator** is someone in top management who articulates the need for innovation, provides funding for innovating activities, creates incentives for middle managers to sponsor new ideas, and protects idea/product champions from suspicious or jealous executives. Unless all of these roles are present in a company, major innovations are less likely to occur.[37]

Companies are finding that one way to overcome the barriers to successful product innovation is by using multifunctional teams with significant autonomy dedicated to a project. See the **Strategy in a Changing World** feature to learn how DuPont used this approach to improve its ability to convert research into successful new products. In a survey of 701 companies from Europe, the United States, and Japan, 85% of the respondents have used this approach with 62% rating it as successful.[38] Research reveals that cross-functional teams are best for designing and developing innovative new products, whereas the more traditional bureaucratic structures seem to be best for developing modifications to existing products, line extensions, and me-too products.[39] Chrysler Corporation was able to reduce the development time for new vehicles by 40% by using cross-functional teams and by developing a partnership approach to new projects.[40] International Specialty Products, a maker of polymers, used "product express" teams composed of chemists

Table 11.1 Five Stages of New Product Development

The Product Development & Management Association, based at Indiana University, has identified five stages of new product development:

- **Stage One: Idea Generation.** A new product concept is identified and refined. A team is formed to determine the idea's validity and market opportunity.

- **Stage Two: Concept Development and Screening.** The concept undergoes a feasibility study. Preliminary market research is conducted and a strategy is developed. If the product is not feasible, it's dropped.

- **Stage Three: Design and Development.** Using computer-aided design techniques, engineering and manufacturing turn the concept into a functioning product.

- **Stage Four: Market Testing.** Prototypes are now tested in the marketplace to learn if anyone is willing to purchase the product and at what price. Suggestions from consumers are fed back to the design team for possible inclusion.

- **Stage Five: Commercialization.** The entire company is energized to launch the new product.

Source: B. W. Mattimore, "Eureka! How to Invent a New Product," *The Futurist* (March-April 1995), p. 38.

and representatives from manufacturing and engineering to cut development time in half. "Instead of passing a baton, we bring everyone into the commercialization process at the same time," explained John Tancredi, Vice-president for R&D. "We are moving laterally, like rugby players, instead of like runners in a relay race."[41]

Organizing for Innovation: Corporate Entrepreneurship

Corporate entrepreneurship (also called *intrapreneurship*) is defined by Guth and Ginsburg as "the birth of new businesses within existing organizations, that is, internal innovation or venturing; and the transformation of organizations through renewal of the key ideas on which they are built, that is, strategic renewal."[42] A large corporation that wants to encourage innovation and creativity within its firm must choose a structure that will give the new business unit an appropriate amount of freedom while maintaining some degree of control at headquarters.

Burgelman proposes (see Figure 11.3) that the use of a particular organizational design should be determined by the *strategic importance of the new business* to the corporation and the *relatedness of the unit's operations* to those of the corporation.[43] The combination of these two factors results in nine organizational designs for corporate entrepreneurship.

1. **Direct integration.** A new business with a great deal of strategic importance and operational relatedness must be a part of the corporation's mainstream. Product champions—people who are respected by others in the corporation and who know how to work the system—are needed to manage these projects. Hal Sperlich, for example, championed the development of the minivan both at Ford and Chrysler Corporation.

2. **New product business department.** A new business with a great deal of strategic importance and partial operational relatedness should be a separate department, organized around an entrepreneurial project in the division where skills and capabilities can be shared. Maytag Corporation did this when it built a new plant near its current Newton, Iowa, washer plant to manufacture a wholly new line of energy and water efficient front-loading dishwashers.

3. **Special business units.** A new business with a great deal of strategic importance and low operational relatedness should be a special new business unit with specific objectives and time horizons. General Motors did this with Saturn because GM wanted to set up an entirely new management, manufacturing, and marketing system.

DUPONT USES CROSS-FUNCTIONAL TEAMS TO IMPROVE INNOVATION

Once CEO Edgar Woolard pointed out the failure of DuPont to convert research into successful new products, the company began to change the way it conducted its R&D. To speed up the new product process, departments created small, interdisciplinary teams to deal with all new product ideas. These teams were allowed just two weeks to make a go or no-go decision. If they decided to go ahead with the concept, they were given two more weeks to form another team to begin the project. This cut the time needed to move from idea to prototype stage to just two months.

The company also started working more closely with its customers to do a better job of handling their requests. For example, Fluorware,

Inc., wanted DuPont to make a purer version of a Teflon basket that Fluorware used to hold silicon wafers during production. The two companies formed a joint team to find a solution. DuPont later brought out a commercial version of the product to sell to other companies. According to John Goodman, Fluorware's senior director for corporate technology, the Fluorware-DuPont team continues to hold regular meetings, "which we hope will lead to breakthroughs in materials science."

Source: S. McMurray, "DuPont Tries to Make Its Research Wizardry Serve the Bottom Line," *Wall Street Journal* (March 27, 1992), pp. A1, A4.

4. **Micro new ventures department.** A new business with uncertain strategic importance and high operational relatedness should be a peripheral project, which is likely to emerge in the operating divisions on a continuous basis. Each division thus has its own new ventures department. Xerox Corporation, for example, uses its SBUs to generate and nurture new ideas. Small product-synthesis teams within each SBU test the feasibility of new ideas. Those concepts receiving a "go" are managed by an SBU product-delivery team, headed by a chief engineer, that takes the prototype from development through manufacturing.

5. **New venture division.** A new business with uncertain strategic importance that is only partly related to present corporate operations belongs in a new venture division. It brings together projects that either exist in various parts of the corporation or can be acquired externally; sizable new businesses are built. R.J. Reynolds Industries, for example, established a separate company, R.J. Reynolds Development, to evaluate new business concepts with growth potential. The development company nurtures and develops businesses that might have the potential to become one of RJR's core businesses.

6. **Independent business units.** Uncertain strategic importance coupled with no relationship to present corporate activities can make external arrangements attractive. Hewlett-Packard established printers as an independent business unit in Boise, Idaho (far from its Palo Alto, California, headquarters) because management was unsure of the desktop printer's future. According to Richard Belluzzo, head of HP's printer business, "We had the resources of a big company, but we were off on our own. There wasn't central planning . . . , so we could make decisions really fast."[44]

7. **Nurturing and contracting.** When an entrepreneurial proposal might not be important strategically to the corporation but is strongly related to present opera-

Figure 11.3
Organizational Designs for Corporate Entrepreneurship

Source: Reprinted from R. A. Burgelman, "Designs for Corporate Entrepreneurship in Established Firms." Copyright © 1984 by the Regents of the University of California. Reprinted/condensed from *California Management Review*, Vol. 26, No. 3, p. 161. By permission of The Regents.

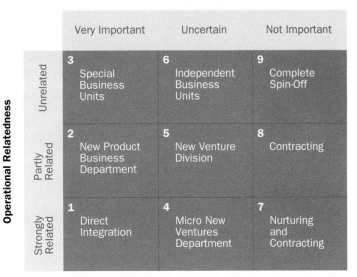

tions, top management might help the entrepreneurial unit to spin off from the corporation. This allows a friendly competitor, instead of one of the corporation's major rivals, to capture a small niche. Techtronix has extensively used this approach. Because of research revealing that related spin-offs tend to be poorer performers than nonrelated spin-offs (presumably owing to the loss of benefits enjoyed with a larger company), it is especially important that the parent company continue to support the development of the spun-off unit in this cell.[45]

8. **Contracting.** As the required capabilities and skills of the new business are less related to those of the corporation, the parent corporation may spin off the strategically unimportant unit, yet keep some relationship through a contractual arrangement with the new firm. The connection is useful in case the new firm eventually develops something of value to the corporation. For example, B.F. Goodrich offered manufacturing rights plus a long-term purchasing agreement to a couple of its managers for a specific raw material Goodrich still used (in declining quantities) in its production process, but no longer wanted to manufacture internally.

9. **Complete spin-off.** If both the strategic importance and the operational relatedness of the new business are negligible, the corporation is likely to completely sell off the business to another firm or to the present employees in some form of ESOP (Employee Stock Ownership Plan). The corporation also could sell off the unit through a leveraged buy-out (executives of the unit buy the unit from the parent company with money from a third source, to be repaid out of the unit's anticipated earnings). Because 3M wanted to focus its development money on areas with more profit potential, it decided to spin off its money-losing data storage and medical imaging divisions in 1996 as a new company called Imation.

Organizing for innovation has become especially important for those corporations that want to become more innovative, but their age and size have made them highly bureaucratic with a culture that discourages creative thinking. These new structural designs for corporate entrepreneurship cannot work by themselves, however. The entrepreneurial units must also have the support of management and sufficient resources. They must also have employees who are risk takers, willing to purchase an ownership interest in the new venture, and a corporate culture that supports new ventures.

11.5 Evaluation and Control

Companies want to gain more productivity at a faster pace from their research and development activities. But how do we measure the effectiveness or efficiency of a company's R&D? This is a problem given that a company shouldn't expect more than 1 in 20 product ideas from basic research to make it to the marketplace. Some companies measure the proportion of their sales attributable to new products. For example, 72% of Hewlett-Packard's revenues come from products introduced in the past three years.[46] At BellCore, the research part of seven regional Bell telephone companies, the effectiveness of basic research is measured by how often the lab's research is cited in other scientists' work. This measure is compiled and published by the Institute for Scientific Information. Other companies judge the quality of research by counting how many patents are filed annually.

Pittiglio Rabin Todd McGrath (PRTM), a high-tech consulting firm, proposes an **index of R&D effectiveness.** The index is calculated by dividing the percentage of total revenue spent on R&D into new product profitability, which is expressed as a percentage. When applying this measure to 45 large electronics manufacturers, only nine companies scored 1.0 or higher, indicating that only 20% received a positive payback from their R&D spending. The top companies kept spending on marginal products to a minimum by running frequent checks on product versus market opportunities and canceling questionable products quickly. They also moved new products to market in half the time of the others. As a result, revenue growth among the top 20% of the companies was double the average of all 45 companies.[47]

A study of 15 multinational companies with successful R&D operations focused on three measures of R&D success: (1) improving technology transfer from R&D to business units, (2) accelerating time to market for new products and processes, and (3) institutionalizing cross-functional participation in R&D. The companies participated in basic, applied, and developmental research activities. The study revealed 13 **best practices** that all of the companies followed.[48] Listed in Table 11.2, they provide a benchmark for a company's R&D activities.

11.6 Global Issues for the 21st Century

- The **21st Century Global Society** feature in this chapter illustrates not only how distinctive competencies in R&D can affect a company's competitive strategy, but also how emerging markets, such as China, are crucial to corporate growth strategies. Toto Ltd. is able to get from design to market quickly, but American Standard is able to design a product to better suit the needs of a new market. Expect both of these global competitors to do very well in China in the near future.

- Companies throughout the world are beginning to realize the benefits from cross-

Table 11.2 Thirteen "Best Practices" for Improving R&D

1. Corporate and business unit strategies are well defined and clearly communicated.
2. Core technologies are defined and communicated to R&D.
3. Investments are made in developing multinational R&D capabilities to tap ideas throughout the world.
4. Funding for basic research comes from corporate sources to ensure a long-term focus; funding for development comes from business units to ensure accountability.
5. Basic and applied research are performed either at a central facility or at a small number of labs, each focused on a particular discipline of science or technology. Development work is usually performed at business unit sites.
6. Formal, cross-functional teams are created for basic, applied, and developmental projects.
7. Formal mechanisms exist for regular interaction among scientists, and between R&D and other functions.
8. Analytical tools are used for selecting projects as well as for on-going project evaluation.
9. The transfer of technology to business units is the most important measure of R&D performance.
10. Effective measures of career development are in place at all levels of R&D.
11. Recruiting of new people is from diverse universities and from other companies when specific experience or skills are required that would take long to develop internally.
12. Some basic research is performed internally, but there are also many university and third-party relationships.
13. Formal mechanisms are used for monitoring external technological developments.

Source: I. Krause, and J. Liu, "Benchmarking R&D Productivity," *Planning Review* (January/February 1993), pp. 16–21, 52–53, with permission from The Planning Forum, The International Society for Strategic Management and Planning.

functional teams in product development activities. This should become the dominant design model in the coming years.

• To be competitive, companies must find the proper mix of product and process R&D. Even though the key to the success of the U.S. major home appliance industry has been its emphasis on process innovation, significant product innovation is more likely to result in a first mover advantage. For example, the first company to successfully use sound waves to clean clothes (instead of water and detergent) may very likely change the entire dynamics of the industry. At this moment, the Japanese appear most likely to develop product innovations in this industry.

• The inability of standard marketing research to properly evaluate the market potential of novel products suggests that many firms will be adopting Sony's approach of continually developing new products to be tested in the marketplace with sophisticated information systems market feedback. If it sells, make more. If it doesn't, cancel production and try another product.

• The inability of established firms to be as innovative as smaller firms indicates that companies may continue to break themselves down into smaller units to encourage creativity and innovation. The next issue will deal with balancing the efficiency rationale for centralizing R&D at corporate headquarters with the effectiveness rationale for decentralizing R&D to the business units. This has serious implications for multinational corporations.

Projections for the 21st Century

• From 1994 to 2010, the number of communications satellites worldwide will grow from 1,100 to 2,260.

• From 1994 to 2010, the number of McDonald's fast food restaurants will increase from 14,000 to 31,000—many of them outside the U.S. [49]

Discussion Questions

1. How should a corporation scan the external environment for new technological developments? Who should be responsible?

2. What is technology research and how does it differ from market research?

3. What is the importance of product and process R&D to competitive strategy?

4. What factors help determine whether a company should outsource a technology?

5. How can a company develop an entrepreneurial culture?

Key Terms

absorptive capacity (p. 272)
best practices (p. 278)
corporate entrepreneurship (p. 275)
index of R&D effectiveness (p. 278)
market research (p. 266)
orchestrator (p. 274)
process innovations (p. 269)
product champion (p. 274)

product innovations (p. 269)
product/market evolution matrix (p. 273)
R&D intensity (p. 267)
sponsor (p. 274)
stages of new product development (p. 273)
strategic alliance (p. 270)

technological competence (p. 272)
technological discontinuity (p. 266)
technology research (p. 266)
technology sourcing (p. 269)
time to market (p. 268)

Strategic Practice Exercise

Mary Clare had to make a decision on a new product idea and wasn't sure how to proceed. She worked as an Editor in the Business and Economics College Textbook Division of Addison Wesley Longman Publishing Company. Two of her current authors, David Hunger and Thomas Wheelen, had proposed an idea for a new book project to her. They were the authors of the successful hard-bound *Strategic Management and Business Policy* textbook. Based on their sense of the marketplace, they were proposing that the company publish a slimmed-down, paperback version of just the chapters (no case studies) of the hard-bound textbook. This new book would be called *Essentials of Strategic Management*. It was to be fairly short at about 200 pages (the current chapters had about 400 pages) and inexpensive—selling to students at around $20–$25. It would include no boxed examples or exercises and would be printed in simple black type. This was compared to the usual 1,000-page strategy textbook that included both text chapters and cases printed in multiple colors and selling for around $60 in campus bookstores. *Essentials* would be half the length of Hunger and Wheelen's paperback, *Strategic Marketing*, which was composed of the complete 14 chapters from *Strategic Management and Business Policy*, and selling at around $35–$40 retail.

Essentials would have a minimal Instructor's Manual compared to the usual large manual provided free to instructors who adopted a text.

The authors felt that there was a market for this product based on certain observations. First, they believed that some instructors preferred to select cases from other sources and didn't want a book that included cases. Second, they felt that some instructors at both the graduate and undergraduate levels wanted a small book that students could read quickly. The instructors could then spend most of the course analyzing cases and/or conducting a management simulation. Third, some instructors were heard to comment that students were no longer bringing their books to class because the books were too large and heavy to carry. The push to make textbooks more user-friendly had meant the addition of so many "bells and whistles" that the books had doubled in size over the past few years. Fourth, they felt increasing pressure from students who wanted cheaper textbooks.

Mary Clare wondered if Wheelen and Hunger were seeing the whole picture. She knew from previous market research that both students and professors strongly preferred textbooks done in multiple colors and including a lot of interesting boxed stories and exercises over the more traditional (but duller) textbooks. Unfortunately these improvements added considerably to both the cost and size of books. The breakeven point for a new textbook was getting higher and higher. An editor could no longer base a decision on a new project just on gut feel. A new book had to pay its own development costs.

One problem was: *What if the market doesn't accept this new type of strategy textbook?* Other publishers had been successful with *Essentials* books in the "Introduction To . . . (Management, Marketing, etc.)" markets, but no one yet had tried an *Essentials* book in strategy. Should Addison Wesley Longman be the first? Maybe it

would be better to let some other publisher try this idea first. On the other hand, *what if the* Essentials *book is a big success?* It might cannibalize the hard-cover textbook if current users of *Strategic Management and Business Policy* converted to the less expensive *Essentials* book. The company makes three times as much money on the large hardcover book than it would on the smaller paperback. But what if the market switches to smaller, simpler, cheaper textbooks and Addison Wesley Longman is left behind with no competitive products?

What should Mary Clare do?

Notes

1. S. McMurray, "DuPont Tries to Make Its Research Wizardry Serve the Bottom Line," *Wall Street Journal* (March 27, 1992), pp. A1, A4.
2. S. J. Towner, "Four Ways to Accelerate New Product Development," *Long Range Planning* (April 1994), p. 57.
3. R. Garud, and P. R. Nayyar, "Transformative Capacity: Continual Structuring by Intertemporal Technology Transfer," *Strategic Management Journal* (June 1994), p. 379.
4. C. A. Ferland, book review of *Third Generation R&D—Managing the Link to Corporate Strategy* by Roussel, Saad, and Erickson, in *Long Range Planning* (April 1993), p. 128.
5. C. Power, K. Kerwin, R. Grover, K. Alexander, and R. D. Hof, "Flops," *Business Week* (August 16, 1993), pp. 76–82.
6. B. R. Schlender, "How Sony Keeps the Magic Going," *Fortune* (February 24, 1992), p. 77.
7. G. C. Hill, and K. Yamada, "Motorola Illustrates How an Aged Giant Can Remain Vibrant," *Wall Street Journal* (December 9, 1992), pp. A1, A14.
8. N. Snyder, "Environmental Volatility, Scanning Intensity and Organizational Performance," *Journal of Contemporary Business* (September 1981), p. 16.
9. G. Hamel, and C. K. Prahalad, "Seeing the Future First," *Fortune* (September 5, 1995), p. 70.
10. J. Wade, "A Community-Level Analysis of Sources and Rates of Technological Variation in the Microprocessor Market," *Academy of Management Journal* (October 1996), pp. 1218–1244.
11. C. M. Christensen, and J. L. Bower, "Customer Power, Strategic Investment, and the Failure of Leading Firms," *Strategic Management Journal* (March 1996), pp. 197–218.
12. G. S. Lynn, J. G. Morone, and A. S. Paulson, "Marketing and Discontinuous Innovation: The Probe and Learn Process," *California Management Review* (Spring 1996), pp. 8–37.
13. W. I. Zangwill, "When Customer Research Is a Lousy Idea," *Wall Street Journal* (March 8, 1993), p. A10.
14. D. F. Kuratko, J. S. Hornsby, D. W. Naffziger, and R. V. Montagno, "Implement Entrepreneurial Thinking in Established Organizations," *SAM Advanced Management Journal* (Winter 1993), p. 29.
15. L. G. Franko, "Global Corporate Competition: Who's Winning, Who's Losing, and the R&D Factor as One Reason Why," *Strategic Management Journal* (September-October 1989), pp. 449–474; See also P. S. Chan, E. J. Flynn, and R. Chinta, "The Strategies of Growing and Turnaround Firms: A Multiple Discriminant Analysis," *International Journal of Management* (September 1991), pp. 669–675.
16. M. J. Chussil, "How Much to Spend on R&D?" *The PIMSletter of Business Strategy*, No. 13 (Cambridge, Mass.: The Strategic Planning Institute, 1978), p. 5.
17. J. S. Harrison, E. H. Hall, Jr., and R. Nargundkar, "Resource Allocation as an Outcropping of Strategic Consistency: Performance Implications," *Academy of Management Journal* (October 1993), pp. 1026–1051.
18. S. B. Graves, and N. S. Langowitz, "Innovative Productivity and Returns to Scale in the Pharmaceutical Industry," *Strategic Management Journal* (November 1993), pp. 593–605; A. Brady, "Small Is as Small Does," *Journal of Business Strategy* (March/April 1995), pp. 44–52.
19. D. H. Freedman, "Through the Looking Glass," in "The State of Small Business," *Inc.* (May 21, 1996), pp. 48–54.
20. N. Nohria, and R. Gulati, "Is Slack Good or Bad for Innovation?" *Academy of Management Journal* (October 1996), pp. 1245–1264.
21. M. A. Hitt, R. E. Hoskisson, and J. S. Harrison, "Strategic Competitiveness in the 1990s: Challenges and Opportunities for U.S. Executives," *Academy of Management Executive* (May 1991), p. 13.
22. T. F. O'Boyle, "Steel's Management Has Itself to Blame," *Wall Street Journal* (May 17, 1983), p. 32.
23. M. Silva, and B. Sjogren, *Europe 1992 and the New World Power Game* (New York: John Wiley and Sons, 1990), p. 231.
24. E. Mansfield, M. Schwartz, and S. Wagner, "Imitation Costs and Patents: An Empirical Study," *Economic Journal* (December 1981), pp. 907–918.
25. G. Stalk, Jr., and A. M. Webber, "Japan's Dark Side of Time," *Harvard Business Review* (July-August 1993), p. 99.
26. A. Deutschman, "If They're Gaining on You, Innovate," *Fortune* (November 2, 1992), p. 86; O. Port, A. Reinhardt, G. McWilliams, and S. V. Brull, "The Silicon Age? It's Just Dawning," *Business Week* (December 9, 1996), pp. 148–152.

27. M. Robert, "Market Fragmentation versus Market Segmentation," *Journal of Business Strategy* (September/October 1992), p. 52.

28. K. Kelly, and M. Ivey, "Turning Cummins into the Engine Maker That Could," *Business Week* (July 30, 1990), pp. 20–21.

29. Silva and Sjogren, *Europe 1992 and the New World Power Game*, pp. 239–241. See also P. Nueno and J. Oosterveld, "Managing Technology Alliances," *Long Range Planning* (June 1988), pp. 11–17.

30. P. R. Nayak, "Should You Outsource Product Development?" *Journal of Business Strategy* (May/June 1993), pp. 44–45.

31. M. A. Hitt, R. E. Hoskisson, R. A. Johnson, and D. D. Moesel, "The Market for Corporate Control and Firm Innovation," *Academy of Management Journal* (October 1996), pp. 1084–1119.

32. W. M. Cohen, and D. A. Levinthal, "Absorptive Capacity: A New Perspective on Learning and Innovation," *Administrative Science Quarterly* (March 1990), pp. 128–152.

33. "The Impact of Industrial Robotics on the World of Work," *International Labour Review*, Vol. 125, No. 1 (1986). Summarized in "The Risks of Robotization," *The Futurist* (May-June 1987), p. 56.

34. Hitt, Hoskisson, and Harrison, "Strategic Competitiveness in the 1990s: Challenges and Opportunities for U.S. Executives," p. 9.

35. D. Dougherty, and C. Hardy, "Sustained Product Innovation in Large, Mature Organizations: Overcoming Innovation-to-Organization Problems," *Academy of Management* (October 1996), pp. 1120–1153.

36. C. A. Lengnick-Hall, "Innovation and Competitive Advantage: What We Know and What We Need to Know," *Journal of Management* (June 1992), pp. 399–429.

37. J. R. Galbraith, "Designing the Innovative Organization," *Organizational Dynamics* (Winter 1982), pp. 5–25.

38. P. R. Nayak, "Product Innovation Practices in Europe, Japan, and the U.S.," *Journal of Business Strategy* (May/June 1992), pp. 62–63.

39. E. M. Olson, "Organizing for Effective New Product Development: The Moderating Role of Product Innovativeness," *Journal of Marketing* (January 1995) as reported by K. Z. Andrews in *Harvard Business Review* (November-December, 1995), pp. 12–13.

40. D. Rowe, "Up and Running," *Journal of Business Strategy* (May/June 1993), pp. 48–50.

41. N. Freundlich, and M. Schroeder, "Getting Everybody Into the Act," *Business Week* (Quality 1991 edition), p. 152.

42. W. D. Guth, and A. Ginsberg, "Corporate Entrepreneurship," *Strategic Management Journal* (Summer 1990), p. 5.

43. R. A. Burgelman, "Designs for Corporate Entrepreneurship," *California Management Review* (Spring 1984), pp. 154–166; R. A. Burgelman and L. R. Sayles, *Inside Corporate Innovation* (New York: The Free Press, 1986).

44. S. K. Yoder, "How H-P Used Tactics of the Japanese to Beat Them at Their Game," *Wall Street Journal* (September 8, 1994), pp. A1, A6.

45. C. Y. Woo, G. E. Willard, and S. M. Beckstead, "Spin-Offs: What Are the Gains?" *Journal of Business Strategy* (March-April 1989), pp. 29–32.

46. J. B. Levin, and R. D. Hof, "Has Philips Found Its Wizard?" *Business Week* (September 6, 1993), pp. 82–84.

47. O. Port, "Rating R&D: How Companies Get the Biggest Bang for the Buck," *Business Week* (July 5, 1993), p. 98.

48. I. Krause, and J. Liu, "Benchmarking R&D Productivity," *Planning Review* (January/February 1993), pp. 16–21, 52–53.

49. J. Warner, "21st Century Capitalism: Snapshots of the Next Century," *Business Week* (November 18, 1994), p. 194.

Chapter 12

Strategic Issues in Entrepreneurial Ventures and Small Businesses

Debbie Giampapa was at a party juggling her food plate and drink. "This is ridiculous," she thought. "Why doesn't somebody make something to hold this?" When she got home she pulled a piece of cardboard out of the trash and cut a hole large enough to hold a standard 10-ounce plastic cup. Then she added a smaller hole for a wine glass. After much trial and error and a lot of perseverance in obtaining funding, plus deciding how to make and market her product, she established her own company, Fun-Zone. She went to die cutters and machinists to learn how machines could make her product. She told them she was doing door hangers because she didn't want them to steal her idea. Said Giampapa,"The more I understand what the machine can do, the better I can design the product." Giampapa is now selling thousands of "Party HOLDems" to customers like American Express, Walt Disney Company, and Coopers and Lybrand. When asked the secret of her success, she responded:

> It's not having the idea. It's believing in yourself and your product enough to put up the money and time for that. I've put in 16-hour days, seven-day weeks for two years.[1]

12.1 *Importance of Small Business and Entrepreneurial Ventures*

Strategic management as a field of study typically deals with large, established business corporations. However, small business cannot be ignored. There are 22 million small businesses—over 95% of all businesses in the United States. According to Dun & Bradstreet, 170,475 entrepreneurial ventures created 846,973 new jobs in the United States during 1996.[2] Research reveals that not only do small firms spend almost twice as much of their R&D dollars on fundamental research as do large firms, but also that small companies are responsible for a high proportion of innovations in products and services.[3] For example, new small firms produce 24 times more innovation per research dollar than do the much larger Fortune 500 firms.[4] The National Science Foundation estimates that 98% of "radical" product developments result from the research done in the labs of small companies.[5]

Despite the overall success of small businesses, however, every year tens of thousands of small companies fail. According to the U.S. Small Business Administration, 24% of all new businesses fail within two years and 63% fail within six years.[6] Similar failure rates occur in the United Kingdom, The Netherlands, Japan, Taiwan, and Hong Kong.[7] Although some studies are more positive regarding the survival rate of new entrepreneurial ventures, new businesses are definitely considered risky.[8] The causes of small-business failure (depending on the study cited) range from inadequate accounting systems to inability to cope with growth. The underlying problem appears to be an overall lack of strategic management—beginning with an inability to plan a strategy to reach the customer, and ending with a failure to develop a system of controls to keep track of performance.[9]

Definition of Small-Business Firms and Entrepreneurial Ventures

The most commonly accepted definition of a small-business firm is one that employs fewer than 500 people and that generates sales of less than $20 million annually.

Although the meanings of the terms "small business" and "entrepreneurship" overlap considerably, the concepts are different. The **small-business firm** is independently owned and operated, not dominant in its field, and does not engage in innovative practices. The **entrepreneurial venture**, in contrast, is any business whose primary goals are profitability and growth and that can be characterized by innovative strategic practices.[10] The basic difference between the small-business firm and the entrepreneurial venture, therefore, lies not in the type of goods or services provided, but in their fundamental views on growth and innovation. According to Donald Sexton, an authority on entrepreneurship, this explains why strategic planning is more likely to be present in an entrepreneurial venture than in the typical small-business firm:

> Most firms start with just a single product. Those oriented toward growth immediately start looking for another one. It's that planning approach that separates the entrepreneur from the small-business owner.[11]

The Entrepreneur as Strategist

Often defined as a person who organizes and manages a business undertaking and who assumes risk for the sake of a profit, the **entrepreneur** is the ultimate strategist. He or she makes all the strategic as well as operational decisions. All three levels of strategy—corporate, business, and functional—are the concerns of this founder and owner-manager of a company. As one entrepreneur puts it: "Entrepreneurs are strategic planners without realizing it."

The founding of FunZone described earlier captures the key elements of the entrepreneurial venture: a basic business idea that has not yet been successfully tried and a gutsy entrepreneur who, while working on borrowed capital and a shoestring budget, creates a new business through a lot of trial and error and persistent hard work. Similar stories can be told of other people, such as Debbie Fields, who created Mrs. Fields Cookies, and Will Parish, who founded National Energy Associates. Both were ridiculed at one time or another for their desire to start a business. Friends and family told Debbie Fields that starting a business to sell chocolate chip cookies "was a stupid idea." Will Parish, who built a power plant in California's Imperial Valley that burns "pasture patties," is called an "entre-manure." Every day the plant burns 900 tons of manure collected from nearby feedlots to generate 15 megawatts of electricity—enough to light 20,000 homes. The power is sold to Southern California Edison. Parish got the idea from a trip to India where the fuel used to heat a meal was cow dung. Now that the plant is earning a profit, Parish is building a larger plant nearby that will burn wheat straw and other crop wastes. The plants provide an environmentally sound as well as profitable way to dispose of waste. Very interested in conservation, Parish says, "I wanted to combine doing well with doing good."[12]

12.2   *Use of Strategic Planning and Strategic Management*

Research shows that strategic planning is strongly related to small-business financial performance.[13] A survey of the high growth *Inc. 500* firms revealed that 86% performed strategic planning. Of those performing strategic planning, 94% reported improved profits.[14] Nevertheless, many small companies still do not use the process. The reasons often cited for the apparent lack of strategic planning practices in many small-business firms are fourfold:

- **Not enough time.** Day-to-day operating problems take up the time necessary for long-term planning. It's relatively easy to justify avoiding strategic planning on the basis of day-to-day crisis management. Some will ask: "How can I be expected to do strategic planning when I don't know if I'm going to be in business next week?"

- **Unfamiliar with strategic planning.** The small-business CEO may be unaware of strategic planning or may view it as irrelevant to the small-business situation. Planning may be viewed as a straitjacket that limits flexibility.

- **Lack of skills.** Small-business managers often lack the skills necessary to begin strategic planning and do not have or want to spend the money necessary to import trained consultants. Future uncertainty may be used to justify a lack of planning. One entrepreneur admits, "Deep down, I know I should plan. But I don't know what to do. I'm the leader but I don't know how to lead the planning process."

- **Lack of trust and openness.** Many small-business owner-managers are very sensitive regarding key information about the business and are thus unwilling to share strategic planning with employees or outsiders. For this reason, boards of directors are often composed only of close friends and relatives of the owner-manager—people unlikely to provide an objective viewpoint or professional advice.

Degree of Formality

Research generally concludes that the *strategic planning process should be far more informal in small companies* than it is in large corporations.[15] Some studies have even found that too much formalization of the strategic planning process may actually result in reduced performance.[16] It is possible that a heavy emphasis on structured, written plans can be dysfunctional to the small entrepreneurial firm because it detracts from the very flexibility that is a benefit of small size. *The process of strategic planning, not the plan itself, is probably the key to improving business performance.*

These observations suggest that new entrepreneurial ventures begin life in Mintzberg's entrepreneurial mode of strategic planning (explained in Chapter 1) and move toward the planning mode as the company becomes established and wants to continue its strong growth. If, after becoming successfully established, the entrepreneur instead chooses stability over growth, the venture moves more toward the adaptive mode so common to many small businesses.

Usefulness of Strategic Management Model

The model of strategic management (presented in Figure 1.2) is also relevant to entrepreneurial ventures and small businesses. This basic model holds for both an established small company and a new entrepreneurial venture. As the research mentioned earlier concluded, small and developing companies increase their chances of success if they make a serious attempt to work through the strategic issues embedded in the strategic management model. The key is to focus on what's important—the set of managerial decisions and actions that determines the long-run performance of the company. The list of informal questions presented in Table 12.1 may be more useful to a small entrepreneurial company than their more formal counterparts used by large established corporations.

Usefulness of Strategic Decision-Making Process

As mentioned in Chapter 1, one way in which the strategic management model can be made action oriented is to follow the strategic decision-making model presented in Figure 1.5. The eight steps presented in that model are just as appropriate for small companies as they are for large corporations. Unfortunately the process does not fit new entrepreneurial ventures. These companies must develop new missions, objectives, strategies, and policies out of a comparison of its external opportunities and threats to its potential strengths and weaknesses. Consequently we propose in Figure 12.1 a modified version of the strategic decision-making process; this version more closely suits the new entrepreneurial business.

The proposed **strategic decision-making process for entrepreneurial ventures** is composed of the following eight interrelated steps:

1. **Develop the basic business idea**—a product and/or service having target customers and/or markets. The idea can be developed from a person's experience or generated in a moment of creative insight. For example, Debbie Giampapa conceived of the beverage-holding party tray long before such a product was feasible.

Table 12.1   Informal Questions to Begin the Strategic Management Process in a Small Company or Entrepreneurial Venture

Formal	Informal
Define mission	What do we stand for?
Set objectives	What are we trying to achieve?
Formulate strategy	How are we going to get there? How can we beat the competition?
Determine policies	What sort of ground rules should we all be following to get the job done right?
Establish programs	How should we organize this operation to get what we want done as cheaply as possible with the highest quality possible?
Prepare *pro forma* **budgets**	How much is it going to cost us and where can we get the cash?
Specify procedures	In how much detail do we have to lay things out, so that everybody knows what to do?
Determine performance measures	What are those few key things that will determine whether we can make it? How can we keep track of them?

2. **Scan and assess the external environment,** to locate factors in the societal and task environments that pose opportunities and threats. The scanning should focus particularly on market potential and resource accessibility.

3. **Scan and assess the internal factors** relevant to the new business. The entrepreneur should objectively consider personal assets, areas of expertise, abilities, and experience, all in terms of the organizational needs of the new venture.

4. **Analyze the strategic factors** in light of the current situation using SWOT. The venture's potential strengths and weaknesses must be evaluated in light of opportunities and threats. Develop a SFAS Table (Figure 5.1) of the strategic factors.

5. **Decide go or no go.** If the basic business idea appears to be a feasible business opportunity, the process should be continued. Otherwise, further development of the idea should be canceled unless the strategic factors change.

6. **Generate a business plan** specifying how the idea will be transformed into reality. See Table 12.2 for the suggested contents of a strategic **business plan**. The proposed venture's mission, objectives, strategies, and policies, as well as its likely board of directors (if a corporation) and key managers should be developed. Key internal factors should be specified and performance projections generated. The business plan serves as a vehicle through which financial support is obtained from potential investors and creditors. Starting a business without a business plan is the quickest way to kill a new venture. For example, one study of 270 clothing retailers found that 80% of the successful stores had written a business plan, whereas 65% of the failed businesses had not.[17]

   The *strategic audit* (see Table 10.5 on pages 252–259) can be used to develop a formal business plan. The audit's sections and subsections, along with the questions within them, provide a useful framework. Instead of analyzing the historical events of an existing company, use the questions to project the proposed company's future. The questions can be reoriented to follow the outline in Table 10.5. A crucial building block of a sound business plan is the construction of realistic scenarios for the pro forma financials. The pro formas must reflect the impact of seasonality on the cash flows of the proposed new venture.

Figure 12.1
Strategic Decision-Making Process for New Ventures

Source: T. L. Wheelen and C. E. Michaels, Jr., "Model for Strategic Decision-Making Process for New Ventures." Copyright © 1987 by T. L. Wheelen. Reprinted by permission.

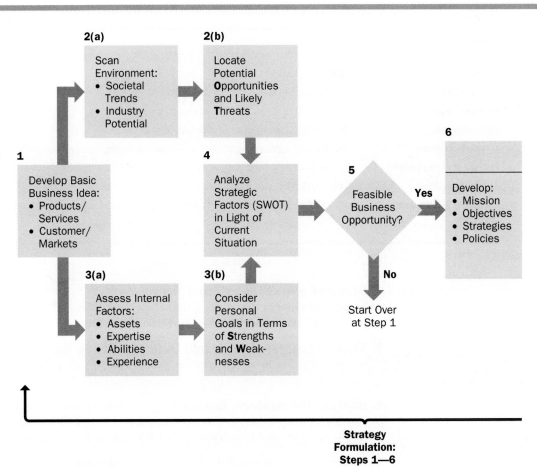

7. **Implement the business plan** through the use of action plans and procedures.

8. **Evaluate the implemented business plan** through comparison of actual perform-ance against projected performance results. This step leads to Step 1(b) of the strategic decision-making process shown in Figure 1.5 on pages 20–21. To the extent that actual results are less than or much greater than the anticipated results, the entrepreneur needs to reconsider the company's current mission, objectives, strate-gies, policies, and programs, and possibly make changes to the original business plan.

12.3   *Issues in Environmental Scanning and Strategy Formulation*

Environmental scanning in small businesses is much less sophisticated than it is in large corporations. The business is usually too small to justify hiring someone to do only envi-ronmental scanning or strategic planning. Top managers, especially if they are the founders, tend to believe that they know the business and can follow it better than any-one else. A study of 220 small rapid-growth companies revealed that the majority of CEOs were actively and personally involved in all phases of the planning process, but

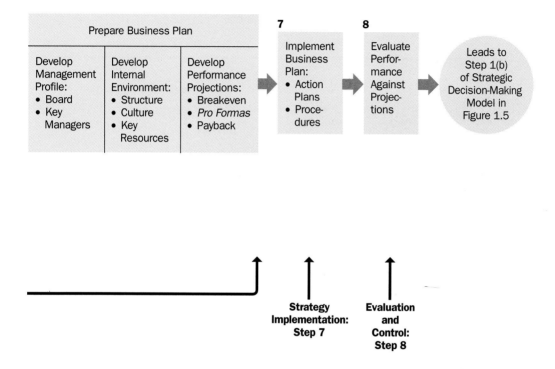

especially in the setting of objectives. Only 15% of the companies used a planning officer or formed a planning group to assist in the planning process. In the rest of the firms, operating managers who participated in strategic planning provided input only to the CEO, who then formulated the plan.[18] Unfortunately the literature suggests that few small businesses do much competitor analysis.

A fundamental reason for differences in *strategy formulation* between large and small entrepreneurial companies lies in the relationship between owners and managers. The CEO of a large corporation has to consider and balance the varied needs of the corporation's many stakeholders. The CEO of a small business, however, is very likely also to be the owner—the company's primary stakeholder. Personal and family needs can thus strongly affect the company's mission and objectives and can overrule other considerations.[19] For example, the **21st Century Global Society** feature illustrates how Anita Roddick's personal social and environmental values determined the policies and mission statement of her entrepreneurial venture, The Body Shop.

Size can affect the selection of an appropriate corporate strategy. Large corporations often choose growth strategies for their many side benefits for management as well as for shareholders. A small company may, however, choose a stability strategy because the entrepreneur is interested mostly in (1) generating employment for family members, (2) providing the family a "decent living," and (3) being the "boss" of a firm small enough

Table 12.2 **Contents of a Strategic Business Plan for an Entrepreneurial Venture**

I. Table of Contents	X. Human Resources Plan
II. Executive Summary	XI. Ownership
III. Nature of the Business	XII. Risk Analysis
IV. Strategy Formulation	XIII. Timetables and Milestones
V. Market Analysis	XIV. Strategy Implementation—Action Plans
VI. Marketing Plan	XV. Evaluation and Control
VII. Operational Plans—Service/Product	XVI. Summary
VIII. Financial Plans	XVII. Appendixes
IX. Organization and Management	

Note:
The strategic audit can be used to develop a business plan. It provides detailed questions to serve as a checklist.

Source: Thomas L. Wheelen, "Contents of a Strategic Business Plan for an Entrepreneurial Venture." Copyright © 1988 by Thomas L. Wheelen. Reprinted by permission.

that he or she can manage it comfortably. Thus the goals of a small business are likely to be the same as the goals of the owner-manager.

The basic SWOT analysis is just as relevant to small entrepreneurial businesses as it is to established large ones. Both the greatest strength and the greatest weakness of the small firm, at least in the beginning, rest with the entrepreneur—the owner-manager of the business. The entrepreneur is *the* manager, the source of product/market strategy, and the dynamo who energizes the company. That is why the internal assessment of a new venture's strengths and weaknesses focuses in Figure 12.1 on the founder's personal characteristics—his or her assets, expertise, abilities, and experience. Just as an entrepreneur's strengths can be the key to company success, personal weaknesses can be a primary cause of failure. For example, the study of clothing retailers mentioned earlier showed that the owner-managers of 85% of the failed stores had no prior retailing experience.

Sources of Innovation

Peter Drucker, in his book *Innovation and Entrepreneurship*, proposes seven sources for innovative opportunity that should be monitored by those interested in starting an entrepreneurial venture, either within an established company or as an independent small business.[20] The first four **sources of innovation** lie within the industry itself; the last three arise in the societal environment. These seven sources are:

1. **The unexpected.** An unexpected success, an unexpected failure, or an unexpected outside event can be a symptom of a unique opportunity. When Don Cullen of Transmet Corporation spilled a box of very fine aluminum flakes onto his company's parking lot, he discovered that their presence in the asphalt prevented it from turning sticky in high temperatures. His company now produces aluminum chips for use in roofing. Sales have doubled every year since the product's introduction and his company will soon dominate the business.

2. **The incongruity.** A discrepancy between reality and what everyone assumes it to be, or between what is and what ought to be, can create an opportunity for innovation. Realizing that the real costs of ocean freighter haulage were not in crew wages but in the time spent loading and unloading at port, Sea-Land changed the entire industry by introducing efficient containerized shipping to reduce handling time and costs.

21ST CENTURY GLOBAL SOCIETY

MISSION AND POLICIES OF THE BODY SHOP REFLECT ENTREPRENEUR'S PERSONAL VALUES AND EXPERIENCES

Anita Roddick wanted to open a shop of her own to sell cosmetics and lotions. She had been dissatisfied with her inability to try a cream or a lotion before purchasing it in a large bottle. She wanted to sell naturally based cosmetics in five sizes so her customers could have a choice. Although the environmental "green" movement had not yet begun in Britain, Roddick was worried about the use of synthetic chemicals in cosmetics.

Roddick opened her first Body Shop in Brighton in 1976. Two nearby funeral homes threatened to sue her over the shop's name. Roddick then informed the local newspaper about the controversy. The resulting article was free publicity for her new shop. Based on this experience, Roddick developed a company policy of never spending a cent on advertising. The focus was instead to be on publicizing company values. Even though marketing experts in the United States doubted if The Body Shop could be successfully established in America without advertising, Roddick refused to change her policy. (By 1995, there were 235 shops in the United States plus hundreds more throughout the world!) Because Roddick used her firm as an expression of her concerns on social issues and the environment, the company received around 2,000 pounds

worth of free publicity annually. The company's mission statement is an extension of Anita Roddick's personal philosophy. It clearly tells that this now-global company is in business for more than just the sales of naturally based cosmetics.

- To creatively balance the financial and human needs of our stakeholders.

- To courageously ensure that our business is ecologically sustainable, meeting the needs of the present without compromising the future.

- To meaningfully contribute to local, national, and international communities in which we trade, adopting a code of conduct that ensures care, honesty, fairness and respect.

- To passionately campaign for the protection of the environment and human and civil rights, and against animal testing within the cosmetics and toiletries industry.

- To tirelessly work to narrow the gap between principle and practice, while making fun, passion, and care part of our daily lives.

Source: *Our Reason for Being.* Handout from The Body Shop.

3. **Innovation based on process need.** When a weak link is evident in a particular process, but people work around it instead of doing something about it, an opportunity is present for the person or company willing to forge a stronger one. For example, Alcon Laboratories was developed based on the discovery that a specific enzyme could enable doctors to avoid cutting a particular ligament when performing eye surgery.

4. **Changes in industry or market structure.** A business is ready for an innovative product, service, or approach to the business when the underlying foundation of the industry or market shifts. Black Entertainment Television, Inc. (BET), was born when Robert Johnson noticed that no television programmer was targeting the increasing number of black viewers. Johnson then successfully expanded into print with *Young Sisters & Brothers*, a monthly magazine aimed at black teenagers.

5. **Demographics.** Changes in the population's size, age structure, composition, employment, level of education, and income can create opportunities for innovation. For

example, Pam Henderson started a company called Kids Kab to shuttle children and teenagers to private schools, doctor and dental appointments, lessons, and extracurricular activities. With the trend to dual careers, parents were no longer always available to provide personal transportation for their own children and needed such a service.

6. **Changes in perception, mood, and meaning.** Opportunities for innovation can develop when a society's general assumptions, attitudes, and beliefs change. For example, the increasing dominance of a few national brewers have caused beer drinkers to look for alternatives to the same old national brands. By positioning Yuengling, a local Pennsylvania beer, as a full-flavored beer and providing it with an artsy, nostalgic-looking label, the small company was able to catch the fancy of young, trendy consumers who viewed it as Pennsylvania's version of Anchor Steam, the successful San Francisco beer.

7. **New knowledge.** Advances in scientific and nonscientific knowledge can create new products and new markets. Advances in two different areas can sometimes be integrated to form the basis of a new product. For example, Tuck Rickards opened The Virtual Emporium in Santa Monica's trendy Third Street Promenade shopping area to combine retailing excitement with information technology. The shop has a decor of an overgrown "Friends" TV set with 30 Gateway personal computers that connect to 80 Internet shopping sites. According to Rickards, "Most people are still intimidated by the Internet and many still want to go to a fun place to shop."[21]

Factors Affecting a New Venture's Success

According to Hofer and Sandberg, three factors have a substantial impact on a new venture's performance. In order of importance, these **factors affecting new venture success** are (1) the structure of the industry entered, (2) the new venture's business strategy, and (3) behavioral characteristics of the entrepreneur.[22]

Industry Structure

Research shows that the chances for success are greater for entrepreneurial ventures that enter rapidly changing industries than for those that enter stable industries. In addition, prospects are better in industries that are in the early, high-growth stages of development. Competition is often less intense. Fast market growth also allows new ventures to make some mistakes without serious penalty. New ventures also increase their chances of success when they enter markets in which they can erect entry barriers to keep out competitors.

Contrary to popular wisdom, however, patents may not always provide competitive advantage, especially for new ventures in a high-tech or hypercompetitive industry. A well-financed competitor could examine a newly filed application for a patent, work around the patent, and beat the pioneering firm to market with a similar product. In addition, the time and cost of filing and defending a patent may not be worth the effort. According to Connie Bagley, author of *The Entrepreneur's Guide to Business Law*:

> It might take 18 months to get a patent on a product that has a 12-month life cycle. By the time you finally get the damn thing litigated, it's meaningless. So people are focusing less on proprietary assurance and more on first-mover advantage. . . . The law is just too slow for this high-speed economy.[23]

Research further reveals that a new venture is more likely to be successful entering an industry in which one dominant competitor has a 50% or more market share than entering an industry in which the largest competitor has less than a 25% market share.

To explain this phenomenon, Hofer and Sandberg point out that when an industry has one dominant firm, the remaining competitors are relatively weak and are easy prey for an aggressive entrepreneur. To avoid direct competition with a major rival, the new venture can focus on a market segment that is being ignored.

Industry product characteristics also have a significant impact on a new venture's success. First, a new venture is more likely to be successful when it enters an industry with heterogeneous (different) products than when it enters one with homogeneous (similar) products. In a heterogeneous industry, a new venture can differentiate itself from competitors with a unique product; or, by focusing on the unique needs of a market segment, it can find a market niche. Second, a new venture is, according to research data, more likely to be successful if the product is relatively unimportant to the customer's total purchasing needs than if it is important. Customers are more likely to experiment with a new product if its cost is low and product failure will not create a problem.

Business Strategy

According to Hofer and Sandberg, the key to success for most new ventures is (1) to differentiate the product from those of other competitors in the areas of quality and service and (2) to focus the product on customer needs in a segment of the market in order to achieve a dominant share of that part of the market (Porter's focused differentiation competitive strategy). Adopting guerrilla-warfare tactics, these companies go after opportunities in market niches too small or too localized to justify retaliation from the market leaders.

To continue its growth once it has found a niche, the entrepreneurial firm can emphasize continued innovation and pursue natural growth in its current markets. It can expand into related markets in which the company's core skills, resources, and facilities offer the keys to further success.[24]

Entrepreneurial Characteristics

Four **entrepreneurial characteristics** are key to a new venture's success. Successful entrepreneurs have:

1. *The ability to identify potential venture opportunities better than most people.* They focus on opportunities—not on problems—and try to learn from failure. Entrepreneurs are goal oriented and have a strong impact on the emerging culture of an organization. They are able to envision where the company is going and are thus able to provide a strong overall sense of strategic direction. See the **Strategy in a Changing World** feature for Cherrill Farnsworth's ability to spot new entrepreneurial opportunities.

2. *A sense of urgency that makes them action oriented.* They have a high need for achievement, which motivates them to put their ideas into action. They tend to have an internal locus of control that leads them to believe that they can determine their own fate through their own behavior. They also have a significantly greater capacity to tolerate ambiguity and stress than do many in established organizations.[25] They also have a strong need for control and may even be viewed as "misfits who need to create their own environment." They tend to distrust others and often have a need "to show others that they amount to something, that they cannot be ignored."[26]

3. *A detailed knowledge of the keys to success in the industry and the physical stamina to make their work their lives.* They have better than average education and significant work experience in the industry in which they start their business. They often work with partners to form a new venture. (70% of new high-tech ventures are started by

STRATEGY IN A CHANGING WORLD

CHERRILL FARNSWORTH'S ENTREPRENEURIAL PERSONALITY

Cherrill Farnsworth is an example of a classic entrepreneur. She likes to form new ventures. Farnsworth is currently the CEO of TME, Inc., the fifth company she has founded. She founded her first company, a bus line, in 1974. After her husband was transferred to Houston in 1970, she noticed that people had no way to get downtown from her northwestern suburb. "Wherever there's angst, there's an opportunity," comments Farnsworth. Despite heavy opposition from major bus operators, she won a franchise to run a bus line. Soon, however, running the bus line became boring. After two years, she sold it for a profit. Remembers Farnsworth, "I realized at that point what value you could get by working hard and creating something new—especially if there's no competition." In her next three new ventures, she leased luxury vehicles, office equipment, and then oil field equipment.

In the early 1980s, Farnsworth was attracted to MRI machines—expensive machines used by hospitals to view the inside of a person's body without the use of x-rays. At the time, hospitals couldn't buy the machines because Medicare had not yet approved reimbursements from health insurers for the service. According to Farnsworth, when she first proposed to hospital administrators that she provide the service, "they found the idea shocking. They giggled and rolled their eyes." Once they reviewed the financials, however, they agreed. Financial backers soon followed.

In assessing her skills as an entrepreneur, Farnsworth sees herself not so much as a manager, but as someone who builds something and then moves on to another challenge. She comments on the future of TME, Inc.:

> I'm not a 20-year player. I've got to develop an exit strategy, probably by going public. I'm very transaction oriented. I love to put something together, build stockholder value, and then raise money again for another venture. Nothing makes me happier.

Source: C. Burck, "The Real World of the Entrepreneur: The Rewards of Angst," *Fortune* (April 5, 1993), pp. 64–65.

more than one founder.)[27] More than half of all entrepreneurs work at least 60 hours a week in the start-up year, according to a National Federation of Independent Business study.[28]

4. *Access to outside help to supplement their skills, knowledge, and abilities.* Over time, they develop a network of people having key skills and knowledge whom the entrepreneurs can call upon for support. Through their enthusiasm, these entrepreneurs are able to attract key investors, partners, creditors, and employees. For example, Mitch Kapor, founder of Lotus Development Corporation, did not hesitate to bring in Jim Manzi as President because Manzi had the managerial skills that Kapor lacked.

In summarizing their conclusions regarding factors affecting the success of entrepreneurial ventures, Hofer and Sandberg propose the guidelines presented in Table 12.3.

12.4 Issues in Strategy Implementation

Two key implementation issues in small companies are organizing and staffing the growing company and transferring ownership of the company to the next generation.

Table 12.3   **Some Guidelines for New Venture Success**

- Focus on industries facing substantial technological or regulatory changes, especially those with recent exits by established competitors.
- Seek industries whose smaller firms have relatively weak competitive positions.
- Seek industries that are in early, high-growth stages of evolution.
- Seek industries in which it is possible to create high barriers to subsequent entry.
- Seek industries with heterogeneous products that are relatively unimportant to the customer's overall success.
- Seek to differentiate your products from those of your competitors in ways that are meaningful to your customers.
- Focus such differentiation efforts on product quality, marketing approaches, and customer service—and charge enough to cover the costs of doing so.
- Seek to dominate the market segments in which you compete. If necessary, either segment the market differently or change the nature and focus of your differentiation efforts to increase your domination of the segments you serve.
- Stress innovation, especially new product innovation, that is built on existing organizational capabilities.
- Seek natural, organic growth through flexibility and opportunism that builds on existing organizational strengths.

Source: C. W. Hofer and W. R. Sandberg, "Improving New Venture Performance: Some Guidelines for Success," *American Journal of Small Business* (Summer 1987), pp. 17, 19. Copyright © 1987 by C. W. Hofer and W. R. Sandberg. Reprinted by permission.

Substages of Small Business Development

The implementation problems of a small business change as the company grows and develops over time. Just as the decision-making process for entrepreneurial ventures is different from that of established businesses, the managerial systems in small companies often vary from those of large corporations. Those variations are based on their stage of development. The stages of corporate growth and development discussed in Chapter 8 suggest that all small businesses are either in Stage I or trying to move into Stage II. These models imply that all successful new ventures eventually become Stage II, functionally organized companies. This is not always true, however. In attempting to show clearly how small businesses develop, Churchill and Lewis propose five **substages of small business development:** (a) existence, (b) survival, (c) success, (d) take-off, and (e) resource maturity.[29] A review of these small-business substages shows in more detail how a company can move through the entrepreneurial Stage I into a functionally oriented, professionally managed Stage II.

Stage A: Existence

At this point, the entrepreneurial venture faces the problems of obtaining customers and delivering the promised product or service. The organizational structure is simple. The entrepreneur does everything and directly supervises subordinates. Systems are minimal. The owner *is* the business.

Stage B: Survival

Those ventures able to satisfy a sufficient number of customers enter this stage; the rest close when their owners run out of start-up capital. Those reaching the survival stage are concerned about generating the cash flow needed to repair and replace capital assets as they wear out and to finance the growth to continue satisfying the market segment they have found.

At this stage, the organizational structure is still simple, but it probably has a sales manager or general supervisor to carry out the owner's well-defined orders. A major problem of many small businesses at this stage is finding a person who is qualified to supervise the business when the owner can't be present, but who is still willing to work for a very modest salary. Entrepreneurs usually try to use family members rather than hiring an outsider who lacks the entrepreneur's dedication to the business and (in the words of one owner-manager) "steals them blind." A company that remains in this stage for a long time is often called a "mom and pop" firm. It earns marginal returns on invested time and capital (with lots of psychic income!) and eventually goes out of business when "mom and pop" give up or retire. This type of small business is viewed more as a **lifestyle company** in which the firm is purely an extension of the owner's lifestyle. Over 94% of small private companies are in this category.[30]

Stage C: Success

By this point, the company's sales have reached a level where the firm is not only profitable, but has sufficient cash flow to reinvest in itself. The key issue at this stage is whether the company should be used as a platform for growth or as a means of support for the owners as they completely or partially disengage from the company. The company is transforming into a functionally structured organization, but it still relies on the entrepreneur for all key decisions. The two options are disengagement and growth.

C(1) Disengagement. The company can now successfully follow a stability strategy and remain at this stage almost indefinitely—provided that environmental change does not destroy its niche or poor management reduce its competitive abilities. By now functional managers have taken over some of the entrepreneur's duties. The company at this stage may be incorporated, but it is still primarily owned by the founder or founder's family. Consequently the board of directors is either a rubber stamp for the entrepreneur or a forum for family squabbles. Growth strategies are not pursued because either the market niche will not allow growth or the owner is content with the company at a size he or she can still manage comfortably.

C(2) Growth. The entrepreneur risks all available cash and the established borrowing power of the company in financing further growth. Strategic as well as operational planning is extensive and deeply involves the owner. Managers with an eye to the company's future rather than for its current situation are hired. This is an entrepreneurial high-growth firm aiming to be included in the *Inc. 500*. The emphasis now is on teamwork rather than on the entrepreneur's personal actions and energy. As noted in the **Company Spotlight on Maytag Corporation** feature, a corporate culture based on the personal values and philosophy of the founder begins to form as the founder hires and trains a dedicated team of successors.

Stage D: Take-Off

The key problems in this stage are how to grow rapidly and how to finance that growth. By now the firm is incorporated and has sold or is planning to sell stock in its company via an initial public offering (IPO) or via a direct public offering (DPO).[31] The entrepreneur must learn to delegate to specialized professional managers or to a team of managers who now form the top management of the company. A functional structure of the organization should now be solidly in place. Operational and strategic planning greatly involve the hired managers, but the company is still dominated by the entrepreneur's presence and stock control. Vertical and horizontal growth strategies are being seriously

COMPANY SPOTLIGHT

Impact of F. L. Maytag on Maytag Corporation

On March 21, 1997, Maytag introduced its new "Neptune" horizontal axis washing machine at New York's Lincoln Center. This was the culmination of a five-year effort to build a new front-loading washer that uses 40% less water and 65% less energy than the usual vertical axis top-loading washer. The new washer began as a response to anticipated government standards. When those standards were delayed, Maytag went ahead with the horizontal axis washer, even though Whirlpool and GE stopped their efforts and continued to focus on vertical axis top loaders. Why did Maytag choose to go ahead with the concept? Part of the reason comes from values ingrained in the company by its founder, F. L. Maytag. This entrepreneur made a lasting impact on the Maytag Corporation's corporate culture through his commitment to quality, innovation, and hard work.

- **Commitment to quality.** In the company's first year of operation (selling attachments to threshing machines), almost half the products sold were defective in some way. F. L.'s insistence on fixing or buying back the faulty products resulted in losses for the new company, but it set a strong example in emphasizing the importance of quality. F. L. commented that *"nothing was actually 'sold' until it was in the hands of a satisfied user."*

- **View of innovation.** In the company's early years when the factory itself sent service people out to far-flung dealers to repair defective products, F. L. Maytag noted that few calls ever came from a Minnesota dealer that employed a mechanic named Howard Snyder. Consequently he hired Snyder to improve the company's products. Snyder was not interested in cosmetic changes for the sake of sales, but in internal improvements related to quality, durability, and safety. This emphasis became the company's dominant view of research and development.

- **Dedication to hard work.** Imbued with the strong work ethic of the Midwest, F. L. Maytag spent huge amounts of time to establish and maintain the company. His trip West while Chairman of the Board to personally sell a traincar load of washers set an example to his sales force and became a permanent part of company lore.

- **Emphasis on performance.** F. L. Maytag did not like to boast about himself or his company. Preferring to be judged by his work rather than by his words, he was quoted in a company newsletter as saying: *"It's a good idea for a fellow to have a fair opinion of himself. . . . But it doesn't sound well to hear him broadcast it. It's a better idea to let his associates discover it by his deeds."*

MAYTAG CORPORATION

considered as the firm's management debates when and how to grow. The company is now included in the *Inc. 500* select group of firms.

At this point, the entrepreneur either is able to manage the transition from a small to a large company or recognizes personal limitations, sells his or her stock for a profit, and leaves the firm. The composition of the board of directors changes from dominance by friends and relatives of the owner to a large percentage of outsiders with managerial experience who can help the owner during the transition to a professionally managed company. The biggest danger facing the firm in this stage is the owner's desire to remain in total control (not willing to delegate) as if it were still a small entrepreneurial venture, even though he or she lacks the managerial skills necessary to run an established corporation.

Stage E: Resource Maturity

It is at this point that the small company has adopted most of the characteristics of an established, large company. It may still be a small-to-medium-sized company, but it is recognized as an important force in the industry and a possible candidate for the *Fortune 500* someday. The greatest concerns of a company at this stage are controlling the financial gains brought on by rapid growth and retaining its flexibility and entrepreneurial spirit. In terms of the stages of organizational growth and development discussed in Chapter 8, the company has become a full-fledged Stage II functional corporation.

Transfer of Power and Wealth in Family Businesses

Small businesses are often **family businesses.** Even though the founders of the companies are the primary forces in starting the entrepreneurial ventures, their needs for business support and financial assistance will cause them to turn to family members, who can be trusted, over unknown outsiders of questionable integrity, who may demand more salary than the enterprise can afford. Sooner or later, the founder's spouse and children are drafted into business operations either because the family standard of living is directly tied to the business or the entrepreneur desperately needs help just to staff the operation. The children are guaranteed summer jobs, and the business changes from dad's or mom's company to "our" company. The family members are extremely valuable assets to the entrepreneur because they are often also willing to put in long hours at low pay to help the business succeed. Even though the spouse and children might have no official stock in the company, they know that they will somehow share in its future and perhaps even inherit the business. The problem is that only 30% of family firms in the United States make it to the second generation, and just 13% survive to the third generation.[32]

Churchill and Hatten propose that family businesses go through four sequential phases from the time in which the venture is strictly managed by the founder to the time in which the next generation takes charge.[33] These phases are detailed in Table 12.4. Each of these phases must be well managed if the company is to survive past the third generation. Some of the reasons why family businesses may fail to successfully transfer ownership to the next generation are (1) inherited wealth destroys entrepreneurial drive, (2) the entrepreneur doesn't allow for a changing firm, (3) emphasis on business means the family is neglected, (4) the business' financial growth can't keep up with rising family lifestyles, (5) family members are not prepared to run a business, and (6) the business becomes an arena for family conflicts.[34] In addition, succession planning may be ignored because of the founder's or family's refusal to think about the founder's death, the founder's unwillingness to let go of the firm, the fear of sibling rivalry, or intergenerational envy.

12.5 Issues in Evaluation and Control

As a means by which the corporation's implementation of strategy can be evaluated, the control systems of large corporations have evolved over a long period of time in response to pressures from the environment (particularly the government). Conversely the entrepreneur creates what is needed as the business grows. Because of a personal involvement in decision making, the entrepreneur managing a small business has little need for a formal, detailed reporting system. Thus the founder who has little under-

Table 12.4 Transfer of Power in a Family Business

Phase 1.	**Owner-managed business.** Phase 1 begins at start-up and continues until the entrance of another family member into the business on a full-time basis. Family considerations influence but are not yet a directing part of the firm. At this point, the founder (entrepreneur) and the business are one.
Phase 2.	**Training and development of new generation.** The children begin to learn the business at the dining room table during early childhood and then through part-time and vacation employment. The family and the business become one. Just as the entrepreneur identified with the business earlier, the family now begins to identify itself with the business.
Phase 3.	**Partnership between generations.** At this point, a son or daughter of the founder has acquired sufficient business and managerial competence so that he or she can be involved in key decisions for at least a part of the company. The entrepreneur's offspring, however, has to first gain respect from the firm's employees and other managers and show that he or she can do the job right. Another issue is the lack of willingness of the founder to share authority with the son or daughter. Consequently a common tactic taken by sons and daughters in family businesses is to take a job in a large, established corporation where they can gain valuable experience and respect for their skills.
Phase 4.	**Transfer of power.** Instead of being forced to sell the company when he or she can no longer manage the business, the founder has the option in a family business of turning it over to the next generation as part of their inheritance. Often the founder moves to the position of Chairman of the Board and promotes one of the children to the position of CEO. Unfortunately some founders cannot resist meddling in operating affairs and unintentionally undermine the leadership position of the son or daughter. To avoid this problem, the founder should sell his or her stock (probably through a leveraged buy-out to the children) and physically leave the company and allow the next generation the freedom it needs to adapt to changing conditions.

Source: N. C. Churchill and K. J. Hatten, "Non-Market-Based Transfer of Wealth and Power: A Research Framework for Family Businesses," *American Journal of Small Business* (Winter 1987), pp. 51–64. Reprinted with permission.

standing of accounting and a shortage of cash might employ a bookkeeper instead of an accountant. A formal personnel function might never appear because the entrepreneur lumps it in with simple bookkeeping and uses a secretary to handle personnel files. As an entrepreneurial venture becomes more established, it will develop more complex evaluation and control systems, but they are often not the kind used in large corporations and are probably used for different purposes.

Financial statements, in particular, tell only half the story in small, privately owned companies. The formality of the financial reporting system in such a company is usually a result of pressures from government tax agencies, not from management's desire for an objective evaluation and control system. For example, the absence of taxes in Bermuda has been given as the reason why business owners keep little documentation—thus finding it nearly impossible to keep track of inventory, monitor sales, or calculate how much they are owed.[35]

Because balance sheets and income statements do not always give an accurate picture, standard ratios such as return on assets and debt-equity are unreliable. *Cash flow is widely regarded as more important for an entrepreneurial business than is the traditional balance sheet or income statement.* Even though a small business may be profitable in the accounting sense, a negative cash flow could bankrupt the company. Levin and Travis provide five reasons why owners, operators, and outside observers should be wary of using standard financial methods to indicate the health of a small, privately owned company.[36]

- **The line between debt and equity is blurred.** In some instances, what appears as a loan is really an easy-to-retrieve equity investment. The entrepreneur in this instance doesn't want to lose his or her investment if the company fails. Another condition is that retained earnings seldom reflect the amount of internal financing needed for the company's growth. This account may merely be a place in which cash is left so that the owner can avoid double taxation. To avoid other taxes, owner-managers may own fixed assets that they lease to the corporation. The equity that was used to buy those assets is really the company's equity, but it doesn't appear on the books.

- **Lifestyle is a part of financial statements.** The lifestyle of the owner and the owner's family is often reflected in the balance sheet. The assets of some firms include beach cottages, mountain chalets, and automobiles. In others, plants and warehouses that are used for company operations are not shown because they are held separately by the family. Income statements may not reflect how well the company is operating. Profitability is not so important in decision making in small, private companies as it is in large, publicly held corporations. For example, spending for recreation or transportation and paying rents or salaries above market rates to relatives put artificially high costs on the books of small firms. The business might appear to be poorly managed to an outsider, but the owner is acting rationally. The owner-manager wants dependable income or its equivalent with the least painful tax consequences. Because the standard profitability measures such as ROI are not useful in the evaluation of such a firm, Levin and Travis recommend return on current assets as a better measure of corporate productivity.

- **Standard financial formulas don't always apply.** Following practices that are in contrast to standard financial recommendations, small companies often use short-term debt to finance fixed assets. The absence of well-organized capital markets for small businesses, along with the typical banker's resistance to making loans without personal guarantees, leaves the private owner little choice.

- **Personal preference determines financial policies.** Because the owner is often the manager of the small firm, dividend policy is largely irrelevant. Dividend decisions are based not on stock price (which is usually unknown because the stock is not traded), but on the owner's lifestyle and the tradeoff between taking wealth from the corporation and double taxation.

- **Banks combine personal and business wealth.** Because of the large percentage of small businesses that go bankrupt every year, bank loan officers are reluctant to lend money to a small business unless the owner also provides some personal guarantees for the loan. In some instances, part of the loan may be composed of a second mortgage on the owner's house. If the owner does not want to succumb to this pressure by lenders to include the owner's personal assets as part of the collateral, the owner-manager must be willing to pay high interest rates for a loan that does not put the family's assets at risk.

12.6 Global Issues for the 21st Century

- The **21st Century Global Society** feature in this chapter illustrates how an entrepreneur's personal values and beliefs can become part of a new venture's mission statement and policies. In this way, entrepreneurs are change agents—leading the way to the future. Anita Roddick incorporated concern for the environment long before it became fashionable. The founders of Apple Computer changed an industry (and perhaps the world) in their effort to make a user-friendly computer widely available.

- Entrepreneurship is becoming increasingly important throughout the world. True to economist Joseph Schumpeter's view of entrepreneurship as "creative destruction," much of the world from Eastern Europe to South America to Asia envisions entrepreneurial ventures as the means to build successful free market economies. New entrepreneurial ventures are emerging daily in these countries.

- Given the inability of large corporations to adapt successfully to technological discontinuities, current technological advances should provide an increasing number of opportunities for entrepreneurial ventures in the near future. For example, entrepreneurs worldwide are using the Internet to advertise and sell their products as well as to find suppliers and distributors.

- Multinational corporations have discovered that forming a joint venture with a local entrepreneur is an excellent strategy to enter a country. Developing nations, in particular, are very wary of foreign-owned companies that don't use their profits to further develop the country. The globalization of industries can thus stimulate entrepreneurial ventures worldwide.

- The inability of most entrepreneurial ventures to have access to financial and other resources means that they need to engage in strategic alliances to obtain adequate supplies and distribution. IBM, for example, invests in new ventures working to develop new technologies in order to gain access to the technologies when they are developed.

Projections for the 21st Century

- From 1994 to 2010, the number of golf courses in the U.S. will increase from 14,648 to 16,800.

- From 1994 to 2010, gambling revenues will grow in the U.S. from $39.5 billion to $125.6 billion.[37]

Discussion Questions

1. In terms of strategic management, how does a new venture's situation differ from that of an ongoing small company?

2. How should a small entrepreneurial company engage in environmental scanning? To what aspects of the environment should management pay most attention?

3. What are the characteristics of an attractive industry from an entrepreneur's point of view? What role does innovation play?

4. What considerations should small-business entrepreneurs keep in mind when they are deciding if a company should follow a growth or a stability strategy?

5. How does being family owned (as compared to being publicly owned) affect a firm's strategic management?

Key Terms

business plan (p. 287)
entrepreneur (p. 284)
entrepreneurial characteristics
    (p. 293)
entrepreneurial venture (p. 284)
factors affecting new venture
    success (p. 292)

family businesses (p. 298)
lifestyle company (p. 296)
small-business firm (p. 284)
sources of innovation (p. 290)
strategic decision-making
    process for entrepreneurial
    ventures (p. 286)

substages of small business
    development (p. 295)

Strategic Practice Exercise

In December 1991, after a day of snowboarding at Squaw Valley, Erik Anderson and Jeff Sand sat on the cold ground working to remove their boots from the large, complicated bindings holding their feet to the snowboards. As they released their boots from the plastic straps, they wondered if there was a better way to attach boots to a snowboard, say, a simple step-in method. Alpine skiers had been using step-in bindings for more than 20 years, but nothing like it had yet been developed for snowboarding—an industry with sales of $750 million in 1996 and projected to top $2 billion by 2000. Although the primary users of snowboards, teenage boys, so far didn't seem to care much about the inconvenient strap-in bindings, a step-in system might attract more people to the sport.

During the spring of 1992, Anderson and Sand began two years of evening and weekend research and development (keeping their day jobs designing retail stores), funded primarily by $200,000 in loans from family and friends. Their goal was to make a product that would eliminate the complicated straps and high-backed plastic frames of conventional bindings, yet provide enough support to preserve control and flexibility. They developed a design incorporating a steel rod on either side of the boot to hold the rider's boot tightly to the board. Because the new binding did away with the high-backed frame, the boots would now have to furnish all the support. This meant that Anderson and Sand's newly formed company, Switch Manufacturing, would have to produce not only the *Autolock binding*, but also its companion, *Flexible boot*, as well.

Anderson and Sand brought their pioneering product to market in early 1995, but competition was not far behind. The giant American ski-maker K2, in partnership with the Japanese bicycle maker Shimano, introduced a step-in product, the *Clicker*. At about the same time, two other step-in systems, *Device* and *T-Bone*, were introduced by other competitors.

Step-in sales grew to 5% of the snowboard-binding market by 1995. Even though Anderson optimistically expected step-ins to soon account for 95% of the market, serious snowboarders had their doubts. Steve Klassen, world extreme snowboarding champion, felt that the product was not yet perfected. "As soon as I find a step-in binding that equals the performance of the strap systems, I'll switch myself. Switch's current design, which has metal bolts hanging off the side of the boot, won't become the standard. But that's not to say that Switch might not come up with the right system in the future."

Because of retailer reluctance to stock multiple lines of step-ins, Anderson predicted that the market would soon have to settle on only three to four step-in systems. Success for Switch meant that it had to be one of these basic standards or face being closed out of distribution.

With little money to spend on marketing, Anderson and Sand decided to license their boot technology to a large number of boot makers as a way to establish the Autolock binding as the de facto standard in this fast-growing industry. Shimano had successfully done this in 1990 when it had licensed its integrated shoe-and-pedal clip-in system to makers of bike shoes around the world. Even though Switch would receive a $5,000 licensing fee plus a $1 royalty on each pair of boots sold, the founders realized that this would cut into sales of Switch's own Flexible boot line. Commented Anderson, "by licensing their technology, Shimano lost a lot of shoe sales, but it was offset incredibly by the increase in their pedal sales." If the boot makers would use Switch's boot technology, they would have to buy the step-in binding from Switch—and success would be assured.

Switch Manufacturing had 1995 sales of $1.5 million. Anderson and Sands projected sales of $9 million for 1996 and $19 million for 1997 with a projected pretax 1997 profit of $2.8 million. Co-founder Anderson claimed that his company's sales and market share in 1996 were the same as those of K2. By year-end 1996, Switch's system was being used by the boot makers Vans, Gordo, Nice, Titan, Duffs, and Flexible.[38] (See Switch's web site at *Switch-sf.com*.)

1. What do you think of Switch's chances to make its binding one of the industry standards?

2. What has Switch done right?

3. Should it have done anything differently?

4. Will Switch survive the competition?

5. What are your recommendations to Switch's management?

Notes

1. J. Norman, "Great Idea? That's the Easy Part," *Des Moines Register* (November 12, 1995), p. 3G.

2. "StartUps: Still a Job Engine," *Business Week* (March 24, 1997), p. 26.

3. *The State of Small Business: A Report to the President,* (Washington, D.C.: U.S. Government Printing Office, 1987), p. 117.

4. B. Keats, and J. Bracker, "Toward a Theory of Small Firm Performance: A Conceptual Model," *American Journal of Small Business* (Spring 1988), pp. 41–58; D. Dougherty, "A Practice-Centered Model of Organizational Renewal Through Product Innovation," *Strategic Management Journal* (Summer 1992), pp. 77–92.

5. J. Castro, J. McDowell, and W. McWhirter, "Big vs. Small," *Time* (September 5, 1988), p. 49.

6. B. Bowers, "This Store Is a Hit But Somehow Cash Flow Is Missing," *Wall Street Journal* (April 13, 1993), p. B2.

7. M. J. Foster, "Scenario Planning for Small Businesses," *Long Range Planning* (February 1993), p. 123; M. S. S. El-Namacki, "Small Business—The Myth and the Reality," *Long Range Planning* (August 1990), p. 79.

8. According to a study by Dun & Bradstreet of 800,000 small U.S. businesses started in 1985, 70% were still in business in March 1994. Contrary to other studies, this study only counted firms as failures if they owed money at the time of their demise. Also see J. Aley, "Debunking the Failure Fallacy," *Fortune* (September 6, 1993), p. 21.

9. R. N. Lussier, "Startup Business Advice from Business Owners to Would-Be Entrepreneurs," *SAM Advanced Management Journal* (Winter 1995), pp. 10–13.

10. J. W. Carland, F. Hoy, W. R. Boulton, and J. A. C. Carland, "Differentiating Entrepreneurs from Small Business Owners: A Conceptualization," *Academy of Management Review* (April 1984), p. 358; J. W. Carland, J. C. Carland, F. Hoy, and W. R. Boulton, "Distinctions Between Entrepreneurial and Small Business Ventures," *International Journal of Management* (March 1988), pp. 98–103.

11. S. P. Galante, "Counting on a Narrow Market Can Cloud Company's Future," *Wall Street Journal* (January 20, 1986), p. 17.

12. D. Fields, "Mrs. Fields' Weekends," *USA Weekend* (February 3–5, 1989), p. 16; M. Alpert, "In the Chips," *Fortune* (July 17, 1989), pp. 115–116.

13. J. S. Bracker, B. W. Keats, and J. N. Pearson, "Planning and Financial Performance Among Small Firms in a Growth Industry," *Strategic Management Journal* (November-December 1988), pp. 591–603; J. Kargar and J. A. Parnell, "Strategic Planning Emphasis and Planning Satisfaction in Small Firms: An Empirical Investigation," *Journal of Business Strategies* (Spring 1996), pp. 1–20.

14. W. H. Baker, H. Lon, and B. Davis, "Business Planning in Successful Small Firms," *Long Range Planning* (December 1993), pp. 82–88.

15. A. Thomas, "Less Is More: How Less Formal Planning Can Be Best," in *The Strategic Planning Management Reader,* edited by L. Fahey (Englewood Cliffs, N.J.: Pren-

tice Hall, 1989), pp. 331–336; C. B. Shrader, C. L. Mulford, and V. L. Blackburn, "Strategic and Operational Planning, Uncertainty, and Performance in Small Firms," *Journal of Small Business Management* (October 1989), pp. 45–60.

16. R. B. Robinson, Jr., and J. A. Pearce II, "The Impact of Formalized Strategic Planning on Financial Performance in Small Organizations," *Strategic Management Journal* (July-September 1983), pp. 197–207; R. Ackelsberg and P. Arlow, "Small Businesses Do Plan and It Pays Off," *Long Range Planning* (October 1985), pp. 61–67.

17. V. Fowler, "Business Study Focuses on Failures," *Des Moines Register* (August 9, 1992), p. G1. For information on preparing a business plan, see J. T. Broome, Jr., "How to Write a Business Plan," *Nation's Business* (February 1993), pp. 29–30, and P. D. O'Hara, *The Total Business Plan* (Boston: Wiley & Sons, 1990). For information on business plan software, see B. McWilliams, "Garbage In, Garbage Out," *Inc.* (August 1996), pp. 41–44.

18. J. C. Shuman, and J. A. Seeger, "The Theory and Practice of Strategic Management in Smaller Rapid Growth Firms," *American Journal of Small Business* (Summer 1986), p. 14.

19. S. Birley, and P. Westhead, "Growth and Performance Contrasts Between 'Types' of Small Firms," *Strategic Management Journal* (November-December 1990), pp. 535–557; J. L. Ward and C. E. Aronloff, "How Family Affects Strategy," *Small Business Forum* (Fall 1994), pp. 85–90.

20. P. F. Drucker, *Innovation and Entrepreneurship* (New York: HarperCollins, 1985), pp. 30–129.

21. "The Virtual Emporium Is Your . . . One-Stop Shop," *GW2k: Gateway Magazine* (Spring 1997), p. 37.

22. C. W. Hofer, and W. R. Sandberg, "Improving New Venture Performance: Some Guidelines for Success," *American Journal of Small Business* (Summer 1987), pp. 12–23. See also J. J. Chrisman and A. Bauerschmidt, "New Venture Performance: Some Critical Extensions to the Model," Paper presented to *State-of-the-Art Symposium on Entrepreneurship,* Iowa State University (April 12–14, 1992).

23. Interview with C. Bagley by J. Useem, "Forget Patents, Says Stanford Prof," *Inc.* (October 1996), p. 23.

24. Some studies do indicate that new ventures can also be successful following strategies other than going after an undefended niche with a focus strategy. See A. C. Cooper, G. E. Willard, and C. Y. Woo, "A Reexamination of the Niche Concept," in *The Strategy Process: Concepts, Contexts, and Cases,* 2nd edition, edited by H. Mintzberg and J. B. Quinn (Englewood Cliffs, N.J.: Prentice-Hall, 1991), pp. 619–628; P. P. McDougal, J. G. Covin, R. B. Robinson, Jr., and L. Herron, "The Effects of Industry Growth and Strategic Breadth on New Venture Performance and Strategy Content," *Strategic Management Journal* (September 1994), pp. 537–554.

25. H. P. Welsch, "Entrepreneurs' Personal Characteristics: Causal Models," Paper presented to *State-of-the-Art Symposium on Entrepreneurship,* Iowa State University (April

12–14, 1992); A. Rahim, "Stress, Strain, and Their Moderators: An Empirical Comparison of Entrepreneurs and Managers," *Journal of Small Business Management* (January 1996), pp. 46–58.

26. M. Kets de Vries, "The Dark Side of Entrepreneurship," *Harvard Business Review* (November-December 1985), pp. 160–167.

27. A. C. Cooper, F. J. Gimeno-Gascon, and C.Y. Woo, "Initial Human and Financial Capital as Predictors of New Venture Performance," *Journal of Business Venturing* (Volume 9, 1994), pp. 371–395; H. R. Feeser, and G. E. Willard, "Founding Strategies and Performance in High-Tech Firms," in *Handbook of Business Strategy, 1991/92 Yearbook*, edited by H. E. Glass, and M. A. Hovde (Boston: Warren, Gorham & Lamont, 1991), pp. 2.1–2.18.

28. R. Ricklefs, and U. Gupta, "Traumas of a New Entrepreneur," *Wall Street Journal* (May 10, 1989), p. B1.

29. N. C. Churchill, and V. L. Lewis, "The Five Stages of Small Business Growth," *Harvard Business Review* (May-June 1983), pp. 30–50.

30. J. W. Petty, and W. D. Bygrave, "What Does Finance Have to Say to the Entrepreneur?" *Journal of Small Business Finance* (Spring 1993), pp. 125–137.

31. See C. Farrell, K. Rebello, R. D. Hof, and M. Maremont, "The Boom in IPOs," *Business Week* (December 18, 1995),

pp. 64–72; S. Gruner, "When Mom & Pop Go Public," *Inc.* (December 1996), pp. 66–73.

32. J. Ward, *Keeping the Family Business Healthy* (San Francisco: Jossey-Bass, 1987), as reported by U. Gupta and M. Robichaux, "Reins Tangle Easily at Family Firms," *Wall Street Journal* (August 9, 1989), p. B1.

33. N. C. Churchill, and K. J. Hatten, "Non-Market-Based Transfers of Wealth and Power: A Research Framework for Family Businesses," *American Journal of Small Business* (Winter 1987), pp. 51–64.

34. J. L. Ward, and C. E. Aronoff, "Shirt Sleeves to Shirt Sleeves," *Nation's Business* (September 1992), pp. 62–63.

35. J. Applegate, "Business People in Bermuda Get Sloppy Without Taxes," *Des Moines Register* (July 6, 1992), p. 8B.

36. R. I. Levin, and V. R. Travis, "Small Company Finance: What the Books Don't Say," *Harvard Business Review* (November-December 1987), pp. 30–32.

37. J. Warner, "21st Century Capitalism: Snapshot of the Next Century," *Business Week* (November 18, 1994), p. 194.

38. C. Caggiano, "Kings of the Hill," *Inc.* (August 1996), pp. 46–53.

Chapter 13

Strategic Issues in Not-for-Profit Organizations

The New York City Chapter of the American Heart Association (AHA) was in a difficult situation. Although it was one of 56 affiliates of the AHA, it had to generate revenue to put into its own projects. In recent years, the number of charitable organizations asking for corporate and foundation funds had proliferated at the same time that government dollars for human services and the arts were being drastically cut. Increasing costs had meant that the chapter would have to either increase its funding through more donations or drop some of its programs. The chapter's board of directors and management was unwilling to cut the chapter's programs on reducing death and disability from heart attacks and strokes. Unfortunately they would then have to raise an additional $1 million on top of the current budget—an impossible goal.[1] What should the organization do?

The American Heart Association was not alone in this situation. By the mid-1990s, most not-for-profit organizations were turning to strategic management and other concepts from business to ensure their survival. This was a significant change because most not-for-profit managers had traditionally felt that business concepts were not relevant to their situation. According to Peter Drucker:

> Twenty years ago, management was a dirty word for those involved in nonprofit organizations. It meant business, and nonprofits prided themselves on being free of the taint of commercialism and above such

sordid considerations as the bottom line. Now most of them have learned that nonprofits need management even more than business does, precisely because they lack the discipline of the bottom line.[2]

A knowledge of not-for-profit organizations is important if only for the sole reason that they employ over 25% of the U.S. workforce and own approximately 15% of the nation's private wealth.[3] In the United States alone, in addition to various federal, state, and local government agencies, there are about 10,000 not-for-profit hospitals and nursing homes (84% of all hospitals), 4,600 colleges and universities, over 100,000 private and public elementary and secondary schools, and almost 350,000 churches and synagogues, plus many thousands of charities and service organizations.[4]

Typically **not-for-profit organizations** include **private nonprofit corporations** (such as hospitals, institutes, private colleges, and organized charities) as well as **public governmental units** or **agencies** (such as welfare departments, prisons, and state universities). Traditionally studies in strategic management have dealt with profit-making firms to the exclusion of nonprofit or governmental organizations. This, however, is changing. Not-for-profit organizations are adopting strategic management in increasing numbers.

Scholars and practitioners are concluding that many strategic management concepts and techniques can be successfully adapted for not-for-profit organizations.[5] Although the evidence is not yet conclusive, there appears to be an association between strategic planning efforts and performance measures such as growth.[6] The purpose of this chapter is, therefore, to highlight briefly the major differences between the profit-making and the not-for-profit organization, so that the effects of their differences on the strategic management process can be understood.

13.1 Why Not-for-Profit?

The not-for-profit sector of an economy is important for several reasons. First, society desires certain goods and services that profit-making firms cannot or will not provide. These are referred to as **public or collective goods** because people who might not have paid for the goods receive benefits from them. Paved roads, police protection, museums, and schools are examples of public goods. A person cannot use a private good unless she or he pays for it. Generally once a public good is provided, however, anyone can use or enjoy it. See the 🌐 **21st Century Global Society** feature for those aspects of society most suited to being served by not-for-profit organizations rather than by profit-making business firms.

Second, a private nonprofit organization tends to receive benefits from society that a private profit-making firm cannot obtain. Preferred tax status to nonstock corporations is given in section 501(c)(3) of the U.S. Internal Revenue code in the form of exemptions from corporate income taxes. Private nonprofit firms also enjoy exemptions from various other state, local, and federal taxes. Under certain conditions, these firms also benefit from the tax deductibility of donors' contributions and membership dues. In addition, they qualify for special third-class mailing privileges.[7] These benefits are allowed because private nonprofit organizations are typically service organizations, which are expected to use any excess of revenue over costs and expenses (a *surplus* rather than a *profit*) either to improve service or to reduce the price of their service. This service orientation is reflected in the fact that not-for-profit organizations do not use the term "customer" to refer to the recipient of the service. The recipient is typically referred to as a patient, student, client, case, or simply "the public."

21ST CENTURY GLOBAL SOCIETY

ASPECTS OF LIFE MOST SUITED FOR NOT-FOR-PROFITS

Certain aspects of life do *not* appear to be served appropriately by profit-making business firms, yet are often crucial to the well-being of society. These aspects include areas in which society as a whole benefits from a particular service, but in which a particular individual only benefits indirectly. It is in these areas that not-for-profit organizations have traditionally been most effective. Libraries and museums are examples. Although most people do not visit libraries or museums very often, they are usually willing to pay taxes and/or donate funds to support their existence. They do so because these people believe that these organizations act to uplift the culture and quality of life of the region. To fulfill their mission, entrance fees (if any) must be set low enough to allow everyone admission. These fees, however, are not profitable—they rarely even cover the costs of the service. The same is true of animal shelters managed by the Humane Society. Although few people want abandoned pets running wild through city streets, fees charged from the sale of these animals cannot alone pay the costs of finding and caring for them. Additional revenue is needed—either in the form of donations or public taxation. Such public or collective services cannot generate a profit, yet they are necessary for any successful civilization.

Many nations throughout the world are attempting to privatize state-owned enterprises to balance their budgets. **Privatization** is (1) the selling of state-owned enterprises to private individuals or corporations or (2) the hiring of a private business to provide services previously offered by a state agency. Problems can result, however, if privatization goes too far. For example, in converting from a communist-oriented, centrally managed economy to a more democratic, free-market economy, Eastern European countries are finding that profit-making business firms are unable to satisfy all of society's needs. What used to be provided by the state free of charge (tax-supported) in Russia and other countries may now be provided only for the rich or not at all. The same problem is evident in the United States in the controversy over the provision of health care.

Some of the aspects of life that cannot easily be privatized and are often better managed by not-for-profit organizations are as follows:

- Religion
- Education
- Charities
- Clubs, interest groups, unions
- Health care
- Government

Although society's need for these aspects of life should continue and even increase in the 21st century, business firms seeking a profit have little incentive to satisfy the needs, with the possible exception of health care.

13.2 *Importance of Revenue Source*

The feature that best differentiates not-for-profit (NFP) organizations from each other as well as from profit-making corporations is their **source of revenue**.[8] The **profit-making firm** depends on revenues obtained from the sale of its goods and services to customers, who typically pay for the costs and expenses of providing the product or service plus a profit. The not-for-profit organization, in contrast, depends heavily on dues, assessments, or donations from its membership, or on funding from a sponsoring agency such as the United Way or the federal government to pay for much of its costs and expenses.

Sources of Not-for-Profit Revenue

Revenue is generated from a variety of sources—not just from clients receiving the product or service from the NFP. It can come from people who do not even receive the services they are subsidizing. One study of Minnesota nonprofits found that donations accounted for almost 40%, government grants for around 25%, and program service fees for about 35% of total revenues.[9] In other types of not-for-profit organizations—such as unions and voluntary medical plans—revenue comes mostly from the members, the people who receive the service. Nevertheless, the members typically pay dues in advance and must accept later whatever service is provided whether they choose it or not, whether it is what they expected or not. The service is often received long after the dues are paid.

In profit-making corporations, there is typically a simple and direct connection between the customer or client and the organization. The organization tends to be totally dependent on sales of its products or services to the customer for revenue and is therefore extremely interested in pleasing the customer. As shown in Figure 13.1, the profit-making organization *(organization A)* tries to influence the customer (through advertising and promotion) to continue to buy and use its services. Either by buying or not buying the item offered, the customer, in turn, directly influences the organization's decision-making process. The business is thus market oriented.

In the case of the typical not-for-profit organization, however, there is likely to be a very different sort of relationship between the organization providing and the person receiving the service. Because the recipient of the service typically does not pay the entire cost of the service, outside sponsors are required. In most instances, the sponsors receive none of the service but provide partial to total funding for the needed revenues. As indicated earlier, these sponsors can be the government (using taxpayers' money) or charitable organizations, such as the United Way (using voluntary donations). As shown in Figure 13.1, the not-for-profit organization can be partially dependent on sponsors for funding *(organizations B and C)* or totally dependent on the sponsors *(organization D)*. The less money it receives from clients receiving the service or product, the less market oriented is the not-for-profit organization.

Patterns of Influence on Strategic Decision Making

The **pattern of influence** on the organization's strategic decision making derives from its sources of revenue. As shown in Figure 13.1, a private university *(organization B)* is heavily dependent on student tuition and other client-generated funds for about 70% of its revenue. Therefore, the students' desires are likely to have a stronger influence (as shown by an unbroken line) on the university's decision making than are the desires of the various sponsors such as alumni and private foundations. The sponsors' relatively marginal influence on the organization is reflected by a broken line. In contrast, a public university *(organization C)* is more heavily dependent on outside sponsors such as a state legislature for revenue funding. Student tuition and other client-generated funds form a small percentage (typically less than 40%) of total revenue. Therefore, the university's decision making is heavily influenced by the sponsors (unbroken line) and only marginally influenced directly by the students (broken line).

In the case of *organization D,* however, the client has no direct influence on the organization because the client pays nothing for the services received. In this situation, the organization tends to measure its effectiveness in terms of sponsor satisfaction. It has no real measure of its efficiency other than its ability to carry out its mission and achieve its objectives within the dollar contributions it has received from its sponsors. In contrast to

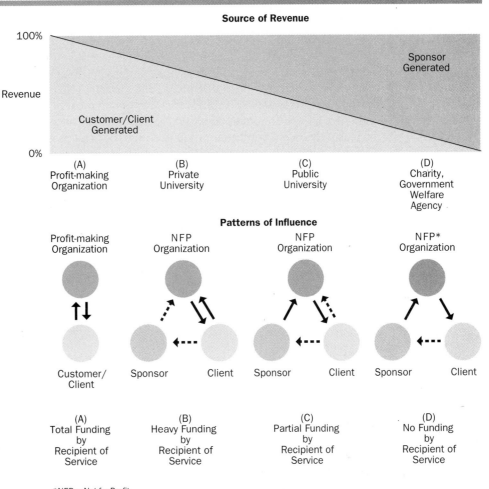

Figure 13.1
The Effects of Sources of Revenue on Patterns of Client-Organization Influence

Source: Thomas L. Wheelen and J. David Hunger, "The Effect of Revenue Upon Patterns of Client-Organization Influence." Copyright © 1982 by Wheelen and Hunger Associates. Revised 1991. Reprinted by permission.

other organizations in which the client contributes a significant proportion of the needed revenue, *organization D* actually might be able to increase its revenue by heavily lobbying its sponsors while reducing the level of its service to its clients!

Regardless of the percentage of total funding that the client generates, the client may attempt to indirectly influence the not-for-profit organization through the sponsors. This is depicted by the broken lines connecting the client and the sponsor in *organizations B, C, and D* in Figure 13.1. Welfare clients or prison inmates, for example, may be able to indirectly improve the services they receive if they pressure government officials by writing to legislators or even by rioting. And students at public universities can lobby state officials for student representation on governing boards.

The key to understanding the management of a not-for-profit organization is thus learning who pays for the delivered services. If the recipients of the service pay only a small proportion of the total cost of the service, strategic managers are likely to be more concerned with satisfying the needs and desires of the funding sponsors or agency than those of the people receiving the service. The acquisition of resources can become an end in itself.

Usefulness of Strategic Management Concepts and Techniques

Some strategic management concepts can be equally applied to business and not-for-profit organizations, whereas others cannot. The marketplace orientation underlying portfolio analysis, for example, does not translate into situations in which client satisfaction and revenue are only indirectly linked. Industry analysis and competitive strategy are primarily relevant to not-for-profits that obtain most of their revenue from user fees rather than from donors or taxpayers. For example, as hospitals find themselves relying increasingly on patient fees for their revenue, they use competitive strategy to gain advantage versus other hospitals. Smaller NFP hospitals stress the "high touch" of their staff over the "high tech" of competitors having better diagnostic machinery.

SWOT analysis, mission statements, stakeholder analysis, and corporate governance are, however, just as relevant to a not-for-profit as they are to a profit-making organization.[10] As with any corporation, nonprofits usually have boards of directors whose job is to ensure that the paid executive director and staff work to fulfill the organization's mission and objectives. Many not-for-profits are finding a well-crafted mission statement not only helps in finding donors, but also in attracting volunteers. Take the example of the mission statement of a local animal shelter:

> To shelter and care for stray, lost, or abandoned animals and to responsibly place animals in new homes and enforce animal laws. We are also here to better educate people in ways to be solutions to animal problems, not causes.[11]

Strategic management is difficult to apply when the organization's output is difficult to measure objectively, as is the case with most not-for-profit organizations. Thus it is very likely that many not-for-profit organizations have *not* used strategic management because its concepts, techniques, and prescriptions did not lend themselves to situations where sponsors, rather than the marketplace, determined revenue. The situation, however, is changing. The trend toward privatizing public organizations, such as converting subsidized community hospitals to independent (nonsubsidized) status, usually means that the clients pay a larger percentage of the costs. As these not-for-profits become more market oriented (and thus client oriented), strategic management becomes more applicable and more increasingly used.[12] Nevertheless, various constraints on not-for-profits mean that strategic management concepts and techniques must be modified to be effective.[13]

13.3 Impact of Constraints on Strategic Management

Several characteristics peculiar to the not-for-profit organization constrain its behavior and affect its strategic management. Newman and Wallender list the following five **constraints on strategic management**:

1. **Service is often intangible and hard to measure.** This difficulty is typically compounded by the existence of multiple service objectives developed to satisfy multiple sponsors.

2. **Client influence may be weak.** Often the organization has a local monopoly, and clients' payments may be a very small source of funds.

3. **Strong employee commitments to professions or to a cause may undermine allegiance** to the organization employing them.

4. **Resource contributors may intrude on the organization's internal management.** Such contributors include fund contributors and government.

5. **Restraints on the use of rewards and punishments** may result from constraints 1, 3, and 4.[14]

It is true that several of these characteristics can be found in profit-making as well as in not-for-profit organizations. Nevertheless, as Newman and Wallender state, the "... frequency of strong impact is much higher in not-for-profit enterprises."[15]

Impact on Strategy Formulation

The long-range planning and decision making affected by the listed constraints serve to add at least four **complications to strategy formulation.**

1. **Goal conflicts interfere with rational planning.** Because the not-for-profit organization typically lacks a single clear-cut performance criterion (such as profits), divergent goals and objectives are likely, especially with multiple sponsors. Differences in the concerns of various important sponsors can prevent management from stating the organization's mission in anything but very broad terms, if they fear that a sponsor who disagrees with a particular narrow definition of mission might cancel its funding. For example, a study of 227 public Canadian hospitals found that over half had very general, ambiguous, and unquantified objectives.[16] According to Heffron, an authority in public administration: "The greater openness within which they are compelled to operate—the fishbowl atmosphere—impedes thorough discussion of issues and discourages long-range plans that might alienate stakeholders."[17] In such organizations, it is the reduced influence of the clients that permits this diversity of values and goals to occur without a clear market check. For example, when a city council considers changing zoning to implement a strategic plan for the city, all sorts of people (including the press) will demand to be heard. A decision might be made based on pressure from a few stakeholders (who make significant contributions or who threaten to stir up trouble) to the detriment of the community as a whole.

2. **An integrated planning focus tends to shift from results to resources.** Because not-for-profit organizations tend to provide services that are hard to measure, they rarely have a net bottom line. Planning, therefore, becomes more concerned with resource inputs, which can easily be measured, than with service, which cannot. Goal displacement (explained earlier in Chapter 10) becomes even more likely than it is in business organizations.[18]

3. **Ambiguous operating objectives create opportunities for internal politics and goal displacement.** The combination of vague objectives and a heavy concern with resources allows managers considerable leeway in their activities. Such leeway makes possible political maneuvering for personal ends. In addition, because the effectiveness of the not-for-profit organization hinges on the satisfaction of the sponsoring group, management tends to ignore the needs of the client while focusing on the desires of a powerful sponsor. University administrators commonly say that people will donate money for a new building (which will carry the donor's name), but not for other more pressing needs, such as the maintenance of existing buildings. In this situation, powerful department heads might wine and dine the donor, hoping to get the money for their pet projects. This problem is compounded by the common practice of selecting people to boards of trustees/directors not on

the basis of their managerial experience, but on the basis of their ability to contribute money, raise funds, and work with politicians. Their lack of interest in overseeing management is reflected in an overall not-for-profit board-meeting attendance rate of only 50%, compared with 90% for boards of directors of business corporations. Board members of not-for-profit organizations, therefore, tend to ignore the task of determining strategies and policies—often leaving this to the paid (or sometimes unpaid) executive director. The larger the board, the less likely it is to exercise control over top management.[19]

4. **Professionalization simplifies detailed planning but adds rigidity.** In not-for-profit organizations in which professionals play important roles (as in hospitals or colleges), professional values and traditions can prevent the organization from changing its conventional behavior patterns to fit new service missions tuned to changing social needs. This rigidity, of course, can occur in any organization that hires professionals. The strong service orientation of most not-for-profit organizations, however, tends to encourage the development of static professional norms and attitudes. As not-for-profits attempt to become more business-like, this may be changing. One study of Minnesota nonprofits revealed that 29% of the program directors and 15% of the staff had degrees or experience in business administration.[20]

Impact on Strategy Implementation

The five constraining characteristics also affect how a not-for-profit organization is organized in both its structure and job design. Three **complications to strategy implementation** in particular can be highlighted:

1. **Decentralization is complicated.** The difficulty of setting objectives for an intangible, hard-to-measure service mission complicates the delegation of decision-making authority. Because of the heavy dependence on sponsors for revenue support, the top management of a not-for-profit organization must be always alert to the sponsors' view of an organizational activity. This necessary caution leads to **defensive centralization**, in which top management retains all decision-making authority so that low-level managers cannot take any actions to which the sponsors may object.

2. **Linking pins for external-internal integration become important.** Because of the heavy dependence on outside sponsors, a special need arises for people in buffer roles to relate to both inside and outside groups. This role is especially necessary when the sponsors are diverse (revenue comes from donations, membership fees, and federal funds) and the service is intangible (for instance, a "good" education) with a broad mission and multiple shifting objectives. The job of a "Dean for External Affairs," for example, consists primarily of working with the school's alumnae and raising funds.

3. **Job enlargement and executive development can be restrained by professionalism.** In organizations that employ a large number of professionals, managers must design jobs that appeal to prevailing professional norms. Professionals have rather clear ideas about which activities are, and which are not, within their province. Enriching a nurse's job by expanding his or her decision-making authority for drug dosage, for example, can cause conflict with medical doctors who believe that such authority is theirs alone. Because a professional often views managerial jobs as nonprofessional and merely supportive, promotion into a management position is not always viewed positively.

Impact on Evaluation and Control

Special **complications to evaluation and control** arising from the constraining characteristics also affect how behavior is motivated and performance is controlled. Two problems, in particular, are often noticed:

1. **Rewards and penalties have little or no relation to performance.** When desired results are vague and the judgment of success is subjective, predictable and impersonal feedback cannot be established. Performance is judged either intuitively ("You don't seem to be taking your job seriously") or on the basis of whatever small aspects of a job can be measured ("You were late to work twice last month").

2. **Inputs rather than outputs are heavily controlled.** Because its inputs can be measured much more easily than outputs, the not-for-profit organization tends to focus more on the resources going into performance than on the performance itself.[21] The emphasis is thus on setting maximum limits for costs and expenses. Because there is little to no reward for staying under these limits, people usually respond negatively to such controls.

13.4   Popular Not-for-Profit Strategies

Because of various pressures on not-for-profit organizations to provide more services than the sponsors and clients can pay for, these organizations are developing strategies to help them meet their desired service objectives. In addition to a heavy use of volunteers to keep costs low, NFPs are choosing the strategies of strategic piggybacking, mergers, and strategic alliances.

Strategic Piggybacking

Coined by Nielsen, the term **strategic piggybacking** refers to the development of a new activity for the not-for-profit organization that would generate the funds needed to make up the difference between revenues and expenses.[22] The new activity is related typically in some manner to the not-for-profit's mission, but its purpose is to help subsidize the primary service programs. It appears to be a form of concentric diversification, but it is engaged in not as part of the mission, but only for its money-generating value. In an inverted use of portfolio analysis, the organization invests in new, safe cash cows to fund its current cash-hungry stars, question marks, and dogs.

Although this strategy is not new, it has recently become very popular. As early as 1874, for example, the Metropolitan Museum of Art retained a professional to photograph its collections and to sell copies of the prints. Profits were used to defray the museum's operating costs. More recently, various income-generating ventures have appeared under various auspices, from the Girl Scouts to UNICEF, and in numerous forms, from cookies and small gift shops to vast real estate developments. A study by the U.S. General Accounting Office revealed that the amount of funds resulting from income-producing activities has significantly increased since the 1970s. Hospitals are offering wellness programs, ranging from meditation classes to aerobics. Some 70% of colleges and universities now offer "auxiliary" services, such as bookstores, conference rooms, and computer centers as sources of income.[23] The Small Business Administration, however, views this activity as "unfair competition." The Internal Revenue Service

(IRS) advises that a not-for-profit that engages in a business "not substantially related" to the organization's exempt purposes may jeopardize its tax-exempt status, particularly if the income from the business exceeds approximately 20% of total organizational revenues. The IRS is enforcing a law requiring charities to pay taxes on income from businesses that aren't related to their charitable activities. Nevertheless, not-for-profits are exempt if their businesses are staffed by volunteers or if almost all their merchandise is donated.[24]

Although strategic piggybacks can help not-for-profit organizations self-subsidize their primary missions and better use their resources, according to Nielsen, there are several potential drawbacks.[25] First, the revenue-generating venture could actually lose money, especially in the short run. Second, the venture could subvert, interfere with, or even take over the primary mission. Third, the public, as well as the sponsors, could reduce their contributions because of negative responses to such "money-grubbing activities" or because of a mistaken belief that the organization is becoming self-supporting. Fourth, the venture could interfere with the internal operations of the not-for-profit organization. To avoid these drawbacks, a not-for-profit should first carefully evaluate its resources before choosing this strategy. See the **Strategy in a Changing World** feature for necessary resources.

Mergers

Dwindling resources are leading an increasing number of not-for-profits to consider **mergers** as a way of reducing costs. For example, the merger of Baptist Health Systems and Research Health Services created Health Midwest in Kansas City. The New York Hospital–Cornell Medical Center and Columbia-Presbyterian Medical Center combined to form the New York and Presbyterian Hospitals Health Care System. Between 1980 and 1991, more than 400 U.S. hospitals were involved in mergers and consolidations— more than half of them happening after 1987.[26]

Strategic Alliances

Strategic alliances involve developing cooperative ties with other organizations. Alliances are often used by not-for-profit organizations as a way to enhance their capacity to serve clients or to acquire resources while still enabling them to keep their identity.[27] Services can be purchased and provided more efficiently through cooperation with other organizations than if they were done alone. For example, four Ohio universities agreed to create and jointly operate a new school of international business. Alone, none of the business schools could afford the $30 million to build the school.

🌑 *13.5* Global Issues for the 21st Century

- The **21st Century Global Society** feature in this chapter describes how some aspects of society may best be provided by not-for-profit organizations than by business firms. As more countries adopt a free market economy and their governments attempt to balance their budgets, expect the debate over what should be business' sphere of influence and what should be that of not-for-profits' to escalate.

- The U.S. National Association of College and University Business Officers predicts that within a few years over 90% of colleges and universities in the United States

STRATEGY IN A CHANGING WORLD

RESOURCES NEEDED FOR SUCCESSFUL STRATEGIC PIGGYBACKING

Based on his experience as a consultant to not-for-profit organizations, Edward Skloot suggests that a not-for-profit should have five resources before engaging in strategic piggybacking:

1. **Something to sell.** The organization should assess its resources to see if people might be willing to pay for goods or services closely related to the organization's primary activity. Repackaging the Boston Symphony into the less formal Boston Pops Orchestra created a way to subsidize the deficit-creating symphony and provide year-round work for the musicians.

2. **Critical mass of management talent.** Enough people must be available to nurture and sustain an income venture over the long haul. This can be very difficult, given that the most competent not-for-profit professionals often don't want to be managers.

3. **Trustee support.** If the trustees have strong feelings against earned-income ventures, they could actively or passively resist commercial involvement. When the Children's Television Workshop began licensing its Sesame Street characters to toy companies and theme parks, many people criticized it for joining business in selling more things to children.

4. **Entrepreneurial attitude.** Management must be able to combine an interest in innovative ideas with business-like practicality.

5. **Venture capital.** Because it often takes money to make money, engaging in a joint venture with a business corporation can provide the necessary start-up funds as well as the marketing and management support. For example, Massachusetts General Hospital receives $50 million from Hoechst, the German chemical company, for biological research in exchange for exclusive licenses to develop commercial products from particular research discoveries.

Source: E. Skloot, "Should Not-for-Profits Go into Business?" *Harvard Business Review* (January-February 1983), pp. 20–24.

will be using strategic piggybacks. Expect a similar trend for other not-for-profits that heavily rely on donations and taxpayer support for their revenue.

- In 1995, the President of the United Way of America was convicted of misusing the charity's money. Although United Way's board of directors was not charged with any wrongdoing, this incident showed that NFP boards could be just as derelict in their duties as were some of the boards of business corporations. This has prompted many nonprofits to evaluate the effectiveness of their corporate governance structure. In the future, expect more nonprofits to be just as concerned about corporate governance as they are about using board members for fund-raising and political connections.

- The privatization of state-owned business enterprises (such as the sale of British Airways stock to the public by the U. K. government) is likely to continue globally because most of these enterprises must expand internationally in order to survive in the increasing global environment. They cannot compete successfully if they are forced to follow inefficient, socially oriented policies and regulations (emphasizing employment over efficiency) rather than economically oriented, international practices (emphasizing efficiency over employment). The global trend toward privatization should continue until each country reaches the point where the efficiency of business is counterbalanced by the effectiveness of the not-for-profit sector of the economy. As political motives overcome economic ones, government will likely intervene in that decision.

- Strategic alliances and mergers are becoming commonplace among not-for-profit organizations. The next logical step is strategic alliances between business firms and not-for-profits. Already business corporations are forming alliances with universities to fund university research in exchange for options on the results of that research. Business firms find it cheaper to pay universities to do basic research than to do it themselves. Universities are in need of research funds to attract top professors and to maintain expensive labs. Such alliances of convenience are being criticized, but they are likely to continue.

Projections for the 21st Century

- From 1994 to 2010, the number of AIDS cases worldwide will grow from 20 million to 38 million.

- From 1994 to 2010, the cost of a Wharton MBA will increase from $84,200 to $257,200.[28]

Discussion Questions

1. Are not-for-profit organizations less efficient than profit-making organizations? Why or why not?

2. How does the lack of a clear-cut performance measure, such as profits, affect the strategic management of a not-for-profit organization?

3. What are the pros and cons of strategic piggybacking? In what way is it "unfair competition" for NFPs to engage in revenue generating activity?

4. What are the pros and cons of mergers and strategic alliances? Should not-for-profits engage in alliances with business firms?

5. Recently, however, many not-for-profit organizations in the United States have been converting to profit making. Why would a not-for-profit organization want to change its status to profit making?

Key Terms

complications to evaluation and control (p. 313)
complications to strategy formulation (p. 311)
complications to strategy implementation (p. 312)
constraints on strategic management (p. 310)

defensive centralization (p. 312)
mergers (p. 314)
not-for-profit organization (p. 306)
patterns of influence (p. 308)
private nonprofit corporations (p. 306)
privatization (p. 307)
profit-making firm (p. 307)

public governmental units or agencies (p. 306)
public or collective goods (p. 306)
source of revenue (p. 307)
strategic alliances (p. 314)
strategic piggybacking (p. 313)

Strategic Practice Exercises

1. Read the **21st Century Global Society** feature in this chapter. It lists six aspects of society that it

proposes are better managed by not-for-profit organizations than by profit-making organizations. Do you agree with this list? Should some aspects be deleted from the list? Should other aspects be added?

2. Examine a local college or university—perhaps the one you may be currently attending. What strategic issues is it facing? Develop a SFAS Table (Figure 5.1) of strategic factors. Is it attempting to use any strategic management concepts? If so, which ones? What sorts of strategies should it be considering for continued survival and future growth? Is it currently using strategic piggybacks to obtain additional funding? What sorts of additional piggybacks should it consider? Are strategic alliances with another college or university or business firm a possibility?

Notes

1. B. Wiesendanger, "Profitable Pointers from Non-Profits," *Journal of Business Strategy* (July/August 1994), pp. 33–39.

2. P. F. Drucker, "What Business Can Learn from Nonprofits," *Harvard Business Review* (July-August 1989), p. 89.

3. G. Rudney, "The Scope and Dimensions of Nonprofit Activity," in *The Nonprofit Sector: A Research Handbook,* edited by W. W. Powell (New Haven: Yale University Press, 1987), p. 56; C. P. McLaughlin, *The Management of Nonprofit Organizations* (New York: John Wiley and Sons, 1986), p. 4.

4. M. O'Neill, *The Third America* (San Francisco: Jossey-Bass, 1989).

5. K. Ascher, and B. Nare, "Strategic Planning in the Public Sector," *International Review of Strategic Management,* Vol. 1, edited by D. E. Hussey (New York: John Wiley & Sons, 1990), pp. 297–315; I. Unterman, and R. H. Davis, *Strategic Management of Not-for-Profit Organizations* (New York: Praeger Press, 1984), p. 2.

6. P. V. Jenster, and G. A. Overstreet, "Planning for a Non-Profit Service: A Study of U.S. Credit Unions," *Long Range Planning* (April 1990), pp. 103–111; G. J. Medley, "Strategic Planning for the World Wildlife Fund," *Long Range Planning* (February 1988), pp. 46–54.

7. J. G. Simon, "The Tax Treatment of Nonprofit Organizations: A Review of Federal and State Policies," in *The Nonprofit Sector: A Research Handbook,* edited by W. W. Powell (New Haven: Yale University Press, 1987), pp. 67–98.

8. B. P. Keating, and M. O. Keating, *Not-for-Profit* (Glen Ridge, N.J.: Thomas Horton & Daughters, 1980), p. 21.

9. K. A. Froelich, "Business Management in Nonprofit Organizations," paper presented to the *Midwest Management Society* (Chicago, 1995).

10. Ascher and Nare, "Strategic Planning in the Public Sector," pp. 297–315; R. McGill, "Planning for Strategic Performance in Local Government," *Long Range Planning* (October 1988), pp. 77–84.

11. Lorna Lavender, Supervisor of Ames (Iowa) Animal Shelter, quoted by K. Petty, "Animal Shelter Cares for Homeless," *ISU Daily* (July 25, 1996), p. 3.

12. E. Ferlie, "The Creation and Evolution of Quasi Markets in the Public Sector: A Problem for Strategic Management," *Strategic Management Journal* (Winter 1992), pp. 79–97; Research has found that for-profit hospitals have more mission statement components dealing with principal services, target customers, and geographic domain than do not-for-profit hospitals. See R. Subramanian, K. Kumar, and C. C. Yauger, "Mission Statements of Hospitals: An Empirical Analysis of Their Contents and Their Relationship to Organizational Factors," *Journal of Business Strategies* (Spring 1993), pp. 63–78.

13. J. D. Hunger, and T. L. Wheelen, "Is Strategic Management Appropriate for Not-for-Profit Organizations?" in *Handbook of Business Strategy, 1989/90 Yearbook,* edited by H. E. Glass (Boston: Warren, Gorham and Lamont, 1989), pp. 3.1–3.8; The contention that the pattern of environmental influence on the organization's strategic decision making derives from the organization's source(s) of income agrees with the authorities in the field. See R. E. Emerson, "Power-Dependence Relations," *American Sociological Review* (February 1962), pp. 31–41; J. D. Thompson, *Organizations in Action* (New York: McGraw-Hill, 1967), pp. 30–31; and J. Pfeffer, and G. R. Salancik, *The External Control of Organizations: A Resource Dependence Perspective* (New York: Harper-Collins, 1978), p. 44.

14. W. H. Newman, and H. W. Wallender III, "Managing Not-for-Profit Enterprises," *Academy of Management Review* (January 1978), p. 26.

15. *Ibid.*, p. 27. The following discussion of the effects of these constraining characteristics is taken from pp. 27–31.

16. J. Denis, A. Langley, and D. Lozeau, "Formal Strategy in Public Hospitals," *Long Range Planning* (February 1991), pp. 71–82.

17. F. Heffron, *Organization Theory and Public Administration* (Englewood Cliffs, N.J.: Prentice-Hall, 1989), p. 132.

18. Heffron, pp. 103–115.

19. I. Unterman, and R. H. Davis, *Strategic Management of Not-for-Profit Organizations* (New York: Praeger Press, 1984), p. 174; J. A. Alexander, M. L. Fennell, and M. T. Halpern, "Leadership Instability in Hospitals: The Influence of Board-CEO Relations and Organizational Growth and Decline," *Administrative Science Quarterly* (March 1993), pp. 74–99.

20. Froelich, "Business Management in Nonprofit Organizations," p. 9.

21. R. M. Kanter, and D. V. Summers, "Doing Well While Doing Good: Dilemmas of Performance Measurement in Nonprofit Organizations and the Need for a Multiple-Constituency Approach," in *The Nonprofit Sector: A Research Handbook,* edited by W. W. Powell (New Haven: Yale University Press, 1987), p. 163.

22. R. P. Nielsen, "SMR Forum: Strategic Piggybacking—A Self-Subsidizing Strategy for Nonprofit Institutions," *Sloan Management Review* (Summer 1982), pp. 65–69; R. P. Nielsen, "Piggybacking for Business and Nonprofits: A

Strategy for Hard Times," *Long Range Planning* (April 1984), pp. 96–102.

23. D. C. Bacon, "Nonprofit Groups: An Unfair Edge?" *Nation's Business* (April 1989), pp. 33–34; "Universities Push Auxiliary Services to Generate More Revenue," *Wall Street Journal* (April 27, 1995), p. A1.

24. E. Skloot, "Should Not-for-Profits Go Into Business?" *Harvard Business Review* (January-February 1983), p. 21; E. Felsenthal, "As Nonprofits Add Sidelines, IRS Takes Aim," *Wall Street Journal* (May 3, 1996), p. B1.

25. R. P. Nielsen, "Piggybacking Strategies for Nonprofits: A Shared Costs Approach," *Strategic Management Journal* (May-June 1986), pp. 209–211.

26. S. Collins, "A Bitter Financial Pill," *U.S. News & World Report* (November 29, 1993), pp. 83–86.

27. K. G. Provan, "Interorganizational Cooperation and Decision Making Autonomy in a Consortium Multihospital System," *Academy of Management Review* (July 1984), pp. 494–504; R. D. Luke, J. W. Begun, and D. D. Pointer, "Quasi-Firms: Strategic Interorganizational Forms in the Health Care Industry," *Academy of Management Review* (January 1989), pp. 9–19.

28. J. Warner, "21st Century Capitalism: Snapshot of the Next Century," *Business Week* (November 18, 1994), p. 194.

Chapter 14

Suggestions for Case Analysis

In July 1996, AlliedSignal's free cash flow measure turned negative. Although the company reported a 16% gain in net income for the second quarter, the *free cash flow* was a negative $90 million. Top management dismissed the cash flow situation as only temporary, arguing that capital spending and increasing inventory during the first part of the year was needed to fuel the company's sales growth expected later in the year. A company spokesman predicted that the free cash flow for the year should hit $300 million and concluded, "There's no problem with cash flow here."

"Not so!" responded Jeffrey Fotta, President of Boston's Ernst Institutional Research. Fotta contended that Allied's growing sales and earnings masked a serious problem in the company. Over the past year, Allied's push to boost sales had caused it difficulty in meeting its cash needs from operations. "They're growing too fast and not getting the returns from capital investments they used to get. Allied peaked in mid 1995, and returns have been deteriorating since." Fotta predicted that without major changes, AlliedSignal would have increasing difficulty continuing its double-digit sales growth.[1]

This is an example of how one analyst used a performance measure to assess the overall health of a company. You can do the same type of in-depth analysis on a comprehensive strategic management case. This chapter provides you with various analytical techniques and suggestions for conducting this kind of case analysis.

14.1 The Case Method

The analysis and discussion of case problems has been the most popular method of teaching strategy and policy for many years. The case method provides the opportunity to move from a narrow, specialized view that emphasizes functional techniques to a broader, less precise analysis of the overall corporation. Cases present actual business situations and enable you to examine both successful and unsuccessful corporations. In case analysis, you might be asked to critically analyze a situation in which a manager had to make a decision of long-term corporate importance. This approach gives you a feel for what it is like to be faced with making and implementing strategic decisions.

14.2 Researching the Case Situation

Don't restrict yourself only to the information written in the case. You should undertake outside research into the environmental setting. Check the decision date of each case to find out when the situation occurred and then screen the business periodicals for that time period. Use computerized company and industry information services such as COMPUSTAT, Compact Disclosure, and CD/International, available on CD-Rom or on-line at the library. On the World Wide Web, Hoover's On Line Corporate Directory (*www.hoovers.com*) and the Security Exchange Commission's Edgar database (*www.sec.gov*) provide access to corporate annual reports and 10-K forms. This background will give you an appreciation for the situation as it was experienced by the participants in the case. See the **Strategy in a Changing World** feature for how to access the World Wide Web for business information.

A company's annual report and 10-K form from that year can be very helpful. Two-thirds of portfolio managers and 54% of security analysts agree that annual reports are the most important documents a public company can produce.[2] They contain not only the usual *income statements* and *balance sheets,* but also *cash flow statements* and notes to the financial statements indicating why certain actions were taken. 10-K forms include detailed information not usually available in an annual report. An understanding of the economy during that period will help you avoid making a serious error in your analysis, for example, suggesting a sale of stock when the stock market is at an all-time low or taking on more debt when the prime interest rate is over 15%. Information on the industry will provide insights on its competitive activities. Some resources available for research into the economy and a corporation's industry are suggested in Appendix 14.A.

14.3 Financial Analysis: A Place to Begin

Once you have read a case, a good place to begin your analysis is with the financial statements. **Ratio analysis** is the calculation of ratios from data in these statements. It is done to identify possible financial strengths or weaknesses. Thus it is a valuable part of SWOT analysis. A review of key financial ratios can help you assess the company's overall situation and pinpoint some problem areas. Ratios are useful regardless of firm size and enable you to compare a company's ratios with industry averages. Table 14.1 lists some of the most important financial ratios, which are (1) **liquidity ratios**, (2) **profitability ratios**, (3) **activity ratios**, and (4) **leverage ratios**.

USING THE WORLD WIDE WEB TO OBTAIN INFORMATION

The **World Wide Web** is a part of the Internet and is an excellent source of information about industries as well as individual companies. To begin, you only need access to the Internet and a browser like Netscape Navigator or Microsoft's Internet Explorer.

Going Directly to the Company's Web Page

If you are looking for information about a particular company, you can first try using a simplified version of the firm's name to directly get to the firm's home (primary) web page. For example, first type in the protocol—the standard first part of the url (uniform resource locator)—*http://www*. Don't capitalize any letters in the url. Then type in a likely name for the firm, such as *maytag, ibm, toyota, hp* (Hewlett-Packard), *ti* (Texas Instruments), or *awl* (Addison Wesley Longman). This is referred to as the company's server name. Follow this name with the suffix *.com*. This is called a domain. In the United States, all business urls end with the domain name .com. University urls end with *.edu*. Government agencies' urls end with *.gov*. Outside of the United States each country has its own suffix, such as *.uk* for Great Britain, *.au* for Australia, *.ca* for Canada, *.de* for Germany, and *.pe* for Peru. This string of words and letters usually completes the url. For example, try typing *http://www.maytag.com* in the location line of your Internet browser and tap the Enter key. This takes you directly to Maytag's home web page. In some instances, the url may also contain a more specific web page beyond the company's home page. In this case, the *.com* is followed by */xxxx.html (xxxx* can be anything). This indicates that this is another web page that uses the html (hypertext markup language) language of the World Wide Web. Sometimes instead of *html*, it is abbreviated to simply *htm*.

Using a Search Tool

If typing in an obvious company name doesn't work, use a search tool. This is especially the case if you are investigating a non-U.S. corporation like AB Electrolux of Sweden. Search tools are services that act like a library's card file to help you find information on a topic. Some of the common search tools are:

- Yahoo (*http://www.yahoo.com*)
- AltaVista (*http://altavista.digital.com*)
- Galaxy (*http://galaxy.einet.net/galaxy.html*)
- Infoseek (*http://infoseek.go.com*)

The url will take you to the search tool's web page where you can type in the name of a company. The search tool uses its search engine to find any references to that firm. One of these references should include the company's url. Use it to get to the company's home web page.

Finding More Information

Getting to the company's home web page does not necessarily mean that you now have access to the firm's financials. For example, Maytag's home page doesn't provide access to its financial reports. In that case, try related business directories such as Hoover's On-Line (*http://www.hoovers.com*) or the U.S. Securities and Exchange Commission Edgar database (*http://www.sec.gov*). If the company's stock is publicly traded and listed on one of the major stock exchanges, these business directories should get you to the database containing the latest annual reports and 10-K reports, as well as quarterly reports. Other sites offering valuable information relating to business firms are:

- All Business Network (*http://www.all-biz.com/srch_abn.htm*)
- Web 100 (*http://www.w100.com*)
- Big Book (*http://www.bigbook.com*)
- Wall Street Research Net (*http://www.wsrn.com*)
- GTE Superpages (*http://superpages.gte.net*)

(continued)

STRATEGY IN A CHANGING WORLD

USING THE WORLD WIDE WEB TO OBTAIN INFORMATION (*continued*)

- International Info (*http://www.nijenrode.nl.nbr/int*)

- Export Hotline & Trade Bank (*http://www. exporthotline.com*)

Additional web sites are listed at the end of Appendix 14.A. Note that web sites constantly change. Just because a particular url works one time does not mean that it will work a year or two later. If the company is doing a good job of managing its web sites, it will leave a message on its abandoned web page sending you to a new web page. If nothing works, simply go to one of the search tools and begin again. Good luck!

Note: Until recently, all Internet addresses in the U.S. ended with one of six domain names: .com for commercial businesses, .org for non-profit organizations, .net for networks, .edu for educational institutions, .gov for governmental bodies, and .mil for the military. Seven endings are being added: .store for businesses offering goods, .info for information services, .nom for personal sites, .firm for businesses, .web for specialized web sites, .arts for cultural groups, and .rec for recreational activities.

For additional information, see C. B. Leshin, *Management on the Web* (Upper Saddle River, N.J.: Prentice-Hall, 1997).

Analyzing Financial Statements

In your analysis, do not simply make an exhibit including all the ratios, but select and discuss only those ratios that have an impact on the company's problems. For instance, accounts receivable and inventory may provide a source of funds. If receivables and inventories are double the industry average, reducing them may provide needed cash. In this situation, the case report should include not only sources of funds, but also the number of dollars freed for use. Compare these ratios with industry averages to discover if the company is out of line with others in the industry.

A typical financial analysis of a firm would include a study of the operating statements for five or so years, including a trend analysis of sales, profits, earnings per share, debt to equity ratio, return on investment, and so on, plus a ratio study comparing the firm under study with industry standards.

- Scrutinize historical income statements and balance sheets. These two basic statements provide most of the data needed for analysis. Statements of cash flow may also be useful.

- Compare historical statements over time if a series of statements is available.

- Calculate changes that occur in individual categories from year to year, as well as the cumulative total change.

- Determine the change as a percentage as well as an absolute amount.

- Adjust for inflation if that was a significant factor.

Examination of this information may reveal developing trends. Compare trends in one category with trends in related categories. For example, an increase in sales of 15% over three years may appear to be satisfactory until you note an increase of 20% in the cost of goods sold during the same period. The outcome of this comparison might suggest that further investigation into the manufacturing process is necessary.

Table 14.1   **Financial Ratio Analysis**

	Formula	How Expressed	Meaning
1. Liquidity Ratios			
Current ratio	$\dfrac{\text{Current assets}}{\text{Current liabilities}}$	Decimal	A short-term indicator of the company's ability to pay its short-term liabilities from short-term assets; how much of current assets are available to cover each dollar of current liabilities.
Quick (acid test) ratio	$\dfrac{\text{Current assets} - \text{Inventory}}{\text{Current liabilities}}$	Decimal	Measures the company's ability to pay off its short-term obligations from current assets, excluding inventories.
Inventory to net working capital	$\dfrac{\text{Inventory}}{\text{Current assets} - \text{Current liabilities}}$	Decimal	A measure of inventory balance; measures the extent to which the cushion of excess current assets over current liabilities may be threatened by unfavorable changes in inventory.
Cash ratio	$\dfrac{\text{Cash} + \text{Cash equivalents}}{\text{Current liabilities}}$	Decimal	Measures the extent to which the company's capital is in cash or cash equivalents; shows how much of the current obligations can be paid from cash or near-cash assets.
2. Profitability Ratios			
Net profit margin	$\dfrac{\text{Net profit after taxes}}{\text{Net sales}}$	Percentage	Shows how much after-tax profits are generated by each dollar of sales.
Gross profit margin	$\dfrac{\text{Sales} - \text{Cost of goods sold}}{\text{Net sales}}$	Percentage	Indicates the total margin available to cover other expenses beyond cost of goods sold, and still yield a profit.
Return on investment (ROI)	$\dfrac{\text{Net profit after taxes}}{\text{Total assets}}$	Percentage	Measures the rate of return on the total assets utilized in the company; a measure of management's efficiency, it shows the return on all the assets under its control regardless of source of financing.
Return on equity (ROE)	$\dfrac{\text{Net profit after taxes}}{\text{Shareholders' equity}}$	Percentage	Measures the rate of return on the book value of shareholders' total investment in the company.

(continued)

Note that multinational corporations follow the accounting rules for their home country. As a result, their financial statements may be somewhat difficult to understand or to use for comparisons with competitors from other countries. For example, British firms such as British Petroleum and The Body Shop use the term "turnover" rather than sales revenue. In the case of AB Electrolux of Sweden, a footnote to the annual report indicates that the consolidated accounts have been prepared in accordance with Swedish accounting standards, which differ in certain significant respects from U.S. generally accepted accounting principles (U.S. GAAP). In this case, 1994 net income of

Table 14.1 **Financial Ratio Analysis** *(continued)*

	Formula	How Expressed	Meaning
Earnings per share (EPS)	$\dfrac{\text{Net profit after taxes} - \text{Preferred stock dividends}}{\text{Average number of common shares}}$	Dollars per share	Shows the after-tax earnings generated for each share of common stock.
3. Activity Ratios			
Inventory turnover	$\dfrac{\text{Net sales}}{\text{Inventory}}$	Decimal	Measures the number of times that average inventory of finished goods was turned over or sold during a period of time, usually a year.
Days of inventory	$\dfrac{\text{Inventory}}{\text{Cost of goods sold} \div 365}$	Days	Measures the number of one day's worth of inventory that a company has on hand at any given time.
Net working capital turnover	$\dfrac{\text{Net sales}}{\text{Net working capital}}$	Decimal	Measures how effectively the net working capital is used to generate sales.
Asset turnover	$\dfrac{\text{Sales}}{\text{Total assets}}$	Decimal	Measures the utilization of all the company's assets; measures how many sales are generated by each dollar of assets.
Fixed asset turnover	$\dfrac{\text{Sales}}{\text{Fixed assets}}$	Decimal	Measures the utilization of the company's fixed assets (i.e., plant and equipment); measures how many sales are generated by each dollar of fixed assets.
Average collection period	$\dfrac{\text{Accounts receivable}}{\text{Sales for year} \div 365}$	Days	Indicates the average length of time in days that a company must wait to collect a sale after making it; may be compared to the credit terms offered by the company to its customers.
Accounts receivable turnover	$\dfrac{\text{Annual credit sales}}{\text{Accounts receivable}}$	Decimal	Indicates the number of times that accounts receivable are cycled during the period (usually a year).
Accounts payable period	$\dfrac{\text{Accounts payable}}{\text{Purchases for year} \div 365}$	Days	Indicates the average length of time in days that the company takes to pay its credit purchases.
Days of cash	$\dfrac{\text{Cash}}{\text{Net sales for year} \div 365}$	Days	Indicates the number of days of cash on hand, at present sales levels.

(continued)

4,830m SEK (Swedish kronor) approximated 5,655 SEK according to U.S. GAAP. Total assets for the same period were 84,183m SEK according to Swedish principle, but 86,658 according to U.S. GAAP.

Common-Size Statements

Common-size statements are income statements and balance sheets in which the dollar figures have been converted into percentages. *For the income statement, net sales*

Table 14.1 **Financial Ratio Analysis (continued)**

	Formula	How Expressed	Meaning
4. Leverage Ratios			
Debt to asset ratio	$\dfrac{\text{Total debt}}{\text{Total assets}}$	Percentage	Measures the extent to which borrowed funds have been used to finance the company's assets.
Debt to equity ratio	$\dfrac{\text{Total debt}}{\text{Shareholders' equity}}$	Percentage	Measures the funds provided by creditors versus the funds provided by owners.
Long-term debt to capital structure	$\dfrac{\text{Long-term debt}}{\text{Shareholders' equity}}$	Percentage	Measures the long-term component of capital structure.
Times interest earned	$\dfrac{\text{Profit before taxes + Interest charges}}{\text{Interest charges}}$	Decimal	Indicates the ability of the company to meet its annual interest costs.
Coverage of fixed charges	$\dfrac{\text{Profit before taxes + Interest charges + Lease charges}}{\text{Interest charges + Lease obligations}}$	Decimal	A measure of the company's ability to meet all of its fixed-charge obligations.
Current liabilities to equity	$\dfrac{\text{Current liabilities}}{\text{Shareholders' equity}}$	Percentage	Measures the short-term financing portion versus that provided by owners.
5. Other Ratios			
Price/earnings ratio	$\dfrac{\text{Market price per share}}{\text{Earnings per share}}$	Decimal	Shows the current market's evaluation of a stock, based on its earnings; shows how much the investor is willing to pay for each dollar of earnings.
Divided payout ratio	$\dfrac{\text{Annual dividends per share}}{\text{Annual earnings per share}}$	Percentage	Indicates the percentage of profit that is paid out as dividends.
Dividend yield on common stock	$\dfrac{\text{Annual dividends per share}}{\text{Current market price per share}}$	Percentage	Indicates the dividend rate of return to common shareholders at the current market price.

Note:
In using ratios for analysis, calculate ratios for the corporation and compare them to the average and quartile ratios for the particular industry. Refer to Standard and Poor's and Robert Morris Associates for average industry data. Special thanks to Dr. Moustafa H. Abdelsamad, Dean, Business School, Texas A&M University–Corpus Christi, Corpus Christi, Texas, for his definitions of these ratios.

represent 100%: calculate the percentage of each category so that the categories sum to the net sales percentage (100%). For the balance sheet, give the total assets a value of 100%, and calculate other asset and liability categories as percentages of the total assets. (Individual asset and liability items, such as accounts receivable and accounts payable, can also be calculated as a percentage of net sales.)

When you convert statements to this form, it is relatively easy to note the percentage that each category represents of the total. Look for trends in specific items, such as cost of goods sold, when compared to the company's historical figures. To get a proper picture, however, make comparisons with industry data, if available, to see if fluctuations are merely reflecting industrywide trends. If a firm's trends are generally in line with those of the rest of the industry, problems are less likely than if the firm's trends are worse than industry averages. These statements are especially helpful in developing scenarios and pro forma statements because they provide a series of historical relationships (for example, cost of goods sold to sales, interest to sales, and inventories as a percentage of assets) from which you can estimate the future with your scenario assumptions for each year.

Z-value, Index of Sustainable Growth, and Free Cash Flow

If the corporation being studied appears to be in poor financial condition, use **Altman's Bankruptcy Formula** to calculate its Z-value. The **Z-value** formula combines five ratios by weighting them according to their importance to a corporation's financial strength. The formula is:

$$Z = 1.2x_1 + 1.4x_2 + 3.3x_3 + 0.6x_4 + 1.0x_5$$

where:

x_1 = Working capital/Total assets (%)

x_2 = Retained earnings/Total assets (%)

x_3 = Earnings before interest & taxes/Total assets (%)

x_4 = Market value of equity/Total liabilities (%)

x_5 = Sales/Total assets (number of times)

Scores below *1.81* indicate significant credit problems, whereas a score above *3.0* indicates a healthy firm. Scores between 1.81 and 3.0 indicate question marks.[3]

The **index of sustainable growth** is useful to learn if a company embarking on a growth strategy will need to take on debt to fund this growth. The index indicates how much of the growth rate of sales can be sustained by internally generated funds. The formula is:

$$g^* = \frac{[P(1-D)\,(1+L)]}{[T - P\,(1-D)\,(1+L)]}$$

where:

P = (Net profit before tax/Net sales) $\times$ 100

D = Target dividends/Profit after tax

L = Total liabilities/Net worth

T = (Total assets/Net sales) $\times$ 100

If the planned growth rate calls for a growth rate higher than its g^*, external capital will be needed to fund the growth unless management is able to find efficiencies, decrease dividends, increase the debt/equity ratio, or reduce assets by renting or leasing arrangements.[4]

Takeover artists and LBO (leveraged buy-out) specialists look at a corporation's financial statements for **operating cash flow**: the amount of money generated by a company before the cost of financing and taxes. This is the company's net income plus depreciation plus depletion, amortization, interest expense, and income tax expense. LBO specialists will take on as much debt as the company's operating cash flow can sup-

IS INFLATION DEAD OR JUST SLEEPING?

Inflation is a recent problem in the United States. Between 1800 and 1940, there was no clear trend up or down in the overall cost of living. A movie-goer in the late 1930s watching a drama set in the early 1800s would not notice prices to be unusual. For example, the cost of a loaf of bread in the late 1930s was roughly the same as in 1800. With the minor exceptions of 1949 and 1955, prices have risen every year since 1945. The Consumer Price Index (a generally used measure of the overall cost of living in the United States) increased nine times from 1945 to 1996. (Watch the movie *It's a Wonderful Life* to see how prices have changed.) From 1970 to 1980, the CPI more than doubled. After an average rate of 7.1% during the 1970s, inflation slowed to 5.5% in the 1980s, and 3.4% during the 1990s.

The rate of inflation in other countries varies and has a significant impact on a multinational corporation's profits. For example, the inflation rate in Brazil during 1987 was 545%. Bolivia's rate during 1985 was an astounding 25,000%! During the 1990s, Western Europe had an inflation rate of around 2%, while Eastern European countries were dealing with a rate ranging from 24% in Hungary to 52% in Russia to 91% in the Ukraine.

A report by the Boskin Commission recommended to Congress that the methodology used by the U.S. Bureau of Labor Statistics tends to overstate inflation and should be changed. Before inflation is declared dead by politicians anxious to reduce cost of living increases to Social Security payments (to reduce government expenditures and thus government debt), note what happens with a relatively constant 3.4% rate of inflation. Through the working of compound interest, the price level has already risen about 25% by 1996 and should reach 40% by the turn of the century. This means that companies have to be constantly monitoring not only their costs, but also the prices of the products they offer. *Unless a company's dollar sales are increasing over 3.5% annually, its sales are actually falling (in constant dollars)!* The same is true for net income. This point is often overlooked by the chief executive officers of troubled companies who are anxious to keep their jobs by fooling both the board and the shareholders.

Source: P. W. Boltz, "Is Inflation Dead?" *T. Rowe Price Report* (Winter 1997), pp. 10–11.

port. Although operating cash flow is a broad measure of a company's funds, some takeover artists look at a much narrower **free cash flow**: the amount of money a new owner can take out of the firm without harming the business. This is net income plus depreciation, depletion, and amortization less capital expenditures and dividends. The free cash flow ratio is very useful in evaluating the stability of an entrepreneurial venture.[5]

Useful Economic Measures

If you are analyzing a company over many years, you may want to adjust sales and net income for inflation to arrive at "true" financial performance in constant dollars. **Constant dollars** are dollars adjusted for inflation to make them comparable over various years. See the **Strategy in a Changing World** feature to learn why inflation is an important issue. One way to adjust for inflation in the U.S. is to use the Consumer Price Index (CPI), as given in Table 14.2. Dividing sales and net income by the CPI factor for that year will change the figures to 1982–1984 constant dollars.

Table 14.2   **U.S. Economic Indicators: Gross Domestic Product (GDP) in Billions of Dollars; Consumer Price Index for All Items (CPI) (1982–84 = 1.0); Prime Interest Rate (PIR)**

Year	GDP	CPI	PIR
1982	3,542.1	.965	14.86%
1983	3,514.5	.996	10.79
1984	3,902.4	1.039	12.04
1985	4,180.7	1.076	9.93
1986	4,422.2	1.096	8.33
1987	4,693.3	1.136	8.21
1988	5,049.6	1.183	9.32
1989	5,483.7	1.240	10.87
1990	5,743.8	1.307	10.01
1991	5,916.7	1.362	8.46
1992	6,244.4	1.403	6.25
1993	6,553.0	1.445	6.00
1994	6,935.7	1.482	7.15
1995	7,253.8	1.524	8.83
1996	7,661.6	1.569	8.27
1997	8,110.9	1.605	8.44
1998	8,537.9	1.630	8.50

Sources:

1. Gross Domestic Product from *Survey of Current Business* (January 1999), Vol. 79, No. 1, Table 1.1, p. D-2.

2. Consumer Price Index from U.S. Department of Commerce, *1997 Statistical Abstract of the United States*, 117th edition, Chart no. 752, p. 487; U.S. Bureau of Labor Statistics, *Monthly Labor Review* (October 1998), Chart no. 28, p. 74.

3. Prime Interest Rates from D. S. Benton, "Banking and Financial Information," Table 1-2, p. 3, in *Thorndike Encyclopedia of Banking and Financial Tables*, 3rd ed., 1998 Yearbook (Boston: Warren, Gorham and Lamont, 1998).

Another helpful analytical aid is **prime interest rate**, the rate of interest banks charge on their lowest risk loans. For better assessments of strategic decisions, it can be useful to note the level of the prime interest rate at the time of the case. (See Table 14.2.) A decision to borrow money to build a new plant would have been a good one in 1992, but less practical in 1989.

In preparing a scenario for your pro forma financial statements, you may want to use the **gross domestic product (GDP)** from Table 14.2. GDP is used worldwide and measures the total output of goods and services within a country's borders. Remember that scenarios have to be adjusted for a country's specific conditions. See the 🌐 **21st Century Global Society** feature for a list of the fastest growing economies in the world. These are the locations making a strong impact on strategic decision making in most corporations.

14.4 *Format for Case Analysis: The Strategic Audit*

There is no one best way to analyze or present a case report. Each instructor has personal preferences for format and approach. Nevertheless, we suggest an approach for both written and oral reports in Appendix 14.B, which provides a systematic method for suc-

21ST CENTURY GLOBAL SOCIETY

THE FASTEST GROWING ECONOMIES IN THE WORLD

Using a sophisticated scoring system based on measures of economic stability, human capital, free market policies, export orientation, and investment ratios, American Express Bank Ltd. publishes a list of the current economic world *tigers*—those countries demonstrating the capacity for rapid, sustained growth. These countries are: China, Hong Kong, Malaysia, Singapore, South Korea, and Thailand. They also calculate a list of *near-tigers*—those countries on the verge of rapid growth. These countries are: the Philippines, Czech Republic, Argentina, Chile, Taiwan, Vietnam, and Indonesia. Expect corporations to be seriously investing in these countries now and in the near future. The following table presents estimated figures for 1997 by country.

Country	GDP	GDP/head	Population	GDP Growth	Inflation
Tigers:					
China	$897 bil	$720	1.24 bil	9.5%	12%
Hong Kong	$171 bil	$27,130	6.32 mil	5%	6.1%
Malaysia	$96 bil	$4,543	21.2 mil	7.8%	3.9%
Singapore	$102 bil	$32,878	3.1 mil	6.9%	1.6%
South Korea	$544 bil	$11,910	45.6 mil	7.3%	4.4%
Thailand	$202 bil	$3,250	62.1 mil	7.1%	4.4%
Near-Tigers:					
Philippines	$86 bil	$1,200	71.2 mil	5.8%	7.5%
Czech Republic	$57 bil	$5,570	10.3 mil	5.5%	8.2%
Argentina	$297 bil	$8,470	35 mil	2.2%	1.8%
Chile	$83 bil	$5,680	14.5 mil	5.5%	6.2%
Taiwan	$305 bil	$14,090	21.6 mil	5.7%	3.5%
Vietnam	$28 bil	$360	77.1 mil	7.9%	8.7%
Indonesia	$246 bil	$1,210	203.3 mil	7.2%	7.0%

Source: G. Koretz, "Look Who's Set to Pounce," *Business Week* (March 31, 1997), p. 30; D. Fishburn (ed.), "The World in Figures: Countries," *The World in 1997* (London: The Economist Group, 1996), pp. 83–89.

cessfully attacking a case. This approach is based on the **strategic audit**, which was presented in Chapter 10 as Table 10.5 (pages 252–259). We find that this approach provides structure and is very helpful for the typical student who may be a relative novice in case analysis. Regardless of the format chosen, be careful to include a complete analysis of key environmental variables—especially of trends in the industry and of the competition. Look at international developments as well.

If you choose to use the strategic audit as a guide to the analysis of complex strategy cases, you may want to use the strategic audit worksheet in Figure 14.1. Make a copy of the worksheet to use to take notes as you analyze a case. **You can also download the Strategic Audit Worksheet, from the *Strategic Management and Business* worldwide web site at http://www.prenhall.com/wheelen.** See Appendix 14.C for an example of a completed student-written analysis of a 1993 Maytag Corporation case *(not the 1996 version in the case portion of this book)* done in an outline form using the strategic audit format. This is an example of what a case analysis in outline form may look like.

Case discussion focuses on critical analysis and logical development of thought. A solution is satisfactory if it resolves important problems and is likely to be implemented successfully. How the corporation actually dealt with the case problems has no real bearing on the analysis because management might have analyzed its problems incorrectly or implemented a series of flawed solutions.

Figure 14.1
Strategic Audit Worksheet

Strategic Audit Heading	Analysis		Comments
	(+) Factors	**(−) Factors**	
I. Current Situation			
A. Past Corporate Performance Indexes			
B. Strategic Posture: Current Mission Current Objectives Current Strategies Current Policies			
SWOT Analysis Begins:			
II. Corporate Governance			
A. Board of Directors			
B. Top Management			
III. External Environment (EFAS): Opportunities and Threats (SWOT)			
A. Societal Environment			
B. Task Environment (Industry Analysis)			
IV. Internal Environment (IFAS): Strengths and Weaknesses (SWOT)			
A. Corporate Structure			
B. Corporate Culture			
C. Corporate Resources 1. Marketing			
2. Finance			
3. Research and Development			
4. Operations and Logistics			
5. Human Resources			
6. Information Systems			
V. Analysis of Strategic Factors (SFAS)			
A. Key Internal and External Strategic Factors (SWOT)			
B. Review of Mission and Objectives			

(continued)

Figure 14.1
Strategic Audit
Worksheet
(continued)

SWOT Analysis Ends. Recommendation Begins:	
VI. Alternatives and Recommendations	
A. Strategic Alternatives	
B. Recommended Strategy	
VII. Implementation	
VIII. Evaluation and Control	

Note: See the complete Strategic Audit on pages 252–259. It lists the pages in the book that discuss each of the eight headings.

Source: T. L. Wheelen and J. D. Hunger, "Strategic Audit Worksheet." Copyright © 1989 by Wheelen and Hunger Associates. Revised 1991, 1994, and 1997. Reprinted by permission. Additional copies available for classroom use in Part D of *Case Instructors Manual* and on the Addison Wesley Longman web site (Use Passport).

14.5   *Global Issues for the 21st Century*

- The **21st Century Global Society** feature in this chapter lists the 13 fastest growing economies in the world. Expect an increasing amount of investment to be located in these countries in the near future. These are attractive locations for outsourcing and for international entry strategies. By the turn of the century, the economic tigers will include not only Asian, but also Eastern European and South American countries.

- Inflation will probably remain at a low but significant level during the near future for much of the developed world. As in the case of the European Union, regional blocs are realizing that inflation must be kept under control if there is to be prosperity.

- Expect the World Wide Web to soon become a dominant source of information throughout the world regarding industries, companies, and countries. It is an excellent way to obtain the latest information for competitive analysis.

- As multinational corporations increase their global presence, there will be increasing pressure for worldwide uniform accounting standards. The coming common currency in the European Union will eliminate some of the currency conversion problems and will support common standards. The next step may be one international stock exchange with subsidiary exchanges in each region or country.

- Standard financial ratios are of limited value for entrepreneurial ventures, especially small/family owned firms. With an increasing global emphasis on new business ventures, expect other measures, such as operating cash flow and free cash flow, to become equally important measures of financial health.

Projections for the 21st Century

- From 1994 to 2010, expect consumer inflation to decline from 4.3% to 2.5%.

- From 1994 to 2010, expect the international value of the U.S. dollar to increase from 1.0 to 9.33.[6]

Discussion Questions

1. Why should you begin a case analysis with a financial analysis? When are other approaches appropriate?

2. What are common-size financial statements? What is their value to case analysis? How are they calculated?

3. When should you gather information outside the case by going to the library or using the Internet? What should you be looking for?

4. When is inflation an important issue in conducting case analysis? Why bother?

5. How can you learn the date a case took place?

Key Terms

activity ratios (p. 320)
Altman's Bankruptcy Formula (p. 326)
common-size statements (p. 324)
constant dollars (p. 327)
free cash flow (p. 327)

gross domestic product (GDP) (p. 328)
index of sustainable growth (p. 326)
leverage ratios (p. 320)
liquidity ratios (p. 320)
operating cash flow (p. 326)

prime interest rate (p. 328)
profitability ratios (p. 320)
ratio analysis (p. 320)
strategic audit worksheet (p. 329)
World Wide Web (p. 321)
Z-value (p. 321)

Strategic Practice Exercise

Convert the following two years of income statements from the Maytag Corporation into common-size state- ments. The dollar figures are in thousands. What does converting to a common-size reveal?

	1992	%	1991	%
Net sales	$3,041,223		$2,970,626	
Cost of sales	2,339,406	_____	2,254,221	_____
Gross profits	701,817		716,405	
Selling, general, and admin. expenses	528,250		524,898	
Reorganization expenses	95,000	_____	—	_____
Operating income	78,567		191,507	
Interest expense	(75,004)		(75,159)	
Other—net	3,983	_____	7,069	_____
Income before taxes and accounting changes	7,546		123,417	
Income taxes	(15,900)		(44,400)	
Income before accounting changes	(8,354)		79,017	
Effects of accounting changes for post-retirement benefits	(307,000)	_____	—	_____
Net income (loss)	$ (315,354)		$ 79,017	

RESOURCES FOR CASE LIBRARY RESEARCH

Company Information

1. Annual Reports
2. *Moody's Manuals on Investment* (a listing of companies within certain industries that contains a brief history and a five-year financial statement of each company)
3. Securities and Exchange Commission Annual Report Form 10-K (annually) and 10-Q (quarterly)
4. Standard and Poor's *Register of Corporations, Directors, and Executives*
5. Value Line's *Investment Survey*
6. *Findex: The Directory of Market Research Reports, Studies and Surveys* (a listing by Find/SVP of over 11,000 studies conducted by leading research firms)
7. *COMPUSTAT, Compact Disclosure, CD/International,* and *Hoover's Online Corporate Directory* (computerized operating and financial information on thousands of publicly held corporations)
8. Shareholders Meeting Notices.

Economic Information

1. Regional statistics and local forecasts from large banks
2. *Business Cycle Development* (Department of Commerce)
3. Chase Econometric Associates' publications
4. U.S. Census Bureau publications on population, transportation, and housing
5. *Current Business Reports* (U.S. Department of Commerce)
6. *Economic Indicators* (U.S. Joint Economic Committee)
7. *Economic Report of the President to Congress*
8. *Long-Term Economic Growth* (U.S. Department of Commerce)
9. *Monthly Labor Review* (U.S. Department of Labor)
10. *Monthly Bulletin of Statistics* (United Nations)
11. *Statistical Abstract of the United States* (U.S. Department of Commerce)
12. *Statistical Yearbook* (United Nations)
13. *Survey of Current Business* (U.S. Department of Commerce)
14. *U.S. Industrial Outlook* (U.S. Department of Defense)
15. *World Trade Annual* (United Nations)
16. *Overseas Business Reports* (by country, published by U.S. Department of Commerce)

Industry Information

1. Analyses of companies and industries by investment brokerage firms
2. *Business Week* (provides weekly economic and business information, and quarterly profit and sales rankings of corporations)
3. *Fortune* (each April publishes listings of financial information on corporations within certain industries)
4. *Industry Survey* (published quarterly by Standard and Poor's Corporation)
5. *Industry Week* (late March/early April issue provides information on 14 industry groups)
6. *Forbes* (mid-January issue provides performance data on firms in various industries)
7. *Inc.* (May and December issues give information on fast-growing entrepreneurial companies)

Directory and Index Information on Companies and Industries

1. *Business Periodical Index* (on computer in many libraries)
2. *Directory of National Trade Associations*
3. *Encyclopedia of Associations*
4. Funk and Scott's *Index of Corporations and Industries*
5. Thomas's *Register of American Manufacturers*
6. *Wall Street Journal Index*

Ratio Analysis Information

1. *Almanac of Business and Industrial Financial Ratios* (Prentice-Hall)
2. *Annual Statement Studies* (Robert Morris Associates)
3. *Dun's Review* (Dun and Bradstreet; published annually in September-December issues)
4. *Industry Norms and Key Business Ratios* (Dun and Bradstreet)

On-Line Information

1. *Hoover's Online*—Financial statements and profiles of public companies *(http://www.hoovers.com)*
2. *U.S. Securities & Exchange Commission*—Official filings of public companies in Edgar database *(http://www.sec.gov)*
3. *Fortune 500*—Statistics for largest U.S. corporations *(http://www.pathfinder.com)*
4. *Dun & Bradstreet's Online*—Short reports on 10 million public and private U.S. companies *(http://www.dbisna.com/dnb/dnbhome.htm)*
5. *Ecola's 24-Hour Newsstand*—Links to web sites of 2,000 newspapers, journals, and magazines *(http://www.ecola.com/news)*
6. *Competitive Intelligence Guide*—Information on company resources *(http://www.fuld.com)*
7. *The Economist*—Provides international information and surveys *(http://www.economist.com)*
8. *Web 100*—Information on 100 largest U.S. and international companies *(http://www.w100.com)*.
9. *Nyenrode University* of the Netherlands— Provides European business information *(http://www.nyenrode.nl)*.
10. *Bloomberg*—Information on interest rates, stock prices, currency conversion rates, and other general financial information *(http://www.bloomberg.com)*

SUGGESTED CASE ANALYSIS METHODOLOGY USING THE STRATEGIC AUDIT

1. READ CASE

First Reading of the Case

- Develop a general overview of the company and its external environment.

- Begin a list of the possible strategic factors facing the company at this time.

- List the research information you may need on the economy, industry, and competitors.

2. READ THE CASE WITH THE STRATEGIC AUDIT

Second Reading of the Case

- Read the case a second time using the strategic audit as a framework for in-depth analysis. (See Table 10.5. on pages 252–259.) You may want to make a copy of the strategic audit work-sheet (Figure 14.1) to use to keep track of your comments as you read the case.

- The questions in the strategic audit parallel the strategic decision making process shown in Figure 1.3 (pages 20–21).

- The audit provides you with a conceptual framework to examine the company's mission, objectives, strategies, and policies as well as problems, symptoms, facts, opinions, and issues.

- Perform a financial analysis of the company using ratio analysis (see Table 14.1) and do the calculations necessary to convert key parts of the financial statements to a common-size basis.

3. DO OUTSIDE RESEARCH

Library and On-line Computer Services

- Each case has a decision date indicating when the case actually took place. Your research should be based on the time period for the case.

- See Appendix 14.A for resources for case research. Your research should include information about the environment at the time of the case. Find average industry ratios. You may also want to obtain further information regarding competitors and the company itself (10-K forms and annual reports). This information should help you conduct an industry analysis. Check with your instructor to see what kind of outside research is appropriate for your assignment.

- Don't try to learn what actually happened to the company discussed in the case. What management actually decided may not be the best solution. It will certainly bias your analysis and will probably cause your recommendation to lack proper justification.

4. BEGIN SWOT ANALYSIS

External Environmental Analysis: EFAS

- Analyze the four societal forces to see what trends are likely to affect the industry(s) in which the company is operating.

- Conduct an industry analysis using Porter's competitive forces from Chapter 3. Develop an Industry Matrix (Table 3.3 on page 71).

- Generate 8–10 external factors. These should be the *most important* opportunities and threats facing the company at the time of the case.

- Develop an EFAS Table, as shown in Table 3.3, for your list of external strategic factors.

- **Suggestion:** Rank the 8–10 factors from most to least important. Start by grouping the 3 top factors and then the 3 bottom factors.

Internal Organizational Analysis: IFAS

- Generate 8–10 internal factors. These should be the *most important* strengths and weaknesses of the company at the time of the case.

- Develop an IFAS Table, as shown in Table 4.2 (page 102), for your list of internal strategic factors.

- **Suggestion:** Rank the 8–10 factors from most to least important. Start by grouping the 3 top factors and then the 3 bottom factors.

5. WRITE YOUR STRATEGIC AUDIT: PARTS I–IV

First Draft of Your Strategic Audit

- Review the student-written audit of an old Maytag case in Appendix 14.C for an example.

- Write Parts I–IV of the strategic audit. Remember to include the factors from your IFAS and IFAS Tables in your audit.

6. WRITE YOUR STRATEGIC AUDIT: PART V

Strategic Factor Analysis Summary: SFAS

- Condense the list of factors from the 16–20 identified in your EFAS and IFAS Tables to only the 8-10 most important factors.

- Select the most important EFAS and IFAS factors. Reconsider the weights of each. The weights still need to add to 1.0.

- Develop a SFAS Table, as shown in Figure 5.1 (page 109), for your final list of strategic factors. Although the weights (indicating the importance of each factor) will probably change from the EFAS and IFAS Tables, the numerical rating (1–5) of each factor should remain the same. These ratings are your assessment of management's performance on each factor.

- This is a good time to reexamine what you wrote earlier in Parts I–IV. You may want to add to or delete some of what you wrote. Ensure that each one of the strategic factors you have included in your SFAS Table is discussed in the appropriate place in Parts I–IV. Part V of the audit is *not* the place to mention a strategic factor for the first time.

- Write Part V of your strategic audit. This completes your SWOT analysis.

- This is the place to suggest a revised mission statement and a better set of objectives for the company. The SWOT analysis coupled with revised mission and objectives for the company set the stage for the generation of strategic alternatives.

7. WRITE YOUR STRATEGIC AUDIT: PART VI

Strategic Alternatives and Recommendation

A. Alternatives
- Develop around three mutually exclusive strategic alternatives. If appropriate to the case you are analyzing, you might propose one alternative for growth, one for stability, and one for retrenchment. Within each corporate strategy, you should probably propose an appropriate business/competitive strategy. You may also want to include some functional strategies where appropriate.

- Construct a scenario for each alternative. Use the data from your outside research to project general societal trends (GDP, inflation, and so on) and industry trends. Use these as the basis of your assumptions to write pro forma financial statements (particularly income statements) for each strategic alternative for the next five years.

- List pros and cons for each alternative based on your scenarios.

B. Recommendation
- Specify which one of your alternative strategies you recommend. Justify your choice in terms of dealing with the strategic factors you listed in Part V of the audit.

- Develop policies to help implement your strategies.

8. WRITE YOUR STRATEGIC AUDIT: PART VII

Implementation

- Develop programs to implement your recommended strategy.

- Specify who is to be responsible for implementing each program and how long each program will take to complete.

- Refer to the pro forma financial statement you developed earlier for your recommended strategy. Do the numbers still make sense? If not, this may be a good time to rethink the budget numbers to reflect your recommended programs.

9. WRITE YOUR STRATEGIC AUDIT: PART VIII

Evaluation and Control

- Specify the type of evaluation and controls that you need to ensure that your recommendation is carried out successfully. Specify who is responsible for monitoring these controls.
- Indicate if sufficient information is available to monitor how the strategy is being implemented. If not, suggest a change to the information system.

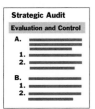

10. PROOF AND FINE-TUNE YOUR AUDIT

Final Draft of Your Strategic Audit

- Check to ensure that your audit is within the page limits of your professor. You may need to cut some parts and expand others.
- Make sure that your recommendation clearly deals with the strategic factors.
- Attach your EFAS, IFAS, and SFAS Tables plus your ratio analysis and pro forma statements. Label them as numbered exhibits and refer to each of them within the body of the audit.
- Proof your work for errors. If on a computer, use a spell checker.

Special Note: Depending on your assignment, it is relatively easy to use the strategic audit you have just developed to write a written case analysis in essay form or to make an oral presentation. The strategic audit is just a detailed case analysis in an outline form and can be used as the basic framework for any sort of case analysis and presentation.

EXAMPLE OF STUDENT-WRITTEN STRATEGIC AUDIT

For 1993 Maytag Corporation Case

I. CURRENT SITUATION

A. Financial Performance—Currently poor, high debt load, first losses since 1920s, and price/earnings ratio negative.

B. Strategic Posture

1. **Mission**—Developed in 1989 for the Maytag Company: "To provide our customers with products of unsurpassed performance that last longer, need fewer repairs, and are produced at the lowest possible cost." Updated in 1991: "Our collective mission is world class quality." This expands Maytag's longstanding belief in product quality to all aspects of our operations.

2. **Objectives**—"To be profitability leader in industry for every product line Maytag manufactures." Choose increased profitability rather than market share. "To be number one in total customer satisfaction," and to "Grow the North American appliance business and become the third largest appliance manufacturer (in unit sales) in North America." Increase profitable market share growth in North American appliance and floor care business, 6.5% return on sales, 10% return on assets, 20% return on equity, beat competition in satisfying customers, dealer, builder and endorser, move into third place in total units shipped per year.

3. **Strategies**—Global growth through acquisition, and alliance with Bosch Siemens, consolidate dealer bases, preserve individual strong quality brand names as competitive advantage, but create synergy between companies, product improvement, investment in plant and equipment.

4. **Policies**—Maytag quality is the standard for the industry; although one goal is to make customer satisfaction second to none, policy to speed delivery is "in process," and Maytag is slow to respond to change in the marketplace or changes in consumer desires.

II. STRATEGIC MANAGERS

A. Board—Fourteen members, of whom 11 are outsiders. Well-respected Americans, most of whom have served on this board since 1986 or earlier...time for a change?

B. Top Management—Promoting from within results in a board that is knowledgeable and experienced in the appliance industry, but no one especially skilled in international business (Asian or Latin American affairs) is on the board—could be a problem.

III. EXTERNAL ENVIRONMENT (*EFAS* see Exhibit 1)

A. Societal environment is unstable but recession is ending, consumer confidence is growing, could increase spending for appliances.

1. North American market mature, but vigilant consumers still want value for money in safe, environmentally sound products—Maytag can do this.

2. NAFTA, European Union, and other regional trade pacts are opening doors to markets in Europe, Asia, Latin America, that offer enormous potential—economy truly becoming global in nature.

B. **Task Environment** very competitive, dominated by Big Global Conglomerates

1. Whirlpool and AB Electrolux have enormous resources and truly global presence.

2. Technology and materials used in manufacture same around the world, no comparative advantage, increased use of robotics.

3. European design impacting everything, as is consumer desire for technologically advanced appliances using fuzzy logic.

4. Quality and safety regulations standardization becoming reality.

5. Super retailers are more important as a distribution channel, mom and pop dealers less.

IV. INTERNAL ENVIRONMENT (*IFAS* see Exhibit 2)

A. Corporate Structure

1. Present structure is conglomerate of appliance manufacturing and vending machine companies in America and Europe, and a loose purchasing alliance with the German firm of Bosch Siemens.

2. Decisions of major impact result from strategic plans made in Newton, Iowa, by Maytag Corporation by corporate staff, with a timeline of about three years.

B. Corporate Culture

1. Quality is the key ingredient and a commitment to quality is shared by executives and workers.

2. Much of corporate culture is based on founder F. L. Maytag's personal philosophy, including concern for quality, employees, local community, innovation, and performance.

C. Corporate Resources

1. **Marketing** efforts streamlined to make them more profitable, combining three sales forces into two, to concentrate on major retailers (took $95 million in charges to do this reconstructing). Hoover also had well-publicized marketing fiasco involving airline tickets.

2. **Finance (see Exhibits 4 and 5)**—Although revenues are up slightly, operating income is down significantly and some key ratios are troubling, such as a 57% debt/asset ratio, 132% long-term debt/equity ratio. Not to mention the fact that net income is 400% less than 1988, based on common-size income statements.

3. **R&D**—Maytag appears to have become a follower, taking far too long to get product innovations to market (competitors put out more in last 6 months than prior 2 years combined) lagging in fuzzy logic and other technological areas.

4. **Operations**—Is where Maytag shines, and continual improvement process kept it dominant in the U.S. market for many years—it's just not enough now.

5. **Human Resources**—Labor relations are strained, with two salary raise delays, and layoffs of 4500 employees from Magic Chef. The unions express concern at new, more distant tone from Maytag Corporation since 1989.

6. **Information Systems** are not mentioned in this case, which makes the reader surmise they are not used efficiently, if at all. It represents another critical area where Maytag seems unwilling or unable to commit resources needed to stay competitive.

V. ANALYSIS OF STRATEGIC FACTORS (*SFAS* see Exhibit 3)

A. Key strategic factors are:

1. Financially Maytag does not have the resources of its competitors, so it must forge alliances with someone (like Bosch Siemens) who does in order to compete in the global market.

2. Technologically Maytag has caught up with everyone else in terms of manufacturing capability, but product design and customer service innovation are areas of serious weakness.

3. Evaluation and control issues, directly related to MIS areas, are only going to become more crucial as the company plants become flung all over the planet. (The Hoover Europe fiasco could happen again!)

4. The good reputation of the Maytag name will continue to serve the company well in North America, quality still is a key factor.

B. Current Mission and Objectives:

1. Current mission appears appropriate.

2. Some of the objectives are really goals and need to be quantified and given time horizons.

VI. STRATEGIC ALTERNATIVES AND RECOMMENDED STRATEGY

A. Strategic Alternatives

1. **Growth Through Concentric Diversification**: Acquire a company in a related industry like commercial appliances.

   a. **Pros:** Product/market synergy created by acquisition of related company.

   b. **Cons:** Maytag does not have the financial resources to play this game.

2. **Pause Strategy**: Consolidate various acquisitions to find economies and to encourage innovation among the business units.

   a. **Pros:** Maytag needs to get its financial house in order and get administrative control over its recent acquisitions.

   b. **Cons:** Unless it can grow through a stronger alliance with Bosch Siemens or some other backer, Maytag is a prime candidate for takeover because of its poor financial performance in recent years and it is suffering from the initial reduction in efficiency inherent in this external growth strategy.

3. **Retrenchment**: Sell Hoover's foreign major home appliance businesses (Australia and UK) to emphasize increasing market share in North America.
   a. **Pros**: Divesting Hoover will improve the bottom line and enable Maytag Corp. to focus on the U.S. while Whirlpool, Electrolux, and GE are battling elsewhere.
   b. **Cons**: Maytag may be giving up its only opportunity to become a player in the coming global appliance industry.

B. **Recommended Strategy**
   1. I recommend the pause strategy, at least for a year, so Maytag can get a grip on its European operation and consolidate the companies it has in a more synergistic way.
   2. Maytag quality must be maintained and continued shortage of operating capital will take its toll, so investment must be made in R&D.
   3. Maytag may be able to make the Hoover U.K. investment work better since the recession is ending and the E.C. countries are closer to integrating than ever before.
   4. Because it is only an average competitor, Maytag needs the Hoover link to Europe to provide a jumping off place for negotiations with Bosch Siemens that could strengthen their alliance.

VII. IMPLEMENTATION

A. The only way to increase profitability in North America is to further involve Maytag with the superstore retailers, sure to anger the independent dealers, but necessary for Maytag to compete.

B. Board members with more global business experience should be recruited with an eye toward the future, especially with expertise in Asia and Latin America.

C. R&D needs to be improved, as does marketing, to get new products on line quickly. IS functions need to be developed for speedier evaluation and control.

VIII. EVALUATION AND CONTROL

A. While the question of controls vs. autonomy is "under review," another Hoover fiasco may easily be brewing.

B. The acquired companies do not all share the Midwestern work ethic or the Maytag Corporation culture and Maytag's managers must inculcate these values into all the new employees.

C. Systems should be developed to decide if the size and location of Maytag manufacturing plants is still correct and to plan for the future; industry analysis indicates that smaller automated plants may be more efficient now than in the past.

Note: The following exhibits were originally attached in their entirety to this strategic audit, but for reasons of space only their titles are listed here:
Exhibit 1: EFAS Table
Exhibit 2: IFAS Table
Exhibit 3: SFAS Table
Exhibit 4: Ratio Analysis for 5 Years
Exhibit 5: Common-size Income Statements

Notes

1. J. A. Sasseen, "Are Profits Shakier Than They Look?" *Business Week* (August 5, 1996), pp. 54–55.
2. J. Fulkerson, "How Investors Use Annual Reports," *American Demographics* (May 1996). Cited from American Demographics web site.
3. M. S. Fridson, *Financial Statement Analysis* (New York: John Wiley & Sons, 1991), pp. 192–194.
4. D. H. Bangs, *Managing by the Numbers* (Dover, N. H.: Upstart Publications, 1992), pp. 106–107.
5. J. M. Laderman, "Earnings, Schmernings Look at the Cash," *Business Week* (July 24, 1989), pp. 56–57.
6. J. Warner, "21st Century Capitalism: Snapshot of the Next Century," *Business Week* (November 18, 1994), p. 194.

Name Index

A

A.C. Nielsen Co., 72
Abdelsamad, M. H., 324
Abraham, S., 23
Ackelsberg, R., 303
Addison Wesley Longman, 280, 281, 327
Adidas, 61
Admiral, 5, 42, 92, 217, 219
Adolph Coors Company, 68
Advanced Micro Devices (AMD), 36, 268
Aerospatiale, 125, 141
Affrim, H., 262
Ainuddin, R., 262
Ajax Continental, 185, 218, 220
Akerson, D., 175
Alamo Rent-A-Car, 115
Alcatel-Alsthom NV, 91
Alcon Laboratories, 291
Aldred, D., 53
Aldred, M., 53
Alexander, J. A., 317
Alexander, K., 281
Alexander, L. D., 204
Alexander, M., 152, 155, 158
All Business Network, 327
Alley, J., 131, 303
Allied Corporation, 134
Allied Signal, 134, 319
Almanac of Business and Industrial Financial Ratios, 335
Alpert, M., 303
Alta Vista, 327
Altman, E, 325
Alto, 95
Amana, 165
Amason, A. C., 181
Amburgey, T. L., 204
America Online, Inc. (AOL), 1, 2, 13, 14, 15, 18
American Airlines, 15
American Can Company, 67
American Cyanamid, 201
American Express, 102, 217, 283
American Heart Association (AHA), 305
American Hospital Supply (AHS), 100
American Productivity & Quality Center, 241
American Standard, 270, 280

Amoco Chemical, 169
AMR Corporation, 139
Anchor Steam, 292
Anderson, C. A., 158
Anderson, E., 302
Andrews, K. S., 131
Andrews, K. Z., 261, 282
Anheuser-Busch, 68, 123, 125, 127, 240
Annual Statement Studies, 335
Ansoff, H. I., 79
Apple Computer, Inc., 63, 95, 145, 161, 191, 240, 245, 300
Applegate, J., 304
Archer Daniels Midland (ADM), 124
Aristotle, 176
Arlow, P., 51, 303
Arm & Hammer Baking Soda, 159, 160, 162, 180
Aronloff, C. E., 303, 304
Arthur D. Little, 67, 267
Ascarelli, S., 262
Ascher, K., 317
Asea Brown Boveri (ABB), 90, 91, 201
Ash, M.K., 37
Ashley, B., 210
Associated Consultants International, 67
Association of South East Asian Nations (ASEAN), 7
AST Research, 118
Aston Martin, 117
AT&T, 122, 128, 161, 180, 211, 217, 236, 265
Atwater, H. B., 152
Aupperle, K.E., 51
Austin-Healey, 117
Aveni, R. A., 80
Avenue Technologies, 335
Avis, 206
Avon Products, 21, 72

B

B.F. Goodrich, 277
Bacon, D. C., 318
Baden-Fuller, C. W. F., 79
Bagley, C., 292, 303
Bain & Company, 241
Baird, I.S., 23
Baker, W. H., 303
Baldwin-United, 191
Baliga, B. R., 50

Balkin, D. B., 262
Ball, F., 102
Bangs, D. H., 344
Banker, R. D., 181
Bankers Trust of New York, 212
Banking Act of 1933, 33
Baptist Health Systems, 314
Bar, P. S., 181
Barkema, H., 158
Barker, III, V.L., 181
Barnevik, P., 91
Barney, J. B., 51, 82, 104, 124, 131
Barrett, A., 23
Barrett, C., 249
Bartholomew, D., 105
Bauerschmidt, A., 303
Baum, J.A.C., 50
Beach, C., 182, 184
Bechtel Group, 21
Beckstead, S. M., 282
Begun, J. W., 318
BellCore, 278
Belluzzo, R., 276
Ben & Jerry's Ice Cream, 41
Bend-Ems, 195
Beneton, 195
Benton, D. S., 328
Berenbeim, R. E., 50
Beresford, L., 202
Berle, A. D., 31
Bernoulli Box, 18
Betamax, 265
Bettis, R. A., 79, 158
Big Book, 327
Bigness, J., 181
Bijur, P., 201
Bill of Rights, 47
Birley, S., 303
Black Entertainment Television, Inc., 291
Black, J. S., 228
Blackburn, V. L., 303
Blackmon, D. A., 181
Bleakley, F. R., 180
Bleeke, J., 131
Blodgett, L. L., 131
Body Shop, The, 289, 291, 324
Boeing, 12, 98, 141
Boeker, W., 228
Boltz, P. W., 321
Bond, M. H., 223, 228
Boroughs, D. L., 105

Borsse, S., 1, 2
Bose Corporation, 169
Boskin Commission, 321
Boston Pops Orchestra, 315
Boston Symphony, 315
Boulton, W. R., 303
Bower, J. L., 281
Bowers, B., 303
Boyd, B. K., 79
Boynton, A. C., 180
Bracker, J. S., 303
Bradford, M., 261
Brady, A., 281
Brady Bunch, 56
Brancato, C. K., 261
Brastemp, 168
Bremner, B., 131
Bridgestone, 142
Briggs, K., 225
British Aerospace, 125, 141
British Airways, 315
British Home Stores, 210
British Petroleum, 85, 136, 324
Broome, J. T., 303
Brull, S.V., 281
Brunswick, 55
Bruton, G. D., 228
Buck, G., 131
Buenos Aires Embotelladora S.A., 183
Buick, 89, 213, 214
Burck, C., 294, 304
Burgelman, R. A., 275, 277, 282
Burger King, 57
Burton, T. M., 131, 224, 228
Busch Gardens, 56
Business Cycle Development, 334
Business Environment Risk Index, 67
Business International, 67
Business Periodical Index, 335
Business Roundtable, 45
Businessland, 128, 161
BusinessLink, 180
Butler, R. J., 24
Bygrave, W. D., 304
Byrne, J.A., 180

C

Cadillac, 89
Caggiano, C., 304
California Public Employees' Retirement System (CALPERS), 26, 34
Campbell, A., 50, 152, 155, 158
Cannavino, J., 229
Cannella, A.S., 228
Cardinal, L.B., 23

Carland, J.A.C., 303
Carland, J. W., 303
Carnival Cruise Lines, 43, 55
Carper, W. B., 158
Carroll, A., 39, 40, 45, 51
Carroll, P. B., 261
Case, S., 18
Casey's General Stores, 106, 116, 177
Castro, J., 303
Cavanagh, G.F., 51
Caves, R. E., 131
CD/International, 320, 334
Celestial Seasonings, 23
Chalmers, J., 202
Chan, P. S., 281
Chandler, A., 187, 204, 209
Charan, R., 51
Charles Schwab, 131
Charmin, 155
Chase Econometric Associates, 334
Chase Manhattan Corporation, 35
Chatterjee, S., 158
Chawla, S. K., 261
Cheerios, 62
Chefs Unlimited, 53
Chesapeake & Ohio, 217
Chevrolet, 88
Children's Television Workshop, 315
Chinta, R., 281
Choudhury, N., 158
Chrisman, J. J., 303
Christensen, C. M., 281
Chrysler Corporation, 15, 31, 98, 99, 110, 166, 194, 266, 274, 275
Church & Dwight, 110, 159, 160, 162, 180
Churchill, N. C., 295, 298, 299, 304
Chussil, M. J., 281
Clark, D., 177, 262
Clark, L.H., 50
Clark, S. M., 79
Clayton Act, 33
Clinton, W., 43
Clorox Company, 124
Coase, R., 137
Coca-Cola, 182, 184, 202, 236, 237, 244
Cohen, B., 210
Cohen, W. M., 282
Colgate-Palmolive, 41, 160, 162, 273
Collins, S., 318
Collis, D. J., 158
Colt Manufacturing, 191
Columbia-Presbyterian Medical Center, 314
Comet, 124

Common Market, 7
Communications Workers of America, 99
Compact Disclosure, 320, 334
Compaq Computer, 63, 118, 143, 145
Competitive Intelligence Guide, 335
Comptronix, 128, 161
CompUSA, 164
COMPUSTAT, 320, 334
ConAgra, 176
Conference Board, 50
Conoco, 136
Construcciones Aeronáuticas, 125, 141
Consumer Price Index (CPI), 321
Continental Airlines, 171
Converse, 61
Cooper, A. C., 303, 304
Coopers and Lybrand, 283
Corfam, 263
Corning, Inc., 198, 208
Corriher, S.E., 51
Cortese, A., 105
Cosby Show, 56
Cosco, J., 24
Cosier, R. A., 181
Cotsakos, C., 129
Council of Logistics Management, 170
Cover Girl, 134
Covin, J. G., 303
Cray, D., 24
CSX Corporation, 140, 217
Cullen, D., 290
Cummings, S., 24
Cummins Engine Co., 110, 270
Curran, J.J., 158
Cypress Semiconductor Corporation, 36
Cyrix Corporation, 122, 268

D

Dacin, T., 204
Daewoo Group, 15, 141, 156
Daily, C.M., 50
Dale, K., 169
Dalton, D. R., 50
Daniels, J. D., 262
Danjou, T., 270
Darling, B. L., 261
Dart Industries of Maryland, 41
Davies, J., 24
D'Aveni, R. A., 8, 23, 69, 70, 120, 121, 131
Davis, B., 303
Davis, R. H., 317
Davis, S.M., 193, 205

Davis, T. R. V., 261
Dayton Hudson, 21, 28, 41
Dean Foods Company, 128, 129, 166
Dean, H., 128, 166
Dean, J.W., 24
Dell Computer Corporation, 56, 63, 118, 143, 145, 245
Dell, M., 143
Deloitte & Touche Consulting Group, 59
Delta Airlines, 15, 16, 102
Demb, A., 50
Deming, W. E., 169
Denis, J., 317
Dependable Drive, 272
DePont Merck Pharmaceutical Company, 127
Despres, C., 79
Deutsche Aerospace, 125, 141
Deutschman, A., 281
Devanna, M.A., 228
Diamond Multimedia Systems, 192
Directory of National Trade Associations, 335
DiStephano, J. J., 131
Dixie-Narco, 42
Dixon, L., 169
Dobrzynski, J. H., 50
Doll Collection, The, 202
Domino's, 119
Donaldson, G., 262
Donnelly, S. B., 105
Dormann, J., 32
DOS, 70
Dougherty, D., 282, 303
Douma, S., 158
Dow Jones, 168
Drazin, R., 227
Drucker, P. F., 142, 290, 303, 305, 317
Due, T., 180
Duffs, 302
Dumaine, B., 104, 181
Dun's Review, 335
Dun & Bradstreet, 284, 303, 335
DuPont Company, 127, 128, 136, 161, 170, 187, 188, 190, 233, 263, 274, 276
Durant, W., 191

E

E*Trade Group, Inc., 130
Eastern Airlines, 171, 191
Eastman Kodak Company, 25, 37, 38, 128, 161
Eckberg, J., 224
Ecola, 335
Economist, The, 335

Eddie Bauer, 43
Edgar, 320, 327
Edwards, K., 18
Eisenhardt, K. M., 31
El-Namacki, M.S.S., 303
Electrolux (AB), 30, 66, 120, 126, 139, 141, 213, 324, 327
Eli Lily, 236
Ellison, K., 188
Elsass, P. M., 181
Elstrom, P., 228
Emerson, R. E., 317
Encyclopaedia Britannica, Inc., 19
Encyclopedia of Associations, 335
Energizer, 186
Eng, P., 23
England, G.W., 51
Enterprise Rent-A-Car, 206
Entrepreneur's Guide to Business Law, The, 292
Erhardt, W., 207
Erickson, 281
Ernst, D., 131
Ernst Institutional Research, 319
Essentials of Strategic Management, 280
Estee Lauder, 56
Ethics Resource Center, 43
European Community, 7
European Union (EU), 6, 7, 57, 242, 243, 331, 332
Eveready, 186
Excel, 62, 172
Export Hotline & Trade Bank, 67, 328

F

Fahey, L., 131, 303
Fang, Y., 199
Fannin, W. R., 262
Farkas, C. M., 228
Farnsworth, C., 293, 294
Farrell, C., 304
Federal Express (FedEX), 63, 100, 170, 179, 245
Feeser, H. R., 304
Fennell, M. L., 317
Ferland, C. A., 281
Ferlie, E., 317
Fiat, 142
Fidelity Investments, 131
Fiegenbaum, A., 79
Field, J. M., 181
Fields, D., 285, 303
Findex:, 334
FIND/SVP, 72
Finkelstein, S., 50
Finsbury Data Services, 72

Fireman's Fund Insurance, 82
Firestone Tire & Rubber, 142
Fishburn, D., 7, 329
Fisher, A. B., 261
Fisher, G., 26, 37, 38, 134
Fleisher, C., 51
Fletcher, J., 79
Flexible, 302
Fluorware, Inc., 276
Flynn, E. J., 281
Flynn, J., 210
Fobrun, C. J., 228
Fogg, C.D., 51
Ford, H., 85, 136, 191
Ford Motor Company, 110, 111, 133, 165, 191, 266, 270, 275
Ford of Britain, 200
Formichelli, J., 145
Forta, J., 319
Foster, M.J., 303
Foster, R., 95
Fowler, K. L., 265
Fowler, V., 303
Frank J. Zamboni & Company, 110
Frank, R., 180, 204, 224, 228
Franko, L. D., 281
Fraser, D., 59
Freedman, D. H., 281
Freeman, R. E., 51, 236
Freundlich, N., 282
Fridson, M. S., 344
Friedland, J., 204
Friedman, M., 36, 39, 40, 51
Frigidaire, 141
Froelich, K. A., 317
Frost and Sullivan, 67
Fuchsberg, G., 261
Fujitsu Ltd., 171
Fulk, J., 79
Fulkerson, J., 344
Fun-Zone, 283

G

GAAP, 325
Gable, M., 51
Gadella, J. W., 204
Galante, S. P., 303
Galaxy, 327
Galbraith, C.S., 181, 262
Galbraith, J. R., 85, 104, 282
Garcia, J., 263
Garud, R., 281
Garvin, D. A., 23, 119
Gates, W., 37, 70, 202
Gateway 2000, 63, 115, 118, 145, 164
Gebelein, C., 23

GEC, 66
General Electric (GE), 3, 4, 14, 35, 66, 91, 98, 120, 125, 126, 139, 149, 162, 165, 170, 177, 190, 208, 211, 236, 237, 240, 251, 297
General Foods, 89
General Mills, 62, 72, 152, 265
General Motors, 28, 88, 111, 125, 126, 136, 146, 176, 187, 188, 190, 191, 192, 213, 214, 215, 223, 237, 275
Geocowets, G., 170
Georgia-Pacific, 169, 236
Gerber, 265
Geringer, J. M., 131
Gerlach, M. L., 50
Gerstner, L., 145
Ghemawat, P., 131
Giampapa, D., 283, 286
Gifford, K.L., 42, 43
Gilbert, D.R., 51
Gillette, 83, 84, 265
Gillooly, B., 158
Gimeno-Gason, F. J., 304
Ginsberg, A., 275, 282
Gioia, D. A., 79
Girl Scouts, 313
Gladwin, T. N., 79
Glain, S., 270
Glass, H. E., 158, 180, 181, 304, 317
Global Information Solutions (GIS), 217
Gluck, F.W., 23
Godrej & Boyce, 126
Goizueta, R., 237
Gomes, L., 18
Gomez-Mejia, L. R., 262
Goodman, J., 228, 276
Goodyear Tire & Rubber, 245
Goold, M., 152, 155, 158
Gopinath, C., 228
Gordo, 302
Gordon, G. G., 228
Gormley, D., 36
Goulet, P. G., 117
Govindarajan, V., 261
Grant, L., 38, 82, 158
Grant, R. M., 104
Graves, S. B., 281
Greco, J., 79
Greising, D., 16
Griffin, R. W., 199
Grimm, C.M., 23, 227
Grossman, L. M., 79
Grove, A., 37, 129, 168, 169, 177
Grover, R., 281
Gruner, S., 304

GTE Superpages, 327
Gulati, R., 281
Gupta, U., 304
Guth, W.D., 51, 79, 275, 282
Guyon, J., 91

H

Hackman, J. R., 199
Hadley, L., 5, 92, 126, 165, 219, 247
Haeckel, S. H., 79
Hall, E. H., 281
Hallmark, 265
Halpern, M. T., 317
Hambrick, D. C., 50
Hamel, G., 180, 281
Hamermesh, R. G., 158
Hames, D. S., 105
Hammer, M., 197
Hansen, M.H., 51
Harback, H.F., 228
Hardee's, 67
Hardwick Stove Company, 5, 42, 194
Hardy, C., 282
Harley-Davidson, 198, 212
Harrell, G. D., 158
Harrigan, K. R., 136, 158
Harrison, D. A., 181
Harrison, J. S., 158, 268, 281, 282
Hatfield, J.D., 51
Hatten, K. J., 79, 298, 299, 304
Hatten, M. L., 79
Hayes, D., 191, 192
Hayes Microcomputer Products, 191, 192
Health Midwest, 314
Healthy Choice, 176
Hedley, B., 158
Heene, A., 180
Hefei Rongshida Group Corporation (RSD), 126
Hegel, 176
Hellriegel, D., 227
Henderson, P., 292
Henkoff, R., 131, 227
Herron, L., 303
Hertz, 206
Hewlett-Packard, 14, 36, 89, 125, 132, 133, 145, 169, 233, 271, 276, 278, 327
Hickson, D. J., 24
Higgins, J.M., 235
Hill, C. W. L., 262
Hill, G. C., 281
Himelstein, L., 131
Hitt, M. A., 158, 180, 228, 268, 281, 282

Hodgetts, R. M., 228, 262
Hoechst AG, 30, 315
Hoerr, J., 227
Hof, R. D., 158, 281, 282, 304
Hofer, C. W., 273, 274, 292, 294, 295, 303
Hoffron, F., 317
Hofstede, G., 222, 223, 228
Holstein, B., 79
Holstein, W. J., 131
Honda, 118, 142
Honeywell, 129, 169
Hoover, 5, 6, 42, 66, 139, 141, 147, 223, 246
Hoover Europe, 223, 247
Hoover's Online Corporate Directory, 72, 320, 327, 328, 334, 335
Hoover, R., 198, 208
Hormozi, A. M., 261
Hornsby, J. S., 281
Hoskisson, R. E., 158, 268, 281, 282
Hotpoint, 66, 139
Hov, F., 303
Hovde, M.A., 158, 180, 181
Howell, W. H., 24
Hoyde, M. A., 304
Humane Society, 307
Hunger, J.D., 20, 71, 76, 102, 109, 174, 280, 309, 317, 331
Husey, D. E., 79, 131, 158, 204, 317
Hwang, P., 262
HyperCompetition, 8

I

IBM, 26, 62, 63, 70, 126, 143, 145, 154, 169, 171, 177, 188, 211, 212, 229, 230, 233, 266
Ibuka, M., 265
Ilinich, A.Y., 158
In Focus Systems, 136
In Search of Excellence, 248
Index of Corporations and Industries, 335
Industry Norms and Key Business Ratios, 335
Infoseek, 327
Ingersoll-Rand, 169
Inkpen, A., 158
Institute for Scientific Information, 278
Intel Corporation, 14, 37, 64, 83, 122, 125, 129, 176, 177, 265, 268, 269
Intercontinental Hotels, 171,
Internal Revenue Service (IRS), 214, 313
International Harvester, 191, 244

International Specialty Products, 274
International Standards Organization, 233, 259
International Strategies, 67
Internet, 327
Internet Explorer, 266, 327
Iomega Corporation, 17, 18
Ireland, R. D., 158
It's a Wonderful Life, 321
Ittner, C. D., 261
Iverson, A., 209
Ivey, M., 281
Izumi, H., 195

J

J.C. Penney Company, 19
J. Crew, 43
Jaguar, 117
Jahera, J. S., 31
James, B. J., 131
Java, 123, 266
Jenn-Air, 5, 42, 139, 165, 194
Jenster, P.V., 317
Jobs, S., 95, 191
Johns, G., 199
Johns-Manville, 191
Johnson & Johnson, 41, 155
Johnson Products, 146
Johnson, R. A., 282, 291
Johnson, W. A., 262
Jones Surplus, 185, 218
Jones, P., 24, 265
Judge, W. Q., 50
Jung, C., 225
Just Toys, 195

K

K2, 302
Kahaner, L., 24, 80, 265
Kaiser, J., 270
Kann, P., 168
Kant, I., 47, 51
Kanter, R. M., 127, 131, 317
Kaplan, R. S., 237, 261
Kapor, M., 294
Kargar, J., 303
Kaske, K., 268
Kaufman, S.P., 23
Kay-Bee Toy & Hobby Shops, 210
Kazanjian, R. K., 227
Keating, B.P., 317
Keating, M. O., 317
Keats, B. W., 228, 303
Keebler, 267
Keels, J.K., 228
Kelleher, H., 37, 249

Keller, J.J., 228
Kelley, B., 180
Kellogg Company, 162
Kelly, K., 131, 227, 281
Keogh, J., 51
Kernaghan, C., 43
Kerwin, K., 281
Kets de Vries, M., 304
Kevlar, 263
Khan, Z. U., 261
Kidney, J. A., 50
Kids Kab, 292
Kiefer, R. O., 158
Kilmann, R. H., 228
Kim, W. C., 262
Kimberly-Clark, 155
KinderCare Learning Centers, 157
Kinloch, J., 99
Kirin, 125
Kirkpatrick, D., 131
Kirsch, R. J., 262
Klassen, S., 302
Klein, H. E., 80
Kliman, D., 82
KLM, 140
Kmart, 43
Kohlberg, L., 44, 45, 51
Kohut, G.F., 51
Kono, T., 228
Koretz, G., 105, 329
Korn/Ferry International, 50
Kotler, P., 93
Kotulic, A. G., 24
Kraar, L., 24
Krause, A., 236
Krause, I., 279, 282
Kremer, L., 168
Krumm, D., 5, 42, 191, 194, 213
Kuczmarski & Associates, 264
Kumar, K., 51, 317
Kuratko, D.F., 23, 281
Kvinnsland, S., 224

L

Labatt, 125
Laderman, J. M., 344
Lamberti, D., 106
Lamont, B. T., 158
Land, E., 191
Langley, A., 317
Langowitz, N. S., 281
Lape, H. W., 131
Larcker, D. F., 261
Lasserre, P., 79
Lau, R. S. M., 23
Laura Ashley, 210

Lavender, L., 317
Lawrence, P. R., 193, 205
Lederman, L.L., 61
Lefvin, J. B., 282
Lehn, K., 261
Lei, D., 158, 162, 180
Lengnick-Hall, C. A., 282
Leontiades, M., 104
Leshin, C. B., 328
Leuchter, M., 181`
Lever Brothers, 160
Levi Strauss, 41, 168
Levin, R. I., 299, 300, 304
Levinthal, D. A., 282
Lewis, J., 218, 220
Lewis, V. L., 295, 304
Lickona, T., 51
Light, L., 50
Lindstrom, G., 79
Linneman, R. E., 80
Lipin, S., 158
Lipton, M., 51
Liu, J., 279, 282
Livingston, R., 170
L. L. Bean, 241
Logistics and Electronic Commerce, 180
Lon, H., 303
Lorange, P., 228
Lorsch, J. W., 51
Lotus Development Corporation, 172, 266, 294
Lozeau, D., 317
LTV Corporation, 145
Lubatkin, M., 158, 228
Lublin, J. S., 50, 51, 228, 261
Lucas, E., 74
Ludwig, P., 129
Luke, R. D., 318
Lussier, R. N., 303
Lyles, M.A., 23
Lynn, G. S., 281

M

M. F. Smith, 261
MacDonald, M., 165
Mack Trucks Inc., 260
Macy, B., 195
Macy's Department Stores, 191
Magic Chef, 5, 12, 42, 92, 139, 194, 217, 219, 247
Mahon, J. F., 131
Mahoney, J.T., 158
Makhiza, A. K., 261
Malekzadeh, A R., 228
Mallinckrodt Group, 28

Mallory, G.R., 24
Manco, Inc., 241
Mansfield, E., 281
Manzi, J., 294
Maremont, M., 304
Mariott, 169
Markides, C. C., 158
Marshall, M., 32
Martinez-Mont, L., 43, 51
Mary Clare, 280
Mary Kay Corporation, 37, 72
Maslow, 45
Massachusetts General Hospital, 315
Masterson, S. S., 228
Matshusita, 269
Mattimore B. W., 275
Maybelline, 56
Maytag Company, 14, 120, 128, 161,
    166, 194, 223, 275
Maytag Corporation, 5, 6, 11, 12, 13,
    41, 42, 65, 66, 76, 89, 90, 92, 101,
    107, 109, 111, 115, 116, 120, 125,
    126, 129, 139, 141, 164, 165, 191,
    194, 213, 217, 219, 246, 247, 272,
    275, 296, 297, 327, 329, 333, 340
Maytag, F. L., 92, 297
McCarthy, M. J., 104
McCartney, S., 104, 249
McDermott, D., 192
McDonald's, 41, 67, 170, 186, 279
McDougal, P. P., 303
McDowell, J., 303
McGill, M., 158
McGill, R., 317
MCI, 122
McKinsey and Company, 95, 149
McLaughlin, D. J., 51
McMurray, S., 276, 281
McWhirter, W., 303
McWilliams, B., 303
McWilliams G., 281
Mead Corporation, 28
Means, G. C., 31
Medley, G. J., 317
Melville Corporation, 210
Mendenhall, M., 228
Menon, K., 228
Mercedes-Benz, 116
Merck & Company, 127, 265
Mercosur (Mercosul), 7, 57
Merrill Lynch, 245
Merrill, G. B., 181
Metropolitan Museum of Art, 313
MG, 117
Michaels, C. E., 288
Micron, 136

Microsoft, 15, 37, 63, 70, 94, 110, 121,
    122, 180, 244, 266, 267, 271, 327
Miles, R. E., 68, 79
Miller Brewing Company, 68
Miller, C.C., 23
Miller, J., 263
Minow, N., 50
Mintzberg, H., 17, 18, 24, 85, 104, 286,
    303
Mitchell, W., 23
Mitsubishi Corporation, 214
Mitsubishi Trading Company, 67
Modelo, 125
Moesel, D. D., 282
Monks, A. G., 50
Monsanto, 146
Montagno, R.V., 281
Moody's Manuals on Investment, 334
Morgan, C., 117
Morgan, H. F. S., 117
Morgan Motor Car Company, 116, 117
Moriata, A., 264
Morone, J. G., 281
Morrison Knudsen, 128, 161
Mosakowski, E., 137
Mothercare Ltd., 210
Motorola, Inc., 26, 98, 134, 136, 177,
    208, 265, 266
Moyer, R. C., 50
Mrs. Fields Cookies, 285
Muir, N.K., 181
Mulford, C. L., 303
Mulvey, P. W., 181
Murphy, D., 228
Murray, E. A., 131
Myers, I., 225

N

Naffziger, D. W., 281
Nahavandi, A., 228
Naisbitt, J., 79, 158
Nare, B., 317
Nargundkar, R., 281
National, 206
National Association of College and
    University Business Officers, 314
National Cash Register (NCR), 98,
    217
National Energy Associates, 285
National Federation of Independent
    Business, 294
National Labor Committee Educa-
    tion Fund, 43
National Organization for Women, 215
National Science Foundation, 284
Navistar, 245

Nayak, P. R., 281, 282
Neff, T. J., 50
Nelson, E., 38
Neptune, 297
Nestlé, 201
Netscape Communications, 121, 122,
    123, 266, 267, 271, 327
Neubauer, F. F., 50
New York and Presbyterian Hospitals
    Health Care System, 314
New York Hospital—Cornell Medical
    Center, 314
New York Stock Exchange, 29
Newman, W. H., 131, 310, 317
Newport News Shipbuilding, 11
Nexel, 175
Nice, 302
Nielsen, R. P., 313, 314, 317, 318
Nijenrode University, 335
Nike, 6, 48, 61, 103, 116, 166, 195
Nissan, 118, 142
Nixon, R. D., 228
Nobody Beats the Wiz, 164
Nohria, N., 281
Nordstrom, 89
Norge, 42
Norman, J., 303
North American Free Trade Agree-
    ment (NAFTA), 7, 57
Northern Telecom, 98, 128, 161
Northwest Airlines, 31, 140
Norton, D. P., 237, 261
Novak, R. S., 180
Noxelle Corporation, 134
Nueno, P., 282
Nummi Corporation, 125
Nutrasweet, 64

O

O'Boyle, T. F., 281
O'Hara, P. D., 303
Ohmae, K., 58, 79
Ohsone, K., 266
Oil of Olay, 134
Oldham, G. R., 199
Oldsmobile, 89
Olive Garden, 67
Oliver, C., 50
Olson, E. M., 282
O'Neal, D., 50
O'Neill, M., 317
Oosterveld, J., 282
Oracle Corporation, 188, 271
O'Reilly, B., 104, 227, 228
Orion Pictures, 191
Orris, J.B., 23

OS/2 Warp, 70
Oster, S. M., 180
Oswald, S. L., 31
Overstreet, G. A., 317
Owens-Corning, 244, 245

P
Pabst Brewing Company, 68
Palo Alto Research Center (PARC), 94, 95
Pan Am Building, 171
Pan American Airlines, 171, 191
Pare, T. P., 261
Parish, W., 285
Parnell, J.A., 228, 303
Party HOLDems, 283
Pascale, R. T., 80
Pascarella, P., 97, 104
Pascual, E., 261, 262
Patterson, M. L., 271
Paulson, A.S., 281
Pearce II, J. A., 50, 158, 303
Pearson, J. N., 303
Pekar, P., 23
Pennings, J. M., 158
Pentium, 14, 83, 125, 168, 177, 268
Pepsico, 182, 183, 184, 202, 241
Peters, T. J., 248, 262
Petty, J. W., 304
Petty, K., 317
Petzinger, T., 23
Pfeffer, J., 317
Pharmacia AB, 223, 224
Pharmacia & Upjohn, Inc., 224
Phatak, A.V., 262
Philcor, 126
Phillips, D., 79
Pickton, D., 261
Pine, B. J., 104, 167, 180
Pittiglio Rapin Todd McGrath (PRTM), 278
Pitts, R. A., 228
Pizza Hut, 119
Platt, L., 132
Playto, 176
Pointer, D. C., 318
Pojman, L. P., 51
Polaroid Corporation, 171, 191, 236
Political System Stability Index, 67
Pollock, E.J., 36
Pontiac, 88
Poon, J.M.L., 262
Port, O., 281, 282
Porter, M. E., 60, 64, 65, 79, 80, 86, 87, 104, 113, 116, 118, 119, 122, 123, 131, 158, 167, 293

Powell, T. C., 228
Powell, W. W., 217, 317
Power, C., 210, 281
Prahalad, C. K., 79, 180, 281
Preece, S., 51
Priem, R. L., 181
Probert, J., 79
Procter & Gamble Company, 41, 58, 62, 72, 84, 85, 117, 124, 126, 134, 155, 160, 162, 188, 194, 209, 215
Provan, K. G., 318

Q
Qiana, 263
Quaker Oats, 236
Quinn, J. B., 19, 24, 85, 104, 162, 180, 303

R
R/3, 244
Radebaugh, J. L. H., 262
Radio Shack, 118
Rahim, A., 304
Rajan, M.V., 261
Ralston Purina, 186
Ramaswamy, K., 227
Ramsoomair, F., 227
Rao, R. S., 50
Rappaport, A., 117
Rasheed, A.M.A., 24
Raynor, M., 59
Raytheon, 66
Rebello, K., 23, 304
Rechner, P.L., 50, 51, 181
Redmond, W., 180
Reebok, 6, 45, 48, 61, 103, 195
Register of American Manufacturers, 335
Reichert, A., 158
Reimann, B. C., 158
Reinhardt, A., 281
Rensi, Edward, 170
Research Health Services, 314
Reynolds, M.A., 79
Richards, B., 105, 262
Richardson, J., 181
Richardson-Vicks, 134
Richmond, T., 181
Rickards, T., 292
Ricklefs, R., 304
Ring, P. S., 137
R.J. Reynolds Industries, 276
Roadway Logistics, 169
Robbins, D. K., 158
Robbins, S. M., 261
Robert, M., 281

Robichaux, M., 304
Robins, J., 158
Robinson, R. B., 303
Rock, A., 177
Rockwell International Corporation, 12
Roddick, A., 289, 291, 300
Rodgers, T. J., 36
Rodrigues, A. F., 262
Rolm and Haas, 28
Roman Catholic Church, 176
Romanelli, E., 24
Ross, D., 207
Ross, J., 181
Roth, K., 51, 228
Rothman, H., 242, 261
Rothschild, W. E., 227
Rousseau, D. M., 104
Roussel, 281
Rowe, D., 282
Royal Dutch Shell, 74, 136
RSD, 125
Rubbermaid, 241
Rudney, G., 317
Rumelt, R. P., 79, 158

S
Saab, 281
SABRE, 15, 139
Salancik, G. R., 317
Sanchez, R., 105
Sand, J., 302
Sandberg, W. R., 181, 292, 294, 295, 303
SAP AG, 244
Saporito, B., 79
Sasseen, J. A., 344
Saturn, 215, 275
Saxton, M. J., 228
Schacht, H., 110
Schendel, D. E., 79, 158, 274
Schiller, Z., 131
Schine, E., 262
Schlender, B. R., 281
Schmidt, D. R., 262
Schmidt, J.A., 232
Schneider, B., 104
Schonberger, R. J., 228
Schroeder, M., 282
Schroeder, R. G., 181
Schuman, M., 141
Schumpeter, J., 300
Schwartz, K. B., 228
Schwartz, M., 281
Schweiger, D. M., 181
Schwenk, C.R., 181

Scott Paper, 155
Sea-Land, 290
Seaboard, 217
Sears Roebuck, 119, 164, 165, 187, 211, 246
Securities and Exchange Commission (SEC), 320, 334, 335, 327
Seeger, J. A., 303
Seitz Corporation, 241, 242
Senge, P.M., 23
Serpa, R., 228
Seven-Eleven, 106
Seward, J. K., 31
Sexton, D., 284
Shanghai Automotive, 214
Shank, J. K., 261
Sharfman, M. P., 24
Sharif, M. F., 261
Shaver, J. M., 23
Shearson, 217
Sheppard, J. P., 50
Sherman, S., 158
Shimano, 302
Shleifer, A., 79
Shook, C. L., 228
Shrader, C. B., 303
Shuman, J. C., 303
Siemens AG, 32, 91, 126, 268
Signal Companies, 134
Silva, M., 281, 282
Simison, R. L., 180
Simmonds, P. G., 158
Simon, J. G., 317
Simpson Industries, 146
Simpson, R. L., 131
Sinha, D. K., 158, 181
Sisters of St. Francis, 36
Sjogren, B., 281, 282
Skloot, E., 315, 318
Slater, R. W., 262
Sloan, A. P., 176, 187, 204
Slocum, J. W., 158, 227, 262
Small Business Administration, 284, 313
Smart, T., 131
Smircich, L., 104
Smith, G., 262
Smith, K. G., 23, 227
Smith, M., 228
Snow, C.C., 68, 79, 262
Snyder, H., 297
Snyder, N., 281
Social Security, 321
Sony Corporation, 84, 264, 266, 279
Soper, B., 261
Southern California Edison, 285

Southwest Airlines, 16, 37, 81, 82, 83, 84, 115, 248, 249
Sperlich, H., 266, 275
Sprint, 122, 236
Squaw Valley, 302
Stalk, G., 281
Standard and Poor's, 334
Standard Oil, 187, 211
Starkey, M., 261
Staw, B. M., 181
Steensma, H. K., 181
Steinmetz, G., 32
Stern, G., 180, 214
Stern Stewart & Company, 236
Stevens, S., 131
Stewart III, G. B., 261
Stewart, T.A., 180, 262
Stobaugh, R. B., 261
Stofford, J. M., 79
Stonich, P. J., 250, 251, 262
Storehouse PLC, 210
Study of Values, 44
Subramanjan, R., 317
Summers, D.V., 317
Suris, O., 131
Switch Manufacturing, 302

T

Tagiuri, R., 51
Taisei Corporation, 21
Tancredi, J., 275
Tandy Corporation, 118
Taylor, A., 207
Taylor, M.S., 228
Techtronix, 277
Teece, D. J., 79, 158
Teknowledge, 126
Teledyne, 236
Templeman, J., 105
Tenneco, 236
Texaco, 85, 136, 210
Texas Gas Resources, 140
Texas Instruments, 273, 327
Thain, D. H. J., 189
Thoman, R., 145
Thomas, A., 303
Thomas, A.S., 227
Thomas, H., 50, 79
Thomas, J.B., 79
Thompson, J. D., 317
Thompson Multimedia, 141
3M (Minnesota Mining & Manufacturing), 11, 14, 41, 172, 201, 233, 264, 273, 277
Tichy, N.M., 51, 228
Tide, 62, 273

TIME, Inc., 294
Time Warner, 15
Timex, 115
Titan, 302
Toccacelli, J., 51
Tomsho, R., 131
Toshiba, 126
Total System Services, 128, 161
Toto Ltd., 270, 278
Towner, S. J., 281
Toy, S., 105
Toyota Motor Corporation, 111, 118, 125, 142, 327
Toys "R" Us, 244
Transmet Corporation, 290
Travis, V. R., 299, 300, 304
Treece, J. B., 158
Trevino, L.K., 51
Trinephi, M., 105
Triumph, 117
Trotman, A., 111
TRW Systems, 194
Tucker, L., 180
Tully, S., 261
Tung, R. L., 228
Tupperware, 52, 53, 58, 73
Turner, T., 37
Tushman, M. L., 24
Tyler, B.B., 181

U

U.S. Bureau of Labor Statistics, 321, 328
U.S. Census Bureau, 334
U.S. Constitution, 47
U.S. Department of Commerce, 328, 334
U.S. Department of Defense, 334
U.S. Department of Justice, 125
U. S. Equal Employment Opportunity Commission, 214, 215
U.S. General Accounting Office, 313
U.S. Internal Revenue Service, 241, 313
U.S. Personal Chef Association, 53
U.S. Robotics, 192
U.S. Securities and Exchange Commission, 320, 327, 334, 335
U.S. Small Business Administration, 284, 313
Ullmann, A.A., 168
UNICEF, 313
Unilever, 162, 212
Union Carbide, 169, 186
United Airlines (UAL), 31, 81, 82
United Auto Workers, 31, 42, 215

United Nations, 334
United Parcel Service (UPS), 161, 170, 180
United Way, 308, 315
Unterman, I., 317
Upjohn Pharmaceuticals, 223, 224
Urschel Laboratories, 164
Useem, J., 303

V
Value Line, 334
Van De Ven, A. H., 137
Vans, 302
Veiga, J. F., 181
Verdin, P. J., 180
Verity, J.W., 180
Versteeg, A., 105
Victor, B., 180
Vidal Sassoon, 134
Virtual Emporium, 292
Viskny, R. W., 79
Vitromatic, 168
Von Bergen, C. W., 261
Von der Embse, T. J., 46, 51
Voss, B., 158, 204

W
Wade, J., 281
Wagley, R.A., 46, 51
Wagner, S., 281
Wall Street Journal Index, 335
Wall Street Research Net, 327
Walleck, A.S., 23
Wallender, III, H. W., 310, 317
Wal-Mart, 43, 106, 115, 143, 241
Walsh, J. P., 31, 208, 227
Walt Disney Productions, 116, 191, 283
Walters, J., 202
Wang Laboratories, Inc., 146

Ward, J. L., 303, 304
Warner, J., 24, 51, 80, 105, 131, 158, 181, 228, 262, 282, 304, 318, 344
Warner-Lambert, 21
Wasson, C. R., 94
Waterman, R. H., 248, 262
Weatherup, C., 183
Web 100, 327, 335
Webber, A. M., 281
Weihrich, H., 112
Welch, J., 35, 177
Welsch, H. P., 303
Westhead, P., 303
Westinghouse, 28, 251
Wetlaufer, S., 228
Weyerhauser, 85
Wheelen, T. L., 20, 71, 76, 102, 109, 174, 280, 288, 290, 309, 317, 331
Wheeling-Pittsburgh Steel, 31, 191
Whirlpool, 28, 66, 120, 126, 139, 161, 165, 168, 236, 272, 297
White Consolidated Industries, 141
White, J. B., 262
White, L., 42
White, M.C., 228
Whitmore, K., 26, 38
Whyte, G., 181
Wiersema, L., 145
Wiersema, M. F., 158
Wiesendanger, B., 317
Willard, G. E., 282, 303, 304
Williams, J. R., 180
Williamson, O.E., 137
Williamson, P. J., 180
Wilson, D.C., 24
Wilson, I., 23, 51
Windows, 70, 94, 123, 266
Winnebago (RVs), 55
Winter, S. G., 137

Woo, C.Y., 282, 303, 304
Woodman, R. W., 227
Woolard, E., 263, 276
Wooldridge, J. R., 262
Word, 62
WordPerfect, 266
World Wide Web, 2, 179, 320, 327, 332
Worthing Technical Center, 141
Wortman, M.S., 262
Wyatt, J., 79

X
Xerox, 94, 95, 161, 212, 240, 276
Xie, J. L., 199

Y
Yahoo, 327
Yamada, K., 281
Yauger, C. C., 317
Yeung, B., 23
Yoder, S. K., 282
Young, S., 213, 214
Young Sisters & Brothers, 291
Yuengling, 292

Z
Zabriskie, 224
Zahra, S. A., 50
Zamboni, 110
Zangwill W.I., 281
Zap Mail, 180
Zeithaml, C. P., 50, 158
Zellner, W., 262
Zenith Electronics Corporation, 28
Ziegler, B., 145
Zip Drive, 18
Zuckerman, L., 23
Zytel, 263

Subject Index

A

Absorptive capacity, 272
Acquisition, 134, 139, 156
Action plan, 217
Active board, 29
Activity ratios, 320, 323
Activity-based costing, 233, 234, 259
Adaptive mode, 19
Advanced manufacturing technology (AMT), 166
Agency problems, 248
Agency theory, 30, 31
Alien territory businesses, 154
Altman's bankruptcy formula, 325
Analytical portfolio manager, 209
Analyzers, 68
Annual report, 320
Arms race, 171
Assembly line, 96
Assessment centers, 211
Assimilation, 217
Assumptions, 73
Autonomous work teams, 98

B

Backward integration, 136
Balanced scorecard, 237, 238, 259
Ballast businesses, 154
Bankruptcy, 146
Bankruptcy formula, 325
Bargaining power of buyers, 64
Bargaining power of suppliers, 64
Basic organizational structures, 87
Basic R&D, 94
BCG growth-share matrix, 147
Behavior controls, 231
Behavior substitution, 246
Benchmarking, 38, 240, 242
Best practices, 278
Blocks to changing stages, 190
Board of director responsibilities, 27
Board of directors continuum, 28
Board qualifications, 36
Board role in strategic management, 27
Boston consulting group, 3
BOT concept, 142
Brainstorming, 73
Broad target, 113
Budget, 15, 186
Budget analysis, 241

Business plan, 287, 290
Business policy, 3
Business process redesign (re-engineering), 39, 197
Business strategy, 12, 113, 293
Bypass attack, 123

C

Capital budgeting, 93
Captive company strategy, 145
Carroll's four responsibilities, 39
Case method, 320
Cash cows, 148
Cash flow, 319, 326
Catalyst board, 29
Categorical imperatives, 47
Cautious profit planner, 209
Center of gravity, 85
Centralization, 201
Codes of ethics, 45
Codetermination, 31
Collusion, 124
Common-size statements, 325
Communication, 215
Company information, 334
Compensatory justice, 47
Competitive activity report, 58
Competitive advantage, 82
Competitive forces, 62
Competitive intelligence, 72
Competitive scope, 113
Competitive strategy, 113, 310
Competitive strategy risks, 117
Competitive tactics, 121
Computer integrated design and manufacturing (CAD/CAM), 166
Concentration strategy, 135
Concentric diversification, 138, 156
Concurrent engineering, 99
Conglomerate diversification, 140, 156
Conglomerate structure, 89
Connected line batch flow, 166
Consensus, 176
Consolidated industry, 65, 119
Constant dollars, 326
Constraints on strategic management, 310
Consumer price index, 326, 328
Continuous improvement, 167, 222

Continuous systems, 96
Continuum of international industries, 67
Continuum of sustainability, 84
Contracting, 277
Controversies in directional growth strategies, 142
Cooperative strategies, 124
Core capability, 160
Core competencies, 38, 83, 160
Corporate capabilities, 83
Corporate culture, 89, 214, 249
Corporate culture pressures, 175
Corporate entrepreneurship, 275
Corporate governance, 26, 310
Corporate parenting, 152, 156
Corporate scenarios, 172
Corporate stakeholders, 41
Corporate strategy, 12, 133
Corporate value-chain, 86
Corporation, 26
Cost accounting, 233
Cost focus, 116
Cost leadership, 115
Cost proximity, 117
Country attractiveness, 150
Creative destruction, 300
Crisis of autonomy, 190
Crisis of leadership, 188
Critical success factors, 153, 248
Cross-impact analysis (CIA), 74
Crossfunctional teams, 274
Cultural integration, 89
Cultural intensity, 89

D

Decentralization, 201, 312
Deculturation, 217
Dedicated transfer lines, 166
Defenders, 68
Defensive centralization, 312
Defensive tactics, 123
Demographics, 291
Demographic trends, 55
Devil's advocate, 176
Dialectical inquiry, 176
Differentiation, 113, 115
Differentiation focus, 116
Dimensions of national culture, 222
Directional strategy, 134
Discretionary expenses, 239

Discretionary responsibilities, 40
Distinctive competencies, 83, 107, 160
Distributive justice, 47
Diverse cultures, 216
Diversification strategies, 138
Diversity, 99
Divestment, 146
Divisional structure, 88, 190
Do everything, 171
Dogs, 148
Downsizing, 211
Downstream, 85
Due care, 27
Due diligence, 27
Durability, 83
Dynamic industry expert, 209

E

Earnings per share, 235
Economic forces, 54
Economic indicators, 328
Economic information, 334
Economic responsibilities, 40
Economic value added (EVA), 236, 237
Economies of scale, 98
Economies of scope, 86, 98
Edge-of-heartland businesses, 154
EFAS table, 75, 76, 107, 112
Employee stock ownership plan (ESOP), 31, 277
Encirclement, 123
Engineered expenses, 239
Engineering (R&D), 95
Entrepreneur, 284
Entrepreneurial characteristics, 293
Entrepreneurial culture, 273
Entrepreneurial mode, 18
Entrepreneurial venture, 284
Entry barrier, 61
Environmental scanning, 9, 53, 265
Environmental uncertainty, 53
EPS (earnings per share), 235
Ethical responsibilities, 40
Ethics, 46
Euro, 243
EVA, 236, 237
Evaluation and control, 15, 278
Executive development, 312
Executive leadership, 35
Executive succession, 210
Executive type, 209
Expense centers, 239
Experience curve, 96
Expert opinion, 73, 74

Exporting, 140
External environment, 9, 174
Extranets, 245
Extrapolation, 73

F

Fairness, 47
Family businesses, 298
Fast-cycle resources, 84
Feedback, 16
Financial analysis, 320
Financial leverage, 92
Financial statements, 321
Financial strategy, 164
First mover, 121
Flanking maneuver, 122
Flexible manufacturing systems, 98, 166
Follow the leader, 171
Forecasting techniques, 73
Formality of planning, 286
Forward integration, 136
Fragmented industry, 65, 119
Free cash flow, 319, 326
Frontal assault, 122
Functional strategy, 12, 160
Functional structure, 88, 189
Fuzzy logic technology, 129, 272

G

GE business screen, 149
Generation Y, 56
Geographic-area structure, 201
Global industries, 66
Global MNC, 244
Globalization, 6
Goal, 11
Goal conflicts, 311
Goal displacement, 246, 311
Golden rule, 47
Green-field development, 142
Gross domestic product (GDP), 326, 328
Growth strategies, 134
Guerrilla warfare, 123
Guidelines for control, 248

H

Heartland businesses, 153
Hierarchy of needs, 45
Hierarchy of strategy, 13
Hiring, 208
Historical comparisons, 241
Hit another home run, 171
Horizontal axis washer, 297

Horizontal growth, 138, 139
Horizontal integration, 138
Horizontal strategy, 155
HRM strategy, 170
Human rights standards, 46
Hypercompetition, 69, 120

I

IFAS table, 101, 112
Imitability, 83
Implementation problems, 184
Independent business units, 276
Index of R&D effectiveness, 278
Index of sustainable growth, 325
Individual rights approach, 47
Individualism-collectivism (I-C), 222
Industry, 60
Industry analysis, 54, 60, 310
Industry evolution, 65
Industry information, 334
Industry intelligence, 72
Industry matrix, 70
Industry scenario, 75
Industry structure, 119, 292
Industry value chain, 85
Inflation, 321, 331, 332
Information systems issues, 100
Information systems strategies, 170
Inside directors, 29
Integration, 217
Interlocking directorate, 33
Intermittent system, 96
Internal customer, 221
Internal environment, 10
International assignment, 213
International entry options, 140
International measurement issues, 241
International portfolio analysis, 150
International risk assessment, 67
International staffing, 212
International transfer pricing, 241
Intranet, 100
Intrapreneurship, 275
Investment centers, 240
ISO 14000, 259
ISO 9000, 233
Issues priority matrix, 59, 61

J

Job characteristics model, 198, 199
Job design, 198
Job enlargement, 198, 312
Job enrichment, 198
Job rotation, 198, 211

Job shops, 96, 166
Joint venture, 126, 140, 214
Justice approach, 47

K

Key performance measures, 238

L

Late movers, 121
Law, 46
Lead director, 34
Leading, 214
Learning organization, 7, 8
Learning process, 16
Legal responsibilities, 40
Leverage ratios, 320, 324
Leveraged buyout, 165
Licensing, 140
Licensing arrangement, 127
Lifestyle company, 296
Liquidation, 146
Liquidity ratios, 320, 322
Logical incrementalism, 19
Logistics strategy, 169
Long-term contracts, 137
Long-term evaluation method, 250
Long-term orientation (LT), 222
Losing hand, 171
Lower cost strategy, 113

M

Management audits, 238
Management board, 32
Management by objectives (MBO), 219
Management contracts, 142
Management directors, 29
Managing corporate culture, 215
Manufacturing strategy, 168
Market development, 162
Market location tactics, 122
Market position, 90
Market research, 266
Market segmentation, 90
Market value added (MVA), 237
Marketing mix, 90
Marketing strategy, 162
Masculinity-femininity (M-F), 222
Mass customization, 56, 98, 167
Mass production, 167
Matrix structure, 193, 194
MBO, 219
Merger, 134, 314
Micro new ventures department, 276
Mission, 10, 111
Mission statements, 265, 310

Model of strategic management, 8, 286
Modes of strategic decision making, 18
Moral development levels, 44
Moral relativism, 44
Morality, 46
Multidomestic industries, 65
Multidomestic MNC, 244
Multinational corporation (MNC), 57, 199,
Multiple sourcing, 168
Multipoint competitors, 155
Mutual service consortium, 126
MVA (market value added), 237
Myers-Briggs type indicator, 227

N

Narrow target, 113
Network structure, 195
New venture division, 276
Niche, 110
No change strategy, 143
Not-for-profit organization, 306, 307
Not-for-profit strategies, 313

O

Objectives, 11, 111
Offensive tactics, 122
On-line information, 334
Operating budgets, 239
Operating cash flow, 326
Operations strategy, 166
Orchestrator, 274
Organization slack, 135
Organizational analysis, 82
Organizational learning, 213
Other stakeholders, 65
Output controls, 232
Outside directors, 29
Outsourcing, 138, 161
Outsourcing technology, 271
Oxymoron, 43

P

Parallel sourcing, 169
Parenting-fit matrix, 153
Pattern of influence, 308
Pause/proceed with caution strategy, 143
Penetration pricing, 164
Performance, 231
Performance appraisal system, 211
Performance gap, 17
Periodic statistical reports, 239
Phantom board, 29
Phases of strategic management, 3

Pioneer, 121
Planning mode, 19
Policy, 14, 177
Political strategy, 175
Political-legal forces, 54
Politics, 221, 311
Portfolio analysis, 147, 310
Power distancer (PD), 222
Primary activities, 86
Prime interest rate (PIR), 326, 328
Private nonprofit corporation, 306
Privatization, 307
Pro forma financial statements, 173
Problems in measuring, 245
Procedures, 15, 186
Process innovations, 269, 272
Process R&D, 95
Product champion, 274
Product development, 162, 264
Product innovations, 269, 272
Product life cycle, 91
Product R&D, 94
Product-group structure, 201
Product/brand management, 194
Product/market evolution matrix, 273
Production sharing, 142
Professional liquidator, 209
Professionalization, 312
Profit centers, 239
Profit strategy, 144
Profit-making firm, 307
Profitability ratios, 320, 322
Program, 14, 185
Propitious niche, 110
Prospectors, 68
Public governmental agencies, 306
Public or collective goods, 306
Pull strategy, 164
Purchasing power parity (PPP), 59
Purchasing strategy, 168
Push strategy, 162

Q

Quality of work life, 99
Quasi-integration, 136
Question marks, 148

R

R&D intensity, 93, 267
R&D mix, 94
R&D strategy, 165
Ratio analysis, 320, 334
Reactors, 68
Reengineering, 39, 197
Regional trade associations, 7

Related diversification, 138
Repatriation of profits, 54, 242
Replicability, 83
Research and development, 269
Researching the case, 320
Resource allocation, 267
Resource-based approach, 82
Responsibility centers, 239
Retrenchment strategies, 144
Retrenchment, 211
Retributive justice, 47
Return on equity (ROE), 235
Return on investment (ROI), 231, 234, 241
Revenue centers, 239
Risk, 173
Rivalry among existing firms, 63
ROE (return on equity), 235
ROI (return on investment), 234, 235
Role of the board of directors, 27
Rubber stamp board, 29

S

Satellites, 279
Scenario planning, 38
Scenario writing, 74
Sell-out, 146
Separation, 217
SFAS Matrix, 107
Shareholder value, 235
Shareholder value analysis, 38
Short-term orientation, 245
Simple structure, 88, 188
Situational analysis, 107
Skim pricing, 164
Slow-cycle resources, 84
Small-business firm, 284
SO strategies, 112
Social responsibility, 39, 40
Societal environment, 9, 54
Sociocultural forces, 54
Sociocultural trends, 54
Sole sourcing, 169
Source of revenue, 307
Sources of innovation, 290
Sourcing, 169
Special business units, 275
Spin-off, 277
Sponsor, 274
ST strategies, 112
Stability strategies, 143
Staffing, 207
Stages of corporate development, 188
Stages of international development, 200

Stages of new product development, 273, 275
Stakeholder analysis, 310
Stakeholder measures, 235
Stakeholders, 236
Standard cost centers, 239
Standard operating procedures (SOP), 15
Standards, 230
Stars, 148
Statistical modeling, 73
Statistical process control, 231
Steering controls, 231
Strategic alliance, 125, 134, 156, 270, 314
Strategic audit, 100, 251, 287, 329, 336, 340
Strategic business units (SBUs), 89, 202
Strategic choice, 171, 176
Strategic decision making, 17, 19
Strategic decision-making process, 19, 286, 288
Strategic decisions, 18
Strategic factors, 9, 59, 82, 101
Strategic financial issues, 91
Strategic flexibility, 8
Strategic group, 67, 69
Strategic human resource issues, 98
Strategic incentive management, 248
Strategic information systems, 244
Strategic management, 3
Strategic management model, 8, 286
Strategic marketing issues, 90
Strategic myopia, 59
Strategic operations issues, 96
Strategic piggybacking, 313
Strategic planning process, 37
Strategic planning staff, 37
Strategic R&D issues, 93
Strategic type, 68
Strategic vision, 11, 35, 37, 216
Strategic window, 110
Strategic-funds approach, 251
Strategic-funds method, 250
Strategies to avoid, 171
Strategy, 12
Strategy formulation, 10, 269
Strategy implementation, 14, 183, 273
Strategy-culture compatibility, 215
Structure follows strategy, 187
Stuck in the middle, 118
Sub-stages of small business development, 295
Suboptimization, 247
Substitute products, 63

Supervisory board, 32
Support activities, 86
SWOT analysis, 9, 107, 310
Synergy, 139, 186

T

Tactic, 121
Taper integration, 136
Task environment, 10, 54
Task forces, 194
Technological competence, 94, 272
Technological discontinuity, 95, 266
Technological follower, 166
Technological followership, 13
Technological forces, 54
Technological leader, 166
Technological leadership, 13
Technology research, 265
Technology sourcing, 269
Technology transfer, 94
Temporary workers, 99
10-K form, 320
Threat of new entrants, 61
Threat of substitute products or services, 63
Time to market, 268
Time-based competition, 39
Timing tactics, 121
Tolerance range, 230
Top management, 238
Top management responsibilities, 35
Total quality management (TQM), 38, 221
TOWS matrix, 111
TQM, 221
Training, 208
Transaction cost, 137
Transaction cost economics, 136, 137
Transfer price, 240
Transferability, 83
Transparency, 83
Trend-impact analysis (TIA), 74
Trends in governance, 34
Triad, 58
Trigger point, 58, 59
Triggering event, 17
Turnaround specialist, 209
Turnaround strategy, 144, 145, 210
Turnkey operations, 142

U

Uncertainty avoidance (UA), 222
Unethical behavior, 43
Union relations, 99
Unrelated diversification, 140

Upstream, 85
Utilitarian approach, 47

V

Valuation and control process, 230
Value chain, 84
Value trap businesses, 155
Value-chain analysis, 39, 84, 233, 259
Value-chain partnership, 128
Values, 44, 291

Vertical growth, 135, 137
Vertical growth strategy, 156
Vertical integration, 136, 137
Virtual organizations, 195
Vision, see strategic vision
VRIO framework, 82

W

Weighted-factor approach, 250
Weighted-factor method, 249

WO strategies, 112
WT strategies, 112

Z

Z-value, 325